'This rich collection of essays initiates and invigorates debates about management education. Ranging widely across history, philosophy and politics, its cast of leading international authors challenge conventional wisdom and provide vital reading for anyone interested in 21st century business schools.'

**Christopher Grey FAcSS**, *Professor of Organization Studies at Royal Holloway, University of London, UK*

'Management Studies is too important to be left to the established patrons of business schools. This comprehensive collection provides immediate resources for educators to expand the political, philosophical and ethical horizon for their work, in the classroom and beyond.'

**Melissa Gregg**, *Intel Corporation, USA*

# The Routledge Companion to Reinventing Management Education

The position and role of the business school and its educational programmes have become increasingly prominent, yet also questioned and contested. What management education entails, and how it is enacted, has become a matter of profound concern in the field of higher education and, more generally, for the development of the organized world.

Drawing upon the humanities and social sciences, *The Routledge Companion to Reinventing Management Education* imagines a different and better education offered to students of management, entrepreneurship and organization studies. It is an intervention into the debates on what is taught and how learning takes place, demonstrating both the potential and the limits of what the humanities and social sciences can do for management education. Divided into six parts, the book traces the history and theory of management education, reimagining central educational principles and outlining an emerging practice-based approach.

With an international cast of authors, *The Routledge Companion to Reinventing Management Education* has been written for contemporary and future educators and for students and scholars who seek to make a difference through their practice.

**Chris Steyaert** is Professor of Organizational Psychology and Director of the Research Institute for Organizational Psychology at the University of St Gallen, Switzerland.

**Timon Beyes** is Professor of Design, Innovation and Aesthetics at the Department of Management, Politics and Philosophy at Copenhagen Business School, Denmark.

**Martin Parker** is Professor of Organization and Culture at the School of Management at the University of Leicester, UK.

## Routledge Companions in Business, Management and Accounting

Routledge Companions in Business, Management and Accounting are prestige reference works providing an overview of a whole subject area or sub-discipline. These books survey the state of the discipline including emerging and cutting edge areas. Providing a comprehensive, up-to-date, definitive work of reference, Routledge Companions can be cited as an authoritative source on the subject.

A key aspect of these Routledge Companions is their international scope and relevance. Edited by an array of highly regarded scholars, these volumes also benefit from teams of contributors that reflect an international range of perspectives.

Individually, Routledge Companions in Business, Management and Accounting provide an impactful one-stop-shop resource for each theme covered. Collectively, they represent a comprehensive learning and research resource for researchers, postgraduate students and practitioners.

*Published titles in this series include:*

**The Routledge Companion to Consumer Behaviour Analysis**
*Edited by Gordon R. Foxall*

**The Routledge Companion to Philosophy in Organization Studies**
*Edited by Raza Mir, Hugh Willmott and Michelle Greenwood*

**The Routledge Companion to Network Industries**
*Edited by Matthias Finger and Christian Jaag*

**The Routledge Companion to Strategic Risk Management**
*Edited by Torben J. Andersen*

**The Routledge Companion to Philanthropy**
*Edited by Tobias Jung, Susan Phillips and Jenny Harrow*

**The Routledge Companion to Marketing History**
*Edited by D. G. Brian Jones and Mark Tadajewski*

**The Routledge Companion to Reinventing Management Education**
*Edited by Chris Steyaert, Timon Beyes and Martin Parker*

# The Routledge Companion to Reinventing Management Education

*Edited by Chris Steyaert, Timon Beyes and Martin Parker*

Routledge
Taylor & Francis Group
LONDON AND NEW YORK

First published 2016
by Routledge
2 Park Square, Milton Park, Abingdon, Oxon OX14 4RN

and by Routledge
605 Third Avenue, New York, NY 10017

First issued in paperback 2021

*Routledge is an imprint of the Taylor & Francis Group, an informa business*



*British Library Cataloguing in Publication Data*
A catalogue record for this book is available from the British Library

*Library of Congress Cataloging-in-Publication Data*
Names: Steyaert, Chris, editor. | Beyes, Timon, 1973- editor. | Parker, Martin, 1962- editor.
Title: The Routledge companion to reinventing management education/ edited by Chris Steyaert, Timon Beyes and Martin Parker.
Description: New York : Routledge, 2016. | Series: Routledge companions in business, management and accounting | Includes bibliographical references and index.
Identifiers: LCCN 2015047041 | ISBN 9780415727372 (hardback) | ISBN 9781315852430 (ebook)
Subjects: LCSH: Business education. | Management--Study and teaching. | Organizational sociology.
Classification: LCC HD30.4.R688 2016 | DDC 658.0071–dc23
LC record available at http://lccn.loc.gov/2015047041

Typeset in Bembo
by Sunrise Setting Ltd, Brixham, UK

ISBN 13: 978-1-03-224243-9 (pbk)
ISBN 13: 978-0-415-72737-2 (hbk)

DOI: 10.4324/9781315852430

Supported by

**HANIEL STIFTUNG**

# The Routledge Companion to Reinventing Management Education

*Edited by Chris Steyaert, Timon Beyes and Martin Parker*

Routledge
Taylor & Francis Group
LONDON AND NEW YORK

First published 2016
by Routledge
2 Park Square, Milton Park, Abingdon, Oxon OX14 4RN

and by Routledge
605 Third Avenue, New York, NY 10017

First issued in paperback 2021

*Routledge is an imprint of the Taylor & Francis Group, an informa business*



Publisher's Note
The publisher has gone to great lengths to ensure the quality of this reprint but points out that some imperfections in the original copies may be apparent.

*British Library Cataloguing in Publication Data*
A catalogue record for this book is available from the British Library

*Library of Congress Cataloging-in-Publication Data*
Names: Steyaert, Chris, editor. | Beyes, Timon, 1973- editor. | Parker, Martin, 1962- editor.
Title: The Routledge companion to reinventing management education/ edited by Chris Steyaert, Timon Beyes and Martin Parker.
Description: New York : Routledge, 2016. | Series: Routledge companions in business, management and accounting | Includes bibliographical references and index.
Identifiers: LCCN 2015047041 | ISBN 9780415727372 (hardback) | ISBN 9781315852430 (ebook)
Subjects: LCSH: Business education. | Management--Study and teaching. | Organizational sociology.
Classification: LCC HD30.4.R688 2016 | DDC 658.0071–dc23
LC record available at http://lccn.loc.gov/2015047041

Typeset in Bembo
by Sunrise Setting Ltd, Brixham, UK

ISBN 13: 978-1-03-224243-9 (pbk)
ISBN 13: 978-0-415-72737-2 (hbk)

DOI: 10.4324/9781315852430

Supported by

**HANIEL STIFTUNG**

# Contents

# Illustrations

## Figures



## Tables

# Contributors

**Kostas Amiridis** is Lecturer at the Lancaster University Management School, Lancaster University, UK.

**Robert D. Austin** is Professor of Management of Innovation and Digital Transformation at Copenhagen Business School, Denmark.

**Götz Bachmann** is Professor for Digital Cultures at the Institute for Culture and Aesthetics of Digital Media, Leuphana University, Lüneburg, Germany.

**Dirk Baecker**, Sociologist, is Professor of Culture Theory and Management at Witten/Herdecke University, Germany.

**Ester Barinaga** is Professor of Social Entrepreneurship at the Department of Management, Politics and Philosophy, Copenhagen Business School, Denmark.

**Daved Barry** is Professor of Creative Organization Studies at Copenhagen Business School, Denmark and Visiting/Adjunct Professor of Management at Jönköping International Business School, Sweden and NovaSBE, Portugal.

**Emma Bell** is Professor of Management and Organisation Studies at Keele Management School, Keele University, UK.

**Timon Beyes** is a professor at Copenhagen Business School, Denmark and at the Centre for Digital Cultures, Leuphana University, Lüneburg, Germany.

**Ulrik Brandi** is Associate Professor of Organizational Learning at Danish School of Education, Aarhus University, Campus Copenhagen, Denmark.

**Steven D. Brown** is Professor of Social and Organizational Psychology at the University of Leicester, UK.

**Robert Chia** is Research Professor of Management at the Adam Smith Business School, University of Glasgow, UK.

**Anne Colby** is Consulting Professor in the Stanford Graduate School of Education, US.

**Bogdan Costea** is Reader in Management and Philosophy at the Lancaster University Management School, Lancaster University, UK.

**Barbara Czarniawska** is Torsten and Ragnar Söderberg Professor of Management Studies at Gothenburg Research Institute, University of Gothenburg, Sweden.

**Christian De Cock** is Professor of Management at Essex Business School, University of Essex, UK.

**Paola Dubini** is Associate Professor of Management at Università Bocconi, Italy.

**Thomas S. Eberle** is Professor Emeritus of Sociology at University of St Gallen, Switzerland.

**Thomas Ehrlich** is Visiting Professor at the Stanford Graduate School of Education and President Emeritus, Indiana University, US.

**Bente Elkjaer** is Professor of Organizational Learning at Danish School of Education, Aarhus University, Campus Copenhagen, Denmark.

**Tara Fenwick** is Professor of Professional Education at the School of Education, University of Stirling, UK.

**Silvia Gherardi** is Senior Professor of Work and Organization at the Research Unit of Communication, Organizational Learning and Aesthetics, University of Trento, Italy and Aalto University, Finland.

**Martyn Griffin** is a Lecturer in Organizational Behaviour at Leeds University Business School, UK.

**Pierre Guillet de Monthoux** is Professor of Philosophy and Management and Director of CBS Art Initiative at Copenhagen Business School, Denmark.

**Daniel Hjorth** is Professor of Entrepreneurship and Organization at the Department of Management, Politics and Philosophy, Copenhagen Business School, Denmark.

**Robin Holt** is Professor of Entrepreneurship, Politics and Society at Copenhagen Business School, Denmark.

**Patrizia Hoyer** is Postdoctoral Researcher in Organizational Psychology at the University of St Gallen, Switzerland.

**Isabelle Huault** is Professor of Organization Studies at Université Paris–Dauphine PSL, France.

**Michael Humphreys** is Professor of Organization Studies at Durham University Business School, UK.

**Rasmus Johnsen** is Assistant Professor at the Department of Management, Politics and Philosophy, Copenhagen Business School, Denmark.

**Ulrike Landfester** is Professor for German Language and Literature and Vice-President at the University of St Gallen, Switzerland.

**Mark Learmonth** is Professor of Organization Studies and Deputy Dean (Research) at Durham University Business School, UK.

**Bent Meier Sørensen** is Professor of Organizational Philosophy at the Department of Management, Politics and Philosophy, Copenhagen Business School, Denmark.

**Stefan Meisiek** is Director of Educational Practice in Business and Associate Professor at the University of Sydney Business School, Australia and Copenhagen Business School, Denmark.

**Jörg Metelmann** is Associate Professor of Culture and Media Studies and Programme Director Leadership Skills in the Contextual Studies, University of St Gallen, Switzerland.

**Christoph Michels** is Postdoctoral Researcher at the Research Institute for Organizational Psychology, University of St Gallen, Switzerland.

**Ajit Nayak** is Senior Lecturer in Strategy at the University of Exeter Business School, UK.

**Daniel Nyberg** is Professor of Management at the University of Newcastle, Australia.

**Ellen S. O'Connor** is Senior Research Fellow at the Institute for Leadership Studies, Barowsky School of Business, Dominican University of California, US.

**Damian O'Doherty** is Senior Lecturer in Organization Analysis at the Manchester Business School, University of Manchester, UK.

**Martin Parker** is Professor of Organization and Culture at the School of Management, University of Leicester, UK.

**Michael Pedersen** is Associate Professor in Business Philosophy at the Department of Management, Politics and Philosophy, Copenhagen Business School, Denmark.

**Véronique Perret** is Professor of Management at Université Paris-Dauphine PSL, France.

**Linda Perriton** is Senior Lecturer in Human Resource Management at the Stirling Management School, University of Stirling, UK.

**Ajnesh Prasad** is Research Professor at Tecnologico de Monterrey's EGADE Business School, Mexico.

**Queralt Prat-i-Pubill** is Researcher on Creativity and Collective Motivations at the School of Humanities and Social Sciences, University of St Gallen, Switzerland.

**Alison Pullen** is Professor of Management and Organization at Macquarie University, Australia.

**Marton Racz** is PhD Candidate and Graduate Teaching Assistant at the School of Management, University of Leicester, UK.

**Elena Raviola** is Assistant Professor at Department of Business Administration, School of Business, Economics and Law, University of Gothenburg, Sweden.

**Bernhard Resch** is PhD Candidate and Assistant at the Research Institute for Organizational Psychology, University of St Gallen, Switzerland.

**Carl Rhodes** is Professor of Organization Studies at UTS Business School, University of Technology Sydney, Australia.

**Perttu Salovaara** is Adjunct Assistant Professor at the Stern School of Business, New York University, US and Senior Researcher at the School of Management, University of Tampere, Finland.

**Nishant Shah** is a Professor of Culture and Aesthetic of Digital Media at the Leuphana University, Lüneburg, Germany and the co-founder of the Centre for Internet & Society, Bangalore, India.

**Amanda Sinclair** is an Author, Teacher and Professorial Fellow at Melbourne Business School, Australia.

**Amritesh Singh** is Postdoctoral Research Fellow at the Institute for Gender Studies, University of South Africa, South Africa.

**Martyna Śliwa** is Professor of Management and Organization Studies at Essex Business School, University of Essex, UK.

**Morten Sørensen Thaning** is Associate Professor in Philosophy and Programme Director of Philosophy and Business Administration, Copenhagen Business School, Denmark.

**Nidhi Srinivas** is Associate Professor of Management at the New School, New York City, US.

**Matt Statler** is Richman Family Director of Business Ethics and Social Impact Programming and Clinical Associate Professor of Business and Society, New York University Stern School of Business, US.

**Chris Steyaert** is Professor of Organizational Psychology and Director of the Research Institute for Organizational Psychology at the University of St Gallen, Switzerland.

**William M. Sullivan** is Senior Scholar at the New American Colleges and Universities and Visiting Professor at the Center for the Study of Professions, University College, Oslo and Akershus, Norway.

**René ten Bos** is Professor of Philosophy at the Department of Management Sciences, Radboud University in Nijmegen, The Netherlands.

**Nicolaj Tofte Brenneche** is Senior Adviser at the Faculty of Humanities, University of Copenhagen, Denmark.

**Russ Vince** is Professor of Leadership and Change at the School of Management, University of Bath, UK.

**Christopher Wright** is Professor of Organizational Studies at the University of Sydney Business School, Australia.

# 1

# Introduction

## Why does management education need reinventing?

*Timon Beyes, Martin Parker and Chris Steyaert*

At a time when a pervasive performative culture encourages scholars who work at higher ranked business schools to invest their energies in their research profiles, that is to say, publication outputs and external funding, why bother to focus on teaching, learning and education? And why in particular on 'The humanities and social sciences in management education', to quote the rather clunky working title that guided us during the creation of this Companion? Why are we trying to conjoin the management school with subjects like philosophy, art, sociology, cultural theory and history? Why does business and management education, characterized by healthy enrolments and a buoyant labour market for academics, need reinventing anyway? Apart from the lazy or cynical response that editing and writing for such a book also yields an entry on the CVs of all the academics involved, we believe there are a number of important reasons to care about the arguments and ideas expressed in this book.

First, for most scholars employed at business school departments or business universities, a significant part of their time is spent on preparing teaching and interacting with students. We hope that this book will work as a handbook that a teacher could turn to and be inspired to integrate the humanities and social sciences into their course design and classroom practice. It provides a reservoir of ideas and concepts, examples and theories, histories and imaginings that might help to reinvent management education, perhaps encouraging us to think of 'management' less as a discipline and more as a topic of inquiry. Indeed as educators, we should all be inquirers into our own practices, narrating and sharing experiences with our colleagues as co-practitioners, altering our own approaches or inspiring those of others.

Second, we presume that for those who, like us, engage with theories, approaches and methods based on the humanities and the social sciences within or connected to the business school curricula, there is a motivation to do so that goes beyond professional research interests. We think, as do others (Gagliardi and Czarniawska 2006), that there is 'something', some particular sensibilities or styles, that the humanities and social sciences can provide for management education and its teachers and students, and we believe that such sensibilities and styles are both worthwhile and relevant. Much of this book is concerned with exploring the nature of this 'something' because we think that it is important to share and spread concepts, thoughts and experiences that can make these contributions more concrete and applicable.

Third, the sheer prominence that the business school and management education have acquired in the recent decades lends this undertaking some urgency. It suffices to point to the last and global financial crisis in order to start reflecting on what kinds of theories and sensibilities might be found wanting in contemporary management education. As the *Wall Street Journal* recently reported in language that radiated astonishment, some business schools now ask their students to read Marx and Kant in courses like 'Why capitalism?' (Korn 2014). Indeed, the movement of critical voices that goes under the name of critical management studies now seems to be spreading far from its northwest European heartlands (Grey *et al.* 2016). Elsewhere on campus, a global network of students of economics has taken matters into its own hands and demanded a curriculum that takes different kinds of knowledge as well as theoretical and methodological pluralism seriously in order to be able to reflect on economics' predicaments (International Student Initiative for Pluralism in Economics (ISIPE) 2014). In other words, it is high time to explore how the humanities and social sciences can intervene in management education precisely because the latter is often understood to be in crisis since it appears so insulated from the everyday concerns of global politics and civil society.

Fourth, we should write 'can *again* intervene in' because all of this is far from new (see French and Grey 1996; Parker and Jary 1995), and yet it is in need of reinvention. In fact, the humanities and social sciences have shaped management education from the get-go. Thinking historically, as several chapters early in this volume do, it seems that management education has been in crisis for quite a while; and the call for a more humanities- and social sciences-based curriculum (Zald 1996), or a return to the liberal arts tradition, is a quite well-rehearsed one. So we need to revisit these prior debates and remember neglected thinkers to think about what we might do anew, or do differently, in terms of reflecting on and practising teaching and learning at the business school.

Fifth, in our experience an interest in the relationship between the humanities, social sciences and management education is clearly growing. Perhaps this is simply because the ever-growing number and size of business schools has ushered in plenty of migrant scholars with different disciplinary backgrounds from what are usually called the 'core' subjects of management education. This may well be one of the causes of this reconsideration and reform of what the study of management should entail because 'outsiders' to the business school bring new ideas and have not yet adopted the common sense that isolates business from other disciplines (Parker 2015). That is why we feel that a more sustained discussion in the form of this Companion is needed to bring these voices, reflections and practices together to make them resound and circulate more widely.

Such is the rationale of this book. We seek to stage an intervention into the debates on what is taught at the business school and how learning takes place, and we aim to squarely position the humanities and social sciences within this discourse – where they belong. Thanks to the generous, thoughtful and eloquent contributions this book demonstrates both the manifold potential and the limits of what the humanities and social sciences can do to and with management education. Before the remainder of the introduction is given over to introducing the respective sections and chapters, we briefly outline the Companion's institutional and discursive contexts and how it originated and took shape.

## The rise and rise of management education

In the field of higher education, the position and role of the business school and its educational programmes have become increasingly prominent, and yet also increasingly questioned and contested. Although management education became a component in European and

North American higher education more than a century ago, the past few decades have seen a massive increase in student intake and, correspondingly, in teaching programmes as well as in the organizational forms of business school departments at universities and specialized business universities all over the world. For instance, the field of management and business studies is now the single largest area of research and education in the UK higher education system (Pettigrew *et al.* 2014). To some degree, the business school has become the institutional home to scholars and teachers with all sorts of disciplinary backgrounds, many of them from comparably more beleaguered departments of the humanities and other social sciences rather than from economics or business studies itself – a fact that is reflected in the professional trajectories of many of the contributors to this book.

The sheer number of students who opt for management programmes corresponds to the managerialization – and, more recently, entrepreneurialization – of all spheres of society. A degree in management is now often sold globally as a prerequisite for a professional career, whether it is sought in the cultural, public and social sector or, of course, the business world itself. What management education entails and how it is enacted has therefore become a matter of profound concern in the field of higher education and, more generally, for the development of the organized world (Pritchard 2012). Fed by successive financial crises, ethical scandals and ecological disasters but also by such evolutions as cognitive capitalism and digital labour (Peters and Bulut 2011), this concern is closely entangled with big questions concerning what kind of knowledge, practices, sensibilities and worldviews are conveyed and on offer in the university sector in general and in its business schools in particular. The scope and direction of management education then becomes a subject matter of great importance because it connects the future of the business school and university to the shaping of tomorrow's society and organizations. This Companion seeks to intervene in these debates and to interrogate if, what and how the humanities and social sciences can contribute to reinventing the education of what, in business school contexts, are routinely addressed as future managers, entrepreneurs or decision-makers.

## Problematizing management education

The business school's rise to prominence and power is accompanied by periodic outbursts of critical scrutiny, self-reflexivity and soul-searching. In recent times, there seems to be at least one so-called 'crisis' per decennium that calls provocatively for 'a debate' (Willmott 1994), that points to 'the end of business schools' (Pfeffer and Fong 2002), that proposes 'a hard look' at management education (Mintzberg 2004), or suggests that business schools have 'lost their way' (Bennis and O'Toole 2005) or sees them 'in ruins' (Starkey and Tempest 2006), followed by calls for rethinking management education (French and Grey 1996), for linking to the social sciences and humanities (Zald 1996), for coupling academic rigour with external relevance (Starkey and Madan 2001), or for developing new agendas (Clegg *et al.* 2011). Against this background of critical attention and sustained insecurity, there is a growing number of works on the historical conditions and development of the business school and management education (Augier and March 2011; Colby *et al.* 2011; Khurana 2007; O'Connor 2012; Pettigrew *et al.* 2014; Starkey and Tiratsoo 2007).

Some of these studies also provide the current debate with new routes to consider as they call for an intensified reliance on what is called liberal arts education in the North American context, giving new prominence to the humanities and social sciences. One of the main ideas concerning the direction and outlook of the educational philosophy, programmes and practices that ground the future of management education is to find solutions for the tension between offering a general, academic education in the tradition of the liberal arts that orients learning towards ethical and political responsibility within a broader sociocultural framework, and the desire for a specialist and practice-oriented learning profile that can draw upon technical skills and practical wisdom. This 'broad' versus 'narrow' metaphor runs through many of the chapters in this book, questioning as it does the epistemological divisions and institutional compartments that produce 'management education'.

We believe that the refreshed focus on the humanities and social sciences and what they might do to reinvent management education is not a secondary or supplementary exercise to the 'real' business of business school teaching and learning. It seems commonplace (and perhaps all too comfortable) to bring in the humanities and social sciences as an add-on and perhaps 'corrective' to what are usually presented as core areas of management education (perhaps echoing the 'compensation thesis' of the philosopher Odo Marquard (1986), according to which the humanities' role is to counterbalance and perhaps atone for the damages wrought by technological–scientific progress). However, one should note that the concerns of the humanities and social sciences have informed and shaped the study and teaching of management education from the start (see Rhodes; and Parker, this volume). The subject of business and management was itself produced as a pot-pourri of ideas from pre-existing disciplines because it could not produce itself from nothing. Simply put, the study of management and organization would look entirely different were it not for the thoughts and categories of, for example, Marx, Durkheim and Weber, or the forms of thought generated in disciplinary categories such as political economy, anthropology and philosophy. Using an insight from the philosopher Michel Serres, we might say that 'management' emerged and developed as a parasite, intercepting and extracting value (in the form of theories, concepts, methods) from humanities-based and social-theoretical thinking, perhaps taking without giving (see Brown, this volume).

The humanities and social sciences have thus infused and shaped what is being taught at business schools, even if contemporary versions of management and organization studies often prefer watered-down and more instrumental accounts of what it means to make sense of organizational life. Attempting to reinvigorate the role of the humanities and social sciences in management education is not a fringe exercise dabbling with exotic concepts and approaches on the margins of the real stuff – it is the real stuff and it has the potential to influence and transform what is taught and learned at business schools and how learning and teaching takes place. This Companion is situated in and seeks to revitalize this tradition of inventing and shaping management education. (For a while, we thought about simply calling this endeavour the 'Companion to Management Education', and let the chapters speak for themselves.)

Although based on a rich heritage of problematizing and reimagining management education, the Companion responds to a climate and debates that are very much of the moment. As noted earlier, there has been an increasing interest in rethinking the theory and practice of management education by encouraging interdisciplinary inquiry with knowledge and practices from the humanities and social sciences. In this sense, this book has profited from a number of conversations and experiments that we wish to foreground in the form of two trajectories. The first is the recent Carnegie II Report on 'The future of business education' (Colby *et al.* 2011), which presents the integration of liberal learning into undergraduate (and graduate) business education as one of the central challenges for business schools and business universities. Notably, the report calls upon the humanities so that business students can better learn to deal with the complexities of a globalized world market and societies under transition, which would require various essential competencies: analytical skills, multi-perspectivism and personal growth and mastery. These are related through integrative practical skills, which will be needed supposedly by a future employee or entrepreneur thrown into the cultural and technical dynamics of worldwide capitalism (see Sullivan, Ehrlich and Colby, this volume).

Following the Carnegie Report, a series of conversations in the North American and European context have turned this most recent call to reconsider the humanities 'for' management education into a broader movement and towards a research agenda that this Companion picks up and unfolds. This began with a Roundtable in 2011 at the Copenhagen Business School, Denmark, and was followed by the Aspen Institute Conference in the US as well as the Professional Development Workshop on 'Integrating liberal learning and business education: putting the Carnegie Report into practice' at the Academy of Management in Boston in 2012. A series of workshops followed: 'Practicing humanities and social sciences in management education' at the University of St Gallen, Switzerland, in 2012, and then events in Copenhagen (2013), at the University of Essex, UK (2014) and at Ca' Foscari University in Venice, Italy (2015).

These four workshops were the outcome of a second and parallel trajectory that emerged from a cooperation between the University of St Gallen and the German Haniel Foundation. Dedicated to the nexus of entrepreneurial practice and social transformation, one of the foundation's main concerns is the support of both students and universities that seek to interrogate the relation between entrepreneurial and sociocultural thought and foster educational programmes and pedagogies that experiment with new ways of connecting management education to matters of societal concern. Since 2003, what is now called the 'European Haniel programme on entrepreneurship and the humanities' has enabled a series of courses and teaching events dedicated to humanities- and social sciences-based concerns and pedagogies at the business universities of St Gallen and Copenhagen, as well as workshops (one of them specifically dedicated to this Companion) and faculty exchanges. This book is the document of these trajectories and conversations; we hope that it provokes their continuation as well as the invention of new debates, cooperations and interventions.

## From histories to futures: the Companion structure and chapters

This volume is divided into six parts. Parts I to V comprise six chapters and Part VI has seven chapters. Part I on 'histories' retraces different elements of the history of management education, touching upon important debates and developments and how they might inform the contemporary situation. Part II on 'philosophies' delves into the works of distinct philosophical thinkers that provoke a reassessment and reimagination of central educational principles that inform teaching and learning at the business school and the university more widely. Part III on 'concepts' is dedicated to important social-theoretical approaches and how these can inform business school pedagogies that are based on an emerging practice-based approach to management education. Although all contributions up to this point in the book in some way or other relate historical and conceptual interrogations to experiences of teaching and learning, Parts IV and V more closely and exemplarily engage with the practices and structures of business school curricula: Part IV moves into (or out of ) 'classrooms' and explores how courses and educational practices can be reinvented. Part V turns to the institutional work of constructing and establishing management 'programmes' based on the humanities and social sciences in the context (or confines) of business schools. The final and sixth part outlines the future challenges that will further influence the ways the humanities and social sciences will be applied and translated in management education.

## Part I: histories

In order to understand the present and shape the future it is always a pretty good idea to try and learn from the past. If we look to the past, we see that the idea that management education is in crisis is not a new one. We can also see that the division between business and management, and the humanities and social sciences, has been seen to be a problem on several previous occasions too. This suggests that it would be productive to begin by trying to understand how the business school has grown and what sort of borrowings and inventions have given it the shape it currently has; however, we also need to be sensitive to national and regional differences because, as many chapters in this book amply demonstrate, the institution has grown very differently in different places.

We begin with a chapter that reviews the 2011 Carnegie Report on the humanities and management education and its impact. In 'The Carnegie Report: looking back and thinking forward', William Sullivan, Tom Ehrlich and Anne Colby reaffirm the importance of liberal learning that underpins all the chapters in this book and suggest (as do many others) that the contemporary US business school has drifted away from its original mission. They begin by summarizing their premises, the plan of their research and their key recommendations that suggest that there is an affinity between the needs of a knowledge-based capitalism and the forms of character and intellect produced by a humanities education. They then move on to describe the book's reception in the US and Europe. It is followed with a view of the future direction of this work and its chief challenges, concluding with several examples of how these challenges can be overcome in a reconstituted model of undergraduate business education.

Ellen S. O'Connor's chapter that follows begins by examining Joseph Wharton's plan for the Collegiate School of Business (CSB), which produced the first business school in the US. In 'The test of time: historical perspectives on management education reform in the US', O'Connor argues that Wharton was interested in the college because of its cultural function and because he wanted to pass on what he and his peers deemed to be valuable. Most colleges had a curriculum that focused on Latin, Greek and classical literature and graduates were intended to take their inherited position in society; however, there was a disconnect because science was growing from an amateur to a highly organized activity and to an economic engine. Wharton deemed that the college's failure to engage with these developments held back and even threatened society. He reformed the college to help change his society's values, but the substantive work of Wharton's college is still relevant to us today in understanding and mastering the creative processes enabled by science, industry and other institutions. O'Connor thus turns to the pioneering work of Follett, Barnard and Bach in the early US business school in order to revisit and revive the original project of building an institution dedicated to understanding collective creativity, including that discovered within the arts and humanities. Early thinkers knew that this focus entails transcending disciplinary and professional boundaries and that the categories that nowadays constitute the field of management and organization as we know it must be rethought and reworked.

Ulrike Landfester, Nicolaj Tofte Brenneche and Queralt Prat-i-Pubill use their chapter to explore the genre of reporting on the present state and crises of management education. In '"Humanities' business" and other narratives: how to read the future of management education' they show how reports on management education perform in the context in which the necessity of changes becomes visible and inescapable. Analysing three recent reports in some detail, including the Carnegie Report, they show how these texts determine which issues are rendered critical and which are marginalized or left out altogether, as well as which purposes of management education are seen as central and which interventions and changes are proposed to accomplish these purposes. They conclude by noting that the institution of the modern university reacted to the explosion of knowledge generated by the Enlightenment by compartmentalizing knowledge into sub-institutional entities in charge of clearly circumscribed smaller fields. This in itself created structural constraints that over the years have hardened into an essentialist notion of disciplinary knowledge with canonical core knowledge at the heart of each discipline. This means that it is hard to imagine such disciplines ceding their mysteries in order to put them at the disposition of any kind of integrationist endeavour. The reports on management education, when understood as texts that achieve effects, often reproduce precisely the problems they diagnose.

In the following chapter, 'Deschooling the manager through the humanities: Mintzberg's amateurish conscience', Nidhi Srinivas explores the work of Henry Mintzberg, who is perhaps one of the most prominent commentators on management education writing at the present time. Srinivas argues that Mintzberg's philosophy of education, combined with his 'late style', has not received sufficient attention. Srinivas makes a convincing case that we can understand this philosophy as an explicit claim to engage with a sensibility that is inherited from the humanities. Mintzberg's claim is for alternative pedagogies to restrain the dangers of corporate power, of technical rationality and societal imbalance that steer away from the certified education offered on MBA programmes. This is work that offers an important provocative critique of management and its prevailing forms of education and research. Ultimately, however, Srinivas argues that it remains unsatisfying for critics (and Ivan Illich is his touchstone here) who wish to take aim at expert power, neoliberal capital and societal inequality. Srinivas assesses Mintzberg's theoretical project in terms of its humanistic potential, particularly as a critique of technocratic knowledge, such as that produced for and by managers. He suggests that is 'it goes some distance but not far enough', largely because it assumes amateurism and common sense will save us from the dominion of MBAs.

Linda Perriton and Amritesh Singh follow this by showing how more self-consciously 'critical' work operates in the context of the management school, particularly in the UK. Like O'Connor, they argue in their chapter that the possibilities for incorporating critical innovation in business schools have been present since their foundation. The broad academic terrain that the management degree covers has allowed space for experimentation and cross-fertilization from other disciplines; however, they suggest that the combined effects of marketization and the narrowing of the perceived purpose of university education to a vocational credentialism are now creating difficulties for established critical approaches. There is a sense that previous ground won for critical management studies and critical management education is under threat. In 'Critical voices in management education in the UK', Perriton and Singh suggest that if the next critical push against technical rational modes of management education is to come in the guise of the liberal arts then the requirement for reflexivity about whose cultural texts is employed is even greater. Not to do so reduces the liberal arts 'approach' to a pirate raid on other disciplines, probably for decorative purposes, rather than the application of critical sensibility to the design of teaching and learning.

The final chapter in Part I by Dirk Baecker explores the paradox of teaching people about something that they need to experience to understand, but that is theorized (in the German context anyway) as being necessarily bracketed away from practice. Drawing on his experience of management and teaching at two German universities, Baecker shows that a great deal of the work of sociology in management education consists in bringing in not only an understanding of the concept of organization but also an understanding of the distinction between organization on one hand and interaction and society on the other. Understanding management therefore begins right under our noses by observing our own institutions. 'A sociology of management in management education' begins with Erich Gutenberg's ingenious foundation of German *Betriebswirtschaftslehre*, which calls for economic efficiency and technological efficacy to rule an organization that is turned into a *Betrieb* by bracketing its complexity. If we reference efficiency and efficacy, we can derive a generalized notion of management as getting action by blocking action. Baecker introduces an understanding of communication to explain the one in terms of the other, and concludes by drawing some consequences for management education, which begins and ends with students gaining a critical knowledge of themselves moving reflexively within different domains of communication.

## Part II: philosophies

The question of the humanities and social sciences in management education takes on a double sense. It is about how philosophical and social–theoretical thought can be brought into the classroom and inform the practices of teaching and learning, and yet there is more to the collision between theories and business schools. There is a rich reservoir of thought that more fundamentally allows and provokes us to ponder the very assumptions that shape the concepts and practices of university education and how we might need to rethink them. Reinventing management education not only means reconsidering what and how we teach, it also means reconsidering education itself. This part is dedicated to such philosophies. It is predicated on the simple, yet perhaps often forgotten point that what we do as educators is entangled with how we implicitly theorize education. Any kind of educational practice is intertwined with theoretical assumptions or regimes of thought. It follows that what problematizes and unsettles such assumptions and regimes can make us rethink – and therefore potentially change – how management education takes place. Rather than offering answers or blueprints, the chapters in Part II raise questions. They problematize what is usually taken for granted, thereby forcing us to think with them (or against them). We might therefore say that the authors invited to contribute to this part present and explore theories and thinkers that pose problems and enable different, sometimes radically different, approaches to how university education is conceived. Their 'lessons' are uneasy, yet productive ones. In this sense, the thinkers that populate the pages of this part – Nietzsche, Whitehead, Jonas, Serres, Rancière and Derrida – are not 'educational theorists'. Although some of them have written on education (Rancière and Serres), they cannot be integrated into or simply read from within any established discourse or practice of education. This is precisely what makes these thoughts provocative, even radical. Either unburdened by or directed against established pedagogical systems, they ask us to think anew about their governing assumptions and tropes. In so doing, they might change the way we teach. In 'Nietzsche as educator', Daniel Hjorth and Robin Holt dwell on some of the writings of the iconoclastic philosopher par excellence to unsettle what seems to be taken for granted, perhaps cynically so, in contemporary management education. Focusing on – and borrowing the title from – Nietzsche's reflections on 'Schopenhauer as educator', Hjorth and Holt quite alarmingly present how the philosopher's untimely thoughts have lost none of their relevance and bite. It is the 'stagnant pools' of money-makers, the state and the university, or the 'threads of money, state power and proven truths', that manage life and are themselves the productions of knowledge and education. Thinking with Schopenhauer and Nietzsche, the authors sketch and probe a notion of education and learning, of provocation and overcoming that goes beyond the safety of managed, stagnant pools. Business schools, it is implicitly suggested in these orderings, might be just the places for experimenting with pedagogies of passion, generosity, cheerfulness and questionability.

Such pedagogies also require a reconsideration of 'relevance', a shibboleth of management education discourse. In 'The art of relevation/revelation: a Whiteheadian approach to management education', Robert Chia and Ajit Nayak turn to the process philosophy of Alfred North Whitehead in order to reconsider the notion of relevance. If management is considered more a science than an art and is more about facts and universal principles than about sensitivity and imagination in dealing with the particularities of concrete situations, then management education becomes 'simply' the task of transmitting expert knowledge to students, and yet this notion of relevance is flawed. Management education, Chia and Nayak argue, ought to also focus on nurturing an art of relevation/revelation amongst students whereby the seemingly irrelevant, the apparently unconnected and the hidden are imaginatively linked together and/or revealed. Such a practice makes meaning and consequence in order that horizons of comprehension are expanded and the possibilities of decision enlarged. Drawing on insights from art education, the authors discuss how such an 'art' is attained by focusing on cultivating empirical sensitivity, refining perceptual awareness and expanding the powers of imagination within the management education process. It is thus associated with an artistic (as opposed to a scientific) rigour that is eminently relevant and useful in the world of management practice.

The next shibboleth in need of scrutiny and reconsideration is 'responsibility'. Can business school classrooms become places to ponder and maintain a meaningful sense of responsibility? In his chapter on 'Responsibility: Hans Jonas and the ethics of business', René ten Bos turns to the thought of this German philosopher in order to pose to management education the one question that, according to Jonas, really matters: 'how do we respond to the demand of survival that life as such poses to us?'. Showing that the very point of management ethics as it is practised and taught is that the idea of responsibility should disappear, ten Bos presents a notion of responsibility that is not difficult to comprehend, but difficult to enact. Rather than reducing the complexity of ethics to codes, lists or the concept of accountability, responsibility is the permanent, straightforward and irreducible imperative to reflect about one's embeddedness in the world and to act towards the conservation, protection and preservation of animated and non-animated beings.

This kind of ecological thinking has interesting links to the reimagination of 'knowledge' that informs Steven D. Brown's chapter 'They have escaped the weight of darkness: the problem space of Michel Serres'. Knowledge, Brown argues, should be seen as a patchwork, locally situated in bodies and in relational practices and encounters. As such, it is non-hierarchical, unbound to epistemological grids that need to be enforced through strategies of violence and hygiene. The implications for thinking and practising management education are radical. Rather than advocating alternative approaches and their own strategies of exclusion, a sideways approach of moving between concepts, practices, idioms and other forms of sense-making emerges. Brown traces different routes of imagining management education through such multiplicity: a dark organizational theory dedicated to the parasitical character of organization and management; detachment as the study of different forms of sustainable living and, perhaps, anti-parasitical organization; and the employment of different archetypes and images to understand and open up the tropes of, for instance, strategy, marketing and finance. Thinking with Serres, he suggests, can be translated into concrete practices of reconsidering management and organization with students.

Reconsidering knowledge, relevance and responsibility and the way they are enacted in the classroom has clear reverberations for the politics of education. In 'Can management education practise Rancière?', Isabelle Huault and Véronique Perret engage with the thought of Jacques Rancière in order to challenge the assumption and practice of inequality and the hierarchy of intelligences that undergird the pedagogical relations of management education. In his book *The Ignorant Schoolmaster*, Rancière mounted both a stinging critique of pedagogical theories and programmes – not least so-called critical ones – and an idiosyncratic case for the equality of intelligences, which an 'ignorant' education would need to assert and actualize rather than suppress different ways of knowing and defer to authority. Can business schools become territories for 'ignorant educators'? Huault and Perret explore how such a radical rejection of the assumed mastery of the educator might be translated into, and re-energize, the practices and politics of management education. To do so, they narrate and ponder an example of an alternative pedagogical design enacted through a collaborative art project.

The meeting of art and philosophy is particularly fruitful for reconsidering the pedagogical principles of management education. Taking their cue from the encounter of Jacques Derrida with the influential jazz musician Ornette Coleman, Mark Learmonth, Mike Humphreys and Martyn Griffin's chapter is dedicated to 'Doing management education with free jazz and Derrida'. The 'doing' is important here: management education is something to be entered into, participated in, experienced and collaboratively shaped. Moreover, the notion of radical improvisation – and its corollaries of risk and uncertainty – can shift and open up sedimented modes of thinking and acting. In what Derrida has called the 'unconditional university', it demands experimenting with collective and democratic participation between students and teachers, but also in academic life more generally. This chapter concludes this part on theory by suggesting that the distinction between theory and practice is a flawed one, and that it is by doing that we come to understand what we have done.

## Part III: concepts

In Part III, we develop some 'guiding concepts' that refer to conceptual approaches that have been prominently developed over the years in the social sciences, and that are adopted and adapted within the context of management education: experimentalism (Brandi and Elkjaer), wisdom (Statler and Salovaara), critique (Vince), imagination (De Cock), sociomateriality (Fenwick) and practice (Gherardi). This part continues and expands the exploration of philosophical approaches from Part II as these social–theoretical approaches – experiential learning theory, psychodynamic theory, critical theory, sociomaterial and practice-based approaches – come with their own philosophical underpinnings: Dewey (Brandi and Elkjaer, Statler and Salovaara), Castoriadis (De Cock), Deleuze and Braidotti (Fenwick, Gherardi). Part III is also programmatic because the connections between these various conceptual approaches, stylishly interrelated and reconstructed by Silvia Gherardi at the end of the part, also point to an emerging practice-based approach to management education. As the chapters can be seen as conceptually focused, they are also excellently illustrated: some authors (Statler and Salovaara, Vince, De Cock) give detailed and in-depth insight into reflections of the social dynamics of their courses, whilst others (Brandi and Elkjaer, Fenwick) exemplify creative ways through which courses and programmes can become reshaped.

Ulrik Brandi and Bente Elkjaer open Part III with a chapter entitled 'Management education in a pragmatist perspective after Dewey's experimentalism', which explores one of the most important educational philosophers in (management) education, namely the US pragmatist John Dewey (1859–1952). Dewey saw education as part of laying the grounds for an engaged population with an ability to deal with the problems at hand and to anticipate what to do next. The terms that Brandi and Elkjaer identify as core to Dewey's work on education are the concepts of 'experience', 'inquiry' and 'experimentalism'. Based on a literature review of recent contributions in the three major journals in the field of management education and learning, the authors suggest that these terms have inspired educationalists to work with an experiential approach to teaching, to use reflection as a way to turn experiences into knowledge and to experiment with different methods of teaching. The authors also identify two versions of the contemporary heritage of pragmatism, one in which individuality and cognition stand out and the other in which we are in the realm of culture and practice. Dewey's experimentalist approach to education maintains a playful, yet reflective pedagogy in which management practice, marked by complexity, comes to life in how we educate for management.

In the next chapter 'Thinking in and of the world: actualizing wisdom and pragmatism in business schools?', Matt Statler and Perttu Salovaara continue to explore the possibilities of Dewey's philosophy of knowledge as they take up questions about how practical wisdom – and the (Ancient) Greek concept of *phronesis* – may be developed among business students. As they focus on the educational practices that involve learning through experience, the authors revisit John Dewey's pragmatic ontology of knowledge and his adage that 'all knowledge is created in and through practical involvement with the world', showing how this conceptualization of experience and its interplay of energies can provide guidance for educators and students seeking to develop wise habits of inquiry. Wisdom is seen as the habit of reflecting critically on the processes of habituation by which we shape our individual and collective experience. The authors develop a normative guide for how wisdom can be developed in business schools. Through a case illustration – richly illustrated with students' experiences with 'consulting' to non-profit organizations – of Dewey's notion of wisdom as the habit of habits, they provide us with striking reflections of students and facilitators on the social dynamics that transform pedagogical practice into wise habits of learning.

In the following chapter entitled 'The art and practice of critique: the possibilities of critical psychodynamic education', Russ Vince also engages with critical reflection and develops one of the themes in critical management education as introduced by Perriton and Singh in Part I (see also Brandi and Elkjaer), offering some reflections on the possibilities of a psychodynamically inspired critical education in the management context. In particular, Vince argues that one way to introduce critique into management education is by reflecting on the emotions and power relations that surround attempts to learn about leading, managing and organizing. According to Vince, the ability to engage with emotions and power relations in the classroom depends on a willingness to 'hold students in the moment' so they can understand their experiences through feeling them. Furthermore, he argues that one should acknowledge the assumption that it is also likely during critical reflection to be mobilizing the power relations that one is seeking to transform. Through three beautiful, yet unassuming experiments with relational and spatial dimensions in the classroom, the author documents how learning for students of management becomes understanding that critical reflection is thus based on the willingness to unsettle current ideas, habits, stuck emotions, defences and prevailing relations of power. This also offers a more general critique of established views of managing and leading as activities focused primarily on positive skills and behaviour that are generally applicable.

In his chapter 'From creativity to imagination with Cornelius Castoriadis', Christian De Cock takes up a personal concern with the inertia of the creativity literature of the past 20 years and proposes to unlock its stalemate by giving more attention to imagination, a concept with a remarkable pedigree historically. De Cock neatly summarizes the problems with the creativity literature and how it lacks creative scholarship itself, and then he leads us on a short historical narrative away from creativity to the neglected notion of the imagination. This is followed by an exposition of the thinking of the Greek–French philosopher and psychoanalyst Cornelius Castoriadis, alongside De Cock's account of how he has shifted the practices of his classes on creativity and innovation to stimulate and develop his own students' imagination. The creative dimension of imagination for Castoriadis is not primarily linked to the generation of ideas, but rather to the capacity to question already given determinations and to reimagine what others have imagined before us. Conceptualizing imagination (and creativity) as profoundly political, historical and social, De Cock makes a crucial move in the context of management education by linking this thinking back to the notion of organization and institutions.

In the next chapter, Tara Fenwick engages with the possibilities of inducting new professionals into the practices and politics into the practices and politics of emerging, dynamic complexity. Taking issue with 'What *matters* in sociomateriality: towards a critical posthuman pedagogy in management education', she takes critical education to another place in an attempt to develop a critical posthuman pedagogy that can also become enacted in the management context as a productive practice-based learning. The author anticipates a radical revision of issues of agency, politics and ontology in management education, turning to a posthuman sensibility that appreciates the entanglements of students, educators and other actants with sociomaterial forces beyond themselves. A materialist analysis of and approach to education is oriented at change through finding and entering the fissures of dominant explanations and institutions, tampering with their weak points and amplifying emergent possibilities. Fenwick is keen to illustrate a sociomaterial approach by developing concepts such as learning 'disruption', 'emergence' and 'difference' that can guide current experiments in the educational landscape. The various illustrations aim for a very different platform of learning as sociomaterial approaches are addressing the most pressing ethical political concerns of our world, and yet they also illustrate some of the crucial parameters for attending to the daily enactment of a critical posthuman pedagogy.

This part collects a range of concepts based on explaining their social–theoretical approaches and philosophical underpinnings to education, but they are also connected by a so-called practice-based understanding of learning and education. In 'The practice-turn in management pedagogy: a cross-reading', Silvia Gherardi traces the various strings that the chapters provide to reconstruct a practice-based pedagogical approach to management education according to three questions: what is taken to be pedagogy; where and how do pedagogical processes take place; and what effects on management education are intended? Gherardi argues that the challenge for experimentation with management education is an open possibility to engage with ways to denaturalize the world of management as we know it in order to keep it open for new practices to emerge and become institutionalized. Furthermore, she believes that these chapters are good examples of what is core to the practice-researcher, namely to value talking, reading and engaging with other co-practitioners and thus to experience the possibility of confronting practices and their local bricolage differently in one's own practice. Practising with others makes our own practice different.

## Part IV: classrooms

In this part, we move from a practice-based understanding of management pedagogy to the various practices that explore how management education can be done differently in the classroom and beyond: film, television and digital social media; activist and spatial experiments; and art and performance. Drawing upon the personal experiences and experiments with a range of communicative, spatial, affective and aesthetic dimensions, the chapters form lively and thick examples of how classrooms can become reshaped and reinvented. Although these examples are all locally embedded, they nevertheless form important inspirations both for individual teachers and also for rethinking the ways we imagine pedagogies and programmes of management education that we will turn to in Part V.

One of the recent changes in the experience of learning is the way in which films, television series, cartoons or documentaries have become shown and reflected upon in management and organization classes (Bell 2008; Bilsberry *et al.* 2012) and which are increasingly complemented by videos and images on YouTube or Instagram or in popular culture generally. In the chapter 'Re-envisaging leadership through the feminine imaginary in film and television', Emma Bell and Amanda Sinclair question how leadership is usually taught in a normative and individualistic way and they look at the possibilities of experiential approaches (as prepared in Part III) through film and television, which can form a substitute for personal experience and help to connect the classroom to a 'here-and-now' moment of critical reflection (see Vince, this volume). Drawing upon feminist film theory, Bell and Sinclair propose a critical view to reading films that enables students to challenge gendered stereotypes and embodied norms and to explore alternative understandings of leadership. In particular, the authors turn to the Danish TV series *Borgen*, which they suggest is important in enabling the representation of female leaders in dynamic and embodied ways. This involves developing images of female characters enacting leadership in ways that through their aesthetic force contest dominant forms and traditional ways of seeing women as leaders and that resist surveillance of how women (are supposed to) appear. In their analysis of some fragments (which could easily be used in a class), Bell and Sinclair discuss some of the embodied responses by the women protagonists in *Borgen* and point to the possibility of a feminine imaginary that disrupts the patriarchal order and highlights the erotic nature of leadership.

With the chapter 'Hacking the classroom: rethinking learning through social media practices' by Götz Bachmann and Nishant Shah, we leave the world of visual media and enter the one of digital social media, whose ubiquity transforms the learning situation as students' presence becomes one with connected devices, streaming data, chatting on personal messaging and sharing information with invisible audiences. Using the metaphor of 'hacking the classroom', Bachmann and Shah show how the classroom can be reconfigured and recreated as 'a multi-modal, multi-media, affective and sharing atmosphere'. In a critical affirmative tone, the authors not only sketch the rise and decline of massive open online courses (MOOC) but they also interrogate and understand the similarities and differences between digital platforms such as Wikipedia, Bulletin Boards, Facebook and Twitter. In their conclusion, the authors point to how the relationships between (digital) technology and pedagogy can become recursive, reminding us that the classroom was always a hybrid of human and technology.

In the following two chapters, we join the idea that we do not need to stay within the classroom spaces that are allocated to us by the administration because the world itself – a particular social site or an urban neighbourhood – can be(come) a classroom. Ester Barinaga, in her chapter 'Activism in business education: making the social sciences practical for social entrepreneurs', explores the possibilities of encouraging students to display activism during her course on social entrepreneurship. In the learning process, the course design connects insightful concepts from social theory, illustrative case examples (developed by the author) and a guide to ethnographic practices through which students can themselves engage with social entrepreneurial processes. Overall, the chapter brings forward a notion of activism with different 'intensities' that varies between engaging with the activism of others in cases, engaging with the life worlds of social entrepreneurs through qualitative research methods, and also engaging with a form of activism based on students developing their own venture. In this sense, Barinaga tries to balance the attraction students might have with the passionate stories of social entrepreneurial initiatives, the focus on relevance and learning about the practice of social entrepreneurship and the necessary emphasis on the political, ethical and ideological aspects of business activity to create a critical awareness of social entrepreneurship.

Christoph Michels and Timon Beyes in their chapter on 'Spaces with a temper: on atmospheres of education' approach classrooms not only as social spaces but also in relation to their material–affective dimensions (see Fenwick, this volume) to understand their affective registers and also their connection to the spatial atmospherics of the university campus. Drawing upon a performative understanding of space (as suggested by Lefebvre and further developed through non-representational theory), Michels and Beyes develop what they call a 'pedagogy of atmospheres'.

As they discuss snapshots from three different courses, the authors exemplify in a specific way the spatial multiplicity of learning spaces, including those of the city around the university. Based on these experiments with and modulations of the contours of the classroom, these small interruptions of the atmospheric conditions make us aware of how learning can become alive and embodied, something that is core in the following chapters.

In the final two chapters of this part, we enter classrooms inspired by artistic and aesthetic practices. Stefan Meisiek, Pierre Guillet de Monthoux, Daved Barry and Robert D. Austin form a wonderful quartet of voices to share experiences that tell us how art and artistic practices have influenced and fundamentally altered how their classrooms look and feel. Their storytelling piece 'Four voices: making a difference with art in management education' is a lively example of how generative a dialogue between art and management can become as they turn their rich experiences into a collage of suggestions: from enacting novels to theatre plays, from exploring artistic styles of famous artists to visiting artists' studios, and from writing a fictionalized case study to designing a (pop-up) studio. Although each author shows how art holds inspiration for understanding management and how this has changed their teaching approach accordingly, they also focus on a different aspect of the artistic process, namely form (Rob Austin), medium (Daved Barry), mirror (Pierre Guillet de Monthoux), and place (Stefan Meisiek).

Finally, the chapter 'Playing and the performing arts: six memos for the future classroom' written by Chris Steyaert, Patrizia Hoyer and Bernhard Resch is focused on the mode of playing that features prominently in the performing arts. Inspired by Italo Calvino's ideas on the future of literature in the form of memos, they try to imagine in a similar way how classrooms might become enacted differently in the future by writing memos on features such as inventiveness, thirdness, playfulness, experimentalism, nimbleness and asceticism/athleticism. Remembering some innovative opera and dance performances in the Brussels art scene, they reflect upon how these artistic companies are engaging with experimentation and how this is mirrored in approaches to art education. Considering the creative bravura of the performing arts and their educational practices, the authors urge us to experiment with how management education can be done with similar danger and daring, giving some inspiration to 'swim along with them' by turning to some illustrative practices from three Master's courses.

## Part V: programmes

In Part V, we move from the practices of teaching to the institutional practices of establishing and working with the humanities and social sciences in the context of business schools, their study programmes and curricula, and not least their power structures. What kind of exemplary models can we discern that have managed to alter the institutional frameworks and study architectures of business schools, enabling and inventing heterotopic spaces of education (Beyes and Michels 2011)? How is such 'other content' related to the allegedly dominant issues of business education? What can we learn from the reflections of colleagues who have many years of experience of both organizing and teaching the humanities and (other) social sciences in the business school context? And finally everybody knows (one might hum along with Leonard Cohen's song of the same name) that every form and practice of teaching that seeks to make a difference is predicated on, and tied to, the institutional labour of carving out and holding on to its own space. Who else but scholars of organization and management should be aware of the organizational struggles around trying to change the education of students routinely addressed as future managers?

In his chapter on 'Permission taking: the humanities and critical pedagogy in the MBA', Carl Rhodes offers quite an ingenious response to these questions, especially to the question of how to make a difference institutionally. Without dismissing the importance of university and educational politics, Rhodes asks us to focus on the very place where we can make a difference – that is the classroom and teaching itself – and thus prepares a perfect transition from Part IV. As teachers of management – and not of the humanities or other social sciences – we can and must 'take permission' to connect with the humanities and bring in critical and unsettling perspectives, thinkers and texts. As the author illustrates through personal examples, this can be done and is acknowledged by the students even in the comparably instrumental setting of an MBA education. Moreover, such permission taking is actually rather easy, Rhodes argues, because 'management' is not a discipline; it has always relied on the import of theorems and concepts from the 'proper' disciplines of the humanities and social sciences. The institutional pressures, here discussed in the form of accreditation agencies and the textbook industry, are much less forceful than often imagined or depicted. Therefore, not to take permission, Rhodes poignantly concludes, is an affront to the profession of scholarly teaching.

In their chapter on 'Knowledge you can't google: teaching philosophy at the business school', Rasmus Johnsen, Morten Sørensen Thaning and Michael Pedersen present and discuss what, following Rhodes, can be called an act of institutional permission taking in relation to the humanities and management education. After outlining the development and the contours of the study programme in 'Philosophy and business administration' at Copenhagen Business School, Denmark, the authors suggest conceiving of philosophy's significant contribution to management education through the notions of problematization and responsibility. On this basis, they reflect upon three concrete examples of the programme's compulsory courses that seek to align philosophical texts and theorems with problems that emerge in a business study context. This kind of 'reciprocal integration' of philosophy and business education, as the authors call it, not only works to establish humanities-based teaching within management education, it also points to a way of learning attuned to reflexivity and responsibility.

From Copenhagen we move to Milan, Italy, and to Bocconi University's degree in 'Management for the arts, culture and communication' at Bachelor's level, founded in 1999, and its more recent Master of Science in 'Economics and management in arts, culture, media and entertainment'. In their chapter on 'Liberal arts in business and business in liberal arts: the view from Bocconi', Paola Dubini and Elena Raviola combine the perspectives of cofounder and programme director as well as former student and then teacher, respectively, to present and reflect upon the programme's history, principles, pedagogies and effects. Dubini and Raviola describe an encouraging and perhaps unlikely success story: the establishment of a popular, in-demand curriculum anchored in the tradition of the liberal arts in the context of a business university guided by managerialist and economistic positions and attitudes. The authors base their discussion on a foundational, unresolved and yet productive tension and debate: do these study programmes specifically educate managers 'for' the arts and the cultural sector, or do they more broadly offer an education in the liberal arts for future managers? Given the programme's results and effects, it seems that the question need not be resolved because a curriculum that takes the humanities and social sciences seriously operates in both directions.

However, the question of how to institutionally integrate the humanities and social sciences in management education can also be answered differently. Thomas S. Eberle and Jörg Metelmann's chapter on 'Integrating humanities and social sciences: institutionalizing a contextual studies programme' is dedicated to the contextual studies programme at the University of St Gallen, Switzerland. Here, curricular innovation did not take the form of a specific degree; rather, the humanities and social sciences were conceived of and established as an integral part of all study programmes on offer at a business university. Taking up a quarter of the overall study time, the contextual studies programme cuts across all specializations and is a mandatory part of every student's trajectory at both Bachelor's and Master's level. After outlining the aims and components of the contextual studies, Eberle and Metelmann reflect on the experiences and major challenges of these integrative efforts by taking up the perspectives of programme organizers, the wider faculty and the students. In identifying the crucial issues of conflicting educational models, disciplinary 'silo thinking' and a university's culture, the authors offer experience-based insights into how to think and practise the integration of humanities and social sciences in business school contexts.

Although the debates and initiatives on the development of management education tend to focus on undergraduate, Master and MBA degrees, much less ink is spilled on the state and future of doctoral programmes. The final two chapters in this part seek to redress this situation and are ideally read in tandem. Barbara Czarniawska frames her thought-provoking comments on 'Survivors of an endangered species: doctoral programmes of the future' as a starting point for a conversation. Marton Racz, himself a doctoral student at the time of writing his chapter, continues and further stimulates what we hope will become an important debate by way of his observations and reflections on 'The researcher's duties: continuing the conversation'. According to Czarniawska, mass higher education no longer offers the means for *Bildung* in the Humboldtian sense; moreover, the social sciences are in greater danger than the humanities. Thus, doctoral and postdoctoral studies in management and organization studies need to reconnect with the humanities and it is here where the classic vision of university education can be upheld. To sketch how such a reconnection can take place, Czarniawska offers a list of courses to be included in future doctoral curricula. Furthermore, she specifically discusses the potential of methodology and writing workshops as well as the need to resist the current publishing frenzy (step forward, tenured scholars). Agreeing with the call to rethink doctoral education that employs the rich potential of the humanities (and social sciences), Racz, who writes from the UK context, paints both a rich and bleak picture of neoliberal university governance and its implications for the state and practices of doctoral education. Against these developments, he urges doctoral scholars in management and related studies to 'turn towards the revolutionary duties' of the researcher. Expanding on Czarniawska's notion of the laboratory, Racz proposes concrete examples and suggestions in order to translate the meeting of humanities, social sciences and doctoral education into more political and transformational concerns and prefigurative practices of knowledge, collegiality and writing.

## Part VI: futures

The final part of the book turns towards to the future, to the possibilities and promises of a management education that might be reinvented through the humanities and social sciences. The future will arrive anyway, but if we want to have a chance of shaping it then we need to consider actively what sort of futures we would rather live in. Various chapters in this part reflect upon how any imagined future must critically engage with past and present problems such as unequal gender relations (Pullen), colonial exploitation (Prasad), sustainability and natural limits (Wright and Nyberg), student debt and employability (Sørensen and Śliwa), and the nature of the university as a machine that parcels up knowledge (Parker). In addition, the ways in which management education can be reinvented might depend on understanding the nature of the humanities and the social sciences in some surprising and more nuanced ways (Costea and Amiridis; O'Doherty).

We begin with two chapters on power and politics. In her chapter 'Notes on feminist management education', Alison Pullen explores how a feminist sensibility challenges ingrained, gendered power structures and knowledge claims, and how it can open up spaces of greater participation, freedom and communality. Pullen begins with a personal reflection on how feminism exposes her as an educator and makes the classroom always and necessarily political.

In a time when neoliberal modes of governance shape the conduct of universities in general and business schools in particular, such exposure becomes all the more poignant, risky and relevant. Pullen discusses the main elements of feminist pedagogy and shows how they can and should be brought to bear on critical management education. It is precisely in the classroom, she concludes, where an affirmative politics of transformation and the struggle against male dominance within the academy begins.

Ajnesh Prasad's chapter that follows turns to another fundamental form of oppression – that which has been produced by centuries of colonial exploitation, usually in the name of business and free trade. In 'The fact of otherness: towards liberating the subaltern consciousness in contemporary management education', Prasad provides a brief sketch of postcolonial theory, with a particular emphasis on the concept of the subaltern. He then goes on to take Abraham Maslow's canonical 'hierarchy of needs' as an example to show how 'Western' is often inadequate to address different forms of organizing in the non-Western world. In a chapter that is aimed at opening the possibilities for future management education to serve as a site of liberation for colonized subjects, Prasad concludes with some postcolonial caveats – thoughts on what conscientious management educators ought to avoid if they attempt to transform scholarship and the classroom into an emancipatory arena.

Understanding and reflecting upon gender and ethnicity are clearly vital to any reinventing of management education, but the next chapter – 'Engaging with the contradictions of capitalism: teaching "sustainability" in the business school' – concerns a question that could be vital for human life on the planet. Christopher Wright and Daniel Nyberg's chapter explores how sustainability education might contribute to a reimagining of our economic system and the role of business. Based on their experience in developing and teaching sustainability curricula in various business schools, they show how sustainability defies the hierarchy of thought in business schools by placing the environment, not the economy or even society, at the centre of our understanding. Genuine sustainability also confronts the idea of a simple market justification for human action and provokes us to imagine other values and justifications where relations between individuals, society and nature are based on more than just market fetishism. Wright and Nyberg argue that such ideas are often heretical to the established order of business education, and hence that material from the arts and social sciences can be used in order to reframe assumptions about the future relevance of the business school in a rapidly warming world.

In 'Classroom diversity, infinite potential and the *Bildung* of debt', Bent Meier Sørensen and Martyna Śliwa address another pressing issue for today's business and management graduates: debt. Taking as the point of departure a management course given at a UK university in which novels were used to provide students with insights into the world of organization, it became obvious to the authors that the political framing of this endeavour was by no means clear to them. The 'values' of the European, humanistic tradition are not part-and-parcel of everybody's tradition and an attempt to enforce these values upon the students did, to a certain extent, happen without either the students or the educators being aware of it. The chapter reflects on this in the context of the Western tradition of *Bildung* and a philosophy built on Jacques Rancière's ideas about radical equality. The question for many students is not what teachers teach, but what their debts teach them, about themselves, about their prospects and about education.

In the following chapter, Martin Parker tries to understand the ways in which the differences between the business school and the arts and humanities can be understood historically and institutionally. '"This is water": labours of division, institutions and history' assumes that we must think about such matters as organizational questions, as forms of classification which have become concrete in the buildings of the university itself. The problem, Parker suggests, is in the university itself and is not something that is unique to the business school, although it is in the business school that this problem finds a rather intense expression. Beginning with some remarks on the history of the university, Parker moves on to consider the university as a machine for classifying, separating and distributing knowledge. He then considers the ways in which the business school has grown and produced its own divisions, which themselves discipline thought. After a consideration of the relationship between the practical and the liberal justifications for education, he concludes by rejecting (with a certain sadness as a co-editor of this volume) the idea that the humanities can either civilize or radicalize the business school. He suggests that the problem is the classification that produces the business school, and it is that which needs to be dissolved in order for any interdisciplinary project to flourish.

Bogdan Costea and Kostas Amiridis, in 'Management education and the humanities: a future together?', return to the beginning of this Companion by highlighting several aspects of the Carnegie diagnosis that they believe present problems. They do not contest the conclusion, which highlights the intellectual isolation of business schools within universities and their apparent impoverishment, but they do question the manner in which this conclusion is derived. They suggest that a better understanding of the power and cultural force of business schools must try to appreciate how they can carry on despite their continued avoidance of the complex contradictions of the epoch. This means that the humanities might not be the miraculous, humanizing cure for the actual and purported limitations of business education; instead, the humanities may still have access to sources of thinking that could bring students of business to a better understanding of the central determining place that business, as a historical process, occupies within it. Instead of the formation of a perfect character or a better integrated curriculum, business education might benefit from a deeper investigation of the worldview of business itself, provided it can subject itself to uncomfortable reflection. The heritage of the humanities and social sciences, particularly the reading of major classical sources, could be potentially mobilized if 'business' and 'management' are opened up for profound investigation. It is possible to envisage interdisciplinary programmes that would attempt to explore the complexity of the contemporary historical condition in which business and management are so central – this book evidences that. However, in Costea and Amiridis's view, it is less viable to think of the humanities and social sciences as devices for the production of a perfected human character, of a figure that could tower above the dilemmas of its own condition.

Damian O'Doherty concludes our Companion by focusing on those things we usually do not teach in management education, namely the whole question of taste, manners and etiquette. This is another meaning of 'culture' and 'character', and one that is crucial to business practice – think of business dinners, meetings and 'leisure' activities that help to 'seal the deal' or navigate the corridors of power. Rather than to write the next how-to manual (many of which O'Doherty has read), the chapter aims to demonstrate a political diagnostics of taste and manners by interweaving ethnographic material of a professional dinner in the context of the study of an airport with fragments of Jane Austen's *Pride and Prejudice*. Through this insightful connection, the chapter provides several provocative suggestions as to how courses in management education might be redesigned – such as a new corporeal calisthenics of business and management – but, above all, it stimulates us to become more sensitive to features of the world that do not appear and yet form a part of the social. The arts and humanities can become a reflexive and constitutive practice that is inextricably a part of the way in which business and management is carried out, particularly in terms of the reproduction of particular assumptions about class, gender, ethnicity and so on. O'Doherty has plenty to say about how this relates the humanities and social sciences to management education, and this chapter thus forms the ideal way to conclude this Companion, but yet to open up for future experiments in preventing business schools from merely becoming a 'finishing school' for the elite.

## Coda

This Companion could not have been realized without the support and ideas of many. First of all, our gratitude goes out to the contributors to this book. Their ideas and inventiveness speak volumes about the potential of reconsidering and shaping management education through the humanities and social sciences. We would like to thank Haniel Stiftung and Geschwister Horstmann Stiftung, and here in particular Rupert Antes and his team, for enabling the various workshops that accompanied the publishing process of this book. We would also like to thank the many participants at these workshops for sharing their ideas because they formed an important background to the contents and structure of the Companion (even if they were not all included in the end). Martyna Śliwa, Daniele Goldoni, Rasmus Johnsen and Jörg Metelmann not only participated in but also generously made room for the debates and exchanges in Essex, Venice, Copenhagen and St Gallen. Moreover, we are indebted to Sabrina Helmer (University of St Gallen) for her amazing work in organizing the workshops and to Bernhard Resch (University of St Gallen) who was invaluable in supporting our editorial process. We are also very grateful to David Varley from Routledge who responded promptly to our ideas for this Companion and to the many Routledge colleagues who have made the publication process much easier than we ever could hope for.

## References

Augier, M. and March, J.G. (2011) *The Roots, Rituals and Rhetorics of Change: North American Business Schools after the Second World War*. Stanford, CA: Stanford Business Books.

Bell, E. (2008) *Reading Management and Organization in Film*. Basingstoke, UK: Palgrave Macmillan.

Bennis, W.G. and O'Toole, J. (2005) 'How business schools lost their way', *Harvard Business Review*, 83(5), 96–104.

Beyes, T. and Michels, C. (2011) 'The production of educational space: heterotopia and the business university', *Management Learning*, 42(5), 521–36.

Billsberry, J., Charlesworth, J. and Leonard, P. (eds.) (2012) *Moving Images: Effective Teaching with Film and Television in Management*. Charlotte, NC: Information Age Publishing.

Clegg, S., Dany, F. and Grey, C. (2011) 'Critical management studies and managerial education: new contexts? New agenda?', *M@n@gement*, 14(5), 271–9.

Colby, A., Ehrlich, T., Sullivan, W.M. and Dolle, J.R. (2011) *Rethinking Undergraduate Business Education. Liberal Learning for the Profession*. San Francisco, CA: Jossey-Bass.

French, R. and Grey, C. (1996) *Rethinking Management Education*. London: Sage Publications.

Gagliardi, P. and Czarniawska, B. (eds.) (2006) *Management Education and Humanities*. Cheltenham, UK: Edward Elgar.

Grey, C., Huault, I., Perret, V. and Taskin, L. (eds.) (2016) *Critical Management Studies: Global Voices, Local Accents*. London: Routledge.

International Student Initiative for Pluralism in Economics (ISIPE) (2014) *Open Letter*, published 5 May 2014. Available from: www.isipe.net/open-letter/ (accessed 30 September 2015).

Khurana, R. (2007) *From Higher Aims to Hired Hands. The Social Transformation of American Business Schools and the Unfulfilled Promise of Management as a Profession*. Princeton, NJ: Princeton University Press.

Korn, M. (2014) 'Why some Ms are reading Plato?', *The Wall Street Journal*, 30 April. Available from: www.wsj.com/articles/SB10001424052702303948104579533610289092866 (accessed 30 September 2015).

Marquard, O. (1986) 'Über die Unvermeidlichkeit der Geisteswissenschaften'. *In*: O. Marquard (ed.) *Apologie des Zufälligen. Philosophische Studien*. Stuttgart: Reclam, pp. 98–116.

Mintzberg, H. (2004) *Managers not MBAs: A Hard Look at the Soft Practice of Managing and Management Development*. San Francisco, CA: Berrett-Koehler.

O'Connor, E. (2012) *Creating New Knowledge in Management, Appropriating the Field's Lost Foundations*. Stanford, CA: Stanford University Press.

Parker, M. (2015) 'Between sociology and the B school: critical studies of organization, work and employment in the UK', *Sociological Review*, 63(1), 162–80.

Parker, M. and Jary, D. (1995) 'The McUniversity: organization, management and academic subjectivity', *Organization*, 2(2), 319–38.

Peters, M.A. and Bulut, E. (eds.) (2011) *Cognitive Capitalism, Education and Digital Labor*. New York, NY: Peter Lang.

Pettigrew, A.M., Cornuel, E. and Hommel, U. (2014) 'Introduction'. *In:* A.M. Pettigrew, E. Cornuel and U. Hommel (eds.) *The Institutional Development of Business Schools*. Oxford: Oxford University Press, pp. 1–5.

Pfeffer, J. and Fong, C.T. (2002) 'The end of business schools? Less success than meets the eye', *Academy of Management Learning and Education*, 1(1), 78–95.

Pritchard, C. (2012) 'Introduction: what are we to do with higher education?', *Organization*, 19(6), 879–80.

Starkey, K. and Madan, P. (2001) 'Bridging the relevance gap: aligning stakeholders in the future of management research', *British Journal of Management*, 12, 3–26.

Starkey, K. and Tempest, S. (2006) 'The business school in ruins? Is there a role for the Humanities?'. *In*: P. Gagliardi and B. Czarniawska (eds.) *Management Education and Humanities*. Cheltenham, UK: Edward Elgar, pp 101–12.

Starkey, K. and Tiratsoo, N. (2007) *The Business School and the Bottom Line*. Cambridge: Cambridge University Press.

Willmott, H. (1994) 'Management education, provocations to a debate', *Management Learning*, 25(1), 105–36.

Zald, M. (1996) 'More fragmentation? Unfinished business in linking the social sciences and the humanities', *Administrative Science Quarterly*, 41(2), 251–61.

# Part I
# Histories

# 2

# The Carnegie Report

## Looking back and thinking forward

*William M. Sullivan, Thomas Ehrlich and Anne Colby*

---

*Rethinking Undergraduate Business Education: Liberal Learning for the Profession*, which quickly became known as the "Carnegie Report," appeared in 2011 (Colby *et al.* 2011), only five years before the publication of this volume. Its wide reception and the interest it generated came as something of a surprise to its authors, so why did this report about the humanities and business education have such an impact? We had conceived the book as a development of the questions and methods embodied in a set of well-regarded studies of professional education in the US carried out by the Carnegie Foundation for the Advancement of Teaching from the late 1990s through the first decade of the present century. These studies of law, engineering, preparation of Jewish and Christian clergy, nursing, and medicine had made their mark in their respective fields (Benner *et al.* 2009; Cooke *et al.* 2009; Foster *et al.* 2006; Sheppard *et al.* 2009; Sullivan *et al.* 2007). Complementary studies were also carried out by several of us at the Carnegie Foundation in the areas of moral development and civic participation amongst US undergraduates (Colby *et al.* 2011).

Taken together, these studies were efforts to examine important aspects of US higher education, seeking not only to criticize where necessary but also to propose "visions of the possible" based upon educators' most creative and ambitious efforts to address widely perceived challenges. The studies were most concerned about how the educational process can effectively prepare students to develop and bring together knowledge, skill, and moral purpose in ways that advance the aims of the several professions and the education of citizens for a democratic society. The study of liberal learning for business undergraduates was organized in the same way and called the BELL Project (Business, Entrepreneurship and Liberal Learning). The project began in 2006 and ended in 2010.

None of the other Carnegie studies seemed to strike a nerve to the degree that this report did. In part, this reception suggests that the public understands the importance of business in the contemporary world, making the preparation of business professionals a matter of widespread concern. But the strong interest in the study was also a matter of timing. The onset of the financial crash and Great Recession in 2008 provoked widespread anxiety about the quality of business education, in both the US and Europe.

This is not the first time that a Carnegie report on undergraduate business education has elicited widespread interest. In the 1950s, both Carnegie and the Ford Foundation had researched the state of undergraduate business programs in US higher education and found them intellectually weak. Both Carnegie and Ford issued reports that called for raising the academic standards of business education (Gordon and Howell 1959; Pierson 1959). These earlier reports singled out the need to increase business students' knowledge of intellectual disciplines beyond economics and business and to enhance their capacities to think critically and write and communicate more effectively. Their focus on intellectual rigor, however valuable at the time, tended to discourage the blending of business with the arts and sciences, making the recommendations of those earlier studies quite different from the emphasis on intellectual integration that characterizes the 2011 Carnegie Report.

As we began our investigation, we wanted to discover what had become of these aims to introduce liberal education into business programs over the intervening half century of vast educational expansion. We were also intrigued that at the time of the two mid-century reports, the Aspen Institute was organizing a highly successful series of meetings of leaders in business with a focus on the reading of "great books" as the core of liberal learning (Allen 1983). Although we did not know it at the time, we would later join in partnership with the Business and Society Program of today's Aspen Institute to find common ground amongst undergraduate fields of study through common study of the liberal arts, as we will explain later.

We found that although there has been significant upgrading of the academic level of business fields since the mid-twentieth century, the problem of narrowness of preparation remains. Although our proposals for reform are quite different from those put forward in the 1950s, they still center on the continuing challenge of developing business professionals who possess the breadth of outlook and can exhibit the conceptual agility needed for the emerging global century.

In what follows, for the convenience of our readers here and in the rest of this book, we will first summarize our premises, the plan of our research, and our key recommendations. We will then describe something of our book's reception in the US, Europe, and more broadly. We will follow this with a view of the future direction of this work and its chief challenges, concluding with several examples of how these challenges can be overcome in a reconstituted model of undergraduate business education.

## Our premises

The centrality of business in society, the great numbers of undergraduates who choose business as their major field of study, and the even greater numbers who will be employed in business for their working lives demand that higher education do more than just help students acquire tools for advancing their personal careers in business, although this is an important goal. We believe that in order to ensure that graduates develop breadth of understanding and engagement with the life of their times, higher education needs to help students understand the relation of business to the larger world and act on that understanding as business professionals and as citizens.

Simply put, we believe that undergraduates who major in business should have the benefits of a strong liberal education. Business and liberal learning must be woven together to prepare students for their professional roles and also to prepare them for lives of social contribution and personal fulfillment. In this sense, we propose an integrated vision of undergraduate education. The question, therefore, is how to do this. What should undergraduate business education provide for students?

It is worth noting that business is the most popular field of undergraduate study in the US. In 2011/2012, the most recent academic year for which national data was available, 21 percent of all undergraduates were business majors. When business is combined with other vocational majors such as engineering, education, and nursing, the total rises to 68 percent of all undergraduates (National Center for Education Statistics 2013). For students in the US, about one-third of all courses taken are in the major field. About one-half of all courses are taken in what is often called "general education" courses. In the typical college curriculum, general education is the domain of liberal education. Students are most often required to take courses, often two or three, in three categories of disciplines – the humanities, the social sciences, and the natural sciences. Many institutions use various categories to help promote breadth in a student's curriculum to complement the depth that comes from courses in the major. Business curricula usually follow this pattern.

We began our research with an understanding that was subsequently reinforced by our observations – that business majors typically experience the liberal arts and science disciplines in ways that are weak or episodic. Undergraduate business seems to be widely understood as a kind of simplified Masters in Business Administration (MBA) program. In institutions that offer both MBA and undergraduate degrees, the undergraduate program rarely has its own faculty or dean and its curriculum mimics that of the graduate program. A more distinctive identity for undergraduate programs would acknowledge that this is their students' college experience as well as their professional preparation. In the US tradition of liberal education this means that students should be prepared for their futures as citizens and persons as well as entrants into the workforce.

## From the barbell to the double helix curriculum

The overall undergraduate program for business majors in the US, as it stands now, might be thought of as a curricular barbell. One end supports the "weight" of the courses students must take in the business program whilst the weight at the other end comes from the required general education courses just described. Each end of the barbell carries a significant weight of intellectual subject matter but the connection is slender. On the two ends of the barbell, students encounter courses taught by different groups of faculty, often from different schools within the university or college, who have little contact with their colleagues on the other end of the curricular barbell. The linkage between the two ends of the barbell receives little explicit attention in the ways that the curriculum is organized or in how courses are taught. Students are mostly on their own when it comes to figuring out how to lift and balance these two disparate sets of weights.

For business students, who tend to focus very intently on career preparation, general education courses are often seen as marginal to their real educational purpose. This means that, for them, the curricular barbell is tilted sharply toward the business end. The tilt may be accentuated by the fact that core subjects in business, such as accounting and finance, emphasize forms of analysis that, although cognitively demanding, present students with problems that have clear, right-or-wrong answers. By contrast, in many courses in the arts and sciences, particularly in the humanities, students encounter and must manage significant ambiguities and uncertainties. Actual business practice, of course, is full of ambiguous and uncertain situations. We heard from many business students that they avoid courses that focus on open-ended questions involving significant interpretation and reflection. This effectively tilts the barbell for these students even further toward business and away from liberal education.

In writing our book, we were seeking to stimulate and contribute to what has become an international conversation about the future of business education by focusing on approaches that work to integrate the two ends of the barbell curriculum. Rather than a barbell, we propose a curriculum shaped like a double helix. Borrowing the image from the famous DNA model developed by Watson, Crick, and Rosalind Franklin, we propose the double helix as a metaphor for an undergraduate business curriculum that explicitly and continually links students' learning in business to their learning in the various arts and sciences disciplines, which can provide a larger, complementary view of the world.

This is not simply an imagined possibility. As we describe in our book, we observed courses and entire programs that explicitly put the disciplinary insights and tools of the social sciences and humanities to use in this way. We saw the liberal arts and sciences used to provide an understanding of the other institutional sectors that business depends upon, such as effective public education organized by governments, and the ways in which business affects those other institutional contexts. Through these double-helix approaches, faculty as well as students can develop facility in navigating the pluralism of values and operating logics that mark the actual lives of their graduates both as business professionals and as citizens.

## The plan of our research

The BELL Project began with a literature review as part of our effort to survey undergraduate business programs broadly. Based on this review, we sought a range of campus types. We chose ten campuses for intensive site visits during the academic years 2007/2008 and 2008/2009. We sought programs that were committed to bringing liberal learning and business disciplines together in an intentional and integrated curriculum with pedagogies designed to facilitate the transfer and integration of knowledge and skills across the fields. To ensure that we grasped the range of issues involved, we visited a variety of program types.

We visited several large university business schools. One of these was the Kelley School of Business at Indiana University and also the Liberal Arts and Management Program housed in the College of Arts and Sciences at Indiana. Besides the public sector, we also visited three large private university business schools: the Wharton School of the University of Pennsylvania, Stern School of New York University, and the Program in Management Science at the Massachusetts Institute of Technology's Sloan School of Business. We visited Babson College and Bentley University, institutions begun as business colleges that have evolved into full four-year institutions, as well as Morehouse College and Franklin and Marshall College among predominantly liberal arts institutions. Our sites also included Santa Clara University, a Jesuit institution in California, and Portland State University, a broad-access, public, urban university in Oregon.

Typically, our research team spent several days on each campus. Whilst there, we had conversations with a wide range of academic personnel. We also spoke extensively with students. We visited classes in both the business disciplines and the arts and sciences, giving special attention to those forms of teaching and learning that brought the two areas of the curriculum together. We focused on understanding the distinctive ways in which the various disciplines are taught, the kinds of learning and skills that each emphasizes, and how students are assessed. In particular, we were interested in the kinds of moral meaning and professional identity that faculty intend to convey and that students perceive as salient.

Throughout these conversations, our aim was to understand the experience of business education for both students and faculty. We tried to grasp how that experience colored and shaped the way students encounter and make sense of the liberal education aspects of the curriculum. To do this, we also inquired into extracurricular activities and the overall campus climate. From these conversations we formulated detailed conceptions of how the practices of business education form students' sensibilities as well as their ways of knowing. We also drew conclusions about the ways in which integration with the perspectives of liberal learning expands and enriches students' understanding of the nature and role of business in the world and thereby opens new possibilities for them.

## Our recommendations

On the basis of our study, we made four major recommendations. First, speaking within the US context, we recommended that a strong liberal education be part of the undergraduate experience of every business major. We argued that the central aim of liberal education should be to shape the minds and the character of students so that they can make sense of the world around them and their place in it, encouraging their constructive contributions to the world. A liberally educated college graduate should have a broad context of knowledge on which to draw as a business professional. This aim allows for considerable flexibility for various programs to choose specific content from amongst the traditional liberal arts clusters as well as mathematics and the natural sciences, the social sciences, and the humanities that can expand and complement the focus on preparation for careers in business. We tried to provide a fuller description of this aim by reframing these goals as the development of four modes of thinking, which are described in the next section.

Second, we recommended that liberal learning be integrated into undergraduate business courses as well as provided through the general education curriculum. We saw some strong illustrations of how this can be done well and reported on some of those in our book. We also noted that well-constructed active or experiential methods of teaching – the pedagogies of engagement as they are sometimes called – can be particularly helpful in enabling students to understand the kind of expertise they are trying to acquire, as well as providing regular practice and feedback to guide their progressive development along the way (Kuh 2008). Such experiential pedagogy can also make the ways that business interacts with other sectors of contemporary society more salient for students.

Third, we recommended that business education be designed to enhance the ability of business students to grapple successfully with ambiguity and uncertainty, to make sound decisions when faced with incomplete information, and to gain the other attributes so often identified with successful innovation in business – and with liberal learning. We argued that achieving this goal will be greatly aided by ensuring that liberal learning is integrated with the learning of the business disciplines through multiple, mutually reinforcing groups of courses and other educational experiences. Many of the examples in our book are offered as illustrations of how to do this effectively.

Fourth, building on these insights we recommend intentional, systematic approaches to designing curricula, in which liberal learning and preparation for business are thoroughly integrated. This kind of institutional intentionality requires a major shift toward more coherent and collaborative design of curricula, which in turn requires administrative leadership and faculty engagement and creativity to shape a set of mutually reinforcing experiences for students that provide an educational whole that is more than its separate parts, ensuring that learning lasts. This means multiple interventions, including where possible the co-curriculum and campus climate innovations that are carefully developed and coordinated with a clear set of learning objectives. In essence, the most effective programs are "designed backward," beginning with a clear statement of desired outcomes and working back from there to subject matter, pedagogies, and student experiences that are most likely to lead to those outcomes.

## Reframing the liberal learning: professional education divergence

As an aid to thinking about implementing such an ambitious – but we believe essential – agenda, we proposed a reframing of the liberal learning versus professional training divergence that divides many campuses. We proposed that the thinking capacities that all undergraduates should develop through a college education can be described as three modes of thought plus a fourth, integrative, mode which we called practical reason.

The first mode of thinking we called analytic. Teaching this skill is the most basic feature of higher education, apart from the transmission of knowledge. It corresponds to what is commonly known as abstract, higher order, or conceptual thinking.

The second mode of thinking we called multiple framing. This involves learning that there are competing models or perspectives, usually based upon different starting assumptions, that are necessary in order to make sense of complex issues. In cases where this diversity represents fundamental, irreducible differences of perspective, individuals must learn to hold more than one frame of reference in mind and to realize that neither can be said to represent the full "truth of the matter". This kind of intrinsic ambiguity characterizes many questions that business and other practical fields must confront, and so this skill is essential not only as an aspect of intellectual sophistication but also as an essential tool of practice.

The third mode of thinking we termed the reflective exploration of meaning. Such thinking engages with questions of purpose, including matters of personal and collective significance. Its development fosters the capacity to imagine a range of visions of what is possible in situations and in life as a whole and encourages the exploration of the significance of those possibilities for oneself and others.

Taken together, we argued that developing proficiency in all these modes of thought ought to be the overarching goal of all higher education, regardless of discipline. They therefore help define the meaning of liberal learning. The first two modes help in understanding what is reasonable to accept as true or valid. The third mode asks what difference such an understanding makes to personal identity and stance toward life. The first two modes foster reflection in increasingly complex ways; the third mode calls for self-reflection.

But we also argued that liberal learning demands that students develop in a disciplined way their ability to reason practically. The goal of such education, for business students as for others, is the capacity to integrate all three modes of thinking as they draw on their knowledge as the basis of wise judgment applied to actual problems in the world. That means the formation of students who can think and act through a back-and-forth dialogue amongst the modes of thinking as they use the knowledge and skills they have learned in the service of living wisely and well, as professionals, as citizens, and as persons. Practical reasoning's imperatives are well summarized by Rabbi Hillel's famous questions: "If I am not for myself, who will be for me? If I am not for others, what am I? And if not now, when?"

We recognized that many – perhaps even most – undergraduates, regardless of major field of study, leave college without a strong liberal education as we have characterized it. Even so, the rudiments are widely present. As we found in our study, some aspects of all of these critical modes of thinking are being taught in various parts of the curriculum. We believe that, using this characterization of what undergraduate education should be, teaching can help focus these efforts, enabling various faculties and programs to better understand each other and find common ground. The reception of this aspect of our work gives grounds for cautious optimism that this approach may stimulate movement toward the four recommendations we made for strengthening the education of undergraduate business students. The challenge is to develop ways to make this integration intentional, pervasive, and effective, a theme we will return to in the latter part of this chapter.

## Reception of the Carnegie Report: North America

*Rethinking Undergraduate Business Education* was based on a sample of undergraduate business programs in the US. Because the book's focus was entirely on US practice and debates, it is not surprising that it was first noticed in the business press along with articles in the US education press. The authors also took advantage of speaking invitations to present on the findings of the study in a number of venues in the US and Canada. In 2011/2012, the first year after the book's publication, the study received attention in the national business media, with coverage in the *Wall Street Journal*, an article in *Bloomberg Business Week*, mentioning in *The Atlantic Monthly*, as well as in *The Chronicle of Higher Education* and *Higher Education Today*. The Carnegie Foundation collaborated with the publisher, Jossey-Bass/Wiley, in organizing a web-based national workshop with several of the authors. In addition, the authors individually or together made presentations on the study to a range of audiences, including groups within the AACSB (Association of American Colleges and Schools of Business) on a number of occasions, as well as the Canadian Academic Accounting Association. The Academy of Management has also hosted several sessions on the book. In early 2013, it received the prestigious Frederick W. Ness award, given by the Association of American Colleges and Universities for a book that significantly "contributes to the understanding and improvement of liberal education."

The most significant outgrowth of these activities was the organization of a consortium of business schools and programs committed to using the book as a guide to shaping their curricula. This effort was led by the Business and Society Program of the Aspen Institute in consultation with the authors, and financially supported by the participating schools and the Teagle Foundation. Teagle had been a partner with Carnegie in supporting the BELL Project from its beginning. In 2012, the Foundation agreed to provide seed money to enable the formation of an Aspen Undergraduate Business Education Consortium, beginning with 20 institutions, which has subsequently doubled in size, and now includes members from Europe and Asia.

The Aspen Consortium has held two conferences, each of which brought the members of the consortium together for several days of highly interactive dialogue, first in Washington, DC in March 2012, and then in Denver, Colorado in March 2013. These events featured teaching samples of innovative pedagogies that embody the integration of liberal learning with business subjects. Participants from a number of institutions also presented cases of programmatic change. Guests from outside business education brought their somewhat different perspectives to the conversation about enhancing undergraduate education for business students. It is noteworthy that several of the international participants took prominent roles in these workshop sessions. By the end of the second conference, the participating schools committed themselves to further development of the consortium. Consequently, a third conference took place at the University of Richmond, Virginia in June 2014.

## The international reception

In October 2011, within only a few months of the book's publication, the Copenhagen Business School's (CBS) department of Management, Politics, and Philosophy held a Roundtable entitled "Integrating the Humanities and the Liberal Arts in Business Education." Supported by the Haniel Foundation of Germany, the Roundtable announced its intention to extend the focus of the Carnegie Report to include the comparative situation of business education in Europe. The event included participation by the author team, as well as prominent figures in business education in the US, Canada, and various European countries. That event began an ongoing series of international scholarly conversations about integrating liberal arts, particularly the humanities, with undergraduate business programs.

The conversation begun in Copenhagen was continued the following year in another convening, this one hosted by the Contextual Studies faculty at the University of St Gallen in Switzerland in November 2012. Entitled "Practicing Humanities and Social Sciences in

Management Education," this event built upon ongoing collaborations around similar issues that had developed between the CBS and the University of St Gallen in Switzerland (UNISG). There was cross-pollination between the European conversation and the Aspen Consortium group because both UNISG and CBS had joined the consortium, along with ESADE Business School of Barcelona.

In these meetings, it became clear that the European reception of the Carnegie Report had stimulated distinctive responses. One of the most important of these concerned the omission of the visual and performing arts from the Carnegie Report and the small space accorded these fields in US thinking about liberal education more generally. At the St Gallen conference, there were presentations on the topic and the announcement by CBS and UNISG of a joint Carnegie Art Initiative project to give more attention to connecting entrepreneurship, leadership, and creativity through the arts. The European discussion was also enriched by the experience of several of the participating schools with the United Nations' Global Compact and its Principles of Responsible Management Education (PRME). The PRME are consistent with both the Carnegie recommendations and the Aspen Consortium's aims. The European Foundation for Management Development (EFMD) also took up the Carnegie Report at its January 2013 meeting in Istanbul.

The developing European conversation coalesced around several foci. There was great interest in developing and disseminating teaching practices that integrate liberal learning into business. A website was launched to provide a platform for exchanging news, teaching samples, and portfolios (www.practical-reasoning.eu/). There was also a strong sense that in order for this movement to succeed there had to be robust research and scholarship to support its methods as well as its aims. The participants endorsed the preparation of a resource handbook to include original research, a decision that resulted in the present volume. In addition, the University of St Gallen became the sponsor of an ambitious project to design and carry out a "Carnegie study for Europe" (see Landfester, Tofte Brenneche, and Prat-i-Pubill, this volume).

All these strands came together in a second, highly interactive meeting at CBS in June 2013. This meeting included lively student participation along with faculty from a number of institutions across Europe. It defined ongoing areas for development in both teaching and research and called for the inclusion of a larger number of business schools as participants in future work.

In sum, in five years, *Rethinking Undergraduate Business Education* has had a remarkable reception and keeps stimulating new responses. There is now an international network of business schools and universities committed to stronger integration of the humanities and liberal learning, including the arts, into the preparation of business students. A number of projects are underway to test, extend, and improve that common aim. Publications and web-based dissemination are developing and there is a sustained and growing international conversation around the reshaping of business education, particularly for undergraduates. We expect that these ongoing conversations will continue to enrich each other, intersecting at events in various locations across the world.

## Thinking forward: the potential for making a difference

What difference might it make if business preparation in higher education were embedded within a framework of liberal learning like that presented in *Rethinking Undergraduate Business Education* and further developed through the international conversation just described? An immediate answer is sketched in the study itself. In an age in which business places a premium on revitalizing, innovating, and creating new entries into the marketplace – often discussed under the rubric of entrepreneurship – there is a close match between the capacities needed for entrepreneurial thinking and those developed by liberal education. In our book, we profiled studies of innovative business leaders and creative design firms that illustrate this relationship between liberal learning and the ability to innovate by seeing new patterns in data. Such leaders are also able to conceive ways to shape organizations to exploit connections that are often invisible even to highly trained analytical, but routine, thinkers.

Successful entrepreneurial founders and leaders, contrary to the common myth, are more often mutually attuned teams rather than rugged individuals, and a key factor in their success turns out to be the ability of leaders to draw from a wide range of particular kinds of knowledge, weaving these forms of expertise into a sustained, collective performance. Many of the programs involved in the post-Carnegie conversations, including the CBS–UNISG Carnegie Art Initiative, provide examples of ways to educate for such work by integrating business skills within a wider matrix of intellectual capacities. These examples validate the study's premise that such integration adds significant value to the preparation of business professionals.

Besides opening up possibilities for thinking in more complex and creative ways about business problems, there is also a larger, and possibly more significant educational goal. That is the strategy of using perspectives from the liberal arts and sciences to broaden the horizon of undergraduate business students beyond a narrowly instrumental view of their education. This is an especially important and yet uniquely challenging goal for undergraduate business education.

Our study found that students' instrumental attitude toward learning was reinforced by business programs' tendencies to purvey a narrowly utilitarian theoretical orientation as the deep truth about human reality. In contrast to this instrumental orientation, as our informants called it, arts and sciences majors (again excepting pre-meds, engineers, and other competitive pre-professional students) were seen by others and characterized themselves as motivated by intellectual and cultural curiosity. Such students were often described as treating their college experience as primarily an opportunity for *exploration*, calling themselves *explorers*. Used this way, exploration refers to intellectual pursuits not tied to getting a good job, admission to medical school, and so forth, and is thought of as the polar opposite of an instrumental orientation toward study.

Although there is some truth in these stereotypes, such a stark dichotomy between preparing for a definite career versus intellectual exploration for its own sake replicates on the level of student and faculty culture just the kind of division between the professional schools and the arts and sciences departments that works against the vision the Report is urging. More importantly, accepting the dichotomy makes liberal learning a stepchild in its own house, caught between opposing, equally narrow views of higher education. Students often think they have to choose between programs and courses that offer either an instrumental, job-focused set of knowledge and skills, or an academic specialization that provides few career possibilities, although it may offer meaningful knowledge. What does not appear as an option is a path of coherent learning that opens possibilities for both intellectual exploration and vocational engagement.

The instrumental-versus-exploration dichotomy makes it hard for students to conceive of higher education as both intellectually adventurous and yet serious, shaping a life that embraces responsible worldly endeavor but is also open to wonder and exploration. Absorption in the instrumental attitude risks closing students off to experiences of self-transcendence and transformation beyond immediate utility. It suppresses the big questions about what makes any career worthwhile and fails to stimulate creativity and thinking on a large canvas. Conversely, although an exploration orientation has the virtue of openness, students with this orientation are often on the defensive in the face of messages that higher education is really about getting ahead. This makes pursuing an exploratory course of study unappealing to those who are intellectually inclined but also aim to make something of themselves so they can contribute to the world.

Although the more complex conditions of twenty-first-century business and life demand greater flexibility of mind and a broader understanding, the dynamics at work within much of higher education worldwide are moving precisely in the opposite direction (see O'Connor, this volume). The result is a serious problem: a higher education that is weak in a capacity that matters deeply, the ability to prepare citizens who both care about the world beyond themselves and have the wherewithal, through professional skill, to contribute to it.

In the best programs we observed, this contradiction was overcome by bringing into play other perspectives derived from disciplines outside business to enable students to appreciate business as a human enterprise of great potential value for society as a whole, not only for shareholders. For example, an emphasis upon the "social impact" of business woven through the curriculum enables students to place their learning and their thinking about future careers within a larger and longer-term framework than is otherwise likely to be the case. The signal contribution of the liberal arts, and particularly the humanities, lies in providing the wider frameworks, ways of thinking, and skills needed to realize this expansive vision of business education.

Consider, as another example, the field of management. As the understanding of the functions of managers has changed to take account of contemporary practice, the activities of the manager appear more interactive and holistic. In the new understanding, managerial leadership is less a linear decision process, as earlier models of management tended to imagine it, and more a cycle of interpreting situations, devising actions, and then reflecting on the effects of these actions toward achieving goals. The restructuring of many contemporary organizations, as well as the imperative they face to mount flexible responses to fast-changing, competitive environments, have given this alternative approach increasing plausibility.

Organizational effectiveness is therefore gained not so much by having the best managerial techniques for solving problems as by the capacity of managers to formulate problems and portray situations so that the members of their organization can organize effective responses that further their collective goals. This capacity to "frame" experience so as to make it meaningful and amenable to action has come to be recognized as a key dimension of managerial skill. In this alternative picture of managerial decision-making, the manager's function is to lead a team in developing a common understanding of their situation. The manager must not only draw out of the participants in the deliberation their sense of what the organization is confronting, but must also interpret the "facts" in ways that connect to the core purposes of the organization.

At stake in such managerial practice is always the question of the kind of organization that is being formed through the manager's decisions and their consequences. Moreover, these deliberations also shape the sort of person the managers become. Whether they realize it or not, through their decisions managers become agents who bear significant responsibility for the future. This responsibility is unavoidable. It is why management matters so much in the contemporary world. The important question is whether the deliberators accept responsibility for the impact of their decisions or fail to do so. The quality of deliberation therefore matters – to the organization, to its members, and to all those who experience the consequences of the actions taken.

## The potential of liberal learning: the particular role of the arts and humanities

In the aftermath of the financial crash of 2008, there has been increased interest in both the business community and the larger society in enhancing the role of the humanities and social science disciplines in the preparation of managers to broaden and deepen their abilities to think deliberatively. The Association of American Colleges and Universities recently surveyed US employers and found a good deal of support for outcomes of liberal education similar to those described in the Carnegie Report (Association of American Colleges and Universities 2012). There is good reason for this new interest. The financial disaster and the continuing slow recovery can, importantly, be partly traced directly to the abrogation of managerial responsibility at the highest levels of both business and public management. Furthermore, this irresponsibility was rationalized by a naïve confidence in the capacity of purely technical methods to supplant conscious and responsible managerial deliberation. There is a clear fit between this need to strengthen the deliberative capacities of business personnel and the development of what we called the reflective exploration of meaning and practical reasoning. In particular, the humanistic approaches cultivated by the humanities fields, as well as in various areas of historical and social investigation, seem especially well suited to shaping more reflective and widely aware business professionals. Humanistic inquiry carries a distinctive signature that reflects its bifocal vision of knowledge. Like the sciences, humanistic inquiry demands rigor in the application of cognitive tools of analysis and comparison, approaching its subjects critically, from the outside. At the same time, humanistic inquiry is grounded in the stance of a participant. It therefore seeks to understand the meaning of actions and events from within a perspective of engagement. Moreover, humanistic inquiry includes the dimension of self-awareness in the application of this two-fold, bifocal approach.

Because it starts and ends with the engaged stance of a participant, humanistic inquiry can never be solely cognitive. Because it is ultimately concerned with making sense of life and experience, humanistic thinking cannot remain detached, however much it may use intellectual methods of questioning and critical analysis to understand its subject. In this respect, humanistic inquiry is like the arts. It requires and provides training in the cultivation of imagination and empathy, along with aesthetic and moral awareness. It is rooted in participation in what it seeks to understand. These twin foci of critical distance and engaged participation establish a creative polarity for fostering both sharpness of mind and depth of ethical sensitivity.

## Fostering an identity for the twenty-first century

Awareness of living in a more interconnected world reveals some deeply problematic consequences of failing to emphasize the humanistic aspects of higher education, especially in business education. The need to understand social and cultural variation as well as the complex interplay between the economic and political, social, and cultural spheres of modern society is likely to become ever greater in the twenty-first century. What humanistic learning can provide is a disciplined and empathic understanding of others as well as the cultivation of responsibility for the effects of business decisions. These features of humanistic learning, however, cut against the grain of much in contemporary higher education. The reasons for this, as well as its implications, have recently been traced by William Theodore de Bary, a distinguished scholar of East Asian culture who over a long career helped introduce Asian thought to Western audiences. In *The Great Civilized Conversation: Education for a World Community*, de Bary recounts the genesis of "general education" at Columbia University in the years prior to World War I (de Bary 2013). At just the time when the classical tradition of the older liberal arts college had come under threat from growing intellectual specialization in US universities, a new way to address the formative intentions of the older curriculum was put forward by a now nearly forgotten figure, John Erskine, a professor of literature. Erskine's innovation was an experiment, at first open only to selected undergraduates, in which the participants would read and discuss a variety of works translated from many literatures, rather than the earlier canon consisting entirely of Greek and Roman works (de Bary 2013).

The key idea was that the texts would be "classics" – a term de Bary finds especially resonant because it is also what the great works of Chinese thought have long been called in East Asia. De Bary notes that to Erskine "a classic text was a great work of art not only in its literary perfection but in its appeal to the heart, the senses, and the aesthetic imagination" (de Bary 2013: 27). Erskine, according to de Bary,

> . . . resisted the enshrinement of "critical thinking" as the be all and end all of learning, which could only result in the narrowing and impoverishment of the self, unless it included sympathetic appreciation and synthesis as well as critical analysis.
>
> *de Bary 2013: 27*

It is significant that Erskine not only taught literature but was also a creative artist himself, a composer and author of poetry, plays, and novels. In its beginning, the notion of a "general education" curriculum was intended to engage a greater personal bandwidth than the cognitive in isolation. Over time, the works studied expanded to a very rich set of readings in philosophy and history, including the history of science and the arts, as well as literature. Erskine understood and implemented the two-fold quality of humanistic learning. On the one hand, students were to personally assimilate the texts they read and, as these works expanded their imagination, the students were to probe and assess their value for their own lives. In addition, the pedagogy was active discussion rather than lectures. This was to engage students collectively with issues raised in the works with each other as well as the instructor, thereby reinvigorating inherited wisdom by using it to illuminate the contemporary.

Surveying the contemporary academic scene, East and West, de Bary worries about the diminished role and status of humanistic learning – and we might add of the creative arts of all kinds – in today's technologically oriented universities. Along with rigor, he insists, there is a great need to cultivate empathy and imagination, culturally, historically, and morally, to appreciate the global context of contemporary life and identity. For de Bary, however, the key is that humanistic education needs to focus on central human problems and choices, much as the classics of both Europe and Asia did. Such cultivation, he argues, would be a great contribution of higher education toward fostering an educated citizenry able to understand and respond to the massive challenges of the global era.

## Future directions

To the (considerable) degree that business, particularly through its use of simulation and case studies, can provide students with vivid encounters with "central human problems," a business education embedded in a framework of liberal learning may provide unexpectedly fertile ground for developing the kind of humanistic imagination needed to engage the problems of our time. By opening up such questions, an enriched business education may even help refocus and energize the mission of humanistic learning.

These are the implications of this project to reshape business education as both professional preparation and liberal learning. To achieve these large ambitions, however, this movement must be able to overcome the forces of resistance rooted in the mutual ignorance that currently prevails amongst both business and arts and sciences faculties. We have suggested that active collaboration between these two groups within the university will be critical to changing students' too-frequent narrow instrumentalism. Without cooperation across the faculties, the cross-disciplinary perspectives needed to broaden the range of business students' areas of concern simply cannot happen. But the kinds of ideas and initiatives reported and discussed

in this chapter and in this volume are proof that growing numbers within the academy are interested in moving beyond the status quo.

The next steps must be to develop and to test convincing models of such education at the course, program, and finally school level. Second, to become the new norm for undergraduate business education, such integrated liberal arts, humanities and business programs will need a firm organizational base and viable business model. Toward these two overlapping goals, the Carnegie Report has served an important function as catalytic agent. But the future depends upon broadening and strengthening the conversation and action plans that have now begun. As authors of the report, we are proud to have had a role in what promises to emerge as a watershed moment in the story of educating undergraduates for business and for life.

## References

Allen, J.S. (1983) *The Romance of Commerce and Culture: Capitalism, Modernism, and the Chicago–Aspen Crusade for Cultural Reform*. Chicago, IL: University of Chicago Press.

Association of American Colleges and Universities (2012) *Big Questions, Urgent Challenges: Liberal Education and America's Global Future; Strategic Plan 2013–17*. Washington, DC: Association of American Colleges and Universities.

Benner, P.E., Sutphen, M., Leonard, V. and Day, L. (2009) *Educating Nurses: A Call for Radical Transformation*. San Francisco, CA: Jossey-Bass/Wiley.

Colby, A., Ehrlich, T., Sullivan, W.M. and Dolle, J.R. (2011) *Rethinking Undergraduate Business Education: Liberal Learning for the Profession*. San Francisco, CA: Jossey-Bass/Wiley.

Cooke, M., Irby, D.M. and O'Brien, B.C. (2009) *Educating Physicians: A Call for Reform of Medical School and Residency*. San Francisco, CA: Jossey-Bass/Wiley.

de Bary, W.T. (2013) *The Great Civilized Conversation: Education for a World Community*. New York, NY: Columbia University Press.

Foster, C., Dahill, L., Goleman, L. and Tollentino, B.W. (2006) *Educating Clergy: Teaching Practices and Pastoral Imagination*. San Francisco, CA: Jossey-Bass/Wiley.

Gordon, R.A. and Howell, J.E. (1959) *Higher Education for Business*. New York, NY: Columbia University Press.

Kuh, G.D. (2008) *High Impact Practices: What They Are, Who Has Access to Them, and Why They Matter*. Washington, DC: Association of American Colleges and Universities.

National Center for Education Statistics (2013) *Digest of Education Statistics*. Washington, DC: Institute of Education Sciences.

Pierson, F.C. (1959) *The Education of American Businessmen: A Study of University-College Programs in Business Administration*. New York, NY: McGraw-Hill.

Sheppard, S.D., Macatangay, K., Colby, A. and Sullivan, W.M. (2009) *Educating Engineers: Designing for the Future of the Field*. San Francisco, CA: Jossey-Bass/Wiley.

Sullivan, W.M., Colby, A., Wegner, J.W., Bond, L. and Shulman, L.W. (2007) *Educating Lawyers: Preparing for the Profession of Law*. San Francisco, CA: Jossey-Bass/Wiley.

# 3

# The test of time

## Historical perspectives on management education reform in the US

*Ellen S. O'Connor*

> The business man has probably the opportunity today of making one of the largest contributions to society that has ever been made, a demonstration of the possibility of collective creativeness.
>
> *Metcalf and Urwick 1940 [Follett 1925]: 94*

This chapter attaches the US business school to a specific purpose: to understand and master the co-creative processes enabled by organization. I ground this interpretation in Joseph Wharton's (1826–1909) pioneering proposal for the business school and in the works of Mary Parker Follett (1868–1933) and Chester Barnard (1883–1961), who dedicated their lives to this purpose. In a series of reforms throughout the twentieth century, US business schools abandoned the founding vision. Follett and Barnard, working outside the academy, recognized that organization enabled unprecedented creativity but was little understood. They used their experience to generate this new knowledge. Follett developed her theory of creative experience and dynamic relating in organizations such as the city, club, and social movement. Barnard grounded his theory of applied social science in the corporation and specifically as a Chief Executive Officer (CEO), a position he held at New Jersey Bell Telephone, a subsidiary of American Telephone and Telegraph, for over 20 years.

My purpose in this chapter is to revisit and revive the original project to build an institution dedicated to understanding collective creativity, including that discovered within the arts and humanities. Follett and Barnard discovered that this focus entails transcending disciplinary and professional boundaries. In fact, collective creativity is a way of life (Hadot 2009). Thus all categories constituting the field of management and organization as we know it must be rethought and reworked. This volume takes a pivotal step in that regard; and this chapter shows how that step moves forward and backward, to the field's origins, at one and the same time.

I begin by explaining how the business school became institutionalized. Joseph Wharton founded the first school in order to address a crisis in the US economy and society. The college, which educated the nation's best and brightest, did not and could not teach science. Wharton deemed that this failure threatened the future of society. He wrote a visionary plan that was never fulfilled because business schools eventually came to serve narrow specialist interests. I then turn to Follett and Barnard, who recognized that no institution possessed the necessary knowledge.

They further asserted that the nature of this knowledge was such that it could only be developed by using it. I conclude with findings from the test of time. What we know about collective creativity is grounded in personal practice, but the business school has institutionalized such that it cannot integrate either the findings or the method. The next frontier is to integrate the institutional form and the substantive knowledge.

## The project: higher education for business

### *Joseph Wharton and the collegiate school of business*

Today's Wharton School of Business bears little comparison to the Wharton School of Finance and Economy (WSFE) of 1881. The latter, described extensively in "The Project" (Wharton 1881), was bold and radical. It reformed the traditional college and its allied institutions, the gentleman and high society, and the society based on tradition. Since colonial times, the college had been a cultural institution. It replicated Oxford and Cambridge, which initiated generations of young gentlemen into their aristocratic society. Wharton's institution would cultivate a new kind of gentleman for what he saw as a new society.

Throughout his career, Wharton had showed singular appreciation and mastery of these conditions. He amassed great personal wealth by taking advantage of newly won access to vast natural resources through metallurgy, manufacturing, and the creative exploitation of interacting factors that he called business management. Wharton made his fortune four times. He discovered and perfected a process for making zinc, which gave him a 420 percent return on his investment from 1855 to 1862. He rebuilt a bankrupt nickel mine and refinery, and he combined with other industrialists to dictate the price of Bismarck's new coin. This gave him a 300 percent return on his investment from 1868 to 1871. He invested in iron with perfect timing to exploit demand from the transcontinental railroad and led the traditionally Quaker and pacifist Bethlehem Steel into the lucrative armaments business (Sass 1982).

Wharton had learned by experience. He was self-taught in chemistry, and he apprenticed with local chemists. Philadelphia, his home, was the US's scientific center at the time (Baltzell 1979; Bridenbaugh and Bridenbaugh 1942). Working with local merchants and in "counting-houses," Wharton learned accounting, bookkeeping, insurance, banking, foreign exchange, and contracts. Wharton also cultivated political acumen and set policy. To finance the Civil War, the US had imposed a tariff on industrial metals. (An income tax was not passed until 1913.) Wharton organized fellow industrialists and lobbied successfully with members of Congress to extend the tariff. When he founded the WSFE, Wharton had successfully led these campaigns for 15 years. He also wrote, published, and distributed protectionist literature, including an 1875 textbook that he had placed in libraries nationwide (Sass 1982: 15).

A pillar of Wharton's plan for the WSFE was to inculcate protectionist policies. Wharton co-founded a thought school, led by the political economist Henry Carey, in Philadelphia. Until then, the prestigious New England colleges taught free trade, and so protectionism lacked intellectual clout (O'Connor 1994). Wharton's WSFE thus advanced a campaign for regional (for example, Pennsylvania's over New England's) and US economic and ideological autonomy from other countries, particularly British ideas about free trade.

Wharton researched higher education for two years, particularly "the vocationally oriented university" (Sass 1982: 35). This reference captures what Wharton saw as a crisis between the traditional and the emerging society. The former held to the values of permanence, wealth preservation, and bequeathed inheritance; the latter to the values of the new, scientific discovery, and enterprise. Initiates to the new society lacked institutions to cultivate the new values. Wharton's business school would thus be a cultural as well as an economic institution.

When Wharton founded the WSFE, "the business school" was a small proprietary school teaching bookkeeping and penmanship to lowly clerks. As Wharton explained in his strategic plan, a second-rank business could not properly train apprentices because it was second rank, and the heads of first-rank businesses were too busy to spend time educating. Young clerks learned business from fellow novices, and so they quickly fell into routine work of narrow scope. Traditional society called for young men to attend college; but upon graduation, they were too old for clerical apprenticeships and too educated to condescend to menial work. In drafting his plan, Wharton took inspiration from two new educational institutions: the scientific school and the technical institute. They had integrated science and technology courses into the curriculum (O'Connor 2012: 16–22). They improved upon apprenticeship by basing their instruction on "the broad principles deduced from all human knowledge." They "ground in science, as well as in art" pupils fit both "to practice what they have learned and to become themselves teachers and discoverers." Wharton praised these schools' achievements "in the world of matter." His WSFE would pursue the analogue of these in the world of industry.

In fact, Wharton glossed over the difficulties. Only one key element of his plan could be executed: the addition of specialized courses such as accounting, taxation, foreign exchange, business law, and transportation. The other elements – the use of science to solve social problems and the ability of college teachers to teach the skills and inculcate the values for the new society – were far more problematic than Wharton assumed. For example, he instructed the professor of taxation to teach "the proper objects and rates of taxation," "the public ends for which money may properly be raised by taxation," "the influences exercised upon the morality and prosperity of a community or nation" by taxation, and "the extent to which corporations should be encouraged by the State."[1] The law professor would teach "the directions in which improvements may be hoped and striven for with regard to 'harmonizing or unifying' the diverse legislation of the different states." The professor of industry, commerce, and transportation would cover "how industries advance in excellence, or decline, and shift from place to place";

> how by intelligent industry nations or communities thrive; how by superior skill and diligence some nations grow rich and powerful and how by idleness or ill-directed industry others become rude and poor; how a great nation should be as far as possible self-sufficient, maintaining a proper balance between agriculture, mining, and manufactures, and supplying its own wants; how mutual advantage results from the reciprocal exchange of commodities natural to one land for the diverse commodities natural to another, but how by craft in commerce one nation may take the substance of a rival and maintain for itself virtual monopoly of the most profitable and civilizing industries; how by suitable tariff legislation a nation may thwart such designs.
>
> *Wharton 1881: 8–15*

Wharton (1881: 8–15) also prescribed that the curriculum inculcate values such as the "immorality and practical inexpediency" of acquiring wealth "by winning it from another rather than by earning it through some sort of service to one's fellow-men"; the necessity of "system and accuracy in accounts, of thoroughness in whatever is undertaken, and of strict fidelity in trusts"; "caution" in incurring debt and "obligation of any kind" but "punctuality in payment of debt" and in "performance of engagements"; "abhorrence of repudiation of debt" and "commensurate abhorrence of lavish or inconsiderate incurring of public debt"; "the deep comfort and healthfulness of pecuniary independence" and "the consequent necessity of careful scrutiny of income and outgo . . . and of such management as will cause the first to exceed, even if but slightly the second"; "the necessity of rigorously punishing by legal penalties and by social exclusion those persons who commit frauds, betray trusts, or steal public funds, directly or indirectly"; and "the necessity for each nation to care for its own, and to maintain by all suitable means its industrial and financial independence." Wharton took for granted that professors subscribed to these values and could teach them and that students would accept and live them.

Even more ambitiously, Wharton instructed the professor of money and currency to teach "the phenomena and causes of panics and money crises." He stated that the professor of industry should teach "the 'nature and prevention' of strikes" and the principles upon which men "combine their energies for the accomplishment of any desirable object." This last instruction merits elaboration. Wharton wrote his plan for the WSFE from 1880 to 1882 in direct response to an economic and social crisis. From 1873 through 1879, the US had experienced the "Panic of '73," which one economist has called "the real Great Depression" (Nelson 2008). In that year, the entire US economy had collapsed when the leading financier of railroads, Jay Cooke and Company, declared bankruptcy. The railroads were the nation's top non-agricultural employer. The Baltimore and Ohio Railroad, which paid the lowest wages of all railroad lines, asked its workers to take a second pay reduction. This cut their wages in half. They went on strike and workers on other railroad lines joined them, causing the first general strike in US history. It lasted for 45 days and ended only when President Rutherford B. Hayes sent federal troops to the major cities. Estimated revenues lost to each railroad line were US$2 million; estimated wages lost to engineers were US$600,000. Sabotage figures were even higher – approximately US$5 million per line. The country not only suffered for the duration of the strike but the means to recover from it the railroad and facilities, were also destroyed.

The crisis exaggerated the stark contrast between the haves and the have-nots. A few industrialists had enough reserves to withstand the crisis and even benefit from it. They bought out their competitors and grew their businesses. In 1879, the Standard Oil trust was created. Nine people controlled 90 percent of US pipelines and 90 percent of the country's oil refining businesses. These circumstances explain Wharton's aspiration to develop individuals "qualif[ied] ... for the solution of the social problems incident to our civilization." The business school's students would know the principles on which men "combine their energies for the accomplishment of any desirable object," and they had to appreciate "the fundamental fact that the United States is a nation, composed of populations wedded together for life ... and not a loose bundle of incoherent communities."

## *Business school reforms: 1900 through the twentieth century*

Wharton's project called for two levels of knowledge: development not only of the ability to creatively engage science in industry but also of the curriculum to train in this process. This knowledge was not at hand, but in the academy it was known as social science. The University of Pennsylvania used Wharton's money to bring in newly minted social science professors from Germany, the leading provider of PhDs at the time. They were inculcated in a thought school, the *Verein für Sozialpolitik*, which resonated with social-reform movements in the US (O'Connor 2012: 45). The new faculty was initially well met by progressive Philadelphia high society; but as advocates worked more intensively for more radical industrial reform and as the federal government began taking industrial regulation seriously, university trustees and alumni deemed the social science faculty too activist.

The WSFE split between the German and non-German trained faculty. In particular, the accountants resented the status system based on the PhD, which made them second class. They formed their own business school, the New York School of Commerce, Accounts, and Finance (NYUC) in 1900. This move dovetailed with accountants' pursuit of professional status through the Certified Public Accountant (CPA). Rejecting the social scientists' political partisanship and imitating the professionalization of medicine, they formulated higher education for business as a set of specialties. NYUC effectively created a new institution: the Vocational School of Business (VSB). It welcomed those that even Wharton's WSFE had followed tradition by excluding: adults, working people, women, immigrants, adolescents, and dropouts. In a few months and after-hours, students could earn a certificate leading to a job or promotion. Most faculty were full-time practitioners, promoting their businesses and recruiting desirable employees.

The VSB made business school popular in every sense of the word. Society now had a thriving social elevator, but the VSB ignored the task of managing specialists to work together in organization.

Wallace B. Donham, Dean of the Harvard Graduate School of Business Administration from 1919 to 1948, recognized this void. He focused on the executive function of overseeing specialists and a new knowledge field, administration, to support this function. Like the accountants who founded NYUC, Donham objected to the reliance on social science, particularly economics, in business education; but unlike them, he sought an alternative theoretical foundation for administration. Through his collaboration with Elton Mayo and the Human Relations School (O'Connor 1999), Donham added psychology to the mix. Ironically, this move undermined Donham's project by making business a hybrid of other disciplines rather than an autonomous field, but Donham pursued psychology not as an end in itself but as a step in differentiating administration from economics.

Donham drew extensively from his education at Harvard Law School (HLS). He had attended HLS just as the institution reached its ambition to become the nation's leading law school. HLS faculty member Christopher Langdell distinguished the new higher professional education from the old clerical proprietary education. Langdell followed the natural and physical sciences by delineating between basic and applied science. For law to achieve the higher level of professionalization, it needed a basic science. Langdell mined legal decisions for the underlying principles to establish this "basis." Donham decided to do the same for business. But unlike the law, business lacked the corpus of written opinions and the tradition of decision based on precedent. Donham resolved that his faculty would write the cases and extract the core principles at the same time.

By that time, however, the field had already institutionalized and advanced by specialization. Business professors at Harvard Business School (HBS) earned about one-third of their income from their private consultancies. They used the Harvard case method to cultivate professional relationships that built up their practices. HBS went into the case-publishing business and sold pedagogical content based on specialization to business schools eager for models and curriculum. In the end, Donham's vision to develop the field of administration not only succumbed to the logic of specialization but also accelerated it.

As the business school became more popular and wealthy, its coexistence with the mainstream academy became more problematic. Vocationalism was not sustainable. The crisis was solved through another reform, the "New Look" or "Business School Revolution," which outsourced the scientific foundations of business to the disciplines, particularly the social and quantitative sciences (Khurana 2007: 259–78). This move resolved the business school's vocationalism, but it also confirmed that the business school had no unifying purpose.

## Pioneers in collective creativity

### *Mary Parker Follett: dynamic relating and creative experience*

Whereas Wharton remade the college to educate for dynamic industry, Follett saw dynamic industry as one form of dynamic society, which entails a quality of relating that she called consciously creative. This theory may be seen as a social science (Follett 1918), a philosophy (Ansell 2009), and a way of life (Cabot 1934). Drawing from her peer-learning experiences in schools, clubs, and social movements, she posited that collective creativity entails no super-authority or deference but demands more individual responsibility: "I am constantly being acted upon, no one is encouraging me to act . . . Thus am I robbed of my most precious possession – my responsibilities – for only the active process of participation can shape me for the social purpose" (Follett 1918: 235).

Follett came of age in Boston where communities divided along economic, political, and cultural lines. These differences stemmed from immigration, especially the second generation, whose expectations and ambitions exceeded those of their parents. Government, schools, and other institutions did not address the situation, but neither did the youths and their families. Follett studied with the greatest professors at Oxford, such as Henry Sidgwick, and the leading public intellectual at Harvard, Albert Hart Bushnell. She was also educated and inculcated in peer-learning traditions open to women, such as the women's club and the college women's settlement house movement. In these domains as well, she trained with the best: Katherine Bowlker and Pauline Agassiz Shaw (O'Connor 2012: 90–4).

The business school and the academy had not worked out the principles for cooperation. Follett had. "The biological law is growth by the continuous integration of simple, specific responses; in the same way do we build up our characters by uniting diverse tendencies into new action patterns; social progress follows exactly the same law" (Follett 1924: 174). She posited four principles of organization, that is, coordinated action: (1) "direct contact of the responsible people concerned"; (2) "in the early stages"; (3) entailing "the reciprocal relating of all the factors in a situation"; as (4) "a continuing process" (Metcalf and Urwick 1940 [Follett 1933]: 297). The first principle set the foundation for the other three. Responsibility is a relation. It cannot be taught, but without it, creative relating cannot begin and dynamic society cannot grow.

### *Follett's management training*

The document that most extensively probes this difficulty is Follett's management training. Follett gave this teaching to the leaders and managers who ran her community centers in neighborhoods throughout Boston. Club leaders supervised activity-oriented groups such as sports teams and theater troupes. Center managers oversaw internal operations as well as the center's relationship with the neighborhood. Follett said that the centers, to be successful, should become a means "by which the people themselves can furnish the satisfaction of their desires" and "get together to express the best in themselves."[2] She held the managers responsible for achieving this goal.

The center members ranged from 14 to 21 years old. They were not in school and many were unemployed. They often came from neighborhoods that lacked a common language, and so music became "the chief means of stimulating fellowship and making felt the common bond." Follett instructed the club leaders to use subject teaching in order to teach the more important lesson, "the social spirit," the "sense which makes us useful members of society": "how to work and play harmoniously together, and to encourage responsibility." Clubs held regular meetings where they made business and operating decisions. Follett's goal was that each club would govern itself and that eventually, center members would run the center. But when Follett gave her training in 1913, the members were not ready for this. Follett instructed the club leaders to oversee the business meetings and gradually develop members' ability to govern themselves. She instructed them to begin with small but concrete decisions, such as the amount of club dues. The managers had to forfeit their right to veto, allow the discussion to become heated and prolonged, and gradually turn over greater responsibility as more members participated more fully in making harder decisions.

The seed was the acceptance of responsibility by members, and what looks like transfer of responsibility by supervisors is in fact acceptance of the higher responsibility entailed in developing members' responsibility. Everything hinged on discerning and giving the right amount of responsibility at the right time.

Follett's instructions to managers show what is entailed in this higher responsibility. They had to relate to individual members, club leaders, individual clubs, club subjects, club activities, the membership as a whole, the neighborhood as a whole, and the community center movement nationally as well as in Boston. The quality of their relating had to encompass both "surface characteristics" and "underlying forces" that "make for righteousness" and which, if "got hold of and fostered and nurtured," might "come to their full fruition." Finally, they had to relate to immediate concrete goals, such as making sure that the centers upheld their contractual agreements, and the long-term vision to make the center integral to neighborhood and city life.

The center had to become a means for people to satisfy their desires – not just any desires but those associated with "the best in themselves" – by definition, an individual *and* collective orientation. Follett explained that the center held out

> the greatest possibility we have ever had in city life for a full expression of the people by themselves, for all to get together to express the best in themselves, not the best in yourself or the best in myself, but the best in *themselves*.
>
> *Follett 1913: 3–20, emphasis in original*

Also, "the best" has to be a moving target. Managers must discern both readiness and fruition. "Are [neighborhood residents] ready to take an interest in municipal affairs?"; "Do the men need to be aroused to a greater interest in civic affairs, or do they merely need some way of expressing their civic interest?"

Follett linked responsibility and the satisfaction of natural as well as cultivated desires. Participation in club and center activities would help members get what they want, but – as guided by Follett, center managers, and center leaders – these activities would also shape their wants as regards "the social purpose." In turn, by participating in the life of the city, the members would shape the social purpose.

Follett's subsequent writings on management reaffirmed this creative relation between the individual and the collectivity and between want-fulfilling and want-shaping. The growth of specialist knowledge and positions in formal organization called for more personal responsibility and for higher cultivation and satisfaction of desire, even as hierarchical relations encouraged deferring to formal authority (for example, Metcalf and Urwick 1940 [Follett 1925]: 50–70, 146–66, 210–29, 247–69). This dilemma would become Barnard's central focus.

## *Chester I. Barnard's experiments in organization*

With the exception of Henri Fayol, Barnard is the only Chief Executive who wrote seminal organization and management theory. His work influenced Herbert Simon and the Carnegie school, which led the partnership between the business school and the academy (see later). Barnard's less visible but more pioneering contribution is the relationship to experience by which he generated his theory.

Barnard saw the knowledge crisis not only as a lack of understanding of formal organization but more importantly as a lack of understanding of the human condition as playing out in formal organization. He raised the stakes in what Follett theorized as processes to cultivate and fulfill desire: as formal organization becomes more crystallized and widespread, it opens and closes creative possibilities at the same time. It opens possibilities because many people can do what one person cannot do. It closes possibilities because the human condition in organization is to defer to others or to "the organization." Barnard experienced this paradox intimately and made it the central focus and thrust of his inquiry.

Barnard was CEO of New Jersey Bell Telephone from 1927 to 1948. He had joined the company in 1909 and had moved laterally and hierarchically in the organization. When he wrote his classic book *The Functions of the Executive* (1968 [1938]), he had been CEO for ten years. Barnard maintained that little was known about organization and that the generally accepted knowledge was not only false but also destructive (Barnard 1968 [1938]: xxviii). Since management was a lever of value creation in organization, the stakes for society were high (1968 [1938]: 282, 289–90). Barnard placed a high premium on experience and a pragmatic relation to experience that he called "intimate, interested, habitual" (1968 [1938]: xxxiv).

Taking his executive practice as an experimental condition, Barnard recognized that organization called for greater personal responsibility whilst diminishing the individual. This dilemma called for "a culture of the individual ... so that great desires make great effort worthwhile" (Wolf and Iino 1986 [Barnard 1934]: 27). From the organizational viewpoint – a conceptual challenge per se – the task was "to secure the essential degree of coordination of a vast system of activities, while securing the degree of centralization and autonomy essential to initiative and to responsible behavior" (Wolf and Iino 1986 [Barnard 1934]: 17–18). Barnard probed "responsible behavior." Formal organization required an equal but opposite force strengthening the individual and the forces of individualism. The counterbalancing emphasis on the individual had not advanced in tandem with formal organization. The challenge of formal organization was to develop the individual who could use formal organization to develop himself in order to develop organization.

## *The fourth door*

Barnard explained how he came to this view (Wolf and Iino 1986 [Barnard 1934]: 10–11). As a youth, he had cultivated, and been cultivated in, individualism. Due to his father's bankruptcy, Barnard was "thrown on [his] own resources" in his youth. He earned his own living and was accepted to New England's finest schools. Enjoying this success, he compared himself to the farmer who credits the harvest to his own efforts, which are trivial compared with "the energy of the sun, the chemistry of the soil, the vital but undefinable processes of life" – the "true sources." He likewise looked on the family, the "social groups of which I was a part, the schools and universities, the railroads, the organizations of industry, the government, as things made available to me by nature rather than by the deliberate and largely conscious effort of men acting in cooperation."

Barnard then entered "one of the greatest and most complex collective enterprises ever organized on a commercial basis." Hundreds of thousands of investors supplied its capital; hundreds of thousands of employees "carefully arranged in a hierarchy of positions and authorities" conducted its operations. The "collectivity called the State" authorized its legal existence. Its "conduct, rights, privileges" were governed by laws and customs spanning generations. Even the value of the service depended on the number of people using it. Barnard recognized the "tremendous power" of this "collective operation" that "accomplished many things impossible except by cooperation on a grand scale." Barnard experienced a stark contrast between his individualistic values and those of the organization. "Constantly expressed phrases" and what he would later call "moral codes" – whose articulation he later theorized to be the most creative executive function (Barnard 1968 [1938]: 272–82) – prescribed what to do. He experienced these instructions as "repression of the individual who was becoming less and less significant." He also felt this constraint in the "intangible barriers of departments, grades and ranks, policies, appropriations, laws, prejudices and economic limitations of customers." Barnard turned away from the "rugged individualism" he had embraced. Now, "facts and principles and organizations and collective action were everything, and the individual was and could be nothing." But this idea was just as destructive as extreme individualism. Also, his supervisors and society continued to treat him as an individual. "I could not eliminate myself from myself." Barnard described three responses: lethargy due to failure to resolve the dilemma; passivity from being a cog in a wheel; and anarchy from excessive individualism. He credited his supervisors for his escape through the "fourth door": that of "directing my individual efforts not only in conformance with, but in furtherance of the objectives of the organization." He "gradually learned that properly understood and with intelligent adjustment the individual can secure from collective organization great expansion of individual opportunity for accomplishment and for self-expression." However, the tension between "duty to one's self" and "duty to the ever present collectivities of which one is inescapably a part" was constitutive of organizational life (Wolf and Iino 1986 [Barnard 1934]: 11–12). Barnard called this "moral complexity."

Underlying this tension was a conscious response toward experience and life itself that Barnard best articulated in his commencement speeches. Finding one commonality in the universe, nature, collectivities, individuals, and himself, Barnard put forth "a helpful view in accordance with reality": "[T]o consider life essentially a process of attaining a balance between conflicting forces" (Chester I. Barnard Papers [CIPB] Book 8: 1-3257). Therefore "the most important process in developing the capacity to live abundantly is to follow that course under which experience of conflicts of ideas, emotions, and principle successfully resolved, may be richest" (CIPB Book 8: 1-3259). The attitude that conflict is inevitable and normal is "an important personal attribute aiding in the maintenance of balance under conditions of stress which are inescapable and are especially so of those who attempt a life of self-development" (CIPB Book 8: 1-3259).

Barnard cultivated what he called "the feeling mind" (1968 [1938]: 322): the use of the body in living, and the use of the mind in distilling, experience. In the preface to his classic book, he expressed disappointment for failing to convey "the *sense* of organization, the dramatic and aesthetic feeling" that words cannot capture (1968 [1938]: xxxiv, emphasis in original). Organization science required people who could perceive "the significant elements" – the "structure of the symphony, the art of its composition, and the skill of its execution." Barnard played piano. In his youth, he led a dance orchestra. He was president of the Bach Society of New Jersey. For Barnard, the metaphor is sensual as well as conceptual.

William Wolf, who conducted the only documented interview with Barnard, asked how he was able to put his experience into words. Barnard said he had to split his personality and he compared himself to Dr Jekyll and Mr Hyde. He did not take notes because writing distracts from "the stream of events in which you are actively concerned." Barnard wrestled with his ideas. After giving a speech that colleagues encouraged him to publish, he realized whilst rewriting it that "I was not sure I knew what I meant myself" by organization. He began "a long effort" to define it (Wolf 1974: 21). Wolf's interview with Barnard, held two months before Barnard's death, shows him still rethinking (Wolf 1973: 15).

> I'm always carrying on an argument with myself. I can't go to sleep talking about it, and very often the picture that comes up is some other fellow I know very well, and he tackles me . . . . I can't help it. I'm living in a world all the time – a world of imagination.
>
> *Barnard 1946: 26*

Barnard avoided intellectualization and other distractions to engage fully in action. Acting in uncertainty creates "a state of tension . . . which greatly expands the scope and increases the sensitivity of the perceptual processes so that partly consciously and much more unconsciously a much larger proportion of the concrete is absorbed" (CIPB Book 6: 1-2016). When verbalizing, however, Barnard exaggerated phenomena. He thus "orchestrated" his relation to the interacting forces in and around him. This shows in his figurative language. He preferred dilemmas, dualities, bipolarities, and juxtaposition: formal versus informal, abstract versus concrete, individualism versus collectivism. But there is no necessary opposition. Opposition is a trope that infuses ideas with feeling – in this case, tension. Positing two extremes summons the most tension and energy, which may be directed to creative purposes.

## History repeats itself

Despite the creativity and humanism of Follett and Barnard, business schools did not develop in the direction that they indicated. Instead, based at the Carnegie Graduate School of Industrial Administration (GSIA), George Leland Bach (1915–1994) led the "New Look" reform or "Business School Revolution." This reform was a direct response to HBS's failure to develop a theoretical foundation for administration and its resulting perpetuation of what the academy called vocationalism. Bach solved the problem by recruiting a faculty of star researchers from multiple disciplines, but particularly the quantitative and behavior sciences, defined as the "underlying disciplines" or basic sciences of business. But once again, faculty members focused on their own specialties and careers (Khurana 2007: 283–4).

Moving to Stanford, CA in 1962, Bach reflected on the impact of the reform he had led and the future of management education. In 1972, he spoke to the American Association of Collegiate Schools of Business (AACSB). He referenced opinion polls showing that the public did not trust business and its motives. "The decline in trust and esteem has been greater for business than for any other of the major institutions of the past decade," he noted. Bach also reflected on the Vietnam War. Despite its military power, the US could not do much there "because we didn't have a sense of legitimacy. The world wouldn't back us up; we couldn't do it ourselves." Likewise, he asserted, the legitimacy of the market and of business "rests on the fundamental proposition that the system is making an important contribution to the welfare of most people in society." Bach called for business schools to examine their own legitimacy. He also declared the need for "a more basic understanding among businessmen of the complex socio-economic-political interfaces between businesses and all the diverse parts of 'the public'." He noted "the challenge of 'equity'" that "may well dominate the 'efficiency' arguments." Finally, he identified the fundamental case as that "for individual freedom and decentralization of decision making and authority, more than just economic efficiency" (Bach 1972).

Bach's appeals recall Wharton's pioneering vision for the business school in 1881. After retiring from Stanford, Bach convened a study group on the future of management education.

In 1985, he issued a memo to the group calling for "fundamental knowledge," which he described as the only knowledge that "will prove to be relatively useful in dealing with a wide variety of unforeseeable problems in the future." This knowledge would also "clarify what management is, who managers are, and what managers do and are expected to do" (Bach 1984).

Bach's reform took international as well as national scope (Djelic 2001; Mazza *et al.* 2005). Supported by the Ford Foundation, the Centers of Excellence programme designated a new category of institution attached to prestigious research universities. The elite business school was a business model and turnkey method. Simply by hiring PhDs from top-ranked programmes in the quantitative and behavioral sciences, a business school could become elite. This policy grew the university's internal economy as new PhDs obtained jobs in a fast-growing, prestigious new institution – and precisely as transpired with the CSB, VSB, and HBS, these PhDs focused on building their academic reputations in their home disciplines (McGrath 2007).

The university-based business school introduced the idea of an institution devoted to understanding co-creative processes among institutions, between institutions and individuals, among individuals, and within the individual. Joseph Wharton's business school sought to understand and master creative relating between science and industry and between formal education and society. Follett's and Barnard's experiments provided the vision, theory, principles, and methods that Wharton's school and subsequent business schools lacked and could not develop.

As the Carnegie Report shows (Sullivan, Ehrlich, and Colby, this volume), the test of time has exposed a looming gap between the formal organization of the business school on the one hand and the personal knowledge about collective co-creation on the other. The former serves the specialist disciplines and professions. But the first lesson of organization is that it requires a unifying purpose. The business school's structure affords no such purpose. The original and pioneering vision, and even the mere idea of vision, remain lost to time.

The persistence and stakes of this gap raise three questions. First, is the academy the appropriate institution to advance the project? Follett worked in the city, club, and social movement; Barnard in the executive office and in formal organization. But personal knowledge is difficult to pass on, and its transmission depends largely on equally personal relationships. The research university holds out the promise of an institution that can codify and disseminate knowledge on a large scale and over a long time. A close partnership between academics and practitioners would be ideal. But this would require three radical concessions by academics. They would have to have the same respect for practitioners that they do for academics, they would have to co-create as well as study, and they would have to make the collaboration more important than their disciplines.

Second, is it even possible to institutionalize creative relating and experience? Is there an inherent gap between what individuals can know and what institutions can teach? Barnard said he had to split himself in two, like Dr Jekyll and Mr Hyde, in order to formalize his experience; however, there are simply too few examples of this research at present. It is premature to answer this question, and it should be part of the agenda that this book addresses.

Third and finally, should this project be called management or organization, and does it belong in the business school? The work transcends disciplinary and conventional thinking. Follett's work may be considered a politics of desire; Barnard's a poetics of structure. Again, this volume offers encouragement in this regard. In fact, the word "management" remains vague and the field shows little interest in defining it. If a consensus developed that management and organization studies focus on collective creativity, then this name suits the project. But if the words continue to be associated with a privileged group holding itself apart from the social body that gives it life, and if society continues to associate these words with wealth accumulation for the few, then other names and places must be found.

## Notes

1 All citations are from Wharton 1881: 8–15.
2 The following citations are from Follett 1913: 3–20.

## References


Ansell, C. (2009) 'Mary Parker Follett and pragmatist organization'. *In*: P. Adler (ed.) *The Oxford Handbook of Sociology and Organization Studies: Classical Foundations*. Oxford: Oxford University Press, pp. 464–85.

Bach, G. (1972) '*AACSB – Las Vegas*.' George Leland Bach Papers, Stanford University Historical Collections, SC 502, Box 8, Folder 14.

Bach, G. (1984) *'Where does business education stand now? How well does it meet society's needs. What can be done? By whom? How? When?'* George Leland Bach Papers, Stanford University Historical Collections, SC 502, Box 7, Folder 1.

Baltzell, E. (1979) *Puritan Boston and Quaker Philadelphia: Two Protestant Ethics and the Spirit of Class Authority and Leadership*. New York, NY: Free Press.

Barnard, C. (1946) *'Grand Jury case for human relations course, April 18, 1946'*, Chester I. Barnard Papers, Harvard University Historical Collections, Carton 2, Folio 69.

Barnard, C. (1968 [1938]) *The Functions of the Executive*, 2nd edn. Cambridge, MA: Harvard University Press.

Bridenbaugh, C. and Bridenbaugh, J. (1942) *Rebels and Gentlemen: Philadelphia in the Age of Franklin*. New York, NY: Reynal and Hitchcock.

Cabot, R. (1934) 'Mary Parker Follett, an appreciation', *Radcliffe Quarterly*, April, 80–2.

Chester I. Barnard Papers (CIBP) Private collection of William B. Wolf, Seattle, WA.

Djelic, M.-L. (2001) *Exporting the American Model: The Postwar Transformation of European Business*. Oxford: Oxford University Press.

Follett, M. (1913) *Evening Centers: Aims and Duties of Leaders Therein*. Boston, MA: City of Boston Printing Department.

Follett, M. (1918) *The New State: Group Organization the Solution of Popular Government*. New York, NY: Longmans, Green.

Follett, M. (1924) *Creative Experience*. New York, NY: Longmans, Green.

Hadot, P. (2009) *The Present Alone is Our Happiness: Conversations with Jeannie Carlier and Arnold I. Davidson*. Stanford, CA: Stanford University Press.

Khurana, R. (2007) *From Higher Aims to Hired Hands: The Social Transformation of American Business Schools and the Unfulfilled Promise of Management as a Profession*. Princeton, NJ: Princeton University Press.

McGrath, R. (2007) 'No longer a stepchild: How the management field can come into its own', *Academy of Management Journal*, 50(6), 1365–78.

Mazza, C., Sahlin-Andersson, K., and Strandgaard Pedersen, J. (2005) 'European constructions of an American model', *Management Learning*, 36(4), 471–91.

Metcalf, H. and Urwick, L. (eds.) (1940) *Dynamic Administration: The Collected Papers of Mary Parker Follett*. New York, NY: Harper & Bros.

Nelson, S. (2008) *The Real Great Depression*. Available from: Srnels.people.wm.edu/articles/realGrtDepr.html (accessed 1 February 2014).

O'Connor, E. (1999) 'The politics of management thought: a case study of the Harvard Business School and the Human Relations School', *Academy of Management Review*, 24(1), 117–31.

O'Connor, E. (2012) *Creating New Knowledge in Management: Appropriating the Field's Lost Foundations*. Stanford, CA: Stanford University Press.

O'Connor, M. (1994) *Origins of Academic Economics in the United States*. New York, NY: Columbia University Press.

Sass, S. (1982) *The Pragmatic Imagination: A History of The Wharton School, 1881–1981*. Philadelphia, PA: University of Pennsylvania Press.

Wharton, J. (1881) *'Agreement between Joseph Wharton and the Trustees of the University of Pennsylvania'*, 22 June 1881 (1923 reprint, Cat. No. UPP 15.3), University of Pennsylvania Archives (UPA), Philadelphia.

Wolf, W. (1973) *Conversations with Chester I. Barnard*. Ithaca, NY: New York State School of Industrial and Labor Relations, Cornell University.

Wolf, W. (1974) *The Basic Barnard: An Introduction to Chester I. Barnard and His Theories of Organization and Management*. Ithaca, NY: New York State School of Industrial and Labor Relations, Cornell University.

Wolf, W. and Iino, H. (eds.) (1986) *Philosophy for Managers: Selected Papers of Chester I. Barnard*. Ithaca, NY: ILR Press.

# 4

# 'Humanities' Business' and other narratives

## How to read the future of management education?

*Ulrike Landfester, Nicolaj Tofte Brenneche and Queralt Prat-i-Pubill*

> In summary, management education currently is clearly at a crossroads. Many of the observations made by AACSB, EFMD and the Colby Report point to a series of consistent weaknesses in the development of a range of managerial capabilities from creative, critical thinking to integrative problem-framing and solving that would enhance the basic knowledge of business and analytic skills.
>
> *Thomas et al. 2014: 11*

> Every generation thinks it knows what it does, especially the reformers in a generation.
>
> *Locke 1996: 145*

### Introduction

The following remarks present the background to this chapter by outlining the current debate on the integration of the humanities and social sciences into management education. Based on this outline, we establish the historical and systematic framework for an analysis of three selected reports on management education, which is subsequently presented in the manner of a recursive operation. Because the current debate shows an emerging consensus among business schools and other stakeholders of management education that the integration of the humanities and social sciences might be a productive and even necessary factor in the future of management education, the chapter as a whole aims at substantiating this consensus by applying humanities' and social sciences' narratological expertise to the arguments and hypotheses offered by those reports to showcase the potential of such integrational endeavours.

In 2011, the report *Rethinking Undergraduate Business Education. Liberal Learning for the Profession* (Colby *et al.* 2011; see also Sullivan, Ehrlich and Colby, this volume), which was sponsored by the Carnegie Foundation, reacted to the recent financial crises by pointing out that management education could and should be improved by integrating the expertise offered by the liberal arts or, put from a European perspective, by the humanities and social sciences. Since then, this issue has developed into a crucial part of the debate on what Thomas *et al.* (2014) in the passage quoted above describe as the *raison d'être* of business schools worldwide, that is the enhancement of 'the basic knowledge of business and analytic skills' by 'creative thinking' and 'integrative problem-framing' (Colby *et al.* 2011: 11). The debate focusing on such skills in management education, most recently summed up comprehensively by Thomas *et al.* (2014), has identified a number of 'specific skill gaps in particular concerning the teaching of 'creativity and innovative thinking', 'ethical and moral perspectives', 'critical thinking and skills of reflection and integration' and 'skills in cognitive and emotional intelligence' (Colby *et al.* 2011: 23).

The appearance of the Carnegie Report (also known as the Colby Report) is indicative of the fact that for quite some time now this debate has approached the questions as to how those skills could be taught by looking for answers in the humanities and social sciences. Already in 1959 with the publication of the first Carnegie Report on US management education, a strong plea was made to make more and better use of the liberal arts (Pierson 1959). The Carnegie Report of 2011 has shown that in the meantime some US business schools have already moved to tentatively introducing those subjects into management education on several levels – and it has also pointed out systemic problems encountered by such moves. These range from basic organizational difficulties in coordinating curricula and faculty from different disciplines; the seeming impossibility of agreement on the precise disciplinary content of integrated courses and programmes; up to and including the respective institutions' concepts of what the humanities and social sciences exactly are or are not and what they could or should offer to management education.

Two years after the appearance of the Carnegie Report, the Presidency of the University of St Gallen in Switzerland launched the research project 'Humanities' Business'. The project's title is a shortened version of its motto: 'Humanity's Business is the Humanities' Business'. It has to be explained at this point that the term 'humanities', as the project team uses it, programmatically includes the social sciences which, we fully realize, is not self-evident because academic tradition today still views the humanities and the social sciences as separate sets of disciplines. We, however, use the term inclusively for the reason that the term 'social sciences' in management education is usually employed rather broadly for fields and competences that have come to be considered to be part of its core fields and thus are subject to the same normative epistemological standards of research and teaching content. As we are proceeding on the insight that the development these standards went through over recent decades is part of the problem that the integration of as yet non-core fields and competences is trying to solve, we decided on our part to use the term 'humanities' broadly for expertise and practices in the field of humanities and social sciences that are not yet part of the core of management education but are under discussion to be developed in this direction.

The project's motto encodes the collaborating team's leading hypothesis that the humanities and social sciences are indeed offering several specialized types of knowledge that are not readily available to students of management and related disciplines in their core courses but are certainly relevant to their professional education. This hypothesis is based on the assumption – an assumption that seems to be the undisputed core of the consensus emerging from the debate outlined earlier – that the professional practice of management can no longer be taught as merely the efficient application of tools to further the financial success of any single enterprise. Rather, in light of the huge impact that the recent crises have shown management practices to have on global society as a whole, it must be taught as a societal practice that is embedded in an enormously complex web of individual and collective interests, historically grown and culturally informed patterns of thought and behaviour and methodologically diverse approaches to problem-solving, to name but a few of the issues arising from this embeddedness. The institutional background of the project is the university's Contextual Studies programme,[1] which was established in 2001 in the course of the Bologna reform and is currently being restructured by the Humanities' Business project in the role of a conceptual think tank. In this role, we are currently creating a report on European business schools' best practices of the integration of humanities and social sciences into management education, aiming to complement the Carnegie Report, which exclusively covers US business schools' efforts in this field.

The ultimate goal of the project is to offer some constructive perspectives on how to improve on such attempts at integration, ideally involving the stakeholders of both management education and the humanities and social sciences in the process. Preliminary findings gathered by the project team's review of the available literature on this topic, however, suggest that the mere reporting on the status quo – either in US or in European business schools – is unlikely to achieve that because the problems encountered by schools that try for an integrational education are problems not simply of institutional governance or of financial, infrastructural and faculty resources, but rather of how to deal with the notion of knowledge as such (see Parker, this volume). To integrate knowledge or knowledges from other disciplines into curricula, which are in themselves based on a strong certainty about the inviolability of their disciplinary cores, obviously challenges this notion to an extent that goes far beyond the complexities of organization inherent in a serious reform of management education.

Therefore, a report covering this angle clearly needs an approach that performs rather than stipulates the integration of the humanities' and social sciences' expertise. On those grounds, the following deliberations set out the methodological foundations for such an approach by focusing on the genre of reporting itself. They are based on the assumption that the genre of reporting participates in shaping its subject through providing both conceptual input and benchmarking information, thus constructing the future of management education discursively. Their main aim is to understand the normative framework underlying the conceptualizations offered, as well as the selection of the examples used for benchmarking. To achieve this, we will treat the historical and current discourse on management education as a group of texts whose common subject matter has generated specific – genre-typical – techniques of stating their case. In short, we will treat them as narratives aiming to generate coherent concepts of management education, which are not, in and of themselves, necessarily preordained by facts but rather developed through the desire to make sense of those facts by selecting and reframing them according to the respective point of view of their authors and their contexts.

The reshaping of academic education in Prussia during the first half of the nineteenth century according to Wilhelm von Humboldt's concept of cosmopolitanism marked the emergence of a university system that is still today broadly recognized as the standard paradigm of the modern university. Humboldt took the idea of the *studium generale* as it was called in pre-modern universities – a first-year education in the 'liberal arts'[2] that was mandatory to all students regardless of their later specialization – to a whole new level. Indeed, it was Humboldt who first advanced the case for an integrated type of education, arguing that it was the university's mission to make its students into cosmopolitans or citizens of the world by offering them a holistic educational experience compounded of all types of academic knowledge instead of merely a narrow professional training. The practical implementation of Humboldt's ideas, however, came with the institutional segregation of these types of knowledge into academic disciplines, creating boundaries that over the past two centuries have solidified into near-insurmountable abuttals. Born from the conviction that students' education should be able to draw on all areas of expertise available, the Humboldtian university has therefore evolved into a system that today threatens to sabotage its original purpose.

In the framework of this system, dealing with narratives has been firmly within the remit of the humanities' and social sciences' disciplinary domain. This was and still is the case, partly because the data the scholars in this domain work with are mostly embedded in or consisting of narratives, partly because working with those data requires an expertise in the areas of fiction and rhetoric that is traditionally viewed to be incompatible with the standards of rigour professed to by most other disciplines, including economics and management studies. For some decades now, however, the latter has begun to recognize the importance of the role that narratives are playing in the construction of societal reality as a whole, seeing that, as Bruner (1990) points out, they not only provide 'interpretative templates for sense-making' (Czarniawska 2008) but actively create the frameworks of value for making sense of said reality. As Grint (2005) and Fairhurst (2007) have comprehensively shown in their studies on narratives and leadership, the narratives we draw upon and are embedded in affect the way we perceive complex issues and thus affect the way we engage with these issues in practice. The issue in question here is the integration of humanities' and social sciences' expertise in management education. This means that the narratives on this issue, which are created by reports on management education, are affected by previous narratives whose acts of making sense directly or indirectly feed into the framework of values created by those reports, whilst at the same time the reports themselves affect practical reality by imposing such frameworks on the data they present.

In light of these preliminary reflections, the genre of reporting on management education begs a number of interesting questions, the first and foremost being how reports on management education perform the context in which the necessity of changes becomes visible and, indeed, inescapable. Analysing this, it is necessary to determine which issues are rendered critical and which are marginalized or left out altogether, which purposes of management education are seen as central, which interventions and changes are proposed to improve on the accomplishment of those purposes and, finally and perhaps most crucially, what overall logics are used to combine all these factors into a cohesive concept. Indeed, we could say that the Carnegie Report established a landscape that this volume is responding to.

To test the viability of such an analysis, we have chosen three reports – all three of which have already answered at least part of the first question posed earlier in the affirmative because all three reports either have proved or are certainly about to prove their practical impact on the reality of management education. Our first report is by Howard Thomas, who wrote *Securing the Future of Management Education: Competitive Destruction or Constructive Innovation?* (Thomas *et al.* 2014). Thomas is the former Dean of the Lee Kong Chian Business School at Singapore Management University and also former Vice-President of the European Foundation for Management Development (EFMD), which runs the European Quality Improvement System (EQUIS). This is a system that will have a crucial influence on business schools' overall acceptance of the improvement on management education by the integration of the humanities and social sciences. The second report by Rakesh Khurana, Professor at the Harvard Business School and author of the study *From Higher Aims to Hired Hands* (Khurana 2007), has had an important part in the 2009 establishment of the famous MBA oath by which Harvard Business School (HBS) students on graduation publicly commit to professional integrity. Finally, the Carnegie Report by Anne Colby, Thomas Ehrlich, William M. Sullivan and Jonathan R. Dolle has, since its appearance in 2011, become a highly influential motor of the debate on the future of management education, especially concerning the integration of the humanities and social sciences. Only a year after its appearance, it led to the renowned Aspen Institute's founding of a new Undergraduate Business Education Consortium in the context of their Business in Society Program (BSP) closely involving several of the report's authors (Sullivan, Ehrlich and Colby, this volume).

## Reporting for a field in transition: diagnostical, genealogical and programmatic narratives

Recent and current reports in management education practically all implicitly or explicitly subscribe to the idea that was put forth most prominently by Michel Foucault's work, that is that the reality of life is pre-eminently shaped by societal discourse, by linguistic operations that make sense either out of heretofore disordered or even chaotic phenomena or by redefining established frameworks of value (Foucault 1972). At first glance this seems to be stating the obvious, seeing that certainly no author who is concerned with contributing constructively to an issue as important as management education would go to the trouble of working hard on a report if they didn't believe that what they write might make a difference. The most important point of the analysis of discourse as established by Foucault, however, is to stipulate both the writer's and the reader's awareness of the techniques and instruments used by the former. Transposed on to reports on management education, this means that – especially if such reports indeed aim at impacting on the reality of business schools by propagating an education that includes the ability to think critically – they would ideally have to demonstrate and thus invite critical thinking by reflecting explicitly on the ways and means by which they build their argument as a whole.

Most reports, of course, are quite clear in outlining their premises and methodology for harvesting and evaluating data according to the disciplinary methodology taught at business schools to them and by them. But few, if any of them, are – or show themselves to be – aware of the fact that they are aligning their findings by means of discursive operations that have their own crucial part in creating the meaning that those reports aim at. As the historiographer Hayden White has pointed out, however, there is no such thing as a discursive operation without an impact on its content because any such operation is historically fraught, contextually motivated and selectively highlights semantic nuances at the cost of others, to name but a few aspects. It is simply impossible to convey factual substance without its being shaped by the form it is given in language (White 1987). In other words, writing – and reading – a report on management education impacts on reality not only through presenting facts culled by a method of research as such but also by the discursive logic informing their presentation, that is the narrative or narratives chosen to frame their content.

So far, the findings of our review of the discourse on the integration of the humanities in management education have suggested that there are three predominant types of genre-typical narratives: the diagnostic, the genealogical and the programmatic. The diagnostic narrative most prominently uses the presentation of empirical evidence on current management education to show up the flaws and fallacies in the system or systems described, implying that the consequences to be drawn from their findings should be taken as more or less self-evident. In the genealogical narrative, too, empirical evidence plays a major role; this role, however, is determined by a historiographical approach that aims to show by what means and because of what reasons current problems have developed in time, either openly stating or implying that the removal or modification of said means and reasons will solve those problems. Compared with the diagnostic and the genealogical type, the programmatic narrative relies less heavily on factual evidence, usually taking for granted that it is well known by its readers; therefore, it presents an initial thesis as to the ideal future of management education, using empirical data mainly to illustrate a sharply profiled, more often than not deliberately provocative and even controversial argument.

It must be understood that the descriptive separation of these three types of narrative is a heuristic tool constructed for the sake of analysing the genre. There are in fact very few reports that are obviously and sometimes even intentionally representing one and only one of the three types; most of them combine elements of all three narratives. As reports on management education usually aim at getting across a concrete message, it could be said that the genre by definition shares a programmatic approach. This even holds for the diagnostic narrative because already the selection of evidence for presentation from the huge mass of available facts constitutes an act of programmatic interpretation. The same goes for the genealogical narrative: when reconstructing chains of cause and effect to explain what went wrong in the past and thus needs to be remedied in the future, it is not only of necessity equally selective in dealing with its diagnostic material but also imposes a historiographical order, the logic of which is a programmatic construction, leading purposefully to the point of its intent. The programmatic narrative, on the other hand, is always at least implicitly diagnostic and even genealogical in nature to ground its claims to the feasibility of its arguments, whilst it explicitly emphasizes the constructive polemics that the other two types are rather more discreet about.

The point of our heuristic typification, therefore, is not to sort the genre into convenient pigeon-holes but rather to identify the techniques that reports use to state their cases and consider their implications for the ideas on the future of management education that the respective reports offer. To this purpose, we have identified the three reports, mentioned earlier, as characteristic of the field, both for preferential leanings towards one type of narrative and for using elements of the others. After presenting this selected reading, we will offer our conclusions, embedded in a description of our own programmatic agenda.

## The diagnostic narrative: Thomas *et al.* 2014

The objective of the diagnostic narrative is to question established presuppositions as to how management education is provided, but with a focus on diagnosing the different potentials for novelty in ongoing efforts in the field. Contrary to a more programmatic effort, the diagnostic approach does not provide for yet another special change agenda but seeks to stimulate change by showing up heterogeneous developments, which in different ways point towards novel approaches in the construction and delivery of management education. The diagnostic approach, therefore, departs from an understanding of the field of management education as a field in transition, but with multiple potential pathways and multiple efforts taking shape in and actively reshaping the field of management education.

The report *Securing the Future of Management Education. Competitive Destruction or Constructive Innovation?* by Thomas *et al.* (2014) is very explicit about using the diagnostic approach. This is the second volume in a series that started in 2013 with the report *Promises Fulfilled and Unfulfilled in Management Education* (Thomas *et al.* 2013), which 'provided interview and other evidence' about its subject, and it 'focuses much more closely on emerging trends, and uncertain futures in management education [. . .] using an open-ended interview process' (Thomas *et al.* 2014: Foreword). From the start, it is thus made clear that its content is firmly based on evidential matter that needs to be taken seriously as purely factual, leaving no room for speculation or ideology.

Formally, this stipulation is underlined by the report's text being divided into short chapters, which in turn consist of series of short paragraphs interspersed with numerous bullet point lists of conclusions and accompanied on the margins by extracts printed in bold to stress particularly important items. Modelled on the rhetorics of the PowerPoint presentation, which has become one of the most established ways of conveying information in management education – and indeed in the upper echelons of management practice – it serves to induce trust by showing that the report's authors are fully versed in the modes of communication that dominate the field on which they are reporting. This form bulwarks the report against any possible accusation of creating homogeneity where the authors perceive there to be none – or at most very little – narrative construction. In fact, the form chosen by the authors might even be called that of an anti-narrative, aiming to give a tightly built itemization of the status quo without any deliberations on the subjects, which are not directly covered by the evidence quoted.

The report's methodology is thus firmly anchored in positivism, an expression coined in the nineteenth century for the technique with which the academic humanities tried to counteract the suspicion that – compared with the natural sciences – they might be 'soft' in their approach to reality through substantiating their findings by relentless factography. Interestingly, the report's positivism creates an inconsistency between its discursive practice and one of its most stringently advocated programmatic elements: the supremacy of practical relevance over academic rigour in management education. Although its positivistic stance stresses the report's commitment to 'real-life' facts and thus to relevance, the formal structure, together with multiple quotations from other reports and related journal articles, places the report firmly in the camp of academic rigour.

Although the report strives for the utmost diagnostic objectivity both through its formal structure and through safeguarding the evidential quality of the content by means of extensively quoting the interviewed respondents, the strong focus that the report puts on particular problems is in itself a statement of a certain framework of values directing their selection. Chapter 5 'Conjectures: the road travelled and the road less travelled' sheds some interesting light on this framework, stating programmatically that management education's basic 'problem [...] is that business schools were never designed to have a purely academic focus. They were always meant to provide pragmatic, real-life management skills to managers, who after business school, would be going back into the marketplace' (Thomas *et al.* 2014: 125). This statement formulates three presuppositions: (1) it stipulates that business schools were in fact 'designed', invented and built intentionally for a certain purpose, which (2) clashes with 'a purely academic focus' because this focus is incremental to the (3) 'real-life' necessities that management students face after their education – 'real-life' being categorically encoded as 'the market place'.

The first of these presuppositions is a genealogical argument that has been built by the report's authors in their first book (Thomas *et al.* 2013), serving here to maintain that the current problems of management education as a whole stem from its deviation from its original purpose. The nature of this purpose becomes clear in the following presuppositions. Not only is 'academic' education as such unable to provide for practical skills but, even worse, it hampers the students' application of whatever they have learned in a 'real life' outside business schools, the demands of which are obviously perceived as structurally different from the 'real life' to which students of other disciplines have to deal with. These presuppositions are, on the one hand, based on the assessment that management education is more important to 'real life' outside academia than most, if not all, other courses of academic education and, on the other hand, based on the assumption that 'real life' as such conforms to the logic of 'the market place'.

The logic of 'the market place' therefore also informs the report's discourse on the possible use that the humanities' expertise might be put to. There are mainly two areas where the humanities' expertise is expected to impact positively on management education: teaching integrative problem solving and providing for morality. A passage describing a revised MBA programme of the University of Toronto's Rotman School of Management in Canada formulates the hoped-for goals as follows: '[...] the overall aim is to produce a holistic student perspective on management [...] that will encourage the development of integrative thinkers who, in management careers, will be more likely to make decisions with integrity, reflection and an ethical and moral compass' (Thomas *et al.* 2014: 21). Mirrored in one of eight bullet points that sum up the current criticism of business schools – 'the business school does not provide a clear sense of purpose, morality and ethics with respect to its role in society' (Thomas *et al.* 2014: 33) – this view remains consistent in the report's discourse on the humanities, to be recapped in the last chapter 'Uncertain futures: what should business schools do now?' under the heading 'Thinking skills':

> A liberal arts education is said to provide the breadth of knowledge and the ability to view a problem from multiple perspectives and hence better equips the manager. The humanities,

> in particular, have been touted as providing much-needed training in analytical thinking, critical thinking and communication as well as developing a greater awareness of self and society.
>
> *Thomas et al. 2014: 204*

Accordingly, the diagnosis provided by the authors yields a two-fold purpose of integrating humanities in management education: they are to complement the perceived amorality of an education that aims at teaching the most efficient ways to earn money by linking such teaching to its societal context and thus balancing individual profit-mindedness with the awareness of global society's needs. At the same time they are to enhance the portfolio of skills needed by management students to make profits – for themselves, for their businesses or for society as a whole – with such skills as are unique to the humanities' expertise. What exactly these skills are, however, is hard to grasp. Tellingly, one of the bullet points outlining the ideas Gary Hamel offers on the future of management education (Hamel 2007) sums up his demand for '[t]he endorsement of a liberal arts model of management education' as being motivated by the assumption that this model 'makes management education more exciting, less boring and instrumental' (Thomas *et al.* 2014: 57).

In conclusion, the diagnostic narrative of Thomas *et al.* (2014) gives a comprehensive account of the fact that of the main protagonists in the current debate on management education, both practitioners and educators are convinced that teaching and even possibly research in management studies could benefit from integrating the humanities' expertise. The ideas on what this expertise might actually be about, however, are unspecific, centring mainly on issues of morality as already academically codified by the discipline of business ethics, but additionally beginning to explore the notion that there might be additional skills that could be useful for management education, even though – apart from their entertainment value – the community of management educators is not yet clear as to what these skills actually might be.

## The genealogical narrative: Khurana 2007

The genealogical narrative problematizes present ideas on management education, including in particular prevailing conventions and institutionalized 'truths', by reconstructing the historical development of the field. In the context of this article, the term 'genealogical' is basically modelled on Steyaert who employs it for the analysis of discursive strategies used in entrepreneurship (Steyaert 2004), but as the term in our case is applied not to practice but to texts, it also carries a teleological dimension highlighting the discursive logics of a report that presents historical facts in a way which makes them account for the present status quo. Our focus, therefore, is not only on the explicit key question guiding the genealogical narrative – how did management education arrive at the status quo it currently finds itself in? – but again also on the framework of values directing the answers given by the report's author as it appears in the causality informing their presentational logic.

The genealogical narrative has long been a preferred mode of intervention into the field of management education, as represented, for example, by the works of Locke (1989, 1996), Hamel (2007), Khurana (2007), Bottom (2009) and O'Connor (2012; and this volume). Mainly, the authors mentioned share the conviction that current management education has deteriorated due to having lost sight of its roots in an originally productively heterogeneous portfolio of disciplinary skills, having streamlined what today is perceived as the proper disciplinary content of management education at the cost of transdisciplinary interests. Basically joining in with the complaint of management education today being fundamentally estranged from management practices, they define 'practice' as the complexities of management as such, including its ethical, processual, political, entrepreneurial and cultural aspects, criticizing management education as serving an over-specialized system of knowledge production and education which, being bogged down by academic supremacy fights, can no longer adequately answer today's challenges. Therefore, the genealogical narrative aims at reframing management education through contesting the narratives of origins and purposes that guide reformers in their staging of change agendas, exposing their programmatic dimensions and explaining those in their historical contexts.

Rakesh Khurana's *From Higher Aims to Hired Hands* (2007) seeks to reactualize the historical and unrealized project of developing management as a profession. He departs from a reading of the contemporary situation of management and business schools as having lost legitimacy in the wider public sphere and a pressing need to regain legitimacy through institutional reforms. The genealogical pursuit of this agenda takes the reader through a reading of the evolution of US university-based business schools and its intertwinement with changing regimes of corporate governance. Khurana's emphasis is put on the transition from a managerialist model of capitalism to an investor capitalist model of governance. According to him, this transition entails a shift in management ideals (and their associated educational purposes in business schools) from an ideal of being a cultivated 'statesman mediator' between the particular interest of the company and the wider interests of society to an ideal of serving the interests of shareholders focusing predominantly on financial performance criteria. Calling the former *Higher Aims* and the latter *Hired Hands* in the title of his book, Khurana makes it clear from the first that he considers the story he tells to be the story of a dramatic decline in the purpose of management education, which in turn engendered a dramatic decline of the theory and the practice of management.

The possible impact of the humanities' expertise on the solution of the problems deriving from this decline appears on two levels in Khurana's work. One level is that of the profession's loss of morality implicit in his core hypothesis:

> In the course of history, the logic of professionalism that underlay the university-based business school in its formative phase was replaced first by a managerialist logic that emphasized professional knowledge rather than professional ideals, and ultimately by a market logic that, taken to its conclusion, subverts the logic of professionalism altogether.
>
> *Khurana 2007: 7*

The presuppositions implicit in this hypothesis are that (1) university-based business schools have been founded to create and teach academic knowledge about the profession of the manager, thus, as Khurana explains elsewhere, giving societal legitimacy to a profession that before was considered as mainly concerned with administration and therefore, academically speaking, menial. Linked with this presupposition, in fact its very foundation, are two others, namely (2) that it is the academic type of education that provides for the ideals which evolve the manager from an administrator into a creative, cultivated and socially conscious leader and (3) that what Thomas *et al.* (2014) consider to be the 'real life' of management students – that is 'the marketplace' and its practicalities – negatively influence management education if allowed to take over and shape it according to 'a market logic'. Submerged in these arguments, the humanities appear to be part and parcel of the academic type of education as such, explicitly inscribed in the text by Khurana's frequent use of the term 'ideal' which, if today significantly de-branded by colloquial use, is in fact originally a key term of the philosophy of aesthetics that describes the concept of perfection.

Khurana's use of the term 'ideal' is only one example of a rhetorical choice of terminology that conveys much more meaning than its descriptive value in the context makes apparent at first glance. Another example is that on the very first page of his introduction, Khurana twice uses the term 'hero', when he points out 'the dramatic contrast between the CEO as superhero and the CEO as anti-hero' (Khurana 2007: 1), which has structured the public discourse on managers in recent decades. By employing this term, he effectively anticipates the criticism he launches against the type of CEOs produced by business schools later on. The term 'hero', first introduced into Western mythology by the epics of Homer, describes a person who is gifted with exceptional powers and uses them to elevate him or herself above all other members of his or her peer group – not to benefit society, but to be admired unconditionally.

The second level on which Khurana involves the humanities in his work is the discursive logic of his work as a whole. The genealogical narrative as such is obviously informed by the methodology of historiography, drawing on the one hand on historical documents to reconstruct chains of cause and effect and, on the other hand, literally 'making sense' of them by setting them out in a narrative mode that interprets the facts through selection, conjecture and conjointure – and not least through the terminology chosen to represent them. Specifically, Khurana's teleological set-up draws heavily upon one of the grand narratives of nineteenth century historiography by Edward Gibbon, whose monumental *History of the Decline and Fall of the Roman Empire* appeared between 1776 and 1789.

Throughout the nineteenth century – and therefore during the formative period of the Humboldtian university system, which still dominates much of today's academic education – the reasons for the downfall of the Roman Empire were as hotly debated in classical and ancient studies – then one of the most influential disciplines of academic study – as are the reasons for the problems in management education today. The difference that marks Khurana's approach as genealogical as opposed to Gibbon's more conventional adding up of what he perceives as indisputable facts, was introduced by the philosopher Oswald Spengler's equally monumental *The Decline of the West* in 1918 (Spengler 1991). Spengler explicitly adopted the teleology of the previous century's grand narrative on cultural decline, but deviated from it conceptually. Instead of accepting facts as given, he fundamentally challenged the Eurocentric framework of current historiography, maintaining that because it was predisposed to harvest and align facts following the idea that all history was firmly rooted in occidental traditions and value systems, it distorted the past and thus significantly contributed to the problems of the present. Thus, Spengler anticipated much of what Foucault's archaeology of knowledge established later as the criticism of epistemology performed by Khurana – up to and including the latter's use of teleology, not as a complaint about a desperate situation but as an intervention against the situation actually happening.

In conclusion, from the perspective on the humanities and their possible – or in Khurana's case factual – relationship with management education, Khurana's genealogical narrative can be seen as a kind of recursive operation. Setting out to reconstruct the history of management education with a view to make clear how the present problems came about, Khurana's mode of intervening in the current debate doesn't just stipulate the integration of the humanities but employs some of the skills taught by them to bring his point across. By doing this, instead of building up an argument that states his purpose he narratively performs it, situating management education in an evolutionary trajectory formed by changing values of managerial governance and knowledge and thus preparing the ground for such an evolutionary trajectory to take new forms in the future. That way, Khurana shows by the very logic of his discourse that the current debate on the future of management education needs to be aware of both its present and its past contexts to provide solutions for the future.

## The programmatic narrative: Colby *et al.* 2011

The programmatic narrative is perhaps the most popular type of the three as far as debates on reforms are concerned. It is easy to process because it tells its readers from the start exactly what they are supposed to think and ideally implement in their respective professional and/or political practices, being explicitly political in intention and rhetorics. Unlike the diagnostic and partly also the genealogical narrative, it does not harass its readers by challenging them to make sense of an *embarras de richesses* of information. Instead, the programmatic narrative openly puts forth hypotheses and groups its material around them – at least in the text it produces because, of course, these hypotheses are generated ideally by the material collected beforehand.

The programmatic approach thus tends to position itself at an abstract level of field investigation, elevated to the position of the imagined viewer above and beyond the field of study. 'It transforms the bewitching world by which one was "possessed" into a text that lies before one's eyes. It allows one to read it, to be a solar eye, looking down as a god' (de Certeau 1984: 92). The programmatic style of reporting pleases the gaze of the strategist, following the vocabulary of de Certeau, but is always in danger of losing touch with practices and processes whereby the field in question is already multiplying and reinventing itself. The overview perspective totalizes its gaze and collapses diversity and novelty into ideal constructs and categories, such as disciplinary entities in management education, structuralist logics of change, linear causation, dichotomizing boundary constructions and multiple other ways of performing strategic perspectives of and for the field.

In the US context, programmatic narratives on the future of management education have been largely dominated by think-tanks like the Carnegie Foundation (Pierson 1959; Colby *et al.* 2011) and the Ford Foundation (Gordon and Howell 1959), whilst European contributions, far from constituting something like a coherent field, are informed by a heterogeneous composition of institutional and societal frameworks and change dynamics (Engwall and Zamagni 1998; Morsing and Sauquet Rovira 2011), even though historically the developments of the US and the European business schools are closely intertwined (Locke 1989). The think-tank reports coming from the US have provided for important programmatic rationales and visions for business schools to aspire towards (Augier and March 2011; Khurana *et al.* 2011), and as such, the construction of programmatic visions for the field has had a clear US bias in terms of empirical examples, institutional frameworks and traditions guiding the programmatic efforts and perspectives promoted in reports.

The most recent Carnegie Foundation report (Colby *et al.* 2011) is the as yet most openly programmatic narrative on the necessity of integrating the humanities into management education – the report uses the term 'liberal arts'. Like the diagnostic and the genealogical narratives analysed earlier, they see the pressing need to counteract the overspecialization and disciplinary single mindedness characteristic of current educational endeavours by broadening the students' horizons and equipping them not only with instrumental skills for doing business but also to grow into responsible personalities with a clear sense of the needs of society as a whole. The report therefore opens with the emphatic statement that 'Business has never mattered more' (Colby *et al.* 2011: 1), but instead of focusing on the economic necessities of globalization – a point that was stressed heavily by the first Carnegie Report (Pierson 1959) – the authors proceed to expound on the dangers of blundering into the 'fragile interdependence' that links the different sectors of the global economy without the skills to recognize and constructively deal with its complexity. On those grounds, they claim that the resulting 'need to grasp this pluralism of values and contexts is, we believe, a weak link in the current organization of undergraduate business programmes' (Colby *et al.* 2011: 5).

In contrast to both the diagnostic and the genealogical narratives, the programmatic narrative, as exemplified by the Carnegie Report, is not content with describing and, in the case of the genealogical narrative, explaining the status quo, but rather it makes a positive case for integrative programmes that include strong liberal arts components. The results are five decisive recommendations on how to create such programmes, the most striking ones being the last two, which stipulate that on the one hand, the institutions concerned 'should be *intentional* in their integration of the arts and sciences and business education' (Colby *et al.* 2011: 169) and that the arts and sciences themselves on the other hand should profit from such integration because '[b]usiness educators have a great deal to contribute to teaching and learning in the arts and sciences' (Colby *et al.* 2011: 170). These two recommendations mirror the main concerns of the report that integration should be firmly anchored on an institutional level – not left to take place more or less incidentally because there happen to be liberal arts available – and also that the liberal arts components should be tailored to meet the needs of management students. The implication of the last recommendation is that liberal arts teachers are not in and of themselves either willing or able to adjust to such tailoring.

Both concerns are at the heart of most of the case studies presented in the report, owing to the realization that if and where the liberal arts already have a place in management education, then this tends to be either accidental or, if institutionalized on any level, perceived by students as an add-on instead of a crucial part of their professional training. To convey these issues, the first chapter of the report presents them in the shape of two distinctive metaphors. The status quo is described as resembling 'a curricula barbell: each end of the bar carries a significant weight of intellectual subject matter but the connection is slender' (Colby *et al.* 2011: 5), whilst for the future the authors 'envision something more like a double helix', 'a metaphor for an undergraduate business curriculum that explicitly and continually links students' learning of business to their use of various arts and sciences disciplines that provide a larger, complementary view of the world' (Colby *et al.* 2011: 6).

Like the terms 'ideal' and 'hero' in Khurana's book, these metaphors carry a load of meaning, which might not be relevant to their primary descriptive function to outline the difference between unintegrated and systematically and institutionally integrated curricula, but serves to give a telling impression of what implicit frameworks of values the report's authors are working with. The metaphor of the barbell implies that a programme that makes its students go through studies in the liberal arts but does not bring both components together is nothing more than a training course to build up muscle, to be gone through for the effect but not an aim in itself and, when over, leaves the pumped-up muscles to deteriorate again. The metaphor of the double helix, in contrast, casts the perfect integration of management and liberal arts components in a shape that suggests the students going through such a programme acquire something like a genetic makeup which not only remains with them ever after but also enables them to pass the knowledge they have acquired on to future generations.

The choice of these two metaphors is curiously ambiguous. Neither of them is taken from either the field of management education or that of the liberal arts; instead, they are linked to the extracurricular activity of fitness training – the barbell – and, in the case of the double helix, to a research field in the natural sciences, which in recent years has been progressing rapidly. It is a field that represents the so-called 'hard' sciences as opposed to the 'soft' ones like management and liberal arts studies at their most efficient. This seems to suggest that either the latter do not yield any metaphors suitable for encoding the endeavours that the report envisions or, more likely, that its authors by their choice stake the claim that if and when management and liberal arts studies are integrated as well as they hope for, the result will equal the discovery of the double helix, thus finally bringing the 'soft' sciences on to the same level of academic and public appreciation which the 'hard' sciences – funding-wise often to the detriment of the 'soft' ones – have been occupying effortlessly since the end of the nineteenth century.

The self-assurance resonating with the metaphor of the double helix – which, indeed, informs the report's whole discourse on integrated programmes and curricula – correlates with the normative quality of the image of the perfect manager that the authors present in their chapter on 'Emerging agendas', that is 'Successful entrepreneurs need a broad, rich knowledge base, the ability to see patterns, an explorer mentality, intellectual flexibility, and a willingness to question basic assumptions – all characteristics of a liberally educated person' (Colby *et al.* 2011: 157). In at least one instance, this image is at variance with what the report itself puts forward because there are a number of basic assumptions informing it that are not questioned, or at least not elaborated upon. The most important of these assumptions pertains to the disciplinary architecture of current academic education as such. Both the metaphor of the barbell and that of the double helix derive their meaning from a binary structure, suggesting that whatever the future of integrated curricula will be, it will always be that of different fields of knowledge aligned alongside to the purpose of complementing each other – the main question is how to translate between the fields whilst affirming that disciplinary segregation as such is a given of any academic education.

In conclusion, the Carnegie Report can be seen to be a programmatic narrative by virtue of its distinctively normative attitude as to the agenda of future management education, whilst fortifying this attitude throughout by referring to their empirical research on US business schools that are in the process of integrating liberal arts into management education. In contrast to the diagnostic narrative given by Howard *et al.* (2014), however, Colby *et al.* (2011) boldly draw conclusions that aim at the practical educational and institutional impact, proclaiming the integration of liberal arts' expertise into the training of future managers to be a – if not *the* – solution to the problems faced by business schools' loss of societal identity and purpose, and that also offer advice on what needs to be done to further this aim. This includes an issue that has as yet rarely been approached: the very practical problem of convincing the faculty teaching the two components to link their endeavours in an effort to create the hoped-for double-helix effect.

## Conclusions: reading the future of management education

Taking these reports together, the use of narratological means towards the end of finding answers to the set of questions raised in our introduction appears to be justified. Selecting them for the fact of their already evident and, in the case of the study by Thomas *et al.* (2014), the expected impact on the future of management education, the core question of how far the chosen reports perform the reality they aim to effect has in part, as mentioned before, been answered in advance. One important and possibly even crucial point to this answer, however, has only become clear through the narratological analysis itself. Taking together the fact of their impact on the one hand and that of all three adhering rather strictly to the logics of their respectively chosen – diagnostic, genealogical, programmatic – type of narrative on the other, there seems to be a close link between those two aspects, suggesting that the recognizably genre-typical conduct of an argument considerably strengthens its powers of persuasion.

This insight might at first seem redundant because any methodology stipulates adherence to once-set rules as a condition for the yielding of convincing results. What is striking, however, in the case of the reports analysed is that although they certainly spell out the way they respectively go about harvesting and interpreting their data, their adherence to the rules of genre-typical narrating throughout remains implicit, even though it distinctly shapes the results' presentation. All three reports use mainly one of the three types of narrative available, abstaining from options of discursive logics employed by the other two types, but do not explicitly reflect on their narrative dimension, leaving this to be inferred by their performance. On the level of said narrative performance, therefore, it can be argued that the much-cited skills lacking in management education – and to be provided by the humanities and social sciences – are, in fact, already very much practised by the reports' authors, although they are missing conspicuously on the levels of content and even methodological reflection where quite possibly the conscious and intentional acquisition and employment of those skills by the authors might have yielded – if not different, then at least even more convincing and perhaps practical – results for implementing an integrated education.

This impression is mirrored by the lack of clarity on the exact nature of the humanities' and social sciences' expertise, which is characteristic of all three reports and, on the strength of our selection being that of narratives representing typical examples for the ongoing debate on management education, therefore of the debate itself. Apart from the pervading sense that the humanities' main quality consists of providing morality to a profession which, in light of the recent financial crises, is perceived by the public as amoral, there is no clear concept of what else the humanities and social sciences might add to a successful mix of curricula. With great fervour, critical thinking, multi-framing of problems and cross-cultural *savoir faire* are proclaimed to be the accomplishments hoped for in future managers, but throughout the debate these formulae remain without the empirical substance that is provided in abundance by any hypothesis on the disciplinary core of management education itself.

Likewise, the cross-fertilization of teaching techniques over disciplinary boundaries, which might be considered one of the crucial challenges of integrating the humanities and social sciences, remains uncharted territory, most notably so in the recommendation that Colby *et al.* offer to business educators having 'a great deal to contribute to teaching and learning in the arts and sciences' (Colby *et al.* 2011: 170). This implies that the arts and sciences are a priori deficient in their teaching when it comes to educating management students, whilst business educators have nothing whatsoever to learn from arts and sciences teachers, an implication that stands as unsubstantiated as the recommendation's explicit content.

As it is, it becomes very clear that the problem at the heart of the debate on the integration of the humanities and social sciences is a seemingly insurmountable threshold between proclaiming the need for such integration on the one hand and seriously engaging with the content and thus the types of knowledge taught by both management and the humanities' and social sciences' educators on the other. This problem appears to be a structural one inherent in the system of academic disciplinarity as established in the nineteenth century. Implementing this system, the institution of the modern university reacted to the explosion of knowledge generated by the Enlightenment movement's scientific curiosity: because it was no longer possible for any one human to know even something of everything, let alone all, as the early modern *uomo universale* had aspired to do, the institution responsible for managing this knowledge in both teaching and research compartmentalized into sub-institutional entities in charge of clearly circumscribed smaller fields (see Parker, this volume). What was a reasonable and even smart move in administering limited resources then created structural constraints, which over the years have engendered what is basically an essentialist notion of disciplinary knowledge, that is the notion that there is a canonical core knowledge to each discipline that may not, indeed cannot, be put at the disposition of any kind of integrational endeavour.

This notion, it seems, is still going strong – strong enough at least to restrict even the most fervent advocates' visions of a management education integrating the humanities and social sciences to within the boundaries of their own disciplinary comfort zones. At the same time, the near-elementary dynamics of the debate on the future of management education shows a growing awareness of the fact that present day 'real life' professional challenges in all fields – including the humanities – can no longer be met by educational institutions that still cling to the traditional disciplinary segregation. 'We need to engage more deeply with the fundamentals of knowledge', conclude Starkey and Tempest (2008: 385), arguing strongly in favour of what they call the 'hybrid vigour' (2008: 387) of a renewed understanding of management education beyond disciplinary boundaries.

To achieve such an understanding is not the task of one institution or that of one set of disciplines, or those of management education or those of the humanities and social sciences; rather, it needs to grow from the consciousness that the assumptions underlying the academic construct 'management education' need to be as carefully reassessed as those underlying the self-image of the humanities and social sciences in order to make way for innovative developments. For management educators on all levels, from business schools' governing bodies to administrators and teachers, the knowledge of the humanities and social sciences as it has been applied to the field of reporting in this chapter may help towards a first step of such a reassessment – just as it may be helpful to the educators in humanities and social sciences to realize and even to enjoy realizing that humanity's business is indeed the humanities' business.

## Notes

1 For detailed information on this programme and its history, see Eberle and Metelmann, this volume.
2 This concept still informs part of the current debate today; for the use of the term 'liberal arts' in the Carnegie Report see later.

## References


Augier, M. and March, J.G. (2011) *The Roots, Rituals, and Rhetorics of Change – North American Business Schools after the Second World War.* Stanford, CA: Stanford Business Books.

Bottom, W.P. (2009) 'Organizing intelligence: development of behavioral science and the research based model of business education', *Journal of the History of Behavioral Sciences*, 45(3), 253–83.

Bruner, J.S. (1990) *Acts of Meaning.* Cambridge, MA: Harvard University Press.

Colby, A., Ehrlich, T., Sullivan, W.M. and Dolle, J.R. (2011) *Rethinking Undergraduate Business Education – Liberal Learning for the Profession*, The Carnegie Foundation for the Advancement of Teaching. San Francisco, CA: Jossey-Bass.

Czarniawska, B. (2008) *A Theory of Organizing.* Cheltenham, UK: Edward Elgar.

de Certeau, M. (1984) *The Practice of Everyday Life.* Berkeley, CA: University of California Press

Engwall, L. and Zamagni, V. (1998). 'Introduction'. *In*: L. Engwall and V. Zamagni (eds.) *Management Education in Historical Perspective.* Manchester, UK: Manchester University Press, chapter 1.

Fairhurst, G.T. (2007) *Discursive Leadership – In Conversation with Leadership Psychology.* Thousand Oaks, CA: Sage Publications.

Foucault, M. (1972) *The Archaeology of Knowledge and the Discourse on Language.* New York, NY: Tavistock Publications.

Gordon, R.A. and Howell, J.E. (1959) *Higher Education for Business.* New York, NY: Columbia University Press.

Grint, K. (2005) 'Problems, problems, problems – the social construction of leadership', *Human Relations*, 58(11), 1467–94.

Hamel, G. (2007) *The Future of Management.* Cambridge, MA: Harvard University Press.

Khurana, R. (2007) *From Higher Aims to Hired Hands – The Social Transformation of American Business Schools and the Unfulfilled Promise of Management as a Profession.* Princeton, NJ: Princeton University Press.

Khurana, R., Kimura, K. and Fourcade, M. (2011) *How Foundations Think: The Ford Foundation as a Dominating Institution in the Field of American Business Schools.* Working Paper 11-070. Cambridge, MA: Harvard Business School.

Locke, R.R. (1989) *Management and Higher Education since 1940: The Influence of America and Japan on Germany, Great Britain, and France.* Cambridge, MA: Cambridge University Press.

Locke, R.R. (1996) 'Mistaking a historical phenomenon for a functional one: postwar management education reconsidered'. *In*: L. Engwall and V. Zamagni (eds.) *Management Education in Historical Perspective.* Manchester and New York: Manchester University Press, pp. 145–56.

Morsing, M. and Sauquet Rovira, A. (2011) *Business Schools and their Contribution to Society.* London: Sage Publications.

O'Connor, E.S. (2012) *Creating New Knowledge in Management – Appropriating the Field's Lost Foundations*. Stanford, CA: Stanford Business Books.

Pierson, F.C. (1959) *The Education of American Businessmen: A Study of University-College Programs in Business Administration*. New York, NY: McGraw Hill.

Spengler, O. (1991) *The Decline of the West*. Oxford: Oxford University Press.

Starkey, K. and Tempest, S. (2008) 'A clear sense of purpose? The evolving role of the business school', *Journal of Management Development*, 27(4), 379–90.

Steyaert, C. (2004) 'The prosaics of entrepreneurship'. *In*: D. Hjorth and C. Steyaert (eds.) *Narrative and Discursive Approaches in Entrepreneurship. A Second Movements in Entrepreneurship Book*. Cheltenham, UK: Edward Elgar, pp. 8–21.

Thomas, H., Thomas, L. and Wilson, A. (2013) *Promises Fulfilled and Unfulfilled in Management Education*. Vol. 1. Bingley, UK: Emerald Group.

Thomas, H., Lee, M., Thomas, L. and Wilson, A. (eds.) (2014) *Securing the Future of Management Education: Competitive Destruction or Constructive Innovation?* Vol. 2. Bingley, UK: Emerald Group.

White, H. (1987) *The Content of the Form – Narrative Discourse and Historical Representation*. Baltimore, MD: Johns Hopkins University Press.

# 5

# Deschooling the manager through the humanities

## Mintzberg's amateurish conscience[1]

*Nidhi Srinivas*

... what of artistic lateness not as harmony and resolution, but as intransigence, difficulty and contradiction?

*Said 2004a: 3*

## Introduction

In a commencement address at the University of Puerto Rico on October 9, 1969, Ivan Illich urged its graduating students to abandon their education and recognize it not as a marker of enhanced knowledge but of societal inequality. He encouraged them to reject its ascription of enhanced status: "I hope that your grandchildren will live in an island where the majority give as little importance to attending class as is now given to attending the mass" (Illich 1969: 13). A blunt critique of expert power, well represented by Illich, could read: hospitals remind us of our illness, schools our ignorance, cars our paralysis. It is in such a spirit that Illich in this address argued that, "the desire for education has actually given way to the compulsion of schooling" (Illich 1969: 12). Schooling is commodified learning. "Upon the receipt of a diploma the educational product acquires a market value" (Illich 1969: 12). In this way schooling acquires exchange value within the capitalist market, enabling elite specialists. In his characteristic tone, Illich notes that "school attendance in itself thus guarantees inclusion in the membership of disciplined consumers of the technocracy – just as in past times church attendance guaranteed membership in the community of saints" (Illich 1969: 12). Anticipating perhaps the demographic force that in our contemporary moment animates global protests for change, from Tahrir Square to Occupy Wall Street, Illich claims "youth wants educational institutions that provide them with education. They neither want nor need to be mothered, to be certified, or to be indoctrinated" (Illich 1969: 15). It is this slippage between the pedagogic expectations promised and those actually available, that Illich characterizes as our contemporary moment. Whether mobility, education or health, what we actually find is a "paradoxical counterproductivity" (Burkhardt 2002) where the stated purpose of organizations appears defeated by their manner of functioning. Meanwhile, the power of certified experts grows.

About twenty years after that address in Puerto Rico, in 1989, I was becoming a certified expert myself as a student in an Indian business school. One afternoon a book in the library caught my attention. Its cover showed a man in the midst of speaking, right hand poised, the face imprinted it seemed with urgency and acute awareness. The book was *Mintzberg on Management* and its chapters ("On management," "On organizations," and "On the society of organization") presented much of Henry Mintzberg's theories of the manager's job and of the structuring of organizations. The initial chapters read as objective theoretical descriptions of management, but the later chapters are written in another tone, less eager to appear detached, more concerned with the costs of managed life, less hopeful.

> What I have to say here may also strike you as pessimistic. I think it is necessarily so. In my opinion, management as contemporarily practiced and organizations as contemporarily run, the two together in a society of large institutions, pose grave dangers for us all.
>
> *Mintzberg 1989: 335*

Mintzberg declares "what I have written elsewhere in this book, on planning and the role of analysis in general and on the functional aspects of bureaucracy, among other things, outline my views with more balance. This final presentation is meant to be a polemic" (1989: 336). The final chapter, "Society has become unmanageable because of organizations," offers multiple pessimistic theses on the deleterious role of management in generating over-organized societies. This self-described "diatribe" (Mintzberg 1989: 335) marks an important stage in Mintzberg's scholarship as he shifts consciously away from a detached analytical stance and style of writing towards more polemical, engaged writing. The essay at times gestures directly towards criticisms of technocracy and ways of teaching management:

> Managers who claim that as professionals they must take control of that work through planning and other technocratic procedures, like professional teachers who claim they must control the learning process through detailed specification of the curriculum, destroy the need for commitment and spontaneous learning in these activities.
>
> *Mintzberg 1989: 364*

The essay's suspicion, almost despair, with management from this initial point of origin culminates in a sense in *Managers Not MBAs* (Mintzberg 2005), which sharply questions and rejects the value of the MBA degree. To Mintzberg, MBAs are not necessarily managers, nor are managers necessarily defined by MBAs.

At times I have wondered what would have happened if I had been able to study with Illich, educated by one who sought to deschool. But I did have the opportunity to study with Mintzberg, educated by one critical of the elitist impractical ways universities "school" managers. Mintzberg is a celebrated management theorist – to some controversial, combative, dismissive, but to others one of the field's more perceptive and wide-ranging thinkers. In this chapter, I explore one aspect of Mintzberg's work that has not received sufficient attention: his philosophy of education. I am especially interested in the substance of his philosophy and its own interaction with the humanities. Can we understand his philosophy as an explicit claim to engage with the humanities?[2]

Questions of philosophy are impelled by a larger claim we make of knowledge – a claim often named as humanistic or "of the humanities" – which is that fields of learning and the material and symbolic worlds that we inhabit as human beings, offer a basis to pose questions of ethics and politics, for self-understanding, for critical engagement and practice. This is an understanding of humanism less as something intrinsically worthwhile, oriented to claims of "great books" curricula, steeped in cultural expectations and particular limitations (see Costea and Amaridis, this volume). It is in fact humanism "as an ongoing practice and not as a possession, on what humanistic activity is about rather than a list of desirable attributes in a humanist" (Said 2004b: 6). This is humanism as "a useable praxis for intellectuals and academics who want to know what they are doing, what they are committed to as scholars, and who want also to connect these principles to the world in which they live as citizens" (Said 2004b: 6). Illich's address to the students at the University of Puerto Rico, where he is broadly critical of the way education is understood, is a humanistic claim in this sense. The goal of education has become marketized indoctrination, merely schooling; its expected recipients reside within the dominant social order and enjoy its benefits; and education proceeds by reminding students of what they do not know, filling them with required knowledge. Illich's claim is for an alternative approach to education that recognizes the democratic potential of education and steers away from technocratic power.

Similarly Mintzberg (2005) makes a humanistic claim. The goal of management education is to offer concepts and skills that build on reflective processes and intense context-based organizational experience. Its recipients are those with experience and the gumption to make decisions in a variety of such organizations. Such education proceeds by opening up the classroom to a variety of views. Mintzberg's claim is for alternative pedagogies to restrain the dangers of corporate power, of technicization and societal imbalance that steer away from the certified education offered within business schools and the MBA. Mintzberg's work offers an important provocative critique of management and its prevailing forms of education and research. Ultimately, however, I will argue that it remains unsatisfying for those of us wary of expert power, neoliberal capital, and societal inequality. It goes some distance but not far enough. This chapter starts with a description of a critical position on expert knowledge – what I call an anti-technocratic position on education. I then outline Mintzberg's theoretical project and its anachronistic appeal to the classical roots of management. Finally I assess Mintzberg's theoretical project in terms of its humanistic potential. What does this project connote in terms of critiquing expert knowledge? What does this project tell us about the contribution of the humanities to management education?

## Tracking anti-technocracy

There is a long engagement in social theory and the humanities with questions of expert power and the expertise offered by education. Theorists reflected on the challenges of ordering society, ways to ensure progressive growth, to channel industrialism and its consequences (Cowen and Shenton 1996; Harris 1953). "Technocracy" names a precise historical response to the challenge of complex societal growth that entrusted the demands of coordinating society to trained experts, whose sole task would be to ensure societies handled well the changes ushered in by industrial growth. How to train some to guide a society of others? Commitment to technocracy led to pedagogical claims familiar to students of management: the exaltation of detachment and use of data for it; commitment to verifiable assertions and forms of proofs to test them; the expectation that spheres of decision making can and should be transferred to experts trained in them. But there were less well-known claims: exhorting a sense of mission, a commitment to larger goals, a reminder to trained experts of the great responsibilities with which they were entrusted (see O'Connor, this volume). In part due to the disciplinary coherence and knowledge systems that emerged through the early twentieth century, those trained in engineering and later in management were expected to have scientific knowledge and applied skills for their organizational roles. Technical expertise was now tied to teaching methods that emphasized foundational knowledge, subsequent testing and assessment, through lectures and exams, the case method, practical projects and presentations. Critiques of expert power have questioned these tendencies through at least three distinct arguments: the purpose of education, its intended recipient, and pedagogy.

Paulo Freire (1970), the Brazilian educator, argued that the dominant view of education was of knowledge poured into the empty vessel that was the student for the needs of the labor market. The knowledge shared does not change in shape or form, nor is it conducive to reinterpretation or internal questioning. It is knowledge for an instrumental purpose, to equip the student for particular jobs and organizational roles. Counterposed to this understanding was another – of education that responded to problems within that social setting (Schugurensky 2011). Such practical education would have to uncover power structures and make them visible and tractable to change to truly succeed in its vaunted solutions. Nor could knowledge be somehow fixed and unchanging, but rather it would have to be relevant to the problems faced, the actors involved, and the goals sought. Such education could not be neutral. In fact education shaped identities and unequal relationships, and political change required transforming inequality so that there were neither masters nor slaves.

A second argument is concerned with the recipient of education. During the late 1960s, Freire's name was often mentioned in tandem with that of a confederate, and at times rival, theorist Ivan Illich. Trained as a priest at the Vatican's Gregorian University and radicalized by work with Puerto Rican and Dominican laity in New York City, Illich saw accredited education in terms of class inequality (Kahn and Kellner 2007). Accredited education and its regimes of selection ensured artificial scarcities of available knowledge, a monopoly of expertise (Illich 1971). In this sense, MBA degrees "school" management education and maintain decision-making power in a class of actors. Such schooling had little relationship to the actual prowess and understanding expected. In short, schooling prevented education in the same sense as MBA training could prevent effective organizational management. Like sociologists of professions (for instance, Abbott 1988), Illich believed professional power required closure of an occupation, restricting its knowledge and creating a monopoly of expertise.

A third argument is with the pedagogy itself. Because schooling prepares students for competitive labor markets, it also encourages teaching practices that enable easy transmission of knowledge, discourage discussion, conversation, contestation, dispute and related forms of social interaction. But the process of educating itself points also to a different understanding of social life, one that seeks an enlarged realm of agency where people find the means to generate convivial interaction amongst themselves. To Illich (1973), the sustenance of such spaces for social interaction, where a variety of views are shared and discussed, can be encouraged through greater access to information and inclusive forums for sharing it, strengthening the ability of people to make a variety of informed decisions amongst themselves without relying on experts to do so. Rather than presuming the teacher is more knowledgeable than the student, the teacher's role is better understood in terms of spurring the student by acknowledging mutual ignorance. To the French philosopher Jacques Rancière (1991) the teacher–student relationship should begin in a presumption of radical equality. The point of education is to uncover the ways power is naturalized, to uncover such distributions of visibility and audibility, and create an alternative way of sharing power (Chambers 2011; Davis 2010; Rancière 1999; Huault and Perret, this volume).

The implication of these three arguments is that dominant forms of education legitimize social inequality. They have become the primary venue for inculcating skills and values amenable to capitalist growth. There is an affinity between the commitment to certified expert-power, access to competitive labor markets, and the choice of learning goals and pedagogy in classrooms. In the process, students are inured to neoliberal statecraft, the impact of deregulation, ecological degradation, increased social inequality, commodifying a widening range of social life. Education devolves to choices within the realm of necessity, rather than a matter of insight and enlightenment about the world. Methods of teaching where the teacher pours her knowledge into the empty vessel of the student, whether called banking education by Freire, schooling by Illich, or radical inequality by Rancière, seek a pedagogic relation that renders the student ignorant in order to equip her for a labor market.

There is an affinity between such critiques of technocracy and the critical currents within management theory (Grey 2004; Parker 2002; Reynolds 1999). In what follows, I discuss Henry Mintzberg's theoretical project, its "late style" critique of management education, and its consonance with anti-technocratic positions.

## Mintzberg's theoretical project

Henry Mintzberg's theoretical project across four decades is wide-ranging and highly influential. It is not my purpose to document it here, but three broad features of this project deserve closer attention: the commitment to functionalist solutions, acceptance of disorder, and suspicion of professional elites. Here I describe each of these through a suitable aphorism.

*There is an inherent functionalist sense to organized life.* Much of Mintzberg's work revolves around identifying the basic building blocks of organized life. To acknowledge the relevance of modes of coordination, types of decision making, parts of an organization, and configurations is also a moment of recognition – it is the start to improving organizational life. There is an inherent rationality and meaning to organizational life, but it has to be uncovered and is never complete or fully known, and yet there is a gap between the optimal potential of organization and the managerial possibility of achieving this potential, between those establishing the optimal set of decisions and those pursuing their own ends, regardless of larger consequences. Mintzberg's well-known use of typologies (notably Mintzberg 1973a, 1979 and more recently Mintzberg and Srinivas 2010), nested concepts that explain immediate levels of behavior whilst pointing to larger structural and strategic consequences as part of a larger analytical project, retain a functionalist commitment to optimal forms of organizing.

*There is a prevalence of disorder, puzzles, and surprise in organized life.* Where prominent theorists of organizational strategy have often emphasized decisive action, hierarchical command, and analytical methods (Andrews 1987; Ansoff 1991), Mintzberg's (1973b, 1990, 1991) interest has been in moments of surprise that break down expectations and plans, the unanticipated ways decisions and organizing actually happen. Decisions happen in all sorts of places and leaders must find ways to let this free flow of decisions thrive and have the organization learn from its various parts, so to speak (Mintzberg and Waters, 1985). The force of his critique of strategic planning, the distinction of emergent from intentional strategies, and the unstructured and improvised quality to managerial work all stem from the recognition that it is impossible to properly anticipate the contingencies of organized life.

*There is a basis to be skeptical of authority in organized life.* Ultimately, Mintzberg does not show much optimism in the possibility that those who are stewards, guardians, and commanders of organizations will be aware or willing to be aware of the building blocks of organized life. His research casts a skeptical eye on systems of authority. The dire effect of an over-emphasis on hierarchical command of decisions is an unwillingness to learn from the "rank and file" managers who confront the consequences of these decisions. There is unusual attention here to the costs of organized life: procedures that routinize actions and decisions, structures that mask the responsibility of those tasked with implementation, and especially the influence of well-trained but ill-experienced managers. He questions the extent to which expert power is aware of the inherent functionalism and optimality of organizational decisions (for instance, Mintzberg 1990, 1994). Management education poorly equips students for wise management; instead it encourages an unaccountable elite, complacent in their modes of decision making.

## Mintzberg's philosophy and humanism

Since the 1990s, Mintzberg's work has included an increasing number of pointed, argumentative, opinionated, passionate, and critical articles. These are not necessarily addressed to readers of academic journals and have included balancing differing economic systems and their respective imperatives (Mintzberg 1992), assessing management theory in terms of classical commitments such as of Adam Smith (Mintzberg 2014) or addressing the perennially fraught cause of Quebec secessionism (Mintzberg 1995). A concern that cuts across these articles is the need for management to return to a classical ideal of market liberalism.

The classical trajectory of management expected managers, corporations, and business schools to contribute to society, apparent in thinkers such as Herbert Simon, Philip Selznick, and Peter Drucker (Gilman 2006; Krygier 2012; Spender 2013). Management offers knowledge not only for corporations but also for public organizations, government ministries, urban planners, hospitals. In short, the underlying disciplinary goal is in terms of creating a better society, not solely of corporate profit. Such a goal acknowledges multiple freedoms or a variety of social choices in organized life, not solely that of market freedom and goal efficiency. This classical view underlay early management writing, which was part of a commitment to using technocratic means to attain benign social ends. This tradition expected matched commitments from the state. If management theory were to equip technocrats, it would need the support of the government to provide basic underlying infrastructure, citizen welfare and health, thereby protecting people and property, the framework within which these freedoms could be exercised.

As the ideal of the social welfare state continues to unravel, Mintzberg has grown concerned with the state of liberalism. The disquiet and urgent tone of his later polemics is a response to this decline of market liberalism itself. The societal imbalance created, the rise of corporate power, and the declining accountability of the state to its citizens threaten the basic rights and freedom of citizens. Mintzberg is seeking a return to a historical balance between the freedom offered by the market and the protection of the state.

Does Mintzberg wish to deschool management so to speak? What is his position on capitalist power and managerial privilege? As with the classical notion of managers held by Drucker and Selznick, a professional obligation to create a better society, Mintzberg retains an expectation that managers (trained or not) will ensure corporate productivity and contribute to capitalist growth. He does not reject the business school as much as seek its reinvention. Business schools must return to their classical goal of guiding societies towards shared social ends, and management knowledge to its past commitment to reason and rational processes. This would require a consideration of a variety of experience and not solely the authority offered by completing an MBA. His position does not entail a rejection of the discipline of management, but rather its further expansion. This he seeks in terms of domains that interact with the traditional realms of management – domains such as design, social welfare, and non-governmental organizations. Such domains are expected to focus on the interplay of experience and expertise, presenting new opportunities to apply management ideas and to create new constellations of context-based expertise and managerial identities. In these ways they further rejuvenate the discipline of management. Mintzberg's philosophy maintains a middle path, not espousing technocratic capitalism nor condemning it, but rather seeking its rehabilitation. It is a populist suspicion of technocracy.

The concern here is with the extent of power held by certified experts, but less so the larger social inequalities and implications of such power.

As a populist retreat from technocracy, Mintzberg's philosophy is not actually anti-technocratic. Mintzberg's project does offer a commentary on technocratic power but not one willing to describe the contemporary social order and call it what it is. Instead, there is a populist distrust of expert power that is concerned with its implications for inequality, but not a distrust that directly acknowledges the contemporary capitalist order, the global 1 percent elite, the neoliberal state, or the extraordinary violence involved in maintaining this order. To state this is not to fault Mintzberg unduly because these reservations can appear as cavils beside more mealy-mouthed conservative conformist positions within most of the management discipline. As I will now argue, it is possible indeed to perceive a particular stance of humanism in his project.

The well-known Business, Entrepreneurship, and Liberal Learning (BELL) Project of the Carnegie Foundation for the Advancement of Teaching (Colby *et al.* 2011; Sullivan, Ehrlich, and Colby, this volume) has increased the prominence of the humanities in management. It is worth noting the similarities and differences in Mintzberg's philosophy to the "Carnegie approach to the humanities." Both emphasize practicality and forms of contextual reasoning. Both emphasize worldliness and the extent managers should be exposed to a variety of perspectives and perceptions (Gosling and Mintzberg 2003). The shared emphasis is ultimately on efficacy, on achieving results through the manager.

But despite these similarities the differences are striking. The first lines of the Carnegie Report declare: "Business has never mattered more" (Colby *et al.* 2011: 1), making quite apparent the importance of such expectations. However, Mintzberg is less interested in grounding his polemics in appeals to business or beholden to expectations of profits and profitable corporations – his concern appears to be one of broadening the relevance of management to a variety of different organizations. Unlike the Carnegie Report, Mintzberg does state the malign consequences of management education quite directly, wishing to restrain these institutions and offer alternative paths for learning the practices of management.

I am arguing here that Mintzberg's project is not anti technocratic as much as humanistic. Given that this project does not reveal a direct social commentary, takes up no explicit position on class inequality, or devote much space to concerns of imperialism or colonialism, how then to explain its inchoate yet compelling critical tenor? It can be characterized as "late-style theorizing," borrowing a memorable phrase used by Edward Said (2004a, 2006) to discuss a variety of musicians and authors whose later work is distinctive and in some ways quite different from their early work. Said argued that such a creative shift was due not to advanced age but to a mediation of internal conflict. In this sense Beethoven's resolution in the 9th Symphony, as Adorno argued, is episodic and unfinished, "a 'catching fire between the extremes, which no longer allow for any secure middle ground or harmony of spontaneity'" (quoted in Said 2004b: 10). It is not resolution that requires abandoning a side as much as recognizing – belated though it may seem – a theme ever present but not suitably addressed that, at this pointed moment, becomes tractable and can be resolved. It is in this sense that Giuseppe Tomasi di Lampedusa's *Il Gatopardo* (translated as "The Leopard" in English), a novel of a declining aristocrat witnessing the onrush of Garibaldi into Sicily, is described by Said (2004b) as a novel that took a lifetime to generate because its writer reflected on the further decline of the members of his social class in early twentieth-century Italy and struggled to describe it, caught between registers of elegiac regret and ironic observation.

It is this sort of dual resolution – of choosing a side and/or acknowledging a latent discontent that takes time to emerge directly – that I believe characterizes Mintzberg's later theoretical work and its critical possibilities. The tone and scope of his writings have gradually shifted away from an effort to fit within the conventions of academic writing and towards a hybrid genre of polemical writing, characterized by intransigence and deliberate anachronism. In this "late-style" theorizing, rather than casting management knowledge as either inherently oppressive and to be discarded, or inherently benign and to be championed, Mintzberg assesses management knowledge and the pedagogical institutions that cohere around it in terms of whether they meet a larger obligation to create a better society – one that offers multiple freedoms (and not solely market freedom). Mintzberg's late style is, in this sense, a renewed, restless focus on the classical concerns of management in responding to contemporary societal and organizational problems. It is not critical as much as humanistic.

## Conclusion: Mintzberg's "amateurish conscience"

An explicit recourse to the humanities as critical practice, as in Freire, Illich, and Rancière, takes a position where the rule of experts is seen as consonant with industrial capitalism, social inequality, and reinforcing inferiority and powerlessness. To these thinkers, technocracy enforces false claims of expertise and willfully conflates personal prowess, taught expertise, and actual knowledge. The implication is to reject the dominant forms of professional education prevalent at present and to reimagine the professional and professional education. In contrast, Mintzberg's position is more in terms of the limitations of professionalizing management education and reforming it rather than challenging technocratic rule. Accredited managers and business schools disenfranchise other kinds of managers who become excluded from decision making. Accredited managers learn universal concepts but not the essential contexts of practice needed in their work. Accredited managers also displace democracies by contributing to forms of corporate power.

Mintzberg's late-style theorizing remains a compelling critique of the discipline of management and its methods of teaching. Often characterized as a "non-mainstream" thinker (for instance, Witzel 2013), Mintzberg is hardly a marginal figure in terms of the influence, scope, and power of his theoretical project for students, academics, practitioners, and consultants. His theoretical work fits closely into a still-dominant period in the disciplinary history of organizational theory, a period that was and is structural functionalist, market liberal, and modernist. Should it matter that it is not anti-technocratic?

Perhaps the real question to pose is not if Mintzberg's work is anti-technocratic but rather what it signifies in terms of the possibility for an internal critique of management shaped by humanism. At the end of one of his Reith Lectures, Edward Said asked whether the intellectual addresses authority "as a professional supplicant or as its unrewarded, amateurish conscience?" (1994: 83). To Said, the intellectual,

> does not represent a statue-like icon, but an individual vocation, an energy, a stubborn force engaging as a committed and recognizable voice in language and in society with a whole slew of issues, all of them having to do in the end with a combination of enlightenment and emancipation or freedom.
>
> *Said 1994: 73*

Said continues

> The great threat to such intellectual life is the demands of professionalism, thinking of your work as an intellectual as something you do for a living, between the hours of nine and five with one eye on the clock, and another cocked at what is considered to be proper, professional behavior – not rocking the boat, not straying outside the accepted paradigms or

> limits, making yourself marketable and above all presentable, hence uncontroversial and unpolitical and 'objective'.
>
> *Said 1994: 74*

But these pressures of professionalism can be countered by amateurism:

> the desire to be moved not by profit or reward but by love for and unquenchable interest in the larger picture, in making connections across lines and barriers, in refusing to be tied down to a specialty, in caring for ideas and values despite the restrictions of a profession.
>
> *Said 1994: 90*

Re-reading this passage, I recalled Mintzberg's 1977 book review of Herbert Simon's *The New Science of Management Decision*. As I was his doctoral student, it was included in a list of compulsory readings for my comprehensive exam, in fact the only book review in that list. Mintzberg begins the review following the expectations of the genre, summarizing it – "the book celebrates the results of technology, particularly of the information processing variety" (Mintzberg 1977: 342) – and its arguments chapter by chapter. But by the fourth page Mintzberg starts to assess the book in a different light. He points to Simon's untempered enthusiasm for technology and his optimism for the potential to routinize all forms of decision making, including of human judgment (Mintzberg 1977: 345–7). He shifts the discussion from the book's content to the extent its assertions make sense to the social world of the reader. He admits his previous optimism in the ability to anticipate patterns of human judgment, "indeed, I positively shared Simon's vision of the coming managerial revolution" (Mintzberg 1977: 347). This optimism he now feels was unwarranted. "What has changed since then?" He hints at his "own research on the work and decision processes of senior managers" but abruptly dismisses this avenue because "that is beside the point in this review." Instead, he declares: "two fundamental events have taken place in those intervening years which have changed my views but not those of Simon" – these being the war in Vietnam and the research on the role of the left and right hemispheres of the human brain (Mintzberg 1977: 347).

Mintzberg admits,

> Vietnam represented a critical turning point in the perceptions of many of us toward analysis . . . its relationship with management, which began in the factory with Frederick Taylor, flourished in the office with the introduction of Operations Research, and culminated in Robert McNamara's application of the Hitch and McKean (1960) proposals for PPBS and cost–benefit analysis at the policy level, started to come apart in the rice paddies of Vietnam.
>
> *Mintzberg 1977: 347*

The effort to apply analytical methods to "the White House's non programmed decisions" had led to "a war effort both ill-conceived and fundamentally immoral" (Mintzberg 1977: 348).

To Mintzberg, the source of serious error in Simon's work, as well as in the US war in Vietnam, was the unwillingness to recognize that facts are themselves based in values – values that enable us to interpret them and favor some over others.

> What went wrong? Could it have been the inability of analysis to handle the soft data – the expression on a peasant's face as opposed to a body count, the will of the enemy as opposed to the number of bombs needed to de-foliate a jungle?
>
> *Mintzberg 1977: 348*

He also points out that facts need to be disciplined by reason or they become ideological.

> Facts become impregnated with value when they consistently line up behind a single set of goals. In Vietnam they supported the military goals; the humanitarian goals, supported only by soft data, were driven out of the analysis. We see the same thing in corporations when the hard data line up behind the economic goals . . . And in society itself, when pollution endures pending calculation of its costs . . . When these things happen, analysis can no longer be called amoral: it drives even well-intentioned decision makers to make decidedly immoral choices.
>
> *Mintzberg 1977: 348*

That is, not only are facts shaped by values, and indeed biased towards hard data over soft data, but there is also a presumption of facile factuality that gives the illusion of impersonality, preventing expression of ideological intent. In this context, Mintzberg seems to be saying that facts can be used expediently for unethical decisions that violate underlying values. Thus he presents two views of values, both of which shape the interpretation of facts and in that sense taint their objectivity ideologically, and also animate judgment and provide occasions to test facts in resolving moral dilemmas.

Mintzberg's engagement in this review, as in his "late-style" theorizing, moves quite far from disciplinary expectations, sparking connections to the social and political world within which managers, large organizations, corporations, and US power function. In making these connections, he raises troubling questions about the extent to which managerial decisions can be value-less and neutral, and the extent that management as a discipline deserves to be separated from the real ethical consequences of a commitment to disinterested decision making. It is striking that this extent of engagement is ultimately unnecessary and separate from the expectations of the book review, but an engagement he feels impelled to offer, nevertheless. I have wondered if the reason the review was allotted to me and other doctoral students was for just this purpose, to remind us to spill over, to be difficult, to not try too hard to fit calmly and neatly within professional expectations, to retain an "amateurish conscience."

For those of us trained to study organizations, earning a living by publishing about them and by teaching students how to manage them, how far do we wish to go with a critique of technocracy? Mintzberg's "late-style" theorizing points to the limits of such a critical position at present, a fact of relevance especially to those committed to practicing critical management in management education (Perriton and Singh, this volume). Where should we draw the line between the promises of capitalist power offered by applied fields of knowledge, such as management, and the tacit aspirations and hopes for democratic accountability of those trained and teaching within them? To what extent is it possible to think of a way of theorizing management that is anti-managerial – and is that necessarily desirable?

In these senses, Mintzberg's "late-style" theorizing, and the questions it raises, offer, paradoxically, an arresting claim to the humanities, rivaling more deliberate efforts to insert the humanities into the managerialist heart of the discipline. Mintzberg is not interested in an instrumental approach to the humanities. The humanities do not serve the purpose of management or the needs of corporate capitalism; indeed, his explicit interest in the humanities in the broad sense of a study of the "classics," the use of literature or philosophy, appears to be modest at best. It is in the spirit more than the content of his theorizing that a sense of the humanities is present: an impatience with capitalist privilege, a cultivated disdain for the vulgarity of profit seeking, a curiosity for stories and storytelling, and an acceptance that the world around us hides mysterious even impenetrable truths. It is in such ways that his theories about organizations and the people who inhabit them connect to the larger world inhabited by these organizations, their members, and his readers.

Mintzberg's work is a compelling although incomplete call for an amateurish managerial conscience, committed to a vocation rather than a profession, to caring more than authorizing, and focused ultimately on stoking an expansive rectitude regardless of how that fits within the narrower concerns of organizations and the specialists who study and staff them.

## Notes

1 I studied with Henry Mintzberg for many years as a doctoral student and this chapter reflects an understanding of his theoretical work from the overlapping perspectives offered through those years and since. He has read an earlier version of this chapter and offered comments. There is no presumption intended on my part that he necessarily agrees with my interpretation and assessment of his work.

2 Whilst exploring what his scholarship can tell us about the state of human society and the world at large, I wish to note that Mintzberg has rarely used either of the words philosophy or humanities in his own considerable writings on management.

## References


Abbott, A. (1988) *The System of Professions*. Chicago, IL: University of Chicago Press.

Andrews, K.R. (1987) *The Concept of Corporate Strategy*. New York, NY: Dow Jones–Irwin.

Ansoff, I. (1991) 'Critique of Henry Mintzberg's "The design school: reconsidering the basic premises of strategic management"', *Strategic Management Journal*, 12(6), 449–61.

Burkhardt, E.J. (2002) 'From the economy to friendship: my years studying Ivan Illich'. *In*: L. Hoinacki and C. Mitcham (eds.) *The Challenges of Ivan Illich: A Collective Reflection*. Albany, NY: State University of New York Press, pp. 153–62.

Chambers, S.A. (2011) 'Jacques Rancière and the problem of pure politics', *European Journal of Political Theory*, 10(3), 303–26.

Colby, A., Ehrlich, T., Sullivan, W.M. and Dolle, J.R. (2011) *Rethinking Undergraduate Business Education: Liberal Learning for the Profession*. San Francisco, CA: Jossey-Bass.

Cowen, M.P. and Shenton, R.W. (1996) *Doctrines of Development*. London: Routledge.

Davis, O. (2010) *Jacques Rancière*. Cambridge, MA: Polity.

Freire, P. (1970) *Pedagogy of the Oppressed*. New York, NY: Continuum.

Gilman, N. (2006) 'The prophet of postmodernism: Peter Drucker and the legitimation of the corporation'. *In*: N. Lichtenstein (ed.) *American Capitalism: Social Thought and Political Economy in the Twentieth Century*. Philadelphia, PA: University of Pennsylvania, pp. 109–31.

Gosling, J. and Mintzberg, H. (2003) 'The five minds of a manager', *Harvard Business Review*, 81(11), 54–63.

Grey, C. (2004) 'Reinventing business schools: the contribution of critical management education', *Academy of Management Learning and Education*, 3(2), 178–86.

Harris, A.L. (1953) 'Veblen as social philosopher – a reappraisal', *Ethics*, 63(3 Part 2), 1–32.

Illich, I. (1969) 'Commencement at the University of Puerto Rico', *New York Review of Books*, 13(6), October 9, 1969, 12–15.

Illich, I. (1971) *Deschooling Society*. New York, NY: Harper and Row.

Illich, I. (1973) *Tools for Conviviality*. New York, NY: Harper and Row.

Kahn, R. and Kellner, D. (2007) 'Paulo Freire and Ivan Illich: technology, politics and the reconstruction of education', *Policy Futures in Education*, 5(4), 431–48.

Krygier, M. (2012) *Philip Selznick: Ideals in the World*. Stanford, CA: Stanford University Press.

Mintzberg, H. (1973a) *The Nature of Managerial Work*. New York, NY: Harper and Row.

Mintzberg, H. (1973b) 'Strategy making in three modes', *California Management Review*, Winter, 44–50.

Mintzberg, H. (1977) 'Review of "The New Science of Management Decision" by Herbert H. Simon', *Administrative Science Quarterly*, 22(2), 342–50.

Mintzberg, H. (1979) *The Structuring of Organizations: A Synthesis of the Research*. New York, NY: Prentice-Hall.

Mintzberg, H. (1989) 'Society has become unmanageable as a result of management'. *In*: H. Mintzberg (ed.) *Mintzberg on Management: Inside our Strange World of Organizations*. New York, NY: Free Press, pp. 335–73.

Mintzberg, H. (1990) 'The design school: reconsidering the basic premises of strategic management', *Strategic Management Journal*, 11(3), 171–95.
Mintzberg, H. (1991) 'Learning 1, planning 0 (reply to Igor Ansoff)', *Strategic Management Journal*, 12, 463–6.
Mintzberg, H. (1992) 'Learning in (and from) Eastern Europe', *Scandinavian Journal of Management*, 8(4), 335–8.
Mintzberg, H. (1994) *The Rise and Fall of Strategic Planning*. New York, NY: Free Press.
Mintzberg, H. (1995) *Les Propos d'un 'Pur Coton': Essai sur la Problématique Canadienne*. Québec, QC: Stoddart.
Mintzberg, H. (2005) *Managers Not MBAs: A Hard Look at the Soft Practice of Management and Management Development*. San Francisco, CA: Berrett-Koehler.
Mintzberg, H. (2014) *Rebalancing Society: Radical Renewal beyond Left, Right, and Center*. Available from: www.mintzberg.org/sites/default/files/rebalancing_society_pamphlet.pdf (accessed 1 November 2013).
Mintzberg, H. and Waters, J.A. (1985) 'Of strategies, deliberate and emergent', *Strategic Management Journal*, 6(3), 257–72.
Mintzberg, H. and Srinivas, N. (2010) 'Juxtaposing doers and helpers in development', *Community Development Journal*, 45(1), 39–57.
Parker, M. (2002) *Against Management: Organization in the Age of Managerialism*. Cambridge: Polity.
Rancière, J. (1991) *The Ignorant Schoolmaster: Five Lessons in Intellectual Emancipation*. Stanford, CA: Stanford University Press.
Rancière, J. (1999) *Disagreement: Politics and Philosophy*. Minneapolis, MN: University of Minnesota Press.
Reynolds, M. (1999) 'Grasping the nettle: possibilities and pitfalls of a critical management pedagogy', *British Journal of Management*, 9, 171–84.
Said, E. (1994) *Representations of the Intellectual*. New York, NY: Vintage.
Said, E. (2004a) 'Thoughts on late style', *London Review of Books*, 26(15), 3–7.
Said, E. (2004b) *Humanism and Democratic Criticism*. New York, NY: Columbia University.
Said, E. (2006) *On Late Style: Music and Literature against the Grain*. New York, NY: Pantheon Books.
Schugurensky, D. (2011) *Paulo Freire*. New York, NY: Continuum.
Spender, J.-C. (2013) 'Herbert Alexander Simon: philosopher of the organizational life world'. *In*: M. Witzel and M. Warner (eds.) *The Oxford Handbook of Management Theorists*. Oxford: Oxford University Press, pp. 297–357.
Witzel, M. (2013) 'Henry Mintzberg'. *In*: M. Witzel and M. Warner (eds.) *The Oxford Handbook of Management Theorists*. Oxford: Oxford University Press, pp. 462–79.

# 6

# Critical voices in management education in the UK

*Linda Perriton and Amritesh Singh*

This chapter looks back over the past thirty years of the critical management education (CME) project as expressed in the UK academic literature. The UK – with its much shorter experience of business schools and with a distinct social science bias – has had the opportunity in the past to pursue educational approaches that disrupt and destabilize the idea of management as a disinterested skill set. But recent funding changes in the UK higher education sector and the reliance on business schools to generate fee income for the wider institution has started to bring the UK more into line with the US and also other professional school models. The UK educational literature suggests that the scope for overt critical content and processes is narrowing.

Although there is a long tradition of management education engaging with social issues, there has been, as yet, no substantial or systematic catalogue of the pedagogical approaches used (Dart 2008). In practice the distinction between pursuing a conscious 'critical management' education agenda and wider educational strategies of encouraging the sociological imagination (Duarte 2009) or reflection, critical reflection and critical reflexivity is difficult to establish. Some teachers are uncomfortable with the push strategy of confronting students with the social consequences of management practice, conscious of the fact that students believe that covering such topics is irrelevant to their post-graduation employment prospects (Dart 2008). Other teachers may agree that the current technical rationality of the curriculum is problematic but prefer to look for indirect approaches such as removing economics from the business school offering (for example, Parker and Pearson 2013); advocating a dynamic capabilities approach (for example, Teece 2011); or focusing on sustainability as an over-arching objective (Gray and Collison 2002; Springett 2005; Walck 2009; Starik *et al.* 2010; Wu *et al.* 2010; Wright and Nyberg, this volume). When there is a *direct* challenge to the prevailing educational approach, it is easier to distinguish the critical voices in management education and to differentiate practice. There are many different educational paths that can lead to critical engagement with the social impact of management practice; however, when these approaches are framed as *complementary* to normative and technical approaches elsewhere in the business school (Duarte 2009) criticality is subsumed in the general debate around what constitutes 'good teaching', further complicating the search for critical management education as a stand-alone concept.

Those who self-identify as 'critical' teachers in the current context of UK business schools are an identifiable part of a longer tradition of resistance to the received binaries of management education, such as those between 'theoretical' and 'practical' knowledge and between 'writing' and 'doing'. We do not assume that management academics who publish under the broad aegis of Critical Management Studies (CMS) are also critical in their teaching approach and aims. CMS has been an established and successful critical movement within management studies for the past twenty years (Delbridge 2014). The importance of CMS to management research has been its ability to challenge the reality of management and organization as a given rather than a political construction, and in disrupting the idea that objective knowledge about management is being produced and transmitted by business schools (Willmott 2013). The aim of CMS is to establish the legitimacy of management *research* that is concerned with the pervasive social injustices that are mirrored or produced by organizations and managers, not to protect wider ideas of critical education.

The current form of 'uncritical' management studies dismisses CMS as irrelevant or threatening to managers or a sign of bias and political motivation by academics (Willmott 2013). The warrant to attend to issues of power and domination in research (Wray-Bliss 2003) is protected by traditions of intellectual freedom and academic interdisciplinarity. Even as the critical management approach is marginalized within the academy, the academy still provides space for debate about its merits. Noam Chomsky has observed that in his experience business schools are the most open spaces for debate in universities (Fleming and Oswick 2014), although this perhaps is more illustrative of his experience of being the invited speaker, rather than the inherent openness of business schools. There is less perceived freedom for those who wish to explore or expose the problems of market capitalism and its social relations within the management *classroom*, especially given the increase in precarious employment and use of contract instructors in universities. The idea of a critical warrant for management *teaching* that foregrounds social issues and the exercise of power and that views students as active participants in their learning who have a nascent social criticality requiring fostering does not enjoy the same protection as the critical warrant for research (see, for example, Saren 2010; Clegg *et al.* 2011; Solitander *et al.* 2012).

We argue in this chapter that the possibilities for incorporating challenge and critical innovation into business schools have been present since their foundation. The broad academic terrain that the management degree covers has allowed space for experimentation and cross-fertilization from other disciplines; however, the combined effects of marketization and the narrowing of the perceived purpose of university education to a vocational entry ticket are creating difficulties for established critical approaches and there is a sense that previous ground won for criticality is under threat. If the next critical push against technical rational modes of management education is to come in the guise of the liberal arts, then there is still a requirement for reflexivity and an open discussion of design decisions. They remain as important as they have always been in the past when critical management education used either critical theory or critical adult education as a pedagogical base.

In the first section of this chapter, we look back over the drivers of criticality within management education since the formation of the business schools in the UK. In the second section, we consider the diminishing scope for the use of traditional critical approaches within the curriculum, whilst also acknowledging the opportunities for taking a more critical stance to the 'public good' delivered by market capitalism provided by successive business scandals and the global financial crisis. Finally, we cover some sample management modules, which incorporate resources from arts and humanities in their curriculum, to consider the possibilities and challenges that interdisciplinarity presents.

## The history of criticality and management education in the UK

Management education – and the concept of the business school – has a far shorter history in the UK than it does in the US (see O'Connor, this volume); however, the development of management education on this side of the Atlantic in the post-war period was watched closely by the supporters of the spread of the business school in the US. Britain's seeming reluctance to embrace management education in the early twentieth century, even as other nations were enlarging their provision in higher education, was blamed on a number of inherently conservative forces in the country. It was variously attributed to the hostility of trade unions to modern management practice, the failure of management to introduce new procedures and the belated realization that the post-war recovery was going to need 'the introduction of principles and techniques commonly associated with highly trained business managements' (Murphy 1953: 37). Murphy's survey of management education in Britain in the 1950s notes that management education shared the general preference for liberal programmes – noting that the existing management education courses 'were cultural-centred, with liberal education as the objective rather than highly specialized preparation for employment' (1953: 39).

Not all reports on UK management education were as dismayed by the liberal bias in its higher education sector. When Fremont Kast surveyed European management education provision a decade after Murphy, his response to the differences in approaches between countries was more phlegmatic. Kast queried whether a uniform approach was needed in the development of management education across all European countries – as long as the overall trend was towards the establishment of *more* business schools (Kast 1965). As a result, Kast was more interested in the 1963 UK Robbins Report and its call for the establishment of two major schools for postgraduate management education. He also considered the Franks Report as both welcome and revolutionary. However, both the Robbins and Franks Reports were aware of and reflected the liberal versus utilitarian tensions inherent in UK education, especially those programmes that were broadly vocational in nature.[1] Franks in particular had noted that the businessmen he had spoken to feared that business schools would be created in the image of other university departments, concerned with the advancement of knowledge and more suited to creating scholars than managers (Franks 1963, cited in Kast 1965: 82).

Institutional inertia ensured that the liberal approach to management education persisted for far longer than the architects of the post-war business school expansion envisaged. The history of the subject area since the 1950s has been one of a shifting emphasis backwards and forwards between liberal and utilitarian approaches, rather than the outright victory of one over the other. Business schools offered differing rationales for their management degrees over time (and still do) and it is therefore difficult to generalize about what narratives are in use or have been in use. For example, French and Grey (1996) characterized the 1980s as a period in which business schools had finally embraced the utilitarian approach. But, as Macfarlane (1997) noted at the time, at least four studies of the business curriculum of that decade (that is, Boys 1988; Brown and Harrison 1980; Silver and Brennan, 1988; Tolley 1983 as cited in Macfarlane 1997) could not make a definitive judgement as to whether management education had become study *for* business or the study *of* business. The liberal versus utilitarian debate never goes away, it just appears in different guises. For example, there have been discussions about the 'hard' and 'soft' subjects in the curriculum, whether management should seek a quantitative or qualitative research base, the 'application' versus 'theory' tension in research output or whether courses are most useful at undergraduate or postgraduate level. The Carnegie Report (Colby *et al.* 2011;

Sullivan, Ehrlich and Colby, this volume) is arguably just the latest, high status contribution to that debate in the UK.

One explanation for the persistence of the problem of deciding what management education is for, and what values it should embody, is its exponential growth. The expansion of management education from the 1980s onwards has required increasing numbers of academic staff. Not all, and perhaps not even the majority, of the academic staff recruited saw management as their disciplinary home. Rowlinson and Hassard's (2011) institutional history of CMS has argued that many of the key figures responsible for promoting the liberal and critical content within management education in the UK in the past were left wing, arts or social science graduates from working class backgrounds. If that is the case, it is hardly surprising to find them resisting technical rational forms of management education. External political developments also played their part in preventing management education from settling into an entirely utilitarian tradition. The Thatcher Government's antipathy towards sociology in the 1980s resulted in many academics, who might otherwise have been employed in sociology departments, finding congenial niches for their research and ideas in the expanding management schools (Rowlinson and Hassard 2011). The embedding of sociological and political approaches to management studies by 'displaced' academics teaching organizational behaviour or labour relations within the business school allowed first Marxist critiques and then those based in post-structuralism to gain footholds in management education at this time. These footholds were crucial early gains that encouraged the wider critical management approach to establish itself in the 1990s.

The start of the CMS project is dated (for the sake of convenience, if not absolute certainty) to the publication of Alvesson and Willmott's (1992) edited book of the same name. Alvesson and Willmott turned to an analysis of power in management using the work of critical theorists and Foucault, and in doing so broke the existing critical consensus that identified exploitation as the key motive in labour relations (Hassard *et al.* 2001; Rowlinson and Hassard 2011). From its inception, CMS was an umbrella term under which a number of different sociologically based critiques found an identity as opposed to replacing one brand of theoretical orthodoxy with another. The early years of the CMS project were also notable for the degree of interest shown in the pedagogical processes of criticality. The early CMS movement posed a two-pronged challenge to business schools – it was interested in radicalizing the content of the courses *and* questioning the existing aims and objectives of the management programmes they provided.

Willmott's (1994) own 'provocations to a debate' put down an early marker regarding CMS's willingness to look at management education practices. Steve Fox's (1994) 'debate' article, the 'polemic' of Grey and Mitev (1995), and the edited book *Re-thinking Management Education* (French and Grey 1996) followed Willmott's initial contribution in quick succession. CMS was – and remains – a project that is concerned with creating space for critical content and research agendas within the business school – and that includes the classroom space – rather than being focused on pedagogical innovation per se. The CMS umbrella provided the means by which business school academics with an existing interest in management education could join in with a larger movement within management education.

Critical Management *Education* (CME) is therefore a label that was useful for two groups after the emergence of CMS (see Vince, this volume). The first group encompassed management educators who were already associated with research and classroom practice that sought to minimize harmful power dynamics in learning and/or sought to raise the critical consciousness of students. The second group contained those who wanted to explore their own pedagogical practices alongside their critical research but were not primarily researchers of critical education approaches. Perriton and Reynolds (2004) outlined the core indicators of a 'critical' management education approach as:

- A commitment to questioning the assumptions underlying management theory and professional practice.
- Asking questions about management and management education processes that were both moral and technical in nature.
- An interest in how management is achieved and what ends are pursued.
- Classroom discussions that focused on processes of power and ideology, especially in respect of where and how management was reproducing existing disadvantages around race, class, age or gender.
- A community orientation (even if the concept is challenged) that springs from a concern with the social as well as the individual.
- Broadly emancipatory in nature, where changes to how we teach management education are seen as a necessary part of the move towards a more just society.

*Perriton and Reynolds 2004: 66*

Most CME research, and its implementation, has been associated with postgraduate and post-experience programmes in the UK. The reasons for this are two-fold and stem from the centrality of critical reflection in CME, with its assumption that students have already experienced the world of work and its contradictions and the clustering of CME research. Alvesson and Willmott (1992) outlined a model for the facilitation of a critical form of management education. Using an example drawn from his own experience of working with practising managers, Willmott explored a two-stage process of reconstruction (that is, the identification of manifestations of power or ideology at work within the job of management) and critique (that is, a collective form of reflection that identifies where changes need to be made). Critique demands adult behaviour (and collectively understood and appreciated work experiences) if it is to be effective as a pedagogical method and, like the other core principles listed previously, is easier to establish in post-experience programmes. The 'adult' assumptions of CME also reflect the influence of radical adult education theory underpinning the postgraduate programmes at the UK's Lancaster University in the 1980s and 1990s. Lancaster scholars such as Fox (1994) and Reynolds (1998, 1999a, 1999b) have been key nodes in a wider network that can be traced back to the innovative Masters programmes based on CME principles and Lancaster's PhD programme which have helped create a core of CME literature over the past three decades. Researchers with Lancastrian connections who continue to focus on critical approaches include Perriton (2000, 2004), Cunliffe (2001), Elliott (2003), Elliott and Turnbull (2005), Swan (2005) and Trehan (2007). However, the changes to the recruitment focus of many UK business schools towards programmes that recruit large numbers of overseas students have taken them away from small, niche post-experience programmes that operated along critical pedagogical lines. As a result many postgraduate programmes share the same features as undergraduate programmes – large numbers of students, increased expectations of an instructional as opposed to an individual learning approach and the creation of a standardized product that reduces the critical warrant of the educator.

## The removal of the critical warrant in management education

Universities have been historically contingent on external factors – from patronage to funding grants and tuition fees – to ensure their survival and these in turn have determined, to a greater or a lesser degree, what is being taught, how and by whom, and to what end (see Parker, this volume). But in the past thirty years, most Western industrialized states have moved towards the use of market solutions to allocate resources, including the allocation of resources to and within higher education institutions. In turn, universities have been forced to think about their own activities in terms of markets and products. Although some UK commentators date this marketization agenda of universities to the introduction of undergraduate tuition fees, the general trend across European institutions since the 1980s has been for a convergence with the US educational model (Engwall and Lindvall 2012). Indeed, if we are to look for a moment when pedagogical decisions were subjected to central institutional oversight, we need to look to earlier public sector reforms that encouraged the 'teaching and learning strategy' pursued to become the 'business' of university managers as well as academics (Holley and Oliver 2000). Because course design affected the costs and revenue generation of the university, pedagogical decision making became much more of a conscious negotiation between the pecuniary needs of the institution, the aims of the educator and the development needs of the students (Gross and Hogler 2005).

Although the idea of a 'negotiated' design for management education might sound like a welcome development and imagined as a collegial – and congenial – discussion about pedagogy, the reality is somewhat less romantic. The marketized education system only makes sense when there is a presumed link between educational choice and (more or less) guaranteed transition into the labour market. The prospective student is encouraged to calculate the value of a specific qualification to the labour market. It is this assumption of the exchange value of a specific qualification that drives the type and, by extension, the content and style of education in higher education (Lauder 2001: 191). Students and their parents use their estimation of the 'employability' that the educational design appears to offer to make their decisions about what programme to enrol on (Jameson *et al.* 2012). Job destination 'league tables' and hence rankings of employability are therefore one of the drivers of institutional responses and decision making in respect of educational design. The pedagogical design – and its coherence – is key to the purchase decision, regardless of the fact that the prospective student is not in a position to make informed or comparative judgements about pedagogy (Little and Williams 2010). The educators, who *are* in a position to make informed and comparative judgements about the pedagogical choices being made, are constrained in turn by the institutional pressures to deliver 'marketable' courses – those that conform to the received ideas about employability and studying *for* business.

The assumption that business schools offer 'vocational' degrees, but vocational degrees with the advantage of not committing the student to a specific professional identity as is the case with medicine, law or dentistry, has delivered substantial growth in student numbers since the introduction of tuition fees. However, there is increased pressure on business schools to continue to attract students, especially those from overseas paying higher fees, to compensate for fluctuating home student numbers in non-vocational subjects and the reduction in government funding. The need for cost efficiency and guaranteed profit margins is resulting in the removal of high-effort/high-cost modules and programmes (Parker 2013). Universities are turning away from small-scale pedagogical models and are repositioning their teaching practices towards large student cohorts and mass delivery systems. Even with larger class sizes, the consumerist orientation forces universities to react to student demands for vocationally oriented modules that are designed to appeal to their aspirations and lifestyles. Programme content, design and delivery are constantly monitored and adapted to respond to the changing tastes and preferences of students (Parker 2013), not the demands of the subject area. Whereas in the past the educator could rely on their professional status to guarantee the educational design, in the marketized system the design now must 'fit' with wider institutional, discursive and income-generating needs. Any challenges to the idea that education is primarily pursued for the advantages it gives in the labour market are likely to be rejected unless the case for a different approach is compelling and multi-faceted (Dart 2008).

Some critical educators (for example, Bridgman 2007) have sought to use crisis moments in capitalism in order to try and create such a compelling case for a more public role for critical educators *in addition* to curricular change. The first such crisis moment was the collapse of Enron, and then global recession following the banking collapse in 2008. Both events have been used to reinforce the argument that management education needs to attend to the moral and ethical dimensions of management practices (for example, Ghoshal 2005; Baker and Comer 2012) and to question the contribution of the MBA to the financial crisis (for example, Podolny 2009; Wong 2009). Although these 'teachable moments' (Colby *et al.* 2011) provide CME – and critical management scholars in general – with opportunities to briefly enter the public debate about the reproduction of management knowledge, there is little sign that crises are forcing a wholesale re-evaluation of the business school curriculum. Rather than being seen as a systemic issue within capitalism, the crises have been attributed to the absence of ethical or moral behaviour of individuals; a framing that has led to increased calls for business ethics classes to be added to or rethought in the curriculum (for example, Swanson 2005; Alsop 2006; Giacalone and Thompson 2006; Beggs and Dean 2007). Initiatives such as Principles for Responsible Management Education (PRME) are perhaps best read as the latest in a series of distress signals sent out by concerned educators, rather than as a sign of a sustained public debate about the need for critical forms of management education.

Nonetheless, CMS as an idea and as an identifiable movement in business schools has been able to sustain a presence in UK academia in a way that CME has struggled to do. The incorporation of critical process into management education has always been a difficult task, and critical content approaches have probably been the more frequently used out of the two approaches (see Perriton 2014 for a discussion of the lack of empirical studies in this area). A focus on social awareness through process remains a key element of smaller, critical enclaves in management education such as Critical Human Resource Development (for example, Fenwick 2005; Callahan 2007; Stewart *et al.* 2007; Sambrook 2008), but it has become clear that the requirement for CMS in terms of teaching is the introduction of critical ideas to students and not the achievement of critical outcomes in the classroom. This distinction is an important one to understand when it comes to CMS and its relationship to the liberal arts. The default for the wider CMS approach to management education is to prioritize the means of delivering critical ideas into the classroom, and therefore it often sees the arts and humanities as offering new and creative resources in support of that aim rather than the achievement of a new sort of classroom politics.

## The incorporation of the arts and humanities in management education

In their reflection on business schools, Patriotta and Starkey (2008: 323) were amongst the first to suggest that the liberal arts model was an alternative route for management education; an alternative evolutionary path to one that inevitably leads to the development of behaviour that 'sustains and perpetuates the institutions of capitalism'. The liberal arts approach is not an institutional strategy of using business schools to subsidize the arts and humanities but the blending of arts subjects and approaches with managerial subjects. When tackled at the level of institutional pathways in the US, a liberal arts approach is delivered by taking modules in different faculties. But in the UK's less flexible system of taking degrees entirely within subject areas, some academics have sought to introduce a liberal arts approach by incorporating material, and approaches, from other faculties *within* management modules.

Introducing learning materials from arts and humanities to business studies classes has created unorthodox learning environments for teachers and students alike. Resources as diverse as music (Comer and Holbrook 2012), cinema (Bell 2008; Billsberry and Gilbert 2008; Smith 2009; Huffman and Kilian 2011; Comer and Holbrook 2012), art (Chio and Fandt 2007) and poetry (Van Buskirk and London 2008) have demonstrated the potential to facilitate conversations between disciplines traditionally thought to be disparate, reinvigorate the dynamic between the tutor and pupil and deliver exciting new challenges to research and teaching. Fields such as organizational behaviour (Van Buskirk and London 2008; Smith 2009; Colakoglu and Littlefield 2011; Huffman and Kilian 2011; Comer and Holbrook 2012), human resource management (Anderson 2007; Chio and Fandt 2007; Billsberry and Gilbert 2008) and critical thinking in management (Anderson 2007; Stepanovich 2009) have particularly encouraged cross-disciplinary collaborations at both undergraduate *and* postgraduate levels.

Educators have claimed that interdisciplinary pedagogical methods have encouraged reflection by students on their tacit assumptions about culture and identity, in both the workplace and the broader society (for example, Chio and Fandt 2007; Colakoglu and Littlefield 2011), equity (for example, Anderson 2007) and the nature and purpose of education (for example, Van Buskirk and London 2008). The design intention is that when shared and compared amongst class members, the individual reflections simultaneously allow the recognition of shared values and points of difference, even conflict. Such unexpected encounters with the self and the 'other' are designed to encourage a more engaged student who is better positioned to grasp the nuances and complexities of the field of study. These methods are justified on the grounds of equipping students with crucial employability skills by embedding elicitation tools such as Photovoice (Chio and Fandt 2007) and projective techniques (Colakoglu and Littlefield 2011) that are a visible and popular presence in some of the industries studied within the curriculum. Such approaches, therefore, not only challenge the boundaries between disciplines but also attempt to bridge the gap between academia and the 'real world' of work.

Often, however, nurturing criticality in management studies using methods from other disciplines is achieved by adopting a reductive approach to the borrowed resources and perspectives. Individual management teachers are rarely able to master the forms of criticality accepted as critical *within* the arts and humanities, regardless of whether or not their eventual objectives within the management classroom are critical in nature. For example, in their (non-critical) discussion, Billsberry and Gilbert (2008) literalize scenarios in their source text to study recruitment and selection. However, their source text, the 2005 film version of *Charlie and the Chocolate Factory*, is a work of fantasy that does not adapt well to this purpose, not least because the racial slurs in the characterization of Oompa Loompas make the choice of the film and text to teach recruitment and selection (Billsberry and Gilbert 2008) a fraught one. Stepanovich (2009), on the other hand, writes a story, 'The Lobster's Tale', which is essentially a case study that is written specifically for pedagogical purposes and with no pretensions to literary status. 'The Lobster's Tale' parades all conceivable sources of conflict – racism, sexism, generational conflict, state versus the individual, and uprisings against corporate titans by independent traders – and asks leading questions to promote critical thinking. This can make the pedagogical motivation in choosing a work of fiction over a case study difficult to understand. These confrontations between disciplines that have not been traditional allies are understandable; indeed it is to be expected. These conflicts can, however, be reduced by a measured approach to interdisciplinarity where coherent curriculum mapping and pedagogical rationale justify the choice of resources and inform learning outcomes.

The troubling aspect of the appropriation of the liberal arts into management modules as opposed to their teaching in parallel is the apparent lack of pedagogical rationale that informs the choice of material. Van Buskirk and London (2008), for example, do not explain why particular poets and eras that served as the principal objects of study were deemed to be better aligned with their pedagogical processes than others. On occasions where multiple versions of the prescribed film exist, a preference of one version over the other is left to speculation. Huffman and Kilian (2011) do not explain their preference for the 1965 version of *The Flight of the Phoenix* over the 2004 remake. Notwithstanding the fact that both films draw from the same source material, Billsberry and Gilbert (2008) indicate an arbitrary partiality for *Charlie and the Chocolate Factory* (2005) over *Willy Wonka & the Chocolate Factory* (1971). Similarly, the decision to present students with a documentary on the making of Fleetwood Mac's *Rumours* as the ideal material to enrich the understanding of group dynamics is left unexplained by Comer and Holbrook (2012). The mining of other academic fields for resources still requires the articulation and justification of design decisions.

As illustrated earlier, not all the pedagogical borrowings from the arts and humanities are for the purpose of developing criticality in students. The most common learning goals of arts/management hybrids are those of knowledge, retention and application (Smith 2009; Huffman and Kilian 2011; Comer and Holbrook 2012). However important those elements are to the learning process, they do not often reflect the higher-order skills of analysis and challenge what CME has held to be important. It is therefore important to distinguish between the decision to incorporate liberal arts materials because it stimulates and engages students and the use of such material to foster criticality. Students enjoy using stimulating and familiar cultural resources, such as books and film, rather than the less typically joyous academic article. This is reflected in their feedback where film and other literary resources are credited for enabling their understanding of conventional concepts that was not achieved through more traditional academic pedagogies (Smith 2009).

There are, however, examples of where teachers *have* used literary resources to foster critical thinking in students and offer opportunities for teachers to reflect on their practice. Śliwa and colleagues (2013; see also Sørensen and Śliwa, this volume) notably make use of literary texts, principally novels, to develop a richer understanding of organizational behaviour and to nurture a more critical outlook at taught postgraduate level. Students on the course were invited to choose a novel that would explore the key concepts of management and organization theory that were being taught – culture, structure, power and change. These individual choices are complemented by excerpts from texts like *Animal Farm* and *Brave New World* that are chosen by the faculty as being instrumental in facilitating a deeper engagement with the subject. Students are assessed on the strength of their essays (where they were invited to capitalize on the novel(s) they had encountered) *and* their reflective commentaries on the nature and purpose of the course and their experience of immersing themselves in an atypical pedagogical situation. Śliwa *et al.* (2013) chart the manner in which initial hesitation in students led to a reflexive enquiry where the faculty ruminated over unanticipated consequences of their pedagogical decision: the politics of incorporating novels that were not in English in the course when selected by individual students; the pitfalls of a preconceived idea that believes all students have command over and affection for at least one novel; the awkward confrontation between the position of the novel as a literary form in the West where it served as the premise for nation-building and its conspicuous absence from comparative sociocultural discourses outside the West. Śliwa *et al.* (2013) also map the trajectory of their students who overcome their reluctance and capitalize on the unique learning materials available to them to produce striking and incisive critiques on the location of the individual within organizational structures.

Somewhat differently, Kearney *et al.* (2013) advocate the use of documentaries on the Holocaust to facilitate more sober reflections on organizational structuring and behaviour in doctoral students. The choice of material in itself is a strategic pedagogic invention to introduce emotion and subjectivity to the discipline to enable students to use them constructively in their critical reflections. Although the challenges of teaching a course such as this are apparent – Kearney *et al.* (2013) acknowledge how the nature and content of the course required an exceptional degree of 'emotional scaffolding' for students – the rewards of creating an experiential learning environment outstrip them. Students made topical connections between the course materials and contemporary political propaganda on controversial issues such as the treatment of inmates at Guantanamo Bay, thus fulfilling the vision that lies at the heart of the CMS project of creating critical, enquiring democratic subjects. Pedagogical interventions such as those designed by Śliwa *et al.* (2013) and Kearney *et al.* (2013) serve to build a reciprocal learning experience for students and faculty even as they identify areas of growth for the CMS project at large.

One of the limitations of these critical innovations in management education is the extent to which resources – films, literary texts, works of art – are drawn from the Western corpus (see Prasad, this volume). These resources reflect local cultural ideologies and reinforce a particular form of hegemony. Western literature, for instance, frequently centres on an individual sense of being that is harboured in the sacrosanct space of interiority. It is this belief that leads Van Buskirk and London (2008: 301) to regard everyone as maintaining 'an interior dialogue that [is] the "raw material" for poetic meditation', to elicit a sharper understanding of the metaphors that underpin SWOT (strengths, weaknesses, opportunities and threats) analysis in their students. However, the notion of the self that is delicately balanced on the fulcrum of interiority does not fit well with, for example, the supposedly more communal culture of East Asia. Using materials from the arts and humanities needs to be done with reflexive care so as not to ignore the extent to which analytical techniques are specific to particular forms of sociocultural upbringing. Instead of fostering criticality, such approaches may unintentionally create hindrances for (international) students who are unfamiliar with the tacit knowledge that governs the production, reception and canonization of (Western) cultural artefacts. What also escapes attention is the extent to which resources that are products of a particular historical moment may carry with them unexpected nodes of tension. Further, the selection of Western literature (novels, poetry, cinema and art) runs contradictory to most universities' emphasis on internationalization and a (largely shared) pedagogical aim of creating a 'global' citizen.

Our aim here is not to discourage interdisciplinary practices in management education, especially those where new resources for introducing critical ideas create excitement and energy amongst our students. It is evident that a migration from (in terms of the students' perspective) obscure, theoretical academic texts to more digestible forms from popular culture and imagination can make challenging ideas more legible for students, especially during their transition into university education. An early introduction to interdisciplinarity at undergraduate level could provide a useful platform for student engagement and a noticeable appreciation in learning. Later stages of the degree could effectively use that foundation to build more complex structures where criticality and reflexivity would take precedence over the use of the arts and humanities as a student-friendly mechanism for the delivery of critical concepts. Our position is therefore one of broad support for the careful articulation of the aims of using arts and humanities resources in management education settings. We think that where the objective of the module is to increase access to ideas or to enable a transition to criticality or the development of alternative registers of enquiry and expression, these should be transparently recorded in learning design and also that some attempt should be made to move beyond the naïve use of resources.

## Conclusion

This chapter has argued that the wider mission of universities to produce knowledge and innovate protects the warrant to research critically – at least for the time being. Although there might have been general frustration with the failure of CMS to encourage social action and activism (Foster and Wiebe 2010; Haynes 2010; Machold and Huse 2010; Saren 2010), there is still an acknowledgement of its contribution to debates and ideas in management. It might have been thought that the activism that CMS encourages was best expressed through the educational process of business schools; however, the increasing challenges of the marketized environment have reduced the opportunities for process radicalism. The increase in taught postgraduate student numbers combined with overseas recruitment has favoured critical content approaches over resource- and language-intensive critical pedagogy, and latterly also the use of resources drawn from the arts and humanities to help introduce and sustain critical ideas within management.

The constant, restless search for teaching approaches that maintain critical and/or challenging social perspectives within management education is not surprising. Good (and passionate) teaching is a product of the identity and integrity of the teacher (Beatty *et al.* 2009). Regardless of the approach, if that teacher has a teaching philosophy that values social justice or exposure to non-utilitarian perspectives on management, then it will find a way of expressing itself through the pedagogical encounter. The second part of this chapter, however, has argued for a rigorous 'critical' reflexivity when using resources from the arts and humanities within management modules. Not to do so reduces the liberal arts 'approach' to a smash-and-grab raid on another discipline, rather than the application of a critical sensibility to the design and practice of the teaching.

## Note

1 The UK Government commissioned the Robbins Report in 1961. Its terms of reference were to review the pattern of full-time higher education in light of national needs and resources, and to advise on what principles its long-term development should be based. It was also asked to recommend if any new types of institutions were desirable and whether changes were needed in planning and coordination of UK higher education. It reported in 1963. As a direct follow-up to that report, Lord Franks was asked to investigate and make recommendations on the business and management education specifically.

## References

Alsop, R. (2006) 'Business ethics education in business schools: a commentary', *Journal of Management Education*, 30(1), 11–14.

Alvesson, M. and Willmott, H. (eds.) (1992) *Critical Management Studies*. London: Sage Publications.

Anderson, M. (2007) '"Why are there so many theories?" A classroom exercise to help students appreciate the need for multiple theories of a management domain', *Journal of Management Education*, 31(6), 757–76.

Baker, S. and Comer, D. (2012) '"Business ethics everywhere": an experiential exercise to develop students' ability to identify and respond to ethical issues in business', *Journal of Management Education*, 36(1), 95–125.

Beatty, J., Leigh, J. and Dean, K.L. (2009) 'Finding our roots: an exercise for creating a personal teaching philosophy statement', *Journal of Management Education*, 33(1), 115–30.

Beggs, J. and Dean, K. (2007) 'Legislated ethics or ethics education? Faculty views in the post-Enron era', *Journal of Business Ethics*, 71(1), 15–37.

Bell, E. (2008) *Reading Management and Organization in Film*. Basingstoke, UK: Palgrave Macmillan.

Billsberry, J. and Gilbert, L. (2008) 'Using Roald Dahl's Charlie and the Chocolate Factory to teach different recruitment and selection paradigms', *Journal of Management Education*, 32(2), 228–47.

Bridgman, T. (2007) 'Freedom and autonomy in the university enterprise', *Journal of Organizational Change Management*, 20(4), 478–90.

Callahan, J. (2007) 'Gazing into the crystal ball: critical HRD as a future of research in the field', *Human Resource Development International*, 10(1), 77–82.

Chio, V. and Fandt, P. (2007) 'Photovoice in the diversity classroom: engagement, voice, and the "eye/I" of the camera', *Journal of Management Education*, 31(4), 484–504.

Clegg, S., Dany, F. and Grey, C. (2011) 'Introduction to the special issue Critical Management Studies and Managerial Education: New Contexts? New Agenda?', *M@n@gement*, 14(5), 271–9.
Colakoglu, S. and Littlefield, J. (2011) 'Teaching organizational culture using a projective technique: collage construction', *Journal of Management Education*, 35(4), 564–85.
Colby, A., Ehrlich, T., Sullivan, W. and Dolle, J. (2011) *Rethinking Undergraduate Business Education: Liberal Learning for the Profession*. San Francisco, CA: Jossey Bass.
Comer, D. and Holbrook, R. (2012) 'Getting behind the scenes of Fleetwood Mac's Rumours using a documentary on the making of a music album to learn about task groups', *Journal of Management Education*, 36(4), 544–67.
Cunliffe, A. (2001) 'Everyday conversations: a social poetics of managing', *Concepts and Transformation*, 6(3), 295–315.
Dart, R. (2008) 'A commentary on "Piercing the Bubble": should management education "confront" poverty?', *Journal of Management Education*, 32(6), 731–7.
Delbridge, R. (2014) 'Promising futures: CMS, post-disciplinarity, and the new public social science', *Journal of Management Studies*, 51(1), 95–117.
Duarte, F. (2009) 'Rekindling the sociological imagination as a pedagogical "package" in management education', *Journal of Management Education*, 33(1), 59–76.
Elliott, C. (2003) 'Representations of the intellectual insights from Gramsci on management education', *Management Learning*, 34(4), 411–27.
Elliott, C. and Turnbull, S. (eds.) (2005) *Critical Thinking in Human Resource Development*. London: Routledge.
Engwall, L. and Lindvall, C. (2012) 'Leaders of modern universities: primi inter pares or chief executive officers?' *In*: S. Tengblad (ed.) *The Work of Managers: Towards a Practice Theory of Management*. Oxford: Oxford University Press, pp. 206–25.
Fenwick, T. (2005) 'Conceptions of critical HRD: dilemmas for theory and practice', *Human Resource Development International*, 8(2), 225–38.
Fleming, P. and Oswick, C. (2014) 'Educating consent? A conversation with Noam Chomsky on the university and business school education', *Organization*, 21(4), 568–78.
Foster, W. and Wiebe, E. (2010) 'Praxis makes perfect: recovering the ethical promise of critical management studies', *Journal of Business Ethics*, 94(2), 271–83.
Fox, S. (1994) 'Debating management learning II', *Management Learning*, 25(1), 83–94.
French, R. and Grey, C. (eds.) (1996) *Rethinking Management Education*. London: Sage Publications.
Ghoshal, S. (2005) 'Bad management theories are destroying good management practices', *Academy of Management Learning & Education*, 4(1), 75–91.
Giacalone, R. and Thompson, K. (2006) 'Business ethics and social responsibility education: shifting the worldview', *Academy of Management Learning & Education*, 5(3), 266–77.
Gray, R. and Collison, D. (2002) 'Can't see the wood for the trees, can't see the trees for the numbers? Accounting education, sustainability and the public interest', *Critical Perspectives on Accounting*, 13(5), 797–836.
Grey, C. and Mitev, N. (1995) 'Management education: a polemic', *Management Learning*, 26(1), 73–90.
Gross, M. and Hogler, R. (2005) 'What the shadow knows: exploring the hidden dimensions of the consumer metaphor in management education', *Journal of Management Education*, 29(1), 3–16.
Hassard, J., Hogan, J. and Rowlinson, M. (2001) 'From labor process theory to critical management studies', *Administrative Theory & Praxis*, 23(3), 339–62.
Haynes, M. (2010) 'Business schools and economic crisis – a need for a rethink?', *International Journal of Management Concepts and Philosophy*, 4(1), 2–7.
Holley, D. and Oliver, M. (2000) 'Pedagogy and new power relationships', *International Journal of Management Education*, 1(1), 11–21.
Huffman, B. and Kilian, C. (2011) 'The flight of the phoenix: interpersonal aspects of project management', *Journal of Management Education*, 36(4), 568–600.
Jameson, J., Strudwick, K., Bond-Taylor, S. and Jones, M. (2012) 'Academic principles versus employability pressures: a modern power struggle or a creative opportunity?', *Teaching in Higher Education*, 17(1), 25–37.
Kast, F. (1965) 'Management education in Europe', *The Academy of Management Journal*, 8(2), 75–89.
Kearney, K., Krumm, B., Hughes, R. and Satterfield, J.W. (2013) 'Organized for genocide: student reactions and learning from use of emotive documentaries on the Holocaust', *Journal of Management Education*, 37(3), 342–66.

Lauder, H. (2001) 'Innovation, skill diffusion, and social exclusion'. *In*: P. Brown, A. Green and H. Lauder (eds.) *Higher Skills: Globalization, Competitiveness, and Skill Formation*. Oxford: Oxford University Press, pp. 161–203.
Little, B. and Williams, R. (2010) 'Students' roles in maintaining quality and in enhancing learning: is there a tension?', *Quality in Higher Education*, 16(2), 115–27.
Macfarlane, B. (1997) 'In search of an identity: lecturer perceptions of the business studies first degree', *Journal of Vocational Education and Training*, 49(1), 5–20.
Machold, S. and Huse, M. (2010) 'Provocation: business schools and economic crisis – the emperor's new clothes: learning from crises?', *International Journal of Management Concepts and Philosophy*, 4(1), 13–20.
Murphy, M. (1953) 'Education for management in Great Britain', *The Journal of Business of the University of Chicago*, 26(1), 37–47.
Parker, L. (2013) 'Contemporary university strategising: the financial imperative', *Financial Accountability & Management*, 29(1), 1–25.
Parker M. and Pearson, G. (2013) 'Why should business schools teach managers?', *Business and Society Review*, 118(1), 1–22.
Patriotta, G. and Starkey, K. (2008) 'From utilitarian morality to moral imagination. reimagining the business school', *Journal of Management Inquiry*, 17(4), 319–27.
Perriton, L. (2000) 'Verandah discourses: critical management education in organizations', *British Journal of Management*, 11(3), 227–37.
Perriton, L. (2004) 'A reflection of what exactly? Questioning the use of "critical reflection" in management education contexts'. *In*: M. Reynolds and R. Vince (eds.) *Organizing Reflection*. Hampshire: Ashgate Publishing, pp. 126–41.
Perriton L. (2014) 'The (re) negotiation of the critical warrant in critical management education: a research agenda', *Human Resource Development International*, 17(4), 384–99.
Perriton, L. and Reynolds, M. (2004) 'Critical management education from pedagogy of possibility to pedagogy of refusal?', *Management Learning*, 35(1), 61–77.
Podolny, J.M. (2009) 'The buck stops (and starts) at business school', *Harvard Business Review*, 87(6), 62–7.
Reynolds, M. (1998) 'Reflection and critical reflection in management learning', *Management Learning*, 29(2), 183–200.
Reynolds, M. (1999a) 'Grasping the nettle: possibilities and pitfalls of a critical management pedagogy', *British Journal of Management*, 10(2), 171–84.
Reynolds, M. (1999b) 'Critical reflection and management education: rehabilitating less hierarchical approaches', *Journal of Management Education*, 23(5), 537–53.
Rowlinson, M. and Hassard, J. (2011) 'How come the critters came to be teaching in business schools? Contradictions in institutionalization of critical management studies', *Organization*, 18(5), 673–89.
Sambrook, S. (2008) 'Critical HRD: a concept analysis', *Personnel Review* 38, 61–73.
Saren, M. (2010) 'Provocation: business schools and economic crisis – we are all critical now: but critique of what, for whom?', *International Journal of Management Concepts and Philosophy*, 4(1), 28–33.
Śliwa, M., Sørensen, B. and Cairns, G. (2013) 'You have to choose a novel: the biopolitics of critical management education', *Management Learning*, 46(3), 243–59.
Smith, G.W. (2009) 'Using feature films as the primary instructional medium to teach organizational behavior', *Journal of Management Education*, 33(4), 462–89.
Solitander, N., Fougère, M., Sobczak, A. and Herlin, H. (2012) 'We are the champions: organizational learning and change for responsible management education', *Journal of Management Education*, 36(3), 337–63.
Springett, D. (2005) '"Education for sustainability" in the business studies curriculum: a call for a critical agenda', *Business Strategy and the Environment*, 14(3), 146–59.
Starik, M., Rands, G., Marcus, A.A. and Clark, T.S. (2010) 'From the guest editors: in search of sustainability in management education', *Academy of Management Learning & Education*, 9(3), 377–83.
Stepanovich, P. (2009) 'The lobster tale: an exercise in critical thinking', *Journal of Management Education*, 33(6), 725–46.
Stewart, J., Rigg, C. and Trehan, K. (2007) *Critical Human Resource Development: Beyond Orthodoxy*. Harlow, UK: Pearson Education.
Swan, E. (2005) 'On bodies, rhinestones and pleasures: women teaching managers', *Management Learning*, 36(3), 317–33.
Swanson, D.L. (2005) 'Business ethics education at bay: addressing a crisis of legitimacy', *Issues in Accounting Education*, 20(3), 247–53.

Teece, D. (2011) 'Achieving integration of the business school curriculum using the dynamic capabilities framework', *Journal of Management Development*, 30(5), 499–518.
Trehan, K. (2007) 'Psychodynamic and critical perspectives on leadership development', *Advances in Developing Human Resources*, 9(1), 72–82.
Van Buskirk, W. and London, M. (2008) 'Inviting the muse into the classroom: poetic license in management education', *Journal of Management Education*, 32(3), 294–315.
Walck, C. (2009) 'Integrating sustainability into management education: a dean's perspective', *Journal of Management Education*, 33(3), 384–90.
Willmott, H. (1994) 'Management education, provocations to a debate', *Management Learning*, 25(1), 105–36.
Willmott, H. (2013) 'Reflections on the darker side of conventional power analytics', *The Academy of Management Perspectives*, 27(4), 281–96.
Wong, L. (2009) 'The crisis: a return to political economy?', *Critical Perspectives on International Business*, 5(1/2), 56–77.
Wray-Bliss, E. (2003) 'Research subjects/research subjections: exploring the ethics and politics of critical research', *Organization*, 10(2), 307–25.
Wu, Y.-C.J., Huang, S., Kuo, L. and Wu, W.-H. (2010) 'Management education for sustainability: a web-based content analysis', *Academy of Management Learning & Education*, 9(3), 520–31.

# 7

# A sociology of management in management education

*Dirk Baecker*

Treating the sociology of management in management education means first specifying and then generalising the notion of management such that students begin to contextualise the complexity and contingency of management and also to understand the means of communication necessary to meet its expectations.[1] Sociology in this understanding is both an academic discipline describing and explaining what management is about and a reflexive scheme for helping students, future managers and everyone who has to do with managers to find their roles when exercising and undergoing it. Interestingly, sociology thus meddles with management in a way that almost makes it into a management device itself and, accordingly, as limited in range and scope as any management device eventually proves to be.

This chapter explores the paradox of teaching people about something that they need to experience, to understand, and that is theorised (in the German context) as being bracketed away from practice. The following text owes as much to my study of sociology, sociological theory and economics as to my work with students of management at Witten/Herdecke University and Zeppelin University, both in Germany, and to my experience of the management of a university at these two places and elsewhere. It transpires that a great deal of the necessary work of sociology in management education consists of bringing in not only an understanding of organisation but also an understanding of the distinction between organisation, on one hand, and interaction and society, on the other, and of the many hybrids emerging between these social forms in the so-called network society. Understanding management therefore begins right under our noses by observing our own institutions dealing with organising processes, interaction in class and old and new social questions of society. Even one of the most imperative questions of sociological theory – what the units of sociological analysis actually are (Nisbet 1966) – finds its place in management education as soon as one tries to come up with ideas of values, norms, roles, action and communication, and with accounts of inequality, power, the sacred, community, mobility, the individual and protest in the attempt to describe any one event in school.

I emphasise a sociological understanding of management in terms of communication theory. The notion of communication is not one of the most widely received notions in sociology but it fits the present question because it does not lend itself to an understanding of management in terms of rational evidence, technological necessity or individual prowess. Instead, the notion of communication enables us to ask what kinds of problems are solved, or hidden, by turning to the symbols of rationality, necessity or individuality. The notion of communication we rely on is one that emphasises the constative as much as the performative aspects of social action. That is to say, it is about both saying and doing. This fits the present question because management is as much about the confirmation of certain realities as it is about their construction and criticism. We know that management begins and ends with calling certain procedures, products and events suboptimal, thus blocking self-organisation within work and establishing coordination by management within organization. We will begin with the specification of management. Management is a new profession that appears during the aptly called managerial revolution of the nineteenth century as the profession that raises and solves problems of coordination and control in large organisations, mainly in industry and business (Chandler 1962, 1977, 1990). It is a story worth considering in its own right that the management of industrial enterprises both relies on ways of designing, steering and controlling large organisations used for centuries in armies, hospitals, monasteries, courts and city governments and also tries to distinguish itself from the concomitant traditional knowledge, skills and competencies. It is probably no exaggeration to call any notion of management from the very outset a polemical notion that tries to dissociate itself from the use of authority, social embedding and fact-bound motivation to be found in these traditional areas of organising, and to insist instead on a self-defined rationality which allows for a much higher variability in both means and ends – as long as there is a link between means and ends. Management is one of the most important vehicles for switching from value-rational action to purposive-rational action in Max Weber's (1978) terms and thus for replacing traditional values and an understanding of organisations as fulfilling some kind of higher duty by self-found and self-defined purposes and new ideologies of entrepreneurial liberalisation, technological progress and growth of wealth.

The story of the managerial revolution is therefore less about new and large organisations being formed and more about a new understanding of rationality for creating and maintaining competitive organisations in environments that are more dynamic than organisations had ever been used to. Material, social and temporal complexity intertwine, calling for an understanding of a design, steering and control of organisations able to calculate any of these three dimensions in terms of the other two. This is why the single position embedded in work chain, value chain and time planning will eventually appear as the unity of an analysis of organisations that takes account of a management that makes work, cooperation and time constraints into variables that can be measured in terms of each other (Luhmann 1988: 302–23).

This story of a management turning organising into a variable begins as a power play not just between capital and labour but also more specifically between engineers and foremen (Burawoy 1979; Edwards 1979; Boltanski 1987). Management in this sense relies on an understanding of administration not only as the execution of well-defined purposes but also as the process of finding, testing, exploring and dropping more or less uncertain purposes (Fayol 1967; Weick 1979; March and Simon 1993; Burns and Stalker 1994; Simon 1997) It delimits an indifference zone of action, experience and work to be expected from employees without having to spell it out in advance, for example when entering into a contract (Barnard 1968). It also more or less explicitly defines as its main reference point the measurement of the success of its decisions on one or several markets outside and inside the organisation (Gutenberg 1929, 1983; Eccles and White 1986; Leifer and White 1986; Baecker 2001, 2003a, 2006, 2010).

Any of these moves is important for a sociological understanding of management to be introduced into management education, and yet the last is possibly the most revealing because Erich Gutenberg, the founder of modern German business studies, used the heading *Betriebswirtschaftslehre* in order to specify the object of management. Two moves proved to be decisive for this specification. The first is the counterintuitive and ingenious assertion that management is not about organisations or about organising. Gutenberg maintains that management begins by leaving the subject of organisation, due to its complexity, to other sciences better prepared to deal with it, such as philosophy, psychology and sociology. Management proper does not invent or design but adopts and moderates the division of labour, hierarchical order, technological process and individual motivation found in the organisation's societal environment and translated selectively into the organisation. *Betriebswirtschaftslehre* then assumes that organisation functions perfectly; problems stemming from organising are not negated but neutralised in order to develop a theoretical calculus focusing on other problems (Gutenberg 1929: 26). These other problems run under the heading of costs and returns and means and ends, and are to be found not within the organisation but in the markets it deals with and within the technologies it relies upon (Gutenberg 1983).

The second move, which accomplishes the first (that is, bracketing the organisation[2]), consists of re-entering what is found on the market into the organisation that deals with it. More precisely, Gutenberg considers two possible sources of problems that *Betriebswirtschaftslehre* would have to deal with: technological problems of efficacy and economic problems of efficiency. Efficacy is about technical means and ends, efficiency about costs and returns. The academic science, as well as the practical teaching Gutenberg was in search of, addressed ways to design, steer and control an organisation (referred to as a *Betrieb* or business) by applying standards of efficacy and efficiency to its procedures. This means that Gutenberg actually founded two disciplines: the literal *Betriebswirtschaftslehre* (BWL) or theory of business economics, which consists of governing the organisation in terms of monetary categories to be calibrated with respect to markets, and a *Betriebstechniklehre*, which was never formalised or institutionalised. The latter was a subject of study that teaches the techniques for developing a business, consisting of ruling the organisation in terms of categories for attaining technical progress. This subject never actually consolidated as an academic discipline at any university but is taught to this day at university faculties of engineering and, when focusing on applied engineering, at institutes such as *Fraunhofer Gesellschaft* establishments in Germany. It is somehow blended with BWL in more technically minded curricula of MBAs and management colleges and polytechnics.

In Gutenberg's concept of BWL, the teaching of efficacy became supplementary to the teaching of efficiency. Economic categories define what management has to strive after, and technical categories define whether there are the necessary means to actually achieve those economic aims. The picture of management emerging from this foundational act of Gutenberg's thinking is that of a discipline and competence that consists both in bracketing the complexity of the organisation in order to focus instead on both markets and technology and then bringing market demand and the technological possibility to bear on the organisation bracketed in the first place. Management is a two-stroke engine. Its acknowledgement, confirmation and criticism should rely on appreciation of the first and the second stroke, accounting for both their separation and recombination.

Interestingly, it needs sociology to account for this two-stroke activity (see also Baecker 1993, 1999, 2003b, 2011). Gutenberg never came back to the foundational act he spelt out so well in his higher doctorate in 1929 – and *Betriebswirtschaftslehre* never really understood what Gutenberg, an economist (*Volkswirt*), had done. The first stroke of bracketing was lost and the discipline of *Betriebswirtschaftslehre*, as well as that of management science, developed as if the management of an organisation as a business could be exercised from outside, from a market and an engineering perspective, as it were. The status of efficacy as supplementary to efficiency was implicitly accepted as a convenient device for dealing with all problems stemming from the non-convergence of the orders of labour process, hierarchical order and market demands (Luhmann 1977). However, instead of acknowledging the ingenious moves of bracketing the organisation and oscillating latently between efficiency and efficacy, later German *Betriebswirtschaftslehre* called for complexity to be brought back into the teaching of management, either in terms of calling attention to human beings actually doing the organising (Heinen 1968) or in terms of bringing supposedly ancillary disciplines such as psychology, sociology and even economics back into the management sciences (Staehle 1980).

Only aptly called organisation theory rediscovered the complexity of the organisation proper and emphasised that the organisation has to be subjected to the rule of the market and technology *within* and *by* the organising process (March and Simon 1993; Cyert and March 1992; Simon 1997). Both the market and the space of technological possibility have to be *enacted* within the process of organising, as Karl Weick (1979) put it, if they are to be evaluated at all. This enactment is subject to decisions, as is almost everything else in an organisation (except its culture), such that the objectivity of costs and returns, their accounting and auditing, their calculation in terms of cost locations, cost units and time horizons as well as the understanding of the relevant and respective technical progress are a matter of organisational conflict, negotiation and precarious agreement.

Notwithstanding this enactment, it is still the bracketing or the distinguishing issues of the organisation stemming from its environment that define the focus of management. Without this distinction being drawn repeatedly to bring the information harnessed by it to bear on the organisation itself, there would not be any management proper. Without the criteria of both efficiency and efficacy and the concomitant optimising ideas, management proper would have no leverage to count on in an organisation that is complex enough to deal with human passions and myopia, power plays, career aspirations, opportunity seeking, responsibility avoidance, and with a sheer blindness to change, chance, risks and dangers.

Thus, the sociology of management, which I propose should be introduced into management education, calls 'management' any move that subjects an organisation to relevant aspects of its environment, specifically the market and technology environment. However, this sociological understanding adds that in order to subject an organisation to its environment, one must also strengthen the idea of an organisation to allow it to successfully come to grips with its environment. If there is no organisation able to first monitor its environment and then answer the latter's presumed demands, management would fail. Removal of the bracketing completes the managerial wisdom that prompts it in the first place. This sounds paradoxical, but it is in fact only oscillatory – nobody can be surprised that *Betriebswirtschaftslehre* preferred to deal with an organisation from the outside looking in (Steinmann and Schreyögg 1993).

However, not considering the original bracketing led the same *Betriebswirtschaftslehre* and management science to confuse management with any kind of design, rule and control of an organisation. It is not. It stands and falls with efficiency issues concerning markets and efficacy issues concerning technology. Where these issues are lacking, as in all organisations not dealing with markets and not relying on well-defined technologies, there is no management in the sense defined by the discipline of *Betriebswirtschaftslehre* and management science. Just as there are many aspects of business and enterprise organisation that are not self-evidently answered by criteria of costs and returns or means and ends, such as interests, passions, motivations and fears, even management proper cannot be undertaken with exclusive reliance on efficiency and efficacy criteria. The knowledge lost in management science, only to be recovered by the shock of praxis, consists in the necessity to moderate, attune and calibrate any application of these criteria to the organisation. The two-stroke activity of management consists in defending the organisation against the attacks brought upon it by itself. The wisdom and practical knowledge of management consists in being aware of the necessity of both defence and attack, of both subjecting the organisation to its 'outside' and bolstering it to withstand subjection.

In concrete terms, this means that management always has to decide which items, processes, ideas and personnel to subject to criteria of cost and return, means and ends, *and which are to be spared this procedure and for how long*. Not surprisingly, this sparing begins with management trying to avoid being taken to account for the effects it has with respect to costs and returns and means and ends. This is fortunate because, in observing itself, management can learn what it needs to know about the organisation and did not find in management science textbooks. On the other hand, it needs more management and even top management to take the decisions that lead to the hiring and firing of managers and their intelligent allocation within the organisation. It may well need external instances such as capital markets to help fire top managers who are failing to answer costs and return and means and ends criteria.

Any sociology of management taking part in management education must begin with the specification we have discussed in order to explain why nineteenth-century management developed into a profession in the twentieth century that dealt with leadership of all kinds of organisations, and in the twenty-first century is still a core competency, if not the only one, in controlling complex tasks, procedures, organisations and networks. In fact there may be no other way to control complexity if by control we mean accepting complexity as a black box and prudently building up a memory of one's own expectations about which measures prove useful and which do not (Ashby 1958). Management takes off where measures of simple causality and technological determination give way to measures of careful observation and the deliberate cultivation of involvement (Leifer 1991). This is even true when questions of efficiency and efficacy are now being superseded by capital market theory issues such as incentives because these questions still concern the fit between organisational strategy, organisational design and the environment (Roberts 2004; Baecker 2009).

But only by specifying management can we show why management proves successful. Its criteria of efficiency and efficacy drawn from the market and the technological environment of organisations are means to both initiate and stop projects of all kinds. Costs and returns and means and ends are stop-and-go rules, which are enacted as if intervening from outside the organisation. This is exactly what gives the complex organisation – thus rightly bracketed by Gutenberg – its play, range and scope. Management initiates and halts organisational projects for investment, development, production and marketing in such a way that there are no definitively right or wrong ways of doing the organising. Organising is designed, steered and controlled with respect to prospects and results, allowing even for loose coupling between the two because all kinds of intermediate results may change both prospects and the expected results. The only rule determined by management is the rule to optimise at any time what everybody is doing. There is no determining of what kinds of tasks, procedures, division of work, organising and networking are to be optimised if costs are lowered, returns increased, means adjusted and ends intelligently set. This combination of ample space for experimentation, on the one hand, and determinate rules to evaluate its results, on the other, has been the secret of management success ever since the outset of industrialisation.

One may note in passing that the rule of optimisation, which allows management to judge whatever work, planning, prospecting or investing is suboptimal, is a direct heir to the Enlightenment's rule of reason. Just as the Enlightenment's message was to scrutinise human practices, beliefs and ideas for a lack of reason, management's message is concerned with diagnosing deficits. In both cases, deficits are spelt out without necessarily telling anybody what to do to remedy them. To find out how to handle your affairs more reasonably and optimise your work is completely up to you as long as your efforts prove successful – and rest assured that whatever you do, both the enlightened intellectual and the trained manager will find some matters still lacking in reason and suboptimal. At the same time, it can be unmercifully easy and shrewd to point out an unreasonable belief in tradition or a still suboptimal routine. The shrewdness consists in leaving the answer to the problem to the people plagued by it. There is possibly no better way to manage – or control – processes of self-organisation.

But management, therefore, depends crucially on having a stop-and-go rule on hand. If there are no external criteria for measuring suboptima, management finds itself in trouble. This is why non-profit management and processes of innovation in situations of technological indeterminacy pose so many questions for management thinking and education (Drucker 1990; Burns and Stalker 1994). Non-profit and innovation management are forced to evaluate organisation in terms of itself, which amounts to opening the Pandora's box that Gutenberg kept so carefully closed.

This is why more recent attempts to generalise management as a technique for designing, steering and controlling government agencies, hospitals, armies, universities, schools, theatres, non-governmental organisations (NGOs) and other forms of organisation therefore runs into trouble. On the one hand, these attempts failed utterly to take account of more traditional professional administration that already existed in those organisations, modes of administration that interestingly often relied on a professional understanding of the organisation itself in order that government agencies, for example, were governed by both power and legal procedures; hospitals by an understanding of diagnosis and therapy; armies by discipline taking account of deadly dangers; universities by endless debates; schools by a belief in improvement; theatres by aesthetic considerations and artistic self-assertion; NGOs by solving social problems; and so on. On the other hand, management itself proved helpless at intervening in such organisations where there were no external criteria for stop-and-go rules. Industrial organisation took literally centuries to develop accounting procedures able to measure costs and returns in terms of monetary debts and assets (Sombart 1987, Vol. 2; Baecker 1992; Chiapello 2007). How can organisations not attuned to markets (or committed to technological exactitude) be expected to match this development in a few decades or even years?

Any generalisation of the understanding and practice of management must therefore accept a detour. There is no way to anticipate management's provisions for efficiency and efficacy in non-monetarised and technologically indeterminate organisations. The organisational complexity of those organisations is bound to overrule any management not equipped with measures relying on criteria that can be enacted as external (Weick 1977). The detour to be accepted therefore consists in asking what kind of external criteria could apply to non-profit and non-mechanical organisations. A general notion of management cannot be found by applying entrepreneurial management to non-entrepreneurial organisations but by looking for functionally equivalent external references to be applied internally to organisational procedures.

In sociological theory, there are at least four devices for undertaking a heuristic search for externalities: agencies, games, systems and networks. The notion of agency is developed within a more intelligent kind of action theory – it tells us that there are no actions with prospects of being reproduced that cannot refer back to agencies (values, authorities, institutions) legitimating the selections it produces (Meyer and Jepperson 2000). A general notion of management might conclude that the agencies of efficiency and efficacy to be found in monetised and technologically determinate organisations are to be substituted in other kinds of organisations by other agencies of similar externalising value. Since these organisations are at least 'polyphonic' (Andersen 2003), such a search will prove non-trivial, as Drucker's forays into non-profit management have already convincingly shown. The search by any economically over-committed management science for other kinds of agency is rendered more difficult because such organisations come up, on one hand, with professional standards thought to be old-fashioned and, on the other, with pretexts for wasteful procedures. Political, medical, academic, military, aesthetic, pedagogical and other values informing agencies that legitimate action and decisions in organisations will prevail only if they somehow manage to make allowances for costs and returns and means and ends as well.

Another sociological approach to thinking about general management is game theory. Game theory considers any decision to be a strategic move somehow binding the decision maker and opening up a field of opportunistic counter-moves for any adversary. A successful game therefore consists in committing the decision maker in such a way that the adversary is bound to comply with the prospects of the decision (Elster 2000). There are as many ways to pursue such a link between commitment and compliance as there are paths to power, money, persuasion, love, ideological belief or criminal blackmail. Both efficiency and efficacy may be considered in terms of games to be played against the market and technological progress. The question of general management is therefore what games are played by non-profit organisations and against whom. As far as I am acquainted with the literature, there is a stupendous lack of knowledge about this kind of question, but the research prospects for a game theory engaging along these lines with organisation research seem to be rich indeed.

Our third sociological notion that could inform the understanding and practice of general management might help game theory in pursuing this line of research. In fact, systems theory can specifically ask what references an organisation drafts as soon as external perspectives are envisioned for evaluating internal procedures. Sociological systems theory of modern society cherishes the idea that organisations somehow decide which functional subsystems of society are of primary concern to them and then place less, and in any case multi-referential, importance on other functional subsystems (Luhmann 2013: 141–54; Tacke 2014). This idea goes a long way towards determining what external references are considered by government agencies (politics and law), by hospitals (medicine), by universities (education and science), by the military (politics), by theatres (art), by firms (economy) and so on. Those external references may then be spelt out to determine how exactly a possible code of a functional subsystem of society is answered by the programmes of organisations competing with each other for successful operations within or with respect to specific functional subsystems, such that power versus powerlessness, health versus sickness, pass versus fail, victory versus defeat and aesthetic profile versus indecision indicate system references as well as frames of games and accounts of agencies. Any sociological system thinking about general management would then start by looking at how these and other external references are observed, translated and enacted by an organisation trying to design, steer and control itself. Professional standards come into view again, but as soon as multi-referential organisations are to be considered, many more questions about inner organisational differentiation, selective observation, the creative handling of paradoxical demands and the recruiting practices of a diverse membership, affiliation and audience also become important. Management becomes a highly skilled art of maintaining ambivalence, avoiding the clear-cut attribution of both problems and solutions, and harnessing evolutionary balance, which has hitherto only been rarely articulated by sociological research on organisations.

The sociological notion of network may somehow encompass all the preceding concepts because it is also about action and agency and games and strategies, and more recently even about systems (or discourse) references and their benchmark value (White 2008; Latour 2013). Network theory in sociology is considered a first step towards an uncertainty calculus that allows any decision to reckon in terms of a trade-off between social evasion and cultural reinterpretation (White 1992: 17–19). Social action searches for identity and faces situations where any chance for identity constitution and maintenance depends on others trying to control their identity and the agency trying to constitute and maintain its own. Network here means that an actual tie is calculated in terms of how promising other ties are for maintaining an identity.

This means that management, as White puts it (1992: 230–86; 2008: 279–333), has to block and get action across the boundaries of the organisation, across the boundaries of hierarchical levels (see also Parsons 1960; Thompson 1967) and across the power plays that actors engage in to promote and foster their version of the systems from which they draw their agencies as opposed to other versions (see also Crozier and Friedberg 1980).

The advantage of sociological network theory is not only that it takes account of action, game and systems theoretical ideas, but also it is not bound to specifically modern versions of sociological theory, as the systems theoretical concept of a functionally differentiated society self-reflexively happens to be. Network theory may be the kind of sociological theory that can envision the transformation of modern society into a network society whose dominant medium – the distribution of communication – is no longer the printing press but electricity, the computer and the Internet (Baecker 2007; Castells 2010). This means that reference to functional subsystems of society, even if multi-referentially combined and confused, lose their operational acuity without necessarily also losing the status of valid reference for discourses, value commitments and the deliberate discrimination of orientation. Both conceptually and practically, networks may now provide space for hybrid combinations of functional references, types of organisation, team projects, agencies from stories, ideologies and beliefs, and idiosyncratic couplings between local and global references.

Interestingly, the more diverse this functionally messy world becomes, the easier it is to formulate a sociological notion of general management. Following White, a general understanding and practice of management consists in both distinguishing between getting and blocking action and considering the one in terms of the other. This is why a general management as conceived of by sociological theory is both complex and clear-cut. It is complex because in management there is no getting action without blocking action, that is without an apparent paradox arising, which serves operationally only to distinguish the two sides of a coin.[3] It is clear-cut because no other distinction matches that between achieving and blocking action in framing the scope and range of management. It fits our understanding of Gutenberg's notion of the *Bewirtschaftung* of an organisation as a *Betrieb*, management as a verb, an action. It also fits a possible action, game and systems theoretical understanding of management.

This is precisely the point of departure for a general sociological research programme into management practices in different kinds of organisation, project and team. It inquires into what kinds of action are achieved, what kinds are blocked and how the two measures are designed, performed and monitored in terms of each other. The educational value of such research is beyond doubt. It is to be carried out by students and researchers alike and still proves able to yield a knowledge about the management of organising processes incongruent with the organisations' self-description, thus adding value, criticism, reflection and managerial insight to how organisations understand themselves (Luhmann 1966). The educational value moreover consists of disassociating both the student and the researcher from any idea to be able to know what is right and wrong in organisational practices. Complexities such as those resulting from both achieving action and blocking action prevent an organisation from considering its action space in terms of linearity, causality or any other kind of straightforwardness.

Students, by means of theory and anecdote, develop a feeling that complexity should be of the utmost importance and begin to cherish any empirical and practical knowledge that they know they have to rely upon when seeking out one of those few chances to act, which does not prove immediately false or succeeds in providing further insights into the complexity at hand. Ironically, management education therefore begins not by looking at practices of all kinds, which students will not understand due to their usual lack of experience, but by looking at texts, or better, at good texts that manage to convey a sense of the uncertainties of knowledge by giving a rich and lively picture of organisation. Literature of some educational value in that sense usually has some ethnological touch to it. Students by reading the literature must learn to look at organisational realities, to become aware of their own anxieties to get it right, put it right and do it right – that is, their desire for an illusion of control, so to speak – and eventually to recognize some rather simple ideas about the complexity they just started to be able to accept.

Gutenberg's case of bracketing the complexity of organisation in order to subject this same organisation to criteria of efficiency and efficacy, thus blocking any action meeting these criteria and instead encouraging action that is fitting, is the special case of a more general device of management to achieve action by blocking action; however, it is just that sort of tool that students may find easy and helpful to memorise. Again, thanks to BWL and the management sciences, it is a highly elaborate and widely tested case that awaits generalisation to other as yet almost neglected cases using different criteria. Students understanding it might someday realise what they owe to this, their first steps into the uncharted terrains of complex organisations.

A sociological theory, such as the one presented here, is therefore able to solve the mystery of a notion like management, which has no antonym to delineate its meaning by indicating what it negates or any role asymmetry it could rely upon when defining certain areas of action. You know what an expert is if you look at a novice, or what a physician is when you look at a patient; and the same is true for teacher and pupil, priest and believer, artist and spectator, politician and voter, even employer and employee. Those are complementary roles, one of them always asking for the other to be present as well. For management, there is no antonym any more than there is a complementary opposite to manager.

As with other notions that have no antonym like 'world' or 'meaning', the conceptual strategy for nevertheless distinguishing what it is about is to internally differentiate it, which means replacing and explaining it by a distinction. With regard to 'world', one possible version of such a strategy is to distinguish system from environment (Luhmann 1995); and for meaning, one could distinguish the actual from the potential (Whitehead 1979; Deleuze 1990; Luhmann 1995). For management, the distinction between blocking and achieving action is considered to define a complex unity and the unit of a specific complexity. The advantage of such a conceptual strategy is that we do not have to look for specific people, hierarchical levels, departments or programmes doing the management because anybody and anything combining those two sides into one decision is doing it. That is why a notion of top management is necessary to draw a distinction with respect to certain people and hierarchical levels and why a further notion of leadership has to be introduced when action is blocked without action being achieved, or vice versa (which would mean that we would have come up with an antonym to management after all).[4]

Such an understanding of management in terms of one distinction has two further advantages. One is that we are better able to describe the improbability and thereby non-triviality of management, and the other is that there are certain ways to present such a notion of management in management education even before there is any feeling for, let alone understanding of, social, technological and temporal complexity – the shock of practice that provides this understanding is a long time coming because many internships undertaken during studies buffer the student from any serious experience of the reality of organisation.

The improbability and therefore non-triviality of management resides in the fact that its achieving action is to be experienced in terms of blocking action, and vice versa. What are the odds for such an experience to occur? And even more so, what are the chances for managerial action to deliberately make that experience happen? We have to switch to the level of the description of communication if we are to see the problem, let alone deal with it. Communication means that certain experiences are to be attributed to certain actions in order for these actions to be contextualised at all with respect to achieving and blocking action. No action theory and no game or network theory deals convincingly with aspects of the experience of action as a necessary condition for selecting action (see also Goffman 1959; Schütz 1967). We need a sociological systems theory to do just this (Luhmann 1990) because in systems theory communication presupposes action *and* experience in order to describe the range of possible attributions of meaning to system or environment, text or context, people or situation, organisation or network, past or future, lie or truth, trust or mistrust.

There is no way for management to avoid involvement with communication. Managerial decisions are bound to present observers with choices of how to interpret and respond to them, if at all. Any technological understanding of management as somehow the causal reason for others to do as requested amounts to a trivialization of managerial communication, which itself can rely only on this communication. Causes and effects must be communicated as well – again presenting the observer with a choice. Communication oscillates between future choices and is never certain which past understanding to rely upon (Baecker 2013). However, this is not the end of management, or proof of its impossibility as deconstruction would perhaps have it (see Khurana 2002), but rather it is the very condition of its possibility. Management can only achieve action by blocking action when communicating. Communication of the one in terms of the other is how it conditions itself with respect to an unknown future and an always to be reinterpreted past, not to mention an uncertain present (Luhmann 1997).

We do not mean to present this understanding of communication as fully comprehensible in our present context. In fact, we rather invite readers to come up with their own experience regarding the occurrence of what they consider to be instances of management. This is why in our concluding remarks we switch to an understanding of management education that is able to take account of the sociological ideas we have tried to comment on in this chapter. It may already be evident where we are heading. In fact, if there is little chance of experiencing any kind of decent management in school or university, not to mention a chance to undertake it, with the exception of already revealing kinds of self-management (students blocking their own action to achieve it), there is by contrast ample chance to engage in and experience communication.

My experience in doing sociology in general and organisation theory and sometimes management teaching at Witten/Herdecke University, Management Zentrum Witten (with consultants) and Zeppelin University can be summed up as using seminars and workshops to present models of communication, organisation, management and consulting and also to let communication be experienced. Anything is useful that conveys a feeling for complexity, not to be shunned but to be embraced by bold, but reversible decisions. Anything is useful that emphasises the paradox in this recommendation. In Witten/Herdecke we had the idea of teaching future entrepreneurs not only by introducing them to all the relevant elements of BWL, but also by letting them experience risk taking – by themselves and by others, the lecturer included – in seminars when engaging in argument, counter-argument and deceptive consensus. We thought that personalities would thus train themselves to handle ambivalence in communication, ambiguity in decisions and uncertainty in prospects (see Sullivan, Ehrlich, and Colby, this volume). To be sure, to somehow train robust personalities is only the first half of the lesson to be learned, the other half is observation of how others do the same and how alignment is possible between the action of the one and the experience of the other. We talked about second-order observation (von Foerster 2003) and we tried to get involved with it to make tying and linking, binding and decoupling evident issues of social intercourse. My best memory of these times is a research seminar on forms of 'postheroic management' (Baecker 1994, taking up a formulation from Handy 1989: 166), which lasted from winter 1998 to summer 2000 and accepted only presentations by students completely uncertain about the value of the texts, models and case studies they presented.

At Zeppelin University these days we are less courageous. We no longer go into matters of personality formation. Times have changed and students expect other lessons. Perhaps electronic networking platforms have made students more familiar with porous networks, uncertain identity and almost impossible control, and thus they already deal with problems of personality formation on their own. I am not sure. Management education at Zeppelin University turns more to questions of research, to the ability to pose and solve problems, to select and deselect theories and methods. In other words, we opt for explicitly looking at complexity and for talking about how to deal with it and to investigate it. Interdisciplinary studies become the order of the day so that the understanding and combination of different disciplinary perspectives already defines a good deal of the task to be mastered by student and lecturer alike. However, interdisciplinarity has at least two kinds of drawbacks, the first consisting of the idea that doing interdisciplinary studies turns your studies into the right thing to do correctly from the beginning, and the other luring you into an underestimation of the value of disciplinary studies consisting of learning not only about notions and models but also about their limits. It is difficult to control the overconfidence you think you owe to your future employer if you do your research by just patching together lots of bits and pieces from both literature and the Internet without going into the risk of seeing a disciplinary model fail and a theoretical notion becoming blunt.

After years, if not decades, of overconfidence in the proficiency of management, our times are heading towards a less confident understanding of messy situations, unclear motivations, absent interests, indeterminate technology and an uncertain future. Management no longer means having to learn the lesson of communication in order to forego the illusion of control. It now means learning to become more explicit in pointing out precisely which action is to be blocked in order to get what kind of other action. We are so used to action, game, systems and network theory that any sociological reference to complexity becomes almost redundant. If, in the 1980s and 1990s, the idea of a necessary irritation of illusions of control (at least in systemic ideas on management) somehow ruled the day and answered the alarming news about autopoietic systems that operated in cheerfully closed self-reference (Bakken and Hernes 2003), since the turn of the century, it has been more like looking for sociological and other theories that offered substitutes for the boundaries that were apparently lost by the boundaryless organisation, which is now in search of new ways to define its identity in fluid networks (Ashkenas *et al.* 1995; Seidl 2005).

Management education now, as ever, means looking critically at management science concepts and models, organisation theories' understanding of complexity and sociological ways of reconstructing how observers act as actors counting on observations (Duarte 2009). Indeed, blocking action to achieve action begins with the students' critical ability to reflexively observe themselves. If this is done on both sides of the coin, a great deal of education for management may already have been achieved, regardless of whether it provides any sociological value added. If students learn in school that the professional practice awaiting them is richer in every aspect and less reflexive than anything encountered at school, a good foundation will have been laid for using the reflective abilities learned at school to explore that richness.

## Notes

1 English language editing by Rhodes Barrett.
2 Considering Gutenberg's theoretical brilliance it would be no exaggeration to refer to this bracketing as *epoché* in the terminology of Edmund Husserl, with which Gutenberg is very likely to have been acquainted (see Husserl 1980).
3 We apply a notion of complexity to be found in mathematics where complex numbers are numbers that consist of at least two other numbers not to be reduced to each other, such as $\sqrt{-1} = [+1 \mid -1]$.

4 We do not go into such a polemical notion of leadership but it is evident that it would help to understand the almost vacuous state-of-the-art in thinking about that notion, which seems about to be replaced by more intelligent versions of critically combined notions of management, governance, commitment and compliance. Alternatively, one might consider leadership a general art of management referring not to markets and technology but to society, and thus achieving socially responsible action by blocking socially irresponsible action (Baecker 2005).

## References


Andersen, N.A. (2003) 'Polyphonic organisation'. *In:* T. Bakken and T. Hernes (eds.) *Autopoietic Organization Theory: Drawing on Niklas Luhmann's Social System Perspective*. Oslo: Abstrakt, pp. 151–82.

Ashby, W.R. (1958) 'Requisite variety and its implications for the control of complex systems', *Cybernetica*, 1, 83–99.

Ashkenas, R., Ulrich, D., Jick, T. and Ker, S. (1995) *The Boundaryless Organization: Breaking the Chains of Organizational Structure*. San Francisco, CA: Jossey-Bass.

Baecker, D. (1992) 'The writing of accounting', *Stanford Literature Review*, 9, 157–78.

Baecker, D. (1993) *Die Form des Unternehmens*. Frankfurt am Main, Germany: Suhrkamp.

Baecker, D. (1994) *Postheroisches Management: Ein Vademecum*. Berlin: Merve.

Baecker, D. (1999) *Organisation als System: Aufsätze*. Frankfurt am Main, Germany: Suhrkamp.

Baecker, D. (2001) 'Managing corporations in networks', *Thesis Eleven*, 66, 83–101.

Baecker, D. (2003a) 'Management within the system'. *In:* T. Bakken and T. Hernes (eds.) *Autopoietic Organization Theory: Drawing on Niklas Luhmann's Social System Perspective*. Oslo: Abstrakt, pp. 183–212.

Baecker, D. (2003b) *Organisation und Management: Aufsätze*. Frankfurt am Main, Germany: Suhrkamp.

Baecker, D. (2005) 'Wer rechnet schon mit Führung?', *OrganisationsEntwicklung*, 24(2), 62–9.

Baecker, D. (2006) 'The form of the firm', *Organization*, 13(1), 109–42.

Baecker, D. (2007) 'Communication with computers, or how next society calls for an understanding of form', *Soziale Systeme*, 13, 409–20.

Baecker, D. (2009) 'Organisation als temporale Form: Ein Ausblick'. *In:* R. Wimmer, J.O. Meissner and O. Wolf (eds.) *Praktische Organisationswissenschaft: Lehrbuch für Studium und Beruf*. Heidelberg: Carl Auer, pp. 258–88.

Baecker, D. (2010) 'Cross 'n' Call: a general model of enterprise'. *In:* S. Kramer and P. Ludes (eds.) *Networks of Culture*. Münster, Germany: LIT Verlag, pp. 97–119.

Baecker, D. (2011) *Organisation und Störung: Aufsätze*. Berlin: Suhrkamp.

Baecker, D. (2013) 'Systemic theories of communication'. *In:* P. Cobley and P.J. Schulz (eds.) *Handbooks of Communication Science: Vol 1: Theories and Models of Communication*. Berlin: de Gruyter Mouton, pp. 85–100.

Bakken, T. and Hernes, T. (eds.) (2003) *Autopoietic Organization Theory: Drawing on Niklas Luhmann's Social System Perspective*. Oslo: Abstrakt.

Barnard, C.I. (1968) *The Functions of the Executive: 30th Anniversary Edition*. Cambridge, MA: Harvard University Press.

Boltanski, L. (1987) *The Making of a Class: Cadres in French Society*. Cambridge: Cambridge University Press.

Burawoy, M. (1979) *Manufacturing Consent: Changes in the Labor Process under Monopoly Capitalism*. Chicago, IL: Chicago University Press.

Burns, T. and Stalker, G.M. (1994) *The Management of Innovation*. Oxford: Oxford University Press.

Castells, M. (2010) *The Rise of the Network Society*. 2nd edn. Oxford: Blackwell.

Chandler, A.D. (1962) *Strategy and Structure: Chapters in the History of the American Industrial Enterprise*. Cambridge, MA: The Belknap Press.

Chandler, A.D. (1977) *The Visible Hand: The Managerial Revolution in American Business*. Cambridge, MA: Harvard University Press.

Chandler, A.D. (1990) *Scale and Scope: The Dynamics of Industrial Capitalism*. Cambridge, MA: Belknap Press.

Chiapello, E. (2007) 'Accounting and the birth of the notion of capitalism', *Critical Perspectives on Accounting*, 18, 263–96.

Crozier, M. and Friedberg, E. (1980) *Actors and Systems: The Politics of Collective Action*. Chicago, IL: Chicago University Press.

Cyert, R.M. and March, J.G. (1992) *A Behavioral Theory of the Firm*. Reprint. Cambridge, MA: Blackwell.

Deleuze, G. (1990) *Logic of Sense*. New York, NY: Columbia University Press.

Drucker, P.F. (1990) *Managing the Non-Profit Organization: Practices and Principles*. New York, NY: HarperCollins.
Duarte, F. (2009) 'What is a sociologist doing in a school of management? Reflections on the use of sociological concepts in management education', *Journal of University Teaching & Learning Practice*, 6. Available from: http://ro.uow.edu.au/jutlp/vol6/iss1/2 (accessed 19 January 2016).
Eccles, R.G. and White, H.C. (1986) 'Firm and market interfaces of profit center control'. *In:* S. Lindenberg, J.S. Coleman and S. Nowak (eds.) *Approaches to Social Theory*. New York, NY: Russell Sage, pp. 203–20.
Edwards, R. (1979) *Contested Terrain: The Transformation of the Workplace in the Twentieth Century*. New York, NY: Basic Books.
Elster, J. (2000) *Ulysses Unbound: Studies in Rationality, Precommitment and Constraint*. Cambridge: Cambridge University Press.
Fayol, H. (1967) *Industrial and General Administration*. London: Pitman.
Goffman, E. (1959) *The Presentation of Self in Everyday Life*. New York, NY: Anchor Books.
Gutenberg, E. (1929) *Die Unternehmung als Gegenstand betriebswirtschaftlicher Theorie*. Berlin: Späth & Linde.
Gutenberg, E. (1983) *Grundlagen der Betriebswirtschaftslehre. Vol. 1: Die Produktion*. 24th edn. Berlin: Springer.
Handy, C. (1989) *The Age of Unreason*. Boston, MA: Harvard Business School.
Heinen, E. (1968) *Einführung in die Betriebswirtschaftslehre*. 9th edn. Wiesbaden, Germany: Gabler.
Husserl, E. (1980) *Ideas Pertaining to a Pure Phenomenology and to a Phenomenological Philosophy*. The Hague: Martinus Nijhoff.
Khurana, T. (2002) 'Deconstruction is the case: deconstruction in management consulting and organization theory', *Soziale Systeme*, 8, 248–82.
Latour, B. (2013) *An Inquiry into Modes of Existence: An Anthropology of the Moderns*. Cambridge, MA: Harvard University Press.
Leifer, E.M. (1991) *Actors as Observers: A Theory of Skill in Social Relationships*. New York, NY: Garland.
Leifer, E.M. and White, H.C. (1986) 'Wheeling and annealing: federal and multidivisional control'. *In:* J.F. Short Jr. (ed.) *The Social Fabric: Issues and Dimensions*. Beverly Hills, CA: Sage Publications, pp. 223–42.
Luhmann, N. (1966) 'Die Bedeutung der Organisationssoziologie für Betrieb und Unternehmung', *Arbeit und Leistung*, 20, 181–9.
Luhmann, N. (1977) *Zweckbegriff und Systemrationalität: Über die Funktion von Zwecken in sozialen Systemen*. Frankfurt am Main, Germany: Suhrkamp.
Luhmann, N. (1988) *Die Wirtschaft der Gesellschaft*. Frankfurt am Main, Germany: Suhrkamp.
Luhmann, N. (1990) 'Meaning as sociology's basic concept'. *In:* N. Luhmann (ed.) *Essays on Self-Reference*. New York, NY: Columbia University Press, pp. 21–79.
Luhmann, N. (1995) *Social Systems*. Stanford, CA: Stanford University Press.
Luhmann, N. (1997) 'The control of intransparency', *Systems Research and Behavioral Science*, 14, 359–71.
Luhmann, N. (2013) *Theory of Society*. Vol. 2. Stanford, CA: Stanford University Press.
March, J.G. and Simon, H.A. (1993) *Organizations*. 2nd edn. Cambridge, MA: Blackwell.
Meyer, J.W. and Jepperson R.L. (2000) 'The "actors" of modern society: the cultural constitution of social agency', *Sociological Theory*, 18(1), 100–20.
Nisbet, R.A. (1966) *The Sociological Tradition*. New York, NY: Basic Books.
Parsons, T. (1960) 'A sociological approach to the theory of organizations'. *In:* T. Parsons (ed.) *Structure and Process in Modern Societies*. New York, NY: Free Press, pp. 16–58.
Roberts, J. (2004) *The Modern Firm: Organizational Design for Performance and Growth*. Oxford: Oxford University Press.
Schütz, A. (1967) *The Phenomenology of the Social World*. Evanston, IL: Northwestern University Press.
Seidl, D. (2005) *Organisational Identity and Self-Transformation: An Autopoietic Perspective*. Aldershot, UK: Ashgate.
Simon, H.A. (1997) *Administrative Behavior: A Study of Decision-Making Processes in Administrative Organization*. 4th edn. New York, NY: Free Press.
Sombart, W. (1987) *Der moderne Kapitalismus: Historisch–systematische Darstellung des gesamteuropäischen Wirtschaftslebens von seinen Anfängen bis zur Gegenwart*. 3 vols. Munich, Germany: Deutscher Taschenbuch Verlag.
Staehle, W.H. (1980) *Management: Eine verhaltenswissenschaftliche Perspektive*. 6th rev. edn. Munich, Germany: Vahlen.
Steinmann, H. and Schreyögg, G. (1993) *Management: Grundlagen der Unternehmensführung: Konzepte – Funktionen – Fallstudien*. 3rd edn. Wiesbaden, Germany: Gabler.
Tacke, V. (2014) *Soziologie der Organisationen*. Bielefeld, Germany: transcript Verlag.

Thompson, J.D. (1967) *Organizations in Action: Social Science Bases of Administrative Theory*. New York, NY: McGraw-Hill.
von Foerster, H. (2003) *Understanding Understanding: Essays on Cybernetics and Cognition*. New York, NY: Springer.
Weber, M. (1978) *Economy and Society: An Outline of Interpretive Sociology*. Berkeley, CA: University of California Press.
Weick, K.E. (1977) 'Re-punctuating the problem'. *In:* P.S. Goodman, J.M. Pennings and associates (eds.) *New Perspectives on Organizational Effectiveness*. San Francisco, CA: Jossey-Bass, pp. 193–225.
Weick, K.E. (1979) *Social Psychology of Organizing*. 2nd edn. Reading, MA: Addison-Wesley.
White, H.C. (1992) *Identity and Control: A Structural Theory of Action*. Princeton, NJ: Princeton University Press.
White, H.C. (2008) *Identity and Control: How Social Formations Emerge*. 2nd edn. Princeton, NJ: Princeton University Press.
Whitehead, A.N. (1979) *Process and Reality: An Essay in Cosmology*. New York, NY: Free Press.

# Part II
# Philosophies

# 8

# Nietzsche as educator

*Daniel Hjorth and Robin Holt*

> If any one has felt what it means to find, in our present world of Centaurs and Chimaeras, a single hearted and unaffected child of nature who moves unconstrained in his own road, he will understand my joy and surprise in discovering Schopenhauer.
>
> *Nietzsche 1873/1976 §1: 179*

Our title is a play on Nietzsche's *Schopenhauer as Educator* first published in his essay collection *Unfashionable Observations*. Within the setting of teaching and studying management practice our chapter is also unfashionable. It argues for a primacy of honesty in feeling in a practice that can encourage the rational selection and manipulation of viewpoints. It argues for cheerful and generous expression in a practice where performance is associated with possession, pre-eminence and competitive advantage, and it argues for a steadfast capacity to question norms and expectations in a practice that values assurance and compliance.

## Management practice: *maneggiare* (to control a horse; dressage)

On 3 January 1889 Nietzsche saw an exhausted horse being whipped by a cabman trying to ply the streets of Turin. Distraught, he threw himself about the animal's prostrate neck and whispers into its ear, before himself collapsing. Onlookers overheard Nietzsche apologising to the animal, explaining that the cabman, being human, could do little else. Embarrassed, the cabman moved on as soon as he could, cussing his lazy horse for placing him, a decent, honest trader, in proximity with such an unseemly and unregulated display of passion. The horse will be taught not to err in the future, it will be given blinkers, it will have its bit tightened and its bridle strengthened, it will, in short, be better managed – or replaced and sent to the knacker's yard. Nietzsche in the meantime was taken back to his lodgings, examined by doctors and slipped into catatonic insanity until his death in 1900.

This apocryphal tale of Nietzsche's fall into madness upon witnessing a managerial event is revisited in Bela Tarr's film *The Turin Horse*, but here we find the eponymous animal less a victim of management practice than an ironic observer. There is no abuse of the horse, and yet it too resists, refusing the work to which horses are typically put, before removing itself from human commerce and taking to its stalls, watching on as all about small human worlds unravel.

Emptiness becomes increasingly present as lives are shown being stripped back to minimal events. Slowly movement itself stalls. The surrounding fields are shrouded in mist and a persistent wind presses into every expression. Have even the crops stopped growing? Buds hesitate to deliver themselves to the world. With people and animals no longer behaving habitually, the once familiar places in which they live also cease to function normally. As spaces they are shown constraining rather than sustaining lives, the simplest of acts becomes a significant event, the viewer contemplating every loaded moment: and under this compression all the fragility and strangeness of these now basic lives becomes more visible. The active management of land, animals and human beings has stopped. What then? Is this the end? No. Beyond the postures of managerialism – everything can and should be managed – Tarr shows life still occurring: things still happen even if they are not being directed, instructed or overtly organised. There is still life, strange and bleak perhaps, but still there.

As a riff on Nietzsche's unfashionable demise, Tarr's film reveals both the persistence of management practice and how life persists beyond management. In showing, and not telling, Tarr exemplifies a specific form of learning – habits and their limits are made apparent without presenting alternatives (for another analysis of a Tarr film, see Brown, this volume). Instead the viewer has to think, to work at meaning, to make sense with the film, to recognise what life is like with and without its management. Tarr's film brings us up close to the basic patterns of life made visible when horses stop, crops stop, decisions stop and the wind cannot be stopped. In this cold, indifferent, unmanaged space of shadows it still goes on.

Tarr learns from Nietzsche, and Nietzsche, in turn, had found an equally powerful exemplar in Schopenhauer, who also showed him images of raw life and the possibilities thereafter.

## Schopenhauer

Nietzsche likens reading Schopenhauer to entering a high forest in which we can breathe with deep, uninhibited naturalness (Nietzsche 1873/1976 §2: 182). Here is a thinker at home with himself, unafraid to confront life stripped back to its unmanaged form. This form is nothing more than a gathering of drives, impulses, urges, movements that when bundled we might call 'will', and which we humans share with all life forms, whether horses, root crops or the soil from which they are pulled. With Schopenhauer 'life appears as instinct for growth, for survival, for power' (Nietzsche 1895 §6). The world is will, nothing more.

For Nietzsche, Schopenhauer is able to think these difficult things through what he identifies as qualities of character: Schopenhauer 'is honest because he speaks and writes to himself and for himself, cheerful because his thought has conquered the most difficult thing, and steadfast because he cannot be otherwise' (Nietzsche 1873/1976 §2: 183). Honesty comes from self-awareness, an inquiry uninhibited by social manners or establishment opinion. There is little that is stylish and smooth in Schopenhauer's writing; he leaves the silver-plating for others; his argument is simple, unadorned and rigorous in its structure. Cheerfulness or joy does not find Schopenhauer full of gaiety, but with a capacity to take the serious in his stride, horror included, and to continue to find life an arresting, passionate and precious experience. Steadfastness shows both constancy and integrity, qualities enabling Schopenhauer to carry himself from place to place, learning all the while, growing, without ceding to the demands of a situation in such a way that you become blameless as a mere victim of circumstance.

There are dangers in having qualities of honesty (openness), cheerfulness (joy) and steadfastness (consistency) – they encourage thoughtfulness, and thinkers tend to have a rough time. The thinker incurs loneliness. This is not isolation. A thinker is to live publicly by virtue of being thrown into countless human ties that elicit thought and by always requiring a readership. However, honesty, cheerfulness and steadfastness bring with them an unusual aura; Schopenhauer is lonely because he presents the world in its primal form and his audience recoil. Nietzsche remembers his own encounter with Schopenhauer's stark image of a world unified by will: 'This is the picture of life; learn from it the meaning of your life' (Nietzsche 1873/1976 §3: 189).

To learn is to take Schopenhauer's image and to place it in your own world. Here we become aware of dangers specific to an age (hence Nietzsche finds his thinking 'unfashionable'). Schopenhauer's thought shows a thinker educating himself against the age, stripping back opinion and style to articulate a simpler human condition of willing we too often ignore. Nietzsche marvels at the occasional and yet persistent way Schopenhauer does this – there are few grand gestures or oppositional dogmas being posited. Instead, we have subtleties whose power comes from their suggestiveness. For example, Nietzsche recalls Schopenhauer's praise of antique vases whose naturalness and naïvety expressed directly what they were meant to be; if nature tried to make a vase it would look like this. Schopenhauer bemoans what follows. The vases of later ages have lost this naturalness, becoming instead an extravagance of arbitrary forms accumulated in the name of fashion and good manners. Nineteenth-century versions were the very worst: fussy, overly decorated, assertive and gaudy (Nietzsche 1873/1976 §7: 238). Look at the evolution of something as ordinary and simple as vases and you see civilisation as a story of loss. This is how it has gone everywhere: vases, manners, architecture, families, leaders. To be educated is to learn how the production of knowledge in learning has already been organised, how it has become culture and with what effects.

Nietzsche learns from Schopenhauer, finding his age still suffering the same problems as Schopenhauer's; indeed it has become worse because religion – that great lie that had for centuries passed itself off in profundities that flooded the mortal, earthly world with their evening promise of life eternal – was ebbing away: '[O]ur age is characterized by the disappearance of contemplation and simplicity; the floodwaters of religion are receding and leaving behind swamps or stagnant pools' (Nietzsche 1873/1976 §4: 198). These stagnant pools are what remains of knowledge, of education, of civilised attainment, and Nietzsche isolates three he finds especially noxious: the pools of money-makers, the state and of the universities. To learn from Schopenhauer, and become educated, is to act against all three.

The pool of money-makers organises knowledge and learning under logics of production and consumption. To be educated in this pool is to be 'fashionable in one's needs and their satisfaction', whilst mindful of the most efficient ways of attaining fashionability, because that way you make money (Nietzsche 1873/1976 §6: 218). The effect of such commerce is to create 'current' people, happiness being a function of how one uses knowledge to appraise oneself of what one is capable of 'now', and in an immediate future, and thus how to maximise available pleasures and profits. In the service of such knowledge and happiness education is speedy, technical and meritocratic, and its goal is to insert people into a life of money-making as rapidly and productively as possible.

The pool of the state finds knowledge being used to cultivate the kinds of predictability and refinement by which established orders organise and distribute culture to transform their apparent pre-eminence into natural forms. This distribution is only ever partial and it is always heavily managed. As a river might be diverted into a mill race to drive looms, so culture might be tamed and employed to animate the machinery of state whose bureaucratic processes have been learnt rote fashion, with thought only for their transparent density. Too much cultured and scientific attainment and this proper education in state machinery risks a deluge and being overwhelmed; too little and the state appears bare, mechanical, even dowdy. An educated state is one of well-funded academies, professions and established salons by whose channels the energy and unruliness of creative expression is siphoned and so allowed to froth gently, confined by manners, directed by protocols and reviewed by the nomenclature for its authority and enhancing quality, whilst all the time the technicalities of administration continue to be passed on through stiffening apprenticeships and examinations of compliance.

Finally, the pool of the universities is one of baked-hard scholarship configured as an intellectual game. The game proceeds by dissecting the world into small, lifeless pieces that are laid out and moved, apparently to discover some pre-ordained order, as bones might be arranged and rearranged in a charnel house in pale acknowledgement of divine purpose. The game is played with dialectical intrigue where players submit to only those questions promising an advance in career and esteem, using disciplinary standards as scaffolding to construct small eminences from details, with little concern for feeling, mystery or suffering (after all, 'a mole is happier in a molehill' (Nietzsche 1873/1976 §6: 227)). In all this, scholars remain conservative, splitting and categorising nature with 'arid self-satisfaction', content that 'their thoughts bloom peacefully in the shade of tradition' (Nietzsche 1873/1976 §8: 31).

With money-makers, officials and scholars, education becomes a means for accruing economic rents, the distinction of rank and security of classified knowledge, respectively – none of which expand life and indeed all of which curtail and fix experience, would we know it. And yet we do not, so tightly woven by envy are the threads of fashion and money, state power and factual truths, and so attractive is the raiment made from these materials of possible success. The will and the striving of those educated in the three pools have been tidied and dressed in a uniform called the good and the proper. These blasé people have created a vast comfort zone into which everyone is invited, provided they corral their association of happiness to that offered by money-makers (possessions, spending-power), state officials (citizenship, patriotism) and scholars (facts) – indeed to everything that is missing from Tarr's film, whose emptiness now appears quite full.

The most secure source of comfort is short term: 'the pursuit of happiness is never greater than when the quarry must be caught between today and tomorrow' (Nietzsche 1873/1976 §4: 199). This haste has a double function. It encourages the association of will with the desire to possess things, status and facts that one currently lacks. Haste also conceals the real nature of our world as one of base willing, a nature that Schopenhauer is striving to reveal, and from which people often run:

> [H]aste is universal because everyone is fleeing from himself; universal too, is the timid concealment of this haste, because we want to appear satisfied and deceive the most perceptive observers about our wretchedness; universal as well, the need for new-sounding word-bells with which life can be adorned and lent an air of noisy festivity.
>
> *Nietzsche 1873/1976 §5: 211*

Nietzsche wants to show us how to quit our happiness and quieten this haste, notably by revealing modern (bourgeois) desires as narrow (concerned with style and status); immediate (they never gestate and are rarely questioned, so lack maturity); and selfish (configured around interests of a solitary ego). To think with Nietzsche is difficult because it dispenses with those civilised accomplishments and prejudices that distinguish us amongst ourselves (attaining refinement) and from the rest of nature (the hierarchy of human over nature). It is hard to relinquish the comforts of money-making, the state and the academies, and be placed back among the animals and trees (Nietzsche 1873/1976 §4: 206). Where we humans are distinguished only by the illusion of control (of management), animals and trees suffer no illusion, they simply desire in desiring. To expunge the age from within begins, therefore, with bringing into relief the apparent naturalness with which life is managed within and between the 'stagnant pools' and to recognise that this management of life – found in fighting wars, writing edicts, following rituals, consuming goods – is but an extension and continuation of an animal and natural will to live, albeit one couched in the illusory frame of being of an entirely different, distinctly human quality.

For Nietzsche even Schopenhauer falls prey to such illusions. Schopenhauer's world is not entirely one of animalistic willing and striving – he finds art, especially music, offering temporary escape. Nietzsche (1895 §14) jumps on Schopenhauer here. Those educated in money-making, public administration and scholarship tend towards the comforts offered by truth, and in Schopenhauer's enthusiasm for music this tendency receives faint and beguiling expression. It is no accident that Schopenhauer isolated music as the best medium of escape. Of all means to reach truth, aesthetics is the least weighty and assertive, and of all aesthetic modes, music is the least freighted with material presence. Music cannot be owned and traded, screwed on to walls or held in safes; it is illocutionary, it permeates things and affords all those with the feeling and patience to perform and to listen a glimpse of beauty preserved in its almost immediate, ephemeral death. Nietzsche has also been tempted by such escape – especially through music – and yet he resists. We are alone, god is dead, things may occasionally appear eternal and unalloyed and this tempts us to believe in the possibility of purer realms; but look hard and stay with our senses and we find things are always moving in cycles of decay and birth, attraction and repulsion, without release. Nietzsche's twist on Schopenhauer is that rather than recognise and then bemoan this situation (finding temporary relief in moments of aesthetic bliss), we can make much of this base condition of willing if we stay with it – it is a much richer scene of possibility than that left to us by Schopenhauer.

## Willing

Schopenhauer shows us a turbid, restless world punctured with rare moments of heavenly light; a realism that Nietzsche takes on by snuffing out the heavenly bit. If there is light, it comes from and remains with us – we are our own lanterns and we create our own shadows. There is no value in the world save our own evaluating power, our own will. Schopenhauer's will becomes transformed into Nietzsche's will to power – the capacity to put value into the world. In feeling this and in sensing this 'putting' power, we vivify the world and we give it the colour, light and tone by which it gathers itself as a place of substance, frustration and possibility (Nietzsche 1873/1976 §3: 204). If will is all there is, then all value emanates from will, and what is valued currently – the values prevailing in stagnant pools – can be overcome with new values.

Through Schopenhauer, Nietzsche therefore not only learns something of content (the world is grounded in willing) but something exemplary: to learn is to be provoked into struggling beyond yourself, using rare examples of fruitful genius as provocations, such as Schopenhauer (Nietzsche 1873/1976 §6: 216). Nietzsche describes this provocation as 'the first sacrament of culture', presaging a second sacrament, for in striving, in recognising and absorbing one's comparative lack of potency when compared with fruitful genius, it is not enough to feel it inwardly – it also requires public acknowledgement through will to power. A twisted form of *Bildung*, self-development, is set in train: one should look to an image – like Schopenhauer in Nietzsche's case, or antique Greek vases in Schopenhauer's case, or Nietzsche in Tarr's case – without genuflection. Allow oneself to be challenged by these rare examples of flourishing genius and yet not be crushed by them as burdens, so one might say eventually 'ah, now I can go on'. There is no way around the hard work; one can only go through them, and thereby also liberate oneself from their thrall.

Here we arrive at the association of will and overcoming, the becoming-overman [*sic*], which is an overcoming of values (whilst working through them) in order to reach a different human sensibility (Deleuze 2006: 94). Thus it is that Nietzsche – or his character Zarathustra (Nietzsche 1887/8 prologue: 44) – praises those wanting to learn from others how to go beyond themselves, coping with the suffering endured in wandering away from oneself, with a shadow always in tow: 'I love him who lives for knowledge and who wishes to know that one day the overman may live. And thus he wills his own downfall.' Zarathustra announces to the unhearing people of the marketplace:

> Even the wisest of you is only a conflict and a mix of plant and ghost. But do I bid you become plants or ghosts?
>
> Behold, I teach you the overman.
>
> The overman is the meaning of the earth. Let your will say: 'The overman shall be the meaning of the earth!'
>
> *Nietzsche 1887/8 prologue: 13*

Unlike a money-maker, the overman eschews the efficient pursuit of fashionability; unlike a state administrator, the overman avoids the status of office; and unlike a scholar, the overman refuses the call of knowledge to split the world into constituent parts. The overman stays with the earth where all things are mixed and being mixed, and avoids looking up to the stars, save those falling and splintering on the ground.

What then for us, who are schooled in business and management studies and educated into the deadening, managed pools of money-makers, administrators and scholars? Evidently, the occupants have become tired of willing and opt instead for a kind of 'hibernation' in the safety of comforts. For this to happen, averages, protocols and definitions have taken over the work of struggling with truth, and this inertness is concealed by the busyness and haste with which comforts are pursued. This is, in fact, management. Can it, should it, be overcome?

Overcoming is a result of having *become* active (affirmation), implicating oneself in the inevitable contingency of having to create one's sense of self again and again, without end. Nietzsche's role is to instil in readers a sense that they no longer know what to do, having to work beyond routine at the undefined job of becoming what one is not, a transformative job, replete with potential. The upshot is an affirmative will to power, and this, by extension, is where life is made difficult and hard (which is what we learn in Tarr's film). That is Nietzsche's contribution: to make life problematic and questionable, to resist the question of how best to make life last the longest and most pleasantly and instead to exemplify the possibilities for transformation in everyday situations (Nietzsche 1887/8 IV §3: 13). Here, overcoming is a negation – a nihilism – which snaps the ties that bind; it is an affirming power by which the habits, expectations and requirements by which all human lives are structured and ordered are worked at along the edges to see whether there might be places from where to jump. To overcome is to shed the weight accumulated in life – a process Nietzsche describes in his parable of metamorphosis in which the spirit changes from camel, to lion and then child. To overcome, the spirit first becomes a load-carrying camel. Prepared to be lonely it wanders into the open desert, self-sufficient and responsible for managing affairs, carrying the weight of fact on its own back. Then, in the loneliness of the desert, the spirit becomes a lion who roars 'no' to all established values and duties, who resists the 'thou shalt' (of managers) with an assertive 'I will'. However, this roar remains oppositional, dogmatic even, as the 'I will' tends to sediment into yet another version of 'thou shalt'. The third metamorphosis finds the spirit becoming a child who, recalling the characteristics Nietzsche imputed to Schopenhauer, acts with a capacity for honesty, playfulness and steadfastness. This is the child who plays, throws herself into the world in joyful action. We thus find a power to affect – a spontaneity – in Schopenhauer's writings as Nietzsche reads them; a spontaneity expressed in the honest, cheerful and steadfast manner with which Nietzsche is moved by, learns from and overcomes Schopenhauer's text and then himself. Nietzsche responds to Schopenhauer affirmatively: 'As soon as I open him I seem to grow a pair of wings' (Nietzsche 1873/1976 §1: 179); education opens lines of flight with little consideration for effectiveness and efficiency. There is neither a pre-determined goal nor a design maximising the chances of realising such, no ground even, beyond that being made in affirmative experimentation.

## Provocation

Nietzsche learns from Schopenhauer's spirit – it is through provocation that one learns, not through the adoption and protection of positions. *Provocare* (meaning 'to call out' and *provocatio* meaning 'to call forth, to summon') has an expressive and courageous quality. *Educere* similarly has this meaning of 'to bring out, lead forth', as in the prefix *ex-* or standing alongside, that is, the expressive child of the metamorphoses. Provocation generates affect and potentially opens the body and increases its power to be affected (receptivity) (Hjorth 2011; see also Michels and Beyes, this volume). We read something like an outcome of this as we go through Nietzsche's reading of Schopenhauer. He is stirred by what he discovers and is moved to action. His receptivity is increased by Schopenhauer's pen, a feeling he then shamelessly exploits: Schopenhauer's word is *pro-vocare*, calling forth, and in summoning, you then go on. Nietzsche's receptivity (power to be affected) responds to Schopenhauer's spontaneity (power to affect) by attesting to the fact that he has become educated in the sense of being 'brought out', 'led forth', that is brought to a state of *ex-*. He has learnt to live in the service of excess, affirming the spilling over quality of life and overcoming who he was.

Provocation is associated with risk – learning is risky, if by learning we mean taking what adds to life rather than imitating what already exists. In fact, it is beyond risk in the economic, calculable sense. It is genuinely uncertain, ambiguous and unlike life in the comfort zone of the pools. For it is difference that is sought after. It is overcoming, overtaking oneself as someone shaped by the templates and the established routes to increased efficiency. Whether learning this way, in the end, still equates to pedagogy in the way we traditionally understand this term, is moot. In the original Greek *paid* – *paido* meaning child and *agôgos* meaning leader, that is someone escorting or accompanying children to school – we can at least begin to understand this as a guiding role rather than an instructing one.

We find in Nietzsche a rare provocation to become-active by increasing one's power to be affected (receptivity) and to affect (spontaneity). This is something like the passion of learning where the passionate learners are led towards making their own way. Affectively engaging what is 'other' in learning (rather than instructing people in what is safe, familiar, comfortable) is a way to overcome the spread of 'last men'.

Such learning perhaps carries overtones of elitism – a strident claim to be different, to rid oneself of common sense, to be a rare, free spirit. Might learning through provocation dispense with tradition and discipline in ways that encourage vainglory?

> If Zarathustra emerges with his language of self-and-world-affirmation, this language must convey the pressure of provocation through its radical self-eulogistic and 'wanton' form. The impact of Nietzsche's sayings and arrows, which take the form of pure dictates, become for easily provoked readers a therapeutic insult eliciting an immune reaction. [. . .] Nietzsche, to be sure, is anti-egalitarian, but this is not in order to make common cause with revenge-hungry populists, as German moral philosophers, whose differences can no longer

> impress, avidly continue to assert in the wisdom of their years. Instead, it is in order to defend the freedom of self-enhancement against the consumerdom of last men.
>
> *Sloterdijk 2013: 61, 72*

The secret of *educere* is this setting against the commodity-fed contentment. Education releases a laughter directed simultaneously against the certainties of learned facts (the stagnant pool of the university), the status and status quo loving weight of political and social institutions (the stagnant pool of the state) and the comforts of possession (the stagnant pool of money-makers). However, education cannot empty those pools – they will persist and indeed in many small ways they are necessary to attain an organised condition of collective human survival. In Safranksi's (1998) biography for example we find Nietzsche sometimes delighting in material possession, as we all do. He writes to his mother asking her to send sausages and socks that help alleviate the Spartan surrounds of the Swiss Alps, and he is a veritable ball of excitement on buying an early typewriter invented by Malling Hansen in Copenhagen as a writing device for the blind; Nietzsche's eyesight was never good. He relies on productions made by the money-makers. He also relies on the university at Basel which continues to pay him a small pension, and on the Swiss cantons and Italian cities through which he is always travelling and whose taxes and bureaucracies see to the upkeep of the roads and enforce the laws of passage that facilitate as well as restrict his physical movement. Nietzsche is no back-to-the-woods mountain man: possessions, the state and the university still influence his life, utterly. His advocacy of learning as transforming provocation is one of perspective; to get up high, breathe clear air in order to see and recognise our conditions of reliance and 'consumerdom', and so look beyond without ever leaving the empirical world. The learning experience is transfiguration, transmutation, a morphing of what is encountered which can be very ordinary, and accidental. So, for example, when Nietzsche's typewriter breaks, he starts to consider how this machine preserves writing in an even, legible script that somehow inscribes itself back into us, rather than us being the scribe; we are being encouraged by the repetitious, neat type and intervals into repetitious, neat behaviour: 'our writing tools are also working on our thoughts' (quoted in Kittler 1999: 210).

In such ways, Nietzsche was always overspilling categories (in this case, the category of machine as a mute tool to aid the execution of tasks), reaching for what was hitherto unthought-of provocation (in concealed ways, which are only revealed through breakdown, thought and action are becoming machine-based). He would also overspill his earlier sense of self, for example continuing to recall and think through his youthful passion for the music of Wagner. What was it about this totalising maestro: the sound, the myth, the arrogant ambition, the singularity of vision? How did he, Nietzsche, find himself captured and corralled in such a catatonic state of idolatrous enthusiasm?

The affirmation made in such questioning of things, other people and oneself is one of acknowledging the other, the foreign, rather than of any settled accomplishment.

> In noting that Nietzsche's poetics abolishes the rules of indirect eulogy and substitutes of the foreigner with self-praise, we see only the outer layer of the turmoil created. On a deeper level, Nietzsche's affirmative language remains obliged to praise the foreigner – better, *it praises the non-self such as it has never been celebrated before.*
>
> *Sloterdijk 2013: 80–1, emphasis added*

Nietzsche's self-praise, his excitement in his own sense of willing power, is directed towards becoming other, to moving. All self-praise reached through provocation ought to remain passionately open to the spontaneity of the other as challenging your spontaneity, asking you to overcome what you are. Self-praise is discovering becoming-other from underneath the dowry of heavy words we inherit through tradition. It is to go one's own way, wending and diverse, without ever asking the way, always testing for ways because the way itself does not exist, and so self-love morphs into self-fleeing (Nietzsche 1887/8 §Spirit of Gravity).

Sloterdijk's remark echoes Deleuze's (2006: 9) note on overcoming and transmutation: 'What a will wants is to affirm its difference. In its essential relation with the "other" a will makes its difference an object of affirmation.' Nietzsche opens an empiricism of joy – a 'yes!' to the 'otherness' of the other, and the self's otherness. This challenge of affirming difference by opening up to the other, exercising the power of being affected, extends any sense of self into the non-self, a reaching beyond what one currently is and might become, like a bud overcoming itself by cracking, affected by the warmth of the sun, or a new delicate shoot holding the promise of another branch. Sloterdijk uses the term 'poetic', as do many thinkers provoked by Nietzsche. It is here, perhaps, that we get a sense of how this 'yea-saying' looks. This is not the camel's 'yes', an acceptance to load oneself up without knowing how to say 'no'. It is the 'yes' of the child, the embracing of the other, that which I can affirm or negate – that which will make me differentiate in affirming the vagueness of the virtual, which will make me move.

## The poetic

Education, the leading out or calling forth, occurs in language. Most typically it is a uniform, univocal language of conceptual equivalences called definitions. By definition, these definitions lack the patina of lived history, making for a language for the dead – to define is somehow to die. Given we are not dead – despite the often deadening blandishments of those hard, truthful theories that have become well-tempered by the repeated hammer blows of attempted falsification – we might accept the complicity of educated selves, truth and language, to realise that behind appearance there is appearance, all the way through, and that behind one concept comes another, all the way through. Far from being a vehicle to deliver us to the world, education is complicit with it and the definitions being spoken of are metaphorical associations, nothing more.

The malaise besetting the modern, educated mind so commonly found in the pools of the money-makers, the state and the universities is a failure to accept that there is but one world. Our wanting more than one (and being educated to want more) began with Plato's contrasting an imperfect realm of appearance with a perfect realm of essences visible to philosopher kings, and then found expression in religions like Christianity displacing truth to unknowable realms such as heaven reached through faith, before being exposed to Kant's hint that God might actually be dead, but we ought not loosen our hope for such foundational truth because without it we have no ground to assert either factual or moral certainties. Ironically, the final death knell for truth itself comes with positivism, the search for objective states whose pile-driving urgency has no truck with metaphysical association. If a claim cannot be verified independently, it is invalid and cannot be taught as fact. To counter any ensuing sense of loneliness in this search for objectively existing phenomena, education, in its teaching certainties using fixing representations, encourages students to venerate the mode of approach. Method is sanctified: do the right thing and the correct outcome will necessarily follow.

Nietzsche welcomes the onset of positivism, calling it the cockcrow waking us to the prospect of a new dawn, but he then resists the scientific impulse to always seek firmer, more objective foundations that are sedimented through education. Now we have dispensed with metaphysics by accepting that we cannot properly commit to a world we can never access, why persist with questions of foundational truth at all? We can keep science a pragmatic project of controlling the world materially without having also to commit to an idea about meaning in which the permanent is privileged over the impermanent, the definitive over the suggestive, the clear above the vague. Ironically, positivism opens us up to the constructed manner of truths: stable concepts are not an outcome of investigations into what is true – they are configured as opening assumptions whose idealised setting we are always finding compromised when we look to use them. No matter how hard we strive we can never remove our assertions concerning what 'is' the case from the moving, empirically open life that permits such assertion. Nietzsche's diagnosis derails the ambitions of positivism to replace God with method, and in its stead we are to accept the inevitability of being historical and to work poetically with the figurations of language, with metaphor, with the mobile associations corralled but not captured through concepts. To speak poetically a moment, truth is something that becomes us. Not content with demonstrating how truth is woven with metaphor (and with it education into persuasion), Nietzsche urges us to revel in the mobility this offers to the experience of being educated.

And so we arrive at a fuller awareness of education as being instructed in what transcends the exactitude of measurement, stipulation and entailment, but which still entails inquiry. It provokes poetically and the world opens up or spills over in some way, gives forth without known consequence, but somehow under a gaze. Nietzsche – when writing towards the end of his publishing life and so overcoming his previous encomiums to pragmatic, positivistic science – touches on this in *Twilight of the Idols*:

> You would need to be situated outside life and at the same time to know life as well as someone – many people, everyone – who has lived it to be allowed even to touch on the problem of the value of life; reason enough for realising that the problem is an inaccessible problem to us.
>
> *Nietzsche 1888 V: 5*

This is the place of education, a practice whose exponents are situated inside because only there can the world be touched; to be outside and to consider the objective ground is a problem for gods, not humans. From the inside, what is taught can only ever be puzzles, quandaries and enticements, which, in drawing one in, reveal and conceal at one and the same time without the presumption of there being a right way of doing things or a securing end-point at which to arrive.The late Nietzsche asks us to take truths as they come as they are encountered in their coming again and again:

> How much truth can a spirit *bear*, how much truth can a spirit dare? That became for me more and more the real measure of value ... Error (– belief in the ideal –) is not blindness; error is *cowardice* ... Every acquisition, every step forward in knowledge is the *result* of courage ... of severity towards oneself, of cleanliness with respect to oneself ... I do not refute ideals, I merely draw on gloves in their presence ... *Nitimur in vertitum*: in this sign my philosophy will one day conquer, for what has hitherto been forbidden on principle has never been anything but the truth.
>
> *Nietzsche 1889, preface: 4*

Dealing with ideals rather than imbibing them, staying reticent rather than advancing a position, following the poet Ovid in striving for what is being refused or denied transform our relationships with the knowledge we are taught, and with teaching what is knowledge.

## Education as overcoming (becoming-other)

To reprise, management – the management for which Nietzsche apologises (*maneggiare,* the training of horses, remember the horse in Turin) – configures the world (and language) as a scene of problems that require a (corrective) response where action needs to be governed and participation needs to be anticipated by pre-formed arenas and techniques for saying/doing what, when. In this it aspires to being scientific, to look and find vagueness the enemy, openness a threat, and movement something that needs breaking. The problem of managing bodies and then time is taught typically from Taylor (1911); and the management of desire taught from Mayo's extension of Taylor's invention into the counselling interview (see O'Connor 1999). Béla Tarr's film recalls bodies, time and desire and provokes us into thinking differently about these and how they might be taught differently. It shows a world in which horses can be lazy or indifferent, where the time of seasons seeps back and begins to subsume clock time and where human desire stutters as action becomes spare and basic. Tarr shows the kind of problems that typically a student would be taught to meet head on with solutions, models and systems. They might be those of better timing, investing in new tools or using alternative modes of transport or communication. These managers-to-come are taught a world of effect and effects in which doers and speakers are always acting in the shadow of some kind of lack, needing and expecting a corrective, moving towards the clear (not vague), closed (not open) and still (broken movement). Tarr shows the experience of lack and also our – the audience's – almost instinctual managerial response to it: the urge to correct by supplementing, replacing and controlling things.

If we were instead to think 'with' Nietzsche (and Tarr) about overcoming the naturalness of seeing the problem of emptiness and alertness, and then offering filling and quickening solutions (extending strategic discourse or delivering results in accord with established logics of accountancy) lack would fall away. This is not saying solutions are wrong, but the way they close the world would become questioned by awareness of a world of affect and affects that finds action in an affirmative rather than corrective register. In spare minimal moments, Tarr's film shows a world that may open out, and there could be potential here. Overcoming – a capacity 'to do' – yields excess, a generous spilling over towards new worlds with little sense of what they might be. There is a productive vagueness to be found in the poetically open, in a language and style that brings the learner into a position of needing to figure out how to make use of the wandering, the uncertain (which is the etymology of vague). 'Certain' comes from Latin *certus*, meaning settled, and it is precisely what the vague is not about. It is about moving you (affect) and allows you to move (act). The vague – a new idea, a potentiality, opportunity, problem – elicits a style of speculative affirmation as a way to explore poetically the standards that have been set by thinkers like Taylor and Mayo. The poetic is not in opposition to these standards and it does not produce rival theories and positions – it provokes because it lives with what is vague. Education is haunted by pedagogy-as-instruction in content and process, which in turn has become a technical practice in the service of settling into more (assets, status, fact). Schooling is in this sense the designed rite of passage from the child's world of open curiosity into more settled, adult worlds of doing things effectively and efficiently (see Srinivas, this volume). Becoming adult means unlearning one's child-capacity: one's power of overcoming, one's power to act in an affirmative 'yes' and one's poetic power. Education leads students away from unstructured variety; the wonder of being alive and the newness of encountering a hitherto unseen world are steadily lost under the impress of instruction in knowing that (fact) and knowing how (skill). Business and management schools are at the vanguard of such instrumentality.

Does the overcoming by which we become child-like require a reversal of this process taking us back to natality? Are we advocating returning to a kind of innocent savagery of the kind that found Voltaire accusing Rousseau of wanting to undo all that was civilised and have us once more crawl about on all fours? On the contrary, overcoming is a condition of maturity by which we are able to acknowledge and pursue our affirmative power to act and create outside of the established orders of things. In learning from Schopenhauer, Nietzsche elaborates on these affirmative powers when he talks about honesty, cheerfulness/joy and steadfastness/consistency.

Schopenhauer's power to affect – the spontaneity that moves Nietzsche – increases his power to be affected and pushes him into the productive space of poetic vagueness where Nietzsche has to figure out what style of thinking/writing will help him get a grip on this world. For us there is learning here. The Schopenhauer–Nietzsche relationship helps us learn that affect, generated by provocation, can move us into a poetic vagueness; a vagueness that can become highly productive if we can inhabit becoming-child as a way of dealing with it. Style certainly has something to do with it: 'it is surely in terms of literary style that Nietzsche's debt to Schopenhauer is greatest' (Bishop 2011: 335). He was certainly challenged by Schopenhauer to produce *with* language rather than to reduce language to reproduce (Holt and Hjorth 2014: 212). How would this look for us as educators who are responsible for learning processes?

Honesty, joy and steadfastness come from learning to know one's knowledge, something that Foucault, another thinker who learned from Nietzsche, describes as critique:

> I will say that critique is the movement by which the subject gives himself [*sic*] the right to question truth on its effects of power and question power on its discourses of truth. [...] critique will be the art of voluntary insubordination [...] would essentially insure the de-subjugation of the subject in the context of what we could call, in a word, the politics of truth.
>
> *Foucault 2007: 47*

Learning to know one's knowledge and to be able to speak honestly requires that we understand the positivity of what we know, how it appeared and functioned when it was born and circulated. Foucault called this attending to the genealogy of knowledge – what could be said, seen and done with management knowledge as distinct from other structural forms.

As always with Nietzsche, we learn a hard lesson. He has pushed us, moved us and perhaps also made us move into that vagueness that asks of us – where is your way? What Nietzsche found in Schopenhauer's writing is also there due to a certain style of writing. Nietzsche realises that, having been moved and having been provoked, he stands before the vagueness of the poetic that he seeks to affirm. He does so by producing with language, affirming the productivity of the vague. His style becomes more poetic, aphoristic and metaphorical. As readers, we are brought to the spot where Schopenhauer took Nietzsche: we need to learn in order to find our way. Finding our way is a matter of affirming, speculating and playing in order to transgress, overcome and experiment. We do find the literary text to be useful in this respect. It carries life to the reader, rather than instructs the reader how to behave skilfully or how to think efficiently (see Sørensen and Śliwa, this volume). Literature is full of examples that speak to problems we face in organisations. Problems are also too readily analysed as managerial problems and made subject to management knowledge. This escapes critique in Foucault's sense. Education should be the two-phased voluntary insubordination, which frees up space for play and movement, and the affirmation of a speculative overcoming of who I am. The educator has a role in both phases: providing readings and examples that provoke and move us, and also affirming affirmation by pointing to examples and leading in the sense of *educere* 'to lead out'. Not by instruction – this is the way! Always by challenge: '"This is my way; where is yours?" – thus I answered those who asked me "the way." For *the way* – that does not exist' (Nietzsche 1887/8: 195).

There is no closure to the poetic striving. Events and singularities, their conditions of emergence, the strategies that determine their reproduction or transmutation, the dynamic force field that explains how it achieves being – these are all questions of relations and forces in which the will figures somewhere as either that which asserts negatively against life or that which positively affirms incipient newness, making the virtual leak into the actual without first having controlled the reception through managed expectation. 'Always ask yourself', said Alasdair MacIntyre (1999: 319), in what could have been learnt from Nietzsche, 'what your social order requires you and others not to know'. This asking takes place in the struggle to resist the acculturation proffered by money-makers, officials and academics, held low by their assets, status and facts. MacIntyre felt managers were unable to ask such questions, so mired were they with the technicalities of their role, so implicated in the means-end ordering of resources that there was no room for character. Business schools collaborate in this ordering but through critique are therefore also places where genealogy and playful experiments can be cultivated in (often literary) exemplification, showing ways of going in order that others might be encouraged to nurture and show their own.

## References


Bishop, P. (2011) 'Schopenhauer's impact on European literature'. *In:* B. Vandenabeele (ed.) *A Companion to Schopenhauer*. Chichester, UK: Wiley, pp. 333–48.

Deleuze, G. (2006) *Nietzsche and Philosophy*. New York, NY: Columbia University Press.

Foucault, M. (2007) *The Politics of Truth*. Los Angeles, CA: MIT Press.

Hjorth, D. (2011) 'On provocation, education and entrepreneurship', *Entrepreneurship & Regional Development*, 23(1–2), 49–63.

Holt, R. and Hjorth, D. (2014) '*Nietzsche*'. *In:* J. Helin, T. Hernes, D. Hjorth and R. Holt (eds.) *Oxford Handbook on Process Philosophy and Organization Studies*. Oxford: Oxford University Press, pp. 202–17.

Kittler, F. (1999) *Gramophone, Film, Typewriter*. Stanford, CA: Stanford University Press.

MacIntyre, A. (1999) 'Social structures and the threats to moral agency', *Philosophy*, 74, 311–32.

Nietzsche, F. (1873/1976) *Schopenhauer as Educator in Untimely Meditations*. [Translated by R. Gray]. Stanford, CA: Stanford University Press. 1995 edition.

Nietzsche, F. (1887/8) *Thus Spoke Zarathustra*. [Translated by R.J. Hollingdale]. Harmondsworth, UK: Penguin. 1976 edition.

Nietzsche, F. (1888) *Twilight of the Idols*. [Translated by D. Large]. Oxford: Oxford University Press. 1998 edition.

Nietzsche, F. (1889) *Ecce Homo*. [Translated by R.J. Hollingdale]. Harmondsworth, UK: Penguin. 1992 edition.

Nietzsche, F. (1895) *Antichrist*. [Translated by R.J. Hollingdale]. Harmondsworth, UK: Penguin. 2003 edition.

O'Connor, E.S. (1999) 'The politics of management thought', *Academy of Management Review*, 24, 117–31.

Safranski, R. (1998) *Martin Heidegger: Between Good and Evil*. Cambridge, MA: Harvard University Press.

Sloterdijk, P. (2013) *Nietzsche's Apostle*. Los Angeles, CA: MIT Press.

Taylor, F.W. (1911) *The Principles of Scientific Management*. New York, NY: Harper and Row.

9

# The art of relevation/revelation

## A Whiteheadian approach to management education

*Robert Chia and Ajit Nayak*

### Introduction

> . . . a University training . . . aims at raising the intellectual tone of society . . . at purifying the national taste . . . at giving enlargement and sobriety to the ideas of the age.
>
> *Newman 1996: 125–6*

Business school education has come under a great deal of criticism for being disengaged and largely irrelevant to managerial realities (Ghoshal 2005; Khurana 2007; Mintzberg 2004; Pfeffer and Fong 2002; Starkey and Tempest 2009). From the current ongoing rigour/relevance debates and discussions, it appears that business schools have a problem with simultaneously addressing the urgent needs of business whilst remaining true to their own ethos of academic rigour and scholarship (Bartunek and Rynes 2014; Butler *et al.* 2015; Kieser *et al.* 2015). This need not be the case. Underpinning many of these exchanges is the assumption that academic rigour is somehow fundamentally incompatible and at odds with the more practical and pragmatic aims and concerns of business. This prevalent view has led to a polarising of opinions. On the one hand, there is the blind championing of academic scholarship without any regard as to how this may relate to the practical needs of business and society (Peng and Dess 2010), on the other business schools have been urged to be more sensitive to the immediate, perceived needs of business (Bennis and O'Toole 2005) by changing their curriculum accordingly.

In both instances, there is little realisation that genuine practical relevance is in fact immanent in the uncompromising pursuit of proper scholarship in universities not because of the content, management knowledge, but because of the 'purifying' of social sensibilities and the 'enlargement' of thought and imagination that inevitably takes place amongst students in a properly rigorous university-based education. Education is as much about nurturing empirical sensitivity to the particularities of social situations and about extending the capacity for imaginative generalisation as it is about the transmission of abstract, universal principles. A properly balanced university education, therefore, must include a process of intellectual refinement that produces an alternative *artistic rigour* (Ehrenzweig 1967) that is eminently relevant and useful to the world of practice. Such an artistically rigorous 'habit of mind' (Newman 1996: 77) is characterised, not so much by rigidly following procedural protocols, but by an acute empirical sensitivity and perceptual awareness, and an imaginative playfulness in engaging with the world of ideas and in dealing with practical affairs. It is about the capacity to creatively utilise knowledge (Whitehead 1967); a capacity involving the relentless configuring and reconfiguring of knowledge and facts in fresh and unusual ways to produce genuinely novel insights and by so doing expanding horizons of comprehension. We call this expansionary process *relevation/revelation*.

Relevation/revelation entails the relentless striving to make the apparently remote/irrelevant/unconnected/unrelated relevant and consequential, and the hidden/obscured/overlooked/inconspicuous more significant and pregnant with implications in order to aid better judgement and decision making. Such an emphasis on making the seemingly irrelevant, unconnected and obscured meaningful and significant is inspired by the Heraclitean dictum: '*Harmoniê aphanês phranerês kreittôn*' (The hidden harmony is deeper, the invisible connection stronger, the inconspicuous correspondence more interesting than the apparent) (Parkes 1987: 106, emphasis original). We maintain that it is the cultivation of this unique capacity for relevation/revelation that makes a proper university-based management education highly valuable and indeed indispensable to successful management practice. Furthermore, such a dispositional capacity can be nurtured by drawing on insights from the arts to enrich the management education process.

The central thesis of our argument is that it is this rigorous cultivation of relevation/revelation in academic scholarship that makes for a truly effective and relevant management education programme. What the management student takes away from such a process-based management education is not so much content-expertise because 'knowledge does not keep any better than fish' (Whitehead 1967: 98), but rather what s/he does takes away is a 'learned and imaginative life'; a 'way of living' more than 'an article of commerce' (Whitehead 1967: 97). So much so that any fact learnt 'is no longer a bare fact: it is invested with all its possibilities . . . it is energising as the poet of our dreams, and as the architect of our purposes' (Whitehead 1967: 93). It is this capacity for imaginative generalisation based upon an acute sensitivity of social situations that is invaluable for the world of practice. An effective management education, therefore, is one that engenders an expansion of horizons of comprehension and hence awareness of fresh hitherto unthought-of possibilities in the conduct of business affairs.

Underpinning this capacity is an *artistic rigour* that accounts for the highly valued ability to reconfigure knowledge, information and resources to create novel product/service/initiatives thereby enabling businesses to remain competitive and viable (see Sullivan, Ehrlich and Colby, this volume). Practical relevance, therefore, is immanent in the proper conduct of research and education but only if this kind of alternative artistic rigour is taken into account as being a necessary part of proper academic scholarship. Furthermore, we maintain that such a dispositional quality is best cultivated by drawing on insights from the arts and art education in particular. Art education trains the student to attain a level of pristine seeing and a capacity for imaginative generalisation that is crucial for the production of good art. What a process-based management education ought to do, therefore, is to learn from techniques used in art education to help equip management students to draw sensitively from their lived experiences and to imaginatively link their knowledge and understanding in fresh and novel ways to meet the real challenges and surprises of a fast-changing and globalised business environment.

## Genuine rigour in management scholarship/education is relevant to business

Contrary to prevailing perceptions amongst management academics, genuine rigour in academic scholarship does not simply entail an unwavering commitment to an established set of methodological procedures and protocols that emphasise: thoroughness and precision in terms of familiarity with the extant conceptual literature surrounding a field of study; care and comprehensiveness in terms of the gathering of extensive empirical evidence to support one's contention; and tight logical soundness and justification in terms of the claims being made and the causal relationships imputed. Genuine rigour also requires the relentless striving to attain a level of naïve 'pristine' seeing, an 'innocence of the eye' (Ruskin 1927: 27) in apprehending phenomena. This enables the researcher to achieve a grasp of the concreteness of particulars that is then followed by the imaginative conjecturing of relations based upon such initial close observations. Such a dual emphasis on refining empirical sensitivity followed by disciplined imaginative generalisation makes for a different kind of rigour from that usually associated with much of management research and scholarship. It involves a kind of artistic rigour that is not well acknowledged or understood in the social sciences but is well recognised amongst art scholars (Ehrenzweig 1967: 29); one associated with the 'radical empiricism' that William James (1912: 42) tried to promote as an alternative to the 'false empiricism' he saw pervaded much of philosophy and the social sciences. For James, a genuine empiricism 'must neither admit into its constructions any element that is not directly experienced, nor exclude from them any element that is directly experienced' (James 1912: 42). It must begin with the 'immediate flux of life which furnishes the material to our later reflection' (James 1912: 93). This imperative to dwell within our raw pristine experience, saturating ourselves with it before proceeding towards imaginative generalisation, constitutes a kind of alternative rigour that is very distant and different from the technical rigour currently employed in generating management research outputs.

This revised understanding of 'rigour' – not as rigidly following established methods and procedural protocols but as the relentless striving to attain an 'uncompromising democracy' of vision (Ehrenzweig 1967: 29), which refuses to accept any pre-existent distinctions and categories in the apprehension of phenomena – is what is missing from much of management scholarship today. It points to a determined refusal to be seduced by ready-made professional abstractions and instead to begin from the pristine reality of raw experience and then develop categories therefrom. There is no substitute, says Whitehead (1948: 199), 'for the direct perception of the concrete achievement of a thing in its actuality', and yet there is a widespread tendency to be 'too much preoccupied with intellectual analysis, and with the acquirement of formularised information' (Whitehead 1948: 197–8). We are too 'exclusively bookish in our scholastic routine' (Whitehead 1948: 198) and neglect to 'strengthen habits of concrete appreciation'. As such, the rigorous scientific approach to analysis has 'riveted on men a certain set of abstractions' and this has been 'disastrous in their influence on the modern mentality' (Whitehead 1948: 200), so much so that 'When you understand all about the sun and all about the atmosphere and all about the rotation of the earth, you may still miss the radiance of the sunset' (Whitehead 1948: 199). Rigorously following procedural protocols can lead to 'mental dryrot' (Whitehead 1967: 2).

In proper academic scholarship, therefore, the true process of discovery is more 'like the flight of an aeroplane. It starts from the ground of particular observation; it makes a flight in the thin air of imaginative generalisation; and it again lands for renewed observation rendered acute by rational interpretation' (Whitehead 1929: 5). Empirical sensitivity and imaginative generalisation play an indispensable role in true scholastic rigour. In this Whiteheadian revision of what proper academic scholarship entails, rigidly adhering to formulaic notions of 'rigour' can result in a *rigor mortis* of the mind; an intellectual 'stiffness' that produces inert and lifeless ideas and facts that are incapable of energising action. It is unable to connect and render coherent apparently unrelated phenomena and experiences to create new avenues of possibilities for thought and action.

Within management scholarship, this dearth of useful insights in much of the published work has led the late Sumantra Ghoshal to criticise the 'pretence of knowledge' surrounding this dominant scientifically rigorous approach to knowledge creation for effectively driving out good management practices. He maintains that it is an error 'to pretend that the methods of the physical sciences can be indiscriminately applied to business studies' (Ghoshal 2005: 77) because it ignores fundamental differences between these academic disciplines. He proposed instead that we adopt an alternative 'scholarship of common sense' (Ghoshal 2005: 81) that views the researcher, more like Darwin or Freud, as an adventurer ('conquistador') or detective rather than a mathematician or man of science. Ghoshal's 'scholarship of common sense' is one that intuitively recognises the need for an alternative kind of rigour – an *artistic* rigour that makes proper academic scholarship highly relevant to the world of practice because this same dispositional quality is to be found in the very best of business practices.

In a variety of fields of intellectual/practical endeavour, including especially that of the worlds of academia and business/management practice, what really underpins success and outstanding accomplishment is not the rigid and unimaginative following of an established set of methods and/or procedural protocols in attempting to achieve a desired end; rather, it is the sensitivity, openness and imagination that is brought to bear by an individual in their relentless pursuit of excellence, each in their own domain of concern. This is what really makes the difference between success and failure. Thus, the sensitivity and intellectual/perceptual openness required, the veracity of the end sought and the uncompromising attention to fine details that are required to create ever-novel products/services/processes etc. that enable a business to succeed and prosper are, in principle, no different from those of the kind of imaginative path-breaking scholarship found in proper academia. This commonality is what makes genuine academic scholarship eminently relevant to the world of practice.

Within a proper university-based management education environment, this nurturing of the capacity for artistic rigour therefore constitutes that 'special fruit of education furnished at a University, as contrasted with other places of teaching or modes of teaching' (Newman 1996: 77). By emphasising keenness of observation, perceptual awareness and imaginative generalisation in the knowledge-creation and transmission process, a proper university-based management education exemplifies and mirrors the highest aspirations in the best of academia and also in the world of business/management. This is how relevance is achieved simply by being properly rigorous.

## Whitehead's process-based approach to education

> What education has to impart is an intimate sense for the power of ideas . . . and an aesthetic sense . . . for the direct attainment of a foreseen end, simply and without waste.
>
> *Whitehead 1967: 12*

> Education is the acquisition of the art of the utilisation of knowledge.
>
> *Whitehead 1967: 4*

In *The Aims of Education and Other Essays,* Whitehead (1967) lays out his philosophy of education. Although the collection does not amount to a 'processual theory of education', several scholars have argued for a Whiteheadian 'organic philosophy of education' based on his process thinking (Brumbaugh 1982; Evans 1998; Riffert 2005; Scarfe 2009; Wegener 1957). For Whitehead, education is 'a creative process of mutual growth that potentially leads to the ecstatic flourishing of both students and teachers' (Scarfe 2009: 8). A proper education as such must lead to the 'evocation of curiosity, of judgement, of the power of mastering a complicated tangle of circumstances' (Whitehead 1967: 5). It has to make the 'pupil see the wood by means of the trees' (Whitehead 1967: 6) by imparting an 'intimate sense for the power of ideas . . . based on an admiration for the direct attainment of a foreseen end, simply and without waste' (Whitehead 1967: 12).

Whitehead calls this ultimate achievement of the educational effort 'style'. Style is not so much a fashion or a skill as it is a dispositional acquirement involving the disciplining of the mind to be simultaneously 'more abstract and more concrete'. This is the most 'austere of qualities' in that 'the administrator with a sense for style hates waste; the engineer with a sense for style economises his material; the artisan with a sense for style prefers good work'. Style is the 'ultimate morality of the mind' (Whitehead 1967: 12). The real purpose of education, therefore, is the cultivation of this style; the dispositional power to see through abstractions and to make relevant and useful connections amidst the chaos and confusion that has been brought about by the complexifying effects of modernity. It constitutes an art of utilising knowledge. Education as such entails honing empirical sensitivity and cultivating the capacity for imaginative generalisation in order to enable the acquirement of this style so that desired ends are achieved quietly, effectively and 'without raising undesirable inflammations' (Whitehead 1967: 12).

Such a cultivated style is accomplished by the student undergoing a 'rhythm of education' comprising the stages of romance, precision and generalisation. Like musical notes, these rhythms are conceptualised as an oscillating tension between freedom and discipline. In the stage of romance, 'the subject-matter has the vividness of novelty; it holds within itself unexplored connexions with possibilities half-disclosed by glimpses and half-concealed by the wealth of material' (Whitehead 1967: 17). This stage brings forth an emotional response to education, one that energises and generates a tendency towards elaborating the spark of freedom and the joy of exploration with regards to a subject matter. During this stage the learners experience intense periods of absorption and involvement. As 'romance' suggests, this stage embodies an overwhelming subjective feeling of hope, dreams and the promise of exhilarating experiences. The second, the 'stage of precision', orients the learner more towards the systematic acquisition of facts and techniques. These facts and techniques, infused by romance, are now not simply inert ideas, but carry the learner to know 'the fundamental details and the main exact generalisations' as well as acquire 'an easy mastery of technique' (Whitehead 1967: 34). Having mastered discipline in the precision stage, Whitehead argues for a return to the freedoms of the romantic stage where the learner engages with his/her experiences with discipline and imagination. This is the 'stage of generalisation' where 'details are shed in favour of the active applications of principles, the details retracting into subconscious habits' (Whitehead 1967: 37). It is here that what is learnt through the rhythms of education gives rise, not merely to a knowledgeable person, but to one equipped with a 'noble and courteous bearing' who is ultimately predisposed to respond in a manner that betrays the refinement of thought and action he/she has undergone in the educational process. This is Whitehead's 'style', and hence Whitehead (1967: 26) insists: 'Your learning is useless to you till you have lost your text-books, burnt your lecture notes, and forgotten the minutiae which you learnt by heart for the examination.'

The rhythms of education that Whitehead identified bring to the fore important considerations for the teacher and learner especially in a university setting. For him, the university, in particular, is a place where 'the spirit of generalisation should dominate' (Whitehead 1967: 25). This is something that university-based business schools need to incorporate in their educational curriculum. In his lecture to the American Association of Collegiate Schools of Business (AACSB) in 1927 at Harvard Business School, Whitehead argued that the primary reason for universities 'is not to be found either in the mere knowledge conveyed to the students or in the mere opportunities for research afforded to the members of the faculty' (Whitehead 1967: 92). Instead, he argued:

> The justification for a university is that it preserves the connection between knowledge and the *zest for life*, by uniting the young and the old in the *imaginative consideration of learning* . . . . A university which fails in this respect has no reason for existence.
>
> *Whitehead 1967: 93, emphasis added*

Above all, for Whitehead, university life should constitute an adventure of ideas shared by both young minds and experienced researchers. As the university sector today faces new challenges with trends in separating education from research, and moving education towards Massive Open Online Courses (MOOCs) and corporate universities, Whitehead's words remind us that university education is not merely about the transmission of information and facts that often can be done more cheaply and efficiently by other means; rather, what the university ought to create is an 'atmosphere of excitement, arising from imaginative consideration [which] transforms knowledge' (Whitehead 1967: 93). The university educational atmosphere, unencumbered by the daily pressures of meetings, deadlines and targets that students will face in the workplace, is most conducive to acquiring this habit of imaginatively linking and configuring knowledge in ever-novel ways to create fresh understanding. The classroom affords students the opportunity to 'think rightly and wrongly, and free to appreciate the variousness of the universe undisturbed by its perils' (Whitehead 1967: 93).

It is at this point that Whitehead draws parallels between the best would-be practitioners and the best researchers. By bringing young minds and researchers together, a university provides fertile ground for imaginative leaps. For him, university education is 'discipline for the adventure for life' (Whitehead 1967: 98), where researchers share their intellectual adventure with young minds tinged with romance. He argues that 'it should be the chief aim of a university professor to exhibit himself in his own true character – that is, as an ignorant man thinking, actively utilising his small share of knowledge' (Whitehead 1967: 37). How the professor searches and re-searches for an adequate way of expressing him/herself, often thinking aloud, provides a compelling exemplar for the students to emulate. This intellectual adventure of searching and re-searching relentlessly for an adequate and coherent form of expression constitutes a 'seamless coat of learning' (Whitehead 1967: 11) that joins the various subdisciplines into a connected whole. Learning is about connecting, so that rather than remain stuck in the 'narrow groove' of rigid disciplines it is the broad context within which specialised knowledge is utilised that must be rendered significant. In this sense, a proper educational process aims at cultivating the dispositional quality of 'style' in the student; one that pervades the whole being of the educated person. Within this dispositional 'style' lies the natural merging of rigour with relevance.

To summarise, Whitehead's philosophy of education emphasises the endless learning process of searching for and making ever-newer and creative connections. It culminates in the acquisition of what he calls 'style' – a dispositional capacity for achieving tangible outcomes directly, simply and without waste. This happens when the learner undergoes a rhythm of education involving the stages of romance, precision and generalisation. Within the university environment it is the latter emphasis on generalisation that makes for the proper preparation of the student for the adventures of life outside the walls of academia. Understood thus, education is an interminable process, combining freedom and restraint with the warp and woof of experience. It culminates in the acquisition of an art of utilising knowledge that will be deployed in the world of practical affairs. This 'art' is what we mean by our notion of relevation/revelation.

## Relevation/revelation as the art of utilising knowledge

Instead of the much-exercised debate surrounding the questions of 'rigour' and 'relevance' of business school education, we propose to dispense with this false dichotomy by introducing a new term 'relevate' as an alternative to the term 'relevance'. Borrowing from etymological roots of the term 'relevant' (*reliever* or *relevāre*, in Latin, meaning to lighten, or to raise again) and the medical term *levation* meaning the act of gradually raising up, 'relevate' implies imaginatively creating connections between previously unconnected phenomena and establishing fresh and novel relationships so that what was previously unnoticed, overlooked or unattended becomes increasingly viewed as being pertinent and relevant to decisional considerations. Relevation is inextricably intertwined with its natural other *revelation*, which alludes to the sudden discovery of latent and hidden connections hitherto unexamined, unthought-of or unthinkable. It is this relevation/revelation couplet that underpins the art of imaginatively utilising knowledge. What distinguishes the process of relevation/revelation is the relentless seeking out of difference and otherness in a situation/phenomenon apprehended, rather than conveniently assigning it to pre-established categories of comprehension. It is about deliberately attending to the hidden, the peripheral and the obscured, with a view to reconfiguring our conventional understanding of a phenomenon or situation under investigation. It involves the relaxing of established paradigmatic boundaries of thought and 'escaping' from the clutches of received wisdom and hence expanding the scope and range of issues considered significant to a particular decisional imperative; it effectively re-problematises a given problem, thereby forcing a new comprehension of the situation encountered.

To 'relevate/revelate' is therefore to provoke, through a variety of rigorous scholarly techniques, a heightened sensitivity to hidden relationships, peripheral event-happenings and/or unnoticed emerging trends in the world such that what was initially regarded as unconnected, unimportant or not immediately relevant becomes increasingly perceived as pregnant with implications and hence vital for consideration. Relevation/revelation involves an *art* of discernment that is particularly attuned to creating fresh connections and seeking out hidden relationships and invisible correspondences. It is predicated upon the prior attainment of empirical sensitivity, perceptual awareness and the capacity for imaginative generalisation. It involves detecting and engaging in the imaginative formulation and re-formulation of the relationships between empirical experiences, causal relations and explanatory accounts with a view to producing fresh and novel insights and hence an expansion of the powers of comprehension. Such a power to established fresh and hitherto unthought-of and unthinkable connections is vital to the practice of producing both novel products/services in business and fresh and path-breaking theories in academia.

Within academia, the capacity to relevate/revelate serves to guard against the natural tendency to seek out evidence that reinforces existing established theories and thereby to extend the 'pretence of knowledge' through this convergent process of empirical verification – a tendency that has been labelled 'confirmation bias' (Taleb 2007) in theory building. Similarly, within the business context it serves to guard against organisational myopia: the ever-present tendency within business organisations to single-mindedly focus upon and pursue an immediate end without giving sufficient regard to the wider and longer-term consequences of such actions/decisions. Such an organisationally myopic condition is precipitated by what the sociologist Robert Merton (1936: 901) calls the 'imperious immediacy of interest' and it is this tendency to narrowly focus on the immediately visible and to attend solely to what is at hand that actually precipitates future negative unintended consequences that are often the underlying causes of corporate failures in the longer term (MacKay and Chia 2013). Relevating/revelating, therefore, entails heightening awareness of the potency of *latent* connections already existing in every business situation and alerting decision makers to the 'invisible presence' already motivating 'the movement of being' (Cooper 2005: 1706). Such an ability to discern the *latent* in any relationship lies in the best of academic scholarship, in the most successful of entrepreneurial ventures and in the most astute of political decision making. In what follows, we show how art education, as an example, provides an inexhaustible fount for nurturing this art of relevation/revelation.

## Art and the art of relevation/revelation

> Art does not reproduce the visible but makes visible.
>
> *Klee 1961: 76*

Art, as Klee reminds us, is more about revealing the latent and the invisible than it is about representing the visible and the manifest. Art sensitises us to peripheral effects, to seeing hidden connections and to making fresh imaginative connections. It makes us think in relational terms and to appreciate phenomenal appearances simultaneously in terms of identity and otherness. Art reveals and relevates. In a strict sense, this ability cannot be directly taught but it can be indirectly nurtured through exemplification on the part of educators and sustained practice on the part of students. It is more process than content. It entails an 'education of attention' (Gibson 1979: 254; Ingold 2000) whereby observational powers are sharpened and this paves the way for the imaginative bringing together of 'diverse materials and combining or redirecting their flow in the anticipation of what might emerge' (Ingold 2011: 213). The fundamental underlying feature of this dispositional capacity is a cultivated empirical sensitivity to ordinary, mundane goings-on that are often glossed over by the inattentive observer. As Whitehead has noted, it is about an attention to the fine details that make for the overall impression of a phenomenon being investigated.

Take for instance the seemingly simple and innocuous task of sawing a plank. We usually think of it in result-terms as an everyday operational accomplishment, and yet there is much more than meets the eye. Contrary to the casual observation, it involves much more than just a single operation; instead, it comprises an entire series of ongoing micro-adjustments involving many steps: 'sawing a plank has the character of a journey that proceeds from place to place, through a movement that – though rhythmic and repetitive – is never strictly monotonous' (Ingold 2011: 53). Sawing a plank comprises an inextricably interlinked sequence of virtually spontaneous ongoing adjustments that make for the eventual outcome. It is '*processional* rather than *successional*' (Ingold 2011: 53, emphasis added); a seamless movement whereby each stroke develops from the previous one and is a preparation for the next. It emphasises the *relational* character of everyday human purposive activities, one that is crucial to our appreciation of the ongoing adjustments, adaptations and improvisations that have to be carried out in the seemingly simplest of tasks. It demands an attention to fine details to appreciate how sawing a piece of wood is in fact a monumental accomplishment of establishing, extending and amplifying connections. In the act of sawing, no two strokes are exactly the same:

> [the] force, amplitude, speed and torque of the manual gesture vary, albeit almost imperceptibly, from stroke to stroke. So does the posture of the body, and the muscular-skeletal configuration of tension and compression that keep it in balance. Yet, the outcome, in skilled hands is a perfectly clean, straight cut.
>
> *Ingold 2011: 58*

Close attention to what it means to saw a plank reveals an intricacy of minute variations in posture, movement and rhythm that often escape ordinary attention.

It is this kind of empirical sensitivity and perceptual awareness that is instilled in the arts in general and in art education in particular, and yet much of this kind of fine detail is often overlooked and replaced by the convenient neat black boxes of established categories that we unthinkingly rely upon to describe what we observe. Art and art education therefore helps the student recover this kind of pristine empirical sensitivity – that 'habit of aesthetic appreciation'

(Whitehead 1948: 199) of fine details that go to make up a phenomenal experience. It requires the setting aside of a universal tendency to achieve too quickly a clear gestalt in the apprehension of phenomena.

The art theorist Ehrenzweig (1967: 21) observes that the urge to see clear form and distinct outlines is something deeply embedded in our collective psyche. We tend for the most part to notice simple, compact and precise forms and to generally ignore vague, apparently incoherent and inarticulate forms. Because of deep cultural programming, our eyes are always eager to register a good gestalt – one that exhibits order, simplicity, compactness, coherence and clarity. This tendency towards a good gestalt, however, is something that a good artist must resist because '[o]nly a bad artist will concentrate his attention exclusively on the large-scale composition and treat less articulate . . . elements like textures or the scribbles of artistic "handwriting" as decorative additions that have no structural significance' (Ehrenzweig 1967: 21). Therefore, instead of focusing on figure or ground, a good artist learns to 'scatter his attention and watch the simultaneous shaping of inside and outside areas on either side of the line, a feat which the gestalt psychologists would consider impossible' (Ehrenzweig 1967: 22). This requires what Ehrenzweig calls a 'syncretistic vision' whereby attention is relaxed and allowed to 'oscillate freely between focused and unfocused (empty) states' (Ehrenzweig 1967: 27). It precipitates an 'uncompromising democracy' of vision that simply absorbs what is apprehended, refusing to make any distinction between the various elements that make up that experience. This is the very 'essence of artistic rigour' (Ehrenzweig 1967: 29). Artistic rigour, in contrast to scientific rigour, is therefore about the cultivation of the ability to dwell within the experience of a phenomenon and to absorb it into our being without having an urge to prematurely make sense of it.

According to Ehrenzweig, any kind of creative search for new ideas or new connections relies on 'unconscious scanning' to 'handle "open" structures with blurred frontiers which will be drawn with proper precision only in the unknowable future' (Ehrenzweig 1967: 42). To rely upon the unconscious is not only to unsettle the conscious mind and to disrupt the gestalt tendency in order to be creative and imaginative, but it is also 'indispensable for efficient work' because it is far superior to the process of 'conscious visualisation' (Ehrenzweig 1965: 28). In order for us to become sensitised to the inarticulate and vague forms operating at the level of the unconscious, we have to adopt a mental attitude not dissimilar to that of the artist who has to scatter his/her attention and to diffusely attend to the whole canvas to understand its wider effects on him/her. This reversal of the common-sense attitude of narrowly focusing consciously on already-formed objects enables us to watch for that seemingly fortuitous, unrelated and accidental detail that is more likely to conceal the unconscious content of our everyday experience. Ehrenzweig (1965: 28) shows how art training involves deliberately directing attention *away* from the obsessive focus on form and searching for those seemingly serendipitous and insignificant details, often at the periphery, that contribute immeasurably to the overall visual effect. In painting, for example, it is the 'minute, almost microscopic, scribbles which make up the technique of a great draftsman or the brush work of a great painter' (Ehrenzweig 1965: 30). The 'pupil's attention is turned away from an exclusive concentration on a single surface gestalt and made to branch out to follow several competing form events unfolding at the same time' (Ehrenzweig 1965: 41). This unconscious scrutiny directs attention away from the articulate forms that each scribble and brushstroke conveys towards the apparently accidental emergence of the whole painting.

What Ehrenzweig reveals in his investigations of artistic vision is how a re-education of attention can be achieved through a study of the arts and the extent to which the unconscious plays in our ability to elicit rich details otherwise unnoticed or overlooked in order to expand our peripheral awareness and enlarge our horizons of comprehension. Immersion in the arts helps us to resist premature gestalt closure and to relevate/revelate the invisible, the latent and the inarticulate so that the hidden, the inconspicuous and the apparently unrelated are rendered meaningful and consequential. This heightened sensitivity to the hidden, the obscured and the latent connectedness of phenomena, as well as the imaginative power to integrate all these together into a coherent whole, is what Whitehead (1967: 4) means when he talks about the 'art of the utilisation of knowledge' and what we call the art of relevation/revelation. This is a capability that must form a key aspect of a management education curriculum.

## Cultivating the art of relevation/revelation in management education

Ehrenzweig's approach to developing an artistic sensibility, which is a basic requirement for producing good art, resonates deeply with what is required in management education to produce 'good' management students – students that are equipped with the dispositional capacity for relevation/revelation. His emphasis on achieving artistic rigour by resisting the tendency towards a clear gestalt and instead relentlessly seeking and attaining an 'uncompromising democracy' of vision provides an alternative comprehension of what scholastic rigour might mean. Furthermore, his insistence on scattering attention and cultivating a 'syncretistic approach' to seek out hidden connections and to create fresh new ones by taking 'flying leaps' over large tracts of incomprehension, provides the basis for the imperative of relevation/revelation that we advocate here as being an important missing skill-set in much of the current management education curriculum.

Whereas analytical tools and techniques developed by the science of management bring business ideas and environmental conditions into sharp focus and precision, and hence aid abstract conceptual understanding, art education informed by Ehrenzweig emphasises the importance of enabling the unconscious to work in refining perception and sensitising us to the presence of the vague, the latent, the invisible and the obscured in business situations. This resistance towards too-quickly achieving a clear gestalt creates a space for dwelling in the experience of a phenomenon and critically enables a deeper appreciation of empirical situations apprehended. It opens up fresh possibilities for imaginative generalisation. In art education, this resistance to premature gestalt closure is nurtured by deliberately making 'the student change his medium as soon as he achieves a too conscious and sure control over it' or to 'make the student use accident-inviting techniques' or to 'make him use both hands or only the left hand, or to draw with the eyes closed' (Ehrenzweig 1961: 125–6). These are disruptive educational strategies intended to defamiliarise the art student and to force him/her to set aside familiar approaches and categories of comprehension in engaging with a piece of work. The awkwardness experienced by a student's failure to impose his conscious will on the medium he/she is working with allows his/her unconscious a 'chance to come through the fissures created by accident and failure' (Ehrenzweig 1961: 126). The deliberate unsettling of conscious control and comprehension using such deliberately disruptive techniques is what produces a good artist.

In management education, we can learn much from the important insights regarding the crucial role of disruption and defamiliarisation employed in art education. Equivalent 'disruptive' educational micro-strategies can be incorporated in the management education curriculum to cause students to break out of dominant paradigms of understanding and thus to expand their horizons of comprehension. In stark contrast to teaching that focuses on providing expert-based management knowledge that tends to converge towards 'best practice', the introduction of equivalent paradigm-disrupting strategies to challenging conventional wisdom can and has been employed in executive education with some success (Harrison *et al.* 2007: 5–6; Paton *et al.* 2014). Using techniques that emphasise 'unlearning', 'falsification', 'otherness' and the importance of peripheral awareness through the employment of pieces of art, literary vignettes and philosophical questions, students have been challenged to learn to think otherwise and to arrive at alternative possibilities previously unthinkable. This has helped instil the art of relevation/revelation and expanded horizons of comprehension such that the senior executives involved in these educational efforts have been able to shift dominant mindsets and, by so doing, have successfully created fresh new product offerings/services previously unthought-of or unthinkable within their own respective business divisions (Paton *et al.* 2014: 274–84). In all this, a deliberate resistance to appear immediately relevant to the pressing concerns of the executives involved proved to be the key. Participants were exhorted to set aside their pressing business concerns temporarily to create a space for experiencing and questioning their own thinking, thereby enabling them to learn to see, think and imagine anew.

Although exposure to such fresh and unconventional approaches was necessarily discomforting and unsettling in the first instance, nevertheless it helps stimulate sensitivity to raw empirical realities in a way that made it possible to rethink business purposes and priorities in a way previously unknown. It forced a return to the 'instant field of the present', that 'plain, unqualified actuality' (James 1912: 23) that is raw experience, and to dwell within it without the irrepressible urge to prematurely engage in the sense-making process. Just as the student-artist learns to 'let go' and to 'unlearn' so that 'new ideas will emerge and bring the longed for solution of a problem' (Ehrenzweig 1961: 123), so too must management students learn to 'let go' of what they think they already know in order to be able to see, think and imagine anew. By learning to live with the creative anxiety of not knowing and not being in control, students gradually develop a 'sustained aesthetic discipline' (Ehrenzweig 1956: 37), a kind of 'negative capability' that is able to be content with 'uncertainties, mysteries, doubts' without the 'irritable tendency to reach after fact and reason' prematurely (Keats 2002: 60–1).

What successful business practitioners share with the best of academic scholarship is the artistic rigour needed to be fully 'in touch' with empirical reality and to be able to then take 'flying leaps' over large areas of incomprehension in order to elicit and discover ever-novel connections and hence to forge fresh and innovative responses. This is what defines the art of relevation/revelation. Such an accomplishment is not so much about applying tools and concepts learnt in an academic setting in the 'real' world, but about instilling an innate capacity for re-lat-ing and revealing hidden and latent connections. This is ultimately what will be eminently useful for business and managerial decision making – it is artistic rigour and not so much scientific rigour that makes a proper management education relevant to the world of business practice and especially to the practice of entrepreneurship.

## Conclusions

The central thrust of our argument is that the practical relevance of academic scholarship lies in the liberating capacity of a proper university-based management education to draw from a variety of seemingly unrelated perspectives to stimulate and instil the art of relevation/revelation amongst management students. It is a capacity that helps by re-educating attention towards the peripheral, the seemingly innocuous, the fleeting, the other and the accidental so that these are given greater prominence in the overall comprehension of things. The need for developing such an imaginative capacity in managers and management students was noted by Whitehead in his lecture given at the twenty-fifth anniversary of Harvard Business School in which he wrote:

> To-day business organisation requires an imaginative grasp of the psychologies of populations engaged in differing modes of occupation; of populations scattered through cities,

> through mountains, through plains; of populations on the ocean, and of populations in mines, and of populations in forests. It requires an imaginative grasp of conditions in the tropics, and of the interlocking interests of great organisations, and of the reactions of the whole complex to any change in one of its elements.
>
> *Whitehead 1967: 94*

What Whitehead recognised was that management realities are not simply confined to the immediate and the obvious, but that the remote, the seemingly peripheral and the distant are all pertinent to decisional considerations. Often they defy familiar categories of thought. The challenge for university-based management education is therefore to equip managers with a comprehensive grasp of the realities they face and to engage in imaginative generalisation therefrom. In a world that increasingly demands relevance and impact along narrowly defined objectives and purposes, management educators inspired by Whitehead's philosophy of education face a key challenge: that of paradoxically ensuring relevance by not capitulating to the popular demands for relevance. To pander to such populist demands would be to lead to the inevitable decline of society as Whitehead so vividly warns: 'A great society is a society in which its men of business think greatly of their function. Low thoughts mean low behaviour, and after a brief orgy of exploitation, low behaviour means a descending standard of living' (Whitehead 1942: 99). The power of a Whiteheadian-inspired university education is that it places the 'coming-to-be' of the learner at the heart of the process of education. It is one where the hidden, the latent and the seemingly innocuous is emphasised because they offer greater potential than the explicit, the obvious and the manifest. This is what the art of relevation/revelation is able to accomplish.

## References


Bartunek, J.M. and Rynes, S.L. (2014) 'Academics and practitioners are alike and unlike: the paradoxes of academic–practitioner relationships', *Journal of Management*, 40(5), 1181–201.

Bennis, W.G. and O'Toole, J. (2005) 'How business schools lost their way', *Harvard Business Review*, 83(5), 96–104.

Brumbaugh, R.S. (1982) *Whitehead, Process Philosophy, and Education*. Albany, NY: State University of New York Press.

Butler, N., Delaney, H. and Spoelstra, S. (2015) 'Problematizing "relevance" in the business school: the case of leadership studies', *British Journal of Management*, 26(4), 731–44.

Cooper, R. (2005) 'Relationality', *Organization Studies*, 26(11), 1689–710.

Ehrenzweig, A. (1956) 'The mastering of creative anxiety'. *In:* E.R. Torroja and E. Mundt (eds.) *Art and Artist*. Oakland, CA: University of California Press, pp. 33–52.

Ehrenzweig, A. (1961) 'The hidden order of art', *British Journal of Aesthetics*, 1(3), 121–33.

Ehrenzweig, A. (1965) *The Psycho-Analysis of Artistic Vision and Hearing*. New York, NY: George Braziller.

Ehrenzweig, A. (1967) *The Hidden Order of Art: A Study in the Psychology of Artistic Imagination*. London: Weidenfeld & Nicolson.

Evans, M. (1998) *Whitehead and Philosophy of Education: The Seamless Coat of Learning*, Atlanta, GA: Rodopi.

Ghoshal, S. (2005) 'Bad management theories are destroying good management practices', *Academy of Management Learning & Education*, 4(1), 75–91.

Gibson, J.J. (1979) *The Ecological Approach to Visual Perception*. Boston, MA: Houghton Mifflin.

Harrison, R.T., Leitch, C.M. and Chia, R. (2007) 'Developing paradigmatic awareness in university business schools: the challenge for executive education', *Academy of Management Learning & Education*, 6(3), 332–43.

Ingold, T. (2000) *The Perception of the Environment: Essays in Livelihood, Dwelling and Skill*. London: Routledge.

Ingold, T. (2011) *Being Alive: Essays on Movement, Knowledge and Description*. London: Routledge.

James, W. (1912) *Essays in Radical Empiricism*. New York, NY: Longman Green.

Keats, J. (2002) 'Letters to G. and T. Keats'. *In:* G.F. Scott (ed.) *Selected Letters of John Keats*. Cambridge, MA: Harvard University Press, pp. 60–1.

Khurana, R. (2007) *From Higher Aims to Hired Hands: The Social Transformation of Business Schools and the Unfulfilled Promise of Management as a Profession*. Princeton, NJ: Princeton University Press.
Kieser, A., Nicolai, A. and Seidl, D. (2015) 'The practical relevance of management research: turning the debate on relevance into a rigorous scientific research program', *The Academy of Management Annals*, 9(1), 143–233.
Klee, P. (1961) *The Notebooks Volume 1: The Thinking Eye*. London: Lund Humphries.
MacKay, R.B. and Chia, R. (2013) 'Choice, chance, and unintended consequences in strategic change: a process understanding of the rise and fall of Northco Automotive', *Academy of Management Journal*, 56(1), 208–30.
Merton, R.K. (1936) 'The unanticipated consequences of purposive social action', *American Sociological Review*, 1(6), 894–904.
Mintzberg, H. (2004) *Managers not MBAs: A Hard Look at the Soft Practice of Management*, Harlow, UK: Financial Times Prentice Hall.
Newman, J.H. (1996) *The Idea of a University*. New Haven, CT: Yale University Press.
Parkes, G. (1987) 'Thoughts on the way: being and time via Lao-Chuang'. *In:* G. Parkes (ed.) *Heidegger and Asian Thought*. Honolulu, HI: University of Hawaii, pp. 105–44.
Paton, S., Chia, R. and Burt, G. (2014) 'Relevance or "relevate"? How university business schools can add value through reflexively learning from strategic partnerships with business', *Management Learning*, 45(3), 267–88.
Peng, M.W. and Dess, G.G. (2010) 'In the spirit of scholarship', *Academy of Management Learning & Education*, 9(2), 282–98.
Pfeffer, J. and Fong, C.T. (2002) 'The end of business schools? Less success than meets the eye', *Academy of Management Learning & Education*, 1(1), 78–95.
Riffert, F.G. (ed.) (2005) *Alfred North Whitehead on Learning and Education: Theory and Application*. Newcastle, UK: Cambridge Scholars Press.
Ruskin, J. (1927) *The Complete Works*. London: Nicholson and Weidenfeld.
Scarfe, A.C. (2009) *The Adventure of Education: Process Philosophers on Learning, Teaching, and Research*. Amsterdam: Rodopi.
Starkey, K. and Tempest, S. (2009) 'The winter of our discontent: the design challenge for business schools', *Academy of Management Learning & Education*, 8(4), 576–86.
Taleb, N.N. (2007) *The Black Swan: The Impact of the Highly Improbable*. London: Penguin.
Wegener, F.C. (1957) *The Organic Philosophy of Education*. Dubuque, IA: WC Brown.
Whitehead, A.N. (1929) *Process and Reality: An Essay in Cosmology*. New York, NY: Free Press.
Whitehead, A.N. (1942) *Adventures of Ideas*. Harmondsworth, UK: Penguin.
Whitehead, A.N. (1948) *Science and the Modern World*. Harmondsworth, UK: Penguin.
Whitehead, A.N. (1967) *The Aims of Education and Other Essays*. New York, NY: Free Press.

# 10

# Responsibility

## Hans Jonas and the ethics of business

*René ten Bos*

It is a widely accepted idea that all great philosophers were basically interested in just one central question. What is God? What is power? What is being? Spinoza asked the first question and found out that God equals nature. The second question was asked by Nietzsche and his answer was that there is a close connection between power and desire. The final question was asked by Heidegger and he maintained that we all precisely forgot to ask this all-important question: what is being? It is the kind of question that oozes from every single page of these philosophers and in the end it rises as an immense nebula of meaning from the entire oeuvre. You only have to hear the names of the philosophers who are involved to know that they asked this single question, *their* question.

For the German philosopher Hans Jonas (1903–93) too, there was only one question that really mattered: how do we respond to the demand of survival that life as such poses to us? In this chapter, I am going to discuss this question, first by a fairly close analysis of what Jonas has to say in his major book, *The Principle of Responsibility*.[1] We will see that this question is, according to Jonas, the only question that we should ask about responsibility. In the context of this book, this is also a way of asking how philosophy – as one of the subjects usually seen to be part of the humanities – can help us think about the future of management education. I will then critically link Jonas's ideas to what nowadays has been referred to as the 'ethics of resilience', bringing in some ideas about responsibility of some contemporary philosophers such as Timothy Morton and Jane Bennett. We will see that Jonas has much in common with these eco-thinkers; however, there is one remarkable difference: whereas Jonas clings to the idea of personal responsibility, Morton and Bennett seem to abandon this idea. For reasons that I will have critically embarked on by the end of the chapter, they don't trust responsibility any more.

Before proceeding, I would like to make a small detour and insert some remarks on responsibility as a concept used in business and management education. In the average handbook or encyclopaedia, the authors usually point out that responsibility is a highly ambiguous and difficult term. They also routinely link it to other fuzzy concepts such as duty, blame, praise, integrity, causality and liability (Corlett 2005: 86). Most authors indulge in the ambiguities involved and ask such mind-boggling questions as: 'can there be collective responsibility?', 'is all responsibility ultimately reducible to the individual?' or 'what does reducibility mean in the previous sentence?' Too many ideas, too many twists and turns, and too much reflexivity. The price to be paid for this is that the central idea – the idea of responsibility – evaporates. But this, it should be said, is exactly the point of management thinking. The idea that responsibility *should* somehow evaporate is the gist of its ethics, and so it occurred that this ethics has, in its own indomitable way, taken many things from us. Professionals in hospitals or schools do not work with patients or pupils any more, but with clients. Their jobs as nurses or teachers are not about care or education any more, but about administration. What was once seen as their responsibility has been replaced with accountability or, worse, *corporate social* responsibility. As a consequence, no one knows what responsibility is any more. The situation is perfectly described by Robert Jackall (2005: 359; see also Jackall 1989):

> [D]espite claims to the contrary, bureaucracies also separate people from internal accountability for their actions. Bureaucratic hierarchies generally encourage superiors' usurpation of credit for the work of subordinates. Moreover, few bureaucracies have formal tracking systems to allot blame for mistakes; men and women who are upwardly mobile can outrun their mistakes, leaving others to bear blame for them. At the upper levels of organizations, among men and women of proven and relatively equal abilities, the allocation of credit and blame, and corresponding success and failure, is thus very often experienced as arbitrary, indeed capricious. In short, big organizations often seem to be vast systems of organized irresponsibility – even, perhaps especially, to those within them.

The pre-eminent strategy to create these systems of irresponsibility is, of course, to render the idea of responsibility fuzzy, nebulous and ambivalent. We end up with what Jackall has called 'moral mazes', and in these moral mazes responsibility can have any meaning, and thus no meaning at all.

Management education prepares students to adjust themselves precisely to these mazes. Even though lip service is paid to what are known as ESR-issues (Environment, Sustainability and Responsibility), ethics is often on the wane. At least, this is what management guru Henry Mintzberg (2004: 73; see also Srinivas, this volume) maintains in a classic text on management education. He discusses a survey of the attitudes towards business and society of almost two thousand MBA students and concludes that during their study 'there is a shift in priorities ... from customer needs and product quality to the importance of shareholder value'. If students were showing awareness of ESR concerns at all, it was because they were worried about the public image of their future employers. It is not difficult to refer to more recent studies than Mintzberg's that make the same point about the erosion of ethics in management education. One reason might be that formalism and arithmetic have become its hard core. The former American Secretary of Defense Robert McNamara, a well-known product of the Harvard Business School, made a telling statement in his autobiography about his education:

> The defining moments in my education ... came in my philosophy and mathematics curricula. The ethics courses forced me to begin to shape my values; studying logic exposed me to rigor and precision in thinking. And many mathematic professors taught me to see math as a process of thought – a language in which to express much, but certainly not all, human activity.
>
> *McNamara cited in Mintzberg 2004: 149*

What McNamara found out, I surmise, is that ethics is difficult to express in rigorous and precise logic. Admittedly, it might shape a person's values, but it definitely lacks the conceptual clarity that rational people should show in their endeavours.

A personal remark is in place here. I myself have been involved with management education – inside and outside academia – for many years and it is precisely this constant complaint about the difficulty of ethics or responsibility that I find so frustrating. What we learn from Jonas is that responsibility might be difficult to enact, but that it is definitely not a difficult concept to comprehend. What we should teach students in management education is that the illogical or non-formal nature of an idea does not render it hopelessly complex. The eagerness to formalize ethics (into codes of conduct, lists of things to do, accountability, etc.) is related to a desire to reduce complexity. This eagerness is a massive problem in management education precisely because, in terms of responsibility, there is no complexity to be reduced. Perhaps this is in fact the most stunning idea of Jonas's work: when it comes to responsibility, there is no strategy or stratagem – just straightforwardness.

## Hans Jonas

The question that was an obsession for Jonas during his life is meant to get us out of the murky waters in which managers feel so much at home. Let me repeat this question here: how do we respond to the demand of survival that life as such poses to us? The implacable nature of the question may put off average scholars of business ethics in the sense that this is clearly not the type of question in which they are interested. Too grim, too unforgiving – as if our *survival* or that of a business ethicist is at stake – and yet this is exactly what Jonas alerts us to. Indeed, we will soon see that the only kind of responsibility he acknowledges is deeply intertwined with the notion of survival: human survival, but also the survival of other entities. It is important to understand that the question's implacability is related to Jonas's eventful life. A descendant from a Jewish family in Mönchengladbach, a German city not too far from the Dutch border, he experienced how anti-Semitism and later also Nazism were baleful forces in his country. In 1933, he fled to England. In his memoirs, he writes that an incident with anti-Semitic juveniles was the most important reason. This might be true, but it has also been maintained that the decision of Martin Heidegger, his teacher and master, to become a member of the NSDAP, the National Socialist German Workers Party, played an equally important role. For Jonas, Heidegger's decision, later described by him as 'an insignificant stupidity', was dramatic and bizarre. He immediately grasped that his teacher's central question – what is being? – might perhaps not be the right question. Being, Jonas understood, is not what matters. Surviving is much more urgent and much more fundamental. How does one survive a period completely permeated by a life-destroying nihilism?

That this was not only a philosophical question but also a question that had a high practical priority for Jonas becomes clear if we look at some more details from his biography. After the break with Heidegger, he left academia for a long time. In 1935, he went to Palestine where he joined the Haganah, a Jewish paramilitary resistance movement. Five years later, he returned to Europe in order to become a soldier fighting with the British forces against the Germans and Italians. All in all, Jonas was on battlefields in Europe and the Middle East for more than eight years. In 1945, he returned to Mönchengladbach to find out that most members of his family, including his mother, did not escape the gas chambers. He decided that Germany was no longer a country where he could live and went back to Palestine to fight in the independence war that led to the foundation of Israel. In 1948, at the age of 45, he decided to move to the US. In 1955, he became a professor in New York, the city where he would die almost 40 years later.

This brief story of a life serves to show the reader that Jonas actually '*lived*' his central question. For him, the question about responsibility was far from formal, logical or abstract. Moreover, it was a question that had something heroic about it. Life and survival as such are heroic: people should fight for a cause even if this means that their own lives will be jeopardized. Throughout his life Jonas insisted that ethics and philosophy must have their roots in a life that is lived heroically. In fact, the very idea that people can turn ethics and philosophy into a solid job in academia was repulsive to him. A job, after all, distances the individual from real life and therefore also from thought. The recurrent theme in all his writings, no matter whether they are about ancient philosophical currents such as Gnosticism or contemporary issues such as bioethics or technology, is life and survival. He rejected Gnosticism because in his mind it does not value life on earth and instead wagers on a different, transcendental life. More importantly in the present context, he also has nagging doubts about science and technology, both of which tend to see nature as a completely value-free and objective domain. In the 1960s, he expressed his doubts in a most dramatic vein:

> That nature in one way or the other does not care about anything is the true abyss. That only human beings care [...] is an unprecedented situation.
>
> *Jonas 2001: 229*

Since both technology and science fell into this abyss, they have become, in spite of their undeniable merits, a threat to nature – indeed to life as such.

As a soldier, Jonas knew no fear or anxiety. Even more so, his behaviour as activist and soldier exemplified a heroism that bordered on downright temerity. Already as a child he mused about 'well-muscled Judaism' and he decided to live this dream. But the philosopher in him, one has to say, was made of different stuff. Fear and anxiety played crucial roles in Jonas's books. Nowhere does this become clearer than in *Das Prinzip Verantwortung*, the book that is generally considered to be his most important, even though Jonas himself emphatically denied this. *The Imperative of Responsibility* (or *IR*) can be seen as a search for a different and new ethics, one that matches much better with the technological and scientific achievements of our time. Jonas would never be entirely sure about the results of his own quest. A year before he passed away – he was 88 years old – he would denounce certain tenets of *IR*. We have to ask ourselves why this might be the case.

## The imperative of responsibility

The general attack launched in the 1960s against the idea of a carefree and indifferent nature is continued in *IR*. Everything in the world, Jonas claims, has only one goal – it wants to continue its existence, it wants to survive. This holds not only for human animals, but also for non-human animals, and even for unanimated objects. A rock resists its own destruction, an animal does the same, and under normal conditions human beings do not act differently. In this sense, nothing and nobody is carefree or indifferent. Nothing can be fully indifferent towards its own being. This simple idea forms the basis of Jonas's entire ethical framework. He goes so far as to argue that the absence of indifference that beings have towards their own being is nothing else than *the* good. Our world, he adds, becomes completely incomprehensible if we cannot accept that animated *and* non-animated beings make a difference (see Brown, this volume). The claim of a being to exist is something that must convince all sensitive and moral creatures. They understand or sense that existence as such is vulnerable and that this is the single most important reason why it has value. To sense and to understand what this vulnerability means must stir up a sense of responsibility.

The age-old gap between fact and value, or between 'is' and 'ought', '*sein*' and '*sollen*', is jettisoned by Jonas. In his worldview, there is no room for a realm of value-free facts. Earth, he maintains, is not an object unable to provoke a moral response. Jonas resists what has been referred to as the 'instrumentalization' of our planet by means of technology and science.

The vulnerability of all entities – organic and inorganic, natural and artificial – is absolutely crucial for him (see Wright and Nyberg, this volume). This is why they need to be protected. This is also why his ideas became interesting for ecology movements all over the world, most notably the Green Party in Germany.

In fact, what he tries to do is to ground the domain of ethics in the domain of being, that is, in an ontology. He embarks on such a highly ambitious and disputable project basically because he does not want to propose an ethical system that stands accused of relativism. To embed his ethical system in ontology is, in other words, a way to provide it with a rational fundament. This is the critical point on which Jonas's moral philosophy hinges. Is an ontology that takes the vulnerability of all beings as an objective point of departure really convincing? Perhaps, one might argue, that Jonas's wish to immunize his ethical system against relativism and to provide it with a rational anchor has been too strong. He does not want the ethics he proposes to be left dangling in mid-air, but critics have argued that his ontological reflections amount to nothing other than the umpteenth appeal to right-minded people to change their way of thinking. But an appeal is not the same as a compelling argument. That he wasn't capable of offering something more compelling, especially not in *IR*, was precisely the reason why Jonas could never overcome the nagging doubts he had about his own ethics until his dying day. I will return to this point later.

Even more important than these musings about how to bridge the gap between ethics and ontology, however, is the insight that what is good in the world is not dependent on our will. As we already saw, good is what matters, what makes a difference, what cannot remain indifferent towards its own being. As such, it does not submit to *our* desire for the good. Jonas is adamant about this: what is solely the object of our will, he argues, must lack the authority of the good. That is to say, we do not determine when the vulnerability of human and non-human others makes a moral appeal to us. They can do that even when it is against our wishes. The good cannot coerce our will to see it as the most important thing in life, but it can make clear that there are obligations or imperatives that are more important than our wishes or desires. Under such circumstances, we might become aware of the fact that we owe something to what is good. This is precisely the moment when responsibility overwhelms us: we understand that the good is more important than our own wishes or desires. It is only this understanding that allows for a moral existence, a '*sittliches Sein*'. Morality always implies a certain selflessness.

The first paradox looming here is, of course, that doing the good can and perhaps should be at the expense of the self. This is a point that we will not easily encounter in Hellenistic or utilitarian ethics, let alone in the management ethics I briefly touched upon earlier, but again Jonas does not mince his words: the good is something that belongs to the world and not to ourselves. The second paradox looming here is that if you do good in such a way that it is not good for yourself, then you will inevitably get a different self, a different individuality or identity. Jonas's ethics is grounded in a belief that moral transformation is possible and necessary. But this transformation is definitely not related to certain personal goals that you may have set for yourself. On the contrary, morality requires that you are capable of abandoning such goals. It is not difficult to see how this idea can be seen as an *ex post facto* justification for the decision once made by Jonas to join the army. Such an act bespeaks precisely the selflessness that provides morality with a certain kind of heroism. This selflessness has another implication as well. Responsibility is not just about serving the world by abandoning your own interests. The very idea of giving up your interests is so important because it allows you to collaborate with others. Only a selfless morality can develop into a shared morality – and such a shared morality is indispensable in a world in which human beings are, by dint of technological developments, more than ever depending on each other. It is therefore not just about your own family, your own clan, or your own nation. Wherever you are, you will inevitably affect others and also those who do not belong to the narrow circle of people you know. When Jonas argued for his famous 'heuristics of fear', he not only argued for a moral restraint with respect to decisions of which we cannot foretell the consequences, but he also wanted us to develop a sense for what might occur to unknown others. Responsibility is not just about stakeholders we have identified. It is not about you and me. It is, in a veritable sense of the word, global.

Technology has created unknown possibilities for human beings. This state of affairs requires us to think about new sorts of responsibilities. The discussion should be about a responsibility that is not only global but also future-oriented, that does not expect any reciprocity and that plays a permanent role in our daily existence. This accent on permanence is based on the idea that survival is also a permanent affair. Jonas expresses the point as follows: whoever feels responsible cannot take a holiday. That is, whoever takes up responsibility cannot brush this aside, for example, when it is convenient. Permanent responsibility is, for Jonas, primarily related to conservation, protection or prevention and not to planning, excellence, formalism or perfection. In this sense, Jonas argues for a completely anti-utopian ethics, something that only becomes clear in the latter parts of *IR*. That such an ethics is not well received in management education should be clear by now.

How should we think of this permanent responsibility? Do we have examples? For Jonas, there are only two significant paradigms of responsibility: one is parental and the other is political. That he speaks about such a day-to-day affair as parental responsibility might come as a surprise after all the talk mentioned earlier about moral transformation, global thinking and heroism. Jonas, however, points out that in parental responsibility vulnerability becomes intertwined with an element that people often forget when discussing responsibility: power. Even though parents can never fully control their children, a point Jonas stresses over and over again, they do exert a certain influence on their offspring. The same holds, at least to a certain extent, for politicians. No matter how fragile it might be, it is precisely this power that makes parents or politicians responsible. Strictly speaking, we cannot assume responsibility when we lack power or influence. In other words, for Jonas, relations of responsibility are by definition asymmetrical.

All this is not to suggest that there are no differences between parental and political responsibility. The aim of parental care, if we are to believe Jonas, can only be a relatively autonomous and content human being. This implies that the child's 'natural' processes of development need to be accepted. These processes are absent in politics. When we talk about political development, we can only say that they can go in all sorts of directions. This is precisely what Jonas experienced throughout his life. There is no premeditated *telos* for political communities. Here, we see again how strongly he distanced himself from utopian design. Again, we emphasize that his ethics, also his political ethics, is all about protection and prevention and not in the least about perfection or excellence. Exactly for this reason, parental responsibility matters to him most. A newborn infant is morally appealing to us. The very fact of its existence creates a certain imperative. It is here that we finally see how the gap between 'is' and 'ought' is not so much bridged as rendered irrelevant. Earlier, we saw that our very survival is a central theme in Jonas's thought. Now, we see the full dimensions: survival is protection and preservation. Every parent knows exactly what this means – and what it does not mean. It does not mean, for example, that raising a child is to perfect him or her. These stunningly simple intuitions about responsibility are completely glossed over in management education. When it comes to managerial responsibility, it is generally preferred to beat about the bush.

Jonas's most famous gesture in *IR* is the formulation of a new categorical imperative that should apply in a global and technological world: 'Act so that the effects of your action are consistent with a continuing genuine life on earth' (Jonas 2011: 39). This in fact means that we should not act destructively for future generations *and* the totality of their life conditions. At face value, the way he phrases his categorical imperative might appear to be somewhat shallow. Indeed, no corporate advocate of an idea called 'sustainability' would have anything against this. Students of business administration meanwhile appear to have become familiar with these ideas. But do they really get the gist of it? At face value, it seems as if Jonas strongly relies on Kantian ethics. This ethics only applies to human beings and famously follows an inner logic that can be tested in specific cases. This is also why Kant has become palatable in management education. Popular questions such as 'are you allowed to indulge in white lies?' or 'should one blow the whistle under any circumstances?' are frequently discussed and students learn that Kantian answers to these questions will be different from utilitarian answers. Here, it is interesting to note that even though Jonas phrases his own version of the categorical imperative, he clearly does not concur with Kant when it comes to his emphasis on sensitivity or empathy. Kant routinely dismissed emotional elements as mere inclination ('*Neigung*'). His ethics is therefore more acceptable in a world where reason and logic are key virtues. Jonas is more difficult to accept. Earlier, we saw that the profundity of his effort to base ethics in an ontology can only be sensed if we think of how parents cherish their newborn child. They do not know yet how it will develop, but it is precisely this openness and ambiguity, or this indelible potentiality of a human life that we have to protect at all costs. The value of human existence does not lie in its perfection, but in the plethora of possibilities that it entails.

## Implications

Jonas provides the discussion with certain intuitions that are no doubt unsatisfactory for utilitarian or Kantian diehards in philosophy, science, politics, but also in management education. Like so many insights from the humanities, his ideas about responsibility cannot be accepted by the managerial world because they wager on something that business life cannot – and will not – always provide: protection and preservation. He is, as he himself once acknowledged, too much a thinker who is 'against the current' ('*gegen der Strom*'). But as precisely such a thinker, he has definitely incited interest, not so much in the managerial world, but in the world of ecology and ecosophy.

It is not difficult to see why. Many commentators have pointed out that Jonas's work has deep biological roots. This is not to say that he is a hard-boiled Darwinist or a reductionist like the English evolutionary biologist Richard Dawkins. However, when he speaks about the vulnerability of all things in the world, he assumes that such things, both living and non-living, are characterized by a striving, a kind of freedom, an inner force that philosophers have described as '*conatus*' (from the Latin *conatur* meaning to strive). In *Ethics*, Spinoza (2002: 236 or Part III, Prop. 6) wrote that '[e]ach thing, as far as it can by its own power, strives to persevere in its own being'. It is this will to persevere that unites all animate and non-animate things. Spinoza (2002: 224 or Part III, Preface) also writes that 'anything whatsoever, whether it be more perfect or less perfect, will always be able to persist in existing with that same force whereby it begins to exist, so that in this respect all things are equal'. In other words, there is continuity between humans and non-humans, between animate and non-animate things, between what people usually refer to as culture and nature. This continuity does not lie in the genes or in some other form of matter, but in the will of all things to persevere in their being. For both Spinoza and Jonas, this will to persevere is a virtue, also in the sense of power (*virtu*). It is also what gives life as such its dignity. This dignity resides not only in human beings, but in non-human beings and things as well. In fact, Jonas applies the Kantian concept of dignity to all living and non-living beings.

Only if we are willing to respect this dignity, will we be able to 'belong' to the world. The same holds for related ideas such as 'freedom' or 'autonomy': the will to persevere in being is a token of freedom and autonomy.

Jonas's philosophy is, like Spinoza's, monistic. At all costs, he tries to avoid dualist notions, which grant an exceptional place to the human being. Rather than locating humans outside the world of things, he argues that they belong to this world. Without such a belonging, that is, without such an embedment in the world, responsibility is simply impossible. For him, responsibility rises out of this feeling of belonging and it is exactly this feeling that makes responsibility something that is not the same as accountability.

These ideas resonate with some insights of philosophers who have argued for a new type of ecological awareness. The claim that responsibility can only originate in a feeling of embedment implies, for example, that we do not have to see human beings as mere animals or, worse, as things – but that we have to treat animals and things as human beings. The British philosopher Timothy Morton (2008: 77) boldly claims that all living creatures are people: 'There is no nature, only people, some of whom are human beings.' Morton bases his claim on ideas developed by French philosophers, such as Nancy, Blanchot or Derrida, who coined the concept of 'singularity' in order to express the fact that with animals one can have feelings of intimacy. Such feelings of intimacy are what counts, not a mystic feeling of being one with nature, let alone the idea that we only need to take care of our social embedment, that is to say, our relations to other human beings.

But will intimacy and a sense of belonging do the job? To an average parent, an animal is, after all, not the same as their progeny. Morton is well aware of the difficulties involved. He does not opt for sentimental or romantic relationships with the world. Our subjectivity, after all, cannot be denied. Even though we are interconnected and embedded in the world around us, we would be very naïve if we assume that this is all good and great fun. To be interconnected, Morton (2008: 92) argues, is often not pleasurable at all. As long as we eat fish, we will find traces of the sea's plastic in our bodies. As long as we purchase teabags or T-shirts, we will be profoundly related to the people working on the slopes of the Himalayas who get the raw materials for us. Interconnection is not nice. What we used to refer to as nature is not somewhere out there; it is in us, it interferes in our lives and it does so in ways that are not romantic. Jute, plastic, fish or anything else that seems not us is difficult and is asking obnoxious questions, questions that we are all – not only in management education – only too keen to dodge. It is one thing to call for a community with things that we have hardly anything in common with; it is a very different thing to wring out of all these ideas a remotely meaningful concept of responsibility.

Jonas's unrest about his own ideas about responsibility is an important reminder here. I think that Morton is also a thinker struggling with responsibility. Not too long ago, he produced an article in which he boldly claims that the age of agriculture is 'responsible' for a kind of thinking that has reigned supreme for thousands of years (Morton 2012: 17). Why? Agriculture has changed the landscape in 'domination-ready chunks of parceled out space waiting to be filled and ploughed by humans' (Morton 2012: 16). The very idea of ploughing is violent. Morton does not use the word 'violence', but prefers words such as 'uncanny' or '*unheimlich*'. We do not know exactly what farmers throughout the ages have done, but somehow their work is so gruesome and spine chilling that we are hardly willing to think of it. In fact, agriculture stands accused of fostering 'a metaphysics of presence'. I will not enter into what this means here, but it is enough to point out that farming is deemed responsible for a wrong way of thinking.

However, in a later publication, Morton (2013: 141) points out that we no longer live in a transparent world where ethical courses of action are relatively straightforward. When we talk about global warming, radioactivity or the problems of extinction, we find ourselves in constantly shifting positions or in what he refers to as 'zones', where events are already happening and where the Kantian appeal to autonomous reflection on ethical decisions simply cannot be upheld. He is right in this, no doubt. Ecological issues tend to overwhelm us and are rendering every firm ethical position groundless or, as Morton himself argues, 'weak'. This weakness, we may infer, does not resonate at all with the kind of heroism to which Jonas emphatically appealed. It is difficult to see how under these circumstances we ourselves should maintain a strong sense of responsibility. Throughout the history of mankind, farmers did what they did and were not thinking at all about 'wrong ways of thinking'. In some sense, our situation has not changed at all. In a zone, we are not capable of providing the right response and this clearly erodes the idea of what responsibility might mean to us.

Yes, the example provided by Jonas is as clear as it is simple – the mother who is taking responsibility of her newborn baby – but responsibility becomes much more difficult when it comes to ecological problems. The big companies in the world, Morton points out, can easily maintain that hydrocarbons do not really damage the world or at least that there is no scientific proof for this, but the point is that there are so many data for or against the claim that these things do harm the world that any ethical decision made here 'feels like an uncanny leap into the void' (Morton 2013: 183). Under these circumstances, the meaning of the concept of responsibility will shift significantly: it is not me who is responsible for all the wrongs in the world; it is a collective called mankind. Morton writes:

> And we know that we are responsible simply because we can understand what global warming is. We don't really need reasons – reasons inhibit our responsible action, or seriously delay it. No neonatal or prenatal infant is responsible for her mother's toxic body. Yet, that is the situation we find ourselves in . . .
>
> *Morton 2013: 183*

Here, we see the kind of tinkering to which the concept of responsibility is frequently exposed: no single individual is responsible but all of us are. I suggest that this is precisely what troubled Jonas so much and this is why he made a moral appeal to all of us. If we replace the idea of individual responsibility with some sort of collective responsibility, we lack a perspective on action. Or to put it more succinctly: shared responsibility cannot be a responsibility. I am alone in my responsibility.

But perhaps thinkers like Morton would argue that the proclivity to put ideas into action is wrong. Perhaps, we should merely think differently. Old ways of thinking are no longer acceptable in a world that has changed. Before we turn to action, it might be better to rethink and ruminate on our embeddedness in the world (see Costea and Amiridis, this volume). This position has been referred to, not without some underlying tone of irony, as 'an ethics of resilience'. David Chandler (2013: 176) refers to this ethics as follows:

> In a world of complexity, ethical responsibility tends to be reformulated to take account of the fact that the consequences of our actions are dependent upon the socio-material processes into which they are inserted. The field of ethical and political responsibility is therefore defined less by our personal or our public choices and more by our embeddedness in emergent chains of causality. In a global relational ontology, our ethical responsibilities stem from the unintended consequences of our relational embeddedness and our ethical duty to become reflexively awareness of this.

So, ethics can no longer be based on rather haughty ideas about freedom or autonomy, let alone on the superiority of Christian faith or Western institutions, such as the market or the state.

The only thing left for responsible people to do is to muse about their embeddedness in the world and then to become reflexively more and more aware about what is going on around them and what that might mean for them. What it might mean is indeed a glimmering understanding of how our pride has been wounded in the past couple of centuries. We do not hold a special place in the universe, we do not differ very clearly from non-human animals – we are in fact things (for example, gene pools). The problem so far is that we have not adjusted our ethics to this state of affairs. It is therefore time that we humbly accept, for moral reasons, that in the ontologies of the world we do not hold a special place.

This position is definitely not, I assume, what Jonas had in mind, but it is a position that his fans might find increasingly difficult to avoid. Jonas believed that dignity could be found everywhere. For him, it was not so much a matter of degrading the human animal, but of uplifting everything that is not human. And he makes an appeal to us as individuals. It is our sense of belonging that, for Jonas, opened up the possibility of responsibility. But we have seen that Jonas kept harbouring nagging doubts about his position. In the end, the question that haunts the complex problems of our age is as straightforward as it is difficult: is it still possible to maintain a meaningful sense of responsibility?

Take, for example, Jane Bennett, an American philosopher. She argues that it is often very difficult 'to grasp just what the sources of agency are that make a particular event happen' (Marres cited in Bennett 2010: 36). It is generally not a single person who can be held responsible for global warming, extinction or relentless carbon emissions. No, we read that the 'locus of political responsibility is a human–nonhuman assemblage'. It is the 'confederations of tools, microbes, minerals, sounds, and "other" foreign materialities' that contribute to a certain state of affairs (Marres cited in Bennett 2010: 36). The idea of assemblage is derived from Deleuze and Guattari who, according to Bennett, have introduced the concept (the French equivalent for 'assemblage' is '*agencement*') in order to express a weaker kind of agency or autonomy than the traditional ones we find in theology, deontology or existentialism. Human beings, we read, are not special, ontologically or ethically. One interesting effect of the age of assemblages is that the moral blaming game is over. We see Bennett (2010: 37) quoting a group of directors belonging to FirstEnergy, an Ohio-based energy corporation: '*[No] one is really to blame*' (Bennett 2010:37, emphasis added), and with this, Bennett finds herself not in a disagreement:

> Though it is unlikely that energy traders shared my vital materialism [the kind of philosophical thinking Bennett is defending, RtB], I, too, find it hard to assign the strongest or most punitive version of moral responsibility to them. Autonomy and strong responsibility seem to me to be empirically false.
>
> *Bennett 2010: 37*

To be sure, Bennett understands that individuals are 'simply incapable of bearing full responsibility for their effects' (Bennett 2010: 37). She is not a cynic, nor is she stupid – and she is definitely correct when she argues for a subtler form of moral reasoning. But it is quite baffling that in the end her position is the same as the managerial position I alluded to earlier when I said that the very point of management ethics is that the idea of responsibility should evaporate. This is a position I do not believe that Bennett really wants, and yet it seems to me that she provided the best licence possible to managers who want to dodge responsibility. Somehow, I think that these ideas would find a warm welcome in the business schools of our world.

The very point of Jonas's idea of responsibility is exactly that one might endorse it in spite of its blatant absurdity, against the odds, against the current. That is what philosophy – as one of the humanities – can do for management education: to remind us that 'management' is not the only way of thinking about the world and our actions within it. There are sound philosophical reasons for jettisoning the idea of responsibility, as Jonas himself was very well aware, but the vulnerability of things, non-human animals and human animals prevented him from doing so. There are no ethics without jumping into the void.

## Note

1 I have used the Dutch translation of the original German version: Jonas 2012. The translation of this book was undertaken by my sister Ingrid ten Bos. For this translation, I wrote a critical introduction: ten Bos 2012. Parts of the present chapter are derived from this introduction. The original German version is: Jonas 1979. There is also an English translation: Jonas 1984.

## References


Bennett, J. (2010) *Vibrant Matter. A Political Ecology of Things*. Durham, NC: Duke University Press.

Chandler, D. (2013) 'Resilience ethics: responsibility and the globally embedded subject', *Ethics & Global Politics*, 6(3), 175–94.

Corlett, A. (2005) 'Collective responsibility'. *In:* P. Werhane and E. Freeman (eds.) *Business Ethics. The Blackwell Encyclopedia of Management*. Vol. II. Oxford: Blackwell, pp. 85–9.

Jackall, R. (1989) *Moral Mazes. The World of Corporate Managers*. New York, NY: Oxford University Press.

Jackall, R. (2005) 'Moral mazes'. *In:* P. Werhane and E. Freeman (eds.) *Business Ethics. The Blackwell Encyclopedia of Management*. Vol. II. Oxford: Blackwell, pp. 359–60.

Jonas, H. (1979) *Das Prinzip Verantwortung: Versuch einer Ethik für die technologische Zivilisation*. Frankfurt, Germany: Suhrkamp.

Jonas, H. (1984) *The Imperative of Responsibility: In Search of an Ethics for the Technological Age*. Chicago, IL: University of Chicago Press.

Jonas, H. (2001) *The Phenomenon of Life. Towards a Philosophical Biology*. Evanston, IL: Northwestern University Press.

Jonas, H. (2012) *Het Principe Verantwoordelijkheid. Onderzoek naar een Ethiek voor de Technologische Civilisatie*. Utrecht, The Netherlands: IJzer.

Mintzberg, H. (2004) *Managers Not MBAs. A Hard Look at the Soft Practice of Managing and Management Development*. London: Prentice Hall.

Morton, T. (2008) 'Ecologocentrism: unworking animals', *Substance*, 37(3), 73–96.

Morton, T. (2012) 'The Oedipal logic of ecological awareness', *Environmental Humanities*, 1, 7–21.

Morton, T. (2013) *Hyperobjects. Philosophy and Ecology after the End of the World*. Minneapolis, MN: University of Minnesota Press.

Spinoza (2002) *Ethica*. Amsterdam: Prometheus/Bert Bakker.

ten Bos, R. (2012) 'Inleiding'. *In:* H. Jonas (ed.) *Het Principe Verantwoordelijkheid. Onderzoek naar een Ethiek voor de Technologische Civilisatie*, pp. 9–15.

# 11

# They have escaped the weight of darkness

## The problem space of Michel Serres

*Steven D. Brown*

### Production has come to an end

The final scene in Béla Tarr's *Werckmeister Harmonies* is a single uninterrupted shot following the character György Eszter into the main square of the small Hungarian town where he lives. The square is oddly calm after the riots and chaos of the previous evening. Debris lies everywhere. At its centre is the colossal body of a whale, perched in the broken shell of the circus truck that brought it into the town the day before. Eszter slowly approaches the rotting body and gazes into its milky, decaying eye. We recall the words he has previously spoken to Valuska: 'Nem számít semmi. Semmi nem számít' ('Nothing counts. Nothing counts at all').

Tarr's film echoes the apocalyptic tone of the novel on which it is based, Lázló Krasznahorkai's *The Melancholy of Resistance* (1998 [1989]). The novel depicts a world that is quite literally sinking into its own pollution. Refuse lies compacted on the streets of the town. Public services and transport are erratic and appear improvised. An old tree has been mysteriously uprooted overnight, as though it has clawed itself out of the ground in order to die. Even the weather seems to have come to a halt. As Mr Eszter tells Valuska, 'No more snow. Snow production has come to an end' (see also Hjorth and Holt, this volume, on another film by Tarr). Into this gradual winding-down of rural life comes a travelling circus, promising to display 'an extraordinary spectacle' – what it claims is 'the biggest whale in the world'. The circus attracts followers – outsiders – who gradually fill up the main square, waiting for a sign. When it comes, they unleash a torrent of violence that overwhelms the entire town.

These are end-times – but also opportunities. In the shadow of the impending dissolution of the town, the three central characters pursue different paths. Tünde Eszter, the embittered President of the Women's Committee, interprets this strange conjunction of signs as indicating the moment when her long nurtured plans to seize power can be enacted, and in so doing she can take revenge upon her estranged husband. For his part, György Eszter seeks only to detach himself further from civic and personal life, to withdraw as far as possible into near solitude. Finally, there is János Valuska who despite his disconnected and shambolic appearance feels no separation between himself and his environment, and is compelled to pace the town at all hours, visiting all its points. Both film and novel end in the same way. A military takeover of the town secures Tünde Eszter's position. György Eszter submits himself to his wife's machinations, unable to see any alternative. Valuska is committed to a psychiatric hospital. The whale lies abandoned to rot.

## Thinking the apocalypse

Throughout the sixty or so books he has written since 1968, Michel Serres has articulated a uniquely non-hierarchical view of knowledge. Serres demonstrates a lateral approach of travelling between practices, of translating across languages and sense making. Knowledge is treated as a patchwork, a scattered collection of pockets of order and sense that emerges from the noise of the world. There can be no formal hierarchy within epistemology outside of strategies of violence or hygiene. Knowledge is rooted in the local, in bodies and practices and their encounters with one another.

Born the son of a bargeman on the Garonne River, and having served for a time in the French maritime service, Serres has regularly claimed that his early years of sailing underpin his notion of 'voyaging' between bodies of thought. He famously once likened the epistemic gap between the human and the natural science to the Northwest Passage, which connects the Pacific and Atlantic Oceans (Serres 1980). Navigating this passage requires considerably more than just a good map. It is an unpredictable 'adventure', wherein all of the embodied skills and know-how of the voyager will be put to the test, and the ultimate goal is uncertain (see Serres and Latour 1995 [1990]). Things do not always turn out well, hence the recurring theme of catastrophe in his work, which often takes the form of reference to being trapped aboard a sinking ship (notably Serres 2008 [1985]: 17–21). However, Serres suggests that it is through these most difficult of experiences that we arrive at novel personal and metaphysical disclosures.

The literary scholar Steven Connor (2005) has noted the importance of the thematic of the 'hard' and the 'soft' across Serres's work. This can used to appreciate something of his intellectual trajectory over the past forty years. His early studies are concerned primarily with translations between the exact sciences (that is, physics, mathematics) and philosophy and culture (that is, literature, art, myth), where this is understood in terms of transformations in the movement of ideas. These early works are fairly tough going for readers who lack the encyclopaedic turn of mind that Serres celebrates. Things become a little easier in relation to his work from the 1980s, which abandons extended exegesis in favour of a more poetic and often autobiographical style of exploring ideas. This culminates in *Angels: A Modern Myth* (1995 [1993]) and *Variations on the Body* (2011 [1999]), both resembling art catalogues in their structure. His millennial work has more or less abandoned formal referencing in book-length extended essays written in an accessible style resembling the extemporaneous and bearing the mark of his public lecturing and broadcasting. *Thumbelina* (2015 [2012]), for example, reads like a series of blog posts – precisely the media of thought that forms the intellectual object of concern in the book.

But at the same time, there is also a progressive hardening of intent. One finds little of the spirit of '68 across the early *Hermes* books, which feel quite disconnected from the social and political conditions under which they were written (1969–80). But from 1980 onwards, Serres became focused on the notion of the foundations of social order in violence – announced by Serres, referring to *The Parasite* (1982 [1980]) as 'the book of evil' and *Rome* (1991 [1983]) as 'the book of foundations'. The terms henceforth become synonymous in his work. *The Natural Contract* (1995 [1990]) raises the stakes higher still. Using the pivotal example of Goya's painting 'Fight with cudgels', Serres argues that whilst we are busy killing one another in the name of a better world, we have failed to take into account that the Earth is a third party to these battles. From this point on, the urgency of thinking on the ecological becomes central to Serres's work, arriving at his recent statement *Biogea* (2012 [2010]). In this work, Serres meditates on the urgent philosophical–practical tasks that accompany the human transition from the Holocene (11,700 BP to the present) to the present Anthropocene, the period where humanity has accomplished more or less complete power, as a species, over the environment. But that power comes without control. The environment, compromised by human activity, perhaps fatally, is responding in ways that will require colossal adaptation if we are to survive (see Wright and Nyberg, this volume). As Serres once put it, if the Ancients distinguished between things that depend on us and those that do not depend on us, then the current situation is one where it no longer depends upon us that *everything* depends upon us (see Serres and Latour 1995 [1990]).

The thematic of the hard and the soft can be complemented by a second relationship between the 'apocalyptic' and the 'ecstatic' that runs throughout Serres's work. The systematic and structural push towards violence is a recurrent motif for Serres. This is summed up in his invocation of the Roman Cult of Diana at Nemi in *Detachment* (1989 [1983]).[1] Legend tells of how a warrior-priest protects the shrine of a sacred tree in the woods above the town. Whoever seeks to control the shrine must first kill the current guardian. But in doing so, the burden – and inevitable fate – passes to the newcomer. The lesson Serres draws from this is that power depends upon and begets violence and murder. His Foundations Trilogy (*Rome* 1991 [1983]; *Statues* 2014 [1987]; *Les Origines de la Géométrie* 1993) develops this further into an account of the mythical foundations of human relations in ritualized violence and sacrifice. Serres argues that technoscientific cultures inherit and accelerate this tendency to found order through death, with the stakes played out around Hiroshima and weapons of mass destruction demonstrating the ultimate horizon.[2] This raises the question of how it is possible to find a space of liberty for non-proprietorial living when all the positions are already colonized by the logic of violent appropriation.

From the beginning of his work, Serres already knew that the search for space was a matter not simply of finding uncolonized territory, but rather of seeking out new relationships to space. The demi-god Hermes, who presides over five early works (*La Communication*; *L'Interférence*; *La Traduction*; *La Distribution*, *Le Passage du Nord-Ouest*), invents new means of transport and communication (along with music and trade). Hermes can pass outside of existing networks and nodes, to find and exploit unexpected relations and points of contact. He is the living embodiment of the ecstatic – literally outwith (ex-) place (stasis). This allows Serres to read across the history of science and technology, and to identify places of unexpected passage, such as between the development of thermodynamic principles and the art of J. M. W. Turner, or between the cybernetic reformulation of the body and the Freudian unconscious (see Serres 1982). The enthusiasm for information technology expressed in Serres's later work (which led him to appear as a media advocate for telecommunications companies), can be understood as a search for the ecstatic, for new modes of movement and hence an evasion of the inherent violence of human relations under the ever-present shadow of apocalypse. In his current work, the figure of 'the bomb' is replaced with the 'pollution' pumped out by a mass of humanity bearing down upon the world with seeming little sense of the short- and long-term consequences. Discovering new means of communicating with the planet itself is the most urgent task.

In this chapter, I will explore the relevance of thinking the hard and the soft, the apocalyptic and the ecstatic, for management education. The pedagogic value of Serres's programme of 'voyaging' has been much explored (for example, Steyaert 2014) and, more generally, enthusiasm has been widely expressed for Serres's classicism and willingness to overcome disciplinary divisions (for example, Abbas 2005; Paulson 1997). However, it seems to me that the lasting message of Serres's work is to be found in the tension between the two statements 'time is running out' and 'nothing new under the sun'. On the one hand, we live in uncertain times where the disconnection of the global financial system from the greater part of humanity and the ravaged planet on which we subsist is as breathtaking as it is ultimately fatal. As Serres notes in *The Natural Contract* (1995 [1990]), sailing lore has it that one should piss from the side of a ship in order not to pollute the vessel. But that option does not exist at a planetary scale. On the other hand, the coming financial, social and ecological catastrophes need not paralyse our thinking.

There are resources within ancient history, myth and philosophy, Serres suggests, that can inform and enrich our efforts to find a way through these times of perpetual crisis. As I will go on to argue, management education needs to be imbued with the paradoxical character of being both firmly forward looking (for example, beyond existing epistemic and political divisions) and simultaneously intensely backward looking (for example, to ancient questions of property and foundation).

In the following sections, I first of all attempt to situate Serres's work in relation to contemporary social science, in order to highlight the problems faced around working philosophical issues into curriculum delivery. I then map out the scope of the problem space that Serres offers, before proceeding to sketch out three routes through that space and their relevance for management knowledge. Finally, I end with some reflections on the practicalities of thinking with Serres.

## The scribblers of social science

There are numerous ways of delivering philosophy within management education and many of the best contemporary practitioners of this dark art are contributors to this volume. Many would, I hope, agree that the strategies for delivering philosophy to management students are limited and difficult. It is possible to imagine offering a whole course on philosophy within a management programme.[3] But there are numerous barriers, from the pressure on space within the curriculum arising from the need to comply with accreditation bodies, through to difficulties in persuading management students of the value 'liberal education', especially when international students constitute either a significant part or the majority of the class.[4] The alternative is to do philosophy by stealth, embedding it across the entire curriculum in the form of conceptual discussions of first principles or ontological presuppositions for the topic in hand. This approach derives from the well-known 1980s 'paradigm' debates within organization theory (see Burrell and Morgan 1979).

The success of this latter approach depends upon being able to convince students that the roots for a workable programme for social science can be surfaced from a given philosopher's work. In the case of Serres, however, this is somewhat hampered by the outright antagonism he displays to the very idea of social science in general (let alone business and management studies). *Malfeasance* contains a disparaging example of 'some scribbler of a social science dissertation' (2011 [2008]: 65) who considers studying dirt. Since the immediately preceding example concerns a 'Peeping Tom' who maps the 'ejaculatory stains on a sheet' (2011 [2008]: 65), Serres's general view of the standing of social scientists is pretty clear here. What makes this all the more puzzling is the emphasis on the comparative that runs through books such as *Rome* or *Statues*. For example, George Dumézil's studies of religion (for example, *The Destiny of a King* 1988 [1971]), which extract grand structural relations organized around the figures of Jupiter (religion), Mars (war) and Quirinus (commerce), are a major touchstone for Serres. But the works of, say, Claude Lévi-Strauss or Gregory Bateson are entirely absent, despite their obvious resonance with Serres's concerns around patterns and connections within the social fabric. Most baffling of all is the lack of reference (to my knowledge) to Mary Douglas (1985), despite Serres continuously revisiting the problem of 'dirt' in relation to the founding of belief systems.

When pressed on this lack of engagement, such as in the dialogues with Latour (Serres and Latour 1995), Serres has presented himself as one of the few 'true structuralists'. What he means by this is taking the principles of set theory and the algebraic topology as guides for speculative investigations of human relations rather than positing abstract structural laws and axioms. Take, for instance, his early essay 'The Wolf's Game'[5] (see Serres 1982). This piece describes La Fontaine's fable of the wolf and the lamb in terms of algebraic ordering relations that constitute a directional flow. Serres argues that the logic of pushing one's opponent into a relation that is 'upstream' whilst simultaneously positioning oneself 'downstream' creates the most powerful position. He then extrapolates towards a discussion of Cartesian reason and the birth of modern science, ending with the portentous phrase 'Western man is a wolf of science' (Serres 1982: 28). In this piece, we see one of the sources of the generalized model of parasitism that becomes central to Serres's approach to relationality from *The Parasite* onwards.

In effect, Serres's move is to create a space that looks remarkably like social science through bypassing the existing traditions of scholarship in the area altogether to create an alternative passageway from the exact sciences to the humanities.[6] His work then resembles a ghostly doppelganger that is at once oddly familiar to social scientists and utterly alien. This can be clearly seen in the uptake of Serres's work in Actor–Network Theory (ANT). Michel Callon's (1980) formulation of translation explicitly marks its debt to Serres, and in particular to the essay 'Betrayal: the thanatocracy' from *Hermes III* (Serres 1974). What Callon does in his piece is to begin to develop his hugely influential model of how rival material semiotic orders become held together in networks (see Callon 1986 for the best initial formalization). Specifically, in this case, how different versions of what constituted an electric car were temporarily made to cohere by Renault and other stakeholders for the duration of an ultimately failed project. Callon's work addresses the problem within the sociology of scientific knowledge of rethinking the nature of 'interests', which acquire a socio-material rather than ideological character in ANT. But what Serres is up to in his piece is both vastly different in scope and tone, and yet strangely similar. He argues that the history of science has rendered itself unworkable because its own historicity is effaced as it seeks to translate the energies of the world into networks. This question, for Serres, is one of the dramatic changes of scale involved. For science to proclaim itself master of nature required a colossal series of conversions, transformations and ruses (hence 'betrayal'), the consequences of which are found in the violence of Hiroshima.

Bruno Latour's engagement with Serres follows similar lines. In his extraordinary 'infra-history' of the relationship between people and things, Latour (1994) draws upon Serres's (2014 [1987]) notion of 'pragmatogony' to describe a genealogy of the various forms of social/political ecology that have emerged as artefacts have mediated and reshaped human relations. The key idea of the exchange of properties between people and things, through translation, has become central to the 'material turn' in the kind of social science that ANT has helped to inaugurate. However, in Serres's work the recognition of our status as subjects through encounters with objects carries with it considerable risk. In *The Natural Contract* (1995 [1990]), Serres recalls the etymology of subject in Latin – *sub* (under) *jacere* (throw). The subject is thrown under, or cast before, the object, exposed to its material affordances and valences upon which she or he subsequently comes to depend. This line of argument is developed in Serres's writing on quasi-objects/quasi-subjects. In the game of rugby, for example, the status and fate of each player – as hero or villain, victor or vanquished – depends upon how they are positioned in relation to the ball (see Serres 1982 [1980]). In a sense, it is the ball that 'decides', in the old meaning of the word to make a path or make a cut. Our standing as subjects is fatally linked to the movement of objects.

## Serres's problem space

Serres's influence on contemporary social science has been, in a manner of speaking, 'methodological'. It is his procedures for working with diverse materials that have been appropriated rather than the broader metaphysical and ethical arguments that serve as their underpinnings. But it is precisely this dark core to Serres's work that speaks to the difficulties of teaching would-be 'Masters' of the modern business world. For example, in *The Parasite* (1982 [1980]),

Serres argues that appropriation – taking without giving – is at the origins of human relations. He models this as a series of interceptions where production is interrupted and redirected, using the fable of the town rat and the country rat as example. From a Marxist perspective, what Serres has to say merely repeats, in a different language, the process of the real subsumption of labour within capital. Everything becomes exchange-value. One could imagine using this point as a jumping off point to a discussion of 'cultural economy' or something similar.

However, what Serres proceeds to do is to push parasitism back beyond production itself. For Serres, agriculture is a kind of parasitism because it is redirecting the energies of nature; it is a form of appropriation, albeit one that humanity has practised since Neolithic times. If production is parasitic, then it follows that before use-value there is 'abuse value'. This is the outcome of applying thermodynamics to political economy:

> Life works; life is work, energy, power, information. It is impossible to translate this description into an ethical discourse. It is thus, it must be thus; I really don't know. The work of life is labour and order but does not occur without borrowing from elsewhere. It makes order here but undoes order there. And it reinforces disorder and noise . . . One parasite chases out the other, as one disorder chases out the other.
>
> *Serres 1982[1980]: 88*

What is at once both fascinating and terrifying about this argument is that it immediately problematizes the idea of a space outside of violence in which to ground some form of ethics. Life itself has a parasitic dimension. Order is created and sustained by interrupting and 'chasing out' prior forms of order. An ethical discourse cannot rely upon some unspecified 'otherness' or supplementary site for its salvation because all the possible positions are already occupied. Which is to say that a business ethics informed by, say, Derrida or Levinas would be of little use. There is no space outside the boat to piss into.

This relentless line of argument is applied in Serres's recent work on the financial crisis. *Times of Crisis* (2014 [2009]) has a rather cheeky subtitle appended to the English translation – 'What the financial crisis revealed and how to reinvent our lives and future'.[7] The reader who takes this to mean that an analysis is to follow of modern financial systems and their manifold failings will be bitterly disappointed. Serres's opening gambit is to confirm what we all know about this least opaque event in recent history: 'I simply think there is a gap between the numbers reached in the volatile stock market casinos and the weightier and slower reality of labour and goods' (2014 [2009]: 1). He then likens the relationship between the 1 per cent and 99 per cent as akin to that between gods and mortals in Greek or Roman culture. But this particular gap, the scale of monetary values, is simply a point of departure. There are numerous measures related to recent human activity that reflect similarly astronomical leaps in scale, such as demographics, health, transportation and media connectivity. Serres argues that taken together, these runaway measures reflect a fissure, a tectonic movement in human history or 'hominization'.

Hominization can, for Serres, be understood in terms of a transformation in the nature of appropriation. Modern forms of appropriation – with the financial crisis being the apotheosis – are rooted in 'natural' acts of territorialization (Serres 2011 [2008]). Dogs mark the boundaries of their respective territories with urine, placing chemical signs to one another. Urine and excrement are dirt, but rather than being 'matter out of place', as Mary Douglas argued, this kind of dirt is a marker of place. It indicates that space is now owned. Conversely, the 'clean' designates that which is provisionally not-yet-owned or temporarily unmarked space (hence, Serres argues, the obsession with white sheets in hotels, inviting the guest to mark it out with their own filth). The dirt of others is disgusting, but our own dirt feels very different. It grounds us in place and hence accords identity. Consider, for example, Tracey Emin's infamous artwork, *My Bed*, consisting of an unkempt bed with soiled sheets, strewn with menstrual blood-stained knickers and condoms. For the viewer, the piece has a 'hard' exterior – it is challenging to look at it too closely – but for the implied subject of the artwork, it has a 'soft' interior, it is an inhabited space that marks out the subjectivity of its user/creator. Dirt is pollution for those outside the territory, and a boundary marker for those within who appropriate it through their acts of soiling. In this way it has both a material 'hard' dimension and a 'soft' symbolic status:

> Let us define two things and clearly distinguish them from one another: first the hard, and second the soft. By the first I mean on the one hand solid residues, liquids, and gases, emitted throughout the atmosphere by big industrial companies or gigantic garbage dumps, the shameful signature of big cities. By the second, tsunamis of writing, signs, images, and logos flooding rural, civic, public and natural spaces as well as landscapes with their advertising. Even though different in terms of energy, garbage and marks nevertheless result from the same soiling gesture, from the same intention to appropriate, and are of animal origin.
>
> *Serres, 2011 [2008]: 41*

Pollution is not a by-product, or an unintended consequence of social and business activity. It is the deliberate marking, occupying and appropriating of space. We need to advise our business ethics students to start their deliberations from this point. The spread of 'hard pollution', as humans seek to mark out the entire planet as their property, is the obvious cause of environmental damage. Hard pollution shows the 'weight' of humanity on the Earth, the way in which humans have become a collective 'global subject' (Serres 1995 [1990]). But 'soft pollution' in the form of the vast proliferation of textual and visual markers is no less problematic. It clearly states that there are no longer any unmarked spaces – everything is property:

> (N)ature is perishing under 'culture'. In the first deluge, on which Noah floated, culture disappeared beneath nature. In this final flood, the reverse of the first one, will there be a single dense point left where a work of art can be found, one last diamond dense with meaning? Who doesn't see that the only thing left floating will be the homogeneous excrement of the victorious Great Owner, Sapiens sapiens?
>
> *Serres 2011 [2008]: 70*

The disappearance of nature under the deluge of culture is the final act in several centuries of ecstatic 'objectivizing', driven by the so-called hard sciences that render the world into 'passive and submissive object, reduced to a few dimensions of space, time, mass, energy and power' (Serres 2012 [2010]: 33) and completed by the soft sciences of management, marketing and finance. What the financial crisis reveals, for Serres, is that finally we are masters of the planet, no longer reliant upon a mystical dependence on the old gods of earth and sky. Our modern science is able to produce 'world objects' that possess 'a dimension commensurable with one of the world's dimensions' (Serres 2011 [2008]: 53). For example, a satellite turns at the speed of the moon; human-made radioactive waste has a lifespan closer to that of the Earth than to that of any given human; financial markets trade sums of money greater than the GDP of most nations. Serres coins the phrase 'hominiscence' to name the kind of creature we have become as we arrive at complete appropriation of the entire planet (that is, from the Holocene to the Anthropocene). Humanity is the most successful parasite of any invasive species although, as Serres (2012 [2010]) notes, our success may simply be the 'disembarkation' point for other more nimbler parasites, such as viruses.

But at the very moment that the world becomes a 'trash-can Earth' of objects to be consumed and disposed, something new happens. For Serres, climate change in all its myriad forms – rising temperatures, 'peak soil', water crises, increased 'natural' catastrophes – are utterances, forms of speech through which the Earth is addressing us directly, and yet we no longer have the means to understand this speech. The ancients subjectified the Earth through symbolic transformation (for example, Neptune came to embody storms at sea, Vulcan's hammering tamed the unpredictability of earthquakes). This transformation allowed recognition of there being actors outside human relations – third parties – whose speech and actions needed to be taken into account. Our survival henceforth depends, once again, upon developing the means to hear and interpret this speech:

> The game with two players that fascinates the masses and opposes only humans, the Master against the Slave, the left versus the right, Republicans against Democrats, this ideology against the one, the greens versus the blues . . . this game begins to disappear when a third party intervenes. And what a third party! The world itself. Here, quicksand, tomorrow the climate. This is what I call 'Biogea', an archaic and new country, inert and alive, water, air, fire, the earth, the flora and fauna and all living species. The game with two players is over and we start a game with three. This is the contemporary global situation.
>
> *Serres 2014 [2009]: 31*

The idea of humanity as a global subject gained its modern form many years ago, when Hobbes and Rousseau set out that only a compact between humans, a social contract that elevated individuals to be so many parts of a single actor, could ward off the war of all-against-all. A third party to our disputes now emerges, which Serres names Biogea (from *bio* 'life' and *gea* 'earth'). The question is not whether we ought to recognize this third party because as a global subject 'the world objectivises us' as it 'falls on our heads and becomes the formidable residual reality that keeps us alive, transcends us and can eradicate us' (Serres 2014 [2009]: 48). Instead, we need to open up a negotiation with this new global subject, Biogea, to find the legal and political means – in effect broker a *natural contract* to be woven into our existing sense of the social contract (Serres 1995 [1990]) – whilst dialogue is still possible.

## The social science of thirdness

In the early 1990s, Serres wrote an influential text, *The Third-Instructed* (1997 [1991][8]), which argued that learning begins when we recognize an intermediate space between two apparent sides. The term 'instructed' is important here because it deliberately echoes Gaston Bachelard's (1986 [1934]) argument for a hierarchy of knowledge, with physics placed at the top, where each discipline needs to take 'instruction' – that is, model its own practices and methods of deliberation – from those higher up. Bachelard's argument was underpinned by the widely shared view in the early twentieth century that only physics, which had reformulated its fundamental terms of reference several times, could lay claim to being a genuinely 'revolutionary' science. From his very earliest work, Serres has rejected this notion of a hierarchy in knowledge, and indeed the concomitant Bachelardian idea of progress through 'ruptures' or 'breaks'. To say that instead we must take our instruction from the spaces between, from 'thirdness' (see Steyaert, Hoyer and Resch, this volume) is, in effect, to argue for multiplicity, mixture and the as-yet-unappropriated.

This kind of thinking chimes well with what we might call a 'soft' form of interdisciplinarity, which sees the expansion of the intellectual palette around problem definition as an unalloyed good. But consider again that word 'instruction'. Serres is not simply recommending that good pedagogy should embed alternative approaches. He is demanding that we place ourselves under the direction of thirdness, of a continuous disciplining of thinking through multiplicity. If, as we have seen, the dark core of Serres's work consists of articulating human history as violence and appropriation, then it will not be enough to merely celebrate alternatives or the inherent value of crossing intellectual borders. Serres insists upon a peculiar new synthetic procedure that arrives from giving oneself over entirely to multiplicity:

> Our analytical hate bursts into these little puzzle pieces, into these texts armoured with compelling, aggressive, defensive citation. In fragmented lives, we think a world burst into technologies, sciences, separated languages. Our meaning lies in scattered limbs. By dint of quartering the subjective, the cognitive, the objective and the collective, how can I say the right word and live a happy life? The analysis that unties these four components comes from the hate that divides them. What love will reunite them?
>
> *Serres 2012: 75*[9]

How might such an extraordinary proposal be put into practice? Very roughly, I think there are three routes through the apocalyptic problem space that Serres has systematically worked out. I will try to describe each in turn with reference to how it might be operationalized in management education.

## *Dark organizational theory (Tünde Eszter)*

The logic of the parasite is the motor of human relations. The parasite takes without giving; it intercepts an existing set of processes and finds a way to extract value (see Serres 1982 [1980]). The parasite produces nothing by themselves – everything they have is borrowed or stolen from others – but because they act as 'irritant' to a prior system, they are nevertheless catalysts of change. Parasitism is a challenge to appropriation; its omnipresence amongst human relations has provoked powerful strategies of re-appropriation. For example, the founding of the great city of Rome was done, Serres argues, to solve the complex inheritance problems – that is, swarms of parasites – around the existing city of Alba Longa (Serres 1991 [1983]). In Serres's language, a new 'white space' or owned site needed to be created. This was done through a sacrifice that converted pollution into purification. Romulus kills Remus, and the city is constructed on the site drenched with his blood. Serres sees the origins of modern religion in this foundation through sacrifice – 'death designates the site and often its limits' (2011 [2008]: 10). When the time comes for a new foundation for Rome, as Romulus's power ebbs away, he is in turn murdered by the Roman senators, legend has it, and is replaced by Numa, who formalizes Roman religious principles ('On the heels of the first murder come religions', 2011 [2008]: 15). The strategy of the Cult of Diana at Nemi becomes the foundation of pre-modern statecraft.

Social order and institutions are founded through violence. Murder and sacrifice cleans the site, opens it up for re-appropriation. Blood replaces urine as the marker of property. This idea bears the imprint of René Girard's work on 'scapegoating' (for example, Girard 2005). Girard – to whom *Rome* is dedicated – posits that human desires have a mimetic structure. We want what the other wants, and when our desires are mutually frustrated, we seek to collectively destroy the elusive object that is the source of our frustration. Thus envy and jealousy are fundamental drivers of collectivity, bringing with it the ongoing threat of violence. The scapegoating mechanism is a solution to the collective descending into the 'war of all-against-all'. Our mimetic desires for the same thing invert into a collective hatred against the same object. This is embodied by the ritual victim – Romulus in the myth of the foundations of Rome, Christ in the foundations of

Christianity – whose sacrifice puts a temporary halt to violence. In doing so, the sacrificial victim, the scapegoat, becomes sacred because they are now attributed with the power to preserve social order.

The scapegoat is the first example of what Serres refers to as 'quasi-objects'. These are objects that confer identity upon subjects. We recognize who or what we are through a relationship to the quasi-object (that is, Christians are those who are both complicit in and redeemed by Christ's sacrifice). For Serres, the emergence of the quasi-object – which is also a quasi-subject by virtue of its powers to act upon the collective – inaugurates the subject/object dichotomy that will prove so pivotal to hominization (an argument made more fully in *Genesis* (1995 [1982]). But quasi-objects are unstable – they only put an end to violence temporarily and they require an institutional structure to be placed around them in order to continue to secure social order. Here Serres turns to George Dumézil's studies of archaic Indo–European societies. Dumézil (1988 [1971]) claimed that social order coheres around three distinct functions – worship, war and commerce. In Roman mythology these are embodied in the gods Jupiter, Mars and Quirinus. On Serres's reading, each institutional group houses its own quasi-subject – *fetishes* (traces of the body of the scapegoat) for religion, *stakes* (polluting and purifying blood) for the military and *merchandise* (circulating signs of soft pollution) for producers. The goal of each institution is to keep their respective quasi-object moving to ward off the threat of total violence and the destruction of the collective.

In contemporary terms, what this means is that the securing of social order requires evermore relics, blood and money to be put into circulation in an ecstatic movement. The financial crisis is a testament to this: the solution to the failure of legitimacy of financial institutions is to pump more money into them, in the same way that the solution to conflict in the twentieth century was to invent technologies to exponentially increase actual or potential death toll. For a time, notably in *Angels: A Modern Myth* (1995 [1993]), Serres appeared to be championing a fourth god – Hermes or communication – as the source of a new-quasi object of 'information'. And yet this too seems to be tending towards hyperbolic breakdown where social and political problems are treated as reducible to the need for more data, whatever the (social, political) cost.

In pedagogic terms, the lesson to be drawn here is that organization is always parasitic upon prior forms of order. Contrary to the routine and tiresome claims made for extraordinary entrepreneurial success *ex-nihilo*, instead we may enquire about the extensive chains of parasitism and appropriation through which this is accomplished. The curriculum may speak of innovation or creativity, but what we are referring to is always theft and violence. Parasitism is the rule, not the exception. But parasites come in many different forms, and their strategies may vary greatly. For example, parasites that kill their hosts tend in general to be less successful and, by definition, are unable to gain numerical superiority over host organisms. Endoparasites that dwell within the body of the host are themselves dependent on other parasites that serve as their vector of transmission (recall how Serres speculates that humanity may ultimately have been the vector for other, as yet unknown parasites to implant themselves). Symbionts exist in mutually parasitic relationships with other species in semi-stable arrangements. If organization is parasitic, then a central task is to describe the precise forms that such parasitism takes.

Equally pressing is the task of analysing the movement of quasi-objects. Here we can usefully begin by dispensing with the idea that there is an economic logic at the core of finance, or a legal–political rationale to war or, indeed, an existential/spiritual need being played out in religion. Which is not to say that there is nothing 'economical' about economics and so on, but rather that these institutional practices are founded in the administration and regulation of violence. Thus 'management' itself becomes the modern domestification of an ancient logic of sacrifice and scapegoating. From urine to blood to spreadsheets. Recognition of the persistence of archaic violence in modern management practices means that the study of recent and ancient history, and of myth and fable, is no less important than contemporary theories and concepts. As Serres's mantra goes: 'nothing new under the sun'.

## *Detachment (György Eszter)*

One of the most curious of Serres's works is a small volume of essays from the mid-1980s, *Detachment* (1989 [1983]). The four pieces contained within it meander between myth, real, or perhaps false, autobiographical remembering and a haunting sense of loss and despondency. The guiding thread between them is of the nature of endurance and what it means for something to persist in time. Commonly we think of this in terms of the historical – the chronological succession of events, one succeeding the other – and yet, as we have seen, the history of human relations is, for Serres, the continuous evolution of violence and the strategies that contain it. Historical endurance therefore amounts to an interplay of parasitism and (re)appropriation. Is this all that can be hoped for?

In one of the essays, 'Trees of Death, The Tree of Life', Serres speculates on the symbolism of trees. As sacred symbols, trees appear as sources of life and rebirth, germination and the continuity of species. The spreading out of branches serves as a potent representation of division and distribution through the growth of successive generations. Small wonder then that the image of a 'tree of life' finds its way into many different religions. To give but one example, the Jewish Kabbalah provides a representation of the emanation of God into the created world, and hence of the ways in which humans may come to know God's creation. The tree of life is also, typically, a tree of knowledge, a diagrammatic representation of the principal distinctions within what is knowable. In this way, the tree structure mediates between the sacred and the profane. Finally, the tree of life and knowledge is also, inevitably, the site of power. In the Christian Bible, transgressing the prohibitions around the tree of life constitutes 'original sin'.

The intertwining of life with the growth of knowledge and the play of power renders the tree structure as a key symbol of the unfolding of history. Serres recounts an experience of standing before a Sequoia tree, one of the largest living organisms on earth. The current form of this tree, with its powerful attributes of longevity and fire-resistance, speaks to a long evolutionary history (dating back to the Jurassic period). It may even be directly speaking *to us* of this history because, as Serres observes elsewhere, the 'things of the world' communicate with one another through chemical and elemental processes far faster and more effectively than we do (Serres 2012 [2010]: 128–30). Serres fantasizes that at some point the Sequoia was planted by an ancient culture whose intentions, knowledge and practices are now lost. This is not an entirely fanciful idea because the marks of cultivation and domestication date back at least to the Neolithic era:

> Four thousand years ago some gifted ancestors – I did not keep track – bequeathed to us plants and animals on this side of the world, on the other slope of the sun. Today we eat lamb, are clothed with wool; my father raised cattle, we taste wheat-bread, we drink wine from the vine, thanks to their immortal genius ... [B]reeding and cultivation perpetuated themselves without shortcoming ... [O]ur forefathers of forty centuries ago trained phylogeny. They forever domesticated the species. They formed the matrix of all matrices. They awakened their genealogy, we only know how to lull it to sleep, they created it to serve them, we can only kill it.
>
> *Serres 1989 [1983]: 58–9*

Serres here observes that some of the most ancient technologies invented by our ancestors in the deep past – viticulture, animal husbandry, milling – continue to shape our world. In this sense, a kind of 'immortality' akin to the growth of the Sequoia has been bequeathed. Serres contrasts this with the forms of longevity that the modern world accomplishes – hazardous radioactive waste with an enormous half-life, huge carbon footprints, irreversible soil erosion. It seems, Serres argues, that we have lost the ability to disappear into the world, to 'live on' in perpetuity through techniques that foster life. Our technologies seem, by contrast, remarkably short-sighted and impose a problematic history that future generations will be forced to endure:

> Why do we no longer invent durable traditions? Why do we only foment revolutions lasting hardly one generation? Why do we no longer discover new know-hows cutting through time? What did we lose to allow us to enter history, this myth of death?
>
> *Serres 1989 [1983]: 61*

Long-term species survival – the immortality accomplished by the ancients – depends upon escaping history, understood here as the continuous violence played out around the tree of knowledge/life. Serres points to the pre-modern condition of China, where mass labour-intensive agriculture created a traditional culture seemingly unchanged by the centuries: 'No time, no history, for millennia agricultural China shows the end of history, the end of time – an adapted eternity – the absorption of humanity into the loam' (Serres 1989 [1983]: 9–10). Chinese farmers were detached from history, Serres muses, because they were sunk into an enduring landscape in which there was no space for change.[10]

We may then propose to our students the importance of the 'off grid' – forms of sustainable living that deliberately try to extricate themselves from history and seek a different relationship to the environment. Detachment is accomplished here by a withdrawal, as far as possible, from existing circuits of production and consumption (which Serres would see as inherently parasitic in nature). This is not to say that there is some clearly defined space outside of parasitism; rather, that it may be possible through anti-parasitic technologies, such as open-source development and production, to find a way to disconnect and effectively 'disappear' into the fabric of social space, into the loam. For decades we have been telling our students of the power and value of networks. Now we need to champion the necessity for partial disconnection, for cutting oneself out of the ecstatic circulation of fetishes, stakes and merchandise.

## *Cords (Janos Valuska)*

Language has a complex status throughout Serres's work. For a thinker who revels in the use of archaic language, who celebrates dialect and local idiom, Serres also displays ire at the manner in which speech is given priority over the body. From classical times onwards, the tongue that speaks is deemed of greater importance than the tongue that tastes or that kisses – 'Socrates, Agathon and Alcibiades speak of love without ever making love, or sit down to eat without actually eating or drink without tasting' (Serres 2008 [1985]: 165). A central concern of one of Serres's key mid-period works, *The Five Senses* (2008 [1985]), is the liberation of the body from language and reconstitution of knowledge and empiricism in our sensuous embodied engagements with one another and the world.

A repeated image of a mountain climber, a body shorn of language, recurs throughout Serres's work. In *Variations on the Body* (2011 [1999]), a series of images of mountains accompanies a strange gymnastic experiment, where the author invites readers to stretch out and trace the edges of a geometric shape formed by their furthest physical extension. 'Who climbs a rock face?' Serres asks. 'Not a visible body exposed to the void, but, precisely, this mobile extensible ball inside of which the simian organism reposes' (Serres 2011 [1999]: 5). Physical activity demonstrates to us that our bodies are not solid containers set against the world, but are instead a dynamic and mutable mixture of forces and surfaces that become mingled with the environment. At one moment the climber is spread taut against the rock, now held to others by ropes, then curled tightly into the snow. All bodies – whether human or non-human – are, in essence, mixtures or 'minglings' of constituent parts rather than discrete entities separated from their environment: 'the state of things becomes tangled, mingled like thread, a long cable, a skein' (Serres 2008 [1985]: 82). The climber is, in some sense, a part of the mountain for the duration of the ascent, the corporeal and the elemental flowing together. They are knotted together like the ropes or cords that attach the climbing party to one another.

The terms 'cord' and 'contract' converge upon the idea of 'drawing together' parties. *The Natural Contract* (1995 [1990]) expounds the idea that we need not only to arrive at a better legal and political framework around the environment, but also to find a new understanding of the manner in which we are jointly attached. The first issue is to reframe our relationship to property. Humanity is no longer the owner-occupier of Biogea, but a tenant: 'we should no longer be the masters and possessors of nature. The new contract becomes a rental agreement' (Serres 2011 [1999]: 72). On this formal basis, we need to develop better means to understand what Biogea is saying when it speaks. This gives a pragmatic rather than a principled priority to the life sciences, which are able to engage with the processes wherein things code and become coded by one another:

> Whether fluid or of air – even solids communicate – things respire together, they conspire with their different breaths, but in a constant and total circulation that's chancy, torn, chaotic and consenting. These breaths have rhythms, *tempi*, a music, waves, codes. Caused, causing, certainly, but coding, coded, I say again. The world adds up the codes.
>
> *Serres [2012] 2010: 129*

The life sciences are best placed to act as legislative counsels on behalf of Biogea. Serres calls for a political–legal forum in which the resulting natural contract can be negotiated, to which he gives the title that translates into rather unfortunate English: WAFEL (Water, Air, Fire, Earth, Living). Much as with Latour's (1993) call for a 'parliament of things', what is interesting about this proposition is not so much the details of how it is put into practice, but rather the new relationship between law, politics and ecology that it asserts as necessary.

The life sciences are, of course, not the only knowledge practices that will be needed. From his very earliest works, Serres has argued for a kind of 'synthesis' or 'encyclopedic' approach to knowledge (see Serres 1982; Serres and Latour 1995 [1990]). Who is to say what we will need to know in order to negotiate with Biogea? If epistemology has previously been in thrall to appropriation and division, alternating between the gods Jupiter, Mars and Quirinus, then the kind of knowledge now required is a 'thinking with' rather than a 'thinking against'. It is skills in mediation and translation – thinking from the middle – that become important in the attempt to unite 'the fields of knowledge amongst themselves the way the things are connected among themselves' (Serres 2012 [2010]: 131).

Ultimately, this amounts to a self-transformation. Serres (1982: 7) once defined the human as the greatest of all parasites in the following way: 'Man is a wolf for man, an eagle for sheep, a rat for rats. In truth, a *rara avis*.' But parasitism alone will not preserve us for much longer. A new relationship with Biogea is required:

> To attempt to open talks with [Biogea] and negotiate together, thanks to the codes shared in this way, a mutual aid and benefit pact, so that we can pass from parasitism to symbiosis

> together. That's why I want to listen to the voices of Biogea while comparing them with ours. Communication, interferences, translation, distribution, passages and bridges.[11] How can the invasive order become a reciprocal dialogue? How can the object become subject? In what language does this mute world speak?
>
> *Serres 2012 [2010]: 171)*

Serres is much taken with Aldo Leopold's phrase 'thinking like a mountain'. To think amongst Biogea, with Biogea, like Biogea means finding ways of encountering wind, sea, fire and earth and being exposed to their contingencies, hence the text *Biogea* is composed of numerous narratives – reliable and unreliable – where extraordinary events overtake the author. At the close of one, he offers the gnomic phrase 'Rare, these moments of being on the lam. Most often, everything is decided at the crossroads' (Serres 2012 [2010]: 150). To be 'on the lam' is to travel as a fugitive, away from home, towards an uncertain destination. It is to offer oneself up to events, to contingencies. There is the chance of unexpected hospitality, the risk of sudden hostility. And, most of all, there are the uncertain moments in between, at the crossroads, where decisions have to be made. That is perhaps something like what it means to 'think like Biogea'.

The goal of management education is typically framed around some desired archetype – the reflective practitioner, the effective manager, the servant leader, etc. What Serres proposes is that we dispense with these kinds of images and recommend thinking like more-than-humans. 'Thinking like Biogea' means understanding strategy from the perspective of a tree, marketing from the belly of the snake, finance amidst the excess of frogspawn, innovation amongst coral. Management education needs to be 'de-hominized' if we are to understand how we can live with rather than against Biogea.

## Thinking with Serres

Let me conclude by trying to develop some practical implications of Serres's work for management education. I have suggested that the problem space that Serres draws up between the hard and the soft, the apocalyptic and the ecstatic, sees the roots of modern organization and human relations in violence and its future in ongoing pollution. One possibility is to develop this argument further into a counter-narrative of organizational and institutional life. In *The Parasite* (1982 [1980]), Serres develops his generalized model of parasitism in opposition to an account of systems, with their guiding principles or equilibrium and feedback. What Serres describes are systems that are being leached, subject to interference and drawn down unpredictable pathways, but which still, nevertheless, 'work'. He asks what we should make of this relationship between apparent order and the parasitical: 'What happens would be the obscure opposite of conscious and clear organization, happening behind everyone's back, the dark side of the system. But what do we call these nocturnal processes?' (Serres 1982 [1980]: 12). Elsewhere, I have suggested the phrase 'dark organizational theory' as a way of treating parasitism not as an exception, but as the very central motor of organizational life (Brown 2013).

Dark organizational theory is a myth, a fable, a tall tale. But it is one that is satisfying to narrate and, I hope, to hear. Rather than convince students that organization is our defence against noise, our means of securing our common interests, we should tell them instead of how it is founded on excrement and murder, that organizations only 'work' because of the continuous movement of parasites up and downstream in relation to one another. Instead of telling them a Kantian or a neo-Derridean fairy story about the (im)possibility of ethics, we should let them know what history tells us, that 'the collective collects itself by killing' (Serres 2012 [2010]: 21). Organization is founded upon theft, appropriation. It is, in the one sense, inherently evil.

The translator of Serres's *Le Mal Propre* settled upon 'malfeasance' as a means of capturing the play on evil and property at work in this fable. But it seems to me that, at least in a management context, the direct rendering of 'clean evil' better articulates the hard and soft pollution piled up by the modern corporation. It would seem a little ambitious to suggest that our students take the oath that Serres recommends to not serve any of Dumézil's three gods – religious, military and economic interests. But we could at least invite them to consider how to place the interests of Biogea above all else.

Another possibility. In *The Five Senses* (2008 [1985]), Serres argues for the corporeal lived dimension of knowledge. We learn through encounters, through physical engagement with the world. The metaphor of the voyage, the adventure has always been central to Serres's work. It is what one learns along the way, at the crossroads, perhaps 'on the lam' that matters. Our students come to us through a variety of routes, some with more or less interesting stories to tell, but all of them come from somewhere, from a place in which their knowledge, their language, their experience is rooted. How might this be mobilized, liberated as central rather than as peripheral to teaching? It is not simply a matter of adding a few cultural references to leaven out the lecture, but instead something more far-reaching. Why not give over sessions to the discussion of ancient and modern mythology? Or to explorations of local practices of brewing, culinary arts, rituals of consumption? Instead of speaking and writing, why not making or creating – fashioning objects, the use of craft skills, visual arts, demonstrations of aesthetic preferences? Serres argues that ultimately it is not 'hard' analytic knowledge that gains immortality, but instead 'soft' technologies:

> [F]or the two economic systems known to this day, not taking any account of this world, have only taken a few decades, negligible at the scale of Biogea, to exhaust the mines, the rivers, the entirety of the available stocks, destroying the seas, polluting the air, laying waste to the Earth, killing, at a lightning-fast pace, the living species, in a word, devouring all earthly capital, hard accumulated over millions of years, not without drowning what's left of human cultures under a flood of ugliness; better, said sustainable development serves as deceptive advertising for them to finish the plundering. What is left that's lasting? Yes, the soft. Water lasts longer than earth, air longer than water . . . signs longer than fire. Here is my theorem in full: the hard does not last, only the soft lasts.
>
> *Serres 2012 [2010]: 192*

Finally, why remain in the classroom itself? Donna Haraway has developed a pedagogic strategy she refers to as 'implosion' (see Ghelfi 2015). Students are asked to pick an object and use it as a starting point for a discussion of the histories that may be tied together within it. For example, a cotton shirt may lead to the history of pesticides and Californian water projects. However, to follow Serres's suggestion of 'going on the lam', why not just leave the lecture hall altogether and explore the myriad objects and sites in nearby surroundings (see Michels and Beyes, this volume)? Architecture can lead to accounts of social history, of the parasitism of social space. Gardens can provoke discussion of the shaping of human and non-human relations. Observing the skyline can reveal more about global communication networks than most textbooks. We need to free the eye of PowerPoint, liberate the ear from lecturing and release the body from the torpor of management education.

## Production has come to an end

The opening scene of *Werckmeister Harmonies*. It is closing time at the Peafeffer inn. One of the drunks advances towards the camera, holding their drink precariously. Valuska is summoned: 'Come on',

'Show us'. Tables are pulled away to make a space. Valuska moves the drunks into position one by one, assigning to each the role of a planetary body. 'The Sun' sways on his feet, wiggling his fingers to imitate solar rays. 'The Earth' is slowly waltzed around 'the Sun', gently spun in its rotation by Valuska. With greater effort 'the Moon' is drawn together into what is now a crowded space and set on its course around 'the Earth'. Valuska tells of the immortal, unchangeable vastness of space, of the power and weighty darkness of an eclipse. The remaining drunks join, forming a moving, turning throng in which Valuska becomes lost. His face is rapturous, ecstatic. The landlord intervenes, shows the door. Valuska leaves with the words 'But Mr Hagelmeyer, it's still not over.' He walks away, the camera following him until he becomes lost in shadow.

## Notes

1 The example is also central to Frazer's *The Golden Bough* (2009).
2 Geometry has long served as an example of 'Martial' science in Serres's works – the mathematical technology of division and control over space.
3 The degree programmes in Business Administration and Philosophy run from the Department of Management, Philosophy and Politics at Copenhagen Business School are excellent examples of this practice (see Johnsen, Sørensen Thaning and Pedersen, this volume).
4 This has been a significant issue around our provision of philosophy and rhetoric on the undergraduate Business and Management Studies programme at Leicester.
5 This has recently received a new translation by Randolph Burks (the best translator to date of Serres in English) along with a set of other short pieces from Hermes IV as 'Streams'.
6 I cannot resist mentioning here a phrase coined by my former doctoral supervisor, Rex Stainton Rogers, who referred to the site connecting the great divisions of the science and the humanities as the 'isthmus' of social science, akin to the place of Panama between North and South America. Serres (1980) famously offers the alternative metaphor of exploring the Northwest Passage to get between the great divisions, rather than taking the more obvious route of the Panama canal.
7 This may have been added because the original French title, *Le Temps des Crisis*, is a rather satisfying pun on *Le Temps des Cerises* ('Cherry Season'), a song associated with the Paris Commune ('I will always cherish the season of cherries, It is that time that I keep in my heart ...'). The French edition reinforces this with an image of the fruit on the cover. In addition, the dual meaning of *le temps* as 'time' and 'the weather' suggests the link between history and ecology that is important to both this text and *The Natural Contract*. Anglophone readers are denied these hooks into the text.
8 The English translation title is the rather unhelpful but perhaps more catalogue-friendly *The Troubadour of Knowledge* (1997 [1991]).
9 I leave it to the reader to decide whether quoting this section is itself an instance of a compelling, aggressive defensive citation.
10 The example is clearly not unproblematic – or even perhaps historically accurate – and is an instance of tendency towards romantic idealization of supposed rural idyll that recurs throughout Serres's work.
11 These are in order the subtitles of the five *Hermes* books from 1968 to 1980.

## References

Abbas, N. (ed.) (2005) *Mapping Michel Serres*. Ann Arbor, MI: University of Michigan Press.
Bachelard, G. (1986 [1934]) *The New Scientific Spirit*. Boston, MA: Beacon Press.
Brown, S.D. (2013) 'In praise of the parasite', *Informática na Educação: Teoria e Prática*, 16(1), 83–100.
Burrell, G. and Morgan, G. (1979) *Sociological Paradigms and Organisational Analysis*. Portsmouth, NH: Heinemann Educational Publishers.
Callon, M. (1980) 'Struggles to define what is problematic and what is not: the socio-logic of translation'. *In:* K.D. Knorr, R. Krohn and R. Whitley (eds.) *The Social Process of Scientific Investigation: Sociology of the Sciences*. Vol IV. Dordrecht, The Netherlands: D. Reidel, pp. 197–219.
Callon, M. (1986) 'Some elements of a sociology of translation: domestification of the scallops and fishermen of St Brieuc bay'. *In:* J. Law (ed.) *Power, Action, Belief: A New Sociology of Knowledge?* London: Routledge and Kegan Paul, pp. 196–223.

Connor, S. (2005) 'Michel Serres's les cinq sens'. *In:* N. Abbas (ed.) *Mapping Michel Serres*. Ann Arbor, MI: University of Michigan Press, pp. 153–69.
Douglas, M. (1985) *Purity and Danger: An Analysis of the Concepts of Pollution and Taboo*. London: Ark.
Dumézil, G. (1988 [1971]) *The Destiny of a King*. Chicago, IL: University of Chicago Press.
Frazer, J.G. (2009) *The Golden Bough: A Study in Magic and Religion*. Oxford: Oxford University Press.
Ghelfi, A. (2015) Worlding politics: justice, commons and technoscience. Ph. D., University of Leicester.
Girard, R. (2005) *Violence and the Sacred*. London: Continuum.
Krasznahorkai, L. (1998 [1989]) *The Melancholy of Resistance*. New York, NY: New Directions.
Latour, B. (1993) *We Have Never Been Modern*. Cambridge, MA: Harvard University Press.
Latour, B. (1994) 'Pragmatogonies. A mythical account of how humans and non-humans swap properties', *American Behavioral Sciences*, 37(6), 791–808.
Paulson, W. (1997) 'Writing that matters', *SubStance*, 83, 22–36.
Serres, M. (1974) *Hèrmes III: La Traduction*. Paris: Éditions de Minuit.
Serres, M. (1980) *Hèrmes V: Passage du Nord-Ouest*. Paris: Éditions de Minuit.
Serres, M. (1982) *Hermes: Literature, Science and Philosophy*. Baltimore, MD: Johns Hopkins University Press.
Serres, M. (1982 [1980]) *The Parasite*. Baltimore, MD: Johns Hopkins Press.
Serres, M. (1989 [1983]) *Detachment*. Athens, OH: Ohio University Press.
Serres, M. (1991 [1983]) *Rome: The Book of Foundations*. Stanford, CA: Stanford University Press.
Serres, M. (1993) *Les Origines de la Géométrie*. Paris: Flammarion.
Serres, M. (1995 [1982]) *Genesis*. Ann Arbor, MI: The University of Michigan Press.
Serres, M. (1995 [1990]) *The Natural Contract*. Ann Arbor, MI: The University of Michigan Press.
Serres, M. (1995 [1993]) *Angels: A Modern Myth*. Paris: Flammarion.
Serres, M. (1997 [1991]) *The Troubadour of Knowledge*. Ann Arbor, MI: The University of Michigan Press.
Serres, M. (2008 [1985]) *The Five Senses: A Philosophy of Mingled Bodies*. London: Continuum.
Serres, M. (2011 [1999]) *Variations on the Body*. Minneapolis, MN: Univocal.
Serres, M. (2011 [2008]) *Malfeasance: Appropriation Through Pollution?* Stanford, CA: Stanford University Press.
Serres, M. (2012 [2010]) *Biogea*. Minneapolis, MN: Univocal.
Serres, M. (2014 [1987]) *Statues: The Second Book of Foundations*. London: Bloomsbury.
Serres, M. (2014 [2009]) *Times of Crisis: What the Financial Crisis Revealed and How to Reinvent Our Lives and Future*. London: Bloomsbury.
Serres, M. (2015 [2012]) *Thumbelina: The Culture and Technology of Millennials*. London: Rowman & Littlefield.
Serres, M. and Latour, B. (1995 [1990]) *Conversations on Science, Culture and Time*. Ann Arbor, MI: The University of Michigan Press.
Steyaert, C. (2014) 'Michel Serres (1930b)'. *In:* J. Helin, T. Hernes, D. Hjorth and R. Holt (eds.) *The Oxford Handbook of Process Philosophy and Organization Studies*. Oxford: Oxford University Press, pp. 549–66.

# 12

# Can management education practise Rancière?

*Isabelle Huault and Véronique Perret*

This chapter aims to contribute to management education by engaging with Jacques Rancière's philosophy.[1] From this perspective, management education is less about training technical experts who put a set of techniques and skills validated by science into practice. Rather it positions itself as contributing to the creation of a more democratic society through the training of active citizens who have the potential to voice their opinions (Dehler 2009).

Jacques Rancière's philosophy is particularly useful in challenging a view of pedagogic relations that places the inequality and asymmetry of positions as a starting point (Huault and Perret 2011). First, Jacques Rancière's thinking invites one to fundamentally challenge the expert/non-expert polarity through the assertion of the hypothesis of *equality*; however, this hypothesis is removed from any idea of collaboration because it places *dissensus* at the heart of emancipation. From this angle, the intention is neither to expose the mechanisms of domination associated with management to an ignorant public nor to reach a consensus on the basis of pragmatic learning geared towards emancipation. Rather, its main goal is to reject both the appropriation inherent in the notion of 'expert' knowledge and the assignation of positions that it presupposes, and also to help in giving voice to those who have no voice.

Accordingly, our chapter reflects on what Rancière's thoughts might 'do' to management education, as well as how they could be brought into it and perhaps be 'taught'. Jacques Rancière, however, emphasizes the impossibility of conceiving of forms of *institutionalized* emancipatory practices. The lack of interest that his work has shown in both the issue of collective forms of organization and practical answers to the strategic questions that they raise could signal the difficulty in mobilizing Rancière's thoughts in the field of management. For example, Rancière's work fails to provide direct or mechanical answers to management education, particularly in relation to which teaching methods should be institutionalized. It also does not provide a solid educational tool whose effects can be imagined in advance (see also Srinivas, this volume). For Rancière, democracy occurs without planning or pre-design. As such, management education cannot be based on the principle of necessity; rather it should be based on the principle of randomness, chance and the unexpected, even though this might undermine its initial purpose (Ben Hassel and Ravelleau 2011; Hjorth and Holt, this volume).

Our point, therefore, is precisely *not* to propose a new pedagogy or recipe because Rancière's notions of equality and politics 'do not necessarily want to go to school' (Whittaker 2011: 70; see also Bingham and Biesta 2010). Rancière's thought is a particularly challenging and indeed radical way of thinking education. Building on Whittaker's approach (2011: 72), we aim not only to search for moments of equality and dissensus, when the power of anybody emerges, but also to pay attention to how these moments might cause trouble for the field of management education and for our ways of seeing and doing as educators.

Our chapter is divided into two parts. We first explore management education in light of Jacques Rancière's thinking, by focusing specifically on the egalitarian postulate and the concept of emancipation as a re-politicization of the social arena. We also discuss how Rancière's thinking on education might be fruitful in the context of management education today. In the second part of the chapter, we examine an art-based installation that took place in Paris as a means of reinventing the spaces of the university, which accordingly can displace and reposition actors and knowledge (Lambert 2012) and enact alternative pedagogic practices that might ultimately reconfigure the sharing of the sensible (Rancière 2000). More precisely, we describe the pedagogical content as the result of collaborative research and the exhibition itself as a 'dis-ordering' educational experience. By considering pedagogy and learning as aesthetic practices, we structure our analysis around the following questions (Whittaker 2011: 13): who are 'not really speaking beings' in scenes of management education? What becomes visible, sayable and audible in educational contexts when we position teachers and participants as political subjects acting upon their own equality? What might it look like to practise equality as educators? Our objective is to document some 'moments when the power of anybody emerges most significantly' (Rancière 2009a: 118) in management education.

## Rancière's philosophy: equality and dissensus

Born in 1940, Jacques Rancière, Emeritus Professor at Paris VIII University, is one of the most renowned French philosophers of his generation. A post-Marxist philosopher, he has published on the issue of working-class identity and ideology (for example, Rancière 1981). Furthermore, he is one of the rare philosophers to have taken an interest in the issue of education in his treatise entitled *The Ignorant Schoolmaster* (2004 [1987]), which is an account of the controversial teaching methods used by Joseph Jacotot. Rancière's work subsequently focused on the status of the intellectual and the expert. Although based on specific historical situations – such as Jacotot's interventions in Restoration-era France or nineteenth-century Parisian workers' activities beyond the workplace – his work takes on a universal character that is relevant to situations in which the question of emancipation is at stake.

Rancière's work does not shy away from questions that run through management education. For one, it points to the failure of critical studies to provide a truly democratic notion of emancipation because emancipation is considered as an ideal that is to be attained, is always set in the future and is contingent upon the knowingness of 'teachers'. Rancière does not consider equality as an ideal to aspire to, but rather as a principle that is to be actualized. With this in mind, emancipation does not relate to what allows us to reach any ideal of equality, but instead refers to a set of practices that are guided by the premise of equality of anyone with anyone else, as well as by a continual drive to confirm this assumption. Second, the central tenet of Rancière's work is not so much the idea of consensus, but rather that of dissensus. Thus, emancipation is a disruption of the so-called natural order whereby institutionalized frameworks are challenged and equality is asserted.

### *Rethinking the educator's position: the radicalism of the equality principle*

Far from the position of the enlightened intellectual who 'teaches' the masses as a means of making them aware of the domination that they are being subjected to, Rancière formulates the hypothesis of equality with conviction, condemning the hierarchy of intelligences, and thus opening the path towards a reinterpretation of the role played by the educator.

The educational experience that Rancière related in *The Ignorant Schoolmaster* (2004 [1987]) provides an empirical reference point for this thesis. *The Ignorant Schoolmaster* tells the story of Joseph Jacotot, a revolutionary French teacher forced into exile in Holland in 1818. During his exile, Jacotot had to teach students who did not speak his language. In order to do this, he asked them to read a bilingual edition of *The Adventures of Telemachus* (1699) by Fénelon. He then asked them to tell him in French what they had understood. The method, which consisted of learning part of the text in French whilst comparing it with the Flemish version, proved to be very successful. The students needed no explanations, nor a teacher to guide them: they had learned by themselves to combine words and form sentences in French. Rancière argued that by associating the known with the unknown, much like when learning one's mother tongue, the need for explanation disappears. The teacher had doubtlessly filled a different function to that of transmitting knowledge. As Rancière (2004 [1987]: 25) explains, Jacotot was a teacher in that he gave them 'the command that enclosed his pupils in a circle from which they alone could escape, and by removing his own intelligence from the picture, he allowed their intelligence to come to grips with that of the book'. What the schoolmaster had successfully made students aware of was their own intelligence: the aim was not to see students move from ignorance to science, but to start with something already known, already acquired, and to move towards new knowledge and new input. Thus, the 'ignorant' schoolteacher is merely ignorant of inequality and is someone 'who wants to know nothing about the reasons for inequality' (Rancière 2009b: 416).

Of course, Rancière does not refute the asymmetry of power, power struggles or unequal access to resources; however, he stresses that the only way to establish equality in a given society is to assert it, that is to apply it in order to ensure its realization. This kind of equality is not a goal to strive for, but rather a hypothesis that is to be actualized. This fundamental reversal, which Rancière calls an *egalitarian syllogism* (2006: 509), is one of the major contributions of his work insofar as equality is declared and it is never a mere component of a programme.

Rancière's observations thus go against the champions of a position of authority in the teacher–learner relationship and an elitist and dominant conception of the educator. This view also tends to depict the learner as a passive victim in the presence of an omnipotent and enlightened teacher (Wray-Bliss 2003). On the contrary, attempts at equipping students as independent learners support a conception that places faculty and students on the same epistemological ground (Dehler *et al.* 2001).

Renouncing the position of authority and asserting equality does not necessitate the search for consensus or collaboration with the publics concerned. Although Rancière's philosophy denies all positions of authority, this does not mean that it recognizes the consensual concepts of democracy as defended by partisans of an ethical, egalitarian or collaborative approach to management education. The political and ethical ideals of management education – which themselves are firmly rooted in Habermasian thought – are based on the search for dialogue and the construction of consensus as being the conditions for democracy (Habermas 1981). Consensus is considered as the art of pacification, as a lever used to ensure agreement, as a means to erase dissent and conflict. Such ideals thus radically oppose the political definition outlined by Rancière, who considers dissensus to be the ultimate expression of democracy. Politics exists when dissensus is expressed. The shared world that can be built through the repetition of the egalitarian principle is polemic, in that it involves underscoring the contentious aspects of realities that are considered as obvious, natural and taken for granted.

## *The aesthetico-political implications of* The Ignorant Schoolmaster

Rancière maintains that politics is determined by the invention and emergence of different and heterogeneous positions. In his book *On the Shores of Politics* (1998), he defines 'police' as a structure that regulates the social field, and 'politics' as the implementation of the egalitarian principle, and therefore as emancipation. The 'police' maintains order, assigns roles and places, and legitimizes the structuring of existing social space. 'Politics' is essentially anarchic: it disrupts the traditional democratic order structured around 'those who are entitled to govern' due to their birthright or knowledge, and invites those who do not 'count' – in other words those who 'have no part' – to take part in the debate. The egalitarian postulate involves undermining the separate worlds of the dominant and the dominated, creating a space for polemic whenever the art of 'police' seeks to de-politicize and to neutralize debate.

The discussion is underpinned by the fact that the subject of the debate could be a source of controversy (Rancière 2007). According to Rancière, consensus reflects the idea of objectivity and the univocity of sensitive information, and yet as long as we disagree about the facts of a situation, politics are involved. Politics should be understood here as a transgression of the rules defined by the official oligarchies, a struggle between worlds of perception, and a combat between the world of experts (who naturalize the elements of a problem) and the world of those who 'have no part', that is, those who must struggle to define what the topic of discussion should be.

Politics therefore implies breaking with the configuration of the sensible and instead materializing itself through interruption. This is highlighted in the emblematic scene of the plebeian secession on the Aventine Hill in Rome to which Rancière often refers:

> The patricians do not hear the plebeians speak. They do not hear an articulated language coming out of their mouths. The plebeians must not only argue their case but must also set a stage on which their arguments will be audible, on which they are visible as speaking subjects, referring to a common world of objects that the patricians are required to see and to recognize as encompassing both parties.
>
> *Rancière 2009a: 176*

The plebeians' words transform the 'map' of what is conceivable, speakable and doable by taking them out of the places that they are assigned to in order to make them visible and audible. This way of organizing people and things refers to an aesthetic phenomenon that reconfigures what is visible and expressible in a spatio-political order. In this sense, aesthetic discourses and practices destabilize hierarchies and oligarchies, as well as their continuous attempts to put (and keep) everything in its 'proper' place (Beyes 2010).

## *Rancière's 'lesson' for the practices of management education*

Of course, Jacotot's experience is tied to a specific socio-historical context that is wholly different from management education today. More importantly, it does not constitute an educational method to be imitated in the first place; however, it does highlight the conflict between egalitarian thinking and the position of authority. This egalitarian conception seeks to avoid the mere transmission of knowledge, and instead creates a learning opportunity. For example, Dehler *et al.* (2001) have illustrated one faculty member's struggle to 'decentre' her classroom (see also Pullen, this volume). This teacher developed her role as an 'expert in not knowing': she refused to 'tell' in an effort to encourage students to depend on their own knowledge and experience, a conception in which the figure of the student is one who already speaks (Whittaker 2011). Rancière's philosophy reflects the tension present in a certain educational tradition, which has at its heart the notion of emancipation (Reynolds 1998), but at the same time shapes (and at times dictates) course agendas and the general intellectual environment (Hagen *et al.* 2003: 247). Fenwick (2005, and this volume) has questioned the potentially repressive nature of such a dominant position. The relationship it implies (with authority and exteriority) prevents it from concretely changing the hierarchical relationships that hamper the emergence of democratic spaces and dialogue. For example, Hagen *et al.* (2003) analysed the disruptive consequences of introducing a critical management perspective into MBA programmes. In their study, the objective was to avoid the notion of the teacher as the expert dictating the programme and imparting knowledge to passive students. Accordingly, the teachers refused to present the syllabus as a finite body of knowledge and proposed an elective that signified a contested arena, which itself was open to various interpretations. For this purpose, the teachers attempted to adopt a 'power with' approach in their relationships with students, 'a stance that views democratic participation as a right rather than a privilege, to ensure participants' voices to be heard, without the teachers falling silent themselves' (Hagen *et al.* 2003: 248).

Rancière's thoughts also offer some insights for management education in a digital era.[2] A digital pedagogy tool, such as a 'discussion forum', can be considered as a 'scene' in which students and teachers interact in creative and unexpected ways; however, some see such digital technologies as 'police' tools through which draconian regulations for the quantity and quality of posts have prevented students and teachers from being creative, inspired or even engaged (Morris and Semmel 2013). These learning management systems (LMS), which propose pre-designed categories and frame the posts, seem to sterilize debates rather than encourage them. Students, therefore, sometimes escape from these LMS by participating in more diverse and expansive open forums and meetings, thereby challenging, questioning and connecting to communities that require them to engage themselves. In stark contrast to LMS characterized by password-protected forums, these environments see students speaking with other students, professionals and even people outside academia, which can lead all parties concerned to develop radically different opinions. Moreover, in these situations, individuals have the resources to create a counter-world (Whittaker 2011) in which they can be seen as translators and counter-translators speaking together under the sign of equality. From a Rancièrian perspective, this can be considered as a democratization of learning and authority that supports students' voices.

It seems that by extending the field of management knowledge construction and teaching it to other stakeholders and other recipients (as a means of serving other goals), the principle of equality can be actualized (Huault and Perret 2009) and management can be positioned as a common good (Grey 2004).

In sum, in the field of management education, Rancière's philosophy implies rejecting the authorized form of expert knowledge and instead 'building stages' upon which silenced or discredited voices can become audible and where the subjects who are excluded or ignored can become visible. In what follows, we will present and analyse a pedagogical experience aimed at challenging the dominant pedagogical logic in terms of the asymmetry of positions between students and teachers. In doing so, we will analyse the pedagogical content of this experience as being the result of a collaborative research project, as building on a dissensual community of inquirers and as using artwork as a mediating artefact through open and emergent design. Rooted in an art-based exhibition, we consider this 'disruptive' experience as an alternative pedagogical space in which the aesthetic dimension of learning is essential. Much like Jacotot's experiment, the attention paid here to the aesthetic dimension assumes the intellectual and creative equality of the participants involved, and also explores what can be achieved under such a supposition (Lambert 2012: 216). By addressing an 'emancipated spectator'

(Rancière 2009c) – be it a student, scholar, unionist, unemployed person or manager – this case can be seen as a reconfiguration of the sharing of the sensible.

## A disruptive pedagogical experience

First, we will analyse the pedagogical content of the experience as the output of a collaborative research project, which is constituted by heterogeneous actors. We will then describe the art-based exhibition as a dis-ordering educational experience in which pedagogical spaces are conceived in a new way and where learning is seen as an aesthetic practice.

### *Investigating restructurings through an alternative pedagogical design*

The experience presented in this section was developed as part of a larger European research project entitled 'Art and Restructuring', which took place between January 2011 and April 2012 (ABRIR 2012; Mairesse *et al.* 2013). By promoting discussion and reflection among a community of actors based on artwork, this project aimed at providing new insights and new pedagogical content and tools concerning social and organizational change. Restructuring practices[3] are part of today's organizational life; in fact, the current economic crisis has amplified their frequency and increased their magnitude and stakes. Furthermore, their economic, social and human consequences weigh heavily on society, whereas dominant discourses conceal or minimize them.

The 'Art and Restructuring' project therefore aimed at opening the black box of restructuring issues and at challenging the dominant pedagogical logic in terms of the transmission of instrumental knowledge and problem-solving design. A main objective was to conceive an approach that could aid in grasping the hidden yet major aspects of restructuring, such as emotions, identities, temporal dimensions and lived experiences.

In order to overcome these issues, a specific research design was implemented during 2011 and an educational experience called 'RestructurARTion' based on this work was conducted over a two-day period in March 2012. The working process of this project was based on three main characteristics.

First, an initial choice was made to form a group that would display a high degree of both heterogeneity and potential dissensus in regards to the actors involved and the topics to be explored. The project focused on recruiting participants based on their experience, age, gender, nationality and expertise vis-à-vis restructuring. Each participant had her/his own view on artwork/organizational restructuring and spoke a language specific to her/his professional and cultural background. The project was therefore original, notably because it brought together participants that would typically be seen as having opposing view points due to their roles and social positions (artists versus managers, unionists versus corporate leaders, students versus teachers, practitioners versus researchers). The encounters between artists, researchers, teachers, students, managers, unionists and workers were geared towards supporting the co-construction of a wider range of issues and visions, making more room for social polyphony and heterogeneity, giving voice to groups, mental perceptions and feelings that would otherwise not have been heard (Berthoin-Anthal *et al.* 2011). As a result, the original situation that this group of actors faced was indeterminate, puzzling and unpredictable because it disturbed the habitual course of action and thought of each participant.

The second characteristic was to use artwork as a mediating artefact. The project proposed analysing and 'teaching' through different artworks that told the story of restructuring cases, both real and fictitious. The general idea was to consider different art forms as soon as they were identified as dealing with a restructuring situation in one way or another. The whole range – from realism to fiction and metaphor – was explored. The choice to examine restructuring through art had one main motivation. Art has a long history with organization studies (Strati 2000; Guillet de Monthoux 2004; Barry and Meisiek 2010) and is considered as a means of introducing expression, polyphony and non-verbal representations within the field (Linstead and Höpfl 2000). An artwork preserves the 'living' side of situations, and through this mediating artefact, the 'spectator' can gain access to the 'hot side' of restructuring situations. Furthermore, art enables one to keep track of invisible, subtle and ephemeral signals, which in turn grant access to the complex and hidden dimensions of specific phenomena. In dealing with the uniqueness of situations by using a universal language, art allows one to identify both recurrences and contingencies. Accordingly, in the spirit of the project, artwork may contribute to the construction of a transversal community of inquirers, thereby opening a dialogical process and creating unique educational content on restructuring.

The third characteristic was to build on an open and emergent design. This heterogeneous group of actors was placed in a loosely framed situation faced with ambiguous and unusual objects. This design – based on artwork, heterogeneity, loosely framed seminars and multiple conversational devices – gradually succeeded in creating new knowledge about restructuring. During the process, the increasingly active role of the group's members was observed. Across the network, one-to-one interactions with artwork and artists rapidly gave way to a more direct, open and sometimes conflictual experience of the art-restructuring theme. At the same time, a mounting number of individual creative initiatives were observed that were inspired by or were in response to the work, people and situations encountered.

The pedagogical exhibition that served as an end to the project was both a result of and a tool for the learning process about restructuring. This exhibition was designed as a location where knowledge that had been created would be visible, and also as a space where this knowledge would be exchanged, taught and come face-to-face with a wider learning community. We present this innovative pedagogical experience, called 'RestructurARTion', in the following section.

### *'RestructurARTion' as a dis-ordering educational experience*

The 'RestructurARTion' exhibition took place in Paris between 9 and 10 March 2012 in a highly symbolic location: the Maison des Métallos. Intended for a large, eclectic audience (researchers, students, managers, consultants, artists, unionists, the general public), this exhibition attracted roughly 400 people over two days. The alternative space-time of this pedagogical experience also carried an aesthetic ambition. The hybrid nature of the event – as a pedagogical experience, an art exhibition and a means of valorizing and disseminating research, but also the multiple and accessible modes of sensory engagement it offered (it was outside the space of the university and its doors were open to the public) – meant that a large variety of people heard and saw it. Moreover, with 'RestructrurARTion' the roles, authority, expertise and skills of both the 'spectators' and the 'authors' of the exhibition were re/distributed. Accordingly, some of the 'authors' of 'RestructurARTion' were themselves students, artists, unionists or unemployed workers, whose voices were rarely heard or counted in the context of higher education in management. We therefore analyse the dis-ordering educational experience by way of its spatial set-up, its aesthetic learning practices and its address of an 'emancipated spectator'.

## Conceiving an 'other' pedagogical space

The spatial dimension was key in the conception of the 'RestructurARTion' project. The consideration of this dimension is implicit in the continuity of research works that suggest spatial interventions facilitate critically affirmative engagement by offering an imaginative approach to management education (Beyes and Michels 2011; Michels and Beyes, this volume). According to these authors, management education would benefit from experimenting with spatial interventions, as well as from their potential to unsettle taken-for-granted practices and to provoke the emergence of what they call 'imaginative geographies'. Building on these authors, 'RestructurARTion' could be seen as a pedagogical experience that attempts to become part of imaginative geographies that might enable heterotopic spaces in higher management education. In this vein, Beyes and Michels (2011: 523) recall that 'the notion of heterotopias [is] opposed to utopias: whereas the latter denotes unusual, consoling, coherent spaces that do not exist, the former are real, disquieting spaces that violate coherence'. In this sense, 'RestructurARTion' can be considered as an 'other' space, a heterotopic space in so far as it disturbs dis-ordering places and spaces of educational practice, as well as those that are supposed to take part in such practice.

The specific attention paid to the spatial dimension of this pedagogic tool was especially evident in both the symbolic location in which the exhibition took place – that is, outside the typical confines of the university – and in how the pedagogical content was conveyed, a process that broke with normative spatial and temporal organization.

The Maison des Métallos, located in a working-class district of Paris, was originally a musical instrument manufactory. From 1936, it transformed into a centre for union activity and the headquarters for a great deal of political activity. Interestingly, in 1946 the street on which it is located was renamed after Jean-Pierre Timbaud, who was a famous member of the resistance during WW2 and a communist militant. Today, the Maison des Métallos is a cultural establishment of the city of Paris, and the Director, Philippe Mourat, has underlined its ambition to combine artistic standards with societal concerns and art with politics:

> The goal of the Maison des Métallos is to intertwine the poetic and the political. [...] In looking to create a poetic gap, the artist seeks to spark imaginations, to grant others a new view of the world, and to reflect on what can make the world a better place. The Maison des Métallos is thus a space for those who give themselves to this authorization, this imagination, this freedom and this energy.
>
> *P. Mourat, interview, 2012*

The 'RestructurARTion' project is neatly aligned with this spirit, and in its own way carries with it the same goal. The 400m$^2$ exhibition hall at the Maison des Métallos (that is, the 'light room') provided the grounds for an 'other' teaching space in which participants/spectators were invited to engage in a different aesthetic mode of learning and knowledge sharing. Spectators were invited to move about, free of a predefined route, from one space to another, witnessing diverse installations along the way. As Lambert (2012) notes, this shift from a classical pedagogical space to a showroom intended to change how both aesthetics and 'knowledge' were coded and interpreted.

## Experimenting learning as an aesthetic practice

The space's layout allowed visitors to move through various visual, auditory, temporal, sensory and intellectual installations. By adopting an aesthetic dubbed 'under construction', these islands were constructed using planks, trestles and blocks and featured an assemblage of texts, photos, film clips and interviews centring on various themes in relation to restructuration (see Figures 12.1 and 12.2). Visitors were able to read, listen to, watch and interact at their own pace thanks to a particular interactive device (see Figures 12.3 and 12.4). Each spectator was also

*Figure 12.1* The '*under construction*' installations. Each installation dealt with a theme related to restructuration.

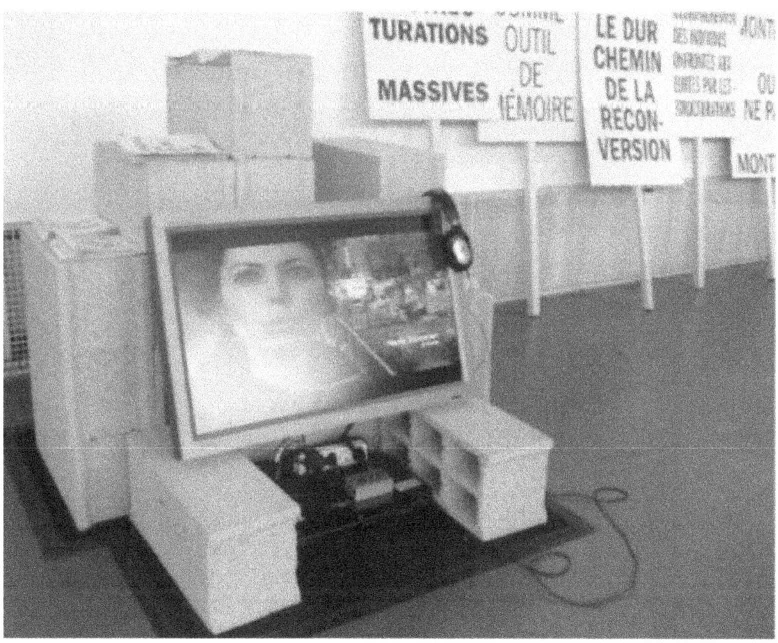


*Figure 12.2* Audio-visual installations. These installations diffused clips from larger works and/or interviews dealing with restructuration.

*Figure 12.3* The '*under construction*' installations. The collection of texts and the assemblage of photos were chosen by the exhibition's 'authors'.

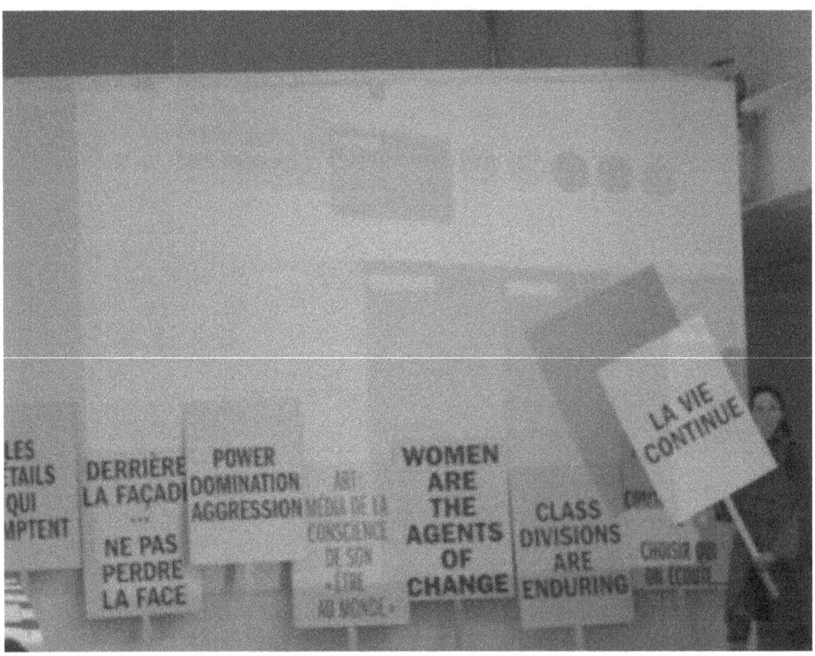


*Figure 12.4* The '*boîtes à écrire*'. Created by artists Anne-Marie Cornu and Nathalie Haran, this installation allowed visitors to interact in real time. The comments that were received were projected on the walls of the exhibition.

able to collect (at his/her discretion) the tracts, images and slogans that were being disseminated, thus creating his/her own 'manual of restructurARTion'.

Besides the exhibition space itself, the event was home to a number of workshops and events organized by artists, practitioners, academics or students.[4]

Confronting the points of view was a key feature of this exhibition. The idea was not to judge, choose or compare the legitimacy of the different perspectives on the subject, nor was it to decide which perspective on restructuring was right or wrong. Moreover, gathering such a heterogeneous group of individuals and materials was not an attempt to unify them: the different logics at work had to coexist and the diverse means of representation that were mobilized offered different methods of reading restructuration by integrating affective, symbolic, experiential and embodied experiences of the sensible. One of the project's major aims was to create a pedagogical space-time in which the multiple dimensions of the sensible could be represented, felt, expressed and potentially redistributed.

## Addressing an 'emancipated spectator'

By addressing a spectator 'whose interpretive and emotional capacity is not only acknowledged but called upon' (Rancière cited in Carnevale and Kelsey 2007: 263), the experiential and collective methodology of 'RestructurARTion' hypothesized an equality of intelligence in both the production and the reception of the pedagogical content. Both the design and the content of this experience blur the lines between teacher/student, active/passive and cognitive/sensory. In comparison with ordinary pedagogical forms in management, 'RestructurARTion' gave way to a different mode of talking and teaching about restructuring in which multiple engagements were possible simultaneously. In particular, one can underline two characteristics that actively take part in the blurring of such boundaries.

The first characteristic is the artistic nature of the project. The emotional impact of the artwork revealed the importance of participants' subjective involvement, not from a theoretical perspective, but from an individual perspective. This triggered a desire to modify the approach to restructuring in order to better address its complex and ambiguous dimensions. As one visitor commented:

> Thanks to artworks, it should be possible to accomplish more when analysing the ambivalence between pain and its disastrous effects and, at the same time, the life that goes on.
>
> *GS, management researcher*

Furthermore, the fictional nature of some of the art presented during the exhibition led to a more critical approach among participants:

> Watching [a film] together here brings the same pleasure as it does in a movie theatre, and, at the same time, the research environment makes me think of things from a critical perspective, as I know we will be discussing the film later on. [. . .] That was the most interesting part, as it led to discussions and critical thinking about the method and about the tension between reality and fiction.
>
> *AL, artist*

Finally, a number of the art pieces deliberately played on the double positioning of the participants. For example, as practitioners they had to install and manage the restructuring processes as part of their professional activity; as participants in a pedagogic project on restructuring they had to reflexively and critically think about their actions. As several participants mentioned, the methodological device allowed them to experience what they were only supposed to observe. In so doing, some of the most intimate, tacit or hidden aspects and mind-sets underlying the phenomena were unveiled by telling how each – as teachers, researchers, artists, managers, workers, students, etc. – proceeded in order to grasp restructuring by investigating and experiencing the art. Through this reflexive process, participants came across conflicting arguments and complex interconnected analyses and emotions, discovering within their own process of inquiry key aspects of the mind-sets and taken-for-granted subgrounds of restructuring phenomena.

The second characteristic of the 'RestructurARTion' exhibit is that it provided the spectator with very few explanations. Nothing was imposed on spectators; only a schedule was proposed that drew on participants' willingness and abilities to engage, to listen and to make something of what he/she was viewing, hearing or experiencing. This mode of pedagogy, characterized by 'uncertainty' and 'adventure', depends on an 'interpreter' and a 'translator'. As Lambert (2012: 223) points out, 'teaching can aspire to be a work of art by enacting a pedagogy of narration and translation over one of explication and attempting to re/organise the aesthetics through which our sense perception, and hence our understanding of the social world, is organised'.

These two characteristics emphasize the usefulness in mobilizing Jacques Rancière's thoughts and works as a means of both developing alternative pedagogical spaces in management and of inviting one to reflexively examine the nature of reconfiguration that such experiences are likely to produce.

### *Getting back to the 'RestructurARTion' experience*

Our account of the 'RestructurARTion' exhibition cannot make empirical claims regarding the sensory engagements of audiences and the kinds of knowledge and identities that may be (de-)constructed through the resulting teaching and/or research. Our experience can, however, highlight the possibilities for redistributing the partitioning and sharing of the sensible.

## Towards a transformation of participants' representations and identities?

Owing to the project's collective dialogic, reflexive and collective dimensions, it undoubtedly led to several outputs in terms of ways of thinking and teaching restructuring processes. Generally speaking, several participants mentioned that the project 'changed the way [they] look at things'. It even seems that many of them felt that they had changed as individuals or professionals. More precisely, most of the participants asserted that the experience would likely affect their professional practice: it introduced new teaching methods to scholars, inspired consultants to create or use new concepts and tools, and strengthened and affirmed artists' involvement in the social field. The researchers claimed that following the exhibition they would introduce more reflexivity and sensitivity into both their teaching and their work in general. Other participants emphasized the fact that the project's main output relied more on the experience itself rather than on acquiring new knowledge about restructuring. Meanwhile, other participants claimed to have developed a better grasp of the object in both their way of thinking about and practising restructuring. As one expert argued:

> I would be able to reap the benefits of this project if I could make crystal clear for an organization what is invisible in the restructuring process, as this dimension should be looked after with the greatest care. The project reinforced my conviction that what matters most is to go with the process, not to evaluate the outcome.
>
> *EBSG, expert*

However, the exhibition also led certain participants to express varying forms of misunderstanding or to critique what was on display. Many visitors spent very little time in the exhibition, expressing little interest in the event. Others voiced concerns vis-à-vis the content, which they claimed demanded 'too much effort to be understood'. One visitor addressed one of the exhibition's authors in detailing the difficulty he was having in understanding the exhibition:

> It's not clear what direction we're supposed to go in, or how we're supposed to go. There are also too many things to read, so in the end I didn't read a lot and wound up leaving relatively quickly.
>
> *VB, student in management*

Others questioned the aesthetic choices of the exhibition:

> But why this kind of 'under construction' installation? Why isn't the work's value emphasized more concretely? The photos are very small, the screens are uncomfortable and difficult to use. On the whole, it's uneven and lacks beauty.
>
> *LG, artist*

These and other remarks force one to question the risks and limits of such pedagogical devices. Moreover, they underline the difficulty in presuming? the effect of such an approach, an acknowledgement that is fundamental in Rancière's thought.

## Art and pedagogy on the edge

The blurring of the boundaries between art, teaching and research enables us to rethink certain pedagogic principles. However, as Lambert (2012) has emphasized, there is little point in teaching being replaced with art if the pedagogical mode and objectives remain the same: that is, pedagogy should not seek to explicate and art should not be instrumentalized for this purpose.

The question of art and its role was a main feature of the project as a whole, encapsulating the risk of instrumentalizing art as a transparent window to reality on the one hand (the naïve gaze) and the risk of instrumentalizing restructuring for art's sake without any social motives (the pure aesthetic gaze) on the other. One participant explained the extent to which this type of project could increase the art's social and economic legitimacy:

> Both the economic and academic worlds need art. The point is to manage to influence each other mutually and reciprocally in order to move beyond our own frameworks and create a new language. Of course, language has a functional role in that it enables the world to reproduce itself. It is interesting when we produce new realities that trigger the need for unification as means of representing what is going on. It is also interesting that we need to discuss them with others in order to understand what is going on.
>
> *AT, artist*

Another participant expressed that he still fears that art could easily be instrumentalized, whereas its mere function is to help emancipation:

> I am still worried when I see that some people use art as a funny and or nice 'thing', which makes it possible to swallow an otherwise hard pill. It scares me when artistic expression is not used for the purpose of emancipation. I have become aware of the dreadful instrument of power that art can be.
>
> *NH, artist*

Finally, many of the comments received during the exhibition outlined the move by participants who felt that they had experimented in an atypical and increasingly transversal and cumulative manner: the exhibition transformed their initial intuition into a consciousness and formulation of a specific knowledge on restructuring. Such participants outlined the specific role of art that must be considered on its own terms, as well as being considered as an object. This role necessitated that all participants make a critical move (which all of them recognized in their interviews) and remain willing to continue a 'beautiful collective adventure', which was, according to them, still in its infancy.

As Rancière states, this critical move – which itself is an aesthetic rupture – involves moving past a form of 'teaching overload' that attempts to always act under the assumption that a result can be predetermined.

> In the pedagogical relationship, the master speaks but never passes his/her knowledge into the mind of the student. In the same way, the artist develops broad strategies but ultimately only provides what elements he/she can, while it is the spectators that come and choose how to reassemble these elements. Emancipation truly begins when there is a true rupture between cause and effect: the activity of the spectator lies within this gap.
>
> *Rancière 2009d: 1*

The 'RestructurARTion' experience brings new questions to pedagogy. Because of its form and its content 'RestructurARTion' voluntarily abandoned the tools of control typically found in management education. On the contrary, the pedagogical content favoured disparity, ambiguity and polyphony rather than a coherent, ordered and homogeneous message. In the space-time of 'RestructurARTion', the knowledge created depended on the multiple possible journeys that participants could take through the materials and the time that they spent with them. However, as Lambert (2012: 222) notes with regard to a different example, if the hierarchy of the classroom was radically displaced, 'the sensory possibilities for engagement offered new challenges [...] Assumptions of an equality of intelligences did not, in practice, make the space feel more equal, but instead very unequal'.

In addressing the experience to a presumably emancipated spectator and in leaving the mastery of space and time in that spectator's hands (rather than in those of its creators), the experience also had to accept the possibility that spectators might not read, participate or intervene in the exhibition. As such, this experience radically called the concept of educational assessment into question.

By voluntarily abandoning control and mastery, 'RestructurARTion' bore witness to the impossibility of teaching, a critical step in the renewal of management education. As Whittaker (2011) has underlined, this is not a cause for defeatism or despair, but is a new starting point for politics: we must put our faith in discontinuity, in the promise of something coming.

## Conclusion

In this chapter, we have argued that Rancière's philosophy constitutes a stimulating means of rethinking management education. We have explored management education in light of his thinking, by focusing specifically on the egalitarian postulate. This perspective calls into question both the expert knowledge conveyed by management and the position held by experts and authority within the traditional educational setting. Indeed, Rancière's conception of management education as outlined in this chapter is principally defined by an assertion of the postulate of equality of intelligence, whilst at the same time undermining of the role of the expert–educator emancipator. This perspective is also characterized by the extension of management education to a great number of various producers and recipients, which in turn promotes the emergence of dissensus, effectively ruling out the search for consensus between the different players. Like Rancière, we can thus envision the educator's role as someone who works towards asserting the intellectual capacity of all, as well as the construction of a space for the voices of those otherwise rendered inaudible by institutionalized frameworks. This does not entail the transmission of management knowledge to an ignorant public through a purely 'expert' relationship because this would risk reproducing present hierarchies and systems of domination. Moreover, it does not position management as an exclusive form of expertise reserved uniquely for the elite, nor does it imply an overvaluing of participation and collaboration with students within a purely consensual design. This perspective also presumes that management education can be seen as a place that is favourable to the emergence of dissensus and to an interruption of the general scheme of things, with a clear statement that each player – teachers, students, practitioners, etc. – has the right to express his/her opinion.

These analyses allow us to better comprehend the individual and collective actions that seek to actualize equality. We have demonstrated that by introducing discontinuity, some students at times put mainstream teaching practices at risk and challenge ordinary scenes of schooling. For teachers, this often implies developing new material (and sometimes virtual) spaces that can incorporate dissensus, and then 'politics'. More specifically, we have illustrated this point by focusing on a 'disruptive' educational experience in which an art-based exhibition was used both as a means of reconsidering the spaces of the university and to enact new practices. Its design presumed an equality of intelligence both in the production of the pedagogical content and in its dissemination (Lambert 2012) by addressing a political participant. In the exhibition, the spectator acts, observes, selects, compares and interprets. Moreover, in doing so, he/she participates in 'a human collective [that] is an intertwining and twisting together of sensations' (Rancière 2009c: 56). But the way people can participate in such a community of sensation is to interject themselves into it. This leads not only to a transformation of the participants' sense of the world in the here and now, but also to a potential transformation of the regime of the sensible (Huault *et al.* 2014). In this way, learning is considered as an aesthetic practice where the emotional and sensory experience of pedagogy (through artworks) is particularly highlighted. This aesthetic effect is also an effect of dis-identification (Rancière 2009c: 62) – that is, aesthetic experiences can emancipate us from identities that we take to be frozen or fixed (such as being a student, a teacher, an artist, a manager, a unionist or an unemployed worker) and open up space for exploring new identities. These kinds of ruptures provoke a shift from a given sensible world to another sensible world that defines different capacities and incapacities (Rancière 2009c: 79). The 'RestructurARTion' exhibition refused the distribution of roles and transgressed intellectual, spatial and disciplinary boundaries. Furthermore, it emphasized the importance of asserting the power of equality in every place, disturbing the social and physical order of things, transgressing rules and interrupting the normalized debate. In this conception of educational practices, emancipation involves reconfiguration in the here and now through the immediate experience of engaging in aesthetic activity (Huault *et al.* 2014: 34). By engaging with Rancière's philosophy, we are able to develop powerful resources for constructing alternatives for, and for 're-energizing', management education.

## Notes

1 The translations of Rancière's work are by the authors.
2 For digital pedagogies and tools, see Bachmann and Shah, this volume.

3 We define restructuring as any reorganizing process that affects activities, work organization, methods, capital or skills or that has an impact on (or poses a threat to) employment on either a quantitative or qualitative level (ABRIR 2012).
4 See the interview with Howard Becker and the commentary in Schmidt *et al.* (2015) for another element of this event.

## References


ABRIR (2012) 'An art-based, collective and dialogic ethnographic method – unveiling corporate restructuring practices'. 28th EGOS Colloquium, Sub-theme 22: New forms of organizational ethnography. Helsinki, Finland.

Barry, D. and Meisiek, S. (2010) 'Seeing more and seeing differently: sensemaking, mindfulness, and the workart', *Organization Studies*, 31(11), 1505–30.

Ben Hassel, F. and Raveleau, B. (2011) 'Les dimensions critiques de l'enseignement de la GRH: plaidoyer pour un management renouvelé'. *In:* L. Taskin and M. de Nanteuil (eds.) *Perspectives Critiques en Management. Pour une Gestion Citoyenne.* Brussels: de Boeck, pp. 210–24.

Berthoin-Antal, A., Brydon-Miller, M., Friedman, V. and Gaya Wicks, P. (2011) 'The changing landscape of arts and action research', *Action Research*, 9(1), 3–11.

Beyes, T. (2010) 'Uncontained. The art and politics of reconfiguring urban space', *Culture and Organization*, 16(3), 229–46.

Beyes, T. and Michels, C. (2011) 'The production of educational space: heterotopia and the business university', *Management Learning*, 42(5), 521–36.

Bingham, C. and Biesta, G. (2010) *Jacques Rancière: Education, Truth, Emancipation.* London: Continuum.

Carnevale, F. and Kelsey, J. (2007) 'Art of the possible: interview with Jacques Rancière', *Artforum International*, 7, 257–69.

Dehler, G. (2009) 'Prospects and possibilities of critical management education: critical beings and a pedagogy of critical action', *Management Learning*, 40, 31–49.

Dehler, G., Welsh, A. and Lewis, M. (2001) 'Critical pedagogy in the "New Paradigm": raising complicated understanding in management learning', *Management Learning*, 32(4), 493–511.

Fenwick, T. (2005) 'Ethical dilemmas of critical management education within classrooms and beyond', *Management Learning*, 36(1), 31–48.

Guillet de Monthoux, P. (2004) *The Art Firm: Aesthetic Management and Metaphysical Marketing.* Stanford, CA: Stanford University Press.

Grey, C. (2004) 'Reinventing business schools: the contribution of critical management education', *Academy of Management Learning and Education*, 3(2), 178–86.

Habermas, J. (1981) *Theorie des kommunikativen Handelns.* Frankfurt am Main, Germany: Suhrkamp.

Hagen, R., Miller, S. and Johnson, M. (2003) 'The "disruptive consequences" of introducing a critical management perspective onto an MBA programme. The lecturers' view', *Management Learning*, 34(2), 241–57.

Huault, I. and Perret, V. (2009) 'Extension du domaine de la stratégie. Plaidoyer pour un agenda de recherche critique', *Economies et Sociétés*, 1(12), 2045–80.

Huault, I. and Perret, V. (2011) 'Critical management education as a vehicle for emancipation. Exploring the philosophy of Jacques Rancière', *M@n@gement*, 14(5), 281–309.

Huault, I., Perret, V. and Spicer, A. (2014) 'Beyond macro- and micro-emancipation. Rethinking emancipation in organization studies', *Organization*, 21(1), 22–49.

Lambert, C. (2012) 'Redistributing the sensory: the critical pedagogy of Jacques Rancière', *Critical Studies in Education*, 53(2), 211–27.

Linstead, S. and Höpfl, H. (2000) *The Aesthetics of Organization.* London: Sage Publications.

Mairesse, P., Beaujolin, R., Begon, E., Perret, V. and Schmidt, G. (2013) 'Three cases of identity (re)construction through art interventions: the role of the "sensible". 29th EGOS Colloquium Sub-theme 09: Identity in Art, Design and Organization. Montréal, Canada.

Morris, S.M. and Semmel, J. (2013) 'The discussion forum is dead; long live the discussion forum', *Hybrid Pedagogy*, 8, May. Available from: www.hybridpedagogy.com/journal/the-discussion-forum-is-dead-long-live-the-discussion-forum/ (accessed September 2015).

Rancière, J. (1981) *La Nuit des Prolétaires. Archives du Rêve Ouvrier.* Paris: Fayard. [Translated by J. Rancière (1989) *The Nights of Labor. The Workers' Dream in the Nineteenth Century France.* Philadelphia, PA: Temple University Press].

Rancière, J. (1998) *Aux Bords du Politique*. Paris: La Fabrique. [Translated by J. Rancière (2007) *On the Shores of Politics*. London: Verso].
Rancière, J. (2000) *Le Partage du Sensible. Esthétique et Politique*. Paris: La Fabrique.
Rancière, J. (2004 [1987]) *Le Maître Ignorant, Cinq Leçons sur l'Emancipation Intellectuelle*. Paris: 10/18. [Translated by J. Rancière (1991) *The Ignorant Schoolmaster*. Stanford, CA: University Press].
Rancière, J. (2006) 'La méthode de l'égalité'. *In:* L. Cornu and P. Vermeren (eds.) *La Philosophie Déplacée. Autour de Jacques Rancière*. Colloque de Cerisy, Bourg en Bresse: Horlieu Editions, pp. 507–23.
Rancière, J. (2007) 'Jacques Rancière: les territoires de la pensée partagée'. *In:* J. Lévy, J. Rennes and D. Zerbib (eds.) *EspacesTemps.net* Available from: www.espacestemps.net/articles/jacques-ranciere-les-territoires-de-la-pensee-partagee/?output=pdf (accessed January 2016).
Rancière, J. (2009a) *Et Tant Pis pour les Gens Fatigués. Entretiens*. Paris: Editions Amsterdam.
Rancière, J. (2009b) *Moments Politiques. Interventions 1977–1999*. Paris: La Fabrique.
Rancière, J. (2009c) *The Emancipated Spectator*. London: Verso.
Rancière, J. (2009d). 'Jacques Rancière: l'Art, Debord et l'émancipation intellect'. *Forum Anarchiste*, 3 August. Available from: http://forum.anarchiste.free.fr/viewtopic.php?f=12&t=2550&start=0&st=0&sk=t&sd=a#p42600 (accessed September 2015).
Reynolds, M. (1998) 'Towards a critical management pedagogy'. *In:* J. Burgoyne and M. Reynolds (eds.) *Management Learning: Integrating Perspectives in Theory and Practice*. London: Sage Publications, pp. 312–28.
Schmidt, G., Bobadilla, N., Debenedetti, S. and Mairesse, P. (2015) 'About art, social science . . . and restructuring: an interview with Howard S. Becker', *Organization*, 22(6), 756–68.
Strati, A. (2000) 'Putting people in the picture: art and aesthetics in photography and in understanding organizational life', *Organization Studies*, 21(1), 53–69.
Whittaker, M. (2011) 'Restaging Rancière. New scenes of democracy and equality in education'. Unpublished dissertation, Ohio State University.
Wray-Bliss, E. (2003) 'Research subjects/research subjections: exploring the ethics and politics of critical research', *Organization*, 10(2), 307–25.

# 13

# Doing management education with free jazz and Derrida

*Mark Learmonth, Michael Humphreys and Martyn Griffin*

## 'Track 1: Deconstruction and X' or 'Song X'[1]

In an intriguing juxtaposition, amongst a list that puts 'some order into all the sentences or all the texts which would come forward in the name of "Deconstruction and X"' (Derrida 2000: 283), Jacques Derrida mentions management and music almost, as it were, in the same breath:

> deconstruction *and* literature, deconstruction *and* right, or architecture, or management, or the visual arts, or music, etc.
>
> *Derrida 2000: 283, italics in original*

We find his juxtaposition of management with 'the visual arts, or music, etc.' productive. We think it is productive, even though neither the discipline of organizational studies and management, nor the field of music is especially prominent in Derrida's work. As far as we can determine, Derrida never mentioned organization, business and management explicitly anywhere else in the whole corpus of his work and, although he said a little more about music, what he *did* say on the subject often stressed his own lack of musical knowledge and competence. Once, for example, Derrida reflected:

> I like cinema very much; I have seen many films, but in comparison with those who know the history of cinema and the theory of film, I am, and I say this without being coy, incompetent. The same holds true for painting, and it is even more true for music.
>
> *Derrida et al. 1994: 9*[2]

Incompetent, perhaps, but his incompetence should not be taken to imply a lack of interest in the musical. Far from it. Later, in the same interview, he went on to say:

> [M]usic is the object of my strongest desire, and yet at the same time it remains completely forbidden. I don't have the competence, I don't have any truly presentable musical culture. Thus my desire remains completely paralyzed. I am even more afraid of speaking nonsense in this area than in any other. Having said that, the tension in what I read and what I write,

> and in the treatment of the words I just spoke about, probably has something to do with a nondiscursive sonority, although I don't know whether I would call it musical. It has something to do with tone, timbre, voice, something to do with the voice.
>
> *Derrida et al. 1994: 21*[3]

Although he never studied it in detail or wrote about it much, music was nevertheless something that Derrida was passionate about – especially, as we shall see, free jazz. Indeed, Wills (2006: 31), a personal friend of his, recounts how after discovering that he and Derrida shared a love of jazz, 'from then on [in their personal conversations] jazz became as much a point of reference as cinema had before'. It is not altogether unsurprising, therefore, that in spite of his fear of speaking nonsense about music Derrida publicly provided another angle on his relation to the object of his 'strongest desire' during a question and answer session with the audience after the premiere of the film 'DERRIDA'[4] at Film Forum, New York, in October 2002. Answering the question 'What kind of music do you listen to, and why do you listen to it?', Derrida gave the following response, albeit with reluctance – or at least with reluctance at first:

> JD: No, no, no, no – I usually don't answer such questions. What would that mean? I love jazz and Bach and Mozart. You shouldn't ask such a question. I love music but I'm not an expert or anything. I have no real musical expertise, in the professional sense, but I love music and I listen to music all the time. And well, free jazz or Bach or Mozart.
>
> Speaking of free jazz, once in Paris I appeared in public with Ornette Coleman. He asked me to come to one of his performances. We met in a hotel. There was a big discussion and he told me he was interested in my texts, so we met. Then he invited me to come to one of his concerts and to say anything I wanted and he would accompany me, improvising. So, I was quite scared ... Finally, I said yes. Although against it, I said yes. So I prepared a text, and Ornette Coleman started the concert and, as we agreed upon, at some point he called me onstage. And once onstage, I started reciting this special text that I'd written for this occasion as he accompanied me, improvising. But his fans were so unhappy with this strange man coming onstage with a written text that they started, uh, whistling? Sorry ...
>
> KD [Kirby Dick, one of the directors of DERRIDA]: Cat-calling? Booing?
>
> JD: So it was a very painful experience. But finally it turned into a happy event because the day after, in the newspapers, everyone mentioned this as something interesting. But, in fact, it was a painful experience for me.
>
> So, I love Ornette Coleman – he's a good friend of mine – and that's the kind of music I like, among others.
>
> *Dick and Ziering Kofman 2005: 115*

The aim of this chapter is to read the encounters between Coleman and Derrida in a manner orientated towards the interests of those concerned with management education. Many business school scholars before us have attempted to make jazz relevant to an organizational audience (see especially the 1998 special edition of *Organization Science* as well as, for example, Bastien and Hostager 1988; Hatch 1997, 1999; Humphreys *et al.* 2012; Kamoche *et al.* 2003; Lewin 1998; Mantere *et al.* 2007; Moorman and Miner 1998; Weick 1989, 1993). However, we seek to extend this literature by considering the more radical version of jazz improvisation associated with Ornette Coleman. Similarly, the implications of Derrida's work for praxis have been developed by Laclau and Mouffe (2001: 112), who emphasize the emancipatory potential in Derrida's championing of 'the impossibility of an ultimate fixity of meaning ... [to allow] the flow of differences'. As Laclau argued,

> [i]f people think that God or nature have made the world as it is, they will tend to consider their fate inevitable. But if the being of the world which they inhabit is only the result of the contingent discourses and vocabularies that constitute it, they will tolerate their fate with less patience and will stand a better chance of becoming political 'strong poets'.
>
> *Laclau 1996: 122*

Deconstruction, therefore, is particularly interesting in the context of management scholarship and education because it aims to produce a tension between what a text purports to claim (its intended meaning) and a double or multiple range of meanings that cannot be contained within the text's intended meaning. This tension is what creates an experience of the impossible (Boje 1995; Cooper 1989; Kilduff 1993; Kilduff and Kelemen 2001; Kilduff and Mehra 1997; Learmonth *et al.* 2012; Martin 1990; Weiss 2007; Weitzner 2007).

There is a sense, therefore, that we shall be working (or to use a more musical and perhaps a more Derridean metaphor: *playing*) on the margins – the margins of Derrida's philosophy (although see Royle 1998), as well as on the margins perhaps of both music and management education (although see Cobussen 2001, 2003; Rhodes 2007; Subotnik 1996). Nevertheless, in the end we trust that to play on these margins will be to do the kinds of things Derrida did, as well as to perform something new, in our own language and in our own voice (Derrida 1996: 217–18). In particular, we propose a way to increase creative improvisation within management practice and education in a manner that may (we hope) be both radically participative and ethical (see also Cunliffe 2002; Hansen *et al.* 2007). In doing so we have tried to draw out the potential for democratic collaboration with regard to management education, whilst remaining faithful to Derrida's work in being able to show:

> a future which [like free jazz] does not allow itself to be modalised or modified into the form of the present, which allows itself neither to be foreseen nor programmed; it is thus ... the opening to freedom, responsibility, decision, ethics and politics [while it is] ... also the *experience of the impossible* ... the least bad definition of deconstruction.
>
> *Derrida 1992: 200, italics in original*

First, we examine improvisation as *the* core ingredient of jazz before introducing free jazz and Coleman's harmolodic approach to music. We do this in order to make a space in which we can discuss some of the organizational significance of Derrida's initial meeting with him, which included an interview (Coleman and Derrida 2004), as well as the concert a week later at which Derrida improvised 'vocals'[5] onstage with the Coleman group.[6] In particular, we explore the notion of improvisation as practice – something that has to be performed, *done* (in fact, Derrida *did* an improvisation onstage with Coleman, despite how much it scared him to do so). As practice, we link improvisation to learning about managing in organizations – something else one must also *do* rather than merely read about. As Mintzberg (1975: 50; see also Srinivas, this volume) has famously shown: 'managers work at an unrelenting pace ... their activities are characterized by brevity, variety and discontinuity, and ... they are strongly orientated to action and dislike reflective activities'.

We read Derrida's/Coleman's practice of improvisation – something that Derrida referred to as a 'unique event that is produced only one time [but which] is nevertheless repeated in its very structure' (Coleman and Derrida 2004: 322–3) – in ways that might contribute to *doing* in the context of management learning. We achieve this through an example based on what we think was an 'experience of the impossible' that one of us has had as a manager. The intent is to show how Coleman's form of improvisation, adapted for a management learning context, has the potential to help us through experiences of the impossible in order to produce unique participatory events – similar to the event between Derrida and Coleman – unique, if still repeated (that is, codified) in their very structure (Ramshaw 2006).

## Track 2: improvisation, Ornette Coleman and Derrida

Hatch (1999: 78), in her paper on the value of the jazz metaphor in the study of organizations, argues that improvisation 'constitutes the distinguishing feature of Jazz'. She went on to describe a typical performance as:

> structured around the playing of tunes which themselves are loosely structured via partial musical arrangements called heads. The head of a tune defines, at a minimum, a chord sequence, a basic melodic idea, and usually an approximate tempo . . . Improvisation centres around the head, which is usually played through 'straight' (without much improvisational embellishment) at the beginning of the tune, then improvised upon, and finally returned to and played again as the ending. The head gets a tune started by suggesting a particular rhythm, harmony and melody. The tune is then built from this starting point via improvisation within which different interpretations of the initial idea are offered and new ideas and further interpretations can be explored.
>
> *Hatch 1999: 78*

This description represents the broad structural context of improvisation within a range of 'traditional' jazz styles variously described by critics as New Orleans, Swing, Be-Bop and Modern. However, as Hatch (1999: 84) notes, 'with the advent of Free jazz, structure became so subtle as to be practically undetectable to any but the most sophisticated listener, including many traditional jazz musicians'. Berliner (1994: 338) further explains that 'Free Jazz groups express concern for democratizing jazz [and] minimize or eliminate the distinctions between soloists and accompanists at times involving band members in constant simultaneous solos throughout performances'.

One of the leading figures in the free jazz[7] movement is Ornette Coleman, an African American musician, who (eventually) found fame in the late 1950s and early 1960s with landmark recordings such as *The Shape of Jazz to Come* and the eponymously titled 1960 album *Free Jazz: A Collective Improvization.* Coleman expressed his approach to music (and life) by coining the term 'harmolodics', which, in a rare (and brief) article in the jazz magazine *Downbeat,* he defined as:

> one's own logic made into an expression of sound to bring about the musical sensation of unison executed by a single person or with a group . . . harmony, melody, speed, rhythm, time and phrases all have equal position in the results that come from the placing and spacing of ideas.
>
> *Coleman 1983: 54*

This 'harmolodics' approach has proved difficult to define for those seeking to categorize Coleman's work – as Kernfeld (1995: 484) explains:

> [I]nsofar as Coleman's explanation can be understood it [harmolodics] apparently involves the simultaneous sounding, in different tonalities and different pitches (determined by, for example a notional change of clef), but in otherwise unchanged form, of a single melody

> or thematic line; the procedure produces a type of simple heterophony. More generally the harmolodic theory espouses principles already well established in Free jazz, namely equality among instruments (rather than the traditional separation between soloist and accompaniment) in harmonically free collective improvization . . . the term derives from a conflation of the words 'harmony', 'movement' and 'melody'.
>
> *Kernfeld 1995: 484*

Coleman's harmolodic approach to music offers 'an aesthetic (but not aestheticized) democracy like that which operates within his performing ensembles' (Murphy 1998: 90). And as Heble (2000: 50–1) further explains, before free jazz:

> most improvisation in jazz was confined to a harmonic and rhythmic framework. Then Coleman came along and swept away[8] the set harmonic structures and tightly knit patterns . . . which had dominated the music of his contemporaries (2000: 49) . . . Melody, then, [in free jazz] is privileged over harmony to the extent that the tune itself becomes the pattern of the composition. (We might be tempted here to make an analogy with Derrida's *différance* . . .) [because] Coleman's jazz is a proliferation of meanings, a valorization of the signifier.

Indeed, just as it may be possible, however tentatively, to link free jazz with Derrida's neologism *différance* – in that they both capture the undecidability of representation and the juxtaposition of otherwise oppositional and incompatible themes – we might also be tempted to make a range of other analogies between the two figures themselves. For example, both have a substantial fan base (let's use that term for each of them) across the world – just as both have also attracted deep controversies within their respective 'mainstream' communities (Nettlebeck 2004). Coleman, for example, has been publicly castigated by his peers for allegedly lacking technical proficiency in basic musicianship and advocating an 'anything goes' approach to improvisation (Wills 1998). As Collier (1978: 462) commented on Coleman's early career, 'his attempts to sit in with jazz bands . . . were met with hostility. Sometimes musicians walked off stands when he came on to play. Dexter Gordon once peremptorily ordered him off the stand'. Such stories, in many ways, echo the *ad hominem* attacks Derrida received from the analytical mainstream in philosophy when the University of Cambridge proposed to award him an honorary degree (Derrida 1995: 399–421). Indeed, the cat-calling Derrida received from Coleman's fans – a response that proved sufficient to cut Derrida's improvisations well short from what he had planned to say – might also link the two. As the translator's note to Derrida's improvised performance at the Coleman event points out: '[t]he irony of this [Derrida being jeered off stage] was undoubtedly not lost on Coleman, who has himself been the object of more abuse and ridicule than perhaps any other musician in the history of jazz' (Derrida 2004: 331).

In autobiographical terms, too, there are similarities, some of which they discussed at their interview. Both were born in 1930 within marginalized communities (Coleman grew up in an underprivileged black family in Texas, US; Derrida was an Algerian Jew) and both suffered from the effects of racial prejudice as young men. It seems likely therefore, that both might be seen as visionaries who were driven by their shared experiences as marginal outsiders. Thus, as Nettlebeck (2004: 199) observes, Coleman and Derrida are:

> 'outsiders' who, paradoxically, have come to be seen as highly representative of the cultures they have attempted to reform. Coleman, as the principal voice of the free jazz, 'New Thing' movement, had reclaimed for jazz its territory of radical creativity.

> Derrida was not just France's leading revolutionary philosopher, but a thinker whose theories of deconstruction and difference had helped to redefine, globally, the parameters of epistemology in the humanities and social sciences.
>
> *Nettlebeck 2004: 199*

On the other hand, it is equally possible to see *contrasts* between the two figures. For example, unlike Derrida, Coleman has produced little written output in the way of books, etc. beyond the sleeve notes that accompany his recordings.[9] Indeed, Collier (1978: 463) notes of Coleman that '[l]ong after he had become a major figure in jazz he still did not know how to read or write music correctly' arguing that 'he must be seen as a primitive artist ... who develops his method and manner independent of the main line'.

Derrida's interview with Coleman is therefore different in tone when compared with, say, the published conversations between Daniel Barenboim and Edward Said (Barenboim and Said 2002). Barenboim has written on music and its relationship with wider political issues, and one gets a sense of the meeting of similar minds – conversations between two individuals who share comparable orientations towards, and understandings of, the world (see also Guimaraes-Costa *et al.* 2009).[10] Derrida and Coleman, however, appeared to have had less in common – at least in terms of their respective temperaments and approaches to life. For example, in his interview with Derrida, Coleman emphasizes the importance of *doing*; thus, in response to Coleman's statement:

> [f]or me, being an innovator doesn't mean being more intelligent, more rich, it's not a word, it's an action. Since it hasn't been done, there's no use talking about it ... [Derrida says] ... I understand that you prefer doing [*faire*] to speaking.
>
> *Coleman and Derrida 2004: 327*

One detects the same kind of contrasts in Coleman's responses to the following questions from Derrida:

> JD: ... last night I read an article that was in fact a conference presentation given by one of my friends, Rudolph Burger, a musician whose group is called Kat Onoma. It was constructed around your statements. In order to analyze the way in which you formulate your music, he began from your statements, of which the first was this: 'For reasons I'm not sure of, I am convinced that before becoming music, music was only a word.' Do you recall having said that?
>
> OC: No.
>
> *Coleman and Derrida 2004: 328*

We enjoy Wills's (2006: 36) wry aside, therefore, in which he suggests of their encounter, that 'one can imagine . . . the serious philosopher preparing himself early in the morning . . . while the Bohemian musician gets up just in time for the meeting, presuming he can take it as it comes'. Indeed, it is of interest to note, that in the context of the others who have collaborated with Derrida (ordinarily, academics or writers with broadly similar interests and orientations), Coleman's particular understanding of, and emphasis on, *doing* is unusual, indeed, almost alien. This contrast seems to have been noticed by Derrida – in a letter to Catherine Malabou, written shortly after the gig, Derrida told her that the encounter with Coleman: '[w]as in Paris, [that is, in Derrida's home city] but no voyage will have ever taken me so far away, myself and my body and my words, onto an unknown stage, without any possible rehearsal or repetition' (Malabou and Derrida 2004: 97(n)).

But it is for this very reason we think that Coleman's preferences – for doing and action (a preference that Derrida acknowledged, and with which he complied by actually appearing onstage with Coleman) – will resonate not only with students, who might learn more effectively through 'doing', but also with the attitudes of many teachers and 'practical' managers (Byers and Rhodes 2004). Indeed, in their interview, Coleman and Derrida talked at length of Coleman's necessary involvement with the music business, as Derrida (2004: 333–4) put it in his vocals:

> In the long conversation I had with him the other day, he never stopped repeating to me, as he always does, that he didn't want to have anything to do with the institutions and powers of the music business, and that even when he deals with the commodity, he never gives in to it; and when that power of marketing or the media is too strong, he doesn't wage war against it, for Ornette is a free[11] man, a sort of non-violent revolutionary, innocent and wounded, so he does not respond to violence, he leaves . . . he goes and plays elsewhere and creates elsewhere, which he has done all his life: going elsewhere and arriving elsewhere, and always here, like tonight.
>
> *Derrida 2004: 333–4*

That Coleman *is* different from a more typical Derridean collaborator – both as a doer (as opposed to a writer) and as someone intimately connected with (the music) business (even as he resists some of the implications of his connections) – represents a reason in itself for suggesting that Derrida's encounters with him may be of special interest for readers with an interest in management education. In the next section, we therefore consider how *doing* jazz improvisation – as understood by Coleman and Derrida – might inform the way we might *do* management.

## Track 3: Coleman's music lesson for free organization

*Doing* – making things happen – is what any kind of jazz performance is all about. As Hatch (1999: 82) puts it, '[j]azz happens. It is an activity, not just an abstract category. As an activity, jazz is something to be entered into, participated in, experienced'. Indeed, in the lyrics of his own performance with the Coleman group, Derrida started by talking of his uncertainties and fears – along with the necessity of improvisation in this context – as well as emphasizing what is *happening*:

> Qu'est-ce qui arrive? What's happening? What's going to happen, Ornette, now, right now? What's happening to me, here, now, with Ornette Coleman? With you? Who? It is indeed necessary to improvize well . . . I knew that Ornette was going to call on me to join him tonight, he told me so when we met one afternoon last week. This chance frightens me, I have no idea what's going to happen. It is indeed necessary to improvize, it is necessary to improvize but *well*, this is already a *music lesson*, your lesson, Ornette.
>
> *Derrida 2004: 331–2, italics in original*

Derrida's emphasis on being unsure – even frightened – and his consequent need to improvise well is resonant for us of the kind of dilemmas that can similarly frighten us in their production of a certain experience of the impossible, both as managers and as teachers. For the former, we illustrate the kind of dilemma we have in mind through retelling a story from a time (almost 20 years ago) when, as a UK National Health Service manager, Mark was asked to introduce a computer system into clinical areas, an introduction that involved changes to the way that nurses worked:

> What I had assumed would be minor changes in nurses' work in exchange for substantial gains in terms of the management systems was seen very differently by the nurses themselves. They argued that looking after patients would be seriously compromised, to an extent that far outweighed what they thought were the cosmetic gains in having a slicker administrative system. Whatever the rights and wrongs, it was clear that the political benefits to the top managers in being seen as leaders in MIS [management information systems] meant that there was no question of not implementing the new system. During the implementation, I happened to overhear two nurses expressing to one another their strong personal animosity against me because of my involvement. The realization of their hostility left me quite shocked and hurt. I had not anticipated it, and at the time, could not work out why it should have been so vociferous.
>
> *Learmonth 2007: 111*

We tend to think this sort of situation – one where you are damned if you do and damned if you don't – is commonplace in organizational life, and we suspect that the feeling of shock and hurt experienced is also one that is common among managers: for example, managers often report suffering from sleepless nights because of their dilemmas (Parker 2004).

We think that one important reason why these situations have the impact they do on our emotional life is because they represent encounters with the other. We follow Attridge (2004: 30) in thinking of the other in the sense of 'that which the existing cultural order has to occlude in order to maintain its capacities and configurations, its value-systems and hierarchies of importance; that which it cannot afford to acknowledge if it is to continue without change'. Encounters with the other are necessarily surprising – and often shocking – because they destabilize our sense of personal coherence in that we become aware of how the exclusions of possibilities through our habitual ways of thinking are being subjected to challenge. Through our exchange with the other, our vision of them is altered as we hear 'rumbling menacingly *a whole other world*, which is the world of the other' (Barthes 1978: 26, italics in the original).

In this case, therefore, the encounter with the nurses was an encounter with the other that made Mark uncomfortably aware of a set of values that he could not acknowledge without changing his own view of self (Connor and Becker 1994). At the time, in trying to ignore their concerns he attempted to ensure that their otherness did not affect his own self-conceptions. Even today, this handling of the situation troubles him. In terms of 'conventional' jazz improvisation, this situation might be thought of as what Hatch (1999: 83) calls a 'trainwreck': 'where the musicians so interfere with one another that they cannot go on playing the tune'.

If we continue the analogy with jazz, conventionally, what a skilled manager might have been expected to do in such a situation is to come up with a brilliant solo that brings everyone back into the groove. But this would not be the approach Coleman's free jazz would encourage. For him, such recourse to power might represent the tyranny of the brilliant soloist imposing his/her will on the group. Rather, Coleman's harmolodics suggests that an alternative would be an improvised response that is collective and democratic. It would be a response allowing for the possibility of everyone soloing together. *Together* – albeit with different melodies, melodies that don't necessarily have to be in the same key or even share the same time signature. In other words, in our example a free jazz ethos would have suggested working with the nurses and the other people involved to explore different alternatives, where all of them would be allowed to be soloing at the same time, even when they disagree – an experience of the impossible, perhaps?

What, then, might a harmolodic approach have meant for management education if Mark had acted following its inspiration in this particular situation? We suggest, most fundamentally, that it would have necessarily involved getting all those in the situation together – the minimum condition of being able to jam. Of course, something approaching jamming never happened in this case. There wasn't even a pretence of a jamming session by management or any indication that they were trying to engage with staff and give the impression that they were listening – what Pateman (1970) called pseudo-participation. A decision was taken by the top manager (the virtuoso or leader) and people, like nurses, were expected merely to play in the background supporting the star – a practice known to jazz musicians as 'comping'.[12]

But if they were all together, the radical improvisation implied by harmolodics suggests, by analogy, the encouragement of a *free* exchange of views. We think that such a free exchange might well have involved arguments, shouting, tears – the expression of emotion (see Habermas 1996) – as well as prompting a consideration of systems, efficiency and other more codifiable issues (Griffin 2012). As Hatch (1999: 89) argues, '[t]he jazz metaphor suggests that whenever we interact, communication rests as heavily upon emotional and physical feeling as it does on the intellectual content of the messages involved'. In order to fully capture this range of learning, we suggest that the harmolodic improvisation would be employee-led and be more radical than traditional managerialist approaches to participation, such as employee voice (Wilkinson *et al.* 2014). The shared risks of such improvisation and collaboration are vividly evoked by Mengelberg who argues that:

> Part of improvisation, of the act of improvising, playing with other people, has very much to do with survival strategy. You have, of course, all your expectations and plans destroyed the moment you play with other people. They all have their own ideas of how the musical world at that moment should be. So there are two, three, five, six composers there at the same time destroying each other's ideas, pieces.
>
> *Mengelberg cited in Corbett 1995: 236*

So, in our example of the MIS system, would a resolution necessarily have been found? Would the computer system have been implemented more quickly – or at all? Well, we just don't know. The important point is that the managerially defined aspects of the problem would not be allowed to solo over the nursing or other interests – including each individual's own views. In other words, harmolodic improvisation should not be thought of as a way of finding 'answers'. Such improvisation cannot replace uncertainty with confidence; indeed, improvisation always has a significant degree of risk and uncertainty.

In free jazz (or in free management learning), there will always be a significant element of risk involved – which is to say that improvising may well not succeed and so there is necessarily a need to trust to the future. Not, as Derrida explains, 'a future which is predictable, programmed, scheduled, foreseeable. But . . . a future, l'avenir (to come) which refers to someone who comes whose arrival is totally unexpected. For me, that is the real future. That which is totally unpredictable' (Dick and Ziering Kofman 2005: 53). In this future, there will always inevitably be a certain helplessness in the face of what might happen. As Derrida said to Catherine Malabou about his encounter with Coleman: '[t]he brief "rehearsal" that preceded the improvization, Coleman or my own, in no way resembled what took place before the audience, in the conditions I've told you about. You know what happened subsequently, the event comes as always, after the event' (Malabou and Derrida 2004: 97(n)).

Thinking about these sorts of dilemmas in a harmolodic approach to free management learning might achieve, rather, a shifting and an opening-up of our settled modes of thinking and feeling that may be thwarting our capacity to be creative in order that we may be able to welcome the other and the possibilities of democratic collaboration more readily (Argote 2005; Bailey *et al.* 2009). Good, creative, harmolodic improvisation, after all, involves trying hard not to try too hard – which is to say that it calls for us to be both active and passive. Preparedness is absolutely necessary and yet it is also the case that, for it to be successful, free jazz improvisation is a collective activity that requires the musicians to be surprised by the music that emerges. Harmolodics, therefore, has two necessary conditions: it can occur only if we have prepared for it, and yet it will work only if the event of the improvisation exceeds our preparations and takes us unawares. As Coleman told Derrida:

> What's really shocking in improvized music is that despite its name, most musicians use a 'framework' . . . as a basis for improvizing. I've just recorded a CD with a European musician, Joachim Kühn, and the music I wrote to play with him, that we recorded in August 1996, has two characteristics: it's totally improvized, but at the same time it follows the laws and rules of European structure. And yet, when you hear it, it has a completely improvized feel.
>
> *Coleman and Derrida 2004: 321*

As managers in difficult organizational situations, should we also be aiming at a similar 'completely improvized feel'? We hope that free jazz read in the light of deconstruction might inspire a move towards what one might call free organizations – as places that have a completely improvised feel, whilst not abandoning conventional organizational forms.

## Coda

So what might free organization mean for management education? We could, as teachers, aim for a completely improvised feel within the classroom in a way that shifts and opens up settled modes of thinking and challenges managerialist assumptions. However, as all three of us have found within our own teaching, this approach is far from straightforward. Indeed, those of us working from a Critical Management Studies (CMS) perspective within business schools (see Perriton and Singh, this volume) – trying to introduce thinkers from across the humanities and social sciences like Derrida – often find ourselves encountering our own experiences of the impossible. Situations in which, due to the demand of the school (or the students), we are compelled to use more traditional textbooks and mainstream ideas rather than offering something quite as radical or something that we actually believe in (Rowlinson and Hassard, 2011).

Despite difficulties of this kind, however, we feel that free organization can (as Coleman found in the jazz industry) help us to work within a wider hegemonic system to open up spaces of resistance. As Adam Shatz wrote of what happened at Coleman's funeral in July 2015:

> In speech after speech, Coleman . . . was remembered as a man who embodied a set of values – freedom, independence, improvisation, cultural survival – that transcend music. . . . 'I had a very interesting father,' his son, the drummer Denardo Coleman, said, in the understatement of the day. 'It's not that he thought outside the box. He just didn't think there were any boxes.'
>
> *Shatz, 2015: 38*

How do you think that there are no boxes? We don't know. We can only say that in our own case as academics in higher education, free organization would involve us refocusing our efforts to share critical approaches to management education. It would provide the conditions for us to 'jam' with our fellow teachers in our community and, in doing so, find techniques and methods of integrating radical thinkers and ideas in to the curricula. Free organization can also provide the platform for us to introduce our own perspectives that challenge the status quo through increased empirical research in alternative organizations. Finally, it can lead us to a step into the unknown with our students to develop a critical approach to teaching through increased dialogical participation in the classroom.

All of this amounts to a collective harmolodic approach towards improvisation that is filled with risk and uncertainty. It would require collective and democratic participation between students and teachers, but also universities more generally. For us, it calls to mind the 'unconditional university' in which Derrida (2002: 24) suggests we as educators would 'have the right to say publicly all that is research, knowledge, and thought concerning the truth'. Like Derrida, we certainly want to avoid blueprints on how best to achieve this, especially in informing themes such as creativity and ethics, but ideas such as free organization are offered as a new way of thinking about management and education.

Now, it's over to you . . .

## Notes

1 'Deconstruction and X' brings to mind Ornette Coleman's 1986 album, with Pat Metheney: *Song X*.
2 Who knows, had Derrida ever been asked explicitly about organization, he might have talked similarly of his incompetence in that field too!
3 Perhaps it is of interest to compare Derrida's statement with the account given by Green Gartside (lead singer of the post-punk band Scritti Politti), who met Derrida following the release of the Politti track, 'Jacques Derrida' (available on *Songs to Remember* [Virgin Records, 1982]): '[w]e were talking about music and I asked him why he had never written a book about music expressly, and he said that it is the most difficult thing. In a slippery Derridean way, he said something to the effect that his books aspire to the condition of musicality, that's the loftiest aim he had' (Interview by John O'Reilly, available from: www.aggressiveart.org/sp_uk/interviews/spuk_1999_6.htm [accessed 3 February 2008]).
4 Directors: Kirby Dick and Amy Ziering Kofman.
5 An English version of Derrida's (French) vocals (as he drafted them) has been published (Derrida 2004).
6 The event took place at a Coleman performance held at La Villette in Paris on 1 July 1997 (Malabou and Derrida 2004).
7 Readers of Derrida might be particularly sensitive to the possibilities for double readings of the formulation 'free jazz'. For example, 'free' can be read as both an adjective and a verb. Murphy (1998: 88) points out that read as a verb: 'the title would act, not as a description of the performance, but as the guiding purpose of the performance: the musicians do not play "Free jazz" they play in order to "free jazz". But to free jazz from what? From itself, I would claim, from its presumed identity.' Furthermore, in our contemporary music downloading culture, 'free jazz' might also imply free in the sense of free-of-charge. Although his recordings are not free in this sense, Coleman, nevertheless, has a complex relationship with the commercial aspects of his work – see endnote 11.
8 We would not entirely agree that Coleman 'swept away' the musical structures of his contemporaries. We suspect that Heble's statement is something like saying of deconstruction's influence on the social sciences that it has 'swept away' positivism.
9 Even in the jazz community, Coleman is seen almost as an anti-intellectual.
10 It is interesting to speculate as to the potential conversation Derrida may have had with another contemporary free jazz pioneer Archie Shepp who was, 'A college graduate with a special interest in literature . . . a spokesman for the young black avant-garde musicians of his time' (Collier 1978: 471).
11 Again, the ambiguity of the word 'free' here is significant. Is this, for example, a statement of Coleman's jazz preferences or an indication that he considered himself free from constraining management influences of the major record labels? See Mackey (1995: 77), in which jazz is discussed as the 'erasure of black inventiveness by white appropriation'.
12 Hatch (1999: 79) explains comping as follows: '[w]hile one musician solos, others may accompany them . . . providing rhythmic or harmonic support to the soloist's improvization, and occasionally offering (or feeding) the soloist ideas which may or may not be incorporated into the solo'.

## References


Argote, L. (2005) 'Reflections on two views of managing learning and knowledge in organizations', *Journal of Management Inquiry*, 14(1), 43–48.

Attridge, D. (2004) *The Singularity of Literature*. London: Routledge and Kegan Paul.

Bailey, J.R., Ford, C.M. and Raelin, J.D. (2009) 'Philosophical ties that bind practice: the case of creativity', *Journal of Management Inquiry*, 18, 1–12.

Barenboim, D. and Said, E. (2002) *Parallels and Paradoxes: Explorations in Music and Society*. New York, NY: Vintage Books.

Barthes, R. (1978) *A Lover's Discourse: Fragments*. London: Random House.

Bastien, D.T. and Hostager, T.J. (1988) 'Jazz as a process of organizational innovation', *Communication Research*, 15(5), 582–602.

Berliner, P.F. (1994) *Thinking in Jazz: The Infinite Art of Improvisation*. Chicago, IL: University of Chicago Press.

Boje, D.M. (1995) 'Stories of the storytelling organization: a postmodern analysis of Disney as *Tamara*-Land', *Academy of Management Journal*, 38(4), 997–1035.

Byers, D. and Rhodes, C. (2004) 'Justice, identity and managing with philosophy', *ephemera*, 4(2), 152–64.

Cobussen, M. (2001) 'Derrida's ear', *Deconstruction in Music*. Interactive Online Diss. Erasmus University, Rotterdam, The Netherlands. Available from: www.deconstructioninmusic.com/ (accessed 11 March 2008).

Cobussen, M. (2003) 'Ethics and/in/as silence', *ephemera*, 3(4), 277–85.

Coleman, O. (1983) 'Prime time for harmolodics', *Down Beat*, 7, 54–5.

Coleman, O. and Derrida, J. (2004) 'The other's language: Jacques Derrida interviews Ornette Coleman, 23 June 1997', *Genre*, 36(2), 319–28.

Collier, J.L. (1978) *The Making of Jazz: A Comprehensive History*. Boston, MA: Houghton Mifflin.

Connor, P.E. and Becker, B.W. (1994) 'Personal values and management: what do we know and why don't we know more?', *Journal of Management Inquiry*, 3(1), 67–73.

Cooper, R. (1989) 'Modernism, postmodernism and organizational analysis: the contribution of Jacques Derrida', *Organization Studies*, 10(4), 479–502.

Corbett, J. (1995) 'Ephemera underscored: writing around free improvisation'. *In:* K. Gabbard (ed.) *Jazz among the Discourses*. Durham, NC: Duke University Press, pp. 217–40.

Cunliffe, A.L. (2002) 'Social poetics as management inquiry: a dialogical approach', *Journal of Management Inquiry*, 11, 128–46.

Derrida, J. (1992) 'Afterw.rds or, at least, less than a letter about a letter less'. *In:* N. Royle (ed.) *Afterwords*. Tampere, Finland: Outside Books, pp. 197–203.

Derrida, J. (1995) *Points . . . Interviews, 1974–1994*. Stanford, CA: Stanford University Press.

Derrida, J. (1996) 'As if I were dead: an interview with Jacques Derrida'. *In:* J. Brannigan, R. Robbins and J. Wolfreys (eds.), *Applying: To Derrida*. Basingstoke, UK: Macmillan, pp. 212–26.

Derrida, J. (2000) 'Et cetera . . . (and so on, und so weiter, and so forth, et ainsi de suite, und so überall, etc.)'. *In:* N. Royle (ed.) *Deconstructions: A User's Guide*. Houndmills, UK: Palgrave, pp. 282–305.

Derrida, J. (2002) 'The future of the profession or the university without condition (thanks to the "Humanities", what could take place tomorrow)'. *In:* T. Cohen (ed.) *Jacques Derrida and the Humanities*. Cambridge: Cambridge University Press, pp. 24–57.

Derrida, J. (2004) 'Play – the first name: 1st July 1997', *Genre*, 36(2), 331–40.

Derrida, J., Brunette, P. and Wills, D. (1994) 'The spatial arts: an interview with Jacques Derrida'. *In:* P. Brunette and D. Wills (eds.) *Deconstruction and the Visual Arts: Art, Media, Architecture*. Cambridge: Cambridge University Press, pp. 9–32.

Dick, K. and Ziering Kofman, A. (2005) *Screenplay and Essays on the Film: Derrida*. Manchester, UK: Manchester University Press.

Griffin, M. (2012) 'Deliberative democracy and emotional intelligence: an internal mechanism to regulate the emotions', *Studies in Philosophy and Education*, 31(6), 517–38.

Guimaraes-Costa, N., Pina e Cuhna, M. and Viera Da Cunha, J. (2009) 'Poetry in motion: songwriting as strategic resource (Portugal, 1974)', *Culture and Organization*, 15(1), 88–108.

Habermas, J. (1996) *Moral Consciousness and Communicative Action*. Cambridge, MA: MIT Press.

Hansen, H., Barry, D., Boje, D.M. and Hatch, M.J. (2007) 'Truth or consequences: an improvised collective story construction', *Journal of Management Inquiry*, 16(2), 112–26.

Hatch, M.J. (1997) 'Jazzing up the theory of organizational improvisation', *Advances in Strategic Management*, 14, 181–91.

Hatch, M.J. (1999) 'Exploring the empty spaces of organizing: how improvisational jazz helps redescribe organizational structure', *Organization Studies*, 20(1), 75–100.
Heble, A. (2000) *Landing on the Wrong Note: Jazz, Dissonance and Critical Practice*. New York, NY: Routledge.
Humphreys, M., Ucbasaran, D. and Lockett, A. (2012) 'Sensemaking and sensegiving: stories of jazz leadership', *Human Relations*, 65(1), 41–62.
Kamoche, K., Pina e Cunha, M. and Viera Da Cunha, J. (2003) 'Towards a theory of organizational improvisation: looking beyond the jazz metaphor', *Journal of Management Studies*, 40(8), 2023–51.
Kernfeld, B. (1995) *The New Grove Dictionary of Jazz*. London: Macmillan.
Kilduff, M. (1993) 'Deconstructing organizations', *Academy of Management Review*, 18(1), 13–31.
Kilduff, M. and Kelemen, M. (2001) 'The consolations of organization theory', *British Journal of Management*, 12, 55–59.
Kilduff, M. and Mehra, A. (1997) 'Postmodernism and organizational research', *Academy of Management Review*, 22(2), 453–81.
Laclau, E. (1996) *Emancipation(s)*. London: Verso.
Laclau, E. and Mouffe, C. (2001) *Hegemony and Socialist Strategy: Towards a Radical Democratic Politics*. London: Verso.
Learmonth, M. (2007) 'Critical management education in action: personal tales of management unlearning', *Academy of Management Learning and Education*, 6(1), 109–13.
Learmonth, M., Lockett, A. and Dowd, K. (2012) 'Promoting scholarship that matters: the uselessness of useful research and the usefulness of useless research', *British Journal of Management*, 23(1), 35–44.
Lewin, A.Y. (1998) 'Special issue: jazz improvisation and organizing', *Organization Science*, 9(5), 539–624.
Mackey, N. (1995). 'Other: from noun to verb'. *In:* K. Gabbard (ed.) *Jazz among the Discourses*. London: Duke University Press, pp. 76–99.
Malabou, C. and Derrida, J. (2004) *Counterpath: traveling with Jacques Derrida*. Stanford, CA: Stanford University Press.
Mantere, S., Sillince, J.A.A. and Hämäläinen, V. (2007) 'Music as a metaphor for organizational change', *Journal of Organizational Change Management*, 20(3), 447–59.
Martin, J. (1990) 'Deconstructing organizational taboos: the suppression of gender conflict in organizations', *Organization Science*, 1(4), 339–59.
Mintzberg, H. (1975) 'The manager's job: folklore and fact', *Harvard Business Review*, July–August, 49–61.
Moorman, C. and Miner, A. (1998) 'Organizational improvisation and organizational memory', *Academy of Management Review*, 23, 698–723.
Murphy, T.S. (1998) 'Composition, improvisation, constitution: forms of life in the music of Pierre Boulez and Ornette Coleman', *Angelaki: Journal of the Theoretical Humanities*, 3(2), 75–102.
Nettlebeck, C. (2004) *Dancing with De Beauvoir: jazz and the French*. Melbourne: Melbourne University Press.
Parker, M. (2004) 'Becoming manager: or, the werewolf looks anxiously in the mirror, checking for unusual facial hair', *Management Learning*, 35(1), 45–59.
Pateman, C. (1970) *Participation and Democratic Theory*. Cambridge, MA: Cambridge University Press.
Ramshaw, S. (2006) 'Deconstructing jazz improvisation: Derrida and the law of the singular event', *Critical Studies in Improvisation*, 2(1), 1–19.
Rhodes, C. (2007) 'Outside the gates of Eden: Utopia and work in rock music', *Group and Organization Management*, 32(1), 22–49.
Rowlinson, M. and Hassard, J. (2011) 'How come the critters came to be teaching in business schools? Contradictions in the institutionalization of critical management studies', *Organization*, 18(5), 673–89.
Royle, N. (1998) 'Jacques Derrida, also, enters into heaven', *Angelaki: Journal of the Theoretical Humanities*, 3(2), 113–16.
Shatz, A. (2015) 'Diary', *London Review of Books*, 37(14), 38–9.
Subotnik, R.R. (1996) *Deconstructive Variations: Music and Reason in Western Society*. MN: University of Minnesota Press.
Weick, K.E. (1989) 'Organizational improvisation: 20 years of organizing', *Communication Studies*, 40, 241–8.
Weick, K.E. (1993) 'Organizational redesign as improvisation'. *In:* G.P. Huber and W.H. Glick (eds.) *Organizational Change and Redesign*. New York, NY: Oxford, pp. 346–79.
Weiss, R.M. (2007) 'Derridada. A response to Weitzner', *Journal of Management Inquiry*, 16(1), 55–9.
Weitzner, D. (2007) 'Deconstruction revisited: implications of theory over methodology', *Journal of Management Inquiry*, 16, 43–54.
Wilkinson, A., Donaghey, J., Dundon, T. and Freeman, R. (2014) *The Handbook of Research on Employee Voice*. London: Edward Elgar.
Wills, D. (1998) 'Jazz annotations: negotiating a discursive limit', *Paragraph*, 21(2), 131–49.
Wills, D. (2006) 'Notes towards a requiem: or the music of memory (Jacques Derrida)', *Mosaic*, 39(3), 27–46.

# Part III
# Concepts

# 14

# Management education in a pragmatist perspective after Dewey's experimentalism

*Ulrik Brandi and Bente Elkjaer*

> Unless professional philosophy can mobilize itself sufficiently to assist in this clarification and redirection of men's thoughts, it is likely to get more and more sidetracked from the main currents of contemporary life.
>
> *Dewey 1917 [1980]: 4*

## Introduction

When we teach organization studies and organizational learning in our fields to part-time students (who have a proper job) and full-time students (who often work different odd jobs), we try, as pragmatist inspired researchers and teachers, to teach students to see themselves as part of an organization, which could be the classroom or the university campus. We do so because we want to provide students with a "feeling for the organization" (Keller 1983). Sometimes we use artistic methods, for example by asking students to make drawings of where they are positioned in their organization or to take photos of a phenomenon that we have asked them to "see" in an organization (for example, organizational learning). The idea is to make students present the photos and drawings in class and with these means enter an experimental, playful discussion into how their position could be different and how a representation of an organizational phenomenon reflects a certain theoretical understanding thereof. We believe that it is through our joint working with these experiments, which speaks to the aesthetic and emotional aspects of experiences, that we can guide students to work with theories and concepts in an "instrumental" (discussed later) way as "tools to think" with.

We use these ways of teaching not as "tricks of the trade," although they may be, but rather because they are inspired by the pragmatist philosophy as developed by John Dewey, whose pragmatism was explicitly linked to education: "Since education is the process through which the needed transformation may be accomplished and not remain a mere hypothesis as to what is desirable, we reach a justification of the statement that philosophy is the theory of education as a deliberately conducted practice" (Dewey 1916 [1980]: 342). In Dewey's understanding, education is a "deliberately conducted practice," which we believe emphasizes teachers' responsibility in guiding students to be better at dealing with problems in order to navigate (in) their lives and work. In other words, when pragmatist philosophy is translated into educational practice, John Dewey stands out amongst his fellow pragmatists as the main protagonist, which is the reason why we put emphasis on his work and its impact and potential for management education. It is to Dewey's pragmatist scholarship that we turn when in need of concepts to guide our own educational practice. But let us back up and make a brief introduction to pragmatist philosophy.

Pragmatism emerged from mid-nineteenth-century American philosophy. The classical proponents of pragmatism were Charles Sanders Peirce (1839–1914), William James (1842–1910), John Dewey (1859–1952), and George Herbert Mead (1863–1931). Even though there have been lots of introductions to pragmatism, Dewey gave in his article *The Development of American Pragmatism* (1925 [1984]) a lucid and thorough introduction to its historical foundation as well as to some of its core principles.

In pragmatism there are no a priori propositions or categories and no universal cognitive structures or mental models that shape learning and knowledge. Meaning and meaning making derive from lived experience, where humans are at work with their environments in an entangled manner and on a continuous basis. Rather than understanding theory and action as two different activities and phenomena, pragmatism regards concepts as tools for actions and, as such, instrumental in coping with situations and events, which may lead to (re-)constructing meaning and action by working with concepts in an experimental way. All educational aspirations, however, begin with an emotional sense that "something is not right." We are as humans embedded in the world and it is as participants (and not spectators) that we have experiences, which are not just our own personal experiences but are also experiences that come from being enmeshed in the world. Experiences provide us, through learning, with abilities to act in a mindful ("intelligent") way using the present and history to anticipate the future. Another Deweyan concept – inquiry – is a method for constructing knowledge in a systematic way from experience. Dewey called his pragmatism "experimentalism" in order to stress the playfulness between ideas and action. He also termed his pragmatism "instrumentalism" to emphasize that he views concepts and theories as "tools" that act as "instruments" in our pursuit to understand and communicate with selves and others. This latter also reminds us that different ways of framing actions lead to different solutions and consequences.

Our way of reading the contemporary reception of pragmatist concepts in literature on management education in this chapter is inspired by the Deweyan spirit in the way that we are searching for a variety of consequences for management education of Dewey's theories on education. These theoretical ideas can be coined as the concepts of experience, inquiry, and experimentalism and then translated into the notions of "experiential learning," "reflection," and "teaching methods" (Armstrong and Fukami 2009b). The purpose of the chapter is to show how these latter concepts have worked as inspiration for contemporary management education, as well as how they may do so in the future. We propose that it is possible to read the translation of Dewey's concepts of experience and inquiry, and experiential learning and reflection, in two overall ways: one leaning more towards individualism and cognition; the other more towards culture and practice. We also propose that it is Dewey's experimentalism and instrumentalism that hold the potential for the future of management education because these pragmatist notions speak to a contemporary management practice, which is less driven by routines and therefore requires methodologies that meet the complexities of management practice.

We have interpreted the contemporary influence of pragmatism in management education through a review of the three most influential journals on management education: *Journal of Management Education* (JME); *Academy of Management Learning and Education* (AMLE); and *Management Learning* (ML) (Armstrong and Fukami 2009a; Beatty and Leigh 2010; Korpiaho *et al.* 2007). A closer reading of the abstracts from articles in JME, AMLE, and ML, and a further refinement of the overall pool of potential articles from the initial search, was conducted, resulting in ten articles on experiential learning, five on reflection and learning, and ten on some version of action and problem-based learning.[1]

We have therefore organized our chapter around these three core concepts in Dewey's pragmatism by first presenting the concept, followed by the concept's reception in contemporary literature on management education. We begin each section with a brief introduction to the relevant concept, followed by a section on how the concept has been interpreted within the management education papers that we worked with.

## Experience

Dewey's understanding of experience is a notion to help bring together a living and historical view of human beings: "[. . .] experiencing means living; and that living goes on in and because of an environing medium, not in a vacuum" (Dewey 1917 [1980]: 7). Experience is not just a process of adjustment; experience is "creative integration," which involves a spatial and a historical meaning (Follett 1924: 228; see O'Connor, this volume). This means that humans (subjects) are embedded in worlds (social and "natural") and integrated in past (reflection), present, and future (anticipation). We are, however, always situated in the present, which is the starting point for Dewey's concept of learning and knowledge:

> We always live at the time we live and not at some other time, and only by extracting at each present time the full meaning of each present experience are we prepared for doing the same thing in the future. This is the only preparation which in the long run amounts to anything.
>
> *Dewey 1938 [1988]: 49*

Dewey's understanding of the notions of experience and learning reflects a relational ontology in which humans and worlds are mutually constituted and constituting in a dynamic way (it is not necessary that humans act first; the world can also "act" and thereby invite humans to re-act). Experience is, in this pragmatist frame of reference, construed on the underlying assumption that we as humans are committed to "doings" in and with the situations at hand just as much as we have to endure and suffer what is given by the relevant situations. A possible scenario, for example, is for a newly employed manager to show initiative and provide direction whilst at the same time reflecting existing values and historical meanings of what is expected of managerial practice in a particular enterprise. The example illustrates that experience is an association between what you as a manager bring to a situation and the situational affordances. Dewey stresses that experience is situated and is also a passive and an active process; it is not first and foremost an inner cognitive process:

> Experience is primarily a process of undergoing: a process of standing something; of suffering and passion, of affection, in the literal sense of these words. [. . .] Experience is no slipping along in a path fixed by inner consciousness. [. . .] Since we live forward; since we live in a world where changes are going on whose issues mean our weal or woe; since every act of ours modifies these changes and hence is fraught with promise, or charged with hostile energies – what should experience be but a future implicated in the present!
>
> *Dewey 1917 [1980]: 8–9, Dewey's punctuation*

Here we see that Dewey's concept of experience departs from an everyday understanding of experience in which experiences are often regarded as an inner personal accumulation of the past (Dewey 1917 [1980]); instead, Dewey's notion of experience is more in line with the current notion of practice in practice theory in the meaning of both practicing, and doing so in an institutionalized practice (Corradi *et al.* 2010; Nicolini 2013). For example, practicing management in a conventional way of management practice. We believe, however, that pragmatism brings important dimensions to practice theory when the issue is management education, given the complexities of contemporary management practice, because of its explicated focus upon the relation between experience and learning, as well as its anticipatory focus.

### *From experience to experiential learning*

Kolb's notion of experiential learning is a major heritage from pragmatist philosophy in management education. Kolb explicitly refers to Dewey's concept of experience, but it is in his own translation and understanding thereof that Kolb takes his point of departure. Kolb's definition of experience is reflected in his definition of learning: "Learning is the process whereby knowledge is created through the transformation of experience" (Kolb 1984: 38). Thus, for Kolb, experience is mainly a foundation for the creation of knowledge, whereas Dewey's notion of experience is "everything," and knowledge is just one kind of experience.

Kolb's model of experiential learning is often represented as a circle with four boxes held together by arrows (Kolb 1984: 21). The four boxes consists of "concrete experience" followed by the box "observations and reflections," which is again followed by a third box "formation of abstract concepts and generalizations" leading up to the fourth box "testing implications of concepts in new situations." Kolb stressed two aspects of his experiential learning cycle. First, that concrete experiences are valuable for creating meaning in learning, as well as for validating the learning process: "Immediate personal experience is the focal point for learning, giving life, texture, and subjective personal meaning to abstract concepts and at the same time providing a concrete, publicly shared reference point for testing the implications and validity of ideas created during the learning process" (Kolb 1984: 21). For Kolb, therefore, experiential learning means that education should start with students' experiences and it should create a motivation for learning, rather than the foundations for life as it is for Dewey (see also McDermott 1973 [1981]). Second, Kolb writes that each stage in the model fits into different forms of adaptation to reality, which in turn reflects different individual learning styles, which has been Kolb's foundation for the development of his "Learning Style Inventory" (LSI).

Kolb's experiential theory of learning has been extremely influential not only in management education but also for schools in general where the notion of learning styles is widely accepted. Kolb's theories have been read, reread, discussed, and criticized, as well as empirically tested by different means. Reading through the selected articles on the reception of Dewey's idea of experience, primarily through Kolb's work, we have identified two recurrent themes associated with management education.

First, we see an emphasis on students' learning styles as a fundamental "toolkit" for understanding and improving learning processes. Many proponents within management education, as well as Kolb himself, have worked from the idea that students exhibit different learning styles. For example, "the Kolbs" (Klimoski 2005; Kolb and Kolb 2005) set out to expand Kolb's experiential learning theory to include the concept of "learning space" to encompass the interface between students' learning styles and the institutional learning environment. Mainemelis *et al.* (2002) were also grounded in experiential learning theory when they set out to empirically test the three instruments derived from this theory defined as the learning style inventory, the adaptive style inventory, and the learning skills profile. Building upon Kolb and Kayes, Armstrong and Mahmud (2008) want to determine whether levels of accumulated managerial tacit knowledge are associated with managers' dominant learning styles, and they find that "it may be *how* people learn from experience rather than the length of experience that matters" (2008: 200, our emphasis). Finally, Li *et al.* (2013) relate to Kolb's work in their development of a term called "cultural intelligence," which is argued to be useful in management education of global leaders. Cultural intelligence is correlated with executives' learning styles because they were developed in Kolb's experiential learning theory.

Second, we have analyzed another pool of texts, which also have their starting point in experiential learning theory but with the explicit intention of modifying Kolb's theory of learning, and in which the notion of experience is interpreted in light of a social and cultural understanding of the term. These interpretations include that of Kayes (2002) who wants to revitalize the Deweyan concept of experience in light of a poststructuralist analysis based upon Lacan, which includes the role of language in the construction of experience. Kayes (2002: 146) discusses how we are to understand experiential learning and points to the importance of developing a precise vocabulary for how to develop a new language of management learning. He proposes a language that adopts experiential learning as dependent on existing social knowledge and thus challenges the dominant cognitive translation of Dewey's notion of experience that we see at work in the Kolb-inspired adoptions. A similar approach that underscores the importance of the social and cultural aspects of experience is that of Baker *et al.* (2005) who argue in favor of a theoretical framework for conversational learning as an "experiential learning process through which people construct meaning together from their experiences" (2005: 426). The idea of Baker *et al.*'s proposal is to create a conversational space that enables "those in the conversation to remain engaged with each other so that differing perspectives can catalyze learning experientially and promote individual learning and organizational learning" (2005: 411).

Some scholars explicitly criticize Kolb's notion of experiential learning, including Conklin (2012) who argues for a more encompassing inclusion of students' experiences, but does so from the perspective of the adult autonomous learner who comes with this concept (Knowles 1973 [1990]). The critical voices also include Reynolds (2009) who discusses experiential learning in light of post-heroic conceptions of leadership and defines this kind of leadership as a relational practice, as a social and political process with the focus as much on the interactions of the people involved as on the characteristics of the individual or management role. Reynolds elaborates on Kayes's translation of experience, arguing for an emphasis on leadership as a relational practice entailing aspects of power and politics grounded in the social interactions of people involved in organizational practices. For both Kayes and Reynolds, management education is more than a process for the individual mind; it is a process embedded in management culture and practice.

Kolb's experiential learning theory brings forward the idea that it is important to include learners' (for example, management students) experiences, and although it is experience understood as individual and mostly cognitive experiences, it is nevertheless an attempt to bring in management practices by way of bringing students' experiences forward to be worked on in class. The consequences for how to construct and design teaching sessions are, however, quite different for the two interpretations of experiential learning. For example, in a course on organizational theory for undergraduate students, we have deployed both the traditional and the critical Kolb-inspired approach in our way of preparing the students for reading texts and presentations in class. We have done so by encouraging students to use their own personal experiences from being members of organizations (see the example in the introduction) and also by asking them to connect their experiences to issues of power in organizations. For example, when discussing how we can understand organizational values and culture, a discussion about the differences between espoused values and values-in-use is often triggered. These are difficult issues to comprehend without establishing a link to students' own experiences of organizational culture, but we also need to encompass wider issues to get beyond organizational functionalism to be able to see how organizational cultures are embedded in negotiations and politics.

## Inquiry

Inquiry is considered by Dewey (1938 [1968]: 108) as a way to acquire knowledge. Dewey defines inquiry as "the controlled or directed transformation of an indeterminate situation into one that is so determinate in its constituent distinctions and relations as to convert the elements of the original situation into a unified whole." Inspired by Darwinism and evolutionary theory, Dewey emphasizes that inquiry is about adaptation to the conditions provided by the environment, but inquiry is also a creative and experimental way to deal with uncertainties when habits are impeded. Inquiry is about handling uncertain situations and felt experiences that may turn into knowledge through the use of ideas and concepts to comprehend and communicate the experiences had. In *Logic: The Theory of Inquiry*, Dewey (1938 [1986]) explicates the content and structure of the process of inquiry that is outlined as a process that sets out with an emotional sense that something is not right. This starting point is followed by a process of discovering provisional facts and employing possible solutions in order to settle the indeterminate situation.

When inquiry leads to new knowledge, thinking and reflection about the relation between the definition of the problem and its solution has been put to work by way of mind and intellect. It is not until a new relation between actions and their consequences is made that new experience and new knowledge may occur, which, in turn, may lead to more informed ("intelligent") future actions. It is important not to reduce inquiry to a mental process because inquiry is not only a matter of thinking but also a way of being in the world. In Dewey's own words: "The significant distinction is no longer between the knower *and* the world; it is between different ways of being in and of the movement of things; between a brute psychical way and a purposive, intelligent way" (Dewey 1917 [1980]: 42, Dewey's emphasis). Dewey argued that inquiry in everyday life has the same structure as scientific inquiry. Inquiry, however, cannot be reduced to a response to purely abstract thoughts because it is anchored in everyday situations, in practices. It is part of living practices and educational activity to inquire, to mull things over, to draw conclusions, and make evaluations.

For Dewey, inquiry, or "critical reflection" as he sometimes called it, is more than a cognitive activity. Inquiry is to be conceptualized as a method that includes emotions, bodies, experiences, knowledge, propositions, values, attitudes, reasoning, decisions, as well as continuous testing of hypotheses and results. In this line of thought, knowledge (being one of the results of inquiry) is not representing truth as such, but rather it is constituted by the interplay between subjects and worlds and action and thinking throughout the process of inquiry.

### *Inquiry transformed into reflection*

If Dewey's notion of experience is the source of inspiration for experiential learning, it is his notion of inquiry that inspires the many contributions within management education that stress reflection as important for the production of knowledge. Based on our interpretation of the texts that connect to inquiry and reflection, we identified issues of reflection understood as an individual and cognitive process, as well as one of interaction, which also includes critical aspects of reflection. Hedberg (2009), for example, speaks directly to an individual understanding of reflection and reflective learning through asking what reflection can bring to management learning. She explores the classroom as a place for reflective learning, and proposes (in line with Kolb) that it is through reflection that experience gains meaning and helps management students to make sense of their world and the concepts and theories that are in use. Hedberg, who cites Dewey and credits him for bringing reflection to education, defines reflection as a cognitive process of "active, persistent and careful consideration of any belief or supposed form of knowledge" (2009: 12).

In contrast to Hedberg, Vince (2002; also this volume) argues for understanding reflection as an organizing (collective) process and points to critical reflection as questioning assumptions and being about the social power relations within organizations. Reynolds and Vince (2004a) continue this line of argument and combine reflection with action-based management learning. The theme of their work is the potential connection between critical management perspectives and action-based learning because, although critical management questions power, control, and vested interests, action-based learning suggests that management students' experiences are as valid as academic theory. Their intention is to develop propositions for a critical approach to managers' learning and to see management learning as an integrated aspect of work-based action. Gray (2007) continues the line of reasoning from Reynolds and Vince in making a distinction between individual development ("the reflective practitioner") and critical reflection as a route to collective action and a component of organizational learning and change in which power and political processes are included.

When we consider contemporary changes of work practices that appear to be increasingly marked by a focus on fluidity and collaboration within and across organizational boundaries (Blackler and Regan 2009; Heizmann 2011; Kauppila *et al.* 2011; Reynolds and Vince 2004b; Vince 2002), a notion of reflection understood as an individual feature may constrain ideas of management education. It therefore seems relevant to ask how this complexity of organizational work practices is to be captured in management education. Based on our experience with designing educational activities, we have tried to meet this challenge by adjusting and aligning our ways of teaching and assessing students by enacting and facilitating more group-oriented ways of working in class.

We wanted, for example, to provide our students with a deeper and more nuanced understanding of how organizational dynamics and complexities are influencing organizational decision making, and we thought it necessary to connect theory on decision making, their personal experiences, and some actual work practices of an organization. We experimented with this in a graduate class on "organizational development and human resource management" through constructing a real-time case, which we designed in close collaboration with a large Danish enterprise. Enterprise representatives visited the class for a whole day during the course and presented different organizational development scenarios in combination with interviews conducted by the students. We found that this way of working brought to light experiences of the complexities of management practice but also organizational life and work. This elucidated how the theoretical conceptual constructs on decision making were put to work and came to life for students as "tools" to think and act with in their work with the case organization.

## Experimentalism

Inquiry is an experimental method by which new experiences may be acquired not only through action but also by using ideas, concepts, hypotheses, and theories as "tools to think with" in an instrumental way. This means that ideas, theories, and concepts work as instrumental for actions: "[. . .] thinking is a process of inquiry, of looking into things, of investigating. Acquiring is always secondary, and instrumental to the act of inquiry. It is seeking, a quest, for something that is not at hand" (Dewey 1916 [1980]: 148). Thinking works in order to generate working hypotheses, the consequences of which are tested in actions and, as such, are experimental. Experimental actions are not merely examples of "trial-and-error"; they are actions governed by an idea or a hypothesis.

The notions of experience, inquiry, experimentalism, and instrumentalism cannot be taken apart practically as we do here for explanatory reasons because inquiry is also an experience and experience is an experimental endeavor that connects past, present, and future:

> To "learn from experience" is to make a backward and forward connection between what we do to things and what we enjoy or suffer from things in consequence. Under such conditions, doing becomes a trying; an experiment with the world to find out what it is like; the undergoing becomes instruction – discovery of the connection of things.
>
> *Dewey 1916 [1980]: 147*

For Dewey, the experiment necessarily implicates some sort of change of the situations or events in which it is embedded, and experimenting and trying things out is a way to find out what the world is like.

In Dewey's conceptual world, a pragmatist theory of learning considers inquiry as a method in an experimental playful way in which inquiry into uncertain situations is the basis for having an experience. Having an experience may, however, also be turned into knowledge through its infusion with ideas and concepts to make the experience meaningful and communicable. The transformation of an uncertain situation that triggers inquiry is dependent on the modification or change of the existing experience, and this transformation can only happen through experimentation with different solutions in the world. We have translated this part of Dewey's pragmatism into teaching methods within the management education literature, and it is to this issue we now turn.

### *Teaching methods*

From our literature review, we find several proponents of different teaching methods in the management education literature under different names, such as problem-based learning, collaborative learning, action learning, and action research. In this section, we present some of the ideas we found for how teaching methods can be worked with in an experimental way in management education. As in the previous two sections on the application of experience and inquiry, we illustrate and discuss how experiments described in the literature can be deployed in an educational setting.

Most work with teaching methods takes issue with the question of how to construct organizational contexts in management education. When Innes (2006), for example, provides an overview of the theoretical rationale for problem-based learning, the focus is upon the implications of two key assumptions: authenticity of the problem context and the quality of the dialogue established. Likewise, Sherwood (2004) writes about the question of how to design a context for problem-based learning in management education. The starting point is that the term "context" is a critical ingredient of problem-based learning in order for successful learning to occur. In his paper, Sherwood begins with Leavitt's "diamond": participants, social structure, goals, and technology supplemented with Scott's 5th element: environment. He further categorizes these into social (participants and social structure) and physical (goals and technology) dimensions and uses this distinction as a framework for designing a problem-based context for management education. Sherwood (2004) also points to the need for more knowledge on the effect of organizational context in the learning process, as well as knowledge on how to adapt the organizational context to geographically dispersed groups of students and teachers.

For Raelin and Coghlan (2006), the proposal is to combine action learning and action research. They deal with the question of how to use the experiences of working managers in management education to produce learning and knowledge, and they propose two pedagogical approaches: action learning and action research. The wish for Raelin and Coghlan is to create contemporary management practice as a context for including management experience and to be able to use that as a point of reference in their work with management learning:

> In this paper, we explore how action learning accomplishes our first objective of converting experience into practical learning, and how action research accomplishes our second of engaging in research on experience that can produce actionable knowledge.
>
> *Raelin and Coghlan 2006: 671*

In another paper, Raelin (2006) studies how action learning can promote collaborative leadership. The assumption is a model of leadership as concurrent (share power), collective (team), mutual (everyone counts), and compassionate (democratic), which is a change from the individual hero-leader. The idea of learning is that it "occurs in the midst of practice and is, indeed, a concurrent by-product of practice" (Raelin 2006: 157).

Action learning is also an important term for Blackler and Kennedy (2004) when they describe their action-learning programme to "renew and refresh" senior (primarily non-medical) management in the National Health Service in the UK. Dehler and Edmonds (2006) regard action research as an answer when both action learning and action research are used in management education, which is also the issue for dealing with the challenge of developing pedagogies that confront the complexities associated with the practice of managing. Joshi *et al.* (2005: 674) also seek to bring organizational contexts to life when teaching undergraduates through an experimental learning process that applies experience as a "vehicle for learning." Thus, the focus upon teaching methods seems to be upon how to design learning processes in more formal settings, taking into account the organizational context in which management students are to practice.

Based on the two previous discussions on experience and reflection within management education, the focus has been on the learning potential of different ways of constructing contexts. It is in these many ways of experimenting with different teaching methods for including organizational contexts that we find the inspiration from Dewey most vivid and challenging. It appears a real struggle for educators to bring organizations to life for management students. Following the argument from the tradition of action learning presented by, for example, Dehler and Edmonds (2006), Raelin (2006), and Raelin and Coghlan (2006), we see the main debate evolving around how to balance and find a "middle way" between a conventional teaching design based on a traditional learning curriculum (see also Welsh and Dehler 2013) and learning situated in management practice. This is in other words seeking to pave a way for pedagogy in management education that takes into account that the field has a well-established research literature and is also moving along with organizational practice, which is in line with Dewey's idea of education between a situated pedagogy and a curriculum-led one (see also Dewey 1902 [1976]).

## Summing up and discussion

Our guiding question in this chapter has been to find out how management practice is brought to life in management education. Over the years, the works of John Dewey have inspired us, particularly his ideas related to learning and education, the concepts of experience, inquiry, and experimentalism, as well as Dewey's understanding of pragmatism as instrumentalism. We have in this pursuit made a review of recent literature within management education as it is published in three major journals on management education. Inspired by scholars on management education, we have translated the Deweyan notions into experiential learning, reflection, and teaching methods (Armstrong and Fukami 2009b).

In relation to the issues of experiential learning and reflection, we saw two main roads in the newer literature: a version marked by individualism and cognition, and the other where culture and practice were more prevalent. We pointed to Kolb's experiential learning theory as very important for management education and, although he makes use of a notion of experience, which is far away from Dewey's encompassing notion of experience, his work has been and continues to be important when including participants' personal experiences in teaching in order to make it more meaningful for students to learn. This means that it is possible to see Kolb's experiential learning theory more as a motivation theory for learning than Dewey's account of experience as the fundamental building block for living lives and acquiring knowledge.

Here it may be relevant to recall Dewey's original impetus to coin the notion of experience as an opposition to the use of a priori concepts (rationalism) or pure sense data (empiricism) in philosophy and his coining of the denotative method (Alexander 2004; Dewey 1925 [1981]). The concept of experience was a way to understand knowledge and its production in relation not to rationalism or empiricism but to a "middle road" (a "via media") (Dewey 1939) or to "restore rationality, agency, and responsibility to the sphere of human action" (Biesta and Burbules 2003: 22). Dewey, however, became increasingly aware that the concept of experience is one that creates much confusion because it is easily conflated with an understanding of experience as only a result of past actions leading to tacit individual knowledge. Thus, when we understand experience as a "tool for motivation" for learning, we risk failing to see the concept as embedded in a larger philosophical discourse. The latter may also prevent us from seeing reflection as transcending individual cognitive activity and lead us to exclude the culture and practices of the smaller (organizational) and larger (institutional) social and natural worlds, of which both experience and reflection are a part.

We have presented our own examples, trying to organize teaching in a way that includes culture and practice in relation to the notion of experience and reflection, as well as bringing other scholars within management education into the picture. This endeavor has also pointed us towards collective and critical understandings of reflection and to a need to bring in work and organizational contexts as a meaningful framing for reflection.

In relation to the literature on teaching methods, it is here that we find the most inspirational ideas of how to bring management practice to life through work on how to provide understandings of organizational contexts for students in class. Organizational contexts encompass a dynamic and complex environment that is linked to management practice relevant for management education. Changes in the organizational context, for example by implementing new technologies, language, values, or strategies, lead to new requirements for management practice and, in turn, management education.

## Debates and future challenges

How can we practice a contemporary pragmatist approach in management education? We began this chapter by including a brief example of how we, in our own teaching, worked with methods that speak to the emotions and aesthetics of students' imaginations or lived experiences of being part of an organization as a framing for helping them see and understand organizations in a conceptual way. This involved ways to try and connect their abstract ideas of organizations and also to remind them that their "bodies" are living and working in these organizations. This may be compared with how we talk about Kolb's experiential learning as a motivation theory for learning, and be seen as a way for us to "motivate" students to include organizational contexts. Even if this is so, it also allows a way to teach students to be sensitive and to act upon their feelings of uncertainty, to make inquiries, and to openly test and validate their solutions to the "felt" problems. This is our way of adhering to an understanding of organizations not only as work and structures but also as a way for them to understand that:

> [...] to study organizations involves thinking about philosophy, politics, ethics and much more. And behind or beyond these abstractions are the lived experiences of people not just working together but joking, arguing, criticizing, fighting, deciding, lusting, despairing, creating, resisting, fearing, hoping or, in short, organizing.
>
> *Grey 2005 [2013]: 2*

Looking ahead, we propose to work with management education stemming from these felt "real-life" uncertainties, and an embodied concept of learning, including emotion and cognition, knowledge as open-ended (fallible), and ethics (which intends to make organizations "better" places to work in) and politics (which acknowledges that power "games" are always an inherent part of organizations). Seeing management education as part of management practice and embedded in organizational practices should not, however, lead to "practicism" because concepts matter as instruments in action too. To avoid this and in order for management education to take a point of departure – not "in" managers but in management practicing organizational management practices – the following questions may be asked: "what does practicing management mean?" and "why does it matter?" (Nicolini 2013)

We believe that a pragmatist perspective on management education should include experimental playfulness because management practices are complex and often include a portfolio of rationales that can be played out "only" in a pragmatist-inspired version of management education and management learning in which, not only organizational contexts like the division of labor and coordinating mechanisms matter, but also that people interacting with selves, others, and materiality matter too. It is in this complexity that Dewey's instrumentalist understanding of pragmatism may help students work with different solutions and always consider the different consequences for different people in organizations. To see that living and working in organizations means different things to different people is, in our view, extremely important for management education because these differences are important for management practicing management practice.

## Note

1 The papers reviewed are, in alphabetical order: Armstrong and Mahmud 2008; Baker *et al.* 2005; Berggren and Söderlund 2011; Blackler and Kennedy 2004; Conklin 2012; Dehler and Edmonds 2006; Gilmore and Anderson 2012; Gray 2007; Hedberg 2009; Hoover *et al.* 2012; Innes 2006; Joshi *et al.* 2005; Kayes 2002; Klimoski 2005; Kolb and Kolb 2005; Li, Mobley, and Kelly 2013; Mainemelis *et al.* 2002; Raelin 2006; Raelin and Coghlan 2006; Reynolds 2009; Reynolds and Vince 2004a; Sherwood 2004; Smith 2005; Vince 2002; Welsh and Dehler 2013. They are not all mentioned in the text.

## References


Alexander, T. (2004) 'Dewey's denotative–empirical method: a thread through the labyrinth', *Journal of Speculative Philosophy*, 18(3), 248–56.

Armstrong, S.J. and Fukami, C.V. (2009a) 'Past, present and future perspectives of management learning, education and development'. *In*: S.J. Armstrong and C.V. Fukami (eds.) *The Sage Handbook of Management Learning, Education and Development*. London: Sage Publications, pp. 1–22.

Armstrong, S.J. and Fukami, C.V. (eds.) (2009b) *The Sage Handbook of Management Learning, Education and Development*. London: Sage Publications.

Armstrong, S.J. and Mahmud, A. (2008) 'Experiential learning and the acquisition of managerial tacit knowledge', *Academy of Management Learning and Education*, 7(2), 189–208.
Baker, A.C., Jensen, P.J. and Kolb, D.A. (2005) 'Conversational learning: an experiential approach to knowledge creation', *Management Learning*, 36(4), 411–27.
Beatty, J.E. and Leigh, J.S.A. (2010) 'Taking stock of management education: a comparison of three management education journals', *Journal of Management Education*, 34(3), 367–92.
Berggren, C. and Söderlund, J. (2011) 'Management education for practicing managers: combining academic rigor with personal change and organizational action', *Journal of Management Education*, 35(3), 377–405.
Biesta, G.J.J. and Burbules, N.C. (2003) *Pragmatism and Educational Research*. Lanham, MD: Rowman and Littlefield.
Blackler, F. and Kennedy, A. (2004) 'The design and evaluation of a leadership programme for experienced chief executives from the public sector', *Management Learning*, 35(2), 181–203.
Blackler, F. and Regan, S. (2009) 'Intentionality, agency, change: practice theory and management', *Management Learning*, 40(2), 161–76.
Conklin, T.A. (2012) 'Making it personal: the importance of student experience in creating autonomy-supportive classrooms for millennial learners', *Journal of Management Education*, 37(4), 499–538.
Corradi, G., Gherardi, S. and Verzelloni, L. (2010) 'Through the practice lens: where is the bandwagon of practice-based studies heading?', *Management Learning*, 41(3), 265–83.
Dehler, G.E. and Edmonds, R.K. (2006) 'Using action research to connect practice to learning: a course project for working management students', *Journal of Management Education*, 30(5), 636–69.
Dewey, J. (1902 [1976]) 'The child and the curriculum'. *In*: J.A. Boydston (ed.) *Middle Works 2*. Carbondale, IL: Southern Illinois University Press, pp. 271–91.
Dewey, J. (1916 [1980]) 'Democracy and education. An introduction to the philosophy of education'. *In*: J.A. Boydston (ed.) *Middle Works: 1899–1924*. Vol. 9. Carbondale, IL: Southern Illinois University Press, pp. 1–370.
Dewey, J. (1917 [1980]) 'The need for a recovery of philosophy'. *In*: J.A. Boydston (ed.) *Middle Works: 1916–1917*. Vol. 10. Carbondale, IL: Southern Illinois University Press, pp. 3–48.
Dewey, J. (1925 [1981]) 'Experience and nature'. *In*: J.A. Boydston (ed.) *The Later Works, 1925–1953*. Vol. 1. Carbondale, IL: Southern Illinois University Press, pp. 1–328.
Dewey, J. (1925 [1984]) 'The development of American pragmatism'. *In*: J.A. Boydston (ed.) *Later Works 2*. Carbondale, IL: Southern Illinois University Press, pp. 3–21.
Dewey, J. (1938 [1986]) 'Logic: the theory of inquiry'. *In*: J.A. Boydston (ed.) *The Later Works, 1925–1953*. Vol. 12. Carbondale, IL: Southern Illinois University Press, pp. 1–539.
Dewey, J. (1938 [1988]) 'Experience and education'. *In*: J.A. Boydston (ed.) *Later Works 13*. Carbondale, IL: Southern Illinois University Press, pp. 1–62.
Dewey, J. (1939) 'Experience, knowledge and value: a rejoinder'. *In*: P.A. Schilpp (ed.) *The Philosophy of John Dewey*. Evanston, IL: Northwestern University, pp. 515–608.
Follett, M.P. (1924) *Creative Experience*. New York, NY: Longmans, Green and Co.
Gilmore, S. and Anderson, V. (2012) 'Anxiety and experience-based learning in a professional standards context', *Management Learning*, 43(1), 75–95.
Gray, D.E. (2007) 'Facilitating management learning: developing critical reflection through reflective tools', *Management Learning*, 38(5), 495–517.
Grey, C. (2005 [2013]) *A Very Short, Fairly Interesting and Reasonably Cheap Book about Studying Organizations*. 3rd edn. London: Sage Publications.
Hedberg, P.R. (2009) 'Learning through reflective classroom practice. Applications to educate the reflective manager', *Journal of Management Education*, 33(1), 10–36.
Heizmann, H. (2011) 'Knowledge sharing in a dispersed network of HR practice: zooming in on power/knowledge struggles', *Management Learning*, 42(4), 379–93.
Hoover, J.D., Giambatista, R.C. and Belkin, L.Y. (2012) 'Eyes on, hands on: vicarious observational learning as an enhancement of direct experience', *Academy of Management Learning and Education*, 11(4), 591–608.
Innes, R.B. (2006) 'What can learning science contribute to our understanding of the effectiveness of problem-based learning groups?', *Journal of Management Education*, 30(6), 751–64.
Joshi, M.P., Davis, E.B., Kathuria, R. and Weidner, C.K. (2005) 'Experiential learning process: exploring teaching and learning of strategic management framework through the winter survival exercise', *Journal of Management Education*, 29(5), 672–95.
Kauppila, O.-P., Rajala, R. and Jyrämä, A. (2011) 'Knowledge sharing through virtual teams across borders and boundaries', *Management Learning*, 42(4), 395–418.

Kayes, D.C. (2002) 'Experiential learning and its critics: preserving the role of experience in management learning and education', *Academy of Management Learning and Education*, 1(2), 137–49.
Keller, E.F. (1983) *A Feeling for the Organism: The Life and Times of Barbara McClintock*. San Francisco, CA: Freeman.
Klimoski, R. (2005) 'The voice(s) of experience on experiential learning', *Academy of Management Learning and Education*, 4(2), 174–5.
Knowles, M. (1973 [1990]) *The Adult Learner: A Neglected Species*. Houston, TX: Gulf Publishing Co.
Kolb, A.Y. and Kolb, D.A. (2005) 'Learning styles and learning spaces: enhancing experiential learning in higher education', *Academy of Management Learning and Education*, 4(2), 193–212.
Kolb, D.A. (1984) *Experiential learning. Experience as the Source of Learning and Development*. Englewood Cliffs, NJ: Prentice Hall.
Korpiaho, K., Päiviö, H. and Räsänen, K. (2007) 'Anglo-American forms of management education: a practice–theoretical perspective', *Scandinavian Journal of Management*, 23(1), 36–65.
Li, M., Mobley, W.H. and Kelly, A. (2013) 'When do global leaders learn best to develop cultural intelligence? An investigation of the moderating role of experiential learning style', *Academy of Management Learning and Education*, 12(1), 32–50.
McDermott, J.J. (1973 [1981]) *The Philosophy of John Dewey. Two Volumes in One: 1. The Structure of Experience; 2. The Lived Experience*. Chicago, IL: University of Chicago Press.
Mainemelis, C., Boyatzis, R.E. and Kolb, D.A. (2002) 'Learning styles and adaptive flexibility. Testing experiential learning theory', *Management Learning*, 33(1), 5–33.
Nicolini, D. (2013) *Practice Theory, Work, and Organization. An Introduction*. Oxford: Oxford University Press.
Raelin, J. (2006) 'Does action learning promote collaborative leadership?', *Academy of Management Learning and Education*, 5(2), 152–68.
Raelin, J.A. and Coghlan, D. (2006) 'Developing managers as learners and researchers: using action learning and action research', *Journal of Management Education*, 30(5), 670–89.
Reynolds, M. (2009) 'Wild frontiers – reflections on experiential learning', *Management Learning*, 40(4), 387–92.
Reynolds, M. and Vince, R. (2004a) 'Critical management education and action-based learning: synergies and contradictions', *Academy of Management Learning and Education*, 3(4), 442–56.
Reynolds, M. and Vince, R. (eds.) (2004b) *Organizing Reflection*. Aldershot, UK: Ashgate.
Sherwood, A.L. (2004) 'Problem-based learning in management education: a framework for designing context', *Journal of Management Education*, 28(5), 536–57.
Smith, G.F. (2005) 'Problem-based learning: can it improve managerial thinking?', *Journal of Management Education*, 29(2), 357–78.
Vince, R. (2002) 'Organizing reflection', *Management Learning*, 33(1), 63–78.
Welsh, M.A. and Dehler, G.E. (2013) 'Combining critical reflection and design thinking to develop integrative learners', *Journal of Management Education*, 37(6), 771–802.

# 15

# Thinking in and of the world

## Actualizing wisdom and pragmatism in business education?

*Matt Statler and Perttu Salovaara*

### What should people learn in business schools and how?

Historians of business school education (see Friga *et al.* 2003; Khurana 2007; Augier and March 2011; O'Connor 2011; Thomas and Wilson 2011) note that although the roots of business education grew from the traditions associated with trades and professional guild associations, when activists and administrators sought to establish business studies as a proper academic discipline in the context of the university (initially, the University of Pennsylvania), they downplayed the practical, normative, and embodied aspects of those traditions. Instead, the subject was constituted with reference to the theoretical, value-neutral, and cognitive aspects of what was widely understood, in the late nineteenth and early twentieth centuries in the US, to constitute empirical science. As critics reflecting on this history have pointed out (Bartunek and Seo 2002; Pfeffer and Fong 2002; Starkey *et al.* 2004; Ghoshal 2005; Pfeffer 2005; Starkey and Tempest 2005), the emphasis on "scientific management" in business schools has had the unintended consequence of diminishing the importance of ethical, moral, or otherwise normative value-laden considerations for several generations of graduates (Colby *et al.* 2011).

As a counter-weight to this pervasive (and many would say, destructive) bias, scholars have been arguing that business schools should re-orient toward the teaching of practical, not scientific or theoretical, reasoning (Colby *et al.* 2011; Sullivan, Ehrlich, and Colby, this volume; see also Bailey and Ford 1996). This term, practical reasoning, is based on the Greek concept of *phronesis*, which has been translated and interpreted variously over the centuries as prudence, *prudentia*, *sapientia*, practical wisdom, and wisdom. Most recently scholars have tried to reframe the overall purpose of the business school as the development of practical wisdom (Bierly *et al.* 2000; Nonaka and Toyama 2007; Chia and Holt 2008; McKenna *et al.* 2009; Antonacopoulou 2010; Nonaka and Takeuchi 2011), but the question remains: how is it possible?

Our response to this question draws on the pragmatic philosophy of John Dewey. Dewey's basic notion that human knowledge involves iterative cycles of action and reflection has provided the foundation for theories of learning (Kolb 1984; see Brandi and Elkjaer, this volume) and organizational learning (Schon 1983; Senge and Sterman 1992). Scholars have revisited this foundation and argued that Dewey's work places greater importance on the critical aspects of reflection than has been appreciated by most business school professors (Elkjaer 2004; Antonacopolou 2010). We wholeheartedly agree and, beyond that, we believe that Dewey's ontology of human experience – that is, his account of what experience is and how we can learn from experience – can guide business educators as they seek to help business school students to develop practical wisdom. In the following section, we present an account of Dewey's conceptualization of wisdom as the habit of forming good habits, and then we discuss a case illustration of how wisdom can be developed and practiced in a business school.

## What is the relationship between knowledge and action? Reviving Dewey

### *Experience and the ontology of knowledge*

Plato commences the Western philosophical tradition by nominating the philosopher as king of an ideal republic. If a person has knowledge of the highest abstractions, then according to Plato he or she should also have the capacity to deal with all the complex and concrete circumstances of human social life. *Sophia* is superior to *phronesis*, and can effectively guide it. Aristotle (1962) by contrast argues that there can never be a science of ethics or politics (or organization, for that matter) because human society is so complex that the future cannot be predicted even from perfect knowledge of the past. The subsequent philosophical tradition – including the epistemological debates about whether business should be considered primarily as a value-neutral, objective science, or as an exercise of normative, value-based practical wisdom – unfolds within the spectrum of difference between Plato and Aristotle.

Pragmatic American philosophy generally occurs on the Aristotelian side of this spectrum, and some pragmatists, including John Dewey, make the unique and radical claim that all of human knowledge, including the most abstract philosophical speculations as well as the most basic scientific theories, is practical in one way or another, serving the interests of the people who have generated it or recognize it as such. As we explain in more detail later, Dewey suggests that all knowledge is created in and through practical involvement with the world; indeed, all *thinking* is *in* and *of* the world in the sense that it involves more than just purely intellectual or cognitive activity and deals with more than just abstractions or ideas. By pursuing this line of argument, and by articulating Dewey's ontology of experience, we can develop a different account of how practical wisdom may or may not be developed in a business school.

Dewey (1964: 390) claims that "[e]xperience, in short, is not a combination of mind and world, subject and object, method and subject matter, but is a single continuous interaction of a great diversity (literally countless in number) of energies." On this account, experience is not merely a subjective phenomenon, interior to the mind or sensory body of any individual. Subjects do not merely perceive and experience objects, just as scientists do not merely use methods to gain knowledge about the world. Instead, experience is an immanent, holistic phenomenon that involves the complex interplay of human and non-human energies. Dewey formulates this point in both ontological as well as psychological terms, claiming that in many activities such as "skating, conversing, hearing music, enjoying a landscape – there is no consciousness of separation of the method of the person and of the subject matter" (1964: 389) – so too, we should add in anticipation of the case illustrations later, with consulting. Of course, in order to understand what learning, conversing, or skating involves, we commonly make analytic distinctions between the person and the action, but Dewey points out that "we are apt to regard it [mistakenly] as a separation in existence and not as a distinction in thought" (1964: 390).

Within the complex interplay of energies involved in "experience," theoretical knowledge of the world and practical action in the world cannot be so easily separated. The point of differentiation between theory and practice itself cannot be known abstractly or with any value-neutral objectivity. Instead, Dewey suggests that people strive collectively to establish knowledge – about the difference between theory and practice as well as other matters of concern – that helps them to deal productively with the complexity of their experiences.

## *Wisdom as the habit of habits*

Dewey's ontology does differentiate between primary experience and reflection on that experience. He claims that the sciences as well as the arts and humanities exemplify "fundamental . . . attitudes and operations" that "express and illustrate in their most concrete form that of which simple and common modes of thought-activity are capable when they work under satisfactory conditions" (1964: 329). In other words, we are capable of reflecting on our experiences, and our reflective capacities allow us to develop elaborate systems of understanding. These systems of understanding remain in and of the world, as do the criteria for judging whether any knowledge they might generate is true.

According to Dewey, "truth" can never be objectively determined in an amoral or value-neutral way; instead, truth can be judged only by those who have an interest in it and only in view of practical consequences. Dewey's notion of pragmatic truth holds that "in the proper interpretation of 'pragmatic', namely the function of consequences as necessary tests of the validity of propositions, *provided* these consequences are operationally instituted and are such as to resolve the specific problem evoking the operations, the text that follows is thoroughly pragmatic" (Dewey 1938: iv). Again, theoretical claims ("propositions") are subjugated to practical understanding because propositions need to be validated by trying out whether they solve the proposed problem or not. The precondition ("*provided*") is that only when they stand the test will they be valid, and the only way to test the claim is to try it out by putting it into operation. The context for that operation, as well as the judgment whether the operation was effective, is shaped by our own interests and values.

For Dewey, whenever we make a claim to have scientific knowledge, we are also making a judgment of value. We can reflect on and gain knowledge about these value claims – and importantly, our values can be "true" in the same sense that our claims to knowledge about them can. Dewey (1929: 278) argues that:

> [a] moral law, like a law in physics, is not something to swear by and stick to at all hazards; it is a formula of the way to respond when specified conditions present themselves . . . [and i]ts claim to authority rests finally upon the imperativeness of the situation that has to be dealt with, not upon its own intrinsic nature.

We develop and refine these "formulas" (including claims to truth and value) iteratively over time, and through our interactions with others.

People can furthermore reflect on their own knowledge and values deliberately in response to the complexity of experience. Dewey uses the term "habit" to describe how we can engage intentionally in the iterative process of acting and reflecting. Habits according to Dewey are not accidental or mindless patterns of action, but are instead acquired through an active involvement with the social environment in which others "approve, disapprove, protest, encourage, share and resist" (Dewey 1922). Through this process, individual habits become "energetic and dominating ways of acting" (Dewey 1922) and shape our experience.

Dewey calls the habit of reflecting critically on the processes of habituation by which we shape our individual and collective experience *wisdom*.

Dewey defines wisdom not as a psychological trait or as a recognizably discrete body of knowledge, but as a particular kind of habit that can develop over time. Wisdom is the habit of habits, the habit of self-habituation. Wisdom involves the use of "thought-activities" (again, Dewey blurs the distinction between thinking and acting) to shape, adjust, and innovate other habits, and thereby, to attain well-being over time. Through such processes of habituation, people can reflexively and intentionally act in ways that bring about the ends that they desire.

So if indeed the purpose of the business school can be reframed as the development of wisdom, Dewey provides interesting guidance regarding how we might proceed as educators. Here we phrase this guidance in explicitly normative terms, as a set of distinct possibilities for "thought-action" among business school professors and students.

## *Zombie Dewey becomes a B-school dean*

To begin, business school professors and students should all recognize and accept that experience is not merely a subjective or human phenomenon – it involves all the animal, vegetable, and material complexity of our environment as well. Therefore we need to become more broadly and deeply aware of the complexity of our world and the contingency of our human existence. As we expand the horizons of our inquiry, we become much more humble about what we think we know, and more critical of the limitations of our commonly accepted theories and research methodologies. We recognize that we cannot simply appeal to some abstract or otherworldly standard of truth or value, but must accept that we are, for better or worse, muddling through life together, interacting in ways that promote our well-being or not.

Beyond that, we need to recognize and accept that when we traffic in "knowledge," whether as researchers trying to generate it, as teachers trying to give it away, or as students trying to get as much as our precious tuition fees can buy, we are developing and perpetuating nothing more or less than a habit of inquiry. This habit includes social and material dimensions even in spite of what appear to be relatively solitary and cognitive activities of reading and writing and calculating regressions. The social dimensions of the activity of knowing involve multiple iterations of reflection and action, multiple collective determinations of what matters to speak or inquire about – and again, this activity does not occur independently from the rest of the world, but in and of the world. Wisdom is not merely socially constructed, floating somehow untethered to materiality; instead, wisdom is seen as the habit of habits and it involves multiple ongoing iterations of reflective action. Wisdom is in this sense not merely an individual-level character trait or cognitive capacity, but a plural or multiple phenomenon that emerges (or not) at different times and for different durations.

Finally, even though we have portrayed wisdom as a kind of meta-habit, this "meta" or "beyond" should not be misunderstood as some kind of absolute hierarchy existing statically in time. Instead, the "habit of habits" conceptualization temporalizes wisdom and frames it as an ongoing and open-ended or aleatory process, unfolding within a similarly mutable and contingent context. How we define wisdom as well as how we perform it may change over time and in different contexts. This claim should be read not as an affirmation of some kind of cheap moral relativism, but instead as an emphasis on the processual ontology of wisdom. Wisdom is something that changes and unfolds differently in different contexts, and for this reason we must continue to reflect critically on our own assumptions about the historical and institutional contexts that frame our own thought-actions as business school professors. In this sense, we echo Socrates's claim that he was the wisest man in Athens because he alone knew that he knew nothing, and therefore engaged in an unceasing process of inquiry. However, as pragmatists we focus critically on the consequences of this inquiry – can business school students actually develop the habits associated with wisdom?

## A case illustration: developing wise habits

In response to that question, we present a case illustration drawn from our own experience as faculty teaching at a large business school in the US. Traditionally, a case shows "how the conceptual argument might actually be applied to one or more empirical settings" (Siggelkow 2007: 22), but in keeping with Dewey's ontology of knowledge, we can instead give a critically reflective account of our own experience collaborating with each other, with other faculty, and with students. We focus on a full semester (14 week) elective course – "Experiential Learning Seminar: Social Impact Consulting" – in which undergraduate students engage in strategic consulting projects with nonprofit organizations as their clients. As of this writing, we are currently teaching this course for the sixth time, and so our experience includes interactions with hundreds of students and dozens of nonprofit clients. In support of the present inquiry, we have gathered the teaching materials (including syllabi, teaching notes and presentation slides, emails to students and clients, etc.) that we have produced over the past years as well as the final reflection papers that students have submitted as their final assignment for the course. Following Dewey, we can present our account of this experience as an iteration of a cycle of action and reflection regarding the emergence of wisdom as the overall purpose of the business school.

### *Background and context*

The course "Social Impact Consulting" was developed in response to an invitation by the faculty curriculum committee to provide business students with occasions to learn by engaging in, and reflecting on, experience. Support for the course is provided by a philanthropic foundation, and the funding allows us to have four faculty members teaching a class of no more than 24 students. Additionally, a programme manager from the foundation and an administrative staff member at our university help to coordinate the logistics involved with the course.

Each offering of the course begins two to six months prior to the start of the semester, with the identification and recruitment of the nonprofit organizations whose strategic issues the students address. In general, the projects are strategic in the sense that they involve consideration of potential future scenarios, the analysis of current realities both within the organization and in the broader landscape, and the development of recommendations for how the organization might fruitfully proceed. More specifically, the projects often include landscape mapping, benchmarking, marketing and media strategy, feasibility studies, digital technology strategy, etc. The nonprofit organizations themselves work on a variety of social issues, including education, the arts, health and well-being, human rights, etc. Within focus areas such as these, the projects are scoped so that they might be undertaken feasibly by teams of undergraduate students who have little or no prior experience working as consultants, but who have elected to gain some of that experience by registering for the class.

On the first day of class, the nonprofit executives attend and present their organizations and the projects to the students. Students listen to these presentations and then rank the projects in terms of their own interest, and based on those rankings we organize the students into teams of three or four individuals. Each team has a dedicated faculty mentor to provide guidance as the semester unfolds. The class meets once a week for 2 hours 45 minutes, and the sessions consist of moderated discussions on the assigned readings, team building and leadership development exercises, and team meetings. In the class sessions, student teams are held responsible for establishing a shared understanding with the client about the overall objectives of the project, for the activities they undertake over the course of the semester, and for the deliverables they will generate to complete the project at the end of the semester.

The explicitly stated objectives of the course are to generate meaningful learning outcomes for the students, and to produce value for the nonprofit clients. In the following description, we will focus primarily on the first of these objectives because it bears directly on the overall focus of our inquiry. The quotes from students have been excerpted verbatim from their journals and reflection papers. The truth of their claims would, from a pragmatic perspective, need to be considered in light of the consequences that their actions had for the clients. We will however leave that line of inquiry for a subsequent series of written reflections.

So what habits do the students develop? And do they contribute to the development of wisdom?

## *Engaging in humble inquiry*

Before coming to the first class session, students are required to read an interview with Ed Schein that focuses on the process of "humble inquiry" (Lambrechts *et al.* 2011). Schein assumes that organizations are irreducibly complex, that individual articulations of such complexity can never accurately represent the whole, and that it is therefore impossible to standardize any kind of method for intervening in that complexity (Schein 2003). Given these assumptions, Schein suggests that consultants (as well as leaders) are most helpful and most effective when they adopt an attitude of humility, deferring to the client's understanding and experience of the situation, and yet striving to help by posing questions to the client that elicit new insights. Thus the consultant's role is framed as a coordinator and facilitator of organizational processes rather than an expert or decision maker.

To initiate the development of this habit, students are invited to begin the process of humble inquiry on the first day of class by listening to the clients presenting their projects, and by posing questions in response. Following these presentations, students are grouped into project teams, and in the following week they reach out to their client and schedule an initial meeting in which they continue the process of questioning. They seek to gain a better of understanding of the client organization and the context within which the project has significance. They then refine the scope of the project as necessary in dialogue with the client and draft a work plan for the semester that will guide them as they seek to fulfill the project's objectives.

In subsequent class sessions, they practice humble inquiry with each other in a variety of ways. They interview each other in small groups, posing open-ended questions and taking turns playing the role of interviewer and interviewee. Faculty members "role model" this habit by continually posing questions about everything from the overall purpose of the project to the specific means that students might use to achieve the ends desired by the client. The process continues throughout the course with an iterative series of feedback loops with the client that takes place when the final deliverables are being developed and presented. One student reflected on the process this way:

> Through humble inquiry I learned that pushing for a particular solution is not always ideal. The solution needs to be revealed through a dialogue, almost like peeling away layers of an onion. I always viewed consulting as a process of identifying the problem and providing its solution. Humble inquiry forced me to shift my mindset. I realized that an effective consultant is not one who speaks more; rather it is one who listens more.

Another student's voice echoed this shift from a pre-existing habit of pushing solutions on to the client to a new habit of listening attentively to the client's needs:

> You have to submit your own goals to client's goals. While I tried to explore [my own] new ideas, I was not receptive to existing strategies. As we kept talking to the clients and discussing as a group, my goals for the project changed. Through the process of humble inquiry, the [client's] goals became my goals.

Students reflected explicitly on their own prior habituation to assume the epistemological primacy of a particular theory or model – indeed much of business education involves learning to apply particular theories to empirical practice – and the value of the newly acquired habit of remaining humble about the limits of any particular theory or concept. One student wrote:

> We were not trained in any consulting frameworks or methodologies prior to being thrown into client interactions. Because we did not have an analytical toolkit, we listened to our client first. Listening allowed us to figure out our clients' challenges and fully understand the organization before jumping to conclusions. Not having frameworks guide our thinking also allowed us to design and test solutions that pushed our creative limits. As our clients said during the reflection session after the final presentation, they appreciated the "listen first" mentality of our class.

Another student emphasized that the consulting project generated value for the client precisely because the students did not employ the kinds of analytic techniques traditionally associated with consulting:

> I realize now that in practice, it is best not to narrow one's vision by using a framework. In this sense, I can understand why we were not taught any frameworks in class; had I applied the frameworks I used during my consulting interviews, I would have lost the kind of flexibility necessary to provide recommendations that were both practical and appealing to the cultural aspect of [the client].

Another student offered this extended meta-reflection on the process of becoming habituated to engage in humble inquiry:

> I knew I was going to have a hard time getting a feel for this class when we were told that we should not be looking for solutions immediately. My first thought was that if we were not there to find solutions, what is the job of the consultant? We were given a problem, and if we were not supposed to figure out how to solve it, what were we doing? As I later learned, the reason for not coming up with solutions immediately was that everyone needed to understand the problems completely first. [...] One thing I learned from this problem-solution exploration is that sometimes when taught a novel concept, the best way to understand it is to keep it at the back of one's head and let it sit until it clicks. It was an odd experience for me. For the entire project, I was struggling to actively understand the concept of not immediately looking for a solution. Now that the project is over, and now that we are reflecting on it, our group actually did exactly what we were told in class, even though I never realized it until writing about it.

Do these quotes provide sufficient evidence to claim that the students truly developed new habits over the course of a 14-week semester? Again, the pragmatic burden of proof hinges upon the consequences associated with the "thought-actions" taken by the students not only in the particular context of the client project, but also in the broader context of their lives as aspiring business professionals and the organizations and institutions in which they work. However, we have quoted the students at some length here in order to hear their voices, which we hear to say that yes, they did develop a new habit of approaching the world more humbly, maintaining critical self-awareness of the limits of any particular theory in its capacity to describe the complexity of the world. We additionally believe that these quotes provide evidence that, through iterative cycles of action and reflection, the students began to reflect deliberately on how those cycles of action and reflection might be shaped or adjusted in order to serve their interests more effectively. By giving voice to this meta-awareness of their own learning process, the students exemplified what Dewey called the habit of habits, wisdom.

### *Collaborating to inquire*

The students taking this course have also explicitly reflected on the normative social dimensions of this process, particularly regarding the dynamics within the project teams. For example, early in the semester, students participate in a tabletop classroom exercise called the "marshmallow tower." In this exercise, project teams are each given twenty sticks of uncooked spaghetti noodles, a meter of string, a meter of tape, and a marshmallow. Then they have 20 minutes to use these materials and construct the tallest freestanding tower that they can with the marshmallow placed at the top. The goal of the exercise from a pedagogical perspective is of course not to see which team wins the competition and has the highest freestanding marshmallow tower, but instead to trigger a subsequent discussion between and among teammates about how their construction process unfolded, and how that process might shed light by analogy on the process of their interactions as a project team. One student reflected that:

> Even though we did not have the tallest tower, we made a tower that stood up and had fun while doing it. I think that was when we started feeling more comfortable with each other. Looking back, I also realize just how much that day can be reflected in our whole group dynamics.

Another classroom exercise that takes place at or just after the midpoint of the semester gives the project teams an occasion to gather and sit quietly, reflecting and writing down answers to the following questions: what actions has each member of your team taken that you have found productive?; what actions has each member of your team taken that you have found unproductive?; and what actions will each person need to take in the coming weeks in order for the project to succeed? Then, in turn, individuals sit quietly and take notes whilst the other members of their team discuss their answers to these questions in the third person, as if they were not actually present. For example, three of four students speak amongst themselves about the fourth student, pretending s/he is not there, and discuss the student's actions in terms of how productive or unproductive they have been for the project thus far. The fourth student has the opportunity to listen quietly to what the other members of the team think about the role s/he has been playing thus far, and what they think s/he should do in the coming weeks to contribute to the success of the project. This peer feedback process encourages all participating students to reflect on their own actions in terms of how they are experienced and judged by the other members of the team. One student reflected about the way in which this feedback process supports and feeds into the process of humble inquiry described above:

> Getting peer feedback is a humbling experience. During our group's first peer review session, the biggest constructive criticism I received was that I needed to dominate conversations less.

The peer feedback exercise has different meaning for each student who participates in it, but from the perspective of curriculum design, the exercise helps to establish and reinforce the habit of engaging in dialogue about the various interpersonal dynamics that may or may not be contributing to the success of the project. Of course, many business school classes involve teamwork, but typically – as one student noted in a reflection paper – it is possible to divide the project work somewhat equally and then combine the parts into a whole without any major problems. By contrast, in this class some students realize that they cannot meet with their clients unless all team members are present. For example, if one member of the team is late or absent without excuse, then it casts a bad light on the team in front of the client, raising doubts about the extent to which they share a common understanding and engage in collaborative action. One student reflected as follows on the value of regular, in-person meetings of project team members:

> But something our team realized early on was that by meeting in person, not only could we keep each other accountable, but we could also bounce off ideas from each other. It was weird, but when we were in a room together, we always seemed so much more passionate about the project and had more ideas, rather than the awkward video chatting or emotionless emails that we exchanged back and forth.

These quotes provide some indication of how the students, whilst they are developing the habit of engaging in humble inquiry, are also developing a related but distinct habit of working together collaboratively. As they collaborate to inquire into the project-related issues presented by the client organization, they often confront difficulties, including a lack of shared understanding, trouble scheduling meetings, different levels of comfort with communication technologies, etc. At a very basic level, they have the occasion to reflect on the limits of their own locus of control – as one student wrote, "just because you have a good idea does not mean everybody else thinks it is a good idea." At the same time, this apparent failure of the all-conquering ego is accompanied by a recognition of the value of other people's interests. One student reflected that she now takes "time to really listen to people and hearing their thoughts, feelings, and ideas before I interject my own."

Our sense is that the process of team-based experiential learning, including the iterative cycles of action and reflection, made the students explicitly aware of how the creation of any knowledge or understanding involves normative social dimensions. As students collaborate to inquire and as they develop knowledge that is shared and affirmed, they realize that judgments of fact as well as judgments of value are shaped by the normativity of social relations. They also develop a meta-awareness of how team dynamics can be intentionally adjusted so that they serve the interests of the team (and its client) more effectively. Again, by giving voice to this meta-awareness of their own learning process, the students exemplified Dewey's account of wisdom.

### *Engaging in an open-ended process of inquiry*

Compared with other, more traditional business school courses that involve sitting and taking notes whilst a professor lectures, this course tends to have a different significance in the lives of the students. The primary point of differentiation may in fact be physically embodied. Not only are the students up and out of their chairs, interacting in an open-ended and fluid manner with their peers and the faculty, they are also leaving the classroom behind, exiting the institutional university setting (see Michels and Beyes, this volume) and entering the context of the client's organization, including the client's own offices as well as the spaces where the client serves its beneficiaries. As mentioned earlier, on the first day of the class the client organizations pitch their projects to the students. Following these pitches, we ask students to rank the projects in terms of which ones they would most prefer to work on, and then we compose the teams based on these preferences as well as other demographic criteria (for example, gender, age, etc.).

Thus as the students move physically into the client's spaces, they are going somewhere that they are intrinsically motivated to go. Many times students choose a particular project because they have some personal connection to the set of issues that the nonprofit seeks to address – for example, one student chose to work for an organization focused on early childhood learning disabilities because she has a brother who suffers from such disabilities. The general point here is that the course triggers a level of personal involvement that differs dramatically from more traditional courses. In the voice of one student:

> I went into the class expecting it to be like any other class I have taken at [this business school] where the work and the teachings were very much contained within the classroom. Instead, the majority of my learning took place outside the classroom and with both my client and my team.

The experiential pedagogical approach is based not on the traditional knowledge "transfer" from teacher to students, but on the notion that knowledge is co-constructed by the students through practice, and because the students understand their role as consultant to be a facilitator in "perpetually changing environments" (Schein 2003: 83), the final outcomes, "deliverables," of the project cannot be predicted in advance. This sort of open learning environment contrasts starkly with their regular classes, where all the materials are available or accessible within the class-room context and where "it's been easy to determine your success – do this a certain way so you can achieve a high grade in your exam/paper/project," as a student commented. The habit of inquiring collaboratively is not easy to predetermine because it is not produced by the teacher, but instead is created by the students themselves. One student wrote:

> We did not really have a complete syllabus that told us what to do at every turn. We had to meet with the clients and come up with the project proposal, then see it through until the very end. It was very liberating having a class where in order to impress the clients, you had to showcase your own ideas instead of regurgitating facts that you learned from lecture. Even though I really enjoyed learning a lot of things from my other lectures, I feel like this taught me something that most people have to wait until after college to experience.

So not only are the students given an opportunity to work on something that they care about, they are additionally given the freedom and encouragement to reflect on how they can improve and enhance their own learning process. With this open-ended freedom, students can develop in many different directions, and they can sometimes surprise themselves. One student wrote:

> I didn't expect this class to have such a profound effect on myself, but I am walking away from this semester a little more cultured, a little more mature, and all-in-all, a better person.

Another student emphasized the personal implications of the experiential learning process:

> I think that this newfound self-awareness and knowledge will be truly helpful to me as I work towards my goals in life.

Another acknowledged the transformative effects of the process:

> I can say with certainty that this class changed me as a person. Some of the most important lessons I learned were not necessarily about consulting specifically, but about . . . accountability, commitment to others, and communication.

Again, these quotes provide some indication that the students developed new habits. Just as they became more humble about their own knowledge, and became more able to inquire collaboratively, they also began to recognize how open-ended, collaborative inquiry can have transformative effects on their own lives far beyond the client projects, the course, and the university context. This reflexive habit of seeking to develop and adopt new habits that have positive effects on one's own life and the lives of others appears to exemplify wisdom as defined by Dewey.

## Wise teaching practices? Implications for business school pedagogy

According to John Dewey, wisdom is the habit of habits, the habit of intentionally shaping, adjusting, and innovating other habits to enable human thriving over time. Through such processes of habituation, wise people can reflexively and intentionally act in ways that bring about the ends that they desire. In the experiential learning seminar described earlier, students engage in humble, collaborative inquiry, serve the clients' interests, and reflect deliberately on how they might improve their own lives through the process. Working within Dewey's pragmatic ontology of knowledge, we cannot say objectively or with any absolute certainty that the students became wiser; we must instead continue the process of inquiry, experimenting to see whether the consequences of our understanding have positive effects.

In keeping with the spirit of "humble inquiry" (Lambrechts *et al.* 2011) that we shared with our students in the earlier case, we should acknowledge several rather significant limitations of this inquiry. We have not made any effort to problematize the professional discipline (consulting) that the case illustrations dealt with, nor have we said much about the social issues that the non-profit organizations struggle to address (see Barinaga, this volume), nor have we considered the role that the students' age and stage in life (19–22-year-old undergraduates) might play in the learning process. Building on work done around these issues (see Richter and Schmidt 2008; Robinson *et al.* 2010; Sachau and Naas 2010), future research could shed light on these dimensions of the case.

These limitations notwithstanding, we believe that the students' voices suggest that the course helped them become more reflexive and intentional about their learning habits, and more aware of how learning takes place in and of the world, with cognitive, social, emotional, and material dimensions all intertwined. If indeed students may cultivate wisdom through experiences like those described, what then are the implications for business school educators?

### *Reflection and action are both embodied*

As we noted earlier, Dewey's work has provided the foundation for Kolb's influential theory of learning (see Kolb *et al.* 2000). The reflection papers cited at length in our case illustration convey clear signs of double-loop learning (Argyris and Schön 1974), and the experiential learning process seems to have provided students with an "unfreezing" impulse that desettled or contradicted previous assumptions (Lewin 1947), disconfirmed data (Schein 1992), or fractured their adult learners' framework (Malinen 2000). However, it has been argued that "Kolb gives an inadequate interpretation of Dewey's thought and [. . .] the very concept of immediate, concrete experience proposed by the experiential learning approach is epistemologically problematic" (Miettinen 2000: 54; see also Brandi and Elkjaer, this volume). In other words, educators should not assume that reflection and action are wholly distinct and separated in linear time as a sequence or cycle of events. Phrased positively, we should focus on the embodiment of both reflection and action.

In this regard, there are other more holistic approaches to learning that can provide guidance, including action learning (Revans 1980; Morgan and Ramirez 1984; Marquardt 1999); the various literatures dealing with the "reflective practitioner" (following Schön 1983; Vince, this volume); "*withness*-thinking" (Shotter 2006); "presencing" (Scharmer 2007); "action research" as practiced in the classroom (see Taylor *et al.* 2008); the recent literature on arts and aesthetics as learning tools (see Taylor and Ladkin 2009; Meisiek, Guillet de Monthoux, Barry, and Austin, this volume); etc. Inspired by these approaches, rather than just encouraging students to strike a "work–life" balance, we could help students realize that just as thinking occurs in and of the world, work occurs in and of life. What work habits improve life, and what habits detract from it? Questions such as these could be woven into the entire business school curriculum – in our experience they remain almost entirely absent.

## *Assessing collaborative inquiry*

How can we as business school faculty assess whether someone becomes a better person, generates newfound self-awareness, or a changes as a person? How can we give students grades based on the extent to which they have developed wise habits?

In the course described above, we emphasized the effects of actions within the context of the client projects, and in the final assessment process we considered the clients' estimation of individual student performance as well as students' estimation of their peers' and teammates' performance. We considered a range of factors, including whether students were punctual for team meetings and client calls; whether teams hit progress milestones throughout the semester; whether individual students engaged constructively with each other within the project team; whether students appeared to help and support the success of other students on their team; whether students took leadership roles in the client interface, etc.

We also asked ourselves a basic question of "fit," formulated as: if I were running a consulting business, would I hire this person to join my team? Because there are four of us serving as faculty, our discussions about assessment of student performance involve a distinct path of inquiry that can reveal unexpected results. For example, a clever, well-articulated high achiever might be perceived as too eager and not really willing to listen to or learn from other people's opinions; a shy, less visible person might contribute significantly to team cohesion; another student who remains calm, positive, and resourceful in difficult situations may be seen by fellow students as an extremely reliable and valuable partner; still another student who is disregarded by the faculty as a "slacker" (trying to benefit from the work of others whilst contributing little) may be highly regarded by the client.

We are aware of the bias involved in this assessment process (including faculty members' personal likes and dislikes), and we tend to employ the "fit to consultancy" criterion only to cases that seemed otherwise ambivalent. At the same time we acknowledge that aesthetic approaches in organization studies have been recognized and legitimized as a valid source of knowledge (Strati 1999, 2007; Linstead and Höpfl 2000; Ropo and Parviainen 2001). In this light, rather than trying to eliminate sense perceptions and aesthetic judgments of fit from academic assessment procedures, we should integrate them more systematically and reflect on them more critically. Indeed, following Dewey's ontology of experience, any claim to objective truth always involves an implicit statement of interests or values, and so we should not try to pretend that we can make objective, value-free, or value-neutral assessments of whether students actually develop wisdom or not.

### *Reflecting critically on our own performances*

Within the recent stream of organizational research focused on the development of practical wisdom in business schools, Chia and Holt (2008) have drawn a useful distinction between "knowledge-by-representation" and "knowledge-by-exemplification" – that is, between what can be made explicit in language and what instead remains tacit, embodied, and pre-reflexive (see also Chia and Nayak, this volume). If we apply this distinction to the case illustration earlier, it seems that not only did the students gain knowledge through the embodied and pre-reflexive experiential process, but additionally that the activity of reflecting on the process itself has tacit dimensions that may never be made fully explicit. In other words, even as we may try to articulate a comprehensive and meaningful account of how our students developed wise habits, this representation of those habits might exemplify other forms of knowledge. This exemplified knowledge may be coherent with or contradictory to the knowledge that we attempt to represent. Phrased most poignantly, our account of wisdom may turn out to be unwise.

In this light, although it may not be particularly pleasant, it is fair to note that we as management educators may be unwittingly exemplifying certain kinds of knowledge by our wardrobe or hairstyle, or by the unconscious postures and gestures that we adopt as we move around the classroom, or by virtue of our position within particular schools, in particular places, with particular reputations, stakeholders, and endowments, etc. Thus we suggest that we could reflect differently by adopting an attitude of radical, critical self-reflexivity (see Chia 1996; Alvesson 2003; Cunliffe 2003; Humphreys 2005; Alvesson and Sandberg 2011; Maclean *et al.* 2012; Steyaert *et al.* 2012; see Vince, this volume) toward our work as business educators. In one sense, we cannot aspire to predictive empirical knowledge about all the different knowledge that we may exemplify (or not), and yet in another sense, perhaps to the extent that we become more aware and intentional about our work as educators, we might discover room for improvement. Indeed, if we humbly aspire to exemplify the wise habits discussed here, and if following Dewey we seek pragmatically to improve our own thinking and action, then we should "maintain the state of doubt and . . . carry on systemic and protracted inquiry" (Dewey 1910: 13) about the purpose of the business school as well as the pedagogical practices designed to achieve it.

## References

Alvesson, M. (2003) 'Beyond neopositivists, romantics, and localists: a reflexive approach to interviews in organizational research', *Academy of Management Review*, (28)1, 13–33.

Alvesson, M. and Sandberg, J. (2011) 'Ways of constructing research questions: gap-spotting or problematization?', *Organization*, 18(1), 23–44.

Antonacopoulou, E.P. (2010) 'Making the business school more "critical": reflexive critique based on phronesis as a foundation for impact', *British Journal of Management*, 21, 6–25.

Argyris, C. and Schön, D. (1974) *Theory in Practice: Increasing Professional Effectiveness*. San Francisco, CA: Jossey-Bass.

Aristotle (1962) *Nicomachean Ethics*. Indianapolis, IN: Bobbs-Merrill.

Augier, M. and March, J. (2011) *The Roots, Rituals, and Rhetorics of Change: North American Business Schools after the Second World War*. Stanford, CA: Stanford Business Books.

Bailey, C. and Ford, C. (1996) 'Management as science versus management as practice in postgraduate business education', *Business Strategy Review*, 7(4), 7–12.

Bartunek, J.M. and Seo, M.-G. (2002) 'Qualitative research can add new meanings to quantitative research', *Journal of Organizational Behavior*, 23, 237–42.
Bierly, P.E. III, Kessler, E.H. and Christensen, E.W. (2000) 'Organizational learning, knowledge and wisdom', *Journal of Organizational Change Management*, 13(6), 595–618.
Chia, R. (1996) 'The problem of reflexivity in organizational research: towards a postmodern science of organization', *Organization*, 3(1), 31–59.
Chia, R. and Holt, R. (2008) 'The nature of knowledge in business schools', *Academy of Management Learning and Education*, 7(4), 471–86.
Colby, A., Ehrlich, T., Sullivan, B. and Dolle, J. (2011) *Rethinking Undergraduate Business Education: Liberal Learning for the Profession*. San Francisco, CA: Jossey-Bass.
Cunliffe, A. (2003) 'Reflexive inquiry in organizational research: questions and possibilities', *Human Relations*, 56(8), 983–1003.
Dewey, J. (1910) *How We Think*. Available from http://archive.org/details/howwethink000838mbp (accessed January 7, 2014).
Dewey, J. (1922) *Human Nature and Conduct: An Introduction to Social Psychology*. http://archive.org/details/humannatureconduOOdeweiala (accessed January 7, 2014).
Dewey, J. (1929) *The Quest for Certainty: A Study of the Relation of Knowledge and Action*. New York, NY: Minton, Balch & Co.
Dewey, J. (1938) *Logic: The Theory of Inquiry*. New York, NY: Holt, Rinehart and Winston.
Dewey, J. (1964) *On Education*. Chicago, IL: University of Chicago Press.
Elkjaer, B. (2004) 'Organizational learning: the third way', *Management Learning*, 35(4), 419–34.
Friga, P.N., Bettis, R.A. and Sullivan, R.S. (2003) 'Changes in graduate management education and new business school strategies for the 21st century', *Academy of Management Learning and Education*, 2, 233–49.
Ghoshal, S. (2005) 'Bad management theories are destroying good management', *Academy of Management Learning and Education*, 4(1), 75–91.
Humphreys, M. (2005) 'Natural resources, conflict, and conflict resolution: uncovering the mechanisms', *Journal of Conflict Resolution*, 49(4), 508–37.
Khurana, R. (2007) *From Higher Aims to Hired Hands: The Social Transformation of American Business Schools and the Unfulfilled Promise of Management as a Profession*. Princeton, NJ: Princeton University Press.
Kolb, D.A. (1984) *Experiential Learning: Experience as the Source of Learning and Development*. Upper Saddle River, NJ: Prentice-Hall.
Kolb, D.A., Boyatzis, B. and Mainemelis, C. (2000) 'Experiential learning theory: previous research and new directions'. *In:* R.J. Sternberg and L.-F. Zhang (eds.) *Perspectives on Cognitive, Learning, and Thinking Styles*. Mahwah, NJ: Lawrence Erlbaum, pp. 227–48.
Lambrechts, F., Bouwen, R., Grieten, S., Huybrechts, J. and Schein, E. (2011) 'Learning to help through humble inquiry and implications for management research, practice, and education: an interview with Edgar H. Schein', *Academy of Management Learning and Education*, (10)1, 131–47.
Lewin, K. (1947) 'Frontiers in group dynamics: concept, method and reality in social science; social equilibria and social change', *Human Relations*, 1.
Linstead, S. and Höpfl, H. (eds.) (2000) *The Aesthetics of Organization*. London: Sage Publications.
McKenna B., Rooney, D. and Boal, K.B. (2009) 'Wisdom principles as a meta-theoretical basis for evaluating leadership', *The Leadership Quarterly*, 20, 177–90.
Maclean, M., Harvey, C. and Chia, R. (2012) 'Reflexive practice and the making of elite business careers', *Management Learning*, (43)4, 385–404.
Malinen, A. (2000) *Towards the Essence of Adult Experiential Learning: A Reading of the Theories of Knowles, Kolb, Mezirow, Revans and Schön*. Portland, OR: International Specialized Book Services.
Marquardt, M.J. (1999) *Action Learning in Action*. Palo Alto, CA: Davies-Black.
Miettinen, R. (2000) 'The concept of experiential learning and John Dewey's theory of reflective thought and action', *International Journal of Lifelong Education*, 19(1), 54–72.
Morgan, G. and Ramirez, R. (1984) 'Action learning: a holographic metaphor for guiding social change', *Human Relations*, 37(1), 1–27.
Nonaka, I. and Takeuchi, H. (2011) 'The wise leader', *Harvard Business Review*, 89(5), 58–67.
Nonaka, I. and Toyama, R. (2007) 'Strategic management as distributed practical wisdom (phronesis)', *Industrial and Corporate Change*, 16(3), 371–94.
O'Connor, E. (2011) *Creating New Knowledge in Management: Appropriating the Field's Lost Foundations*. Palo Alto, CA: Stanford University Press.

Pfeffer, J. (2005) 'Changing mental models: HR's most important task', *Human Resource Management*, 44(2), 123–28.
Pfeffer, J. and Fong, C. (2002) 'The end of business schools? Less success than meets the eye', *Academy of Management Learning and Education*, 1(1), 78–95.
Revans, R. (1980) *Action Learning: New Techniques for Management*. London: Blond & Briggs.
Richter, A. and Schmidt, S. (2008) 'The effectiveness of university-level management consulting courses', *Journal of Management Education*, 32(1), 84–99.
Robinson, D., Sherwood, A. and DePaolo, C. (2010) 'Service-learning by doing: how a student-run consulting company finds relevance and purpose in a business strategy capstone course', *Journal of Management Education*, 34(1), 88–112.
Ropo, A. and Parviainen, J. (2001) 'Leadership and bodily knowledge in expert organizations: epistemological rethinking', *Scandinavian Journal of Management*, 17(1), 1–18.
Sachau, D. and Naas, P. (2010) 'The consulting challenge: a case competition', *Journal of Management Education*, 34(4), 605–31.
Scharmer, O. (2007) *Theory U: Leading from the Future as it Emerges*. San Francisco, CA: Berret-Koehler.
Schein, E.H. (1992) *Organizational Culture and Leadership*. 2nd edn. San Francisco, CA: Jossey-Bass.
Schein, E.H. (2003) 'Five traps for consulting psychologist: or how I learned to take culture seriously', *Consulting Psychology Journal: Practice and Research*, 55(2), 75–83.
Schön, D. (1983) *The Reflective Practitioner*. New York, NY: Basic Books.
Senge, P.M and Sterman, J.D. (1992) 'Systems thinking and organizational learning: acting locally and thinking globally in the organization of the future', *European Journal of Operational Research*, 59(1), 137–50.
Shotter, J. (2006) 'Understanding process from within: an argument for "withness"-thinking', *Organization Studies*, 27(4), 585–604.
Siggelkow, N. (2007) 'Persuasion with case studies', *Academy of Management Journal*, 50(1), 20–4.
Starkey, K. and Tempest, S. (2005) 'The future of the business school: knowledge, challenges and opportunities', *Human Relations*, 58(1), 61–82.
Starkey, K., Hatchuel, A. and Tempest, S. (2004) 'Rethinking the business school: a European perspective', *Journal of Management Studies*, 41(8), 1521–31.
Steyaert, C., Marti, L. and Michels, C. (2012) 'Multiplicity and reflexivity in organizational research: towards a performative approach to the visual', *Qualitative Research in Organizations and Management: An International Journal*, 7(1), 34–53.
Strati, A. (1999) *Organization and Aesthetics*. London: Sage Publications.
Strati, A. (2007) 'Sensible knowledge and practice-based learning', *Management Learning*, 38(1), 61–77.
Taylor, S.S. and Ladkin, D. (2009) 'Understanding arts-based methods in managerial development', *Academy of Management Learning and Education*, 8(1), 55–69.
Taylor, S.S., Rudolph J.W. and Foldy, E.G. (2008) 'Teaching reflective practice: key stages, concepts and practices'. *In:* P. Reason and H. Bradbury (eds.) *Handbook of Action Research: Participative Inquiry and Practice*. Thousand Oaks, CA: Sage Publications, pp. 656–68.
Thomas, H. and Wilson, A.D. (2011) '"Physics envy," cognitive legitimacy or practical relevance: dilemmas in the evolution of management research in the UK', *British Journal of Management*, 22(3), 443–56.

# 16

# The art and practice of critique

## The possibilities of critical psychodynamic education

*Russ Vince*

In this chapter, I reflect on learning and critique in the management classroom. *Critique* in management education is sustained through a continuous desire to doubt or unsettle prevailing knowledge, as well as a wish to surface the emotions and power relations that maintain such knowledge. This makes it possible to call into question, for example, the established knowledge of professors; the nature of the knowledge desired by students and practitioners; and the preferred approaches to the delivery of knowledge that have become compulsory within business and management schools. I argue that one way to introduce critique into management education is by reflecting, in a broadly psychodynamic way, on the emotions and power relations that surround attempts to learn about leading, managing and organizing. Such reflection can reveal the complexities of behaviour and action that are integral to management and organization and that are also brought, both consciously and unconsciously, into teaching and learning groups. My main aim in this chapter is to illustrate the relationship between learning and critique through examples from my own practice, as well as encouraging other management educators to be influenced by 'the art and practice of critique'.

In my experience, bringing learning and critique together in the business and management school classroom involves two key assumptions. First, the ability to engage with emotions and power relations in the classroom depends on the management educator's willingness to *hold students in the moment*, to generate 'here and now' experiences from which they can *feel* their reflections as a prerequisite to understanding them. There is an ambiguity in this idea of 'holding'. In part it refers to holding students' (as well as one's own) attention on what is happening here and now. It also refers to the creation of environments in which students' emotional responses to what is happening here and now can be held – which is to say, kept available for critical reflection rather than lost in students' desire to move away from emotion as quickly as possible. Generating 'here and now' experience is a key element of the 'group relations' perspective on management learning (French and Vince 1999). The theoretical roots of this perspective come from the psychodynamic study of organizations (Neumann and Hirschhorn 1999), which stresses the impact of conscious and unconscious, individual and collective emotions on workplace behaviour. More recently, psychosocial studies (Kenny and Fotaki 2014) have provided a more critical edge by recognizing the inseparability of affect and power in organizations.

In practical terms, the reason why critical reflection is important is because it can help to engage with a general problem for managers, which is that they often work in task-obsessed, overly rational and conflict-averse environments (sometimes of their own making). It also helps to dispel the notion that learning can be provided through universally applicable models, through problem-solving tools, or with a set of defined skills and capabilities for successful implementation. The interplay between learning and critique provides the basis for learning about the contradictory, messy, emotion-laden and power-filled environments in which we work, as well as providing a way to make relations of domination transparent.

Second, one of the characteristics of *critical reflection* is that it is likely to mobilize the power relations that it is seeking to transform (Nicolini *et al.* 2004). Critical reflection surfaces a tension at the heart of organizations that management students need to know about – that managers are absorbed in the power relations they are seeking to transform at the same time as they are capable of unsettling established relations of power. Without this insight, managers might believe, for example, that their behaviour and actions are assisted by a defined range of management skills and capabilities rather than also restricted by them. We reproduce the power relations around us at the same time as we attempt to challenge or change them.

The possibilities of critical education depend on the willingness of management educators to help students and practitioners to notice and to interpret emotional and political dynamics in organizations through noticing and interpreting them in the business and management school classroom. As management educators we can provide opportunities for students of management to learn, for example, how organizations are emotional places (*not* how individuals within organizations can 'manage' emotion); how strategies and actions are subverted by unacknowledged emotions; how individuals and groups internalize and enact organizational dynamics; how links between individuals' behaviour and organizational structures are created and recreated; and how initiatives designed for change come to represent or replicate existing anxieties, stuck relations, limited ways of working, or repressive/regressive practices and patterns of compliance and control.

In order to address at least some of this list, it will be important for management educators to utilize the feelings and behaviour that students bring with them (consciously and unconsciously) into the learning environment, how they interact with others from such feelings and behaviour, and the ways in which such feelings and behaviours structure, limit and create opportunities for learning. I argue that holding students in the moment and mobilizing opportunities for critical reflection in order to comprehend emotions and power relations in organizations offers one strategy for connecting learning and critique. This is what I am focusing on in this chapter, but it is important to recognize that my approach is set within a range of broader ways of thinking and working that come under the heading of 'critical management education' (see Perriton and Singh, this volume). In the rest of the chapter, after some brief reflections on critical management education, I discuss ways of connecting learning and critique in large, undergraduate classes, for MBA students and through different spatial arrangements of the postgraduate classroom.

## Some brief reflections on critical management education

The various possibilities and difficulties of bringing critical approaches into business and management schools have already been well explored and explained (see Antonacopoulou 2002, 2010; Brocklehurst *et al.* 2007; Clegg *et al.* 2011; Cunliffe *et al.* 2002; Currie and Knights 2003; Currie *et al.* 2010; Dehler 2009; Grey 2002, 2004, 2008; Hay 2008; Hibbert 2013; Miller *et al.* 2003; Reynolds 1999; Reynolds and Vince 2004; Sinclair 2007; Vince 2010). The importance of critical perspectives has been in their ability to show that managers' capacity to reason is not solely concerned with efficiency and effectiveness, but also bound up with power, control and inequality (Fournier and Grey 2000). Critical management education (CME) has questioned assumptions about managers' learning in terms of both content and processes of management education (French and Grey 1996). A key focus has been on ways in which management education reflects and reproduces the operation of power relations in work organizations (Gherardi and Poggio 2007; Grey 2004; Reynolds and Trehan 2001; Reynolds and Vince 2004).

The teaching and learning that takes place in business schools is never divorced from the complexities of self/other relations, from business school power relations, or from power relations more broadly within society. Existing literature from CME has provided some guiding ideas about the relationship between CME and business schools. First, it is important 'to consider the modes of domination that exist in our own institutions and our own classrooms' (Cunliffe *et al.* 2002: 489) if we are to be able to engage with managers in seeking improved understanding of power relations in organizations. Second, we need to accept 'that management is not about neutral techniques but about values' (Grey 2004: 180). CME reconfigures management education in terms of attention to values and to organizational context. This invites us to question the values and assumptions communicated implicitly and explicitly within business schools. Third, it is important to question the desirability and the possibility of control (Grey 2004) and especially the ways in which control has come to define the role of 'teacher' (see Srinivas, this volume). Finally, because CME seeks to communicate about power, values and control, it can speak clearly on the everyday experiences and political processes involved in practice (Antonacopoulou 2006).

Critical approaches to management raise the possibility of undermining the conventional view of organizations 'as rationally ordered, appropriately structured, and emotion free life spaces, where the right decisions are made for the right reasons by the right people, in a reliable and predictable manner' (Kersten 2001: 452). Studies that have been concerned specifically with the relationship between emotion and power have shown that emotion is essential to control processes, and that emotions need to be understood in terms of the social and political structures of which they are a part (Fineman and Sturdy 1999). Emotions underpin and influence behaviour in organizations in ways that create distinctive political dynamics and organizing processes. For example, I have highlighted how a company's vision of itself as a *learning company* was undermined by defensiveness and the political unwillingness of senior managers to acknowledge learning as an aspect of their own role. This contributed to a 'politics of imagined stability' where a veneer of collegiality covered over behaviour 'based on the personal need to retain control and on collective fear of conflict, failure and loss of authority and influence' (Vince 2002: 1202). Emotions guide individuals in appraising social situations and responding to them, and are therefore part of an interpersonal, meaning-creating process (Antonacopoulou and Gabriel 2001). These organizing processes connect to broader political relations, such as the engineering and marketing of corporate culture (Kunda 1992; Van Maanen and Kunda 1989) and gendered emotions in organizations (Lewis and Simpson 2007; Reynolds and Trehan 2001; Swan 2005).

CME has sought to question modes of domination in the classroom in order to reveal power relations that are part of management and management education. It focuses on values rather than techniques, as well as the consequent need to address the context of both management and management education. CME calls into question the desirability and possibility of control and it emphasizes the link between political processes within management education and the politics of management practice. Because critical reflection mobilizes the power relations it is seeking to transform, the implementation of CME within business and management schools can be challenging to say the least. For example, Amanda Sinclair (2007) has narrated this challenge beautifully in her paper on educational experiences with MBA students. These experiences include both pedagogical heaven ('thrilling and full of risk', 2007: 464) and hell ('intensive and very content orientated', 2007: 465). She highlights the anxiety levels and holding possible in these two environments, one where her methods 'provoked anxiety that I was able to contain with help and within a structure with which I was familiar' (2007: 469) and the other where the same methods 'were a trigger for anxieties that lay present, circulating but largely unprocessed within a new and difficult structure' (2007: 469).

Despite or maybe because of such challenges, CME adds value to the education of management students and practitioners because it confronts what and how individuals and groups expect to learn. It engages with emotions and politics in the classroom in order to connect with the broader institutional context within which such relations and dynamics are created and maintained. Approaches to management education that do not involve the emotions and politics of being a manager are likely to reduce the potential for managers to learn and to be aware of how they (and the organizations they work in) create limits on learning.

Individual managers' feelings, knowledge and behaviour in the classroom are often a reliable mirror of emotions, behaviour and dispositions in the organizations these managers come from (Reynolds and Trehan 2001). Managers bring many things: feelings of anxiety and ambivalence; an eagerness to discover; helpful and unhelpful existing knowledge; defensiveness; care; good ideas and competitiveness (to name but a few). In addition, the temporary organization that management students and management educators co-create in the classroom has an organizational dynamic – it is more than the sum of its individual parts. In learning groups, implicit structures and habits emerge very quickly and without knowing; they become established as rules and relations that determine 'the way we do things here'. Such dynamics are contextually specific and political and they both limit and legitimize behaviour and action. Reflecting on the way this happens in the business and management school classroom provides an opportunity to better understand and work through these dynamics within organizations. In the following section I provide a number of specific examples in order to illustrate these points.

## Some examples from my own practice

### *Undergraduate*

My first example is an exercise that I use often with large, undergraduate groups in lecture theatres. The exercise is designed both to sit alongside and to critique lectures on organizational behaviour that focus on single themes (for example, perception, communication, motivation, group formation, etc.). The aim is to show students the complexity and messiness of behaviour in organizations and, in particular, the emotions that inform both organizational behaviour and action.

The session lasts fifty minutes. When the students come into the lecture theatre I arrange for them each to have one sheet of blank A4 paper. After they have settled down, I say: 'using the resources I have given you, you have ten minutes to create something beautiful'. The students interpret this task in many different ways. For example, paper planes soon start to float across the lecture theatre. Some students sit with the sheet of paper in their hands, unclear what they are meant to be doing. I notice students drawing, using different coloured pens they happened to have with them. Some tear shapes into the paper or fold it neatly. Some make delicate origami figures and others screw the paper into a ball and drop it. They talk with their neighbours ('what is this nonsense?', 'what are we supposed to be doing?', 'do you know what's going on?'). Some have abandoned the A4 sheet and are reading or responding to emails or sending text messages on their phones, others are looking around the room, somewhat bemused.

Students' reaction in class to a request from an authority figure to undertake a task gives them the opportunity for public reflection on the variety of feelings and responses that are mobilized by such requests, for example confusion, ambivalence, creativity, innovation, frustration, excitement and anxiety. Their various emotions and perceptions, as well as the actions they generate, can be used during the remaining time to discuss the complexities of feeling and behaviour that were mobilized. Their reactions as a group of students provide a remarkably accurate picture of behaviour in response to what people imagine is required of them in organizations. For example, paper planes are inevitable; they are a predictable response. In addition, there are ambivalent responses (sending text messages), creative responses (elaborate colour pictures) and inquiring responses (talking with others to clarify or criticize the point of the task).

There are many different possible interpretations of the things we are asked to do in organizations, as well as fantasies and expectations concerning what may be the 'right' and 'wrong' way to do them. This exercise helps undergraduate students of organizational behaviour to understand that managing and being managed often involve complicated relationships, varied interpretations, limited resources and unclear commands. It provides the students with immediate evidence from their own individual and collective experience that behaviour in organizations is messy and complicated. In this exercise, holding undergraduate students in a moment of uncertainty for just ten minutes produces an extraordinarily wide range of responses that illustrate the feelings and reactions that are mobilized by a simple (and yet ambiguous) request.

The critique mobilized by this exercise is twofold. First, the students' notions of organizational behaviour as being a subject (of study) are unsettled by the discovery that they themselves are the subjects of, and that they are subjected to, organizational behaviour. For example, the exercise evokes strong feelings from some students, particularly anger or frustration at the tutor's 'inability to give us clear instruction'. However, moving beyond a passive relationship between tutor and student helps to raise questions about 'us and them' that will be integral to their working lives. Students are able to engage with my position and power in the room as part of understanding the experience of leading/following and managing/being managed in organizations. On one hand, 'we expect you to tell us what we need to know about organizational behaviour' and on the other, 'I realize that the way we reacted in this exercise is just like reactions in the organization I worked in'. Second, students are able to move beyond expectations about learning in didactic ways and to understand better that the feeling they express that 'we don't know what we were supposed to be doing' or 'we didn't know what the outcomes were going to be' is quite usual in organizations. They are able to reflect on a variety of reactions in relation to *how we do things here* – to the emotions and power relations that underpin expectations about behaviour and the structural dispositions that create and are created by such behaviour.

The classroom becomes a temporary organization, with the same sort of relational and political dynamics that students are likely to encounter (or have already encountered) in placements, work experience or the direct experience of work. For example, when one does not know what is expected, it becomes important to ask, interpret or experiment, which is not always easy to do. Expectations are built in the relationship between managers and managed, they might reflect the difficulty that powerful individuals have in delegating authority, or conversely that people within positions of authority can feel out of their depth. The exercise brings the complexities and contradictions of behaviour in organizations to the surface and emphasizes the importance of reflection in the midst of action or incomprehension; it asks students (and the tutor) to reflect on the consequences of their reactions; and it provides an opportunity to raise and discuss the politics of action and inaction.

### *Master of Business Administration*

I run a five-day elective for Master of Business Administration (MBA) students called 'Leadership in Context'. This is open to both our full-time and executive MBA students. The maximum size of the student group is 24. The design uses experiential learning (in the 'group relations' tradition – see

French and Vince 1999) to critically reflect on and to examine group processes and dynamics within the classroom in order to generate insights about leadership and organizations. In particular, the module invites MBA students to notice and to reflect on the emotions and politics of leadership in the context of everyday organizational relations and practices.

There are a number of assumptions about leadership that this approach seeks to get across to MBA students. In effect, these offer a critique of the mainstream approach to leadership, which emphasizes the individual leader in the context of positive skills and behaviour. It is also designed to address the unspoken plea or desire that MBA students inevitably place on to me as the 'professor of leadership', which is to 'give me the skills I need to be a better leader'. The assumptions that inform the module are first, that leadership is not only an individual skill that has a specific set of abilities and competences; rather, it is a practice that changes according to the emotional, political and practical context in which it is situated. Second, organizations and groups create *dynamics* or ways of working that limit as well as support leadership behaviour and action. Understanding these dynamics is important because leaders often experience contradictions in their roles. For example, we are often asked to be *both* the champions of change and the guardians of the status quo. Third, an awareness of the organizational context of leadership helps students to feel and to perceive the complexities of emotions and relations that are part of leadership in practice. They can therefore understand the importance of continuous, critical reflection on leadership practice. This approach can be both challenging and enlightening.

For this example, I am going to talk about an exercise that is designed to be the transition point, halfway through the unit, between students' confusion about the relevance of the two days of experiential exercises they have undergone and their insights that inform the two days they have left to transform their ideas about leadership in practice.

Before I do this, I want to briefly illustrate what students encounter in the build up to this transition point, which involves experiential exercises in small groups, as a whole group, and within an 'institutional' exercise. For example, I ask students to organize themselves into small groups. The process of getting themselves into groups is often interesting in terms of the choices (or the lack of choices) that are made. Once small groups have formed, I ask them to give themselves a name and an identity (I do not specify what I mean by identity). They spend the time carefully and carelessly working out the best name for themselves; and they often highlight particular aspects of their identity – that they are a group where all are equal, a group with a shared interest in learning, a diverse group, a positive group, etc. They give themselves names like 'the A Team', the 'Nice Group' or they devise their own words that are an anagram of their combined names.

I then ask them to say how they as a group are different from the other groups in the room. Each small group quickly develops strong convictions and beliefs about their own labels and (consciously and unconsciously) uses them to reinforce the differences between 'us' and the 'other' groups. Their fantasy of consensus in 'our group' is unstable enough to need to be reinforced through suspicion of the other groups. The force that constructs 'other' groups as different comes from apprehension about unexplored differences within 'my' group. I have found that this exercise is useful in showing how quickly political relations are created and mobilized within and between sub-groups from emotional responses to 'other'; to protect the (at times fragile) distinctiveness that 'we' have made; and to provide an example of why silos develop, why it is often difficult within organizations to move or communicate between sub-system boundaries.

After two and a half days of experiential exercises, students can be feeling confused about their learning. It is at this transition point that they undertake some very specific work in small groups. The aim of their work together in these small groups (three to four people in each group) is to help each other to apply the experience of the experiential exercises they have encountered to their own work experience and practice.

Each member of the group takes it in turn to speak for about five to ten minutes about a real and current work problem or issue. I ask them to choose a problem that really matters; that feels difficult and is not readily amenable to being resolved. (For the full-time MBA students this can be an issue from past experience.) The other group members listen to the problem without interruption. When the individual has finished communicating the problem then the other group members can speak. However, they do not directly question the individual about the problem – *they only talk about their perceptions and experiences of the individual within the experiential exercises they have undertaken in the module.* Therefore, group members do not talk directly about the problem; they communicate what they noticed and how they perceived that particular individual within the specific context of the experiential exercises. The format is intended to allow individuals to think about and to make their own connections between behaviour and experience within the module and behaviour and experience at work.

This exercise is designed as a critique of expectations and practice. The way in which I am holding students in the moment here arises from asking them to focus only on the shared experience of the previous two days, whilst also talking about a significant issue or problem from past experience. Students reflect on their behaviour during the previous two days to support their understanding of behavioural issues at work (that they may or may not be aware of). Students initially expect to give each other the benefit of their opinions about the specific problem presented. However, to do this would limit the ability of all the people involved to engage emotionally with the issue and to provide each other with practical evidence of how their behaviour has been experienced in the learning group. Students also begin to understand how much of their practice is informed by a compulsion to act in habitual ways that limit and exclude many different possibilities for reflection and action. For example:

> My colleagues observed that my desire to be liked, and avoid conflict, may have prevented me from dealing with the situation upfront. I found the exercise powerful, reflecting in three areas: (a) I care about what people think of me and whether I am liked, (b) it is this that often makes me sweep difficult issues under the rug, which may cause adverse effects and (c) a realization that this desire was perhaps in response to negative childhood memories.
>
> In brief, my defensive response is withdrawal that presents itself externally as a sense of removal, of superiority, of arrogance, of unavailability, of unwillingness to compromise. For me this is the last line of defence when I am unable to use humour or charm. I give up and the situation becomes irresolvable.

Asking them to examine how they behaved both individually and collectively in the experiential exercises in order to better comprehend their problem or issue helps MBA students to see with greater clarity how tied up they are in the emotional and political dynamics of the problem.

## *The Master of Arts Degree in Advanced Management Practice*

The Master of Arts Degree in Advanced Management Practice (MAMP) is a Masters level programme with around forty students. The sessions I describe here were undertaken over three days (one each day) and in two-hour sessions. Using the same instruction for each session, I created three different arrangements of the chairs in the classroom to represent (that is, to make visible and manifest) a range of emotional and political dynamics in organizations. In each of the three designs the participants were given the instruction: 'you have an hour to work together as a group on any task and/or issue you want. The only rules are that you stay together as a group and that you cannot move the chairs from their current arrangement.' By creating differences of space and place, each of the three designs for learning aimed to engage with different aspects of emotion and politics in the classroom (as a reflection of emotions and politics in organizations).

The three designs generated differences in the ways in which the space is perceived, which is to say, its 'relative' qualities (Harvey 2005). In addition, emotions and interpersonal politics were mobilized in the lived or relational space of each design. These were particularly visible in the *tensions* that emerged from different spatial arrangements (I discuss these later). After they have ended, all three exercises have around an hour for the participants to reflect together and with the tutor, and to discuss and to make sense of the emotions, relations and politics stimulated within these different spatial arrangements for learning. Here, I am using different designs of the physical space of the classroom in order to hold students in the moment. I am asking them to reflect on the different dynamics that are generated within and by different spatial arrangements and to recognize the different patterns of leadership and interaction that emerge from these spaces.

## Design 1: the lecture theatre

In this, the first of the three sessions, the chairs are arranged in a 'lecture theatre' style. However, I (as tutor) am not standing in front of the participants, but sitting in the rows with them. In order to mark the beginning of the hour I say the instruction (see earlier) and let them know the time when the exercise will end. The students are accustomed to having someone in the role of tutor at the front of the lecture theatre rather than within the rows and we all continue to look towards the front. The most frequent outcome of the 'lecture theatre' arrangement of the chairs in the classroom is that sooner or later someone will get up and go to the front in order to address the group and to attempt to manage their task. The individual that puts him or herself in this place (or who is persuaded to go there by the group) both replaces the missing tutor and temporarily becomes the tutor.

Such an act is double edged because, although other participants are relieved to have someone who will take on this role, the individual is now 'different' and in danger of being punished for her inability to remain 'one of us' or for his hubris at placing himself 'above us'. The act of coming to the front in the class provides much of the material for the final hour of reflection and discussion. It connects with the common experience in organizations where an individual is promoted from being a team member to being a team leader. This individual suddenly has to change from being 'one of us' to being in an authority role.

The act of going to the front (of taking a lead, or being persuaded to do so by the group) does help to reduce feelings of confusion and uncertainty that the tutor's behaviour has caused. The spatial arrangements of the lecture theatre design lend themselves to being dependent on and sustained by the individual or individuals at the front. Such dependency not only relates to the function an individual at the front might perform in helping others to define and decide what they are doing; but the individual at the front also serves the purpose of providing a focal point for blame if and when things disappoint, fall short or go wrong. The shared fantasy that sustains the behaviour of the group is that creating a replacement for the tutor will enable the group to successfully manage the confusion and uncertainty that is present. This is a space where the focus is on activity at 'the front'. In its determination to maintain a focus on the front as the place where learning is generated and delivered, the group rejects its own potential to generate learning.

## Design 2: the circle of chairs

In the second session, the chairs are arranged in a large circle and the tutor is sitting within this circle. The same instruction is given to the group and the exercise lasts the same amount of time. The circle of chairs allows all to see and to be engaged with all other members of the learning group. In this design, the circle means that everyone is *seen* to be a member of the group, and for some members increased visibility and proximity to others means increased uncertainty and discomfort. Like the 'lecture theatre' configuration, the circle of chairs generates anxiety for the students initially as a result of not having a clear task. However, in this place the intensified emotions of visibility and proximity mean that they feel pulled by an imagined responsibility or expectation to achieve a task (however mundane that task may be).

As feelings of anxiety emerge, participants repeat tried and tested strategies for avoiding this anxiety: writing ideas on the flip-chart, going round the group so everyone has a chance to say something, finding an individual from within the group who will be the leader, blaming the tutor, etc. (see Vince 2010). For example, it is very common for someone in the group to say that 'we should all go around and say one idea about what to do' and then lead the exercise by writing the ideas down on the flip chart. There are often group members who want to try to be fair to everyone, at the same time as imposing their suggestion on the group. Such behaviour is an accurate representation of the speed with which implicit structures and ways of working are set up to defend against the anxiety that uncertainty brings to groups and to organizations. In addition, (as the tutor) I am closer, more visible and more present within this space. The failings of the tutor are often discussed in this configuration, and the tutor is used more deliberately as someone 'different' because this helps the group to avoid looking at the differences between group members.

The key managerial tension in this second configuration of chairs is about how (individually and collectively) to avoid or to try to manage conflict and difference. One particular assumption that participants make about this circular design is that it *removes* power differences and emphasizes the equality inherent in learning with and from our peers. In fact, social and strategic power relations and differences are not 'removed'; rather, they are replaced with a shared fantasy of equality that sustains the idea that there are few significant differences in the group. This design encourages the notion that 'we are all the same here' – that we are all learning together in the same way and with the same opportunities. Unconsciously, the group defends itself against the differences (for example, of power, knowledge, understanding, enthusiasm, social and cultural diversity) that are invariably part of the group and may contribute to its effective or ineffective functioning.

This particular arrangement of chairs reveals students' desire to minimize and to avoid conflict and difference. The circle of chairs lends itself to attempts to include everyone in decision making, to emphasize that 'we are *all* here to learn together'. The shared fantasy that sustains the behaviour of the group is that in our group there is togetherness and equality; that we only have to work together in order to defeat confusion and successfully perform our task. However, students also mobilize the potential circularity of collaboration (literally, at times we are all going round in circles). In the determination to make everyone in the group happy, equal or involved, the students collectively reject conflicts and differences that might make a difference to their learning.

The participants' emphasis on the collaborative nature of this design for learning obscures the fact that collaboration *and* compliance are bound together in this format. The fantasy that 'we are all equal', although it begins as a productive response to the discomfort of having to negotiate with others around a task, is a restriction – it eventually discourages differences of behaviour, opinion and action. Tensions emerge from trying to avoid conflict and differences in the group and through the promotion of togetherness. The exclusion of difference and the avoidance of conflict are very common organizational dynamics, where the tendency is to emphasize the need for 'positive' thought and action and to ignore the destructiveness that is part of behaviour in organizations.

## Design 3: The woman sign

In the third session, the chairs are arranged into the symbol for 'woman' (a circle with a cross below it) I am sitting in the circular part of the design. The group receives the same instruction and the exercise lasts the same amount of time. Participants find the material space of this design to be unsettling, especially those individuals who have entered the room last and are positioned in the 'cross' part of the design rather than the 'circle'. The arrangement of chairs in this symbol deliberately reintroduces (gendered) power relations as an underlying aspect of all reflections, decisions and actions that occur within the group. The students are not usually aware of why the chairs are so arranged, and it often takes a while for the symbol to be noticed and acknowledged. This configuration of chairs represents a perpetual emotional and political issue within organizations, the desire to avoid interacting with the dynamics between men and women in the group.

I have been struck by the consistency in different groups' responses to this configuration of chairs. At some point in the exercise, two or three individuals notice the structure as 'the woman sign' but they do not communicate this fact to the whole group. For example, I was sitting near Indira and I heard her whisper to her friend, 'it's the woman sign'. Neither Indira nor her friend mentioned this to the rest of the group. One way to think about this is that the group spends some of the exercise 'knowing' about the spatial design in a sub-group but not in the whole group. In other words, there are participants who know that the design is 'the woman sign' but do not want to say this out loud. However, the structure is sooner or later noticed by or brought to the attention of the group as a whole, but an individual or a sub-group then dismisses the design as unimportant ('that's irrelevant!'), which makes speaking about it more difficult. The shared fantasy inherent in this configuration is that the gendered power dynamics that emerge are at the same time both too obvious and too complicated to discuss. To use an analogy, it is a bit like important interpersonal or organizational issues or relations that get mentioned at the water cooler after the meeting, rather than in the meeting itself.

This arrangement is a complex place, one that reflects the embodied differences that constitute the social. The dynamics of this configuration seem to offer an accurate representation of gendered power relations in organizations, where it is equally difficult to negotiate, comprehend and interact with the way such power relations impact on thought, behaviour, action and inaction. There is a strong desire to ignore, avoid or dismiss gendered power relations, to fight against or flee from having to include such issues as a legitimate aspect of management learning. The significance of the spatial arrangement of the chairs is rejected, even when it is perceived. The shared fantasy that sustains the behaviour of the group is that to talk about gendered power relations would take it to an uncomfortable, unwanted and difficult place where tensions between men and women might explode in the group, thereby destroying it and rendering it incapable of delivering its task. This design is a challenge because it is explicit about the power relations that are part of experience in a group where male and female managers are working together.

The three chair arrangements I use over the three sessions can be thought of separately as different spatial designs for learning. However, it is the emphasis on their interconnection that provides particular insights about the emotions and politics of managing and organizing. All three designs signify spatial arrangements linked to intersecting structures and relations of power. They help managers to understand how power relations are 'part of the medium within which all social relations occur' (Hoggett and Thompson 2002). Each design reveals tensions concerning different processes and relations of power. The lecture theatre design is *hierarchical* – revealing both a need for the charismatic power of individual leadership, *and* the passivity, dependency and compliance that are created from it. Existing power relations within groups tend to be reinforced in this place. It also points to the tension within an individual management or leadership role between being part of 'them' or part of 'us'. The circle of chairs mixes both *collaboration and compliance* – revealing the collective capacity to create something of value together, *and* a fantasy of sameness that avoids conflicts and discourages risk. Avoiding conflict and risk encourages predictability and prescription, which limits the (public) emergence of new knowledge. Differential power relations tend to be ignored or set aside in this place so that the status quo is not disturbed. The 'woman sign' is a *critical* space – it points to the contradictions inherent in organization, *and* at the same time it does not attempt to provide solutions or prescriptions for improvement because the social issues represented here are too complex for solutions.

## Conclusion

If we are going to encourage managers and leaders to use their imaginations (see De Cock, this volume) to connect with personal and social emotions and to broaden their alternatives in practice, then as management educators we should at least be trying to do the same. This raises a broader question concerning what can be done to promote the possibilities of critical education? To conclude, I will summarize what I think this involves.

I have identified two general principles that inform my practice when I am thinking about how to create suitable environments for learning. First, I ask what do I need to do in order to *hold students in the moment,* which is to say to create spaces where students can feel and acknowledge the emotions that underpin both their willingness and their unwillingness to learn? Second, I find that it is important to remember that *critical reflection is likely to mobilize the power relations it is seeking to transform.* For example, if we want to engage with students about their attempts to negotiate power relations in class, then as tutors we need a corresponding willingness to make our own power visible and discussable. This is not the same as relinquishing authority; it is rather about the importance of reflecting on various ongoing and emerging authority relations in public. In this way, a critical approach to teaching managers and leaders mirrors what we might hope to convey about the critical practice of management and leadership.

I have discussed three examples of holding students in the moment and critical reflection. The first provides undergraduate students with direct experience of ten minutes of uncertainty, which produces a wide range of responses that illustrate the complex feelings and reactions that can be mobilized by an apparently simple request. The second shows how a focus on here and now experience in the classroom helps students to reflect on habits and attachments to particular ways of thinking, behaving and acting. The third example illustrates the way in which three spatial arrangements helped to reveal different and intersecting structures and relations of power. Using these examples, I illustrate how I make use of the business and management school classroom as an environment for the study of the emotional, relational and political psychodynamics present in organizations. Such dynamics will vary in how they are felt and expressed, and they will always be contextually specific. However, the examples all try to focus on recurring aspects of individual and collective behaviour in organizations. Reflecting on immediate evidence from their own individual and collective experience in the classroom gives the opportunity for students to view behaviour in the context of wider emotions and power relations.

The possibilities of critical education depend on management educators and management students noticing and interpreting emotional and political dynamics in the business and management school classroom. It is important not to look away as we catch glimpses of the power relations that inform people's creativity and their compliance. In particular, the willingness to unsettle current ideas, habits, stuck emotions, defences and prevailing relations of power offers a more general critique of established views of managing and leading as activities focused primarily on positive skills and behaviour that are generally applicable. Building critique of established views into the learning experience is integral to expanding alternative ideas about managing and leading in practice.

## References


Antonacopoulou, E. (2002) 'Corporate universities: the domestication of management education'. *In:* C. Wankel and R. De Fillippi (eds.) *Rethinking Management Education for the 21st Century*. Greenwich, CT: Information Age Publishing, pp. 185–207.

Antonacopoulou, E. (2006) 'Working life learning: learning-in-practise'. *In:* E. Antonacopoulou, P. Jarvis, V. Andersen, B. Elkjaer and S. Hoyrup (eds.) *Learning, Working and Living: Mapping the Terrain of Working Life Learning*. Basingstoke, UK: Palgrave, pp. 234–56.

Antonacopoulou, E. (2010) 'Making business schools more "critical": reflexive critique based on phronesis as a foundation for impact', *British Journal of Management*, 21, 6–25.

Antonacopoulou, E. and Gabriel, Y. (2001) 'Emotion, learning and organizational change: towards an integration of psychoanalytic and other perspectives', *Journal of Organizational Change Management*, 14, 435–51.

Brocklehurst, M., Sturdy, A., Winstanley, D. and Driver, M. (2007) 'Whither the MBA? Factions, fault lines and the future', *Management Learning*, 38, 379–88.

Clegg, S., Dany, F. and Grey C. (2011) 'Introduction to the special issue critical management studies and managerial education: new contexts? New agenda', *M@n@gement* 14(5), 271–9.

Cunliffe, A., Forray, J. and Knights, D. (2002) 'Considering management education: insights from critical management studies', *Journal of Management Education*, 26, 489–95.

Currie, G. and Knights, D. (2003) 'Reflecting on a critical pedagogy in MBA education', *Management Learning*, 34, 27–49.

Currie, G., Knights, D. and Starkey, K. (2010) 'Introduction: a post-crisis critical reflection on business schools', *British Journal of Management*, 21(1), 1–5.

Dehler, G. (2009) 'Prospects and possibilities of critical management education: critical beings and a pedagogy of critical action', *Management Learning*, 40(1), 31–49.

Fineman, S. and Sturdy, A. (1999) 'The emotions of control: a qualitative exploration of environmental regulation', *Human Relations*, 52, 631–63.

Fournier, V. and Grey, C. (2000) 'At the critical moment: conditions and prospects for critical management studies', *Human Relations*, 53, 7–32.

French, R. and Grey, C. (eds.) (1996) *Rethinking Management Education*. London: Sage Publications.

French, R. and Vince, R. (eds.) (1999) *Group Relations, Management and Organisation*. Oxford: Oxford University Press.

Gherardi, S. and Poggio, B. (2007) 'Tales of ordinary leadership: a feminist approach to experiential learning'. *In:* M. Reynolds and R. Vince (eds.) *The Handbook of Experiential Learning and Management Education*. Oxford: Oxford University Press, pp. 155–68.

Grey, C. (2002) 'What are business schools for? On silence and voice in management education', *Journal of Management Education*, 26, 496–511.

Grey, C. (2004) 'Reinventing business schools: the contribution of critical management education', *Academy of Management Learning and Education*, 3, 178–86.

Grey, C. (2008) *A Very Short Fairly Interesting and Reasonably Cheap Book about Studying Organizations*. London: Sage Publications.

Harvey, D. (2005) 'Space as a key word'. *In:* D. Harvey (ed.) *Spaces of Neoliberalization: Towards a Theory of Uneven Geographical Development*. Heidelberg, Germany: Franz Steiner Verlag, pp. 93–118.

Hay, A. (2008) 'More success than meets the eye – a challenge to critiques of the MBA: possibilities for critical management education', *Management Learning*, 39(1), 21–40.
Hibbert, P. (2013) 'Approaching reflexivity through reflection: issues for critical management education', *Journal of Management Education*, 37(6), 803–27.
Hoggett, P. and Thompson, S. (2002) 'Towards a democracy of the emotions', *Constellations*, 9, 106–26.
Kenny, K. and Fotaki, M. (2014) *The Psychosocial and Organization Studies: Affect at Work*. Houndmills, UK: Palgrave Macmillan.
Kersten, A. (2001) 'Organizing for powerlessness: a critical perspective on psychodynamics and dysfunctionality', *Journal of Organizational Change Management*, 14, 452–67.
Kunda, G. (1992) *Engineering Culture: Control and Commitment in a High-Tech Corporation*. Philadelphia, PA: Temple University Press.
Lewis, P. and Simpson, R. (2007) *Gendering Emotions in Organizations*. London: Palgrave Macmillan.
Miller, S., Hagen, R. and Johnson, M. (2003) 'The disruptive consequences of introducing a critical perspective onto an MBA programme', *Management Learning*, 34, 241–57.
Neumann, J.E. and Hirschhorn, L. (1999) 'The challenge of integrating psychodynamic and organizational theory', *Human Relations*, 52(6), 683–95.
Nicolini, D., Sher, M., Childerstone, S. and Gorli, M. (2004) 'In search of "the structure that reflects": promoting organizational reflection practices in a UK health authority'. *In:* M. Reynolds and R. Vince (eds.) *Organizing Reflection*. Aldershot, UK: Ashgate, pp. 81–104.
Reynolds, M. (1999) 'Grasping the nettle: possibilities and pitfalls of a critical management pedagogy', *British Journal of Management*, 9, 171–84.
Reynolds, M. and Trehan, K. (2001) 'Classroom as real world: propositions for a pedagogy of difference', *Gender and Education*, 13, 357–72.
Reynolds, M. and Vince, R. (2004) 'Critical management education and action-based learning: synergies and contradictions', *Academy of Management Learning and Education*, 3(4), 442–56.
Sinclair, A. (2007) 'Teaching leadership critically to MBAs: experiences from heaven and hell', *Management Learning*, 38, 458–72.
Swan, E. (2005) 'On bodies, rhinestones and pleasures: women teaching managers', *Management Learning*, 36, 317–33.
Van Maanen, J. and Kunda, G. (1989) '"Real feelings": emotional expression and organizational culture', *Research in Organizational Behaviour*, 11, 43–104.
Vince, R. (2002). 'The politics of imagined stability: a psychodynamic understanding of change at Hyder plc', *Human Relations*, 55, 1189–208.
Vince, R. (2010) 'Anxiety, politics and critical management education', *British Journal of Management*, 21(1), 26–39.

# 17

# From creativity to imagination with Cornelius Castoriadis

*Christian De Cock*

## Introduction

The aim of this chapter is to open up creativity teaching and research to the deeper challenges of the humanities and social sciences. It is in part a response to a personal concern, reflecting on my on–off involvement with the field of creativity over a period of twenty-five years, that traditional creativity research and teaching, through the unthinking repetition of an accepted body of knowledge, is in danger of destroying the very object ('creativity') it pretends to grasp and encourages students to learn. This realization first struck home about ten years ago when after a prolonged period away from the creativity field I attended the fifteenth anniversary conference of the journal *Creativity & Innovation Management* in Oxford and found myself in a strange time warp: the same people were talking about the same issues using the same conceptual frameworks and techniques. They all just looked a bit older. But the curious stasis that seems to haunt the academic field of creativity research is perhaps best exemplified by a different kind of personal time warp. In 1994 I co-authored a chapter surveying the field of creativity, which although delivered on time to the editor, somehow disappeared between the cracks of academic life. To my utter incredulity it appeared in a handbook of cutting-edge creativity research some eighteen years later, complete with references to 'recent' research from the early 1990s (Rickards and De Cock 2012).

What I offer in the following pages to counteract this curious stasis is a philosophical–historical narrative, very much inspired by the work of Cornelius Castoriadis (1987). Castoriadis was concerned throughout his work with the key question of how the 'new' can come into being and this required him to focus on the imagination, which has a history that reaches far further back than does that of creativity (going all the way back to Aristotle's *De Anima*). It is my contention that a historical awareness of the rich pedigree of 'imagination' can help students to appreciate better the operant logic in which modern notions of creativity have been captured. One tentative suggestion I will make in this chapter is that we should push the term 'creativity' into the background and focus on developing our students' imagination instead. With Castoriadis, I will advocate an approach to creativity/imagination that is profoundly political, historical and social, which – and this is crucial in the context of management education – links back to the notion of organization and institutions (De Cock 2013). This is a conceptualization of creativity/imagination as a counterweight to the actuality of the (organizational) world, as the capacity to convert the given confines of the here and now into an open horizon of possibilities (Kearney 1998).

In the following section I will problematize popular uses and conceptualizations of creativity using recently published handbooks and review articles. I will then introduce a turn to the notion of imagination, which allows me to provide some historical and philosophical depth to ways of addressing 'the new'. This socio-historical and philosophical exploration culminates in the work of Castoriadis in the third section, the implications of which for creativity teaching and research are explored in the fourth and final part.

## The problems with creativity

In developing my argument I will rely on a number of recent 'handbooks' and review articles to sketch the operant logic that underpins the teaching and researching of creativity in a business context. In doing so I will take care to avoid the straw man arguments we often find in these sources, for example, positioning creativity teaching and research against 'a traditional view that creativity and innovation are simply of little importance to the success of organizations' (Mumford *et al.* 2012: 3). This is often followed by the suggestion that twenty-first-century organizations need creativity and innovation because of the opening up of new global markets and rapid technological developments, and that creativity and innovation are important causes of organizational value, growth and performance in a dynamically changing environment. Managing creativity then becomes about 'putting into place a variety of factors (e.g. person and contextual characteristics) that will consciously lead employees to develop new ideas to solve problems and create new opportunities' (George 2007: 446). Underpinning this effort is the belief in 'the role of the conscious mind and conscious thought', and models of the creative process applied in creativity training workshops and organizations more generally therefore have 'a decidedly rational flavor' (George 2007: 446). An implicit assumption that goes unchallenged in this dominant narrative of creativity is that both novelty and usefulness are constitutive of creativity, with creativity typically viewed as a precursor to innovation (for example, Amabile *et al.* 2005; Rickards and Moger 2006). This leads well-respected creativity researchers such as Sternberg and Kaufman (2010: 468) to suggest, for example, that 'those who are imaginative but whose ideas are useless become frustrated dreamers. Those who have useful ideas that are not imaginative become, whether in name or in deed, technicians'. George (2007) astutely remarked in her overview of the field that questions such as 'what is meant by useful?' and 'useful for whom?' are almost invariably neglected in this mainstream creativity discourse.

Although since the early 1990s creativity has been conceived of as a multilevel construct, operating at the individual, group and organizational levels (Woodman *et al.* 1993; Drazin *et al.* 1999), most research has very much focused on created products and efforts by individuals (Chan 2013) and on rare occasions by groups (George 2007). When considering the organizational level, characteristics and processes at the individual level are largely anthropomorphized (Rickards and De Cock 2012). It should not be surprising therefore that despite a huge amount of research output on the role of 'creativity and innovation' as components of organizational performance over the past 30 years or so, researchers consistently include the rider in their conclusions that 'scholars' understanding of the creative process and the factors influencing it is still quite limited' (Amabile *et al.* 2005: 398). The problem lies not so much in a lack of quality research, but with the stories the field of creativity research tends to tell itself about itself – very often taking Guilford's address to the American Psychological Association in 1950 as the beginning of modern creativity research – whilst projecting the ideal of the field as homogeneous and creativity as a unitary construct. As Chan (2013: 26) pointed out, for historical reasons (organizational) psychologists have dominated the field of creativity research for the past 60 years, and this has meant that 'many creativity researchers are still searching for a "clearer definition of creativity" and ways to improve the scientific validity of their research findings'.

When creativity researchers working in the mainstream tradition do set out to explore 'extended historical changes in the concept of creativity' (Runco and Albert 2010: 3) it leads to some, no doubt unintended, comical effects, such as in the suggestion that 'Aristotle, Kant, and many other luminaries had much to say about creativity, but . . . they did not base their ideas about it on rigorous empirical evidence' (Runco and Albert 2010: 4). Although acknowledging that 'still no concept of "creativity" existed' by the seventeenth century, Runco and Albert (2010: 9) manage to explore pre-Christian views (Aristotle and the Romans) in just over half a page, and then take just a page to get to the eighteenth-century Enlightenment via Locke and Hobbes. Suggesting that eighteenth-century debates on the imagination were 'tedious and tangential', they give thinkers of the time some credit because they came close to the holy grail of creativity in that 'their discussions of "imagination" led as early as the 1730s to the phrase, "the creative imagination"' (Runco and Albert 2010: 9). For good measure they outline their underlying assumption (again, one that is very typical in the dominant narratives of creativity) that 'history is the medium in which ideas and events build up and arrive, with some significant effects rarely going away'. This is a view of history as a 'slow boil', or what Walter Benjamin (1999: 254) describes as 'historicism's bordello', that we need to blast open (also see De Cock *et al.* 2013a).

Only recently has there emerged an acknowledgement of the need to examine critically the discourses of creativity, 'laying bare the institutional interests, ideological assumptions, and social consequences of different constructions of creativity' (Chan 2013: 22), and to open up the concept methodologically and theoretically. In doing so, we must of course be heedful to distinguish between the self-designated field of 'creativity research' and the wider range of intellectual endeavour that has implications for understanding creativity (De Cock 1996; De Cock and Rehn 2006). My suggested turn to the social sciences and humanities, albeit not always grounded in 'rigorous empirical evidence' as Runco and Albert (2010) demand, precisely aims to respond to what is a rather ironic feature of creativity research and teaching in an organizational context: that it is profoundly uncreative on its own terms, offering little novelty and questionable usefulness (Rehn and De Cock 2009). Or as George (2007) put it somewhat more subtly in her conclusion to a substantial state-of-the-art article:

> [O]ne might wonder to what extent the literature on creativity is succumbing to a certain single-mindedness or routinization that, while enriching our understanding of creativity in incremental ways, is not leading to the kinds of breakthrough advances that are the true marks of creativity in the scholarly domain. While perhaps a harsh overstatement, the existing literature has approached creativity in ways that do not always do justice to the very nature of creative endeavours.
>
> *George 2007: 466*

## From creativity to imagination

Attempts to historicize the notion of creativity, as in the effort by Runco and Albert (2010) discussed earlier, are all too rare in the creativity literature. And perhaps there is good reason for this: there is simply not all that much to historicize in the first place. Mason (2003) points out that although the noun 'creativeness' was used in English from the end of the eighteenth century, the term 'creativity' itself appeared late in the nineteenth century and became common only well into the twentieth century. In French and German, the nouns *créativité* and *Kreativität* were actually derived from Anglo-American usage in psychology and came into general use only in the second half of the twenthieth century. What this shows us is that both popular and academic conceptualizations of 'creativity' actually do not come trailing with all that much historical freight behind them. If we want to explore historically how 'the new' comes into being, we thus must engage with the much older and richer concept of 'imagination'. Not that we will find a slow and irreversible build-up of ideas and events (see Runco and Albert 2010) when considering the concept of imagination. Rather, what we encounter are 'successive movements of discovery and covering back over that have marked the history of the question of the imagination' (Castoriadis 1993: 3). Crucial breakthroughs are 'followed immediately by a strange and total forgetting', something Castoriadis (1993: 2) referred to as the 'scandal of the imagination'. Casey (1976: 15) talks in this respect of a negligence by philosophers where few 'convincing and lasting distinctions have been made between imagination and the group of sibling acts that would include memory, perceptual illusion, fantasy, delusion, and hallucination'. Although it would be beyond the scope of this chapter to give an exhaustive historical overview, it is still useful to summarize some of the key intellectual discoveries Castoriadis referred to, if only to build up a rich and thematically organized concept of imagination and open up a space for Castoriadis's very imaginative take on imagination.

Aristotle's early conception of the imagination prefigured later philosophers' interest in the mind's 'functional architecture', which posits a hierarchy of the faculties (usually with reason as the king of the faculties). He proposed *phantasia* (of which *imaginatio* is the Latin translation) as part of a wider faculty, having the role of combining experiences into so-called phantasmata, meaning coherent mental representations (Roth 2007). Aristotle thus allows *phantasia* a certain legitimacy as an aid to practical reason – by recalling past experiences and anticipating future ones it can mobilize our present behaviour in a particular direction – and yet he held on to the view that imagination is for the most part false (Kearney 1998). This negative view of imagination persisted through the ages and led to a neglect of the concept until it became situated again with Hume and Kant (and to a certain extent Hobbes in the seventeenth century) in the uppermost echelons in the hierarchy of mental faculties (Casey 1976). These modern philosophers developed the basic understanding of imagination as a 'presence-in-absence', whilst generally reversing the negative verdict it had received in the tribunal of tradition (Kearney 1998). For Hume (1968 [1739]), imagination mediates between sensory impressions and ideas of memory and judgement, thus placing it in a pivotal role. Imagination is necessary both to our thinking of things when they are not present to our senses and to our thought of them when they are so present, if we are to imbue these objects of perception with any permanence or any existence separate from ourselves (Warnock 1994). The continuity and identity of an object perceived thus can be ascertained only with the aid of the imagination. However, Hume also introduced a negative 'valence' – imagination as the product of an unfortunate 'psychological habit' of believing in a world whose existence cannot be rationally established – that overshadowed the concept's subsequent development. For Kant (2008), in the first edition of the *Critique of Pure Reason* (1781), the imagination becomes the concealed and yet real condition of all knowledge. It is the faculty of representing in intuition an object that is not itself present and the categories of pure reason are therefore creations and representations of an imagination that is only partially presented, and yet ever present. It is the imagination that loosens our relation to, and reliance on, wholly empirical conditions. Imagination is thus acknowledged as one of the most fundamental, if concealed, powers of humankind by Kant (Rundell 1994). If Kant comes close to admitting a sort of primacy of imagination, in the second edition of the *Critique* (1787) he retreats from his discovery and relegates the imagination to a more subaltern intermediary role between intellect and intuition (Bottici 2011).

Twentieth-century phenomenological approaches rediscovered the idea of imagination as presence-in-absence: the act of making what is present absent and what is absent present, and thus to elaborate concepts, images and ideas that do not correspond to current or past reality, and that may never be actualized (Roth 2007). As Kearney eloquently put it:

> The plurality of terms for imagination ... all refer, in their diverse ways, to the human power to convert absence into presence, actuality into possibility, what-is into something-other-than-it-is. In short, they all designate our ability to transform the time and space of our world into a specifically human mode of existence *(Dasein)*.
>
> *Kearney 1998: 4*

For Sartre (2004 [1940]), the ability to imagine is identical, with the ability to detach ourselves from our actual situation and envisage situations that are *non-actual* and thus become the very precondition of human freedom and the possibility of action. The capacity to begin something new depends upon our capacity to mentally remove ourselves from where we are physically located and to imagine that things might well be different from what they actually are (Bottici 2011). It is because we can imagine that we can think about things that are absent, including things that no longer exist or do not yet exist, and that we can anticipate how things might be and that we can envision the world as if it were otherwise (Warnock 1994).

From this brief historical survey we can note a longstanding dialectic of reason and imagination, with imagination seen as a precondition for reason but always becoming subordinated to it (for example, in Aristotle, Hume and Kant). It is only in Castoriadis's work that the basic anthropological trait that distinguishes humans from other species will no longer be the universal innateness of reason but that of the imagination. It is this imagination, furthermore, that enables humans to operate effectively in complex social groupings and contemplate intricate plans for possible future action, by bringing an absent 'non-actual' future into presence (Roth 2007). The imagination therefore is not a single act producing an imaginative output; it is a vital process of communication whereby we pass beyond ourselves towards what is other than ourselves. For phenomenological thinkers like Merleau-Ponty (1968) society itself therefore becomes, in a fundamental sense, an incarnation of human imagining. The triple dialectic of reason/imagination, absence/presence and individual/society provides a platform for Castoriadis's thinking on creation and imagination, which suggests a decisive break with the routinization in our understanding of creativity we referred to in the second section.

## The radical imagination of Cornelius Castoriadis

> It is entirely natural to call *imaginary* and *imagination* this faculty of radical novation, creation, and formation . . . We [therefore] must admit that there is in human collectivities a creative potential, a *vis formandi*, which I call *the instituting social imaginary*.
>
> *Castoriadis 2005: 125*

If, for most social and philosophical thinkers throughout the ages, the exploration of the imagination was perhaps a side project, with Cornelius Castoriadis the concept becomes truly central (Karagiannis and Wagner 2012). The key question that concerned Castoriadis is how the 'new' can come into being. In his magnum opus, *The Imaginary Institution of Society* (1987), Castoriadis elaborates the notion of creation *ex nihilo*, the bringing into existence of forms that did not previously exist – a feature of which is its unmotivated and undetermined character. Castoriadis's aim was very much to develop a way of thinking about 'the fact that something other than what exists is bringing itself into being, and bringing itself into being as new or as other' (1987: 185). Crucial to his project was the concept of *radical imagination*, which states 'that "reality" exists *for us* – exists *tout court* – and exists *as* it exists' (Castoriadis 1997a: 321), and any human being can, in principle, reimagine what another human being has imagined. Creation therefore means the positive rupture of already given determinations and the positing of new determinations, or what Castoriadis calls 'social imaginary significations'. This imagined world of signification allows us 'to create for ourselves a *world* – or to present to ourselves something of which, without the imagination, we would know nothing and we could say nothing' (Castoriadis 1997b: 104). Imaginary significations represent a surplus of meaning, a 'capacity to see in a thing what it is not, to see it other than it is' (Castoriadis 1987: 127), which transcends all determinants and presuppositions (Arnason 1989). They therefore form a creative potential, an a-causal *vis formandi*, that is immanent to the anonymous collective as well as to singular human beings. For Castoriadis (1987: 366), imaginary significations 'are obviously not what individuals represent to themselves, consciously or unconsciously, or what they think. They are that by means of which and on the basis of which individuals are formed as social individuals, capable of participating in social doing and representing/saying'. They articulate the world in the double sense of imposing form on it and giving access to it and function as 'the invisible cement holding together this endless collection of real, rational and symbolic odds and ends that constitute every society, and as the principle that selects and shapes the bits and pieces that will be accepted there'[1] (Castoriadis 1987: 143).

Castoriadis talks about the *instituting imaginary* because it is this imaginary that underpins the instituting of society. Drawing on Merleau-Ponty's work, he sees the imaginary as crucial to both a *mise en forme* (form giving; shaping) and a *mise en question* (putting into question) of any given institution of society (Karagiannis and Wagner 2012). This imaginary is a kind of ultimate that needs society as a medium for its appearance, just as society needs it in order to become institutionalized. Our institutions are symbolic systems that human subjects incorporate into their behaviour, and every individual imagination is charged accordingly by the symbols of society that surround it as it, in turn, recharges these symbols (Kearney 1998). The institution of a society presupposes the institution of imaginary significations that must, in principle, be able to provide meaning to whatever presents itself empirically, and yet this society also depends for its existence on human subjects created by that society. As Bottici (2011: 25) put it, 'Society can exist concretely only through the fragmentary and complementary incarnation and incorporation of its institution and its imaginary significations in the living, talking and acting individuals of that society'.[2]

Aiming to avoid the duality of individual and society, which has marked much of the history of the social sciences and humanities (namely debates around agency and structure), Castoriadis works with the dialectic of the psychical and the social-historical, both of which have the potential for creation (Karagiannis and Wagner 2012) but which cannot exist one without the other and which are irreducible to each other (Castoriadis 1997b). The radical imagination of the psyche is the equivalent form of expression at the individual level of the instituting social imaginary at the social-historical level: 'the question of the psyche . . . is inseparable from the question of the social-historical, two expressions of the radical imagination – here, as radical imagination; there as social imaginary' (Castoriadis 1987: 274). This is a notion of imagination (and creation) that exceeds the psychological horizon, which is so typical of considerations of creativity in business and management studies. To understand imagination we therefore need to look beyond individuals and acknowledge the institutional and instituting dimensions through which humans organize themselves collectively. Imagination is not just a process through which individuals or groups generate creative thoughts and outputs; human beings are in continuous interplay with the institutions they created, and are being sustained and altered by them (Roth 2007). All knowing and acting is for Castoriadis (1997b: 105) indissociably psychical *and* social-historical: 'Man is *psuché*; soul, psyche in its underlying strata, unconscious. And man is society; he *is* only in and through society, its institution, and the social imaginary significations that render the psyche fit for life.'[3]

The radical imagination is, for Castoriadis (1997a), the flux or incessant flow of spontaneously emerging representations, affects and desires within the psyche, which is singular for each human being. If human beings were given over fully to this radical imagination, they would not be able to survive in society because 'the desires that surge forth don't bear the subject toward a life lived in common' (Castoriadis 2005: 128). This flux must therefore be channelled and controlled and when this socialization takes place through the absorption of the instituted society and its significations, the most important manifestations of the radical imagination are, up to a certain point, stifled. It is primarily through language that the psyche receives the totality of the social imaginary significations that language bears, conveys and renders possible, and yet there persists a permanent incommensurability between the social order of imaginary significations and the spontaneous flux of representations that form the creative core of the individual mind (Dews 2002). It is this clash between the psyche and the socio-historical that enables meaning to remain in principle open, or if in danger of closing upon itself, to be reopened through interrogation (Rundell 1994). The presence of the radical imagination thus implies the potential ability to question and lucidly examine social significations as a social discourse as well as a personal identification (Urribari 2002).

For Castoriadis the creative dimension of the imagination is emphatically linked to the capacity to question the existing and the given. This 'given' Castoriadis (1987) refers to as the 'instituted social imaginary', a solidification and crystallization of the instituting imaginary. Social reality, as is constituted for us and by us, is the result of the dialectic between the instituted and the instituting side of the social imaginary as society continually defines and redefines itself (Bottici 2011). For Castoriadis (1987: 108), therefore, the social-historical is the anonymous collective whole which is 'on the one hand, given structures, and, on the other hand, *that which* structures, institutes, materializes. In short, it is the union *and* the tension of instituting society and of instituted society, of history made and of history in the making'. For Castoriadis, the institution of the social-historical and the creation of imaginary significations always involve both the creation of radical otherness (the new) and the workings of what he calls an ensemblist–identitary logic. All social institutions, the foremost of which is language, have what Castoriadis calls an 'ensemblist–identitary' dimension that sits alongside the imaginary dimension, and the operations of the ensemblist–identitary logic are represented through the notions of *legein* and *teukhein*.[4] It is these operations that provide the imaginary with meaning:

> The instrumental institution of *legein* is the institution of the identitary–ensemblist conditions for social representing/saying. The instrumental institution of *teukhein* is the institution of the identitary–ensemblist conditions for social doing. The two institutions mutually imply one another, they intrinsically inhere in one another, and each is impossible without the other.
>
> *Castoriadis 1987: 370*

Society cannot represent things and represent itself, make things and make itself without applying this ensemblistic–identitary logic that establishes institutions and institutes itself only by instituting *legein* and *teukhein* as well. Castoriadis (1997a: 305) sees this 'ensemblistic "part" [as] everywhere dense in natural language'. It is impossible to speak in any context whatsoever without utilizing ensemblistic–identitary operators. He finds this process also at work in the writings of Hegel and Marx, for example, who,

> can say what they have to say that is fundamental about society and history only by transgressing what they believe they know about what being and thinking mean, and who finally reduce it, by forcing it to enter into a system that cannot contain it.
>
> *Castoriadis 1997a: 204*

In Castoriadis's work, we see the interaction of the instituting and the instituted society at work in that new institutions always need to take account of the already instituted. The instituting imaginary has to contend with different orders of constraints, both external (those imposed by the natural strata, especially biology) and historical (the reproductive inertia within the instituted society), but these constraints do not warrant a deterministic reading. Castoriadis does not privilege the instituting over the instituted; rather, the key issue for him that determines the health of any society is the extent to which it recognizes in its institution its own self-creation. Alienation occurs when society does not recognize in the imaginary of institutions something that is its own product, and when it does not see itself as instituting as well as instituted (Castoriadis 1987).

Castoriadis died in 1997, and in his last writings he attacked Western societies because they attempt to cover the traces of their contingent social institution and present themselves as the product of an extra-social, and thus eternal and unchanging source (De Cock *et al.* 2013b). He particularly deplored the fact that collective terrains were being abandoned with people withdrawing into their individual or immediate family existence and not worrying about anything that goes on beyond the very narrow circle of their personal interests. This is what Castoriadis (2010) called the *privatization of individuals*, leaving them isolated and maintained in the illusion of their liberty by mechanisms that have become independent of all social control and are managed by anonymous apparatuses (Castoriadis 1997b). If imagination, and indeed creativity, is to mean anything it must be 'calling into question the institution of society, the representation of the world, and the social imaginary significations it conveys and bears within itself' (Castoriadis 2010: 82). Twenty years later, Jameson (2009) expressed our current predicament rather poetically, without using Castoriadis's vocabulary, and very aptly captured the sentiments expressed in Castoriadis's late work:

> We continue murmuring Kant's old questions – What can I know? What should I do? What may I hope? – under a starry heaven no more responsive than a mirror or a space ship, not understanding that they require the adjunct of an ugly and bureaucratic representational qualification: what can I know *in this system?* What should I do in this new world *completely invented by me?* What can I hope for *alone in an altogether human age?* And failing to replace them by the only meaningful one, namely how can I recognize this forbiddingly foreign totality as my own doing, how may I appropriate it and make it my own handiwork and acknowledge its laws as my own projection and my own praxis?
>
> *Jameson 2009: 608*

What we take therefore from Castoriadis's work is an idea of imagination that is both profoundly individual and profoundly social, with neither being reducible to the other. It is the permanent tension between the two that gives imagination its essentially undetermined character. The creative dimension of imagination is for Castoriadis not linked primarily to the generation of ideas, but rather to the capacity to question already given determinations and to reimagine what others have imagined. Castoriadis sees the world very much as something we have assembled for ourselves to live in, always instituted as well as always instituting (building, transforming and even abolishing), and it is this very basic realization I aim to elaborate on when considering some implications for, and practical examples of, creativity teaching and management education more broadly.

## Educating the imagination?

> We have a duty to educate the imagination above all else.
>
> *Warnock 1976:10*

This final section is in three parts. First I will elaborate on some of the key differences between a Castoriadis-inspired take on creativity and imagination and the one put forward by the 'creativity industry'. These concern the importance of the social, the receptiveness to others' creation and the fundamental subversiveness (in relation to what exists) of the imagination. I will then illustrate how I have tried to integrate some lessons in my own practice of teaching creativity seminars. I conclude by broadening out the significance of Castoriadis's thought to business school education more generally.

Contemporary society supposedly offers individuals a high degree of personal freedom and emphasizes the need to realize a unique creative and productive self, hence the imperative of developing 'creativity' in organizations, and yet the very conditions that create this demand for creativity also deny its fulfilment. The social fragmentation and the ever more attenuated sense of belonging to a wider society have undermined the degree of recognition that can actually validate uniqueness and creativity (Mason 2003). It is here that Castoriadis's conceptualization of the imagination, as not only a psychological or individual phenomenon but also one that is always-already dialectically entwined with the collective, offers an important analytical grip. Castoriadis believed that even in the most original thinkers there is but a minute part of what they say and write that does not come from society, from what they have learnt, from what surrounds them, and is not simply a trivial elaboration. As he put it, 'If one wants, metaphorically speaking, to quantify all that, the kernel of what is truly new in a Plato, an Aristotle, a Kant, a Hegel, a Marx, or a Freud represents perhaps one percent of what they said or wrote' (Castoriadis 2010: 65). Furthermore, whilst it is imagination that allows the creation of the new, what Castoriadis (1997b: 111) calls 'the emergence of forms, figures, original schemata of thought and of the thinkable', this same imagination means that human beings are capable of receiving, welcoming and accepting another's creation. This is also a dimension that is mostly ignored in the mainstream creativity literature. Sternberg and Kaufman (2010: 472), for example, are typical in their suggestion that 'a curiosity of creativity is that the fact that one is oneself creative in no way guarantees that one's reaction to others who are creative will be positive'. For Castoriadis (1997b: 112), however, the imagination has a double dimension in that it both creates the original and makes us capable of gathering it, in effect creating a new subjectivity that is 'critically and lucidly open to the new; it does not repress the works of the imagination (one's own or others') but is capable of receiving them critically, of accepting them or rejecting them'. This chimes with Warnock's (1994: 173) reflections on an educational policy that develops the imagination, where she cautions against the belief that learners should simply be encouraged to be creative or express themselves. There is nothing *uniquely* valuable for her in producing things that are original (although it may have value of course). For Warnock, the main purpose of the imagination is the acceptance and revitalization of shared and continuing values and thus a key societal good to be cultivated. Currie and Ravenscroft (2002) talk about the 're-creative' imagination in this context. They draw a distinction between creative imagination as the capacity to do things in a new way and re-creative imagination as the capacity to put ourselves in the place of another, or in the place of our own future, past or counterfactual self.

It is also significant that Castoriadis (1987, 1997b) talks about radical imagination; unsettled and unsettling imagination, imagination not limited to already given and known forms. This imagination does not allow itself to be held and contained, nor to be put into place in a clear and assignable relation to sensibility and thought. For Castoriadis, every interpretation of the imagination from the standpoint of function is therefore a reduction; its processes can be elucidated and interpreted but not explained, and yet 'function' is precisely what the 'usefulness' criterion that haunts the organizational creativity literature always imposes. But this is really a newness that is always-already boxed in by the demand of dominant (organizational) interests, an outcome of which is that technical innovation totally dominates any social innovation. As Castoriadis (2010: 82) put it: 'everyone is in favor of progress, therefore progressive, and since such progress is always the same thing, it is mere preservation, at the deepest level, of what is'. Furthermore, if we look at the organizational creativity literature with Castoriadis we notice that it is dominated by a methodological individualism of substantial naiveté, with academics continuing to talk and write as if Freud had never existed and as if human beings' motivations were trivially simple and 'rational'. What seems to matter above all is to shore up and assure the creativity theory: of what is valid in its very necessity and determinacy. Imagination, however, is in its essence rebellious against determinacy. If we are to engage seriously with Castoriadis's thought we have to acknowledge in our teaching that the concepts of creativity and imagination can have no definite, uncontested content that gives us somehow privileged access to the new and valuable.

In my own teaching I have gradually started building in more time and space for such a critical and yet practical reflection on the nature and history of the concepts of creativity and imagination. During a typical twenty-hour course (spread over five four-hour days) I devote the first two days to explaining the basic tenets of the creativity literature whilst also introducing basic creativity techniques as found in the practitioner literature (Bills and Genasi 2003; Gogatz and Mondejar 2005; Proctor 2005). After practising some of these techniques on both artificial problems and issues relating to the students' work or educational context, I would then encourage them to apply some of these techniques (around mind-sets, conceptual blocks and reversals in particular) during the second day, with the aim of challenging the very tenets of the creativity literature (that is, its focus on individuals and groups, and on 'containing' and explaining the creative process): what are the mind-sets at work here and how can we reverse some of these basic assumptions? I have found that such techniques from the practitioner literature can be fruitfully used to subvert some of the taken-for-granted creativity discourse. It is important of course to give the students a degree of confidence in applying the techniques whilst complementing this approach with a rich historical narrative around the idea of 'imagination' of the kind outlined earlier, so that they can connect their own 'creative challenging' to this way of thinking. I also use recent videos at the end of day two or the start of day three that link the idea of creativity to wider economic and social issues. *Surviving Progress* (2011) is a recent example of a video that I have used to good effect. It shows how past civilizations were destroyed by 'progress traps' – alluring technologies and belief systems that serve immediate needs but ransom the future – and goes on to challenge basic assumptions of our own society (see also Bell and Sinclair, this volume). Again this allows the students to consider critically the notions of creativity and imagination. Over the years I have therefore made my creativity teaching both more theoretical (in terms of introducing a philosophical–historical narrative around imagination) and more practical (in terms of getting the students to engage with traditional concepts and ideas using basic creativity tools). What becomes squeezed in my classes, and to some extent dismantled, is the mainstream creativity mantra.

However, the point here is that we should not simply reject what is currently being done in creativity research and teaching, but rather we should try and insert an imaginative/instituting dimension into what is quite a petrified instituted field. In Castoriadis's vocabulary, we have to use the resources of an ensemblistic–identitary logic to somehow transgress it. Just as Castoriadis created a language of his own in using terms like 'ensemblistic-identitary', 'legein' and 'teukhein', by shifting the emphasis of the term 'creativity' to the term 'imagination' – and the historical–philosophical intervention it implies – we can bring in 'new' determinations in thinking about 'the new' without immediately subordinating them to the significations and determinations that already dominate the field of creativity. After all, as Bourdieu (1990) already suggested, the struggle to know reality almost always has to begin with a struggle against words.

During the second half of the course I introduce the students to a variant of the Creative Problem Solving (CPS) model (Parnes 1987), namely the MPIA process (Rickards and De Cock 1994; Rickards and Moger 2006). MPIA stands for Map/Mess – Perspective – Idea – Action. Each phase has a diverging (opening up) and converging (closing down) moment. The students are first asked to come up with a collective representation (the Map) of the problem or organizational situation they are facing. The emphasis here is very much on collectively building a platform of understanding. The actual form that this representation can take varies, but the basic version involves the use of flipchart paper and marker pens. Once this platform of understanding is established (and very often it gets adapted throughout the process), the students move on to the Perspectives stage. Here they are encouraged to develop the imaginative capacity of putting themselves in another person's place, to play with counterfactuals, and generate as many perspectives as possible on the given problem or situation. They are also encouraged to use various creativity techniques at this stage. I tend to leave the progression to the Idea stage deliberately vague, using the metaphorical reframing of the problem at hand and the subsequent ideas or solutions for that problem in the metaphorical domain as a launch pad for the Idea stage proper. In the Action stage, basic techniques such as force-field analysis or the impact–ease matrix are used to evaluate ideas. I tend to focus most effort in terms of guidance on the first two phases where students are really trying to take the messy reality they are faced with apart. The latter two stages are more about putting it together again in a different way and it is here that confusion and frustration can become quite productive.

Applying the MPIA model involves a group project where the students work on an organizational problem of their own choosing or that of an invited organization (these have included an investment bank, a housing charity, a hospital, a motorcar franchise, and a local council). Students have a significant amount of scope to structure this assignment within set parameters: they have to move through all the stages of the problem solving model and critically reflect on the overall process using course readings in writing up their report. My approach has shifted over the years from getting students to stick to the stages of the model and generate 'actionable ideas' for changing or improving the organization, to implicitly encouraging them to get 'productively' lost in the stages of the model. I achieve this by taking more of an analyst type role – *le sujet supposé savoir* (or 'the subject supposed to know'; Lacan 1977) – than a facilitator role. Of course I need to inspire confidence in my students (that is, that I am on top of the material and that I understand what they are doing) and I am the one imposing the model on them in the first place, but I very much aim to keep the actual learning at this point subject to the determinations that the students themselves introduce, thus allowing the unbounded and collective dimensions of imagination to come to the fore. To quote from a reflection on a recent group project:

> As we stepped from one part of the model to another we felt that some parts were natural whilst others held us back ... When we broadened out at each stage it felt slightly

> disorienting. At many points in the process we found it difficult to focus and regularly asked ourselves: Where are we? What do we do next? The process felt more manageable closed down . . . Some stages we went over more than once and sometimes we went out of sequence . . . Metaphors and reversals were used at almost every stage of the process even though we knew they were for the ideas stage . . . The process was genuinely useful and will be taken into the real life 'mess' . . .

It is precisely when the students rely on me too much in checking whether they are 'doing the right thing' that perhaps the outcomes are the least interesting. I continuously encourage students to trust the process whilst at the same time trusting their own imagination (again a case of using ensemblistic–identitary logic to somehow transgress that logic). A key factor is also to work on something that genuinely holds their interest and is meaningful to them so they can keep the energy and motivation levels up. Invariably the groups that get seriously stuck at some point deliver the most surprising and genuinely challenging projects. These are the projects that really take a problem or situation apart and reassemble it in fairly idiosyncratic ways. It is this achievement of 'taking reality apart and putting it together again' as a student once commented, even if there is no clear productive 'outcome', that leads to the most rewarding learning experiences. And if students do get temporarily stuck at a particular point in the process, I tend to remind them of a beloved Castoriadis quote:

> To think is to enter the Labyrinth. . . . It is to lose oneself amidst the galleries which exist only because we never tire of digging them; to turn round and round at the end of a cul-de-sac whose entrance has been shut off behind us – until, inexplicably, this spinning around opens up in the surrounding walls cracks which offer passage.
>
> *Castoriadis 1986: ix–x*

Of course Castoriadis's thought has implications for the modern business school beyond the teaching of creativity courses. Imagination, as Castoriadis conceives it, involves projecting oneself into a future situation that is opened up on all sides to the unknown. In this sense its key function could be to provide a counterweight to the actuality of the organizational world and to make us think how we and our organizations might be otherwise, rather than featuring as some kind of super-problem solving device within clearly (even though not explicitly) delineated societal parameters (De Cock *et al.* 2013b). Furthermore, Castoriadis reminds us that we always live in an imaginary relationship to what we believe to be our 'real' organizational world. Social imaginary significations actively create a 'representation' of the organizational world that shapes the psyche of individuals, making them believe that the representation *is* the reality. These imaginary significations create clusters of affects, permeating the whole of organizational life (Castoriadis 1997b). Our institutions and the imaginary significations these institutions bear and convey thus posit and define what is the weight, pertinence and value of some given information at any given time, which organizational actors will act upon (Castoriadis 2010).

Since a business school audience has various levels of interest in, and sophistication about, the theories and examples they are exposed to, management education must necessarily be multi-layered to appeal to various groups. We would be well advised therefore *not* to turn our humanities-inspired teaching into a purely philosophical or historical investigation. Such an investigation always has to be connected to situations students face in the here-and-now, which they then somehow can tinker with; taking them apart and putting them back together again (see Brandi and Elkjaer, this volume). Here existing management tools, which somehow become '*Umfunktioniert*' (rebuilt and re-adapted), to use a Brechtian term, can assist in the process.

Specifically, a humanities-inspired take on creativity as 'imagination' can reclaim and revitalize the 'trash' of creativity training concepts, techniques and examples ('nine dots' anyone?) by putting them on a broader canvas and giving them back their suggestive character, and thus the capacity to produce effects by showing things that students suddenly realize they have never seen or experienced before. Rather than some extra utensil in the modern manager's toolbox, creativity/imagination can therefore become (again) 'a continual regaining of what human beings have never lost' (Iser 1993: 240). More generally, a Castoriadis-inspired business school teaching would be concerned not so much with imparting 'knowledge' as with calling into question our quotidian organized world, the organization of which is always dependent on specific social imaginary significations.

In his exploration of the interplay between the instituting and the instituted imaginary, and the operation of what he calls the ensemblistic–identitary logic (a concept far richer and more suggestive than the over-used 'mind-set'), Castoriadis opens up a space for thinking 'the new' into our historical–organizational moment – he writes about the 'irruption of the instituting imaginary in and through the activity of an anonymous collective' (2010: 333) – a move that is particularly pertinent against the background of almost permanent financial crises and the seeming deadlock in dealing with the huge challenges of climate change. A Castoriadis-inspired business school teaching would therefore induce us to render strange what has become too familiar and aim to unsettle the fundamental social imaginaries that hold us all in thrall.

## Notes

1 Examples of such social imaginary significations include the God of monotheistic religions, the State, the Commodity, Money, the Party, Citizenship (Castoriadis 1997b).
2 In turn, we as individuals only are what we are by embodying the imaginary significations of our respective societies, to the extent that we are these 'walking, working, drinking etc. imaginary significations' (Castoriadis 1997b: 107).
3 Elsewhere Castoriadis (1997a: 367) describes the psyche as 'a massive and monstrous case of inadaptation. This inadaptation is, somehow or other, subdued by the social institution and the socialization of the psyche – which certainly has, in this regard, a value, not "adaptive", but one of survival: if humanity had not created the institution, it would have disappeared as a living species'.
4 As Castoriadis (1997b) pointed out in a article, *legein* and *teukhein* are not concepts of Greek philosophy but Greek words he used to construct new concepts. The main use of 'lego' (from which 'legein' comes) in Ancient Greek and Modern Greek is 'to speak' (*lego*) (and 'speaking' [*legein*]). Its noun is 'logos', which means 'discourse', 'speech'. 'Teukhein' is not really used in Modern Greek, although its noun (*teukhos*) is still used (for example, when we want to speak about the 'issue' of a journal as distinct from other issues). In Ancient Greek, it meant 'construct', 'produce', 'build'. I am most grateful to Yannis Stavrakakis (personal communication) for this particular insight into Modern and Ancient Greek.

## References

Amabile, T., Barsade, S., Mueller, J. and Staw, B. (2005) 'Affect and creativity at work', *Administrative Science Quarterly*, 50, 367–403.
Arnason, J. P. (1989) 'Culture and imaginary significations', *Thesis Eleven*, 22, 25–45.
Benjamin, W. (1999) *Illuminations*. London: Pimlico.
Bills, T. and Genasi, C. (2003) *Creative Business: Achieving your Goals through Creative Thinking and Action*. London: Palgrave.
Bottici, C. (2011) 'From imagination to the imaginary and beyond'. *In:* C. Bottici and B. Challand (eds.) *The Politics of Imagination*. London: Birckbeck Law Press, pp.16–37.
Bourdieu, P. (1990) *In Other Words: Essays towards a Reflexive Sociology*. Cambridge: Polity.
Casey, E.S. (1976) *Imagining: A Phenomenological Study*. Bloomington, IN: Indiana University Press.
Castoriadis, C. (1986) *Crossroads in the Labyrinth*. Harvard, MA: MIT Press.

Castoriadis, C. (1987) *The Imaginary Institution of Society*. Cambridge: Polity.
Castoriadis, C. (1993) 'Merleau-Ponty and the weight of the ontological tradition', *Thesis Eleven*, 36(1), 1–36.
Castoriadis, C. (1997a) *The Castoriadis Reader*. Oxford: Blackwell.
Castoriadis, C. (1997b) 'Anthropology, philosophy, politics', *Thesis Eleven*, 49, 99–116.
Castoriadis, C. (2005) *Figures of the Thinkable*. Available from: www.notbored.org/FTPK.pdf. Edited and published anonymously as public service (accessed 19 January 2016).
Castoriadis, C. (2010) *A Society Adrift: More Interviews and Discussions on the Rising Tide of Insignificancy*. Available from: www.notbored.org/ASA.pdf. Edited and published anonymously as public service (accessed 19 January 2016).
Chan, J. (2013) 'Researching creativity and creativity research'. *In:* K. Thomas and J. Chan (eds.) *Handbook of Research on Creativity*. Cheltenham, UK: Edward Elgar, pp. 21–32.
Currie, G. and Ravenscroft, I. (2002) *Recreative Minds*. Oxford: Oxford University Press.
De Cock, C. (1996) 'Thinking creatively about creativity: what can we learn from recent developments in the philosophy of science?', *Creativity and Innovation Management*, 5(3), 204–11.
De Cock, C. (2013) 'Imagination and organization: a review of Cornelius Castoriadis's *The Imaginary Institution of Society*', *Scandinavian Journal of Management*, 29(4), 406–8.
De Cock, C. and Rehn, A. (2006) 'On novelty and being novel', *Creativity and Innovation Management*, 15(2), 123–6.
De Cock, C., O'Doherty, D. and Rehn, A. (2013a) 'Spectres, ruins and chimeras: management and organizational history's encounter with Benjamin', *Management and Organizational History*, 8(1), 1–9.
De Cock, C., Rehn A. and Berry, D. (2013b) 'For a critical creativity: the radical imagination of Cornelius Castoriadis' in K. Thomas and J. Chan (eds.) *Handbook of Research on Creativity*. Cheltenham, UK: Edward Elgar, pp. 150–61.
Dews, P. (2002) 'Imagination and the symbolic: Castoriadis and Lacan', *Constellations*, 9(4), 516–21.
Drazin, R., Glynn, M.A. and Kazanjian, R.K. (1999) 'Multilevel theorizing about creativity in organizations: a sensemaking perspective', *Academy of Management Review*, 24(2), 286–307.
George, J.M. (2007) 'Creativity in organizations', *Academy of Management Annals*, 1(1), 439–77.
Gogatz, A. and Mondejar, R. (2005) *Business Creativity: Breaking the Invisible Barriers*. Basingstoke, UK: Palgrave Macmillan.
Hume, D. (1968 [1739]) *A Treatise of Human Nature*. Oxford: Clarendon Press.
Iser, W. (1993) *The Fictive and the Imaginary. Charting Literary Anthropology*. Baltimore, MD: Johns Hopkins University Press.
Jameson, F. (2009) *Valences of the Dialectic*. New York, NY: Verso.
Kant, I. (2008) *Critique of Pure Reason*. London: Penguin Classics.
Karagiannis, N. and Wagner, P. (2012) 'Imagination and tragic democracy', *Critical Horizons*, 13(1), 12–28.
Kearney, R. (1998) *Poetics of Imagining*. Edinburgh: Edinburgh University Press.
Lacan, J. (1977) *Ecrits: A Selection*. London: Routledge.
Mason, J.H. (2003) *The Value of Creativity*. Aldershot, UK: Ashgate.
Merleau-Ponty, M. (1968) *The Visible and the Invisible*. Evanston, IL: Northwestern University.
Mumford, M., Hester, K. and Robledo, I. (2012) 'Creativity in organizations: importance and approaches'. *In:* M. Mumford (ed.) *Handbook of Organizational Creativity*. Amsterdam: Academic Press, pp. 3–16.
Parnes, S.J. (1987) 'The creative studies project'. *In:* S.G. Isaksen (ed.) *Frontiers of Creativity Research: Beyond the Basics*. Buffalo, NY: Bearly, pp. 156–87.
Proctor, T. (2005) *Creative Problem Solving for Managers: Developing Skills for Decision Making and Innovation*. London: Routledge.
Rehn, A. and De Cock, C. (2009) 'Deconstructing creativity'. *In:* T. Rickards, M. Runco and S. Moger (eds.) *The Routledge Companion to Creativity*. Oxford: Routledge, pp. 222–31.
Rickards, T. and De Cock, C. (1994) 'Training for creativity: findings in a European context', *Interfaces*, 24(6), 59–65.
Rickards, T. and De Cock, C. (2012) 'Understanding organizational creativity: toward a multiparadigmatic approach'. *In:* M. Runco (ed.) *The Creativity Research Handbook*. Vol. 2. New York, NY: Hampton Press, pp. 1–31.
Rickards, T. and Moger, S. (2006) 'Creative leaders: a decade of contributions from creativity and innovation management journal', *Creativity and Innovation Management*, 15(1), 4–18.
Roth, I. (2007) 'Imaginative minds: concepts, controversies, and themes'. *In:* I. Roth (ed.) *Imaginative Minds*. Oxford: Oxford University Press, pp. xix–xxxvi.

Runco, M.A. and Albert, R.S. (2010) 'Creativity research: a historical view'. *In:* J.C. Kaufman and R.J. Sternberg (eds.) *The Cambridge Handbook of Creativity*. Cambridge: Cambridge University Press, pp. 3–19.

Rundell, J. (1994) 'Introduction'. *In:* G. Robinson and J. Rundell (eds.) *Rethinking Imagination: Culture and Creativity*. London: Routledge, pp. 1–11.

Sartre, J.-P. (2004 [1940]) *The Imaginary: A Phenomenological Psychology of the Imagination*. London: Routledge.

Sternberg, R.J. and Kaufman, J.C. (2010) 'Constraints on creativity: obvious and not so obvious'. *In:* J.C. Kaufman and R.J. Sternberg (eds.) *The Cambridge Handbook of Creativity*. Cambridge: Cambridge University Press, pp. 467–82.

*Surviving Progress* (2011) Directed by Mathieu Roy and Harold Crooks. Available from: www.nfb.ca/film/surviving-progress/trailer/surviving_progress_trailer/ (accessed 19 January 2016).

Urribarri, F. (2002) 'Castoriadis: the radical imagination and the post-Lacanian unconscious', *Thesis Eleven*, 71, 40–51.

Warnock, M. (1976) *Imagination*. London: Faber and Faber.

Warnock, M. (1994) *Imagination and Time*. Oxford: Blackwell.

Woodman, R.W., Sawyer, J.E. and Griffin, R.W. (1993) 'Toward a theory of organizational creativity', *Academy of Management Review*, 18(2), 293–321.

# 18

# What *matters* in sociomateriality

## Towards a critical posthuman pedagogy in management education

*Tara Fenwick*

### Introduction

One of the most common complaints about management education is its continuing reliance on traditional models that students are expected to apply to solve problems of practice. However, the dilemmas that managers increasingly encounter are so chaotic, emergent and multi-faceted that pre-determined models may offer little more than an illusion of certainty and an inadequately linear way to proceed. Other complaints about management education charge a lack of direction, individualistic focus and relatively low level of engagement with actual business organizations (Khurana 2007; Starkey and Tempest 2009; Landfester, Tofte Brenneche and Prat i Pubill, this volume). It might be reasonable to suggest a connection between these problems: due to the fact that management education remains separated from contemporary struggles of management practice on-the-ground, its curricula may not be as helpful as they might for inducting new professionals into the practices and politics of emergent, dynamic complexity.

Similar issues are being discussed in professional education more broadly. Not only is there concern that educators and curricula need to engage more fully with complexity, there is also recognition that what makes the world of practice is not just social or even sociocultural – it is sociomaterial. Professional knowledge and identities, as well as activities, are entangled with materiality – technologies, settings, substances, bodies, devices and texts – that embeds a history of politics and ethics. In education, the material tends to be disregarded or dismissed as mere tools of human intention and action; however, recent emphasis on practice-based learning examines the materiality of practice as enmeshed with social interactions, desires, cognition and so forth. Knowing and doing are understood to be interrelated and practice is situated between the established and the emergent. The focus increasingly is upon 'knowing-in-practice' (Gherardi 2009, and in this volume), performed through what some call assemblages (Deleuze and Guattari 1987/2007) or networks (Latour 2005) that are more-than-human.

For educators, this last point may be the hardest to accept, but it is key to understanding the sociomaterial nature of complexity: human dynamics do not have priority. This is not to diminish human subjectivity in all its unique energies and affects, but to acknowledge the ways that other heterogeneous forces act with and on human dynamics to make things happen in practice. Braidotti (2013) argues that the excesses of global capitalism are already appropriating the posthuman through biopolitical and biotechnological practices: dehumanizing 'social' media, commodified genomes, biocapital, data-mining, drone-led wars, hypersurveillance embedded in everyday objects, environmental sensors and so forth. Braidotti and others introduced in this chapter who talk about our age as 'the posthuman' urge us not only to leave aside illusions of human-driven control and solution, but to mobilize new strategies, new visions and politics that can work more effectively with this complexity. This is an approach that not only acknowledges the more-than-human sociomateriality of our lives and professional work, but that critically and actively interferes with its circulations and assemblings.

If we want to re-envision management education for particular purposes, we need to sharpen our view of what practices and knowings *matter* most. And what matters depends so often on what becomes materialized, or not, and how it acts on the unfolding action – how matter really matters in practice.

This chapter explores what this critical posthuman approach might mean for management education. It takes as its departure point the recognition that sociomaterial conceptions of practices, in management and in learning, can open useful ways of rethinking management education. These reveal management learning as a series of continuing struggles and experimentations performed not by individual human actors but by sociomaterial collectives that are more-than-human. One implication is a radical revisioning of issues of agency, politics and ontology in management practice and education, shifting students and educators to a posthuman sensibility that appreciates their entanglements with sociomaterial forces beyond themselves. Another is attuning students and educators critically to the material forces at play – bodies, substances, settings, devices – as they engage with the world, in practices of management and of education that enact the broader dilemmas that matter most. A third is examining pedagogical implications for teaching that can support productive practice-based learning.

The chapter begins by introducing concepts of sociomateriality, why the material matters, and how these approaches may be useful in analysing management practice and in reconsidering education. The second section discusses issues of criticality in sociomaterial or 'posthuman' orientations, showing the importance of power relations and politics in these analyses. The third section turns to management education, illustrating sociomaterial approaches in three areas that have particular contemporary relevance for management education: digital technologies ('learning disruption'), social responsibility ('learning emergence') and ecological sustainability ('learning difference'). The final section suggests educational principles and approaches for advancing a posthuman sensibility and for promoting practices of critical materialism. The aim of the discussion is to open dialogue on these issues towards developing a critical posthuman pedagogy in management education.

## Matters of the 'sociomaterial'

A sociomaterial approach views the material and the social as mutually implicated in bringing forth everyday action and knowledge. The emphasis shifts away from preoccupation with language, communication, discourses and identity, which many claim have become exhausted in the 'cultural turn' and have proved inadequate for thinking about matter, materiality and politics in contemporary contexts of biopolitics and the global political economy (Coole and Frost 2010; Marres and Lezaun 2011). Instead, materiality is foregrounded as critical forces in relation with the social. 'Material' is the everyday stuff of our lives that is organic and inorganic, technological and natural: bodies, settings, substances and devices. 'Social' is our symbols and desires, human interactions and communication. It is in the relations and entanglings between material and social forces that everyday practices – including practitioners' activities, decisions, responsibilities, etc. – are produced. Capacity is thus viewed as distributed, and agency is not limited to human actors.

In studies of management practice, the rise of 'practice-based' accounts draws attention to the importance of non-human as well as human actors, the material as well as discursive and virtual, as interrelated in knowing and action (for example, Gherardi and Strati 2012; Hager *et al.* 2012; Nicolini 2012). These studies often work with Gherardi's notion of 'knowing-in-practice' (Gherardi 2009), where knowing (including learning processes) cannot be separated from the activity of professional practices, and where practices are understood as enactments that are more-than-human and situated between the established and the emergent. Amidst these dynamics of knowing-in-practice, material things are performative, not inert.

But how can these ideas speak to education? In fact, sociomaterial studies in education have been slowly proliferating in the past two decades or so. In a review of this work, Fenwick *et al.* (2011: 2) explain:

> What socio-material approaches offer to educational research are resources to systematically consider both the patterns as well as the unpredictability that makes educational activity possible. They promote methods by which to recognize and trace the multifarious struggles, negotiations and accommodations whose effects constitute the 'things' in education: students, teachers, learning activities and spaces, knowledge representations such as texts, pedagogy, curriculum content, and so forth. Rather than take such concepts as foundational categories, or objects with properties, they become explored as themselves effects of heterogeneous relations.

In education, studies drawing from these orientations explore ways that human and non-human materialities combine to perform particular purposes, agencies and effects in education. They examine the messy textures woven through different kinds of networks – and the resulting ambivalences – that intersect in pedagogical processes. In fact, the human/non-human distinction becomes very problematic in these sociomaterial conceptions. Most phenomena are understood to be always already hybrid *assemblages* of materials, ideas, symbols, desires, bodies, natural forces, etc. that are always active, always reconstituting themselves (see also Brown, this volume).

'Sociomaterial' is a broad term adopted here to represent a range of theoretical approaches: STS (science and technology studies), including actor–network theory and its many 'post' developments; 'new materialist' and posthuman analyses; geography and complexity theory-based resources (see Fenwick *et al.* 2011 for an extended discussion; also Coole and Frost 2010).

What all of these perspectives tend to share is, first, a *focus on materials* as dynamic and enmeshed with human activity in everyday practices. This is what Orlikowski (2007: 1435) describes as 'the constitutive entanglement of the social and material'. This is an understanding of relationships that pushes beyond assumptions that objects and subjects *inter*-act, as though they begin as separate entities that must then develop connections. Instead, sociomaterial accounts examine what the physicist Barad (2007) describes as *intra*-actions of heterogeneous elements of nature, technologies, humanity and materials of all kinds, that is, these elements and forces penetrate one another – they act together – to bring forth what appears to be the solid, separate, immutable objects of everyday life. People who are being performed as 'students' are sleepy and silent in front of the PowerPoint slides that structure information and enact tutors in very particular ways according to what these people are perceived to need and what the software's latest designer permits (as well as what is measurable for course outcome results). Things emerge according to what Barad calls the 'apparatuses' that we use to observe, work with and make meaning of everyday materials. As we observe and work with them, we create categories that define subjects and objects. These 'cuts' in matter create boundaries that define (subjects and objects, activity and phenomena) but also open new possibilities. This is a rethinking of causality as entanglements with surprising effects, not linear relations between causes and effects.

The second shared understanding is that all materials or, more accurately, all sociomaterial objects, are in fact *heterogeneous assemblages*. They are gatherings of *heterogeneous* natural, technical and cognitive elements. All objects embed a history of these gatherings in the negotiation of their design and accumulated uses, whether instruments, equipment, protocols, evidence, etc. In examining particular practices of medicine or medical education, researchers ask how and why particular elements became assembled, why some elements become included and others excluded, and most importantly, how elements change as they come together, as they *intra*-act, translating each other to create new problems or possibilities.

Third, a sociomaterial perspective views all things – human and non-human, hybrids and parts, knowledge and systems – as *effects* of connections and activity. Everything is *performed* into existence in webs of relations: 'the agents, their dimensions and what they are and do, all depend on the morphology of the relations in which they are involved' (Callon 1998: 8). In the PowerPoint pedagogy, for instance, the effects of the entire assemblage appear to be separate objects but in fact they act together to perform one another: the lecture theatre, the student, the tutor's voice, the presentation software, the bulleted text constructing what knowledge is to be most valued. Materials are enacted, not inert; they are matter and they matter. They *act*, together with other types of things and forces, to exclude, invite and regulate activity.

These three processes – materiality and materialization of power, the ways heterogeneous elements gather or fail to gather, and the working webs of relations that produce particular objects, identities and practices – suggest important learning issues and shifts in the ways managers understand their practices. Sociomaterial studies shift the conversation from issues defined by the personal and the social to questions about the sociomaterial assemblages, how they move and how they produce what may appear to be distinct objects, subjects and events. How and why do certain combinations of things come together, and what particular effects do they perform? What knowledge is produced through patterns of assemblage? How do some assemblages become stable, and what force do they wield? These will be developed further on with specific suggestions for management education. But first let us turn to even more critical questions: how do these assemblages exclude, marginalize and regulate particular practices and how can more oppressive assemblages be interrupted and weakened?

## Critical matters of power and politics in sociomateriality

These are political questions because they interrogate the flows of power and relations of influence. Bennett and Joyce (2010) are among those who argue, through empirical examples, that material relationships purvey powers that are little recognized in social science research. They foreground questions specifically intended to illuminate these in terms of power imbalances: how do material practices mobilize particular human and non-human agencies? What materials have authority and why? On what does their authority rest, within and outside particular systems of practice?

As argued in Edwards and Fenwick (2014), sociomaterial analyses have been criticized over the years for being a-political or merely descriptive, failing to provide a critique to challenge structures of domination. Latour's (2005) response to such attacks is to resist available explanatory categories and examine more closely the controversies and uncertainties about how resources and agency are distributed, the kinds of agencies that are produced in different sociomaterial formations and the ways that actors contextualize one another. His approach registers competing accounts of flows of capital, particularly in the production of inequities and how different actors are rendered more active or more passive through sociomaterial relations. Sociomaterial analyses do not use pre-determined abstract categories such as 'neoliberal capitalism' or 'social structures', which risk totalizing material experience and reducing it to economic relations. This not only denies the materiality of non-economic processes, but also can foreclose empirical surprise or miss important nuances and emergences. Instead, as Holifield (2009) explains, these analyses focus on the circulating forms, standards and relations that do the work of making the tendencies in capital general. They trace how forms and standards connect local sites and interactions to equally local centres of power, thus defining and producing what is taken to be the social 'context' – stabilizing 'social relations' and consolidating 'subjectivities' in relations whose effects may be inequality and domination.

It is these particularities that materialist analyses illuminate in the belief that real change occurs not through critique, but through finding and entering the fissures of dominant explanations and institutions, tampering with the weak joints and amplifying the emergent possibilities. This approach does not ignore the productive forces of capital; it simply refuses to allow all of existence, including future imaginings (see De Cock, this volume), to be captured in a continuing reproduction of its powerful categories. Coole and Frost (2010) argue that what is needed is a new, more open analysis of the flows of capital and their effects, which would incorporate biopolitics and the emergence of new social and economic forms, trace complicated reversible relations that link everyday practices with broader geopolitical developments, examine potential sources of immanent rupture and remain sensitive to global developments that are uneven, contingent and plural.

This centrality of materials and their relations is being directed to reformulate notions of power relations and politics in public life. Bennett (2010), for example, shows how public life is dramatically acted upon by matter, such as food, fat, stem cells, metal and electricity. Her example of the North American electricity blackout of 2003 that affected 50 million people is intended to show the important role played by materials in producing unjust consequences. This incident was the result of a heterogeneous assemblage of power plants (with overprotective mechanisms and understaffing), transmission wires (with limits on their heat capacity), a regulatory commission and policy act (that privatized electricity and separated transmission of electricity from distribution), energy-trading corporations (profiting from the grid at the expense of maintaining infrastructure), consumers (with growing demand for electricity) and a brush fire in Ohio that ignited multiple events. Materiality, Bennett argues, is interpenetrated with human intensities in these assemblages in ways that produce force, distribution of resources, privilege and exclusion.

Distribution and mobilization are particularly important questions of politics that are foregrounded in materialist research. As Law and Hetherington (2003) state, if we want to understand how globalization is achieved, we have no choice but to look at the ways in which it is materially produced. Centres, such as powerful cities or banks, are produced through flows of objects, bodies and devices directed from local settings to single sites, which become strengthened through these multiple redundant tributaries of resources. When centres translate these resources into representations, such as numbers in a database, they can flatten and display them in one space, eliminating their material complexities. Thus decontextualized and reconfigured as non-material, these entities can be calculated and circulated in ways that produce hierarchies of advantage. Think of the processes of financialization, which Stockhammer (2012) claims are the main driver of gross inequality – when massive credit is made available to consumers, particularly those forced on to such low wages that they cannot buy homes and appliances, companies can sell this projected income to financial markets where it is traded against other streams of credit. The materialities disappear as consumers become an interest-bearing conduit for financial income streams, from corporations to car loans and buy-to-let firms, banks, or arrears-collecting local government.

In a different approach to understanding the politics of materiality, Marres and Lezaun (2011) argue that materials themselves enact political participation. Objects, devices and settings – not just subjects – acquire explicit political capacities, such as mediating matters of concern. In their studies of ecological housing experiments, Marres and Lezaun show how the materials of the sustainable house become inscribed explicitly as political actors and work to organize particular forms of human participation. Hawkins (2011) analyses the plastic bottle within recycling practices to show how the bottle itself ensnares humans in particular alliances and obligations. Materials can entangle and also disentangle engagement, and materialist researchers can trace the means through which actors can be excluded and isolated from influence.

In this line of argument, Braidotti (2013) is an enthusiastic exhorter of an affirmative posthuman politics, a transversal and relational materialist conception that expands the limitations of idealist, universalist humanism. Working from Deleuze's conceptions of 'becoming', she advocates a movement of 'becoming more-than-human'. This movement is grounded in lived experience and examines the concrete, complex materiality of bodies immersed in social relations of power; however, it ultimately seeks to extend justice to humans and non-humans, and to understand how to share increasingly complex (and commodified and plundered) environments sustainably, through analysis and promotion of posthuman relational materiality. Bennett (2010) describes this as the 'force of things', 'the agency of assemblages' and 'the vitality of materiality', drawing from a Deleuzian conception of vital materialism of energies coursing through matter.

This approach is reminiscent of deconstruction, which, at least for Derrida, sought to create new possibilities through the interplay of categories, not just to expose how oppositions create hierarchies (see Learmonth, Humphreys and Griffin, this volume). Braidotti distances herself from what she perceived to be deconstruction's preoccupations with representation, but her commitments are similar. Her affirmative politics are not naïvely romantic, but explicitly resistant to the destructive excesses of posthuman global capitalism. The aim is towards constructing sustainable alternative futures, and extending what Braidotti (2012) calls horizons of hope. For Bennett, notions of generative materiality are critical to reformulating a politics of ecology that moves beyond oppositions, blame and self-interest. Similarly, Braidotti eschews the tradition of negative criticality, and argues instead for a 'critical creativity' that 'entails the creation of sustainable alternatives geared to the construction of social horizons of hope, while at the same time doing critical theory, which implies resistance to the present' (Braidotti 2012: 267). Persistent deep social inequalities and other failures of justice and fairness that are evident in globally rampant dehumanizing biotechnological and biopolitical practices are precisely what these writers argue are driving their efforts to seek sharper, more nuanced analytic tools. Barad (2007) is concerned about analyses that reduce every aspect of human life to an effect of social structure. She experiments with alternative tools, such as diffraction, intra-activity and tracing the effects of material-discursive apparatuses, to enable some appreciation of the extent to which social structures are themselves perpetuated through material practices and material inequalities produced through situated everyday practices. Returning to Latour, his empirical approach is focused on keeping open the controversies, or at least slowing down the process of resolving controversies about what the world is made of – the effort of analysis should be 'to highlight the stabilizing mechanisms so that the premature transformation of matters of concern into matters of fact is counteracted' (Latour 2005: 261).

Overall, these analysts argue for new (socio)materialist methodological and theoretical resources that are capable of addressing our most pressing ethical political concerns: food security, climate change, global flows of capital and population, biotechnological engineering of genetically modified organisms, digital virtual technologies saturating everyday life, and so forth. These are raising new questions for us about the nature of matter and matter of nature, the resilience of the planet and the distinctiveness of being human. They should also provoke new ways to think about management education.

## Matters for management education: a sociomaterial approach

Experiments are underway in higher education to engage students in these larger questions, and to attune students to the sociomaterial dynamics influencing them and others in everyday intra-actions. Although these examples may appear to be somewhat removed from the immediate practical concerns of some management education, they are offered here in a spirit of opening new ideas and approaches that reach beyond familiar discourses and models of management, and even beyond the disciplinary walls of management science. Three have been selected, each addressing broad content concerns that should be part of management curricula and simultaneously illustrating important dynamics of learning in a sociomaterial, posthuman pedagogy: digital technologies (learning 'disruption'), social responsibility (learning 'emergence') and ecological sustainability (learning 'difference').

### *Digital technologies: learning 'disruption'*

E-skills are prominent in curricular wishlists for prospective managers, and digital technologies are ubiquitous environments mediating not only management education but also management students' everyday lives and future professional practices (Bachmann and Shah, this volume). Pedagogies that disrupt these technologies, therefore, are useful entry points to teach the sorts of critical capabilities that help students to denaturalize their worlds – to keep open the controversies and disrupt the stabilizing mechanisms, in Latour's (2005) terms. From a sociomaterial perspective, technology only becomes valuable, meaningful and consequential when people actually engage with it in practice (Orlikowski 2010). Technologies are artefacts whose operation and outcomes are not fixed or determining, but always temporally emergent through interaction with humans in practice. When we follow the consequential and mutually constitutive relations between humans and technologies we can examine, for instance, how dynamic materiality configures and reconfigures not only existing practices but also future possibilities for alternative forms of user engagement with technology. In higher education, Gourlay and Oliver (2013) argue that digital literacies need to be understood as sociomaterial – emergent through complex networks of human and non-human actors, through bodies and iPads and dusty libraries or airport lounges and email bombardments, all connecting in different circuits to produce different texts and positionings.

One way for students to begin disrupting their relations with digital media is by critically examining the regulatory codes and openings built into the software itself. These create technological infrastructures of everyday life, or 'codespace' as Kitchin and Dodge (2011) describe it. Code doesn't just mediate existing social forms – it acts, it does things and it interpolates, mixes with and ultimately produces collective political, economic and cultural life (Williamson 2013) in ways that are fundamentally changing professional work and communication as well as higher education processes, amongst others. Existing histories of social media can already be seen to influence particular forms of participation, problem solving or resistance. Facebook algorithms and routines, for instance, shape the content and style of exchange and the nature of what is taken for knowledge. Patterns of 'friending', 'favouriting', following, trending – the 'I like' modes of interaction – have become normalized (Van Dijk 2013). These sociomaterial processes are bound to affect how managers and their staff and stakeholders – as well as students, their peers and educators – engage online.

More broadly, the fundamental imperatives promoted by social media – in particular those of 'openness' and connectivity – deserve disruption. Keen (2012) suggests a return to basic questions: is openness and sharing necessarily a good thing? If we live online and everything is social, what is outside it? Where is privacy? Or what is it that 'privacy' is transmogrifying to become? Such disruptive questions can encourage more systemic thinking amongst students and educators in professional education programmes. Rather than simply learning ways to protect themselves against the hazards posed by 'openness', or how to avoid 'friending' the wrong thing, student managers might critically examine their own patterns of social media participation as part of larger cultural trends. Students can, for instance, trawl back through selected traces of their activity, perhaps relating to a particular theme of interest. They can analyse their tweets/retweets over a period, the photos they have posted or favourited, the friends they have accumulated, etc., thereby analysing the identities, values or ways of relating that they are performing online. They might consider more critically how, in sociomaterial terms, software code is inscribing them and their peers and stakeholders – including those pressuring them to develop 'e-skills' to better serve their clients – into particular ways of relating, representing themselves and acting.

Further expanding this sociomaterial scope, social media platforms need to be understood as merely the visible surfaces of far-reaching networks that tie local or personal practices into powerful centres of capital. Facebook and Twitter are multinational corporations whose commercial profits depend upon content sharing contributed by its users through their free labour. Also controversial is the so-called sharing economy in which citizens sell goods and services peer-to-peer through platforms such as Airbnb (for renting lodging), Uber (ride sharing), ODesk (collaboration among business freelancers) or mechanical turk (a crowd-sourced marketplace of knowledge tasks). These have been shown to profit from precarious and poorly paid work conditions – some are nicknamed digital sweatshops. Of course, user connectivity is continuously trawled, hauled and aggregated in data mining – every tweet and blog post is assembled and recontextualized for purposes and benefits that the people generating them mostly never discover. Social media participants are therefore caught in a central tension, becoming simultaneously both empowered agents supposing themselves to be acting beyond conventional institutional structures and targets for exploitation by global capitalist networks (Curran *et al.* 2012).

These considerations provide important critical balance for the simple exhortations that students and educators should develop more facility in using social media or create more visible online presence and connectivity to increase their professional impact. In the spirit of Braidotti's affirmative politics, students can be prompted to critically interrogate and disrupt their posthuman engagements in these digital media, whilst recreating and refocusing these engagements. Ross (2012) suggests helping students to understand their participation in virtual activities in terms of spectacle, which focuses their attention on the performativity of themselves and others through these engagements. She shows how students can become appreciatively aware of the different ways they become 'present' online (for example, not just through their own actions and postings) and how different identities are performed through how their posted content mingles with others' uses. Bayne (2010) works with students to help them capture, analyse and remix their many 'ghostly' traces in virtual environments, photos, posts and web pages, both recalling and reinventing their past engagements and identities. Drawing from posthuman and sociomaterial perspectives, Bayne engages students in critically examining those 'uncanny' elisions between presence/absence and here/there that they experience through the multiple synchronicities of virtual engagement. This approach of 'productive disruption' (Bayne 2010) encourages students to reconfigure their natural sense of the 'strange' and their participation in distributed agency. Students can learn not only to disrupt and actively resist the perpetuation of material inequities through human–non-human intra-actions, but also to adjust to those surprising possibilities that emerge for creativity, sustainable ecologies and hope.

## *Social responsibility: learning 'emergence'*

A central understanding for managers coping with complexity is *emergence*, that is, understanding how phenomena, events, actors and knowledge emerge together in dynamic and unpredictable structures as mutually dependent and mutually constitutive (Davis and Sumara 2006; Osberg and Biesta 2007). The sociomaterial view is that humans are viewed as fully interconnected with other material and immaterial elements of the systems that are constantly acting upon each other. In higher education, Haggis (2004) argues that this orientation of 'emergence' from complexity science helps move beyond preoccupations with activity and practice, to understand how activity, discourse, intentionality, biology and location interact together to produce emergent effects across a range of embedded and mutually implicated systems. The difficulty for managers is determining, within this orientation, how to act when no clear lines of human intention can be traced from these interactions to their outcomes.

One example of a higher education initiative that immersed students in an emergence orientation was catalysed by the desire to promote students' sense of social responsibility. The initiative, at the University of Guelph in Canada, is particularly interesting for demonstrating that social responsibility and dynamics of emergence are not concepts to be taught, but living forces to be engaged – not just by students, as though they can be separated from the sociomaterial webs of learning practices, but also by educators, administrators and other stakeholders. The initiative is the *School for a Civil Society*, a university-wide commitment to social responsibility through community engagement, rooted in principles of building mutual linkages and deeper engagement between university and communities for community benefit:

> respectful, collaborative interactions among higher education institutions and groups or individuals and communities (or groups within communities) for the greater benefit of the community . . . [that] provide participants with a view to their role in the larger world and their responsibilities as both citizens and professionals.
>
> (*University of Guelph 2012*)

The university's process has been deliberately following principles of emergence, rather than a top–down implementation, drawing explicitly on complexity-derived concepts developed for social innovation: 'co-initiating' or establishing common ground with community stakeholders, 'co-sensing' or attuning critically to emerging dynamics and 'co-creating' alternatives. This iteration is Scharmer's (2009) 'theory U', which is based on a tradition of organization development work originating in the 1970s by researchers Fritz Glasl and Dirk Lemson from The Netherlands Pedagogical Institute. The University of Guelph began with an iterative series of dialogues with students and community organizations, 'perturbations' in complexity terms, generating provocative visions for the university in terms of civic engagement, global citizenship, 'anti-complacency', etc. Multiple possibilities emerged and began to interact. A 'catalyst' team amplified the conversations, convening and highlighting and communicating the results through additional in-person and online gatherings to enable continuing interactions. Experimental pilot projects with stakeholders were conducted on particular ideas, with an emphasis on 'rapid prototyping' and multiple redundant efforts to concretize ideas and experiment with possibilities. Various feedback loops monitor the entire process – the catalyst team convened conversations to connect the parts to the whole (structures, limitations, etc.) and to enable collaborative contemplation and critical reflection on the directions that emerged in terms of the overall aim to benefit the community and also to engage students in deeper understanding of community issues.

The initiative is now spearheading projects on a variety of fronts to engage global and local civil society organizations and individuals as well as students, administrators and faculty in new pathways for teaching, learning, research and service (University of Guelph 2012). The university's Learning Opportunities Trust provides a wide range of awards to enable students to pursue extended community engagement placements: 88 per cent of undergraduates now complete such a placement. A new Certificate in Civic Engagement and Global Citizenship was launched in 2013, and an Institute for Community Engaged Scholarship develops interdisciplinary research in partnership with communities on problems they identify, on issues ranging from agricultural to environmental design. These projects involve postgraduate as well as undergraduate students who are taught community-based research methods and are then supervised on cluster projects by faculty and senior postgraduate students (CSAHS 2012).

In helping students to learn emergence, a complexity sensibility draws attention to the fine-grained relations amongst learners and the community environs in which they become enmeshed. Learning becomes defined as expanded possibilities for action, or becoming 'capable of more sophisticated, more flexible, more creative action' (Davis and Sumara 2006). Civic engagement is not about treating the community as an object to be simply analysed or linked with or learned from. Community engagement initiatives, such as the University of Guelph project, focus on enabling conditions for complexity and emergence – they involve as much diversity as possible, create opportunities for and encourage multiple interactions, amplify perturbations in directions to be encouraged, ensure multiple feedback loops to connect various activities and units, and inject different forms of information. The point is to hold open the spaces of uncertainty and to do whatever is possible to sustain co-sensing (attuning critically) and 'presencing' (acting from the presence of what is trying to emerge) with all participants.

Here is the affirmative politics of 'learning emergence' in management education. It holds open controversy and conflict, resisting the urge for resolution and consensus, inviting students to develop tolerance and even appreciation for such uncertainty. It also permits them to develop strategies for finding the productive openings that conflict makes possible. These may include patience and close attunement, as well as critical analysis of the power circulations and creative reframing. This is part of how students learn to work with complexity in their future practice.

The other part is learning how to work in emergence itself. This discussion suggests two approaches to enable this in management education. One is to create conditions of complexity in different student activities: diversity, interaction, perturbation, feedback loops and decentralized organization. The University of Guelph's example set out to actively attract as much diversity as possible, to provoke multiple dialogues and to provide decentralized scaffolds to encourage, gather and amplify all the interaction and feedback. A second approach involves students actively in bottom–up projects of co-production. This is about encouraging participants – students, staff and administrators – to work together collaboratively with non-academic stakeholders in an initiative of community engagement. These initiatives need to be actively facilitated and supported to engage in ways that attune to emergence and hold open spaces of controversy. This is a pedagogy that slows down the action rather than rushing to solutions, that pushes participants to notice how they are inter-penetrated by complex assemblings of relationships and to recognize radical possibilities and novel patterns that are continually emerging in surprising ways. Rather than relying solely on fixed models and plans and evidence-based knowledge, a posthuman complexity pedagogy prompts people to move forward with hope amidst undecidability in knowing and practice (Osberg and Biesta 2007). This is about learning resilience in radical contingency, but also learning to experiment and improvise, finding the possibilities that are continually emerging in everyday practice. Critical attunement is not left behind but reoriented from dismissal and attack to seeking or inventing alternatives and the spaces where they might begin to flourish.

## *Ecological sustainability: learning 'difference'*

A key area in which managers are increasingly called to help develop radical new possibilities is in ecological sustainability (see Wright and Nyberg, this volume). Somerville (2013) has argued that the goals of education for sustainability cannot be realized using the same ontologies and epistemologies – ways of being and knowing – with which we currently operate. One major challenge for managers lies in somehow connecting multiple interests – industrial, biopolitical, governmental, scientific, local community and environmental – which is typically about working through fundamental differences amongst systems of knowledge and practice at play. Mol (2002), amongst others, has shown how these differences are not simply a matter of diverse perspectives but actually represent different worlds of being.

Somerville (2013) describes in detail one initiative to promote learning of ecological sustainability that clearly demonstrates the difficulties of bridging different material worlds. The project, involving art and storytelling to link academics and students with Aboriginal communities, focused on the rapidly disappearing Murray–Darling basin (MDB) river system, a prominent Australian example of the global crisis in water shortage. Perspectives of government, local towns, businesses, environmental groups and the many Aboriginal peoples affected by the MDB are sharply divided. Somerville, with her colleagues and students, partnered with Aboriginal communities and artists to share knowledge and collectively learn new approaches to respond to the MDB crisis. Using an arts-based research approach that Somerville refers to as 'enabling place pedagogies', the initiative seeks to bridge these knowledges and also to mobilize new knowledge. Paintings and other art pieces were produced to represent the unique Aboriginal knowledges of MDB history and relations with local communitie. These were presented to groups along with accompanying oral stories. Community audiences were invited to engage with the complex, layered meanings embedded in the artworks and stories in a process facilitated to invite new discoveries. Somerville (2012) describes the overall approach as a pedagogical one, working in the space between the different worlds of Indigenous and non-Indigenous knowings to explore how knowledge can travel between them.

For example, one exhibition was launched with a ceremony welcoming non-Aboriginal visitors. The welcome was led by a Wiradjuri Elder wearing the traditional possum skin cloak, which was marked on one side with designs signifying a person's tribal and country connections and is also an important protector and source of warmth. The academics explained the project purpose, underpinning the ideas of place, people and pedagogy. Stories were offered that spoke of the people's different connections to water, and the artworks were displayed as an opening for different ways of thinking about water. One story explained the teller's deep attachment to the threatened Narran Lake and how much she feared it turning into 'a body after an autopsy'. A possum cloak was held out to the audience to reveal the story of country and river identity inscribed on it, and was then placed in the centre of the room and the audience invited to touch it. As Somerville (2012: 93) explains, 'When the many people feel the cloak with their hands they are participating in a ritual of place, touching identity, and touching country. Through the cloak as a sensory object they are offered a bridge into a different way of knowing.' The cloak is a transitional object, an artwork mapping the river, a deeply personal story of body, a symbol of people's bonds with country, a material link between artists, audience and academics, and a connection to energies of birth, renewal and creation. Later, the audience were invited to share their own stories of attachments to the land and memories of the water. Somerville (2012: 93) explains, 'the conversation flowed from the space of the exhibition with its artworks and stories, to larger questions of caring for the environment, to climate change, to the fate of the earth, and to the relationship of all this to global indigenous knowledges of place'.

Learning difference therefore involves students recalling and sharing deep personal embodied experiences of their 'country'. Art making is one approach where students make and share idiographic maps or drawings of significant elements of their own place memories and sense of place. Another starting point is objects or photos of objects that have been brought by students to represent important personal place elements. Through storytelling, students seek to identify not the similarities amongst them, but one another's different material worlds – and the distinct knowledges they each bring from these worlds. From here, students can be invited to discuss a shared issue, perhaps framing a problem of management practice and seeking a solution, or responding to a multi-stakeholder controversy, such as hydraulic fracking or co-productive placemaking. Management students can also undertake case-based projects with students from other disciplines, such as architecture, civil engineering and urban planning, to examine issues of urban design, nursing, social work and psychiatry and teaching to examine issues of child protection, and so forth. If possible, students might become actively involved in, or at least visit, a multi-stakeholder community consultation meeting, such as a controversial initiative to address threats to ecological sustainability. A classroom re-creation of such a consultation might begin by having students research the different participants – how they live in particular materialities and what knowledge they bring from those worlds – and then attempt to role-play a dialogue that gathers these productively.

The point in such activities is to slow down the rush to frame and solve the problem by first concentrating on understanding each other's sense of place – the deep differences in how each are located materially and historically – and to understand and connect the different knowledges that each brings from their location. Somerville's approaches are about recognizing and reaching out to engage with others' artwork, storytelling, ceremonies, field visits, diverse models and material objects of place. The central challenge is to engage meanings and histories across different material worlds in ways that do not appropriate or dismiss the other's world of being. The anthropologist Mol (2002) writes about these practices of moving across different worlds as ontological politics, patching together different knowledge systems in a juxtaposition that may feel incoherent. For Somerville (2013), in the pedagogical undertaking to share water knowledge across diverse cultural groups of students, artists, bureaucrats and scientists, the challenge is to enter another's material world and seek the flows between it and other worlds. For both Mol and Somerville, difference is taken seriously as a difficult and deeply material encounter. Difference is not to be resolved in these crossings, but to be honoured on its own terms as a profound experience that cannot be known prior to engagement.

## Towards a critical posthuman pedagogy

These examples are intended to be illustrative, not prescriptive. Management education is unlikely to be well served by stuffing more topics into its curricula. The point here has been to suggest different ways to engage students, not to propose yet more projects and learning activities. The emphasis has been on reconsidering the content and approaches of management education in terms of the dynamics of sociomateriality, dynamics that constitute students' everyday lives that will configure their future work as managers, wherever they work – in industry, government, health and social care, third sector, arts organizations or small enterprises. The three examples outlined in the previous section illuminate three of these dynamics and their negotiation: disruption and keeping open matters of concern; emergence with its attendant activities of attunement and experimentation; and difference involving the ontological politics of multiple material worlds.

But there are many others, from incorporating critical pedagogies, ethical training and gender sensitivity to introducing fine arts activities or mindfulness therapies. This book presents some of these important approaches. The point is not which one 'works' best because what unfolds in any educative situation relies on *how* particular students are induced to engage with particular materials, questions and opportunities – *what* is the precise nature of that engagement, and *what* is produced in terms of effects. All sorts of things influence this engagement, not just the teacher or curriculum outline, and certainly not just a particular pedagogical activity. The critical issue is how to understand what things are at play in these practices and how they combine to produce what Gherardi (2009, and in this volume) calls particular 'knowings-in-practice'. Management education can look more closely at what material elements most influence how professionals in a particular place do their work, how materials limit or enhance possibilities for practice, why particular practices become stabilized and powerful, and when these black boxes create problems. Reading across the examples and literature outlined here, we might propose that a critical posthuman orientation in management education would incorporate:

- attending to minor, even mundane, fluctuations and uncanny slips,
- attuning to emerging ideas and action possibilities – the intra-actions of ongoing mattering processes,
- noticing one's own and others' effects on what is emerging in terms of sustainability, equity and justice,
- tinkering amidst uncertainty to seek more productive alternatives, and
- interrupting black boxes of practice to hold open their controversies and disturbances.

Orlikowski (2010) emphasizes that we need to challenge the existence of independent objects with given properties and boundaries, and focus instead on situated, relational practices that enact entangled and contingent identities, entities and effects. This would suggest that our curricula cultivate an appreciation of 'dynamic and contingent sociomaterial configurations, entailing the ongoing performance of multiple, distributed, and diverse agencies'. Coole and Frost (2010) suggest practices of 'critical materialism', which present a useful provocation to educators. These practices would integrate politically engaged critical social theory with an analysis of actual conditions of material existence and their inherent inequality, combined with ongoing invention of new concepts/frames to understand the complexities of global capitalism and its diverse, localized effects on everyday lives. Barad (2012: 113) argues for developing new mapping practices, 'genealogies of the material–discursive apparatuses of production which take account of the intra-active topological dynamics that reconfigure the spacetime manifold'.

As can be expected, sociomaterial analysts emphasize different positions about the political role of materials in constituting particular forms of everyday life and learning, and they promote diverse strategies for critical engagement. However, all share a commitment to restore a focus on material bodies, substances, settings and devices to show how these both configure flows of power and mediate forms of political engagement. Second, all advance a commitment to social change through equity and justice. What they tend to resist are normative categories and ideologies imposed to formulate critique of particular phenomena without sufficient attention to their contemporary material dynamics, many of which refute the continuing fitness of these analytic categories. As Law (2012) points out, many critiques of sociomaterial approaches emanate from their threat to deep metaphysical assumptions embedded in Western or Northern common sense. These assumptions are unused to being treated as 'effects', rather than as de facto canons defining the objects, problems and procedures that perpetuate the very problems they purport to solve. To incorporate a critical posthuman pedagogy into management education is to disturb, not just particular management models of practice and assumptions about purposes, but also central foundations and investments.

## References

Barad, K. (2007) *Meeting the Universe Half-Way*. Durham, NC: Duke University Press.
Barad, K. (2012) 'Interview with Karen Barad'. *In:* R. Dolphijn and I. van der Tuin (eds.) *New Materialism: Interviews and Cartographies*. University of Michigan, MI: Open Humanities Press, pp. 48–70.
Bayne, S. (2010) 'Academetron, automaton, phantom: uncanny digital pedagogies', *London Review of Education*, 8(1), 5–13.
Bennett, J. (2010) *Vibrant Matter: A Political Ecology of Things*. Durham, NC: Duke University Press.
Bennett, T. and Joyce, P. (2010) *Material Powers: Cultural Studies, History and the Material Turn*. London: Routledge.
Braidotti, R. (2012) 'Powers of affirmation'. *In:* R. Braidotti (ed.) *Nomadic Theory: The Portable Rosi Braidotti*. New York, NY: Columbia University Press, pp. 267–98.
Braidotti, R. (2013) *The Posthuman*. Cambridge: Polity Press.
Callon, M. (1998) *The Laws of the Market*. Oxford: Blackwell.
Coole, D. and Frost, D. (2010) 'Introducing the new materialisms'. *In:* D. Coole and D. Frost (eds.) *New Materialisms: Ontology, Agency, and Politics*. Durham, NC: Duke University Press, pp. 1–46.
CSAHS (2012) *Institute for Community-Engaged Scholarship*. University of Guelph, ON. Available from: www.cesinstitute.ca/ (accessed 21 September 2015).
Curran, J., Fenton, N. and Freedman D. (2012) *Misunderstanding the Internet*. London: Routledge.
Davis, B. and Sumara, D.J. (2006) *Complexity and Education: Inquiries into Learning, Teaching and Research*. Mahwah, NJ: Erlbaum.
Deleuze, G. and Guattari, F. (1987/2007) *A Thousand Plateaus: Capitalism and Schizophrenia*. Minneapolis, MN: University of Minnesota Press.
Edwards, R and Fenwick, T. (2014) 'Critique and politics: a sociomaterialist intervention', *Educational Philosophy and Theory*, 47(13–14), 1385–404.
Fenwick, T., Edwards, R. and Sawchuk, P. (2011) *Emerging Approaches to Educational Research: Tracing the Socio-Material*. London: Routledge.
Gherardi, S. (2009) 'The critical power of the practice lens', *Management Learning*, 40(2), 115–28.
Gherardi, S. and Strati, A. (2012) *Learning and Knowing in Practice-Based Studies*. Cheltenham, UK: Edward Elgar.
Gourlay, L. and Oliver, M. (2013) 'Beyond "the social": digital literacies as sociomaterial practice'. *In:* R. Goodfellow and M. Lea (eds.) *Literacy in the Digital University: Critical Perspectives on Learning, Scholarship and Technology*. London: Routledge, pp. 79–94.
Hager, P., Lee, A. and Reich, A. (2012) *Practice, Learning and Change*. Dordrecht, The Netherlands: Springer.
Haggis, T. (2004) 'Meaning, identity and "motivation": expanding what matters in understanding learning in higher education?', *Studies in Higher Education*, 29(3), 335–52.
Hawkins, G. (2011) 'Packaging water: plastic bottles as market and public devices', *Economy and Society*, 40(4), 534–52.
Holifield, R. (2009) 'Actor–network theory as a critical approach to environmental justice: a case against synthesis with urban political ecology', *Antipode*, 41(4), 637–58.
Keen, A.J. (2012) *Digital Vertigo: How Today's Online Social Revolution is Dividing, Diminishing and Disorientating Us*. New York, NY: St Martin's Press.
Khurana, R. (2007) *From Higher Aims to Hired Hands*. Princeton, NJ: Princeton University Press.
Kitchin, R. and Dodge, M. (2011) *Code/Space: Software and Everyday Life*. Cambridge, MA: MIT Press.
Latour, B. (2005) *Reassembling the Social*. Oxford: Oxford University Press.
Law, J. (2012) *Knowledge Places*. ESRC Centre for Research on Socio-Cultural Change, The Open University. Available from: www.heterogeneities.net/publications/Law2011KnowledgePlaces.pdf (accessed 19 January 2016).
Law, J. and Hetherington, K. (2003) 'Materialities, spatialities, globalities'. *In:* M. Dear and S. Flusty (eds.) *The Spaces of Postmodernism*. Oxford: Blackwell Publishing, pp. 390–401.

Marres, N. and Lezaun, J. (2011) 'Materials and devices of the public: an introduction', *Economy and Society*, 40(4), 489–509.

Mol, A.-M. (2002) *The Body Multiple*. Durham, NC: Duke University Press.

Nicolini, D. (2012) *Practice Theory, Work, and Organisation*. Oxford: Oxford University Press.

Orlikowski, W.J. (2007) 'Sociomaterial practices: exploring technology at work', *Organization Studies*, 28, 1435–48.

Orlikowski, W.J. (2010) 'The sociomateriality of organizational life: considering technology in management research', *Cambridge Journal of Economics*, 34, 125–41.

Osberg, D.C. and Biesta, G.J.J. (2007) 'Beyond presence: epistemological and pedagogical implications of strong emergence', *Interchange*, 38(1), 31–51.

Ross, J. (2012) 'The spectacle and the placeholder: digital futures for reflective practices in higher education'. *In:* V. Hodgson, C. Jones, M. de Laat, D. McConnell, T. Ryberg and P. Sloep (eds.) *Proceedings of the 8th International Conference on Networked Learning*, Maastricht 2012. Available from: www.lancaster.ac.uk/fss/organisations/netlc/past/nlc2012/abstracts/pdf/ross.pdf (accessed 21 September 2015).

Scharmer, C.O. (2009) *Theory U: Leading from the Future as it Emerges*. San Francisco, CA: Berrett-Koehler.

Somerville, M. (2012) 'Art, community, and knowledge flows'. *In:* T. Fenwick and L. Farrell (eds.) *Knowledge Mobilization and Educational Research*. London: Routledge, pp. 86–99.

Somerville, M. (2013) *Water in a Dry Land: Place Learning through Art and Story*. New York, NY: Routledge.

Starkey, K. and Tempest, S. (2009) 'The winter of our discontent – the design challenge for business schools', *Academy of Management Learning and Education*, 8(4), 576–86.

Stockhammer, E. (2012) 'Financialisation, income distribution and the crisis', *Investigacion Economica*, 71(279), 39–70.

University of Guelph (2012) 'Creating a vision for the school for a civil society', Guelph, ON: University of Guelph. Available from: http://schoolforcivilsociety.ca/Creating_a_Vision_for_the_SFCSE_Apr22.pdf (accessed 19 January 2016).

Van Dijk, J. (2013) *The Culture of Connectivity: A Critical History of Social Media*. Oxford: Oxford University Press.

Williamson, B. (2013) 'Code acts: how computer code configures learning', *Digital Media and Learning Research Hub*, 4 February 2013. Available from: http://dmlcentral.net/blog/ben-williamson/code-acts-how-computer-code-configures-learning (accessed 19 January 2016).

# 19

# The practice-turn in management pedagogy

## A cross-reading

*Silvia Gherardi*

How to match university curricula with the expertise that constitutes the knowledge base of each profession is a problem that concerns all professions and all educational pathways. On the one hand, it requires university courses to anticipate the contingencies that the future professional will encounter in the workplace; on the other, it requires projecting into the future those skills and sensibilities that will form the professional identity of a competent and ethically reliable professional. We may therefore say that this is the core around which the entire issue of pedagogy for professional practice rotates (Hager 2011).

Although the problem is common to psychologists, sociologists, social workers, engineers, architects and other professionals as a problem of education, in the field of management education it assumes distinctive features. The factors that make management education a case different from other professions reside first in the historical process of the recent institutionalization of professional knowledge and its variability among countries and second in the recent undermining by financial scandals of the trust placed by Western capitalist society in 'good managers' and their training. This debate has taken different forms in media communication and business schools. In the latter, it has resulted mainly in reflection (more or less defensive) on the distance between what students learn at university and academics theorize and what practitioners deem to constitute useful and realistic knowledge.

The discussion has often taken the form of an opposition between theory and practice, or between relevance and rigour (Antonacopoulou 2002, 2010; Currie *et al.* 2010), which mobilizes a symbolic universe in which the values of practice are hierarchically subordinate to those of theory, rather than recognizing the ontological diversity of forms of knowledge that presuppose different pedagogies. It is therefore necessary to move beyond the debate on the usefulness or otherwise of decontextualized knowledge in guiding practice, and the role of formal education in preparing professionals critical of practice. This step forward in assuming and theorizing the concept of practice in its autonomy has been taken by the chapters that make up this part of the Companion. More or less explicitly, they all conduct inquiry and reflection that moves towards a pedagogy of practice and they all distance themselves from the assumptions that have been criticized for being focused on a psychological and individualized approach that privileges individual learners, teachers and minds (Fenwick and Landri 2012; and Fenwick, this volume). On the contrary, they move towards the situatedness of pedagogical processes and their many interrelations within a texture of educational practices (Gherardi 2015; Hopwood 2014). These chapters explore the ways in which managerial education and students' learning and knowing are rooted in action and also in the materiality of educational practices. At the same time, the chapters stem from theoretical positions that can be arranged along a continuum between human-centred and post-humanist pedagogy, and they reflect on the teaching experiences of the authors, which have both shared and very different features.

In this brief review I do not intend to focus on the individual chapters; I prefer to leave to the reader the pleasure of discovering each voice and each personal style of approaching the same topic. Nor shall I go into details on the teaching experiments that the authors describe and the experiences that they thus transmit; rather, I shall propose a cross-reading of five chapters (Chapters 14–18) in this Companion organized on the basis of three questions:

- What is taken to be pedagogy?
- Where and how do pedagogical processes take place?
- What effects on management education are intended?

## What is taken to be pedagogy?

When looking for a concise answer to this question, one inevitably returns to Dewey and his conception of pragmatism. Two chapters in this Companion – Brandi and Elkjaer (Chapter 14) and Statler and Salovaara (Chapter 15) – explicitly propose a pedagogical vision grounded on pragmatism. Brandi and Elkjaer propose Dewey's definition of education as a 'deliberately conducted practice', which they believe emphasizes teachers' responsibility in guiding students to be better at dealing with problems in order to navigate their lives and work. In other words, education has to do with the art of deliberately planning a trajectory that assembles all the activities in a practice deemed to guide students on how to live in the social world of management. What is interesting and innovative in Brandi and Elkjaer's reading of Dewey is the clear distinction that they draw between the two versions of the contemporary heritage of pragmatism: one is more traditional in that individuality and cognition stand out, and the other is more promising for future management education grounded in the realm of culture and practice. Not only do the authors develop their understanding of a pragmatist pedagogy along the lines of culture and practice, but they also outline how pragmatism brings important dimensions to practice theory when the issue is the complexities of contemporary management practice. What a pragmatist reading offers is a specific focus on the relation between experience and learning, as well as a focus on anticipation.

Statler and Salovaara's chapter proposes a pedagogical reflection based on Dewey's understanding of educational institutions as inculcators of habits. If the habits formed in business schools are wisely designed and practised, they should enable students to thrive within the relevant context; in this case, to thrive in business. In fact, institutions can reproduce and maintain particular habits for better or worse. The implicit pedagogy proposed by Statler and Salovaara's chapter therefore revolves around the question of how teachers should cultivate the habit of reflecting critically on those habits that enable business people to thrive in, rather than extract rents from, society.

All five chapters deal in different ways with reflection and the ability to transmit a critical capacity. Nevertheless, it is Vince's chapter (Chapter 16) that is explicitly based on a critical education philosophy that owes a great deal to pragmatism (see also Perriton and Singh, this volume). It is in the concept of critique that we can find its pedagogy: critique in management education is sustained through a continuous desire to doubt or unsettle prevailing knowledge, as well as a wish to bring the psychodynamic emotions and power relations maintaining such knowledge to the surface. The aim and competence of teachers therefore consists of their ability to engage students with emotions and power relations in the classroom – holding them 'in the moment' – as anticipatory socialization to the contradictory, messy, emotion-laden and power-filled environments of management practices.

The pedagogy inspired by a continuous doubt and a desire to unsettle prevailing knowledge has an ideal continuation in the concept of social imagination as formulated by Cornelius Castoriadis and elaborated in De Cock's Chapter 17. It contains a telling quote from Warnock (1976) that exemplifies what De Cock means by pedagogy: 'We have a duty to educate the imagination above all else.' What De Cock takes from Castoriadis's work is the creative dimension of imagination, which is not primarily linked to the generation of ideas, but rather to the capacity to question already given determinations and to re-imagine what others have imagined. Imagination is profoundly individual and profoundly social, with neither being reducible to the other. It is the permanent tension between the two that gives imagination its essentially undetermined character. Castoriadis sees the world as something that humans have assembled to live in, always instituted, as well as always in the process of instituting, building, transforming or abolishing because imagination is a societal good to be cultivated. In fact, De Cock elaborates on this very basic realization of our social world for the teaching of creativity in management education, and he argues that a Castoriadis-inspired business school teaching would induce us to render strange what has become too familiar and aim to unsettle the fundamental social imaginaries that hold us all in thrall.

Although we can discern a common human-centred pedagogy in the aforementioned chapters, in Fenwick's contribution (Chapter 18) we find a clear presentation of a pedagogy inscribed in posthumanism, which recognizes that what makes the world of practice is not just sociocultural but also sociomaterial. Within this framework, management learning is conceptualized as a series of continued struggles and experimentations performed not by individual human actors but by sociomaterial collectives that – to use Braidotti's (2013) expression – are more-than-human. Such a critical posthuman pedagogy has the aim of attuning students and educators critically to the material forces at play – bodies, substances, settings and devices – as they engage with the world in practices of management and of education. It implies a radical revisioning of issues of agency, politics and ontology in order that students and educators are shifted to a posthuman sensibility that appreciates their entanglements with sociomaterial forces beyond themselves. Fenwick's proposal is to integrate politically engaged critical social theory with an analysis of actual conditions of material existence and their inherent inequality, in order to understand the complexities of global capitalism and its diverse and localized effects on everyday lives.

## Where and how do pedagogical processes take place?

Although the chapters recognize the classroom as the most common and traditional place for experimenting with various ways of teaching, their ways of conceiving and using the space of the classroom (see Michels and Beyes, this volume) differ. For Brandi and Elkjaer, the classroom is part of the wider university organization in which the students learn to 'feel the organizing' and may experiment with the site's aesthetics; for Vince, the classroom is a temporary organization, and the physical space may become a pedagogical tool when it is designed in different ways that are conducive to specific emotional and political experiences; for Statler and Salovaara, the classroom extends to include experimental consulting projects that students with little or no experience as consultants may undertake; for Fenwick learning is 'located' on heterogeneous platforms because these assemble human and non-human actors around the most pressing 'worldly' concerns.

Within a critical posthuman pedagogy, the 'where' (and the 'how') of the pedagogical project is suggested by three areas of particular relevance to contemporary management education. Digital technologies are ubiquitous environments, and e-skills are critical for future professional practices. They therefore represent the first area in which to experiment with pedagogies for teaching the critical capabilities that help students to de-naturalize their worlds, to keep controversies open, and disrupt stabilizing mechanisms. The process occurring in the relationship between students and digital media (see Bachmann and Shah, this volume) is learning to disrupt their relations with digital media by critically examining the regulatory codes and openings built into the software itself. The second area of engagement is social responsibility, where the students may learn (and live) the meaning of the concept of emergence. Fenwick gives the example of the University of Guelph in Canada, a university-wide commitment to social responsibility through community engagement, rooted in principles of building mutual linkages and deeper engagement between university and communities for community benefit. The third area is ecological sustainability, where students may learn the value of difference (see Wright and Nyberg, this volume). Through another example, which illustrates the idea of 'enabling place pedagogies', Fenwick argues against the habitual way to frame and solve the problem in a rush, and in favour of first coming to understand each other's sense of place in order to acknowledge the deep differences in how people are located materially and historically. Difference, in fact, is not to be resolved, but to be honoured on its own terms as a profound experience that cannot be known prior to engagement.

The processes that actualize management teaching are linked to specific concepts. Within a pragmatist pedagogy they are experience, inquiry and experimentation in Brandi and Elkjaer's chapter and wisdom in Statler and Salovaara's. In the former, experience is a relational concept – an association between what a manager brings to a situation and the situational affordances in it. Experiential learning is thus construed on the underlying assumption that humans are committed to active 'doings' in and with the situations at hand, just as much as they have to endure and suffer what is given by the relevant situations. Experiential learning is thus counterposed to a priori curricula and it is an invitation for students to use their own personal experiences of being members of organizations and to connect their experiences to issues of power in organizations.

The second concept – inquiry – is connected to the process of critical reflection because inquiry is the way to acquire knowledge by handling uncertain situations and felt experiences that may turn into knowledge through the use of ideas and concepts to comprehend and communicate the experiences had. In Vince's chapter, critical reflection constitutes the key for teaching how to connect with emotions, bodies, experiences and politics.

The third concept – experimentalism – sustains the process of experimental teaching methods (like problem-based learning, collaborative learning, action learning and action research) where the main issue is how to construct verisimilar organizational contexts for management education. There is an important lesson to learn from putting together the ideas of experiential learning, critical reflection and experimental teaching: it is the need to make management teaching more meaningful for students to learn. To achieve the goal of co-producing a meaningful context for managerial education, the concept of wisdom may be mobilized.

As illustrated by Statler and Salovaara, wisdom is a kind of habit that develops over time. It involves a self-reflexive, intentional effort to select and develop other good habits. Wisdom is the habit of habits, the habit of self-habituation, that involves the use of 'thought-actions' to shape, adjust and innovate other habits and thereby to attain well-being over time. Through such processes of habituation, future managers can reflexively and intentionally act in ways that should bring about the ends that they desire. Teachers in business education should therefore pay more attention to the knowledge of processes, power dynamics and materiality that is exemplified when teachers and students engage in experiential learning.

Finally, when discussing processes that realize education as an intended and deliberate practice, we should pay attention to temporality, in the form of the past and the historicity of management as a discipline and a codified body of knowledge, and also in the form of the future as anticipated future in the present and as social imaginary. I have already introduced Castoriadis's concept of the imaginary, and De Cock's chapter exemplifies a pedagogy where imagining is the pedagogical process enabling the 'faculty of radical innovation, creation and formation' (to use Castoriadis's words).

On a crosswise reading of the five chapters in Part 3 of this Companion, we can see how pedagogical processes put in motion in the educational experience relate to a future professional identity, to non-representational knowledge, to the assembling of humans and more-than humans within a single practice, and to habits of minds and bodies.

## What effects on management education are intended?

A common implicit agreement exists on a pedagogy positioned 'midway' between the traditional teaching design of traditional learning curricula and learning situated in management practices and valuing personal experiences. It is commonly acknowledged that what counts as 'management practice' is not easily accessible, mainly because its complexity is growing and its uncertainty is constitutive. Nevertheless, management practice is not separate from management education, even if management education should not mirror what managers do because effectiveness is not the only measure of value in education. In my opinion, we can obtain a wider view of the problem when we frame it within the field of practices of education, and when we identify what is specific about management education and what is basic in education as a social practice.

We may say that education as a social practice (Gherardi 2015) is the emergent product (intentional and non-intentional) from a texture of practices where the following actors, materialities and situated ways of doing, informed by specific rationalities and expressed in different discourses, are entangled. If we focus on the main actors and sociomaterial relations, we may distinguish:

- the regulatory bodies, such as the state and its agencies, that through the imposition of standards and certifications of competencies exert a regulatory power aimed at the legitimation and standardization of professional knowledge;
- the institutions and organizations that generate knowledge and transmit it to the practitioner-in-becoming, such as universities or research institutes that mobilize scientific legitimation for professional knowledge;
- the professional associations that exert control over exercise of the profession and have a representative mandate; and
- the organizations – public, private or non-profit – that employ the professionals and mobilize organizational control on how professional competencies are performed.

Each group of actors claims jurisdiction over different domains of professional knowledge and exercises it in their respective practices and according to a regulatory, educational, representative and organizational logic (see Parker, this volume). In so doing, their intertwined practices produce 'education' as a socially constructed epistemic object and perform it as a social practice. Epistemic objects in Knorr-Cetina's (2001: 182) conception are characterized by a 'lack of completeness of being', as knowledge 'always in the making', and the texture of practices may be conceived as the symbolic space in which the negotiation of meanings and the influence of one practice over the others is exerted.

Managerial knowledge can be conceived as an epistemic object always in the making. Profound historical transformations have affected the way in which this knowledge is established and shaped in our culture, and in our contemporary debate there is a tendency to underestimate the historical factors that have produced the current terms of the debate. There is increasing pressure on universities and industries to provide practice-based learning, and students and the professional accrediting bodies are seeking to ensure that these practice-based experiences are embedded and assured as part of university professional programmes. Nevertheless, what makes such experiences desirable is mainly driven by the ideology of economic rationalism in which 'education' is considered as 'investment' and 'university' means 'business' (Kennedy *et al.* 2015). Even if we were to accept this formulation of the problem within a purely economic logic, we would also have to consider how the lifecycle of professional knowledge has grown shorter and the practices and actors that produce knowledge have become ever more diverse and dynamic.

Professional knowledge and professional learning are undergoing profound changes due to what Jensen and Lahn (2005) term 'individualization'. Processes of individualization challenge the embeddedness of individuals in professional communities. Professionals, rather than working in stable communities and relying on existing norms and values, are thus increasingly required to actively form and participate in knowledge networks outside their immediate work. In such a socioeconomic context, is higher education ready to elaborate a copying strategy?

Pessimists would reply that there is no remedy for the spread of neoliberalism in our educational practices; optimists would argue that it could be halted by force of will and critical thought. I am reminded of Donna Haraway's (1997) position as a 'modest witness', and the chapters that make up this part of the book seem to express a similar style. Haraway (2000: 160) conceives modesty as a form of accountability, open-ended dialogue and critical thinking that aims at witnessing, not at judging: 'The approach I am trying to work for is rigorously committed to testing and attesting. To engage in and understand that this is always an interpretative, engaged, contingent, fallible engagement. It is never a disengaged account.' Braidotti quotes Haraway to stress how prophetic, nomadic or visionary minds are thinkers of the future. She writes that,

> future as an active object of desire propels us forth and we can draw from it the strength and motivation to be active in the here and now of a present that hangs on in between the 'no longer' and the 'not yet' of advanced postmodernity. The present is always the future present: it will have made a positive difference in the world.
>
> *Haraway quoted in Braidotti 2006: 206*

## Outlook

The pedagogical principles in the five chapters discussed contribute a distinctive approach to management education and offer a style of presentation that is both rich and rewarding. In assuming a practice-based concept of management pedagogy those involved in planning curricula and those concerned in creating a bridge between higher education institutions and the world of management may find the methodological tools for theorizing on management education as a practice, materially and historically situated.

From a practice-based approach, management knowledge is 'always in the making' and the texture of practices in which it is produced is the symbolic space in which the negotiation of meanings and the influence of imagination of the future are exerted. In the present, there is the need to make management teaching more meaningful for students to learn, and the quest for sense is grounded in an ethical stance that is not external to managerial practices, but is internal to the way in which sociomaterial collectives perform responsibility and care for the world. The challenge for a managerial experimentation with education is an open possibility to engage with ways to de-naturalize the world of management, as we know it, in order to keep it open for new practices to emerge and become institutionalized. In fact, when we consider educational practices in their emergence (Räsänen 2008) we become able to appreciate local experimentations and the autonomous bricolage in renewing academic work.

Moreover, there is an important lesson to learn from the standpoint of a practice researcher and it concerns the value of talking, reading and engaging with other co-practitioners. The possibility of confronting practices and their local bricolage is the possibility to share positive experiences of intervening in teaching and research (Katila *et al.* 2010) and to carve out solutions that work locally. The value of sharing positive experience is seen by Katila and colleagues as 'doing inclusion' in academic work, where inclusion means bringing in new voices, themes and methods in teaching and researching. Questioning the ways in which curriculum, courses and research projects are developed and run means questioning established power relations and privileged knowledges and locally rendering visible alternative understandings and practices.

## References


Antonacopoulou, E. (2002) 'Corporate universities: the domestication of management education'. *In:* C. Wankel and R. de Fillippi (eds.) *Rethinking Management Education for the 21st Century*. Greenwich, CT: Information Age Publishing, pp. 185–207.

Antonacopoulou, E. (2010) 'Making business schools more "critical": reflexive critique based on phronesis as a foundation for impact', *British Journal of Management*, 21, 6–25.

Braidotti, R. (2006) 'Posthuman. All too human: towards a new process ontology', *Theory, Culture & Society*, 23(7–8), 197–208.

Braidotti, R. (2013) *The Posthuman*. Cambridge: Polity Press.

Currie, G., Knight, D. and Starkey, K. (2010) 'Introduction: a post-crisis critical reflection on business schools', *British Journal of Management*, 21, 1–5.

Fenwick, T. and Landri, P. (2012) 'Materialities, textures and pedagogies: socio-material assemblages in education', *Pedagogy, Culture & Society*, 20(1), 1–7.

Gherardi, S. (2015) 'Conclusions: towards an understanding of education as a social practice'. *In:* M. Kennedy, S. Billet, S. Gherardi and L. Grealish (eds.) *Practice-based Learning in Higher Education: Jostling Cultures*. Dordrecht, The Netherlands: Springer International, pp. 173–82.

Hager, P. (2011) 'Theories of workplace learning'. *In:* M. Malloch, L. Cairns, K. Evans and B.N. O'Connor (eds.) *The SAGE Handbook of Workplace Learning*, pp. 17–31. London: Sage Publications.

Haraway, D. (1997) *Modest_Witness@Second_Millennium. FemaleMan©_Meets_OncomouseTM*. London and New York, NY: Routledge.

Haraway, D. (2000) *How Like a Leaf: An Interview with Thyrza Nichols Goodeve*. London and New York, NY: Routledge.

Hopwood, N. (2014) 'Four essential dimensions of workplace learning', *Journal of Workplace Learning*, 26(6/7), 349–63.

Jensen, K. and Lahn, L. (2005) 'The binding role of knowledge: an analysis of nursing students' knowledge ties', *Journal of Education and Work*, 18(3), 305–20.

Katila, S., Meriläinen, S. and Tienari, J. (eds.) (2010) *Making Inclusion Work: Experiences from Academia around the World*. Cheltenham, UK: Edward Elgar.

Kennedy, M., Billet, S., Gherardi, S. and Grealish, L. (eds.) (2015) *Practice-based Learning in Higher Education: Jostling Cultures*. Dordrecht, The Netherlands: Springer International.

Knorr-Cetina, K. (2001) 'Objectual practice'. *In:* T.R. Schatzki, K. Knorr-Cetina and E. von Savigny (eds.) *The Practice Turn in Contemporary Theory*. London: Routledge, pp. 175–88.

Räsänen, K. (2008) 'Meaningful academic work as praxis in emergence', *Journal of Research Practice*, 4(1), article P1.

Warnock, M. (1976) *Imagination*. London: Faber and Faber.

# Part IV
# Classrooms

# 20

# Re-envisaging leadership through the feminine imaginary in film and television

*Emma Bell and Amanda Sinclair*

Leadership is widely seen to be a central, if often inadequately taught, part of the management education curriculum. Although it has traditionally been taught by imparting theories, normative models of what makes a good leader and also case studies of well-known corporate heroes (Doh 2003), there is some doubt as to whether leadership can be effectively taught using such conventional pedagogic methods (Parks 2005; Sinclair 2007a). Some suggest there is a need for alternative ways of conveying the complex, contradictory and embodied pressures associated with the lived experience of trying to 'do' leadership. This includes the use of experiential approaches that use the classroom as an opportunity 'in the here and now' (see Vince, this volume) for participants to embody and experience leadership amongst their peers and do their own leadership 'identity work' (Sinclair 2007b; Carroll and Levy 2010; Nicholson and Carroll 2013).

Experiential approaches to learning about leadership include the use of film and television in management education, which can act as a vicarious substitute for personal experience (Bell 2008; Billsberry *et al.* 2012) and are suggested to represent 'an untapped source of leadership wisdom' (Clemens and Wolff 1999). However, the vast majority of these recommended texts feature male leaders exercising influence in a variety of political and organisational settings and the leadership styles that are represented are heroic and hyper-masculinised. From *The Sopranos* to *The West Wing*, such texts invite audiences to emotionally invest in the morally complex and wayward behaviours of men with power (Martin 2013: 5). On the rare occasions when women are represented doing leadership in film and television, they are often stereotypically and negatively represented (McDowell 1998; Brewis 2004). It is therefore important to challenge the assumption that such texts provide a direct or 'reflectional' correspondence to the 'real' world. Such treatment ignores the ideological aspects of these texts in shaping individual subjectivities in ways that constitute and reinforce power relations. We therefore propose a critical approach to reading film and television texts that enables students to challenge stereotypes and embodied norms and explore alternative understandings of leadership. Such critical readings can provide a means of revealing important aspects of leadership that are often obscured by conventional academic perspectives and methods, including the role of bodies, materiality and physicality (Pullen and Vachhani 2013; Pullen, this volume). This also enables critique of the ways in which women leaders' bodies are represented in positions of leadership.

Our chapter begins by reviewing the use of film and television in management education. We then discuss the media representation of former Australian Prime Minister, Julia Gillard, as an example that illustrates the gendered visibility and critical scrutiny that accompanies women in leadership. Next we turn to representations in film and television, drawing on feminist film theory to explore 'what's going on' when the camera is focused on female leaders, showing how the masculine 'gaze' transforms women's power and sexualities into more benign forms through 'fictionalised' representation. The remainder of the chapter explores the Danish TV series *Borgen*, which we suggest is important in enabling the representation of female leaders in dynamic and embodied ways. This involves female characters enacting leadership in ways that contest dominant forms and convey agency and possibility. Our analysis focuses on three categories of leadership: disrupting the patriarchal order, erotic leadership and acting on a 'feminine imaginary'. We conclude by suggesting that engagement with diverse, innovative texts, such as *Borgen*, opens up opportunities for management educators and students to re-envisage leadership.

## Using film and television to understand leadership

The use of film and television in management education has increased in recent years as a consequence of the influence of the narrative turn. This calls into question the objectivity of scientific conventions that have traditionally guided management studies and advocates the development of new ways of understanding management as a creative, emotional and embodied practice (Czarniawska-Joerges and de Monthoux 1994; Gagliardi and Czarniawska 2006). Our experience as management educators suggests that managers and students may learn more about how to talk and act like a leader through popular culture than from scholarly articles or business school cases (Czarniawska and Rhodes 2006). Film and television are useful in understanding the importance of bodies in leadership because they create a 'sense of active, exploratory touch which involves all the senses simultaneously' and 'demands participation and involvement in depth of the whole being' (McLuhan and Fiore 1967). This enables educators and students to literally and metaphorically 'freeze-frame' vivid moments of leadership-in-action, giving space and opportunity to explore their meanings and impacts.

Popular culture thus provides resources to investigate and challenge representations of leadership in a way that traditional cases and classroom materials do not. As Pullen and Rhodes (2011: 52) suggest, popular culture not only reveals gendered power regimes in organisations but also 'contains within it the resources for the critique and even subversion of those norms'. They draw on Tyler and Cohen's (2008) deconstruction of the UK version of *The Office*, where the self-proclaimed 'transformational leadership' of manager David Brent is parodied, inviting the audience to recognise and critique the effects of ubiquitous leadership jargon. Similar dynamics can be found in other aspects of popular culture including novels. Phillips and Knowles (2012: 422) in their study of fictional entrepreneurial women suggest that novels provide a form of 'cultural fantasy', sites where conventional, gendered 'truths' about entrepreneurs can be upended. Research on the impact of media on young people confirms that audiences are not passive recipients of idealised images, but rather select and reject according to understandings of the norms of image presentation (Coleman 2008). The observer/reader is therefore an active interpreter of the text who is able to explore the processes whereby some characters espouse dominant narratives, whilst others escape straightforward signification within dominant gender discourses. By 'widening the repertoire of representation modes' and exploring their aesthetic force (Czarniawska 2011: 106), students are given space, not only to critique the gender norms that are represented on screen, but also to disrupt them by envisaging ways of doing leadership differently.

To illustrate what is entailed in this, we focus on the Danish TV series *Borgen* (2010, 2011 and 2013), a political drama set and made in Denmark. We suggest that the importance of TV series like *Borgen* arises from their potential as a means of representing lived experience and offering mobilising representations of leadership to audiences. Such narratives are meaning making through offering convincing interpretations (Czarniawska 1999, 2006). They provide spectators with role models of embodied organisational behaviour that they may choose to emulate (Bell 2012; Buzzanell and D'Enbeau 2014). This is particularly useful in understanding gendered power in organisations because of the difficulty of using conventional research methods for studying gender (Martin 1992; Czarniawska 2011). Our reading of *Borgen* focuses on the representation of women leaders as influential embodied protagonists. We suggest that the characters' responses to patriarchal values and practices constitute significant acts of resistance, subversion, reclaiming – and leadership. We use our reading to explore the potential of these portrayals in enabling students to envisage alternative conceptions of leadership and ushering in a fundamental shift towards more diverse and inclusive understandings of what leadership looks like.

## Traditional ways of seeing women leaders

The rise of a minority of women to highly visible positions of leadership provides a rich resource in understanding societal norms that surround the embodiment of leadership subject positions – indeed women experience a disproportionate visibility because of their gender. Examples include women who occupy positions of political leadership (Genovese and Steckenrider 2013) and also those who occupy senior roles in business, public sector and other organisations. For the purposes of this chapter, we adopt a broad definition of leadership, encompassing societal and organisational roles, and including informal as well as formal leadership positions. Our discussion also deliberately blurs the boundaries between 'cinematic' and 'everyday' realities, drawing on examples that illustrate how women leaders are represented in the news media and also in film and television dramas, which are largely fictive. This is because the cultural myths about leadership that sustain these cultural texts are closely interrelated, to the extent that the everyday is defined by the cinematic and vice versa (Denzin 1995).

Research highlights the importance of leaders embodying a leader-ly or leader-like identity, which typically conforms to a masculine stereotype (Eagly 2011; Ely *et al.* 2011). In contrast to white male leaders' bodies, which usually enjoy the privilege of not being 'seen', 'women's identities, gender and bodies are routinely tied together and attributed meanings antithetical to leadership' (Sinclair 2013: 242). Research has also documented how women in senior positions are routinely scrutinised and measured against sex stereotypes that are applied to their bodies, clothes, demeanour and sexuality in ways that conflict with conventional images of 'good' leadership and cause them to be viewed as less leader-like and less successful. Even when senior women are judged as equally competent as male colleagues, they are typically penalised for their success and considered 'less likeable' (Heilman *et al.* 2004; Ibarra *et al.* 2013). A fundamental and deeply embedded tension therefore exists between norms of acceptable female embodiment and notions of effective leadership. This tension is particularly evident in on-screen images (Hall and Donaghue 2013; Sinclair 2011) where women's bodies are often represented in ways that render them disreputable as leaders.

The question of what women leaders should do in response to high levels of visibility, scrutiny and gendered criticism is far from resolved. Women are expected to actively camouflage their gender and sexuality to manage their 'difference' (Sinclair 1995, 1998; Trethewey 1999). This has given rise to a proliferation of analysis and advice about how women should act or manage their image to steer a path through this gendered minefield, often implying that it is the individual woman's responsibility to manage her body and her image to minimise these effects (Hochschild 1990). Academic analyses have identified the double binds that women leaders face, for example the need to mute personal ambition and only focus on the common good (Hall and Donaghue 2013), and the need to do the necessary extra 'identity work' involved in the transition to leadership (Ely *et al.* 2011; Ibarra *et al.* 2013). Although some have argued that women's visibility and consequent scrutiny will eventually subside as more women come into leadership roles and they cease to be remarkable and speculated upon, there is little evidence to support this critical mass argument. Sheryl Sandberg, Chief Operating Officer of Facebook, has recommended that women 'lean in' in order to gain access to organisational leadership opportunities (Sandberg 2013), and yet she has more recently acknowledged that such efforts by women have not substantively impacted the numbers or pay equity of women in leadership. Such discourses of neoliberal individualism (Rottenburg 2014) therefore provide women leaders with few resources to navigate structural obstacles, such as scrutiny of their embodied leadership.

The treatment of former Australian Prime Minister, Julia Gillard, provides a powerful illustration of the role of news and social media in damaging the credibility of a female leader by focusing on her gender and portraying her body as unsuitable for leadership. Gillard was ultimately forced into a contest for leadership within her own party. Many observers argue that this was an inevitable outcome of the orchestrated gendered attack that involved mainstream and social media and included slogans like 'ditch the witch', repeated by the leader of the Opposition.[1] As Gillard (2014) explains in her recent autobiography, throughout her leadership her body shape and clothing were considered newsworthy in ways that did not apply to male counterparts. Cameras were trained on her bottom; news reports focused on her choice of clothes; and a situation when she tripped over in India was reported frame-by-frame in a front page spread of a leading Australian newspaper. In the initial stages of her leadership she ignored negative coverage of her body image, assuming that it would eventually subside, but then later realised that it had 'morphed into a judgement of who she was as a person' (Gillard 2014: 103). Towards the end of her prime ministerial career, she made an impassioned speech to Parliament on just this issue – the concerted campaign of misogynistic, sexist attacks from the opposition party and some of their associates, not just towards herself but towards Australian women in general. Although her speech attracted sour commentary from the established Australian media, it went viral internationally, with more than 2.7 million hits on YouTube. As Gillard now reflects:

> For many people I meet around the world, it is really the only thing they know about me. For many in Australia, even with everything else in my prime ministership, it is the only thing they want to talk about. The speech has been raised with me by world leaders. By mothers who said they watched with their daughters and cried and then watched it again ... By corporate leaders who have told me that it started a huge conversation about gender in their workplace. By union leaders who have told me the same thing about discussions on the shop floor. That speech brought me the reputation of being the one who was brave enough to name sexism and misogyny.
>
> *Gillard 2014: 111–2*

One reason the speech struck a chord with so many (and indeed Gillard's Australian approval ratings went up for some months) was that it named an underbelly of leadership rarely discussed in either academic literature or mainstream media. It exhorted audiences to notice the ways sexism continues in the media and other public platforms to suggest women's ineligibility for leadership.

Gillard's experience illustrates that women who exercise leadership are subject to gendered visibility and critical scrutiny in many media forms, including online and social media. Other recent examples include online abuse directed towards University of Cambridge academic Mary Beard, Caroline Criado-Perez who led a campaign to put more women on UK banknotes and UK MP Stella Creasy – all of whom have been berated not primarily for what they said or did, but for how they looked. Gendered visibility and critical surveillance, including self-surveillance, of the body is thus a pervasive aspect of the lived experience of women in positions of leadership.

## Change and continuity in representing women leaders on screen

Although women leaders are sometimes represented in film and television, they are often represented in negative stereotypical ways. TV series such as *Suits* (2011–14) and *Mad Men* (2007–14) portray senior women as obsessed by work, sexually frustrated or manipulative, lonely and ruthless. For example, in *Suits*, the managing partner of Pearson Hardman, a New York law firm, is a woman who appears statuesque and commanding, wearing tight skirts and stilettos. The camera lingers on her body and the series gives her lines that are full of innuendo, for example she asserts she likes 'playing with tigers' (that is, men in the firm). For all her steely achievement, she is shown to be a tragic figure, lonely and married to the job. She is thereby sexualised by the gaze whilst her own sexuality is rendered impotent by the job. This reinforces the idea that to become a woman leader one must be single-minded and sexually attractive, but without sexual agency. Such on screen images guide in-use understandings of how to behave and dress as a leader in ways that are gendered and highly normative (Kelan 2012).

Similar conventions apply in films where a woman is a leading character in the narrative. Typically shown as torn between passive femininity (the good mother, wife, girlfriend) and active masculinity (the ruthless, aggressive career bitch), women are portrayed as oscillating between the two and unable to achieve a stable sexual identity. Women leaders are also represented disciplining their bodies through fitness, diet and dress into forms that conform to masculine or gendered norms (Trethewey 1999; Kenny and Bell 2011). Although this is often portrayed as a doomed project that ends in failure and a return to more traditional gender role identities (e.g. *Working Girl* 1988). Even in films where the narrative revolves around a strong female character who exercises leadership, such as *Erin Brockovich* (2000), the story of a single-mother's legal fight to expose a corporate cover-up involving contaminated water in a local community, the heroine only succeeds by conforming to masculine values and standards. Moreover, the female protagonist's oscillation between passive femininity and active masculinity often runs throughout the film, and is only ultimately resolved by her rejection of the latter in favour of the former (*The Devil Wears Prada* 2006).

However, more recently women have been placed at the centre of the action in TV series including *Madam Secretary* (2014) and in films, for example *The Hunger Games* (2012, 2013, 14, 2015). These representations and others like them (for example, *Game of Thrones* 2011–14) often feature fantastical worlds, populated by leaders who are only partially identifiable as human. Although we may be inspired by their bravery, there is limited opportunity to identify with or learn from their leadership. Despite representing an ostensibly enlightened world where women can be leaders, characters such as Katniss Everdeen in *The Hunger Games* lead through highly conventional masculine performances, such as winning battles, whilst also being represented as beautiful, selfless and caring for the weak.

Various initiatives have reviewed the treatment of women in the media, such as the Geena Davis Institute on Gender in Media[2] that analyses gender prevalence in on screen representations.

A recent study shows that the percentage of female speaking characters in top grossing movies has not changed in over half a century: 'only 23% of the films had a girl or woman as a lead or co-lead driving the plot' (Smith *et al.* 2014: 2), with few female characters holding occupations of power and importance on screen. It further shows that female characters were twice as likely to be 'shown in sexually revealing clothing, partially or fully naked, thin, and five times as likely to be referenced as attractive' (Smith *et al.* 2014: 2). The documentary film *Miss Representation* (2011) traces the role of the media in shaping the body image of girls and women in ways that severely constrain their participation in political and social life. It is argued that objectification of women in the media encourages women to see themselves as an object, and such self-objectification makes them less likely to engage in leadership practice. Featuring interviews with some of the most powerful women in US society, such as former US Secretary of State Condoleezza Rice, and analysing media portrayals of Hillary Clinton and Sarah Palin, the film exposes processes of 'symbolic annihilation' as these powerful women are systematically attacked by the media, either by being fetishised and 'pornified' in the case of Palin or, in the case of Clinton, labelled as an emotionless 'bitch'. The film portrays this as a backlash because, as women have gained greater power in the concrete realm, attacks on them in the symbolic realm have intensified.

The relationship between on screen images and women's bodies is an enduring preoccupation of feminist theorists in the field of film studies. Feminist psychoanalytic theory suggests that on screen images operate through a notion of male desire, which position women as passive objects of the male subject's gaze. We belong to a visual culture within which fetishised images of female body parts, such as legs, breasts or lips, are used to distract us from something that has the potential to threaten masculine power. In her foundational article, feminist film theorist Laura Mulvey argues, from a psychoanalytic perspective, that mainstream Hollywood cinema is based on a language of symbolic representation that constitutes the woman as *narrative-freezing* spectacle in order to visualise and secure sexual difference (Mulvey 1975). This style of representation codes the erotic into the language of the dominant patriarchal order (Mulvey 2009). The male character is the main controlling figure with whom the audience identifies, whereas the woman is the passive, erotic object of the male character's and the film spectator's gaze. Men are central to narrative flow, advancing the story and making things happen whereas women are 'acted upon rather than active, desired rather than desiring' (Bell 2008: 140). Mulvey distinguishes between different forms of pleasure that audiences derive from their engagement with these representations. Scopophilia is the pleasure of looking and 'taking other people as objects and subjecting them to a controlling and curious gaze' (Mulvey 2009: 17). Mulvey argues that these conventions arise from anxiety that is provoked in the male unconscious by the female image as a castration threat. The response to this involves turning the represented figure into a fetish, building up the physical beauty of the object and transforming it into something satisfying, and yet impotent, for example in the form of a sexualised female movie star. This is a form of sadistic voyeurism that constitutes the woman as the bearer of guilt, 'asserting control and subjugating the guilty person through punishment or forgiveness' (Mulvey 2009: 22). Through her failure to conform to representational norms that constitute her as the passive object of the gaze, and her desire to be seen as the active subject, the woman leader produces a particular form of anxiety in the collective masculine unconscious. This gives rise to sadistic voyeurism, directed towards achieving control and subjugation over the female leader. Theorists such as Mulvey call for the destruction of such oppressive portrayals and the construction of alternative aesthetics that are more favourable to women.

In the next section, we draw on the example of *Borgen*, focusing on the representation of embodied women leaders as influential protagonists. We suggest that the responses of the women leaders to patriarchal values and practices constitute significant acts of resistance, subversion, reclaiming – and leadership. We suggest that, in addition to providing an alternative way of *seeing* women in leadership, this text provides audiences with a means of interrogating and thereby disrupting the notion of leadership, especially its implicit normative masculinity.

## Looking into leadership in *Borgen*

*Borgen* is a political drama that tells the story of Birgitte Nyborg, leader of the Moderate Party, who unexpectedly becomes the first female Prime Minister of Denmark. Aimed at Scandinavian audiences, the popularity of the series with international audiences was unanticipated by the screenwriter, Adam Price, who set out to create a 'strong but feminine central character'[3] in a situation of power. The series was also intended to initiate discussion amongst viewers about the personal and political aspects of the narrative and the moral actions of characters. The narrative revolves around the central character's transformation as she encounters the demands of a developing political career. At the beginning of the first series the mood is triumphant as Birgitte assumes the position of Prime Minister, but by the end of series one and throughout series two, Birgitte's private life is in disarray as she works around the clock (including in bed) and makes trade-offs that leave her family a low priority. She is judged by the media and the public for putting her family second and then, later, for putting them first. The richness of the *Borgen* text as a resource for exploring women in leadership is enhanced by other strong female characters: Katrine, the TV journalist and presenter, who by the third series becomes Birgitte's political 'spin doctor' whilst single-parenting a young child, as well as journalist Hanne, TV producer Pia and other female politicians with whom Birgitte collaborates and competes. These influential women confront their flaws and demons, adapt and learn, but they are shown doing this in embodied ways – ways that do not show simple resolutions or ways forward. The narrative thus powerfully depicts the demands and tensions associated with leadership, including how this impacts on leaders at a personal and relationship level. The viewer is encouraged to vividly experience the material and mundane consequences of leadership choices, revealing the complexity and trade-offs that are part of navigating leadership, for women and, perhaps to a lesser extent, for men.

After filming the second series, Denmark elected female Prime Minister Helle Thorning-Schmidt, in a case perhaps of life imitating art (Crace 2012). Further blurring of the boundaries between fact and fiction occurred when recently appointed Scottish First Minister Nicola Sturgeon commented of the series that is was 'one of the most credible fictional accounts of life in politics that I've seen on television, and it's from a woman's perspective too, which is rare' (Brooks 2014). Our view is that this blurring and interweaving of on screen characters and experience with 'real' life is important in helping to explain how the experiences of notionally fictional characters can be influential in challenging normative models of leadership.

In the following section, we identify three categories of embodied response by the women protagonists in *Borgen*: disrupting the patriarchal order, erotic leadership and creating an alternative, feminine imaginary. We describe and analyse representations, drawing on one or a series of scenes.

### *Disrupting the patriarchal order*

In the run up to the Danish general election, Birgitte is at home with her family preparing for a final pre-election televised leader debate. She puts on a red frilled-front blouse and black skirt suit. Her daughter says: 'Give it up mom – dad, talk to her. She's too fat for that skirt.' Birgitte says to her husband, Philip, 'If I push it here, it doesn't show, does it?' squeezing her bulging waistline and trying to close the zip. 'Do I look OK?' she asks. 'The honest or loving response?' Philip asks. Birgitte demands 'the truth'. Philip: 'Your arse is too big for

> that skirt. You'd need to lose five kilos at best.' He follows up with the loving response, joking that the dry cleaner must have shrunk the skirt and telling her how proud he and the children are of her. Birgitte concludes she will have to wear a purple dress as this is the only item of clothing that fits her; Philip observes that she always puts on weight in opposition. Later, Birgitte gives a brilliant closing speech in the televised debate, going off her prepared speech, and joking that she will be in trouble with her spin doctor for wearing the wrong clothes: 'the trouble is I've got too fat for them', she explains. She goes on to turn this into a political point: 'I believe we should own up to our mistakes . . . I became a politician because I once held strong views on how this world should be – I still do.'

This description is from the first episode of the first series, and the interconnections between embodied self-hood and enacted leadership that shape the overall narrative are immediately established. Rather than being undermined by her out-of-control body, which, according to tradition, must be disciplined and subjugated to masculine norms during the televised speech, Birgitte makes her too-plump-for-the-skirt body the focus of attention. In so doing, she disrupts the patriarchal order, deliberately drawing attention to her own body and its otherness, and acknowledging the effect that wearing the 'wrong clothes' is likely to have on her political career. She then uses this to highlight the triviality of such concerns as articulated by her spin doctor and contrasting them with political ideals of honesty and idealism that form the focus for her leadership.

## *Erotic leadership*

Scholars of leadership have argued the need to recognise – rather than deny or suppress – the body, pleasure and physicality into the influencing and changing work of leadership (see Ladkin 2008; Ropo and Sauer 2008). For example, Buzzanell and D'Enbeau (2014) explore erotic mentoring and 'erotic heroines' in *Mad Men*, showing how women navigate eroticism in their leadership rather than being defined by binaries such as erotic/chaste or feminine/masculine. The female characters are portrayed as 'doing' leadership whilst also allowing audiences to explore aspects of leadership that tend to be obscured.

Erotic leadership in *Borgen* involves women putting a value on their sexual lives, identities and opportunities for erotic pleasure. Although the erotic in organisational life has come to be defined as sexual, its fuller meaning emphasises the importance of pleasure and love as human feelings (Bell and Sinclair 2014) and we suggest that leadership life involves, and should be portrayed as including, these elements. In *Borgen*, an interest in sex, love and pleasure is depicted through, for example, political debates about prostitution and the possibility of women having sex without love and when Birgitte, in a lonely, unguarded moment, gives into sexual desire and sleeps with a driver assigned to her. We are encouraged to see and explore how sex, attraction and the pleasures of physical connection on the one hand and sexual abuse and exploitation on the other are played out for people working in intense, and often lonely, leadership jobs. This theme also draws attention to the materiality of leadership, in both public and private spaces, including how physicality works and doesn't work in leadership, how the body interacts with the cerebral and how it may force change, such as when Birgitte receives treatment for precancerous cells in her breasts. What is distinctive in *Borgen*'s treatment of these issues is that the portrayal is not voyeuristic; rather, it is identifiable and not easily resolved, as illustrated in scenes from the first series:

> Birgitte has been Prime Minister for a hundred days. The demands of the job are causing her to spend less time at home, dropping by briefly around dinnertime to see the children before going back to work again in the evening. When she is at home, she is continually

> taking and making phone calls or working on her laptop, even when in bed, prompting Philip to ask her, if she must work, to at least 'go and do it in the other room'. One evening, she arrives home late in the evening, again. Philip has been waiting up. They are in the bedroom, both apparently interested in sex, despite the hour and their son being in an adjacent room, not yet asleep. Philip starts to pull off her tights. It is a crumpled, urgent, yet mundane sex scene. The following morning, Birgitte is in the kitchen with Philip, who is unloading the dishwasher. She is in her work clothes; he is wearing a vest. Birgitte says, 'it's been three weeks since we last had sex because I've been so busy. What if we had a few regular days, Tuesdays and Saturdays?' Philip: 'I'm having scheduled sex sessions with the Prime Minister?' Later, Birgitte tells Philip, 'your wife loves you'. Philip replies 'I love her too. But I'm not sure about that Prime Minister lady'.

Birgitte's and Philip's demeanours convey the complexity of these changes: her trying to make their sexual arrangements work through problem-solving and rational management, his goodwill being eroded as they come to realise what the leadership role means for their relationship. The sex scene is rushed and awkward, afterwards it is tender and yet fertile in the suggestion that everything they have taken for granted about their private lives is changing. The scene invites our identification with the dilemma: do we side with Birgitte in her regrettable and yet pragmatic response to circumstance, or do we align ourselves with Philip in his regret and resignation? Through both major and minor characters, *Borgen* offers diverse ways of envisaging how the sexual and erotic, how pleasure and love, are experienced and negotiated in and around positions of leadership.

## *Creating an alternative, feminine imaginary*

As we have argued, current discourses of leadership tend to valorise the masculine subject and define leadership according to embodied codes that women literally and figuratively 'cannot master' (Irigaray 1993: 118). The male leader is the subject against which the woman leader's body is compared. By constructing her as different from men but without granting her any positive content, she is defined as the aberrant sex – her sex must therefore be controlled or suppressed. Women's participation in leadership therefore comes at a high physical and psychological price. Changing this involves altering the identity formation of the subject through the construction of a *feminine imaginary*, 'a self-defined woman who would not be satisfied with sameness, but whose otherness and difference would be given social and symbolic representation' (Whitford 1991: 24–5). Irigaray (2002: 60) further argues that in Western traditions, men are the 'guarantors of texts and laws', a regime in which women are told to conquer their bodies. For her, the alternative feminine imaginary involves 'the cultivation of sensible perceptions', the recognition and co-existence of 'the other' based not on patriarchal-generated 'equality' but on love, respect of the body, the natural world and the senses (Irigaray 2002: 55). Construction of a feminine imaginary requires recognition of 'a self-defined woman who would not be satisfied with sameness, but whose otherness and difference would be given social and symbolic representation' (Whitford 1991: 24–5).

Drawing on the work of Irigaray, recent film theorists have suggested a different way of envisaging women – one that escapes the parameters of patriarchal discourse through focusing on genuine sexual difference rather than on traditional male/female binarism, and indicating a 'possible way for women to think about themselves other than phallocratically' (Bolton 2011: 2–3). 'For Irigaray, the female sex is not a "lack" or an "Other" that immanently and negatively defines the subject in its masculinity. On the contrary, the female sex eludes the very requirements of representation, for she is neither "Other" nor the "lack"' (Butler 1990: 16). Through constituting sexual difference as a duality rather than a dualism, these representations provide a basis for altering the status of women in the symbolic realm. Based on analysis of recent films where female characters are central to the narrative, Bolton (2011) suggests that in focusing on the process of transition or transformation, these texts invite consideration of female subjectivity:

> These films are doing something different with female subjectivity: they create space for the female characters to explore themselves and others, using language, the body, and consciousness, offering a vision of a possible alternative way of being for women in cinema. They invite the spectator into dialogue with the female characters and provide open, optimistic endings that enable the future explorations of the characters to be the abiding focus of the films.
>
> *Bolton 2011: 3*

Film and television that shows women acting and conceiving of their actions not according to patriarchal rules but in a world governed by alternative values is a potentially important resource in enabling management students to explore what such alternatives might look like. The following example comes from the first series of *Borgen*, when Birgitte's teenage daughter is struggling with depression:

> Following a period in which her teenage daughter, Laura, experiences mental health problems associated with her high-profile life as the daughter of the Prime Minister, Birgitte addresses journalists at a press conference: 'I am astonished to see how brutal the press coverage of me and my private life has become. It is vital for my family to overcome these hardships – and for the government to get peace to work. And so I implore you, the media, to respect my daughter's need to be left in peace. However, a PM can't avoid the attention of the press. This story has become one of public interest. This has led me to make the difficult, but necessary decision to obtain leave as PM in order to focus on my family and daughter. Vice PM H.C. Thorsen will be taking over my official duties.' Katrine: 'How long will you be on leave for?' Birgitte: 'That depends on my daughter.' Hanne: 'Will you call an election?' Birgitte: 'No. This is only about me, the PM, not Parliament.' Later, in the clinic where Laura is being treated, Birgitte meets with the clinic director, who adds: 'Birgitte, I'm also a mother and I have a career. I've made millions of mistakes. They've made me all the wiser. You can't work 24 hours a day and be a good mother at the same time. But you can't stop working. What kind of role model would that make you?' Birgitte: 'I don't feel like a role model. Sometimes I'm happier working and not having to deal with my family.' Director: 'Join the club. I think all workaholics feel like that.' Moving closer and looking her in the face, the clinic director then says, 'Let me make this clear: Laura did not get ill because you became PM. Do you understand?' Birgitte gives a slight nod, says 'thank you', and leaves.

Birgitte is portrayed in this scene making a different kind of 'deal' with herself, her family and political stakeholders. The binary values associated with patriarchal culture still exist: home versus work, politician versus mother, as do the dominant norms: 'keep private matters private', 'commit to the job 100% or resign'. But rather than take a position within this culture or be defined by press scrutiny and condemnation, she finds an alternative way to be in the space of her daughter's illness, with power, agency and compassion (including for herself and other women).

## Discussion and conclusion

> You can't be what you can't see.
>
> *Marian Wright Edelman*[4]

We have argued that academic and some popular discourses about women in leadership fail to engage with the lived and embodied experiences of women, including the everyday pressures and contradictions that women experience in positions of leadership. These discourses also fail to convey the ways in which leadership continues to be gendered – that is, the norms and conventions that make men seem more 'natural' leaders whilst making women visible and their embodiment as leaders flawed (Sinclair 2013). Despite promoting attention to diversity and gender in leadership, management education has not generally provided ways of teaching and helping students to understand these issues. Instead, it has sometimes colluded in keeping leadership masculine by, for example, maintaining gender as a problem that is about women and suggesting can be fixed by women by 'leaning in' (Sandberg 2013).

In order to re-embody leadership generally and address the distorted ways in which women leaders have been represented and evaluated, we have suggested that a focus on film and television can provide opportunities for a different kind of encounter with being in leadership. As other researchers increasingly argue, men's and women's experiences of leadership and influence may be more readily revealed, critiqued and subverted by engaging with representations in media such as film and television. We suggest that women's struggles to gain and hold leadership positions and be seen as credible leaders cannot be separated from issues of image and representation.

In traditional representations of management and leadership in film and television, women occupy a 'spectacular' role, serving only to interrupt a narrative that is defined and driven by male characters. In this chapter we have focused on a TV series where women are central to the narrative, showing how it makes visible dominant cultural rules regarding gender and offering examples of women doing leadership differently. *Borgen* introduces the possibility of a feminine imaginary that disrupts the patriarchal order and highlights the erotic nature of leadership in the full sense of that term. This involves explicit recognition of sexual differences between men and women, and honouring the connection women potentially have to their bodies, their senses and nature as an alternative basis for living and being, and, we suggest, enacting leadership. Although the central female characters are portrayed as subject to gendered power discourses and are required to perform certain gendered dispositions, they do so in ways that often contest, disrupt or transcend traditional gender distinctions and thereby challenge notions of what good leadership looks like. *Borgen* also starkly represents the trade-offs faced by leaders, their friends and families as they fulfil their roles, including the sacrifices they make in hyper-masculine 'win or die' organisational environments where erotic pleasure and passion is achieved through achieving domination over others in the corporate hierarchy (Acker 2004).

The text also brings to the foreground gendered organisational practices and the gendered nature of power, alongside the multiple, sometimes contradictory ways characters respond to these pressures. It thus shows, vividly and viscerally, the multiple and diverse ways of being in leadership that women adopt. Through this, it gives permission to explore embodied aspects of leadership often neglected in scholarly accounts. *Borgen* does not tell women or men what to do, nor does it offer a single role model of a woman leader; instead, it implies that it is sometimes possible to exercise agency and to resist gendered role expectations. It enables exploration of alternatives to performing gender according to values of hegemonic masculinity or acting 'like a man'. As Panayiotou (2010: 20–1) notes, such representations provide a 'critical testing ground' for exploring alternative gender forms, 'so that popular culture is not merely entertainment but a way of exploring and challenging the dominant ethos of contemporary patriarchy'. Although we have focused on *Borgen* in this chapter, there are other examples of TV series – sometimes made by women writers and directors – that offer non-stereotyped and yet embodied and complex representations of women and men leading. These images have the potential to shape understandings of what it means to be a leader, perhaps more powerfully than academic research, through the potential pleasures that audiences gain from these alternative representations and by encouraging viewers to enact leadership in ways not defined by conventional patriarchal norms or gender binaries.

## Notes

1 See, for example, Moira Rayner, 'Gillard, Bligh and Leadership in a Crisis', *Eureka Street*, 7 January 2011. For more recent commentary, see the November 2012 issue of *The Monthly* by Amanda Lohrey, 'A matter of context: Gillard and the press gallery' and Judith Brett, 'They had it coming: Gillard and the misogynists'.
2 Thanks to Monica Wirz for highlighting this and for commenting on an earlier version of this chapter. See http://seejane.org/.
3 Interview with *Borgen* screenwriter Adam Price in *Nordic Noir Magazine*, Autumn/Winter 2013, p. 10.
4 Quoted in *Miss Representation* (2011).

## References


Acker, J. (2004) 'Gender, capitalism and globalization', *Critical Sociology*, 30(1), 17–41.
Bell, E. (2008) *Reading Management and Organization in Film*. Basingstoke, UK: Palgrave Macmillan.
Bell, E. (2012) 'Understanding audiences'. *In:* J. Billsberry, J. Charlesworth and P. Leonard (eds.) *Moving Images: Effective Teaching with Film and Television in Management*. Charlotte, NC: Information Age Publishing, pp. 119–32.
Bell, E. and Sinclair, A. (2014) 'Reclaiming eroticism in the academy', *Organization*, 2(2), 268–80.
Billsberry, J., Charlesworth, J. and Leonard, P. (eds.) (2012) *Moving Images: Effective Teaching with Film and Television in Management*. Charlotte, NC: Information Age Publishing.
Bolton, L. (2011) *Film and Female Consciousness: Irigaray, Cinema and Thinking Women*. Basingstoke, UK: Palgrave Macmillan.
Brewis, J. (2004) 'Sex and not the city? The aspirations of the thirty-something working woman', *Urban Studies*, 41(9), 1821–38.
Brooks, L. (2014) 'Nicola Sturgeon: Salmond's deputy is on the brink of unpredecented power,' *Guardian*, 5 September. Available from: www.theguardian.com/politics/2014/sep/05/nicola-sturgeon-salmond-deputy-brink-power (accessed 27 January 2016).
Butler, J. (1990) *Gender Trouble: Feminism and the Subversion of Identity*. London: Routledge.
Buzzanell, P.M. and D'Enbeau, S. (2014) 'Intimate, ambivalent and erotic mentoring: popular culture and mentor–mentee relational processes in *Mad Men*', *Human Relations*, 67(6), 695–714.
Carroll, B. and Levy, L. (2010) 'Leadership development as identity construction', *Management Communication Quarterly*, 24(2), 211–31.
Clemens, J.K. and Wolff, M. (1999) *Movies to Manage By: Lessons in Leadership from Great Films*. Chicago, IL: Contemporary Books.
Coleman, R. (2008) 'The becoming of bodies: girls, media effects and body image', *Feminist Media Studies*, 8(2), 163–79.
Crace, J. (2012) 'Sidse Babett Knudsen: "We had no idea Borgen would have any appeal outside Denmark,"' *Guardian*, 1 February. Available from: www.theguardian.com/tv-and-radio/2012/feb/01/sidse-babett-knudsen-borgens-appeal (accessed 27 January 2016).
Czarniawska, B. (1999) *Writing Management: Organization Theory as a Literary Genre*. Oxford: Oxford University Press.
Czarniawska, B. (2006) 'Doing gender unto the other: fiction as a mode of studying gender discrimination in organizations', *Gender, Work & Organization*, 13(3), 234–53.

Czarniawska, B. (2011) 'How to study gender inequality in organizations?'. *In:* E. Jeanes, D. Knights and P.Y. Martin (eds.) *Handbook of Gender, Work and Organization*. Chichester, UK: Wiley, pp. 81–108.
Czarniawska, B. and Rhodes, C. (2006) 'Strong plots: popular culture in management practice and theory'. *In:* P. Gagliardi and B. Czarniawska (eds.) *Management Education and the Humanities*. London: Edward Elgar, pp.195–218.
Czarniawska-Joerges, B. and de Monthoux, P.G. (eds.) (1994) *Good Novels Better Management: Reading Organizational Realities in Fiction*. Abingdon, UK: Harwood Academic Publishers.
Denzin, N. (1995) *The Cinematic Society: The Voyeur's Gaze*. London: Sage Publications.
Doh, J.P. (2003) 'Can leadership be taught? Perspectives from management educators', *Academy of Management Learning & Education*, 2(1), 54–67.
Eagly, A. (2011) 'Female leadership advantage and disadvantage: resolving the contradiction'. *In:* D. Collinson, K. Grint and B. Jackson (eds.) *Leadership*. London: Sage Publications, pp. 251–72.
Ely, R., Ibarra, H. and Kolb, D. (2011) 'Taking gender into account: theory and design for women's leadership development programs', *Academy of Management Learning and Education*, 10(3), 474–93.
Gagliardi, P. and Czarniawska, B. (eds.) (2006) *Management Education and the Humanities*. London: Edward Elgar.
Genovese, M.A. and Steckenrider, J.S. (2013) 'Introduction: women as political leaders: does gender matter?'. *In:* M.A. Genovese and J.S. Steckenrider (eds.) *Women as Political Leaders*. London: Routledge, pp. 1–13.
Gillard, J. (2014) *My Story*. London: Transworld Publishers.
Hall, L.J. and Donaghue, N. (2013) '"Nice girls don't carry knives": constructions of ambition in media coverage of Australia's first female prime minister', *British Journal of Social Psychology*, 52(4), 631–47.
Heilman, M., Wallen, A., Fuchs, D. and Tamkins, M. (2004) 'Penalties for success: reactions to women who succeed at male gender-typed tasks', *Journal of Applied Psychology*, 89, 416–27.
Hochschild, A. (1990) 'Gender codes in women's advice books'. *In:* S.H. Riggins (ed.) *Beyond Goffman: Studies on Communication, Institution, and Social Interaction*. Berlin: Mouton de Gruyter, pp. 277–94.
Ibarra, H., Ely, R. and Kolb, D. (2013) 'Women rising: the unseen barriers', *Harvard Business Review*, September, 61–6.
Irigaray, L. (1993) *Je, Tu, Nous*. London: Routledge.
Irigaray, L. (2002) *The Way of Love*. London: Continuum.
Kelan, E. (2012) 'The becoming of business bodies: gender, appearance, and leadership development', *Management Learning*, 44(1), 45–61.
Kenny, K. and Bell, E. (2011) 'Representing the successful managerial body'. *In:* E. Jeanes, D. Knights and M.P. Yancey (eds.) *Handbook of Gender, Work and Organization*. Chichester, UK: Wiley, pp. 163–76.
Ladkin, D. (2008) 'Leading beautifully: how mastery, congruence and purpose create the aesthetic of embodied leadership practice', *The Leadership Quarterly*, 19, 31–41.
McDowell, L. (1998) 'Fictional money (or, greed isn't so good in the 1990s)'. *In:* J. Hassard and R. Holliday (eds.) *Organization Representation: Work and Organizations in Popular Culture*. London: Sage Publications.
McLuhan, M. and Fiore, Q. (1967) *The Medium is the Massage*. London: Penguin.
Martin, B. (2013) *Difficult Men: Behind the Scenes of a Creative Revolution, from the* Sopranos *and the* Wire *to* Madmen *and* Breaking Bad. New York, NY: The Penguin Press.
Martin, J. (1992) 'Escaping the inherent conservatism of empirical organizational research'. *In:* P. Frost and R. Stablein (eds.) *Doing Exemplary Research*. Newbury Park, CA: Sage Publications, pp. 233–9.
Mulvey, L. (1975) 'Visual pleasure and narrative cinema', *Screen*, 16(3), 6–18.
Mulvey, L. (2009) *Visual and Other Pleasures*. Basingstoke, UK: Palgrave Macmillan.
Nicholson, H. and Carroll, B. (2013) 'Identity undoing and power relations in leadership development', *Human Relations*, 66(9), 1225–48.
Panayiotou, A. (2010) '"Macho" managers and organizational heroes: competing masculinities in popular films', *Organization*, 17(6), 659–83.
Parks, S.D. (2005) *Leadership Can Be Taught: A Bold Approach for a Complex World*. Boston, MA: Harvard Business Press.
Phillips, M. and Knowles, D. (2012) 'Performance and performativity: undoing fictions of women business owners', *Gender, Work and Organization*, 19(4), 416–37.
Pullen, A. and Rhodes C. (2011) 'Gender, work and organization in popular culture'. *In:* E. Jeanes, D. Knights and P. Martin (eds.) *Handbook of Gender, Work and Organization*. Chichester, UK: John Wiley and Sons, pp. 51–64.
Pullen, A. and Vachhani, S. (2013) 'The materiality of leadership', *Leadership*, 9(3), 315–19.

Ropo, A. and Sauer, E. (2008) 'Corporeal leaders'. *In:* D. Barry and H. Hansen (eds.) *The SAGE Handbook of New Approaches in Management and Organization*. London: Sage Publications, pp. 469–78.
Rottenburg, C. (2014) 'The rise of neoliberal feminism', *Cultural Studies*, 28(3), 418–37.
Sandberg, S. (2013) *Lean In: Women, Work and the Will to Lead*. London: WH Allen.
Sinclair, A. (1995) 'Sexuality in leadership', *International Review of Women and Leadership*, 1(2), 25–38.
Sinclair, A. (1998) *Doing Leadership Differently: Gender, Power and Sexuality in Leading*. Carlton, Australia: Melbourne University Press.
Sinclair, A. (2007a) *Leadership for the Disillusioned: Beyond Myths and Heroes to Leading that Liberates*. Sydney: Allen & Unwin.
Sinclair, A. (2007b) 'Teaching leadership critically to MBAs: experiences from heaven and hell', *Management Learning*, 38(4), 461–75.
Sinclair, A. (2011) 'Leading with body'. *In:* E. Jeanes, D. Knights and P. Martin (eds.) *Handbook of Gender, Work and Organization*. Chichester, UK: John Wiley and Sons, pp. 117–30.
Sinclair, A. (2013) 'Can I really be me? The challenges for women leaders constructing authenticity'. *In:* D. Ladkin and C. Spiller (eds.) *Authentic Leadership: Concepts, Coalescences and Clashes*. Cheltenham, UK: Edward Elgar, pp. 239–51.
Smith, S.L., Choueiti, M. and Pieper, K. (2014) *Gender Bias without Borders: An Investigation of Female Characters in Popular Films across 11 countries*. Geena Davies Institute on Gender in Media.
Trethewey, A. (1999) 'Disciplined bodies: women's embodied identities at work', *Organization Studies*, 20(3), 423–50.
Tyler, M. and Cohen, M. (2008) 'Management in/as comic relief: queer theory and gender performativity in *The Office*,' *Gender, Work and Organization*, 15(2), 113–32.
Whitford, M. (1991) *The Irigaray Reader*. Oxford: Blackwell.

# 21

# Hacking the classroom

## Rethinking learning through social media practices

*Götz Bachmann and Nishant Shah*

Social media's ubiquity is transforming contemporary education. Students inhabit classrooms with connected devices, streaming data, chatting on personal messaging and sharing information with invisible audiences. The academic curriculum is challenged not only by social media resources, but also by novel, complex practices of producing, organising, evaluating and distributing knowledge. Some have taken the emergence of these connected learning environments as questioning the very need for a physical classroom. We seek to unpack the dynamics that social media generate in academic teaching, thinking and learning without severely compromising the pedagogic impulse. Consequently, this chapter begins with a look at the rapid rise and even faster decline of massively open online courses (MOOC) with the aim of identifying some of the pitfalls for attempts to rethink higher education in the light of social media. The second part of this chapter proposes that the classroom was historically constructed with and in relationship to technologies of knowledge production, thus questioning the dissociation between the pedagogical practices and technological conditions of learning. This leads to an exploration of some of the modes of engagement in user-generated content platforms, which have potentially fruitful resonances in higher education knowledge infrastructures and pedagogy. We explore this by examining Wikipedia, then look at conditions of speech and assessment through the lens of Bulletin Board Systems, examine registers of sharing and labour through Facebook, and reflect on content curation through Twitter. The third and final part of the chapter argues that analysing and conceptualising social media can become a test bed for experimental knowledge in management education.

As a name for this endeavour we suggest the metaphor of 'hacking the classroom'. Although MOOCs have significantly added to expanding the scope of traditional learning, most MOOCs still anchor in metaphors of the physical classroom. This approach makes sense because it seeks to learn from centuries of innovation in teaching and learning methods that have vitalised the classroom; however, it also produces a pitfall, indeed a paradox. In constructing the classroom as something, which on the one hand is to be protected and on the other hand now extended through technologies, it conceptualises the classroom as a non-technological precursor to the MOOC, constructing a false history of an a-technological past, which then, in turn, is prone to produce impoverished virtual copies. 'Hacking the classroom' contrarily suggests that practices and infrastructures, which have evolved with contemporary technologies, have the ability to hack the classroom in fundamental and productive ways exactly *because* the classroom has always been grounded in technologies (see Fenwick, this volume). Hacking, in physical computation, refers to the dismantling of a system in order to identify the processes and components that make it work as a single seamless unit. Hacking is a process of disarticulation, of locating the joints, of understanding the logic and logistics that go into the making of a system. To hack a classroom is not to break it, replace it or upgrade it, but to understand some of its key functions and to reimagine, reconfigure and recreate them. It is an ongoing process that lays bare the power and privilege of those who can hack, but also imagines users as actors, thus enabling multiple approaches and viewpoints, and offering the 'hackers' new choices between disabling, reassembling and modifying their classrooms.

## After MOOCs: learning from a bursting bubble

Like many Internet trends, the MOOC has had a long history in a very short time. The *New York Times* declared 2012 as the 'Year of the MOOC', celebrating the potential of MOOC to create unrestricted participation in education for a wide range of people by building open educational resources and learning management systems. Looking at the accelerated rate at which prominent and well-funded online open courseware programmes were being launched by some of the largest US universities, as well as private companies like Coursera and Udacity, there was a great excitement at imagining the MOOC as challenging the brick-and-mortar university structure. MOOCs, as new spaces of learning, were quickly posited as replacing the classroom, thus responding to a particular and longstanding narrative of the 'university in ruins' (Readings 1996), which describes the university as inadequate and in need of change to become more 'open' and accessible for new and non-traditional learners.

When Dave Cormier and Bryan Alexander coined the term 'massive open online courseware' in 2008, they drew from various histories of attempts at opening up the gated knowledge compounds that the traditional university had come to embody. Experiments in distance learning,[1] connected learning,[2] distributed learning[3] and other broadcast-based structures that imagined the university at the centre of a hub-and-spoke model all coalesced into an imaginary of how the MOOCs would change and reform the existing university system. As such, MOOCs stand in a long tradition of promises implied in the wedding of the technological and the pedagogical. As Carolyn Marvin (1988) points out, almost all technological innovations tend to evoke the imagination of a dramatic pedagogical and educational impact. This is particularly true of information and communication technologies (ICT) that have premised the opening up of learning possibilities across different information delivery systems like correspondence courses facilitated by postal services and radio-enabled broadcast teaching and direct content delivery mechanisms, ranging from televised classrooms to open educational courseware (OECs),[4] such as Khan Academy and MIT Courseware.

MOOCs set out to harness the power of the web to build a new approach to learning and education. Early MOOCs were extended education experiments. Stephen Downes's course on 'connectivism and connective knowledge' in 2008 included 25 tuition-paying students at the University of Manitoba, along with 2,300 registered online students from the general public who paid nothing for it (Parr 2013). The course content was available through RSS feeds, and the online students were required to participate in the course through collaborative and participative tools like blogs, discussion forums and virtual meetings in Second Life. From such beginnings, MOOCs have emerged at a fast rate to form a new paradigm for a technological and pedagogical merger. Most contemporary MOOCs operate with a logic of didactics and pedagogic value residing in its interface and participatory design; work on a financial model where basic services are free and additional learning opportunity, resources and customisation require the student to pay premium fees (otherwise called the freemium model); and execute an aggregation of online interactive learning resources through information and learning management platforms.

Despite their growing popularity, MOOCs soon ran into a growing wave of critique. Some commentators worried that MOOCs flatten the complexity, granularity and specificity of human learning enshrined in traditional classrooms (Ragman's Circle 2013). Others pointed out that MOOCs increasingly favoured skills and content delivery over committed and engaged learning, thus ending up using 'the least interesting instructional modes' (Kamenetz 2013) and adding to the tendency of conflating higher education with vocational training. For Cathy Davidson (2013), for example, the main reason for MOOCs' popularity with university administrators is that they find their roots in the Industrial Revolution, thus reinforcing rather than questioning the status quo of the contemporary educational structures. This relates not only to the forms of learning, but also to the politics and economy of access. Although it is general consensus that MOOCs can give students from the developing world access to hitherto unaffordable educational resources, Sharmila Rege (2010) argued that the very construction of the crisis narrative that MOOCs are supposed to solve is symptomatic of a new power dynamic that responds to an unprecedented appearance of dalit, female and queer bodies in public learning institutions. For Rege, it is important to understand whose crisis MOOCs are resolving as they rewrite a political question into a technological one to create, once again, an elite educational learning space of physical co-presence that can exclude learners marked by racial, economic, gendered or sexual disadvantage.

A further strand of critique targeted the parasitic arrangements between star academics, universities and, often, private providers. MOOCs looked increasingly like a game only a wealthy few can play. The Department of Philosophy at San Jose State University (2013) argued in an open letter that the ability of universities such as Harvard and Massachusetts Institute of Technology (MIT) to build and develop MOOC environments creates new inequities of elites who have their 'own' professors and the outliers, whose access to public school professors is demeaned and sought to be replaced by the remote access that MOOCs provide. Just as importantly, MOOCs appeared increasingly disenchanting even when measured against their own indicators of success. Extremely high dropout rates caused their effectiveness to be questioned, and a closer look at their participants showed that they were taken mostly by those who already had advanced degrees. In light of such results, even MOOC service providers became cautious about some of the grander visions. The Stanford University-based artificial intelligence professor, Sebastian Thrun, whose for-profit MOOC company Udacity is considered to be one of the largest MOOC service providers in the world, has often emphasised that MOOCs as they function at the moment need to be evaluated not for what they are, but for what they can be. In the face of the research from University of Pennsylvania, which had declared that MOOCs have 'failed', Thrun accepted that MOOCs, in the way that they are currently designed are better equipped for vocational training rather than for higher education. It came as no surprise, therefore, that critical digital scholars and online courseware advocates soon started to make calls to think of learning and education 'beyond MOOCs' (Yuan *et al.* 2014.)

To conflate outreach and opening up of resources with the political and pedagogic practices of learning in one big technological 'solution' might be a mistake. As Wendy Chun and Lisa Rhody (2013: 3) mention in the *Dark Side of Digital Humanities*, MOOCs are characterised by a desire to 'rewrite political and pedagogical problems into technological ones, into problems that technology can fix'. MOOCs have been caught in the paradox where they first emerged as a critique of traditional structures, and are now being subsumed by those very administrative and organisation logics that take MOOCs as easy technological fixes for complex and historically constructed pedagogical, academic and societal problems that need more granularity and specificity (Ayers 2013). Anne Balsamo (2013) succinctly summarises the problem when she says that MOOCs are failed opportunities when they merely rebuild what is available. It is therefore time to remind us of Ashish Rajadhyaksha's (2011) call for making a distinction between digitalisation and virtualisation of the classroom. He argues that virtualisation is merely to render an existing form in a digital format whereas digitalisation offers an opportunity to reconceptualise the form, providing systemic and foundational restructuring of the roles, the processes and the values that our universities stand for. It is Rajadhyaksha's idea of the digitalisation of higher education which we now want to push forward further.

## Pedagogy of social media: what could we learn, if we wanted to?

In this second part of the chapter, we propose that we need to frame our thinking in a much larger historical and technological context for understanding the classroom. If the classroom is a nexus that brings together the various knowledge interactions within the university-based knowledge ecology, we have to realise that the classroom is an amalgamation of learning and technology practices since the days of simple anamnesis techniques, writing tools and systems and rudimentary calculating devices, which were slowly turned into the assemblage of books, furniture, libraries and, indeed, the brick and mortar structures of our universities. In other words, the classroom comes into being not only as a producer of learning practices, but also informed and shaped from its very beginnings by technological models of knowledge production, consumption and distribution. Following this argument, we suggest that it might be useful to look at the classroom in the age of social media, not as something that is an extension of the older form, but as something that can be recreated – hacked, if you will – by looking at some of the key learning principles that describe and shape everyday practices, structures and models of digital social media.

Instead of figuring out how to use social media in the digital learning environment,[5] we therefore propose that the way to conceive of the digital post-MOOC classroom is to begin by looking at some of the learning and knowledge-production principles embedded in influential social media spaces. In a way, we propose going back to the early days of the MOOCs when similar ideas were playing out. These principles offer us new solutions to older problems, and in the process also 'hack' these problems through new interfaces, designs and flows of information and knowledge. The following list of principles is not exhaustive or definitive, nor is it meant to be a critical analysis of these principles. Although busting the ideological claims that accompany social media rhetoric is a necessary task, it is not in the scope of this chapter; therefore, we bracket the rich critical discourse on social media, acknowledging its presence and usefulness, but not engaging with it now. We offer instead a symptomatic and a consciously affirmative list of its learning and knowledge-production principles, with the aim to open up new ways of reconceptualising the classroom in the time of social media. Identifying learning principles and modes of engagement stemming from cyber cultures might help understand the classroom as a multi-modal, multi-media, affective and sharing atmosphere.

### *The question of verification*

As a start, we want to look at one of the toughest questions that the classroom has to solve: verification of sources of learning, evaluation of lessons learned and skills acquired, authentication of the provenance of knowledge and standardising templates by which indicators of learning can be established have all been questions that have structurally informed and shaped how classrooms operate. The ways in which these concerns have been addressed in traditional academia is to create broadcast-based models where the teaching, curating and evaluating are all rolled into the central figure of the teacher, who then transmits information and learning to those in the class. Similarly, centralised authorities like curriculum approval committees and review boards become the meta-centres that replicate this hub-and-spoke model. So endemic is this imagination of traditional learning that all the activities, even those that expect students to take up different collaborative roles, eventually subscribe to the idea of one-to-many communication. Verification and rigour are embedded in everybody looking over/after everybody else, enfranchised to pass judgement of value, worth and relevance.

With the emergence of Wikipedia in 2005, this particular model was quickly questioned. As Wikipedians started engaging with the task of building the 'sum total of all human knowledge', which included not only lofty disciplinary summaries but also the aggregation of all the whimsical, strange and banal things that makes us human, they introduced a different way of thinking about verification. Through self-organisation, detailed discussion, open hierarchies and a unique system of consensus generation supported by the principle of a 'neutral point of view',[6] Wikipedia came and offered new ways of thinking about the verification question. Wikipedia relied on folksonomies of knowledge rather than taxonomies, thus encouraging people to find value in what they already know and love and encouraging them to learn more and contribute to the knowledge entry on Wikipedia. Instead of scouting only for experts, its system of cross-verification and fact-checking allowed for 12–15-year-olds writing for what has become the de facto global referencing system. So strong was this process of multiple layers of iterative verification that it subsumed the different roles of digital systems like identification, authentication, validation and verification, all into one process. It therefore culminated in the famous experiment conducted by *Nature* magazine, which showed that the number of substantial errors in blindly selected Wikipedia articles was almost the same as in articles selected from *Encyclopaedia Britannica* (Giles 2005).

Wikipedia demonstrates the evolution of a model that does not depend upon single narrative structures that lend a stamp of authority to a particular thing; instead, it evolved a knowledge commons built on good faith, endorsing a principle of novice–expert where people with particular passions, interests and knowledge were asked to write about things that they were deeply interested in, and learn about things they had never heard before. Although Wikipedia has come under criticism for not allowing non-textual and oral citations as well as original research in its structure, there is consensus that Wikipedia has contributed to the reworking of knowledge engagements and interaction. It has proposed a new paradigm of learning whilst teaching, and introduced models of discussion, debate and consensus building that remain unparalleled across any other user-generated knowledge website. Taking this paradigm as an inspiration can initiate some immediate changes into the classroom – setting up etherpads, which enable collaboratively produced and edited minutes during class is one simple example, cooperative editing Wikipedia pages as part of assignments is a second one – but it can also lead us into questioning the ways we build our curricula and frame and practise knowledge. A digital classroom that actually takes these principles seriously would look very different, not only in its structure, but also in the ways it would help conceptualise the form and function of the body of knowledge that is opening up, and imagine new roles for the bodies that engage within the knowledge ecologies with each other and the system. The teacher will have to be dismantled to become a co-learner. Students will have to be imagined as stakeholders who construct and add to the curricula-building processes. Wikipedia's form of verification is a two-way process of establishing accountability and responsibility that at least in parts eschews the structures of authority and authorship that continue to inform our academic practice.

## Speech and assessment

Although Wikipedia has content consensus as its ultimate goal and thus places the finished text at its foreground, other platforms thrive on infrastructures of discussion, critique and dissent, which Wikipedia glosses behind the finished 'article' page. The wildest of those platforms oriented towards a multiplicity of positions are undoubtedly the oldest: discussion and image boards, often still named after the long-gone technical solution *Bulletin Board Systems*. They tend to order posts in topical threads, in the order of appearance and sometimes in nested threads that react to an initial thread. In the West, *4chan* received considerable attention due to the big impact of *Anonymous* as a new form of activist collective, but discussion boards are not to be reduced to *4chan*: its prototype, the Japanese board *2chan*, still has an immense influence on the Japanese online discourses. Similarly, the biggest online sphere in the world – the Chinese sphere – is partially ruled by myriad board providers with thousands of boards popping up every day.

Many of these boards prescribe in their architecture, in the interface design, in processes of conflict resolution and the foregrounding of information and conversation, slightly different versions of how information is designed and arranged, censored and contained, and how interaction is accelerated or slowed down. Some boards privilege dialogical, others confrontational and even others mutually affirmative forms of relating posts to each other. Assessment is reorganised in peer-to-peer-structures, based on use as well as on evaluation, and often the collective assessment is fed back to other users in rankings. Providers such as Reddit or Slashdot use the possibilities of gaining status (often named 'Karma') for its contributors as a motivational tool, ordering mechanism, relevance criteria and possibility to further fine tune its inner workings.

All these forms of arranging sociality have potentially huge implications for pedagogy. They can provide us with new ways of enabling dialogue, dissent, affirmation, assessment, status, speed, relevance and ordering of conversations. An example might demonstrate the potential of such an approach: many discussion boards use cultural techniques of anonymity, ranging from the absence of clear names to the lack of pseudonym identity or the choice of making IP addresses accessible or not. Anonymity, in turn, is also a fundamental principle of academic judgement on levels of both scholarly and student work. But regimes of anonymity have much bigger potentials – they provide us with specific conditions for speech as well as for assessment, which can be made fruitful on much larger scales. It is possible to think of knowledge as information without signatures. Allowing students to be identified but still be anonymous, collective rather than an individual, is a good starting point. The possibility of knowledge transactions through avatars, the incorporation of anonymised safe spaces for discussion and comment through online spaces help augment classroom structures and conversations. Similarly, setting up new evaluation patterns that recognise the invisible labour – affective, material, intellectual, social – that learners often perform and rewarding these through badges[7] and documentary practices that move beyond the fetish object of the final academic performance might be ways in which we learn to hack the classroom as a bulletin board.

## Sharing is caring?

A lot of energy in contemporary social networking universes is directed at the values and principles that one abides by in the quest to create a new commons. These values are often reflected in the visionary evangelism of the early web pioneers. Tim Berners Lee, for example, hoped in his romantic manifesto for the World Wide Web that the Internet would become a space for sharing. By now we know a lot about the problematic implications of current structures tailor-built for 'primitive accumulation', big data analysis and mass surveillance produced by this wave of sharing, and yet 'sharing' seems to remain one of the principles that upholds our ubiquitous social networks and the quotidian practices they house. Within the contexts of the traditional classroom, the desire to share and to collaborate has been looked at as a positive outcome of good pedagogy (although the same takes on a sinister note when framed as plagiarism or copying), despite the often competitive models of learning, which gear students towards a cut-throat race for resources both inside and outside the classroom. Entire cultures of secrecy around research work and findings, the extraordinary value put upon individual authorship and the fight against sharing texts by creating exclusionary knowledge spaces have all been a part of knowledge cultures and industries. With the emergence of a sharing networking platform like Facebook, we see a mass return to this idea of the commons – as compromised as it may be – and its processes of sharing are remarkable.

Platforms like Facebook invite users to enumerate, describe, quantify and endorse their daily lives, relationships, thoughts, ideas and politics. The user in the social network is not just a producer of data. The user finds meaning in their articulations through sharing the data they produce. Although sharing is caring, sharing is also currency. Examining the ubiquitous 'Like' button and the 'Facebook Feed', which curates information based on algorithms that determine interest, proximity and relevance, might help us look at sharing as a principle that cuts across a wide range of practices within the classroom. Users share what they produce – content and articulation. What we 'author' on Facebook is the basis of building our communities. Although the sharing of this data – mimicking the principles of open access and open education movements – is not new, Facebook puts equal value on metadata. Metadata is not the content, but the content about the content. Digital content is often understood as merely the information that we see on our screens; however, all digital data is accompanied by other protocols, rules, guidelines and information sets that determine how this data will be read, circulated, shared, distributed, stored and archived. For big data networks like Facebook, the importance therefore is not in the human content but in the algorithms of correlation, curation and customisation that scan this data and create new connections. This provides a second level of sharing: not only what we produce, but also what we 'like' on Facebook is a lead into engaging with knowledge. An iterative cycle of liking that allows students to share resources from their locations and experiences outside classrooms could indeed produce wide-ranging effects.

## Curating data about data

In his optimistic book *Everything is Miscellaneous*, David Weinberger (2007) has proposed that the power of the social web lies in the ability of netizens to take an object and ascribe it meaning, value and circulation, fuelling economies of virality and folksonomies and setting up the hierarchies of attention economies. In the over-produced world of the social web, where multiple digital objects contend for attention and interaction, the micro-blogging platform Twitter produced one of the most intuitive forms of curating information and making it relevant. Twitter is today one of the most powerful tools of distributed conversations that tend to be non-archival and relevant. Its hashtags, unlike Facebook's Likes, are not just metadata. A hashtag has meaning, it carries particular information and it is a tool for generating interest. It is subject to mutation and morphing and often performs bridging roles, bringing together communities and readers in a common tweet. This potential of uniting multi-stakeholder interests in common tags that can travel, be shared and help to filter information is new. The hashtag's ability to filter – not through brute text search but through intelligent interest groups – offers a new way of looking at information parsing and processing in our online and offline classrooms. To imagine the community of learners as producing new filters of querying the knowledge sets available to them and to be able to share those filters with each other, learning from what the others have designed, might lead us to radically rethink inter-learner relationships.

This becomes compounded by the 're-tweet' endorsement that Twitter users get rewarded for. In our traditional classrooms, students are not always encouraged to actually promote each other's work. Despite the strong push for collaboration and participation, the cultures of solo-authorship and individual relationship with work are very strong. To think of a community that is not only pushing out collective work, but also promoting the work of others outside the standard practices of citation and referencing, produces a very networked way of constructing the classroom. Twitter's real-time trending patterns might also help the educators to understand evaluation parameters and processes in a more nuanced way. Getting the students to condense their knowledge into bite-sized responses and making it accessible is a concern that we have historically shared. Putting an artificial restraint to their articulations might help in managing their outreach and access better. With each learning community, based on certain interests and similarities, are there some topics and areas that might start trending within a classroom? Twitter's trending analysis might help the educator to leverage what is of interest to the learning group, but also focus on things that are left out in the group articulations.

Twitter, as a paradigm of thinking about knowledge engagement and acquisition, offers hacks into our classroom teaching and learning processes that can be executed and curated by the students. It produces shared semantic and temporal presence, and allows single short knowledge snippets to form its meaning and value against such a background. If the role of the digital is to convert memory into storage, then we are all archivists and collectors. Students can be made critically aware of their own learning practices by documenting their learning processes in real time, where instead of focusing only on final assignments they learn to think of themselves as resource builders, knowledge infrastructure creators and collaborative research and knowledge producers. Learners often create parallel systems of curricula and conversations that hack their academic practices. Making these hacks visible and encouraging them to participate through live streams in and outside the classroom, through curating content as a critical exercise, and through supporting via sharing are all processes by which the post-MOOC classroom comes into being.

## Social media as organisation: using social media as a means to think

In the second part of this chapter, we made some broad suggestions on how existing social media platforms might provide us with techniques and metaphors that can be employed for re-imagining learning and pedagogy. This approach was based on the assumption that such platforms provide us with new ways of organising experiences, sociality, motivations, (free) labour, resources and knowledge. In our final remarks we want to use these assumptions and read them against the grain: if social media organise experiences, sociality, motivation, resources, labour and knowledge, they can be seen, in fact, as forms of organisations. With 'organisation' we mean here an idea of extended organisation: it includes not only the entities that run the platforms (such as the Wikimedia Foundation or Facebook Inc.), but also, for example, programmer communities that contribute to its development, users sharing content and, indeed, all users, who provide the most valuable forms of all resources at stake: their attention, commitment and data. The key idea of these last remarks is this: if we take this overall complex assemblage as a new form of organisation, looking at *such* an organisation can open up new ways of understanding organisations in general.

Applying such an approach to management education might start simply. Analysing existing social media platforms with such a framework of extended organisation theory might provide students with questions, case studies and insights that extend their existing ideas of leadership, motivation or control, to name just a few examples. A more ambitious approach would equip students in ways that would allow them to conceptualise social media platforms themselves (Lovink and Rossiter 2013). Such a task is not only an easy way of winning students' attention (there are few students who have not dreamed up an app); once it is taken seriously, it also demands from students that they understand and lay out explicitly the forms of sociality they want to pre-organise, the experiences they want to prepare and the incentive structures they want to pre-configure – all of which are necessary to get user interaction going. If such conceptual thinking is pushed further to the level of designing mock-ups, they would be able to start to understand the complex and multiple demands of social media, which have to juggle many such ambitions at once. If they then make the first steps to building prototypes – most likely this would have to be done in project teamwork with students doing computer science degrees – they would also start to understand how programming front- and back-ends of an application or a platform asks them to reduce their conceptual ideas to basic abstract, and therefore programmable logic.

This, in combination with the more predictable business plan, would most likely lead not only to insights that are directly usable in the development of new social media offerings but, more importantly, to a better understanding of organisational change. Although conceptualising social media platforms, students will have to leave at some point the height of conceptual development and work from scratch. This is an experience that will enable them to understand the complex patchwork of different protocols, most of them far beyond control, that makes up any organisation. Understanding social media in such a way will equip students for an age of complex ICT systems, such as logistical software, in which arguably the organisation itself is partially transformed into software (Rossiter 2014). At this point it is important to caution once more against imagining pre-ICT organisations as free of media. As scholars including Cornelia Vismann (2008) and Ben Kafka (2012) have shown, organisations, just as classrooms, have always been partially constituted by media. In understanding social media as organisations, and organisations as partially constituted by media, students – and with them we as academic scholars – might also extend the idea of social media and start to understand *all* organisations as forms of social media.

## Conclusion

It might be the basic featureless character of the classroom as a blank canvas that can be moulded by pedagogic practices that has made it resilient and able to survive the various shifts in the composition of our academic and teaching processes. However, this blank canvas is always shaped by specific media technological conditions. That is not to say that it is a passive site upon which technologies become operative, but neither can the classroom negate changes in such technologies. Instead of only trying to figure out how we accommodate social media in our offline and online classrooms – which can sometimes be reluctant, sometimes frustrating and sometimes serendipitously generative – we suggest that the classroom should be seen as an amalgamation of various technological practices that inform and shape it, give it form and structure, and as such, can be hacked. Here, we have proposed three directions: first, the search for new forms of online learning, which go beyond the limits of existing MOOCs; second, employing in offline as well as online classrooms, with or without the enhancement of digital technologies, social media's methodologies for knowledge-generation and teaching, many of which are participatory, decentralised, collaborative, iterative and constantly subject to morphing and mutation; and third, including in the curriculum the analysis and experimental conceptualisation of social media, which can lead us into understanding not only social media, but also new modes of organising as embedded in technology and organisation alike.

We suggest that these principles can be operationalised in hybrid classrooms, by conceiving of distributed teachers, learners, resources and processes of learning. Hacking the classroom produces recursive relationships between technologies and pedagogy, and as such an infinite set of versions of teaching and learning. The three directions we proposed – online learning beyond MOOCs, learning about learning from social media and understanding social media in novel ways – can reinforce each other. It is hard to predict the outcomes of such positive feedback, but one way to imagine the post-MOOC digital classroom is as a space for distribution. If the premise of the traditional classroom was consolidation – where different learning resources, the interaction between learners, the transfer of knowledge from the teacher to the student, and the performance of academic knowledge and thought were brought together-then the post-MOOC digital classroom can perhaps be thought of as carrying the promise of distribution. Whilst we have already established that the current MOOCs are robust digital information delivery systems harnessing the strengths of the connected web, thinking of the MOOC as the first entry point into hacking the classroom enables thinking about distribution at a different level.

## Notes

1 Keith Harry, Desmond Keegan and Magnus John (1993) point out that despite the technological advancements, the two problems that stay at the centre of distance learning models are (1) the location of the student and (2) the communication between student–student, student–teacher and teacher–student. Lee Ayers Schlosser and Michael R. Simonson (2009) locate four different axes at the heart of distance learning: (1) the academic institution within which the programme is housed, which distinguishes it from 'self-learning'; (2) the separation of the teacher from the student geographically and temporally; (3) asynchronous and distributed interaction between the different participants; and (4) availability of resources and the problems of relevance. These are all questions that the MOOC challenges and addresses in new and different ways.

2 Daphne Koller and Andrew Ng (2012), the founders of the largest MOOC Coursera, talk about 'connected learning' as a shift from the teacher-centric focus of education discourse to a learning-centred approach in their vision of the MOOC. However, Elizabeth Losh (2014) argues that their vision is compromised by both the hierarchical construction of their learning systems as well as the episodic nature of MOOCs that does not support 'life-long learning', which has been at the heart of the interest-based, passion-driven idea of 'connected learning'.

3 Mary R. Lea and Kathy Nicoll (2005) propose that the notions of distributed learning are multiple and varied, and inform the construction of the MOOC in different ways: the breaking down of traditional boundaries of face-to-face and open and distance education; the development of distributed learning environments; the changes in our own understanding of learning and teaching as distributed practices; learning as a shared enterprise housed in multiple individuals and locations; divorcing of learning from formal institutional settings; and the tensions of the global and the local within which learning has to be located.

4 According to the report *Giving Knowledge for Free – The Emergence of Open Educational Resources* by OECD and CERI (2007), the definition of OER currently most often used is 'digitised materials offered freely and openly for educators, students and self-learners to use and reuse for teaching, learning and research'. OER includes learning content, software tools to develop, use and distribute content, and implementation resources such as open licences. The report suggests that 'open educational resources refers to accumulated digital assets that can be adjusted and which provide benefits without restricting the possibilities for others to enjoy them' (OECD and CERI 2007: 10).

5 As is the trend in looking at concepts such as blended learning, connecting learning, extended learning, etc. that seek to incorporate the social media in classrooms, as if the two were discrete and extricable entities.

6 https://en.wikipedia.org/wiki/Wikipedia:Neutral_point_of_view (accessed 22 July 2015).

7 Take the example of Mozilla's Open Badging Initiative, for instance, which allows the learners in an environment to adopt a multiplicity of badges that recognise their different practices of learning. Open Badges like these help the learners to recognise their own modes of learning and also reward different roles of connectors, distributors, nodes or sharers as important.

## References


Ayers, E. (2013) 'A more-radical online revolution'. *The Chronicle of Higher Education.* Available from: http://chronicle.com/article/article-content/136915/ (accessed 22 July 2015).

Balsamo, A. (2013) 'The latest MOOC alternative?: a DOOC'. *The New School News.* Available from: http://blogs.newschool.edu/news/2013/08/the-latest-mooc-alternative-a-docc/#.Vg-1MMuqqkp (accessed 22 July 2015).

Chun, W. and Rhody, L. (2013) 'Working the digital humanities: uncovering shadows between the dark and light'. *In: The Dark Side of the Digital Humanities.* Thinking C21. Available from: www.c21uwm.com/2013/01/09/the-dark-side-of-the-digital-humanities-part-1/ (accessed 22 July 2015).

Davidson, C. (2013) 'Peer learning, online learning, MOOCs, and me: response to the chronicle of higher education'. *hastac.* Available from: www.hastac.org/blogs/cathy-davidson/2013/04/29/peer-learning-online-learning-moocs-and-me-response-chronicle-higher (accessed 10 June 2015).

Department of Philosophy San José (2013) 'An open letter to Professor Michael Sandel'. *The Chronicle of Higher Education.* Available from: http://chronicle.com/article/The-Document-Open-Letter-From/138937/ (accessed 10 June 2015).

Giles, J. (2005) 'Internet encyclopaedias go head to head', *Nature*, 438, 900–1.

Harry, K., Keegan, D. and Magnus J. (1993) *Distance Education: New Perspectives.* London: Routledge.

Kafka, B. (2012) *The Demon of Writing: Powers and Failures of Paperwork.* New York, NY: Zone Books.

Kamenetz, A. (2013) 'Can we move beyond the MOOC to reclaim open learning?' *Huff Post College.* Available from: www.huffingtonpost.com/anya-kamenetz/can-we-move-beyond-the-mooc_b_3451418.html (accessed 20 June 2015).

Koller, D. and Ng, A. (2012) *The Online Revolution: Education for Everyone.* Available from: http://edpolicyinca.org/sites/default/files/Daphne%20Koller-pace-2012.pdf (accessed 4 January 2014).

Lea, M.R. and Nicoll, K. (2005) *Distributed Learning: Social and Cultural Approaches to Practice.* London: Routledge.

Losh, E. (2014) *The War on Learning: Gaining Ground in the Digital University.* Cambridge, MA: MIT Press.

Lovink, G. and Rossiter, N. (2013) 'In praise of concept production: formats, schools and non-representational media studies'. *In:* K. Gates (ed.) *Media Studies Futures. The International Encyclopedia of Media Studies.* Vol. 5. Cambridge and Malden, MA: Wiley–Blackwell, pp. 61–75.

Marvin, C. (1988) *When Old Technologies Were New.* Oxford: Oxford University Press.

Organisation for Economic Co-operation and Development (OECD) and Centre for Educational Research and Innovation (CERI) (2007) *Giving Knowledge for Free – The Emergence of Open Educational Resources.* Paris: Organisation for Economic Co-operation and Development.

Parr, C. (2013) 'MOOC creators criticise courses' lack of creativity'. *The Times Higher Education.* Available from: https://www.timeshighereducation.com/news/mooc-creators-criticise-courses-lack-of-creativity/2008180.article (accessed 10 August 2015).

Ragman's Circle (2013) *20 Things the Matter with MOOCs.* Available from: http://ragmanscircles.wordpress.com/2013/03/12/20-things-the-matter-with-moocs/ (accessed 10 August 2015).

Rajadhyaksha, A. (2011) *The Cultural Last Mile. An Inquiry into Technology and Governance in India.* The Centre for Internet and Society. Available from: http://cis-india.org/raw/histories-of-the-internet/last-cultural-mile.pdf (accessed 14 September 2015).

Readings, B. (1996) *The University in Ruins.* Cambridge, MA: Harvard University Press.

Rege, S. (2010) 'Education as trutiya ratna: towards phule-ambedkarite feminist pedagogic practices', *Economic Political Weekly*, 45(44), 88–98.

Rossiter, N. (2014): 'Logistical worlds', *Cultural Studies Review*, 20(1), 53–76.

Schlosser, L.A. and Simonson, M.R. (2009) *Distance Education: Definitions and Glossary of Terms.* Charlotte, NC: Information Age Publishing.

Vismann, C. (2008) *Files: Law and Media Technology.* Stanford, CA: Stanford University Press.

Weinberger, D. (2007) *Everything is Miscellaneous: The Power of the New Digital Disorder.* New York, NY: Times Books.

Yuan, L., Powell, S. and Olivier, B. (2014) *Beyond MOOCs: Sustainable Online Learning in Institutions.* Available from: http://publications.cetis.org.uk/wp-content/uploads/2014/01/Beyond-MOOCs-Sustainable-Online-Learning-in-Institutions.pdf (accessed 22 July 2015).

# 22

# Activism in business education

## Making the social sciences practical for social entrepreneurs

*Ester Barinaga*

Social entrepreneurship is a hot topic on many campuses around the world. The past decade has seen the birth of many a course on starting up social ventures, the development of whole educational programmes on social innovation, the establishment of university centres for the promotion of social impact and the launch of incubation labs for students who want to make the world a better place. Although some of these initiatives cut across academic faculties, business schools have been swift in embracing the phenomenon and offer a plethora of alternatives for students interested in learning about the social entrepreneurial process or in becoming a social entrepreneur (Kim and Leu 2011; Worsham 2012).

Along with this growing interest in bringing social entrepreneurship to the university campus and in line with the community orientation of the field, scholars are developing teaching practices and openly sharing educational resources (Zietsma and Tuck 2012). Freely accessible repositories for pedagogic materials on social entrepreneurship offer a wealth of cases, readings, course syllabi, podcasts and videos of inspirational social entrepreneurs, webinars, class plans detailed to the minute, and even customizable presentations for faculty to engage their institution on teaching social entrepreneurship (for examples, see Brock and Kim 2011; Leaman *et al.* 2011). From generalist web-based libraries of teaching resources, such as the Aspen Institute's CasePlace.org or the European Case Centre, to institutes specializing in social entrepreneurship, such as Ashoka.org, the Center for the Advancement of Social Entrepreneurship at Duke University or Stanford Center for Social Innovation, all are testimony to the extent that social entrepreneurs' enthusiasm for changing the world is being translated into pedagogic initiatives aimed at igniting and further feeding that passion.

Welcome as this profusion of courses and pedagogic materials may be, recent voices are timidly cautioning against too much enthusiasm. Seduced by passionate social entrepreneurs and a multitude of life-changing stories, these voices fear that teachers of social entrepreneurship could get carried away by individual stories and their accomplishments, and thus forget to ask more critical questions (Dey 2006; Zietsma and Tuck 2012). After all, social entrepreneurship is about finding new ways to address multifaceted social ills such as inequality, environmental damage, lack of universal education or poor healthcare provision (Zahra *et al.* 2009). These necessarily imply changing the status quo (Light 2009), putting together new combinations (Swedberg 2006) and tinkering with the social fabric of our communities (Barinaga 2014a).

How the critical questions are answered therefore becomes central to the shape taken by the new societies that these entrepreneurs are contributing to build. Whose interests are being served by the changes being introduced? Who is the entrepreneur to enact her/himself as spokesperson of a particular community? What are the unintended consequences of meddling with relations, social groups and communities? What are the prejudices implicit in the way social ventures frame the problems being addressed? To what extent are social ventures imposing solutions that are not based on how the vulnerable groups they want to serve define their own well-being? Or to what extent are the solutions offered reproducing the original problem only in a new shape?

Microfinance may serve as a case in point because it is often presented as the epitome of social entrepreneurship. The debates following the aftermath of the Banco Compartamos' IPO (initial public offering) and the wave of suicides among micro-loan takers in Andhra Pradesh, India, raised questions concerning not merely the tools and strategies used by social entrepreneurs in addressing social ills but, more importantly, about the values implicit in those tools and strategies, as well as concerns about the ethos brought by entrepreneurs to the social field (Aitken 2010; Ashta and Hudon 2012; Cull *et al.* 2009; Gruère and Sengupta 2011; Taylor 2011). Greg Dees succinctly formulates such preoccupations when he argues that 'social entrepreneurship [. . .] is not just about starting new ventures. It is about achieving social impact' (Dees cited in Worsham 2012: 446) and calls for teaching methods that develop students' sense of humility and empathy for the people whose situation social entrepreneurs want to see changed.

Attentive to these concerns, this chapter argues that the social sciences introduce that element of critical awareness to the complexity of large-scale social systems that is needed amongst those aiming to ignite change in those systems. It introduces the idea of activism as a pedagogic approach to raise awareness, develop humility and mobilize students as well as to add nuance to the realities that social entrepreneurs aim to change. Based on my experiences of teaching social entrepreneurship to international masters students enrolled in the Organizational Innovation and Entrepreneurship (OIE) Programme at Copenhagen Business School (CBS), this chapter considers the delicate balance between political awareness and practical relevance that teachers of social entrepreneurship need to strike in business schools. More particularly, the chapter presents two ways to introduce the social sciences in social entrepreneurship teaching to sharpen students' sensitivities to the political, social and cultural implications of social change efforts. The chapter is structured accordingly. After exploring the practical–political conundrum in social entrepreneurship teaching in more depth, the chapter deals with how I use the social sciences inside the classroom to develop students' appreciation for the social, political and ethical dimensions of social entrepreneurship. I then discuss aspects of the social sciences that I use to activate and engage students' social and political sensibilities outside the classroom. The chapter ends with a reflection on the lessons learnt that might be useful to the activist educator.

## The practical–political conundrum when teaching social entrepreneurship

According to Swedberg (2006: 21), 'the current literature on social entrepreneurship is richer on inspiring examples and anecdotes than it is on theoretical insights and analytical power'. A reason for this lack of theoretical sophistication may be that the field has tended to idolize the individual entrepreneur and describe the tools that these entrepreneurs suggest in their striving for social change whilst disregarding the social dynamics that catalyse such social change. For instance, important as it is to consider the role of social capital in the formative stage of the social enterprise (Hulgård and Spear 2007), dominant research and teaching has ignored the extent to which social capital can be a tool to break the dynamics of social reproduction. That is, within the context of social entrepreneurship, social capital has been discussed to the extent that it concerns management issues, such as opportunity recognition (Myers and Nelson 2010), mobilization of resources (Evers 2001) or scaling up efforts (Volery and Hackl 2010). Such a focus on the management-related aspects of social entrepreneurship has unfortunately been to the detriment of engaging with the concept of social capital for its role in reproducing (or contributing to break) the very social problems addressed by the ventures. Unfortunate as this may be, it is however not surprising. Researched and taught at business schools, often within programmes with a strong management orientation (such as MBAs) and for students that demand a practical focus, it comes almost as given that the focus is set on the concept's relevance for starting or building the venture. We need to remember, however, that understanding the social dynamics behind a particular social ill is the first step towards overcoming that ill, otherwise the risk is that in their efforts to do good, social entrepreneurs become part of the very problem they are attempting to solve.

Social entrepreneurship educators in business schools therefore face a particular challenge: how are the political, ethical and ideological dimensions of social entrepreneurial efforts to be elicited in the classroom without compromising the managerial focus of business students? How to foster critical thinking amongst practice-oriented students of social entrepreneurship? In an effort to tackle the practical–political conundrum, I take recourse to an activist approach to teaching, an approach that seeks to engage students in the societies they live in, that helps students assess their own – often implicit – beliefs, and that aims to shape our students into becoming aware citizens working for more just, equal and freer societies. In this chapter, I suggest that the social sciences offer excellent theoretical and methodological tools to do this. Through sociological notions and qualitative methods, the social sciences have the potential to help educators shake students out of preconceived truths about the groups whose situation they may want to improve and to start looking critically at what they do.

This chapter is an effort to show how I take advantage of the social sciences to develop students' political awareness and social engagement by presenting how I engage the social sciences in teaching a course called Social Entrepreneurship within a programme addressed to Masters students specializing in entrepreneurship. From the outset, the course puts the 'will to achieve social change' at the core of social entrepreneurship. The organization of efforts to ignite such change is therefore its focus. Mark the words *organization* and *(social) change* because these are key to the design of the course – they guide me through the choice, combination and implementation of pedagogic activities so that the course balances the practical orientation of business students whilst cultivating their critical awareness. As a result, with each pedagogic tool I introduce to the course, I strive to elicit both practical and social science dimensions. Two concerns run throughout the course and translate into its pedagogical design: (1) to promote reflection on the extent to which market rationalities and business tools are appropriate to work with a range of social issues; and (2) to help students deepen their understanding of the social mechanisms at the root of the problems they may be working with inside and outside the classroom – inside the classroom by teaching cases (amongst other things) whilst outside the classroom the pedagogic work is organized around the creation of students' own social entrepreneurial ventures.

## Activism in the classroom

Let me start as I do in my courses – with a few exemplary cases. Those presented in this chapter have been developed either by colleagues from the Stockholm School of Economics or by myself. The material that serves as the basis for the cases comes from longer qualitative research studies of the ventures discussed in them. Please bear with me throughout the somewhat detailed case descriptions because details will be necessary to explain the use of sociological notions to shake students out of their comfort zones.

## *Case 1: Fryshuset*

Fryshuset is one of the first cases I use in my effort to bring forth the social and political dimension of social entrepreneurial efforts (Sjöblom and Wijkström 2011). Started in 1984 in Stockholm by Anders Carlberg, Fryshuset is a non-for-profit organization addressing young people, and it has a particular focus 'on those living or at risk of living under exclusion'.[1] Unique for Fryshuset's way of working is that it employs ex-convicts and teenagers with a background as street fighters to reduce violence. The Easy Street Project is a particularly good example of Fryshuset's involvement of former criminals to reach out to and include violent youth. Initiated after the violence in Stockholm's Water Festival of 1995 had threatened the festivities, the project employed young adults (mainly in their 20s and 30s) from the troublesome neighbourhoods as 'hosts' who patrolled and watched over the public transportation system in Stockholm. Drawing on their standing and contacts in the areas where they now worked and establishing contact with the youngsters hanging around the underground stations in the high-risk areas, the hosts prevented conflicts and managed street aggression. Trained in conflict resolution, group dynamics, leadership skills, anger control and coaching, the hosts used the respect they had amongst the violent youth to reach out and prevent felonies and violence.

Impressed by the success of Easy Street in reducing violence in the Stockholm metro, the headmaster of Tumba's Upper Secondary School contacted Fryshuset after fires, drug dealing, aggressive incidents and recurring police interventions had led to the temporary closure of the school. Fryshuset placed five of its hosts in the school, three of whom were former students. These hosts worked as they had done outside the underground stations, by relating to the various subgroups in the schoolyard. Fryshuset also recruited students to train them as hosts. 'Out of 50 kids who had been extremely problematic, 40 applied to become school juniors' (cited in Sjöblom and Wijkström 2011). These kids turned out to be instrumental in ameliorating the school's climate, reducing bullying, racism and violence.

> [Drug dealers and other criminals] check our track record [. . .] and see if this is something they can ignore or not. And when they see what we have accomplished and see who we have on our side, they generally don't make trouble with us.
>
> *Cited in Sjöblom and Wijkström 2011*

So positive were the outcomes of involving former criminals, that Easy Street extended from the underground line and the school yard to cover entire neighbourhoods. The news spread and soon schools, public agencies and municipal commissioners in other cities were asking Fryshuset to help them improve their social tensions. The case stops at this moment when Anders Carlberg and his team have to decide whether to scale up the Easy Street Project – and with it the organization – to Göteborg and Malmö, the second and third largest cities in Sweden, respectively.

As most educators who use teaching cases already know, the decision is the trigger of class discussion. It brings the complexities and dilemmas of real-life situations to the classroom, prompting students to actively participate in the analysis of the case situation. At the risk of repeating what many have said before (see, for instance, Peterson 2004), the practice-orientation of the case not only satisfies students' demand for relevance, but is also an opportunity to introduce theory in an engaging manner. It is at this point, when social theory is actively engaged in the analysis of the practical issues described in the case, that we educators can bring in the more critical questions, questions that highlight the social, political and ethical aspects of the case.

In the Fryshuset case, having to decide on whether to scale up to other cities and, in that case, what strategy to follow, brings to the centre of the discussion the question of what Fryshuset's social impact was based on. Can Fryshuset's social impact be scaled up to other cities and, in that case, what would the most promising strategy look like? To answer that practical question, however, students first need to understand what aspects of Fryshuset's work are key to its social impact. Students are quick to realize that the *recognition* granted by the troublesome youth to ex-convicts for their accomplishments in their previous illicit endeavours is pivotal in reaching out and attracting the youth into Fryshuset. Students also see the value of a criminal past to keep current criminals in check. And so, the whole class is soon deeply engaged in a discussion on the forms of *social capital* and the role it plays for the efforts of a social initiative to reach out to its target group. This discussion not only raises the distinction between scaling up impact and scaling up the organization, it also helps students gain theoretical sophistication because they can appreciate the distinction between social capital understood as an individual's 'social networks and the norms of reciprocity and trustworthiness that arise from them' – as Putnam would have it (Putnam 2000: 19) – and Bourdieu's sense of that which is recognized by social groups as valuable (Bourdieu 1986).

In an effort to enhance the critical value brought by the sociological notions of recognition and social capital, I reformulate the question and stretch it into students' own everyday lives: how would you look upon employing former prisoners to serve as role models for the violent and criminal youth? Are we able to recognize a criminal past and the knowledge of the criminal culture as a resource to put to work when addressing at-risk youth? Or would you fund former thieves for starting up a social initiative? Such formulations of the idea of recognition most often produce a lengthy moment of silence, which I read as a sign of introspection. A few students seem to appreciate the social and experiential value of a criminal past; others timidly bring examples of cases of prisoners re-offending that they know of or have read about. Some reject altogether the idea that a criminal past can serve as a resource for social purposes. This evaluation of one's values further contributes to developing an understanding of social capital as a resource with value that hinges on the beliefs and classificatory schemes of the person or group looking at it. And so, in a very practical way, students manage to connect the (economic) notion of value to the (sociological) notion of values (Stark 2009).

Furthermore, an evaluation of one's values brings the social and political dimensions of the problem Fryshuset addressed on to a personal level. To what extent are the beliefs that I hold part of a larger system of thought that demonizes ex-convicts and at-risk youth, thus limiting their chances to break out of their situation? Hopefully, this way of pushing students makes them consider their participation in a system of thought that contributes to hamper ex-convicts' insertion in society and makes it harder to reach at-risk youth.

## *Case 2: Voices of the Suburbs (a series of cases)*

A second example I use to elicit the cultural and ideological dimension of social change is that of Voices of the Suburbs, a not-for-profit organization that I started in Stockholm in 2010 to change the stigmatized images of the so-called 'immigrant suburbs' and their residents (Barinaga 2014a). The organization uses the collective production of mural art in public spaces 'to let those who are talked about in the public debate take the power over their own story'. Voices of the Suburbs uses the colourful stories on the painted wall as well as the community-building processes catalysed through the collective production of mural art as platforms from which 'to reformulate Sweden's integration debate'.[2]

Written as a series of teaching cases, each case confronts students with the different decisions faced by the founder (me) throughout the process of starting, building up and expanding the organization. The first case in the series follows the entrepreneurial process from the origin of the idea in similar initiatives in San Francisco to the translation of that idea into the Swedish context, engaging partners, finding funds and carrying out a first pilot project under the umbrella of the Red Cross. The case stops at the moment when the founder has to decide whether to start up a social venture or continue operating under the Red Cross.

Relevant details for the theoretical and activist discussion of this case have to do with the founder's background and social standing. With a PhD from the Stockholm School of Economics, having held positions in several Swedish universities and fully funded by a generous research grant, the founder finds no difficulty in gaining access to potential funders and establishing collaborations with recognized art schools. Indeed, as the official of a major Swedish foundation let the venture's founder know during their first meeting:

> It's very unusual to get a proposal signed by someone from the Stockholm School of Economics and backed-up with research. It's usually ill-defined artists and civil society organizations sending the proposals. This is unusual!

Once more, the practical and theoretical discussions elicited through the case soon lead into issues of critical awareness – on this occasion, it concerns who is perceived as an entrepreneur and who is awarded legitimacy to speak for the vulnerable. At the core of the practical decision to be taken lies the extent to which the founder is able to garner resources outside the protective umbrella of the Red Cross. Early in the discussion students note the foundation official's acknowledgement of the founder's symbolic and cultural capital in the objectified forms of the founder's PhD and university affiliation, and the respect granted to an application grounded in academic research. Although the project lacks economic resources, we come to realize the importance of these other *types and forms of capital* for new social ventures and analyse the various strategies presented in the case to convert these into economic capital.

The activist moment comes when noticing that the founder is given legitimacy for articulating the voices of the immigrant suburbs despite the fact that the founder neither grew up nor lived in any of them. What makes the social entrepreneur a legitimate spokesperson of the vulnerable? What is the recognition of the social entrepreneur based on? To what extent is the target group adequately represented by someone who does not share their socio-economic conditions? These are questions that not only de-mythologize the entrepreneur, thus counteracting the literature's somewhat un-nuanced focus on the individual (Dacin, Dacin, and Tracey 2011; Dey 2006; Mair and Martí 2006), but also critically foreground matters of language and articulation, thus freeing socially divisive lines such as class and ethnicity from essentialism. Such a conceptual movement productively shifts the focus of the discussion from the individual changemaker to the collective nature of processes of social reproduction and social change.

Successive cases in the series take up other practical crossroads that similarly introduce sociological notions to think about. Again, I use these notions to awaken students' political and cultural awareness. For instance, one of the other cases in the series deals with the clash between the City of Stockholm's policies and the methods used by the not-for-profit organization. The vigour of Stockholm's zero-tolerance policy against graffiti becomes apparent one year after the formal starting up of the non-profit organization as permits to paint murals in public walls become enormously difficult to get. This results in a lack of access to permanent outdoor walls to paint on, and yet these walls are central to Voices of the Suburbs' community involvement work in the public space and also to citizen engagement in the public debate.

Whereas the city applies the *frame* of vandalism and criminality to street art produced by the young residents of the suburbs, Voices of the Suburbs frames street art as a platform for inclusive and democratic practices. These differing interpretations are more than a mere conflict of perspectives; they shape the experiences of public space, the interactions and expressions allowed in it, and the futures imagined for the urban sphere. What, for the city, is urban order and citizen security is, for the project, yet another sign of a democratic deficit for the stigmatized residents of the suburbs. The tight connection between the political and the aesthetic is obviated here. 'Who is allowed to express him or herself in the public space and who is excluded from it?' and 'what makes certain forms of art legitimate and others not?' are some of the activist questions that students readily fill with examples, from Banksy to Brigada Ramona Parra in Chile or the politically contentious murals of Belfast.

Other cases in the series are discussed with concepts such as field, habitus or from the point of view of the sociology of worth. I use these to introduce questions such as 'what are the political stakes of entering public–private partnerships?', 'to what extent are we implicated in that which we condemn?' or 'what are the values implicit in assessments of social and aesthetic value?' Reformulating sociological concepts into activist questions instigates a reflection on the values, prejudices and interests implicit in the decisions and actions that are meant to bring about more equal societies. At the heart of such a critical activist stance is an emphasis on the agency of individuals and collectives – a stance that is optimistic about the possibility of overcoming social inequalities.

### *Case 3: Microfinance*

A third example comes from the efforts to introduce microfinance as a tool to work with vulnerable groups in Sweden, more particularly ex-convicts, former drug-addicts and long-term unemployed women of immigrant background – a process that I had the opportunity to study (Barinaga 2014b). Launched in the autumn of 2008, the microfinance initiative was organized following a linkage-banking model in which non-profit organizations team up with financial providers. The case follows the strained relations between the Savings Bank of Sörmland – the savings bank of the pilot project – and Forum for Entrepreneurs from Ethnic Minorities (FEEM) – a small non-profit organization whose mission was 'to mobilize and promote entrepreneurship among women from ethnic minorities' as well as 'to reduce unemployment among [them]' (Barinaga 2013a). This goal was shared at the outset by the bank, which aimed 'to reach individuals outside the labour market and with no relation to the banking system'. However, as the case develops we learn that the bank's and the non-profit organization's different definitions of the target group and different understandings of microfinance result in different assessments of potential loan-takers. The case stops when relations between the parties have become so tense that the project leader within the sphere of the savings banks is considering ending all formal collaboration with the non-profit organization.

Facing the practical decision of whether to continue or cease a partnership focuses the analysis of the case on the quality and dynamics of those relationships. Class discussion starts by noticing that partners differed in the criteria they used to assess the initiative and in the rationalities they used when implementing microfinance. On the one hand, the bank deemed that '[t]he project's success shouldn't be measured in number of micro-loans granted, but rather in number of new companies started as well as number of persons who no longer depend on social welfare benefits'. In other words, for the bank, the microfinance process started before the actual granting of the micro-loan. Accordingly, in its effort to reduce social welfare dependency, the bank put a series of requirements on how the non-profit organization conducted its work with its target group, for example when indicating how the non-profit organization was to identify, train and select potential micro-loan takers; when suggesting the appointment of a loan-officer within the non-profit organization; or when advising the non-profit organization to involve welfare agencies in its programmes. In other words, the tools of calculation and financial practices of the bank – tools such as business plans, market analysis, balance sheets and budgets – were being extended to the *government* of the non-profit organization's conduct and to the management of the non-profit organization's work with its target group. The activist question is close at hand. Advocated as a tool for the financial inclusion of vulnerable individuals, to what extent is microfinance also serving to legitimize neoliberal forms of government that extend the power of the state well beyond its limits to include other economic and social actors (Barinaga 2014b; Rose and Miller 1992)? The sociological notion of governmentality is thus introduced to politicize microfinance as a potential neoliberal tool.

On the other hand, FEEM insisted on the relevance of the ethnic boundary to define its target group – individual entrepreneurs are interesting not because of their situation at the margins of the labour market or because of their social welfare dependency, but because of their immigrant past. As a result, the non-profit organization presented these immigrant women as successful micro-loan takers even though some of them had already been economically and financially independent for several years. It is possible to discuss the sincerity of assessing the success of the microfinance initiative with reference to the ethnic instead of the economic background of the loan-taker. It is also possible to discuss whether, by articulating its target group along ethnic lines, the non-profit might be contributing to the reproduction of the ethnic category that it condemns. However, with a focus on empowering women of foreign background and to overcome the ethnic organization of Swedish society, the way in which the non-profit organization insisted on the ethnic line to turn attention to the social root of economic exclusion can also be discussed or, putting it differently, the non-profit organization resisted the individualization implicit in a neoliberal understanding of microfinance with a definition of the loan-takers as part of an ethnic category, that is although the bank's financial tools turn larger structural problems into a matter of individual business plans, the non-profit organization points back to the social origins of exclusion. In a simpler activist formulation that can stir critical awareness among students: whose interests are being served when serving the vulnerable? To what extent does a focus on individual financial inclusion render large-scale social problems into personal ones? How can a focus on the effects of inequality (such as economic dependency) address its larger social roots?

## *Teaching cases in the classroom*

In sum, the social sciences offer us notions that can be used to focus on the political, cultural and ethical dimensions of entrepreneurs' social change efforts. Amongst those introduced through these cases are the notions of recognition, social capital, symbolic capital, legitimacy and governmentality. If used well, these help students understand the difference between social and economic value, opening the road towards broader discussions on the social value of profit, the social implications of organizational size, or the democratic consequences of starting up and leading a venture that claims to represent the vulnerable.

Two principles are important in aligning these notions and discussions to the practical-orientation of business students. First, cases should centre on a practical decision faced by the social entrepreneur. Second, cases should have the potential to provoke an examination of one's own values and preconceptions. By facilitating students to engage with the activism of others, and by making students examine their own presumptions about the venture's target groups and social challenges, this way of using cases supports a form of activism that works with students' sense of awareness. Applying theories to real-life cases to raise critical questions is a way to push students into considering the political and practical relevance of what they learn. Invariably, they asked for more cases when explaining theoretical concepts: 'I would like to keep working with cases as I think it is always easier to apply theory to real life scenarios', 'They make theories easier to understand', or 'cases helped make sociology concrete and relevant'. Taken together, the activist approach to teaching presented earlier addresses the fear expressed by some observant educators of social entrepreneurship (Zietsma and Tuck 2012) whilst adding nuance to the management focus recommended by others (Tracey and Phillips 2007).

Some may argue that I am being ideological in my teaching and that ideology should be kept outside management education. My response would be that there are values implicit in all knowledge we teach. Asking what the social value of profit is forces us to examine our understanding of profit, for what and for whom. By extension, it pushes us to reconsider the role of the knowledge we teach in performing the societies we live in. By bringing activism to the classroom, we make explicit the particular set of values dominant in business schools, thus questioning the types of societies that such knowledge is contributing to bring about. The hope is to cultivate students into becoming more aware citizens (see Sullivan, Colby and Ehrlich, this volume), conscious of their place in society and their role in it.

## Activism outside the classroom

Productive as teaching cases may be in developing students' analytical problem-solving skills (Corey 1996), on their own they fall short of developing the practical leadership skills required in the world of management (Foster and Carboni 2009). Within the field of social entrepreneurship, one such key skill is the capacity for empathy (Bornstein 2006; Drayton 2012). It is to this end that I once more take recourse to the social sciences. From in-depth interviews to ethnographic-inspired methods, the social sciences offer us a range of methods that are helpful in sensitizing students to the everyday political and cultural manifestations of social ills that social entrepreneurs want to see changed. A tour of the city guided by a homeless person helps students to see the urban space as experienced by them (see Beyes and Michel, this volume), inviting students to appreciate the tacit knowledge of persons who are otherwise seen through the stigma imposed on them. How many of us would survive a freezing winter night without the shelter of a roof? An interview with the refugee woman living in a camp brings immediacy to the life consequences of restrictive immigration policies enacted in the name of labour market protection. A visit to a centre that deals with young people who have social, psychological and drug-abuse problems forces students to realize the privileged lives they may have had. A discussion with the educated man hampered by the stigma that came with his HIV positive diagnosis makes students aware that merits and individual effort are not enough for securing a respected life.

To give coherence to the knowledge developed through the methods and techniques of the social sciences, as well as to give students the opportunity to gain depth on a particular social problem of their interest, the course is organized around the creation of students' own social ventures. Organized in groups, students first need to decide what particular social challenge they will be working with throughout the course. Then, during the course's first half, students are asked to interview individuals living with the challenge they have chosen, experts in the topic and managers working in organizations that address that challenge. They are also asked to conduct ethnographically inspired fieldwork, shadowing the poor or vulnerable or participating in their activities to the extent they are allowed. For instance, if the challenge is homelessness in Copenhagen, why not spend a night on the streets? If it is refugees in the camps, why not go to the camp itself? If it is the unhealthy eating habits of Danish children, why not visit schools in different neighbourhoods to discuss with the children what dinner was yesterday or the way they spend their pocket money (if any)?

Repeatedly, students admit the power of the experience of meeting and talking with those whose situation they aim to improve. Often, such meetings prove to be instrumental for developing students' political, social and cultural awareness: 'I'm ashamed to admit, but I had never before been aware of their situation [refugees]. It's shameful for Denmark to treat them as we do', 'It wasn't until we visited the elderly home that I realized how age-segregated our society is' or 'It was interesting to see how children in the poorer neighbourhoods got soft-drinks and a McDonalds burger when their parents wanted to give them a special evening. Children in the richer areas had different diets'. All these quotes illustrate the role played by social sciences' methods in pushing students' understanding of the economic, political and cultural underpinnings of social challenges. The experiences enabled by qualitative methods force students to question their, at times, implicit assumption that the responsibility for the problem, and thus for its solution, is to be located in the poor and marginalized individual. Instead, student groups start discussing how to solve a problem that is social, and not personal, in its origin. As a result, and invariably, students rate fieldwork among the most powerful elements of the course: '[it] made me reconsider my understanding of the social and what it takes to change the world.'

The lessons learnt through qualitative methods may be critical, but it is just as important to connect these to the practical decisions of students' own entrepreneurial process. Organizing the course around the creation of students' own social ventures gives the lessons (both inside and outside the classroom) a sense of urgency and a deeper personal meaning. 'I really enjoyed working for the homelessness cause. It made me feel good about the fact that I am giving something back to society.' As we saw in the previous section, the conceptual tools of the social sciences can help us as educators in business schools to conjure up the values implicit in the knowledge we teach and the management decisions students will be one day making. Methods common in the social sciences can further contribute to our efforts to get students to understand the performative force of the knowledge they learn (Howorth, Smith, and Parkinson 2012). Fieldwork, ethnographic interviews or other types of qualitative methods that are common in the social sciences have a focus on understanding the world as lived by those studied. They hand us excellent tools to enter the universe of meaning of those who social ventures aim to address, and they allow us to map vulnerable communities and capture their strategies to cope with their vulnerabilities. By directing our attention to local situated knowledges, such methods force future social entrepreneurs to recognize the value of the experiences of their eventual target groups as well as to nuance the, at times, limited and limiting images they may have of the poor, marginalized and excluded. A richer appreciation of those living with the social problems that entrepreneurs may want to address is key to designing ventures that are grounded in local knowledge and that approach the poor, marginalized and excluded as actors of the social change that entrepreneurs so want to see happen (for a similar argument from within economics, see Banerjee and Duflo 2011).

## Lessons for the activist educator

Social entrepreneurship education is most often designed as a combination of descriptions of the contextual background to the development of the phenomenon; heroic stories of social entrepreneurs and their paths to success; and how-to-do discussions through manualized texts and teaching cases (for a review of common resources used in social entrepreneurship courses, see Howorth *et al.* 2012; Moss and Gras 2012; Zietsma and Tuck 2012). Although acknowledging the importance of inspiration and practical orientation in shaping a future generation of social entrepreneurs, this teaching risks forgetting that social entrepreneurship is not just about the practical complexities of starting up new ventures (Worsham 2012). What excites social entrepreneurs and the field alike is a focus on 'destabilizing the status quo' (Light 2009), on 'creating social change' (Dees cited in Worsham 2012; Hjorth 2013) and on bringing about 'systemic change' (Drayton 2002) that creates shared value and transforms capitalism (Porter cited in Driver 2012). This challenges social entrepreneurship scholars to acknowledge the political mileage of social entrepreneurial efforts (Barinaga 2013b; Cho 2006; Dey and Steyaert 2010), and puts a demand on educators to address the ideological dimension of social entrepreneurial processes and initiatives (Howorth *et al.* 2012).

Placing social change at the core of social entrepreneurship, as both scholars and practitioners do, therefore challenges educators to elicit power and ideology as central dimensions of the phenomenon. But how are the political, ethical and ideological aspects of social entrepreneurial initiatives to be elicited in the classroom without compromising the practical focus of students in business schools? On the one hand, the social sciences provide us with a set of concepts to understand the dynamics of social reproduction. Such intellectual tools facilitate an appreciation of both the material and symbolic dimensions of the social issues aimed at by social entrepreneurs. Further, concepts such as those discussed through the teaching cases presented in this chapter – frame, habitus, social capital or governmentality – enable students to acknowledge the larger institutional aspect of the social ills aimed at and help them to realize their own contribution to the making of the problem. This is a humbling exercise that might lead students to desist in their efforts towards social change.

On the other hand, business school students demand a strong hands-on orientation and management educators have excelled at developing strong practical pedagogic methods: teaching cases, study visits, boot-strapping camps, simulations and business plan competitions are widely used to inspire as well as to encourage students to start their own ventures. Productive as these teaching methods are, but often lacking a sophisticated understanding of the social problem addressed, students risk at best not contributing to social impact; at worst, ignoring their own role in reproducing the very problem they aim to address.

The challenge is therefore to help students realize the enormity, complexity and uncertainty of the social ills confronted whilst appreciating the space of action that students have in alleviating those ills. Bringing activism to our teaching is a way to recognize the wider structures limiting action whilst acknowledging our role as individuals and collectives in recreating or contributing to changing those structures. In striving to awaken such critical awareness in my students, I find the social sciences offer excellent tools to bring forth the ideological dimension of entrepreneurs' social change efforts. Using the concepts and tools handed to us by the social sciences to discuss real-life cases and think through students' own venture-creation process allows us to strike a balance between practical relevance and critical awareness. This demands a particular teaching approach, one that addresses the practical–political conundrum through three levels of activism:

1 Developing students' self-awareness. Sociological notions – from social capital and habitus to governmentality and frames – are put to work to encourage students to revise the implicit assumptions they hold regarding the poor, subordinated and marginalized; that is, of those whose lives social entrepreneurs aim to ameliorate.
2 Engaging students in the life-worlds of others. Fieldwork and other qualitative methods give students the opportunity to enter the universes of those addressed by social entrepreneurial initiatives and they help students gain an understanding of the world as lived by those whose lives they want to change. They are therefore excellent tools to train students' empathy and humility for the knowledge of the stigmatized and excluded.

3 Encouraging students to take action concerning one of today's social and political challenges. Through the design of their own ventures, students engage the knowledge they have gained from their target groups, an exercise that often results in a reflection on the role played by everyone – the more and the lesser privileged – in making this world a better place. This is a necessary lesson if we want to involve the poor and marginalized as agents of the social change we want to see happen.

Let me end this chapter by offering some tips for practising such an activist approach in our teaching.

First, in each single session, connect one or two notions from the social sciences to real-life teaching cases. During preparation for the lesson, develop three or four thematic questions that relate the practical challenges faced by social ventures with the ideological underpinnings of sociological observations.

Second, in your lesson plan, translate these thematic questions into activist/politicized ones that probe the values underlying the case's main character and even those of the students – an *ad hominem* style of interrogating that focuses on the person rather than the position they may have.

Third, after asking a question, be patient with prolonged silence (see Vince, this volume). It may be a signal of the productive discomfort created by the question and a sign of students examining their core values and beliefs.

Fourth, introduce elements of experiential learning into your course plan (see Brandi and Elkjaer, this volume). Meeting, interviewing or spending a full morning with a person from the target group of the student venture can be an overwhelming experience for some students because they learn to appreciate the problem from the perspective of the vulnerable. This experience pushes students away from the taken-from-granted preconceived ideas of the poor and marginalized and teaches them to respect the implicit knowledge that the vulnerable may have of the social problem addressed by the venture.

Finally, design the course along a practical project that students need to carry out. It may be the creation of students' own social ventures or a consultancy assignment from an already existing venture. Whatever the project, it is important that students feel that they are working in a real-life project because it gives purpose and a sense of urgency to what they are learning.

Richard Swedberg argues that 'the social sciences have a very important contribution to make, not only to the theoretical understanding of entrepreneurship but also to entrepreneurship as a practical enterprise' (Swedberg 2000: 7). Swedberg argues that this is not because the social sciences are driven by an aim to be practical, but because much of what they have to say about entrepreneurship does have practical implications. This is particularly pertinent in what concerns social entrepreneurship because the social sciences help us to highlight the ideological aspects of entrepreneurial endeavours. The chapter has been an effort to take that insight into our teaching practices.

## Notes

1 From Fryshuset's homepage (http://fryshuset.se/om-fryshuset/). My own translation.
2 From Voices of the Suburbs' homepage (www.forortenicentrum.org). My own translation.

## References

Aitken. R. (2010) 'Ambiguous incorporations: microfinance and global governmentality', *Global Networks*, 10(2), 223–43.

Ashta, A. and Hudon, M. (2012) 'The Compartamos microfinance IPO: mission conflicts in hybrid institutions with diverse shareholding', *Strategic Change*, 21(7–8), 331–41.
Banerjee, A. and Duflo, E. (2011) *Poor Economics*. New York, NY: Public Affairs.
Barinaga, E. (2013a) 'Introducing micro-finance in Sweden to work with vulnerable groups', *Journal of the International Academy for Case Studies*, 19(3), 33–43.
Barinaga, E. (2013b) 'Politicising social entrepreneurship: three social entrepreneurial rationalities towards social change', *Journal of Social Entrepreneurship*, 4(3), 347–72.
Barinaga, E. (2014a) *Social Entrepreneurship: Cases and Concepts*. Lund, Sweden: Studentlitteratur.
Barinaga, E. (2014b) 'Micro-finance in a developed welfare state: a hybrid technology for the government of the outcast', *Geoforum*, 51, 27–36.
Bornstein, D. (2006) *How to Change the World: Social Entrepreneurs and the Power of New Ideas*. Oxford: Oxford University Press.
Bourdieu, P. (1986) 'The forms of capital'. *In:* J.G. Richardson (ed.) *Handbook of Theory and Research in the Sociology of Education*. New York, NY: Greenwood Press, pp. 241–58.
Brock, D. and Kim, M. (2011) *Social Entrepreneurship Education Resource Handbook*. Washington, DC: Ashoka U.
Cho, A.H. (2006) 'Politics, values and social entrepreneurship: a critical appraisal'. *In:* J. Mair, J. Robinson and K. Hockerts (eds.) *Social Entrepreneurship*. Basingstoke: Palgrave Macmillan, pp. 34–56.
Corey, R.E. (1996) *The Use of Cases in Management Education*. Boston, MA: Harvard Business School Publishing.
Cull, R., Demirgüç-Kunt, A. and Morduch, J. (2009) 'Microfinance meets the market'. *In:* T.A. Watkins and K. Hicks (eds.) *Moving Beyond Storytelling: Emerging Research in Microfinance, Contemporary Studies in Economic and Financial Analysis*. Vol. 92. Bingley, UK: Emerald Group Publishing, pp. 1–30.
Dacin, M.T., Dacin, P.A. and Tracey, P. (2011) 'Social entrepreneurship: a critique and future directions', *Organization Science*, 22(5), 1203–13.
Dey, P. (2006) 'The rhetoric of social entrepreneurship: paralogy and new language games in academic discourse'. *In:* C. Steyaert and D. Hjorth (eds.), *Entrepreneurship as Social Change*. Cheltenham, UK: Edward Elgar, pp. 121–44.
Dey, P. and Steyaert, C. (2010) 'The politics of narrating social entrepreneurship', *Journal of Enterprising Communities: People and Places in the Global Economy*, 4(1), 85–108.
Drayton, W. (2002) 'The citizen sector: becoming as entrepreneurial and competitive as business', *California Management Review*, 44(3), 120–32.
Drayton, W. (2012) 'Bill Drayton's five trends for social entrepreneurs', *Forbes*, retrieved from: http://www.forbes.com/sites/ashoka/2012/12/12/bill-draytons-five-advice-for-social-entrepreneurs-what-the-future-holds-and-how-you-should-adjust/#32a2a9df4cc6 (accessed 6 March 2016).
Driver, M. (2012) 'An interview with Michael Porter: social entrepreneurship and the transformation of capitalism', *Academy of Management Learning and Education*, 11(3), 421–31.
Evers, A. (2001) 'The significance of social capital in the multiple goal and resource structure of social enterprises'. *In:* C. Borzaga and J. Defourny (eds.) *The Emergence of Social Enterprise*. London and New York: Routledge, pp. 296–311.
Foster, P. and Carboni, I. (2009) 'Using student-centered cases in the classroom: an action inquiry approach to leadership development', *Journal of Management Education*, 33(6), 676–98.
Gruère, G. and Sengupta, D. (2011) 'Bt cotton and farmer suicides in India: an evidence-based assessment'. *The Journal of Development Studies*, 47(2), 316–37.
Hjorth, D. (2013) 'Public entrepreneurship: desiring social change, creating sociality', *Entrepreneurship and Regional Development: An International Journal*, 25(1–2), 34–51.
Howorth, C., Smith, S.M. and Parkinson, C. (2012) 'Social learning and social entrepreneurship education', *Academy of Management Learning and Education*, 11(3), 371–89.
Hulgård, L. and Spear, R. (2007) 'Social entrepreneurship and the mobilization of social capital in European social enterprises'. *In:* M. Nyssens (ed.) *Social Enterprise: At the Cross-Road of Market, Public Policies and Civil Society*. London: Routledge, pp. 85–107.
Kim, M. and Leu, J. (2011) 'The field of social entrepreneurship education: from the second wave of growth to a third wave of innovation'. *In:* U. Ashoka and D. Brock (eds.), *Social Entrepreneurship Education Resource Handbook*. Washington, DC: Ashoka U, pp. 8–9.
Leaman, M., Fraizer, L., Brock, D. and Leu, J. (2011) *Campus Starter Kit: Resources for Faculty and Staff for Developing Social Entrepreneurship Education on Your Campus*. Washington, DC: Ashoka U.
Light, P.C. (2009) 'Social entrepreneurship revisited: not just anyone, anywhere, in any organization can make breakthrough change', *Stanford Social Innovation Review*, summer issue.

Mair, J. and Martí, I. (2006) 'Social entrepreneurship research: a source of explanation, prediction, and delight', *Journal of World Business*, 41, 36–44.
Moss, T.W. and Gras, D. (2012) 'A review and assessment of social entrepreneurship textbooks', *Academy of Management Learning and Education*, 11(3), 518–27.
Myers, P. and Nelson, T. (2010) 'Considering social capital in the context of social entrepreneurship'. *In:* H. Fayolle and A. Matlay (eds.) *Handbook of Research on Social Entrepreneurship*. Cheltenham, UK: Edward Elgar, pp. 271–85.
Peterson, T.O. (2004) 'So you're thinking of trying problem based learning? Three critical success factors for implementation', *Journal of Management Education*, 28(5), 630–47.
Putnam, R.D. (2000) *Bowling Alone. The Collapse and Revival of American Community*. New York, NY: Simon & Schuster.
Rose, N. and Miller, P. (1992) 'Political power beyond the state: problematics of government', *British Journal of Sociology*, 43, 173–205.
Sjöblom, L. and Wijkström, F. (2011) *Fryshuset*. Center for Social Investment, University of Heidelberg.
Stark, D. (2009) *The Sense of Dissonance: Accounts of Worth in Economic Life*. Princeton, NJ: Princeton University Press.
Swedberg, R. (2000) 'The social science view of entrepreneurship: introduction and practical implications'. *In:* R. Swedberg (ed.) *Entrepreneurship: The Social Science View*. Oxford: Oxford University Press.
Swedberg, R. (2006) 'Social entrepreneurship: the view of the young Schumpeter'. *In:* C. Steyaert and D. Hjorth (eds.) *Entrepreneurship as Social Change: A Third Movements in Entrepreneurship Book*. Cheltenham, UK: Edward Elgar.
Taylor, M. (2011) '"Freedom from poverty is not for free": rural development and the microfinance crisis in Andhra Pradesh, India', *Journal of Agrarian Change*, 11(4), 484–504.
Tracey, P. and Phillips, N. (2007) 'The distinctive challenge of educating social entrepreneurs: a postscript and rejoinder to the special issue on entrepreneurship education', *Academy of Management Learning and Education*, 6, 264–71.
Volery, T. and Hackl, V. (2010) 'The promise of social franchising as a model to achieve social goals'. *In:* H. Fayolle and A. Matlay (eds.) *Handbook of Research on Social Entrepreneurship*. Cheltenham, UK: Edward Elgar, pp. 157–81.
Worsham, E. (2012) 'Reflections and insights on teaching social entrepreneurship: an interview with Greg Dees', *Academy of Management Learning and Education*, 11(3), 442–52.
Zahra, S.A., Gedajlovic, E., Neubaum, D.O. and Shulman, J.M. (2009) 'A typology of social entrepreneurs: motives, search processes and ethical challenges', *Journal of Business Venturing*, 24, 519–32.
Zietsma, C. and Tuck, R. (2012) 'First, do no harm: evaluating resources for teaching social entrepreneurship', *Academy of Management Learning and Education*, 11(3), 512–17.

# 23

# Spaces with a temper

## On atmospheres of education

*Christoph Michels and Timon Beyes*

### Introduction: mixed feelings

> Everything depends on the feel of an atmosphere and the angle of arrival.
>
> *Kathleen Stewart 2010: 340*

*Everything depends on the angle of arrival.* We begin with a small empirical study undertaken by one of our students. It took place at a business university, in a course called "Cities and Creativity." The course was dedicated to and constructed around short, quasi-ethnographic studies that the students conducted on the everyday constitution of urban spaces, the way such spaces afford certain kinds of emotions, perceptions, and practices and the way they are shaped by these emotions, perceptions, and practices in return. Our student took on the university campus itself. Among other things, his study assembled narratives of the campus's atmospheric force based on interviews with and cognitive mappings by a local architect, a researcher, a janitor, a student, and an inhabitant of the city. In their accounts and maps, we found a variety of ways of affectively relating to the campus and its buildings. We learned that the architect was "thrilled" and "fascinated" by the style of the building, that the researcher experienced the campus as "dull" and "boring," that the janitor found the campus a "tense" and "strange" place, that the student "detested" the campus's "unwelcoming atmosphere," and finally that to the inhabitant of the city the university felt "far away" and "a big mystery."

*Everything depends on the feel of an atmosphere.* Reading the interview excerpts and studying the drawings we learn that each of these sensations is attached to, or provoked by, the university's spatial atmospherics – these are spaces with a temper. However, in each account different components form part of these affective atmospheres: specific elements of the campus, such as doors, staircases, or the art collection; other buildings in the city (with which the university's architecture is compared); narratives and images of the university that circulate in the city and shape the interviewees' perceptions; people such as neighbors, students, administrators, and professors (and their respective practices); and, of course, the interviewees' bodies themselves that resonate with the university's sites and sights (and smells, colors, and sounds). As we move through the university in our daily routines, as we study, do research, teach, eat, and meet, we are constantly moving in and out of atmospheric compositions that make us feel, act, and think in specific ways.

These compositions not only comprise the built space that envelops university life but can include a variety of other components such as stories, sounds, lights, colors, technologies, clothes, food, texts, and last but not least other people. Such compositions of university space emerge as sensing bodies start to resonate in various ways, co-producing a university's atmospheres.

Taking our cue from the student's magnificent little study, and building up on earlier work that we undertook on the production of university space (Beyes and Michels 2011, 2014), this chapter inquires into the spatial atmospherics of management education. How can we understand the emergence and effects of pedagogical atmospheres? How can we make space for experimenting with what spaces can do as part of educational practice? To answer our guiding questions, this chapter pursues a twofold aim. First, drawing upon recent philosophical and social-theoretical engagements with the spatial and the atmospheric, we seek to outline a performative notion of spatial atmospherics as a distinct contribution of humanities- and social theory-based thinking for both studying and practicing management education. Second, we offer examples of, and reflections on, how spaces with a temper can become part and parcel of practices of management education. Such educational practice, we argue, can foster a critical sensibility for the atmospheric politics of organizing in the double sense of the managerial practice of atmospheric modulation as a form of power (Böhme 1993; Borch 2010) and of spatial multiplicity as the condition for intervening in and transforming how organization takes place (Beyes and Steyaert 2012).

We believe that this endeavor offers a relevant contribution to the current interest in (re)introducing the humanities and social sciences into business schools (Statler and Guillet de Monthoux 2015). In this context, it productively relates to recent work on the materiality (Taylor and Statler 2014; Fenwick, this volume), the aesthetics and artfulness (Katz-Buonincontro 2015; Meisiek, Guillet de Monthoux, Barry, and Austin, this volume), and the affects and emotions (Vince 2010; Steyaert, Hoyer, and Resch, this volume) of management education. However, we present an approach and a vocabulary to sense and make sense of the business school and its processes of teaching and learning that so far has barely been addressed in the study of management education. Moreover, turning spatial atmospherics into the very material of teaching carries its own criticality and politics. Rather than confronting the malaise of the business school in general terms and perhaps "look[ing] for a mythical 'other' from the status quo" that is "comfortably and comfortingly unattainable" (Volkmann and De Cock 2007: 399), what we tentatively call a "pedagogy of atmospheres" entails inquiries into and enactments of "other spaces" of organization and management.

We proceed in three steps. First, we connect the concept of atmospheres to the bourgeoning interest in a processual or performative notion of space or "spacing." Second, we present exemplary snapshots taken from three courses that we have offered at a business university. Third, we explore conceptual elaborations and empirical vignettes in order to sketch the contours of a pedagogy of atmospheres, and we translate the preliminary implications for management education into tactical slogans for the atmospheric management educator.

## Spatial atmospherics

As the introductory vignette shows, space is multiple. It is never the physical structures alone that provoke a specific sensation; rather, materialities intermingle with objects, persons, practices, narratives, images, and imaginations to produce space. Space, moreover, is invariably atmospheric: it engenders and is shaped by affects that seem to hover between "objects" and "subjects" that engulf and befall human bodies, which then react to, act upon, and thus co-produce such atmospheres. To conceive of space as atmospherically charged, and of atmospheres as spatially constituted, is warranted by both a growing interest in the processual, performative, and affective characteristics of space – or "spacing" – and the recent interest in the notion of atmospheres as "spaces with a mood" (Böhme, Borch, Eliasson, and Pallasmaa 2014: 96). To develop an understanding or a feel for a pedagogy of atmospheres, in this section we therefore connect a performative notion of space to the processes of its atmospheric constitution.

## *Spacing*

We begin with space or spacing. Faced with a proliferation of approaches across disciplines that have sought to unfix, mobilize, and enliven our grasp of the spatiality of human life – constituting the so-called "spatial turn," "the enormous, subterranean revolution in the art of spatial science" (Doel 1999: 2) – it is useful to begin with Lefebvre's seminal meditations on "The Production of Space" (Lefebvre 1991 [1974]). "Encompass[ing] a great deal of what," some 40 years later, "has become stock-in-trade in the social sciences" (Löw 2008: 29),[1] Lefebvre's book begins by countering universal categories of space with a threefold ontology, analytically distinguishing between physical, mental, and social space and stressing their simultaneous interrelations (Lefebvre 1991 [1974]: 11 et seq.). Such spatial multiplicity constitutes an active force and is both produced and producing. "The outcome is a vast moment in terms of which space can no longer be looked upon as an 'essence', as an object distinct from the point of view of (or as compared with) 'subjects', as answering to a logic of its own" (Lefebvre 1991 [1974]: 410 et seq.). In what indeed has become a vast theoretical moment, Lefebvre challenged the spatial scholar to think and experience spatiality as assembled from multiple and intertwined spatial trajectories.

By way of an influential epistemological move, Lefebvre suggested exploring the production of space as entailing the conceived (think of the planned disciplinary ordering of a classroom), everyday spatial practice (consider the routine spatial practices of students and teachers), and the lived (imagine temporary appropriations and transformations of what can be done in a classroom). Importantly, these spatialities constantly mingle. Only in this sense can space be studied as multiplicity, made up of heterogeneous and interrelated spatial trajectories, as "a simultaneity of stories-so-far" (Massey 2005: 9), and as always in-the-making as a processual and performative force of stories-to-come. And it is in this sense that the question of space is held to be an eminently political one. As a "sphere of relations, negotiations, practices of engagement, power in all its forms" (Massey 2005: 99), space is not only an outcome of powerful design and emplacement, of discipline and dressage; it also constitutes a sphere of contestation and difference.

Such spatial sensibility is thus attuned to everyday shifts and reconfigurations of spatial trajectories. As Latour wrote, "[w]e should not speak of time, space, and actant but rather of temporalization, spatialization, actantialization (the words are horrible) or more elegantly, of tim*ing*, spac*ing*, act*ing*" (Latour 2005: 178). From this perspective, the spatiality of business schools cannot be separated from, but is an effect of the heterogeneous everyday performances of their socio-material relations of spacing. Classrooms, for instance, are enacted in various ways that rely on narratives, daily routines, embodied practices, affects, perceptions, and imaginations as much as on the very physical boundaries and objects.

Although Lefebvre already paid close attention to the human body as a "yardstick of spatial practice" (Lefebvre 1991 [1974]: 54), more recent conceptual developments, sometimes grouped under the label of "non-representational theory" (Anderson and Harrison 2010; Thrift 2007), have more thoroughly embraced the "spatial swirl of affects" (Thrift 2006: 143). Broadly put, affects denote relations and intensities at work in all kinds of human and non-human bodies (Seyfert 2012). Confounding subject–object distinctions, they are grasped as impersonal forces that take hold of and condition what human bodies can perceive, feel, and do

(Massumi 2002). They "prefigure encounters, [. . .] set up encounters, and [. . .] have to be worked on in these encounters" (Thrift 2000: 219). It follows that human bodies are seen not as preformed entities but as an outcome of, and the setting for, a play of connections and forces, a "volatile combination of flesh, fluids, organs, skeletal structure and dreams, desires, ideas, social conventions and habits" (Latham *et al.* 2009: 108). In this sense, embodiments, moods, and feelings become fragile effects and amplifiers of the production of space. Moreover, spatial practices are not reduced to human agents but seen as material–relational bundles in which all sorts of stuff is actively participating. "Space is therefore constitutive in the strongest possible sense and it is not a misuse of a term to call it performative" (Thrift 2003: 2023).

## Atmospherics

> Is there anyone who has not, at least once, walked into a room and "felt the atmosphere"?
>
> *Brennan 2004: 1*

Arguably, this turn to spaces with a temper – to the affective constitution of space and to space as a radiating affect – paves the way for an understanding of spatial atmospherics (Anderson 2009, 2014) and thus for our attempt to outline a pedagogy of atmospheres. The notion of atmospheres occupies an increasingly busy place in the contemporary landscape of the humanities and social sciences (Heibach 2012), reflecting a more general aestheticization of the social that is marked by a heightened attention to the design and aesthetic modulation of sensory environments (Böhme 1995; Reckwitz 2012). For instance, in anthropological as well as affect-based thinking, the atmospheric has been linked to the study of everyday life as made up of atmospheric scenes one walks into, senses, and responds to (Brennan 2004; Stewart 2011). In media theory, the notion of "atmospheric media" denotes the effects of today's intelligent environments or ambient technologies, that is the human body's constant connection to imperceptible digital information flows and technical micro-agents (Bachmann and Beyes 2013; Hansen 2012). In an earlier attempt to relate the atmospheric to education, Bollnow (1964) reflected on "the pedagogical atmosphere" (*Die pädagogische Atmosphäre*) in order to obtain an understanding of teaching as relational "mood production" (our term) between students and teachers. More recently, Reckwitz (2012: 254) has stressed that atmospheres offer a "rich potential for an analysis of affects" in general, and noted how "atmospheres are an integral part of [. . .] educational practices with their classrooms and libraries."

How can the atmospheric be apprehended? According to the German neo-phenomenological philosopher Hermann Schmitz (1969), atmospheres resemble moods (*Stimmungen*) that are spatially discharged. Atmospheres constitute "half-things" and "tuned spaces" (*gestimmte Räume*), which are pre-subjective and yet experienced through the "felt body" (*Leib*). Although Schmitz focuses on how atmospheres are experienced and "work" on subjective experience, we can turn to the writings of philosophers Gernot Böhme and Peter Sloterdijk – both of them readers of Schmitz – to shift emphasis to the production and modulation of atmospheres. Moving from Schmitz's phenomenological focus on the experiencing subject to the "a-subjective" and "a-objective" dimensions of atmospheres, Böhme (1993) described the atmospheric as an in-between and intermediary phenomenon that was predicated on the co-presence of objects, all sorts of materialities, and subjects floating between them. Atmospheres emanate from things and yet they aren't the properties of things (hence Schmitz's notion of "half-things," whilst Böhme speaks of "the ecstasies of things"); they resonate with human bodies and provoke moods and yet are not grounded in human actors' sensory apparatuses. Thus, atmospheres become a profoundly social "half-thing." Like Böhme, Sloterdijk (2004a) extended the idea of atmospheres to the socio-political sphere. For instance, he reflected on the design of products and organizational atmospheres as they are modulated in shopping malls or convention centers, their physical architectures as well as their smells, lights, colors, and sounds (see Beyes 2014 and Borch 2010 for attempts to relate this kind of atmospheric thinking to organizational analysis).

As our brief tour through contemporary approaches to atmospheres indicates, the term "spatial atmospherics" amounts to a pleonasm: the emergence and experience of atmospheres is tied to the production of space, and spaces are invariably atmospheric. As Böhme succinctly put it, "atmospheres are spaces with a mood, or emotionally felt spaces" (Böhme *et al.* 2014: 96). Importantly, the notion of atmospheres reflects the multiplicity of spacing. It requires thinking of the coming-together of all sorts of spatial trajectories that assemble sound, light, colors, smell, objects, technologies, architecture, bodies, and embodied practices in specific ways. Exploring the atmospheric thus offers a response to the question of "how to attend to collective affects that are not reducible to the individual bodies that they emerge from" (Anderson 2009: 80). For the purpose of our chapter, educational atmospheres can be grasped as an in-between phenomenon that is both a-objective and a-subjective, whilst emanating from, as well as affecting, the objects and bodies involved in spaces of teaching. Irreducible to subjective state of minds, the atmospheric lends itself to analyses of the complex interplay between teaching environments and the way in which students and faculty experience and act upon them.

Although some work in critical pedagogy has responded to Soja's (2004: ix) demand to take recent spatial theorizing seriously in order to "ignite a radical reconfiguration of [. . .] education theory" (for example, Gulson and Symes 2007; Kitchens 2009), to our knowledge research on management education has so far largely kept away from the "spatial turn" in general and atmospheric analysis in particular (Beyes and Michels 2011; Edenius and Yakhlef 2007). However, the formation of business school graduates is obviously as much a situated process of spatial and atmospheric becoming as it is a cognitive exercise. Such is the guiding assumption of a pedagogy of atmospheres: any intellectual development is entangled with embodied habits as well as interruptions and reconfigurations of ways of dwelling in and appropriating specific environments.

## Snapshots from management education

After the conceptual considerations, we will now turn to the more concrete question of what forms of learning we can invent or experiment with in order to "bring space in" (Kornberger and Clegg 2004). As has been pointed out with regard to organizational analysis, an affective and atmospheric understanding of space calls for a performative notion of research itself, which contributes to and intervenes in spatial settings in order to apprehend their relational configuration and their openness to transformation (Beyes and Steyaert 2012). In this sense our empirical narratives present exemplary interventions by way of two specific courses and a larger-scale, experimental teaching project offered at a Swiss business university. As such, they are limited to situational contexts in their moments of realization and the spatial atmospherics thus unleashed, leaving aside other atmospheric forces that are part of the daily life of the institution (some of which have been touched upon in the introductory vignette). Importantly, our examples stem from a "contextual" study programme that is designed to integrate the humanities and social sciences into management education and its specific "core" programs (see Eberle and Metelmann, this volume). The three courses are dedicated to the nexus of space and organizational life, addressing the topics of city of the future, architecture and organization, and cities and creativity, respectively. As teachers, our backgrounds are in organizational sociology and architecture. The two courses we discuss are regularly offered as electives; the large-scale teaching project was a one-off in the form of the mandatory "freshmen week" for all incoming students (Beyes *et al.* 2006).

What has guided our choice of examples is this chapter's aim to bring a humanities- and social theory-based understanding into business school education, namely spatial atmospherics. This entails a focus on how the atmospheric constitution of learning and teaching can become apparent and can be changed. However, we will also indicate that our matter of concern has reverberations for the students' and our understanding of organization and management. At the risk of oversimplification, we distinguish between three atmospheric practices: first, *bringing in* other, perhaps unconventional, "teaching material"; second, *playing with* the composition and order of existing elements; and third, *leaving* the spaces of the classroom and turning urban atmospheres into the very material of education. Although basing the discussion of each practice on one example, it should be noted in advance that the following courses in some way or other enact all three "spatial tactics." Moreover, the site-specificity of atmospheres and their respective spatial heterogeneities preclude didactical blueprints, as well as straightforward translations to other contexts.[2]

## *Bringing in . . . an abstract wooden structure*

Our first example comes from a large-scale teaching project on imaginations of the city of the future that we have discussed in more detail elsewhere (Beyes *et al.* 2006; Beyes and Michels 2011). It brought together a whole class of first-year students of a business university and confronted them with the quite monstrous task to conceive of and design a city of the future in the space of a week. Notably, it entailed a strange wooden artifact, the so-called "structure," designed by the architect Daniel Libeskind and built by a local Swiss carpenter. Part work of art, part unusual teaching material, this sculptural object consisted of 2,164 single parts forming 98 towers made up of zigzagging elements, eschewing right angles and ranging from 0.2 to 3.8 meters in height (see Figure 23.1). More a contingent assemblage of divergent (if similar) forms

*Figure 23.1* The "raw" "structure" at the beginning of the teaching project

momentarily held together by a spatial ordering than a semblance of unity, stability, and "wholeness," more "organizational diagram beyond congruence and collage" (Kipnis 2001: 12) than readable signifier or symbolization of urban infrastructure, the "structure" radiated a both orderly and disorderly as well as abstract atmosphere. In other words, the students had to come to terms with and appropriate an artistic framework and its material and discursive connotations.

For the purpose of our chapter, it is relevant to focus on what happened next: the students set out to modify the "structure." Its elements or "towers" served as a point of departure for each of the 70 groups, with each group comprising about 12 students. They were asked to gather and discuss ideas, materials, and narratives of their vision of a future city and then to correspondingly transform first "their" element and second the overall structure into a new, collective assemblage. Supported by artists, architects, and researchers, the students set out to explore not only how a future city could function and what it might entail, but also how it could potentially feel. Not being allowed to seriously alter the respective components, the student groups thus embarked on the quest to visualize their ideas of the city of the future on and with the structure's elements. For this, they used all sorts of materials from wherever they could find them, often from the streets.

In their aesthetic work the groups came up with a multiplicity of working processes and compositions. Although some students enacted careful, restrained collages, as if somewhat overpowered by the strength and symbolism of a piece of art, we saw others dancing around their fragment, mocking it, carelessly placing it on the floor, and going on to other things. To briefly relate a particularly poignant outcome: one group invited a street musician to play his violin next to their fragment during the final public exhibition. Quite blatantly selling the surface of their sculptural element to local companies and displaying their logos, the group generated the funding for the musician's performance. Here, the Libeskind "structure" served as a device for composing an urban atmosphere that draws on and reassembles the everyday aesthetics of urban life. The installation interwove different layers of affective capture: the music and sight of a street musician, the visual marketing tools of advertisements, the event of a public exhibition (see Figure 23.2).

As this example indicates, the final assemblage of partly interconnected elements of a future city resembled a cacophony of forms, narratives, sounds, and colors as the "structure" was morphed into a bizarre meshwork of arrangements and connections. Significantly, these expressions experimentally asked what could be done with and to the structure's elements once they had been wrestled from their prior determination: they could be displaced, reassembled into new atmospheric compositions, and released into multiple affective encounters (Anderson 2014).

More important, therefore, than a representation of spatial multiplicity in its own right, the appropriation and construction process was one of multiple spacings in which – to return to Lefebvre's thinking – the conceived space of architecture mingled with everyday spatial practices of learning and lived experimentations that went beyond what conventional educational practice entails, or what we could ever expect. All of this was, of course, shaped by an aesthetic repertoire of playful learning practices (see Meisiek, Guillet de Monthoux, Barry, and Austin, this volume); however, spatial multiplicity does not exhaust itself in playful or artful learning. The "structure" performed an atmospheric intervention that interfered with the everyday atmospheres of the business university itself, as well as its spatial practices of (classroom) teaching – just as much as it called for further atmospheric interventions through strange materials, colors, and sounds. Indeed, all sorts of atmospheric tensions and contradictions emerged (Beyes and Michels 2011), for example around bringing a renowned architect and a massive wooden

*Figure 23.2* Impression from the final presentation of the students' work

structure into a business university, about the politics of the whole endeavor, about what this signaled to the students and the wider public, about what can and cannot be done in classrooms, what management learning entails, about sending students out into the streets, and so forth. In the midst of clashing spaces with a temper, the teaching project invited its participants to enact "a pedagogy of appropriation" – to borrow Lefebvre's term (1991 [1974]: 205) – to collectively engage with the imagination and production of (urban) atmospheres, to take possession of a work of art, to co-construct the spaces of their learning experience, and to self-organize the aesthetic realization of their visions of a future city.

## *Playing with . . . the setting of the classroom*

Our second example presents the spatial modulation of a bachelor-level course on "architecture and organization." The course introduced four metaphors or paradigms of organization (as machine, as symbol, as political system, and as flux) and reflected on the role of architecture in the context of these four paradigms. Taking the organization of the classroom itself as an example for the course's topic (see also Vince, this volume), the sessions dedicated to the metaphors played with the composition of the classroom and involved the participants in a performance of the respective paradigm. The aim was not only to convey an intellectual understanding of the organizational paradigms but also to literally "spatialize" them: to make space for an embodied experience and co-performance of organization as machine, symbol, political system, and flux.

For each of the four sessions the classroom was composed in an entirely different manner. Obviously the participants prepared specific readings, presentations, and questions for each session. Moreover, before each session the room's tables and chairs were rearranged in a way that allowed for different learning styles to unfold. Although for the first three metaphors (machine, symbol, and political system) the spatial layout and the according teaching formats had been preconceived by the lecturer, for the flux metaphor the classroom was turned into a void or open space in which the participants were invited to invent their own learning styles.

So imagine this: 8:15 in the morning (in Switzerland, one gets up early), a huge clock was projected on the classroom's wall, every second was marked with a ticking sound that continued to echo in the background of the entire session. Tables and chairs had been precisely aligned in neat rows and were provided with a pencil and a questionnaire, producing an examination-style setting. Underneath the clock, the lecturer was seated at a clean desk awaiting the incoming students, neatly shaved and wearing a dark suit. The arriving students were asked to leave their jackets and bags at a provisionally installed wardrobe and to find their places in the alphabetically ordered seating arrangement. Fearful questions about if this would be an unannounced exam were clarified by explaining that the only concern would be the efficient and disciplined unfolding of the four hours to come. Tick-tock. Walking up and down the rows of tables, the teacher explained how the layout of the room serves the purpose of transmitting the maximum amount of knowledge from teacher to students, how questions should be noted down and asked in the assigned time frame at the end of the session, how it was utterly important to stick to the session's tight schedule and how the set of multiple-choice questionnaires had been designed to validate and evaluate the knowledge transfer from top to bottom. Students arriving late were welcomed with the precise announcement of the minutes and seconds of their delay and were asked to quickly find their place in the alphabetical order in the classroom. Of course, there were subversive practices. Giggles filled the air with every arrival of late students, smartphones appeared under the tables and some bags did not stay in their assigned wardrobe place. Smirks appeared on the faces of both students and lecturer, who could not quite hold up the performance, adding affective layers that undermined and helped reflect the seeming efficiency of the learning machine.

The sessions' spatial set-ups changed according to metaphor. After the functionalist setting, the second round took place in a classroom charged with symbolic meaning. For instance, the placing and ordering of the tables assigned students different positions according to their performance in the multiple-choice questionnaires of the first session. In the third session the tables were arranged in a circle so as to promote a discourse of democratic learning and sharing of ideas. The fourth and final session was based on a spatial arrangement where all tables were put together to form an elevated surface on one side of the room, leaving the rest of the space empty, all chairs removed and stacked away. Asked to design their own learning environment, the students brought in mattresses, badminton equipment, and other objects from the adjacent university gym (see Figure 23.3). Some left the seminar room to explore other spaces. In groups they gathered some of the teaching materials (texts, images, DVDs) and defined their own spaces of learning. For example, one group projected images from the course presentations on the wall, discussing them whilst engaging in a game of badminton. Another group left the seminar room and started to explore the building, reflecting its role for the everyday organization of university life.

Extending the composition of the seminar beyond the selection of texts, slides, case studies, etc., the course design explicitly included the classroom's spatial modulation. Setting the stage for the performance of the four different organizational paradigms allowed for the sensual immersion of the participants into the course's topic and raised awareness for how spaces with a temper shape organization itself and, concretely, the process of education and its power structures. Experiencing different compositions of the classroom therefore allowed for an awareness of how the classroom is predominantly performed and how it potentially could be recomposed into other atmospheres of learning.

*Figure 23.3* Students playing with learning formats in the flux session

## *Leaving the classroom . . . for a walk*

Our third example brings us back to the beginning of this chapter, to the study on university space done by one of our students. It was realized in a course called "Cities and Creativity," which is offered roughly once every two years as an elective to MA students. By now, the course has taken a turn towards what we suggest can be called a pedagogy of atmospheres, in that affect and atmosphere have become not only empirical material but the thematic focus itself (Beyes and Steyaert 2015; Steyaert 2009). For instance, in 2011, 2013, and 2015, the course was specifically dedicated to "affective cartographies" and "affective atmospheres" of the city of Berlin, where we convened with the students for an intensive seminar. The atmospheric constitution of everyday urban space, what it does to urban dwellers, and what they can do with it, became part and parcel of its unfolding. For this, we needed to leave the classroom and venture on to the streets and squares where the students conducted mini-ethnographies of urban affects and everyday urban creativity by immersing themselves in the movements of urban life (see Figure 23.4). As Pyyry (2014: 2; emphasis in original) has argued with reference to the Situationist practice of "dérive," (photo-) walking and hanging out in the city can "open up new *pedagogical spaces of enchantment* by paying attention to experience as it is experienced." The students practiced, among other things, the fieldwork techniques of thick descriptions, serial photographic images, and different kinds of

*Figure 23.4* Students intervening in urban space

mapping in order to document their encounters. The notion of creativity in the course's title not only refers to the everyday production of urban space, its atmospheric organization, and creative contestation or appropriation; it also refers to the students' quasi-ethnographic performances themselves.

In particular, it is practices of walking that usher in a specific sensibility for learning to apprehend spaces with a temper. As Whybrow writes (2010: xviii; emphasis in original), "moving in and around or *between* the spaces of the city emerges as a possible paradigm for interdisciplinary knowing, for the way in which we may come to know and be transformed by a variety of 'unknown things'." This kind of "learning on your feet" comprises the arts of straying, drifting, and witnessing (Beyes and Steyaert 2015). As a kind of purposeless wandering about, straying not only holds the promise of detecting new and different places to the ones the students expect to find; it also sharpens the sensibility for the atmospheric constitution of places deemed ordinary or well known; it "allow[s] in the unknown by jolting perceptions of the familiar out of any banalising complacency" (Whybrow 2010: xvii). More interventionist, drifting as psychogeographical practice seeks to provoke unplanned encounters and situations and therefore a more pronounced form of irritation that might engender challenging and alternative sensations, perceptions, and usages of urban space (Sadler 1999). Such atmospheric disturbances and reconfigurations offer different representations of the possibilities of urban life that can lead the more adventurous course participants to enact their own interventions and document their consequences. Finally, the students-in-movement become witnesses of manifold encounters and narratives that quite viscerally affect their bodies and provoke all sorts of emotional and, later, reflective responses. This kind of witnessing, and the way the students deal with and try to make sense of it, makes the course moving in a double sense: as teachers, we are on the move between the respective and transient whereabouts of the student groups, where their moving stories and experiences affect us. Again, spatial multiplicity and spaces with a temper are both moved and moving, a generator of atmospheres and a product of atmospheric forces.

Perhaps more radical than the other two examples, this course turns the notion of spatial atmospherics – how they are organized, modulated, and transformed – into the subject matter itself. The students are asked to realize little urban cartographies of space's atmospheric constitution. Of course, this approach is predicated on an acknowledgement of spatial multiplicity – which is nowhere as apparent as when one moves through the city – and on the assumption that leaving the classroom and going for a walk affords the kind of atmospheric modifications and interferences that make the atmospheric present and perceivable.

## Towards a pedagogy of atmospheres

Relating our conceptual deliberations as presented in the first section of this chapter to these observations, course formats, and educational practices, we can now outline tentatively three aspects of a pedagogy of atmospheres and relate them to the business school context. First, it is attuned to spatial multiplicity; second, it both feeds off and generates, or interferes with, atmospheres; third, it turns spatial multiplicity and the everyday production of spatial atmospherics into the very material of management education.

First, the notion of spatial multiplicity cautions against the well-worn architectural fantasy of designing physical space "for" instrumental effects, as if a certain material set-up of buildings, floors, and seminar rooms would in itself suffice to foster desired learning habits: the docile and disciplined student tied to her or his desk, the creative student unleashed through playful environments. If anything, Lefebvre's spatial "triad" of conceived, perceived, and lived space should act as an antidote to narratives of "function follows form." Although the conceived architecture of business school campuses and buildings might set the scene for specific ways of learning, its everyday interplay with the perceived and lived spaces of education engenders contrasts and tensions – in short, spatial multiplicity. In atmospheric terms, the corridors, classrooms, libraries, foyers, cafeterias, and administrative offices are spaces with a temper, co-constituted by the mundane and transient affective encounters that take place. The effects and affects that emerge from these encounters are inherently open-ended and multiple – even if in the everyday routines of university life these encounters become patterned and repetitive – and re-enact, if not identical then at least similar, affective atmospheres.

In this sense, the spatial production of management learning and the situational atmospheres of education can intervene in, collide with, and temporarily transform the spaces of the business school. We focused on how practices of "bringing in," "playing with," and "leaving the classroom" interrupt spatial routines. Bringing in a strange sculptural object, reshuffling the spatial set-up of the classroom, or leaving it behind and venturing into the city are ways of prizing open the repetitive, often rigid spatialities of the business school. Importantly, therefore, the attunement to spatial multiplicity opens up our forms and practices of education to their atmospheric embeddedness and charge. A pedagogy of atmosphere therefore entails an "atmospheric politics" (Sloterdijk 2004b) that is aware of how spaces are conditioned, tuned, and tempered and that enables or fosters the emergence of differently tempered spaces in relation to the conceived spaces and everyday spatial practices of the business school. Quite simply, a pedagogy of atmospheres acknowledges, reckons with, and tries to exacerbate a business school's spatial multiplicity.

Second, upon entering a seminar room – or maybe already in anticipation of entering it – students and teachers are drawn into a specific mood, a way of sensually and physically relating to one another, to their spatial surroundings as well as to the seminar's topic. Obviously this can differ from seminar to seminar, from session to session, from location to location, from body to body. As our examples show, bringing in unconventional objects, playing with the composition of objects at hand, and leaving the classroom for other spaces of learning can constitute interventions that allow for the emergence of different and, to some extent, unpredictable affective resonances, for the redistribution of what can be sensed and therefore acted upon. It is precisely this open-endedness that can contribute to learning experiences that are more alive and more embodied. A pedagogy of atmospheres therefore asks how educational practice reproduces or interferes with the situational atmospheres of teaching and learning. It tries to work on and with these spatial atmospherics, for example by irritating or changing predominant and customary ways of doing education, by rearranging its components, bringing in other objects, or exploring other spaces than the assigned classrooms and lecture halls. In atmospheric analysis as well as pedagogy, attention is directed at those "actants" that "interrupt, modify, interfere, interest" other actants (Latour 2005: 178). It is interruptions of atmospheric conditions that make present everyday spatial multiplicity and allow for their temporary and uncertain transformation.

Third, a pedagogy of atmospheres, as envisaged here, therefore turns to the multiple spatialities and spaces with a temper as "objects" or "matterings" of management education. In this sense, management education is as much about conveying specific forms of knowing as it is about sensitizing for or initiating resonances with the various components that shape the spatialities of organizational life. After all, today's urban and organizational habitats are ever more susceptible to atmospheric modulation and atmospheric politics (Amin and Thrift 2013; Sloterdijk 2004b), and students of management and organization need to be confronted with such processes of "atmospheric management" and its subtle forms of power (Borch 2010); a pedagogy of atmospheres has "the task of making this broad range of aesthetic reality transparent and articulatable" (Böhme 1993: 125). As Vince shows (2010, this volume), the spatial organization of the classroom is tightly interwoven with the affective dynamics of learning and the politics of organizing, with power relations inside and outside management education. In our examples of "Architecture and Organization" and "Cities and Creativity," such experiences are explicitly provoked and reflected upon. The former explores the various paradigms of organizing the classroom and their affective layers; the latter directly thematizes the atmospheric constitution of urban spaces, their modulations, and their creative potentials.[3]

As our vignettes perhaps indicate, we believe that this is a critical endeavor in a double sense. For one, it seems timely – even urgent – to study the pervasive modulation of atmospheres that marks the organization of the social. For the other, a pedagogy of atmospheres can engage with what could be called a minor politics of education. Such a politics of education would allow for and reflect upon the spatial multiplicity of its own performance, turning the classroom into a space – or leaving it for alternative spaces – in which established modes of teaching and learning are altered and alternative forms of organizing may emerge. Working with and on a sculptural structure, playing with the organization of the classroom, or exploring and intervening into the atmospheric compositions of urban life are possible ways of opening up educational spaces and reflecting upon alternative ways of organizing and their specific affective dynamics.[4]

## Slogans for the atmospheric educator

Our examples are specifically situated at the interface between organization studies, architecture, and urban studies, as well as in a – perhaps comparably well-tempered – business university context, which not only allows for but explicitly invites scholars of the humanities and social sciences to bring their concerns, concepts, and methods to management education. However, we would like to suggest that in the wake of (re)introducing the humanities and arts into business schools' curricula and the growing interest in the very material, aesthetic, and affective conditions of learning, a pedagogy of atmospheres can provide further stimulations for experimenting with the spatialities of management education and also a critical reflexivity about how such experiments relate to the spaces of the business school.

How can we broaden our considerations towards implications for the practice of management education that is invariably situated and context-specific? Again, based on our experience and our examples, the contours of a pedagogy of atmospheres can be supplemented with three tactical slogans or "lessons" for the atmospheric schoolmaster, to paraphrase Rancière's *The Ignorant Schoolmaster* (1991), with whom a pedagogy of atmosphere would share the impetus of a teacherly ignorance in terms of not knowing in advance where the teaching process will lead (see Huault and Perret, this volume). Who knows what spacing can do and what atmospheres of management education can become?

First, *enable self-reflexive engagements with the spaces of the business school.* Consider once again the student's explorative study with which we began. It presents an example of problematizing "inside" perceptions of a particular business university. By applying fairly inventive methods to apprehend spatial multiplicity, the project demonstrates how the physical spaces of the business school are entangled with different spatial stories, routines, affects, and experiences, and how they are thus enacted in complex and contradictory ways. Although our examples are framed as educational initiatives on space, the city, and architecture, such explorations of spatial multiplicity lend themselves to other areas of management education, as the course on organizational metaphors suggests. For example, the Lefebvrian distinction of conceived, perceived, and lived space offers students a heuristics to inquire into the everyday complexity and contradictions of organization that play out in, and produce, organizational space – from the managerial design and dressage of atmospheres to the embodied routines of organizational life to playful or resistant appropriations of space or spatial inventions of alternative forms of organizing.

Second, *undo everyday spatial routines of the business school.* This harks back to the large-scale experimental educational project on the city of the future. One of the most striking characteristics of the event was its atmospheric inventiveness, the way the spatial practices of regular university life were (temporally) reconfigured. It seemed to be the aesthetic objects and techniques of learning, further provoked by the presence of architects and artists, which messed with usual business university routines, leading to struggles around the production of educational space and the emergence of imaginative, "lived" spaces through the students' work. Again, we think that such undoing of spatial routines is not predicated on teaching theories of spatial atmospherics – consider studio-based education and its aesthetic props and processes that are put to use in all sorts of management or entrepreneurship modules (Barry and Meisiek 2015; Meisiek, Guillet de Monthoux, Barry, and Austin, this volume).

Third, *leave the spaces of the business school for everyday life.* We are simply very fond of thematizing the city and thus the multiplicity of urban space in our teaching activities on the ordering and disordering of space. Leaving classrooms and campus, we ask students to conduct mini- or quasi-ethnographies of urban spaces and their everyday meshworks of buildings, streets, and sidewalks, and also objects, narratives, images, and imaginations, as well as atmospheric "swirls." Students-as-researchers are thus confronted with, or rather involved in, the constitution and effects of the urban atmospheres; they learn (or so we hope) "by being affected by the intensities, connections and blockages in everyday interactions and practices of urban living" (Steyaert 2009). These affects are not tied to thematizing the urban itself. As platforms of organizing, cities and urban atmospheres are sites for many aspects of management education, from social entrepreneurship (see Barinaga, this volume) to critical inquiries into how contemporary marketing practices and spaces of consumption rely on atmospheric modulations of sense experience, to give just two examples.

## Conclusion: an angle of departure

This chapter has sought to bring the concept and the experience of spatial atmospherics to the question of what the humanities and social sciences can do to management education. To counter what has been diagnosed as a prevailing "pedagogy of placelessness" in higher education (Kitchens 2009: 240), we presented and connected recent spatial and atmospheric thinking based on a performative understanding of space or spacing. Its notions of multiplicity (the co-presence of difference), relationality (the interconnectedness of spatial trajectories), and affect (pre-subjective forces that collide with human bodies, provoking sensations) imply that "an atmosphere is not an inert context but a force field in which people find themselves" (Stewart 2011: 452) – and that there is invariably an excess of space that exceeds the educator's gaze and discourse. What is called for is therefore a more critical and open stance towards what the physical spaces of management learning are designed to accomplish. Some spatial designs might be more conducive to creativity, innovation, and entrepreneurship than others. Provocatively put, however, creativity emerges either outside the conceived spaces of creativity or in tension with these spaces: in the ways that they are appropriated and transformed.

If universities potentially constitute heterotopias *par excellence*, as Sloterdijk (2008) has argued, and are thus potential reservoirs of imagination, then an understanding of space as spacing implies the need for an experimental way of relating to it. To be playful and daring in the performance of business school spaces allows for exploring other ways of assembling them and to reflect on possible alternatives of enacting them. This relates to processes of teaching and learning and the way we bring "space in the making" into the locations and practices of management education. A pedagogy of atmospheres, as outlined here, appreciates and works with this kind of spatial sensibility. It is attuned to spatial multiplicity and relationality; it experiments with atmospheres of learning; and it turns spatial atmospherics into the "object" of education. We formulated three tactical slogans to adumbrate the implications for management education: enable self-reflexive engagements with the spaces of the business school; undo its everyday spatial routines; and leave its spaces for everyday life.

And yet so much depends on the feel of an atmosphere and the angle of arrival, to return to the introductory quote taken from Kathleen Stewart (2010: 340). Our "lessons" are contingent on and limited by our own experiences of and modest interventions on the spaces of a business university. We cannot know what a pedagogy of atmosphere might do to other contexts and spaces of management education. What we can do, however, and what this chapter has tried to elucidate, is to recommend and encourage the everyday spatial reconfiguration of what can be sensed, thought, and done in business school settings, of how learning processes unfold *atmospherically*. As an angle of departure, we end on the call to spatially intervene in the perhaps particularly ambivalent conditions of the business school as an institution of higher learning. But then, quite possibly here more than anywhere else, there is a need for critical and creative practices of education that are guided by the notion of spatial atmospherics: to embed ourselves in; face; help resonate; and add to the relational multiplicity and affective openness of space.

## Notes

1 Lefebvre's theory of the social production of space has also become a well-established point of reference for studies of organizational space (for example, Beyes and Steyaert 2012; Wasserman and Frenkel 2011; Zhang and Spicer 2014), if not in the narrower literature on management education.
2 Indeed, our experience that some of this cannot be frictionlessly translated from one university site to another in continental Europe is a timely reminder that the so-called Bologna Process is also a spatial trajectory, enabling or disabling certain spatial configurations. That it seems to be rather far off the mark

of harmonizing university education in the EU is an indicator that the desired European Higher Education Area (EHEA) resembles a complex institutional landscape of spatial multiplicity.

3 To some degree, all three examples show aspects of what Middleton (2014: 179), drawing upon Lefebvre, identifies as the four principles of pedagogy of appropriation: first, self-management of learning; second, students and teachers are mutually engaged in the critique of everyday life; third, pedagogy centers on contradictions and moments that render critique possible; and fourth, critique can be encouraged through engagement with the arts and through doing spatial histories.

4 We are aware that the practices offered here could be inscribed in a more general valorization of the expressive, the creative, and the experimental that marks contemporary capitalism and the shaping of entrepreneurial subjects. They can correspondingly be classified as relevant and useful "for" management education and are therefore prone to be corrupted into the logic of business that shapes the ordering of the business school (see Parker, this volume). However, we believe there is a need to "work with this emerging spatial grain, in the full understanding that it is both a part of a series of means of opening up new opportunities for the exercise of power and profit *and* a new palette of possibilities" (Thrift 2007: 23; emphasis in original).

## References


Amin, A. and Thrift, N. (2013) *Arts of the Political: New Openings for the Left.* Durham, NC: Duke University Press.

Anderson, B. (2009) 'Affective atmospheres', *Emotion, Space and Society*, 2(2), 77–81.

Anderson, B. (2014) *Encountering Affect: Capacities, Apparatuses, Conditions.* Farnham, UK: Ashgate.

Anderson, B. and Harrison, P. (2010) *Taking-place: Non-Representational Theories and Geography.* Farnham, UK: Ashgate.

Bachmann, G. and Beyes, T. (2013) 'Media atmospheres: remediating sociality/Medien-Atmosphären: Zur Remediation von Sozialität'. *In:* M. Doulis and P. Ott (eds.) *Remediate: At the Borders of Film, Internet and Archives/An den Rändern von Film, Netz und Archiv.* Munich, Germany: Wilhelm Fink, pp. 131–52.

Barry, D. and Meisiek, S. (2015) 'Discovering the business studio', *Journal of Management Education*, 39(1), 153–75.

Beyes, T. (2014) 'Peter Sloterdijk'. *In:* R. Holt, J. Helin, T. Hernes and D. Hjorth (eds.) *The Oxford Handbook of Process Philosophy and Organization Studies.* Oxford: Oxford University Press, pp. 549–84.

Beyes, T. and Michels, C. (2011) 'The production of educational space: heterotopia and the business university', *Management Learning*, 42(5), 521–36.

Beyes, T. and Michels, C. (2014) 'Performing university space: multiplicity, relationality, affect'. *In:* P. Temple (ed.) *The Physical University: Contours of Space and Place in Higher Education.* Abingdon, UK: Routledge, pp. 15–33.

Beyes, T. and Steyaert, C. (2012) 'Spacing organization: non-representational theory and performing organizational space', *Organization*, 19(1), 45–61.

Beyes, T. and Steyaert, C. (2015) 'Der Sinn der Lehre: Ethnographie, Affekt, sensemaking'. *In:* C. Maeder, A. Brosziewski and J. Nentwich (eds.) *Vom Sinn der Soziologie.* Konstanz, Germany: UVK, pp. 197–211.

Beyes, T., Keller, H., Libeskind, D. and Spoun, S. (eds.) (2006) *Die Stadt als Perspektive. Zur Konstruktion urbaner Räume.* Ostfildern, Germany: Hatje Cantz.

Böhme, G. (1993) 'Atmosphere as the fundamental concept of a new aesthetics', *Thesis Eleven*, 36, 113–26.

Böhme, G. (1995) *Atmosphäre. Essays zur neuen Ästhetik.* Frankfurt a.M., Germany: Suhrkamp.

Böhme, G., Borch, C., Eliasson, O. and Pallasmaa, J. (2014) 'The notion of atmospheres'. *In:* C. Borch (ed.) *Architectural Atmospheres: On the Experience and Politics of Architecture.* Basel, Switzerland: Birkhäuser, pp. 90–107.

Bollnow, O.F. (1964) *Die pädagogische Atmosphäre. Untersuchungen über die gefühlsmäßigen zwischenmenschlichen Voraussetzungen der Erziehung.* Heidelberg, Germany: Quelle & Meyer.

Borch, C. (2010) 'Organizational atmospheres: foam, affect and architecture', *Organization*, 17(2), 223–41.

Brennan, T. (2004) *The Transmission of Affect.* Ithaca, NY: Cornell University Press.

Doel, M.A. (1999) *Poststructuralist Geographies: The Diabolical Art of Spatial Science.* Lanham, MD: Rowman & Littlefield.

Edenius, M. and Yakhlef, A. (2007) 'Space, vision and organizational learning: the interplay of incorporating and inscribing practices', *Management Learning*, 38(2), 193–210.

Gulson, K.N. and Symes, C. (eds.) (2007) *Spatial Theories of Education: Policy and Geography Matters.* New York, NY: Routledge.

Hansen, M.B.N. (2012) 'Ubiquitous sensation or the autonomy of the peripheral: towards an atmospheric, impersonal and microtemporal media'. *In:* U. Ekman (ed.) *Throughout: Art and Culture Emerging with Ubiquitous Computing*. Cambridge, MA: MIT Press, pp. 63–88.

Heibach, C. (ed.) (2012) *Atmosphären: Dimensionen eines diffusen Phänomens. Munich*, Germany: Wilhelm Fink.

Katz-Buonincontro, J. (2015) 'Decorative integration or relevant learning? A literature review of studio arts-based management education with recommendations for teaching and research', *Journal of Management Education*, 39(1), 81–115.

Kipnis, J. (2001) 'Preface'. *In:* D. Libeskind (ed.) *The Space of Encounter*. London: Thames & Hudson, pp. 10–13.

Kitchens, J. (2009) 'Situated pedagogy and the Situationist International: countering a pedagogy of placelessness', *Educational Studies*, 45, 240–61.

Kornberger, M. and Clegg, S.R. (2004) 'Bringing space back in: organizing the generative building', *Organization Studies*, 25(7), 1095–114.

Latham, A., McCormack, D.P., McNamara, K. and McNeill, D. (2009) *Key Concepts in Urban Geography*. London: Sage Publications.

Latour, B. (2005) 'Trains of thought. The fifth dimension and its fabrication'. *In:* A.N. Perret-Clermont (ed.) *Thinking Time: A Multidisciplinary Perspective on Time*. Göttingen, Germany: Hogrefe and Hupher, pp. 173–87.

Lefebvre, H. (1991 [1974]) *The Production of Space*. Oxford: Blackwell.

Löw, M. (2008) 'The constitution of space: the structuration of spaces through the simultaneity of effect and perception', *European Journal of Social Theory*, 11(1), 24–49.

Massey, D. (2005) *For Space*. London: Sage Publications.

Massumi, B. (2002) *Parables for the Virtual: Movement, Affect, Sensation*. Durham, NC: Duke University Press.

Middleton, S. (2014) *Henri Lefebvre and Education. Space, History, Theory*. London: Routledge.

Pyyry, N. (2014) 'Learning with the city via enchantment: photo-walks as creative encounters', *Discourse: Studies in the Cultural Politics of Education*, published online, 1–14.

Rancière, J. (1991) *The Ignorant Schoolmaster. Five Lessons in Intellectual Emancipation*. Stanford, CA: Stanford University Press.

Reckwitz, A. (2012) 'Affective spaces: a praxeological outlook', *Rethinking History*, 16(2), 241–58.

Sadler, S. (1999) *The Situationist City*. Cambridge, MA: MIT Press.

Seyfert, R. (2012) 'Beyond personal feelings and collective emotions: toward a theory of social affect', *Theory, Culture and Society*, 29(6), 27–46.

Schmitz, H. (1969) *System der Philosophie, III.2: Der Gefühlsraum*. Bonn, Germany: Bouvier.

Sloterdijk, P. (2004a) *Sphären 3: Schäume (Vol. 3)*. Frankfurt a.M., Germany: Suhrkamp.

Sloterdijk, P. (2004b) 'Atmospheric politics'. *In:* B. Latour and P. Weibel (eds.) *Making Things Public*. Boston, MA: MIT Press, pp. 944–51.

Sloterdijk, P. (2008) 'Die Akademie als Heterotopie'. *In:* M. Jongen (ed.) *Philosophie des Raumes: Standortbestimmungen ästhetischer und politischer Theorie*. Munich, Germany: Wilhelm Fink, pp. 23–32.

Soja, E.W. (2004) 'Preface'. *In:* K.M. Leander and M. Sheehy (eds.) *Spatializing Literary Research and Practice*. New York, NY: Peter Lang, pp. ix–xvi.

Statler, M. and Guillet de Monthoux, P. (2015) 'Humanities and arts in management education: the emerging Carnegie Paradigm', *Journal of Management Education*, 39(1), 3–15.

Stewart, K. (2010) 'Afterword: worlding refrains'. *In:* M. Gregg and G.J. Seigworth (eds.) *The Affect Theory Reader*. Durham, NC: Duke University Press, pp. 339–53.

Stewart, K. (2011) 'Atmospheric attunements', *Environment and Planning D: Society and Space*, 29(3), 445–53.

Steyaert, C. (2009) 'Enacting urban ethnographies of artistic interventions in the entrepreneurial city'. *In:* T. Beyes, A. Deufelhard and S. Krempl (eds.) *Parcitypate: Art and Urban Space*. Sulgen, Switzerland: Niggli, pp. 382–465.

Taylor, S. and Statler, M. (2014) 'Material matters: increasing emotional engagement in learning', *Journal of Management Education*, 38(4), 586–607.

Thrift, N. (2000) 'Afterwords', *Environment and Planning D: Society and Space*, 18(2), 213–55.

Thrift, N. (2003) 'Performance and . . .', *Environment and Planning A*, 35(11), 2019–24.

Thrift, N. (2006) 'Space', *Theory, Culture and Society*, 23(2–3), 139–46.

Thrift, N. (2007) *Non-Representational Theory: Space, Politics, Affect*. London: Routledge.

Vince, R. (2010) 'Anxiety, politics and critical management education', *British Journal of Management*, 21(1), 26–39.

Volkmann, C. and De Cock, C. (2007) 'The Bauhaus and the business school: exploring analogies, resisting imitation', *Management Learning* 38(4), 389–403.

Wasserman, V. and Frenkel, M. (2011) 'Organizational aesthetics: caught between identity regulation and culture jamming', *Organization Science*, 22(2), 503–21.

Whybrow, N. (ed.) (2010) *Performance and the Contemporary City. An Interdisciplinary Reader*. New York, NY: Palgrave Macmillan.

Zhang, Z. and Spicer, A. (2014) '"Leader, you first": the everyday production of hierarchical space in a Chinese bureaucracy', *Human Relations*, 67(6), 739–62.

# 24

# Four voices

## Making a difference with art in management education

*Stefan Meisiek, Pierre Guillet de Monthoux, Daved Barry and Robert D. Austin*

### Introduction

In this chapter, four scholars and teachers write about their practices for altering the classroom and for changing the way that students learn management through engaging with art and aesthetics. Each author describes how he discovered that art forms, materials, works, and practices hold inspiration for teaching management, how they have changed their teaching approach accordingly, and where the journey has taken them so far. Reflections on the practical dos and don'ts of drawing inspiration from the arts accompany the accounts.

This introduction provides a bracket for the four stories, showing where and how they touch upon each other. We then invite the reader to go on a journey through our four stories and to compare it with their own teaching practice and experience. Collectively, the stories represent the breadth of generative links between art and management in the business school classroom. Having said this, we are far from claiming that our four stories cover all possible inspirations and links. They present illustrations of how particular people, interests, and research topics developed into classroom practices. We would be glad if, by placing your story next to ours, we could help you discover your way forward. In this sense, the present chapter is less of a manual and more of a collage of suggestions.

Although the authors have known each other for some 15 years, their classroom practices haven't grown out of a single idea, perspective, or theory. We would probably not even be able to agree on what art is, and yet it is probably no coincidence that all four authors have worked at Copenhagen Business School (CBS) in the Management, Politics, and Philosophy (MPP) department, where the humanities have a legitimate voice in business matters and faculty had the opportunity and freedom to experiment with bringing art and management into a sensible relationship in the classroom. This has attracted faculty appreciative of this freedom and interested in pushing the envelope of business school education. For the five years we stayed together, it allowed us to compare our approaches, teach on each other's courses, learn from one another, and appreciate the differences.

The four inspirations from the arts that we have worked with are form, medium, mirror, and place. Taking inspiration from an art form means to explore how, for example, poetry, literature, graphic novels, theater, choreography, or exhibitions can help to produce management-relevant content that students can appreciate, are drawn into, and learn from. Management content is poured into a form that is more engaging and affords more than one interpretation. The goal is generally to teach for judgment and help students develop practical wisdom through argumentation and discussion. It is an extension of the Harvard case method that runs counter to the recent trend of making cases shorter. Although Harvard Business School (HBS) has developed a number of short cases (seven instead of the usual fifteen pages), Rob Austin took inspiration from other literature forms, wrote case novels, made a graphic novel case, and produced accompanying theater and film material.

Where the art medium instead of its form stands in the foreground, students are invited to practice an art, however amateurishly, to access and understand business problems and develop solutions to them. This goes beyond the common use of artworks to illustrate a concept or theory, for example paintings of great persons might help to understand leadership theory. Questioning whether this is the most powerful way of linking art, business problem, and management theory, Daved Barry developed his concept of analogically mediated inquiry. This entails asking students to make art so as to understand a management topic. Art making is here understood as rigorous research. To ask how to represent a management problem in an art medium means that the students have to understand it not only analytically, but also in its lived, messy, human dimension. It's not scientific research, but a process of inquiry aiming for an understanding that is aesthetically memorable, suggestively rich, and bridges between local problem context and theory. Film, acting, sculpting, making collages, and other media might give access to a more full-spectrum view of a management problem.

Where art is a mirror of business theory and practices, students are taken to museums, performances, and events that have in their nature apparently nothing to do with business. Looking at the artist, the art world, and the art management necessary to produce and present the artwork, however, students find a mirror to the management practices in common organizations. Pierre Guillet de Monthoux has taken students with him to the art world and back to the management classroom for years, and he describes many analogies and inspiring encounters where management learned from avant-garde arts management and production.

Finally, a source of inspiration can also be an artist's studio as a place for inquiry and learning. The previous three approaches might well find their place in such a studio, and it places the student in the middle to work in an experiential, problem-based, and processual way, instead of listening to a lecture or being in a case discussion. Stefan Meisiek founded, developed, and operated the Studio at CBS and had ample opportunity to experiment with a pedagogy that takes its inspiration from art, design, and the crafts.

But enough of summarizing the links between art and management; without further ado, let's come to the four stories.

## Rob Austin: form

I have always loved stories. Having majored in both English and engineering in college, I chose stories over lucrative tech job offers and headed to playwriting grad school at the University of Texas. Although I never finished that program, there theater historian Oscar Brockett guided me through Aristotle's *Poetics*, stirring my already intense interest in plot. When later I took up a PhD in Management and Decision Sciences at Carnegie Mellon, Herb Simon further stoked these interests. My final project in his course was a think-aloud protocol analysis (Ericsson and Simon 1980) of the cognitive processing involved in watching a poker scene in the 1987 David Mamet film *House of Games*. The scene includes a classic plot twist of exactly the sort that Aristotle described in *Poetics*. Simon encouraged me to keep working on this.

Fast-forward to the late 1990s when I'd become a professor at HBS. I learned the school's famous "case method" and immersed myself in stories in a new (to me) literary form – the business school case. On a whim, I reached out to my former theater professor at Swarthmore, Lee Devin, and began a collaborative relationship that would last years. Lee was a former Brockett student and a big Aristotle fan, because he had been taught it by Kenneth Telford. Lee said that Telford argued that an alternative title for *Poetics* might well be *On the Productive Sciences*, suggesting that Aristotle intended his work to be relevant beyond plays and playwriting, and that it might be very relevant to business.

Lee and I wrote a book together, *Artful Making* (Austin and Devin 2003), which won the Elliot Hayes Award given by the Literary Managers and Dramaturgs of the Americas, 'in recognition of exemplary contributions by dramaturgs to the conception, development and production of theater or to educational projects' (Lee was the dramaturg – it was really his award). This business book, it seemed, had earned the respect of a community of practicing artistic storytellers.

With *Artful Making* as a foundation, Lee and I conceived the HBS course called Managing in the Creative Economy. At this point, Shannon O'Donnell (now Shannon Hessel), who had been a director at the highly regarded People's Light and Theater in the Philadelphia area, joined our team. Shannon and I spent the 2005–6 academic year at CBS, which allowed us to write several cases on Danish design for the course. Case subjects included design firms, film companies, visual artists, string quartets, jazz ensembles, and creative teams within aerospace firms.

We offered the new course at Harvard in the spring of 2007 as one of a pair of "half-courses" (the other half was offered by Teresa Amabile). Sixty-plus MBAs signed up for the course, where they participated in exercises led by the Danish conductor Peter Hanke, learned about collaboration from Paul Robertson of the Medici String Quartet, and discussed the innovative ways of Miles Davis with jazz drummer, business consultant, and case co-author, Carl Størmer. The course would have run again at Harvard had I not opted to move to CBS in the fall of 2007. The course has run every year since then at CBS, always drawing substantial numbers of students.

Until about 2008, we worked with cases in mostly conventional formats, focused on artful and creative subjects. Beginning that year, however, we began to play with the form itself. Jeremy Short, now with the University of Oklahoma, and I, together with a number of visual artists, created the first HBS case in a graphic novel format, *iPremier: Denial of Service Attack (Graphic Novel Version)* (Austin and Short 2009).

Other experiments with the case form followed. I had long worked with Harvard professor Richard ("Dick") Nolan on an executive program for information technology (IT) managers. Dick and I started on a book project, seeking to capture the content that we had developed for the IT program. But we lost momentum. After two false starts, we decided to try doing it in an unusual way: we would write a collection of fictional cases about the same company, based on real events, and put them together to make our business book. In essence, we would write a "business novel."

We weren't the first to try this, of course. Goldratt and Cox (1984) succeeded famously with *The Goal*, a novel about operations management that focused on the work and life difficulties of a factory manager. We conceived our novel similarly, around the story of Jim Barton, a non-technical manager who, much to his chagrin, is chosen to become the Chief Information Officer (CIO) of a financial service firm, partly because he has been an outspoken critic of the company's IT department. We had more success with this approach than on our earlier attempts, but still we did not gain full momentum until we invited Shannon into this work.

By this time she had become a CBS doctoral student, and she brought to our team what turned out to be a big idea: what if, she suggested, we applied Joseph Campbell's (1949) "hero's journey," aka "the monomyth," to enhance our narrative and make it more engaging? The monomyth, in which a reluctant hero makes a difficult journey and overcomes obstacles to become transformed, is an archetype for many of the world's most compelling stories from Moses in Exodus, to *Star Wars* and *The Matrix*. Shannon had used this approach in the past as a theater director.

With Shannon onboard, we remade our story and the project came together. We prototyped the teaching approach at the University of Washington, CBS, and Harvard. It worked well, and in 2009 we published *The Adventures of an IT Leader* (Austin *et al.* 2009a). The book invites readers to "walk in the shoes" of a new CIO, complete with teaching notes for each chapter. The publisher, Harvard Business Press, provided budget to commission artist Asaf Hanuka to create Japanese anime-inspired illustrations within the book.

As we detailed (Austin *et al.* 2009b), the pedagogical advantages of this approach were twofold. First, the format is engaging and facilitates a highly participative and discussion-based learning process. Second, the extended narrative format allowed us to develop management frameworks cumulatively, returning to earlier points as later developments in the story arose. Pedagogically speaking, cases access theoretical content inductively, calling on students to extract generalizations ("theories") from specific accounts (cases). Our extended narrative worked the same way, but with continuity that allowed development of a grander, more extended, and nuanced framework. In effect, the approach combines the engagement advantages of a case-based approach with the more cumulative framework advantages more typical of lecture-based approaches.

In the classroom, whether with undergrads, grads, or executives, the approach worked splendidly. In group discussions, we posed some of the key questions raised by each chapter and facilitated a discussion that captured learning points on the board. The format fitted well with role playing and small group exercises. We surveyed the students systematically to gauge the benefits of this approach – students noted that the classes built on each other, pushed thinking beyond memorization, seemed applicable and realistic, and were very interesting. Execs said that the course was riveting, true-to-life, and helped them generate their own frameworks and refine their conceptual ideas.

More recently, we have extended these ideas farther as we offered a course called Leadership in 21st Century Organizations at CBS, based on our new book, *Harder Than I Thought* (Austin *et al.* 2012). In *Harder*, a sequel to *Adventures*, Jim Barton takes his first CEO job. Not content, however, with the book form, we conceived a plan that called for Shannon to travel back to her old theater where she worked with the resident company and a video team to create video versions of scenes from the book. The course was based on these "dramatized episodes." We are still evaluating the results of this experiment, but students seemed to like it. In September 2015, we launched a Massively Open Online Course (MOOC) based on these video episodes, the first, as far as we know, story-based MOOC (see Bachmann and Shah, this volume).

## Daved Barry: medium

My arts and management story starts in the 1980s when I worked as Stephen Carroll's teaching assistant in undergraduate management courses at the University of Maryland. He would lecture to the masses and we teaching assistants would take notes for the smaller discussion sections. Besides being a vivid storyteller, Steve had a strong knack for using art to illustrate his points – much of this is illustrated in his 2010 book with Patrick Flood, *The Persuasive Leader* (Carroll and Flood 2010). When the time came for me to develop and teach my own management courses at Syracuse University, I too started using art in illustrative ways. My hope then was to bring some kind of liveliness to what was otherwise pretty dry material. At that time, I naïvely and metonymically equated art with art museum pieces and artistic practice with the mediums used by professional artists. In other words, I thought that being able to play musical instruments was synonymous with producing musical art, that paint and paintings equaled visual art, and so on. I would use clips from movies like *12 Angry Men* and *Wild Strawberries*, paintings such as Picasso's *Guernica* and Edward Hopper's *Nighthawks*, and musical works from my students' collections to look at things like group decision making, leadership, conflict, and organizational dynamics.

Although art-as-illustration made my courses more provocative, it also piqued my curiosity about what might happen if we were to use art processes in more creational ways. Around this time I delved into art therapy, which primarily uses stereotypical art media to change one situation into another more preferred one. I wondered if such methods could play into the general managerial mandate to make things work better. I also wondered whether such methods could change what "better" meant – not just more efficient but more lifeful workplaces. Hence, I started asking my MBA students – particularly the part-timers – to variously draw, sculpt, story, and dramatize their management problems. I think we were all surprised at how simply changing mediums could reveal new and interesting facets of an issue, sometimes giving form to tacit understandings and sometimes catalyzing completely new perspectives. My students were mostly happy to have new eyes, ears, and even noses, and yet I found myself haunted by the suspicion that what I was doing was nothing more art therapy than art (which, in retrospect, it rather was). Although my experiences convinced me that "material matters" – as Steve Taylor and Matt Statler (2013) nicely discuss – it seemed that material considerations had mostly driven out artistic ones.

Over a decade later, I started to rethink all this whilst researching art interventions in Denmark with Stefan Meisiek. He and I drove around the country studying nineteen cases where professional artists had intervened in various companies with the intent of enhancing company innovation. What struck us both was the high variance in artistic approaches, conceptualizations of what constituted art, and artistic quality. We also saw some exceptionally good interventions, ones that had made a big difference because of their artistic merit. To understand art's effects in these studies, we had to go back to what art was in all its many forms. We read extensively, talked to many professional artists, became more deeply acquainted with Howard Becker's (1982) dizzying *Art Worlds*, and with the differences between what art philosopher Stephen Davies (2007) terms "Big A Art" (works that are deemed art by formal art institutions) and "little a art" (typically local works that have artistic properties and/or intent).

All this rubbed off on my teaching. When I had the opportunity to teach a CBS organizational aesthetics course called Beauty and the Business, I decided it was time to bring Big A Art back in. Maybe there was a way that "Big A" Art appreciation and "little a" art practice could be combined. How might I use formal art in both appreciative and practical ways? After talking with some artist friends and educators, I devised a format where students would address live managerial problems through the aesthetics and methods of famous artists living and dead, classical and contemporary – trying to work out how a given artist might frame and address the problem and then coming up with a personalized response using similar aesthetics and concepts. By using multiple artists and traditions (for example, Michelangelo, Picasso, Hockney, Stravinsky, John Cage, Shakespeare, Dostoevsky, Gaudi), I hoped to avoid getting locked into any particular one. The course turned out to be an eye-opener. For the first time, my students seriously asked the question as to what made the art of these people so special. What did they do that "little a" artists do not? And could they (the students) do the same? Art appreciation began to coalesce with artistic problem solving. The students were not only able to understand a bit of how some of the great artworks were created, but started to apply these modes of thinking to more local problems (for example, how to run some of the CBS student organizations).

I took my new perspectives to Lisbon, where I ran Art of Management courses for MBA and MSc students. After a couple of years, I decided to radically challenge my students' tendencies to equate art with stereotypical art materials. I asked one of my MBA classes to create artistic responses to managerial problems, but this time they had to work mostly with at-hand workplace materials – for example, spreadsheets, office layouts, meetings, planning charts, employees, reporting relationships. This proved difficult. The students complained of headaches. I feared for my teaching ratings and had my own share of headaches. However, in the end many of the students managed to come up with art solutions that usefully improved their work, even though they drew upon traditional art materials after all. An example is that of Catarina, who worked for a pharmaceutical company that had, as she put it, lost its inventive spirit in favor of hitting sales targets. She began making copies of Lewis Carroll's White Rabbit running mindlessly with its stopwatch and had the night cleaning crew place them around the workstations and labs – whilst maintaining her anonymity. This was followed up with a big batch of Easter eggs. She managed to hack the company's intranet and anonymously sent out White Rabbit spam mail. This created a furor in the company, until she finally confessed during a weekly management meeting, saying that the company needed to stop being so mindless and rediscover its original purpose. From there, a "let's re-invent ourselves" campaign was started, which in fact worked so well that she was poached by a rival firm.

Today I employ these artful inquiry methods in numerous ways. Recently, I combined multiple material perspectives and aesthetic approaches by asking the class to develop a play that would respond to a challenge set by Kultur Østerbro (an association of cultural institutions in the eastern part of Copenhagen) – namely, to figure out what skills Kultur Østerbro's employees would need in the upcoming decade. I asked the students to form a theater company, replete with two directors. The problem was that no one had any theater training, including me, and so I invited theater-trained guests Mogens Holm (also the director of Kultur Østerbro), Salman Ahmed (an organizational behavior professor who had performed numerous plays), and Claus Springborg (a choreographer with a PhD in management) to help the students conceive and choose between different performance options. Although unpaid, all three graciously put in considerable time and collectively made a striking difference in the learning that happened. In a memorable thirty-minute session, Claus managed to break up the class's month-long "paralysis by analysis" by having them enact performance alternatives within two minutes or less, and evaluating the enactments on their energetic and aesthetic appeal. The "two minute rule" became the foundation of the entire course, ultimately resulting in a powerful performance that Kultur Østerbro employees still use to inform their operations.

To conclude and perhaps advise, I think that learning how to apply art thinking and practices to management is best accomplished with mixes of professional artists, "Big A" artworks, "little a" art processes, materials, and problem sets. Although each helps a bit, it's the combination that leads to the "ahas." How to concoct these mixes is a hard question, however. As soon as "Big A" artworks are used as examples of artistic merit and exemplars of how students might work, students – and especially business students – can start to despair. They may end up feeling that they don't have a chance of being able to make artful projects that anyone would like, let alone ones that could make a difference. Then there's the frequent remark "but we didn't come to business school to think like this," followed by my inevitable reply "if you want to see and do things differently – to make a difference – it's processes like these that can help you get there." Sometimes I wish it were different, that I wouldn't need to spend so much time rationalizing art's worth in the management classroom. I'd like to simply reply, "you did read the course description before you signed up, didn't you?" But maybe a more constructive way for me to think about this is to return to why I originally brought art into my classrooms – because

I personally find it moving and uplifting and that it has a way of bringing life to overly dry and deadening representations of management. Perhaps that's enough after all.

## Pierre Guillet de Monthoux: mirror

For me it began twenty-five years ago when I received my old world professorship at Stockholm University and I decided to invest my academic freedom in combining art with management, much inspired by how technology and science had successfully entered innovation studies.

I hung out with "artists" and "art managers," and I invited museum curators, film producers, theater directors, and orchestra conductors to my management classes to tell their stories about managing creative people and doing art in organizations. What they told my students, I fed into research seminars, where my doctoral students and I began investigating research-based ways to fuse art practice with management. I was on the lookout for theories articulating how art could enlighten management, and the classes and seminars put us on the track of going to aesthetic philosophy for help. We invited international artists like Michelangelo Pistoletto, continental aesthetic philosophers like Wolfgang Welsch or Gernot Böhme, art sociologists such as Nathalie Heinich, and Ole Fogh Kirkeby (2000) from the Danish Centre for Art and Leadership who supported us in emphasizing the continental philosophical connections. Because I worked on an urban campus, I could take students to art fairs, museums, galleries, theaters, and other venues. We explored the backstage of art work and found material and witnesses about how "regular" management resembled art management. We were able to hint at alternatives to the old industrial way of running firms (Austin and Devin 2003). Heritage and culture is okay, but what I was really after were ideas and unexpected inspiration in contemporary art.

Between 1998 and 2004 our group at Stockholm University profited from a generous research grant that produced thirteen PhDs in Art and Management in Sweden (Guillet de Monthoux *et al.* 2007). Later, a generous Finnish grant made a "nomadic university" possible and we traveled to places like the Venice Biennale, Kassel Documenta, and Cittadellarte (Michelangelo Pistoletto's Italian center for socially responsible art). We could escape the classroom routine for intensive three-day excursions to spaces where art and management were both discussed and exhibited (see Michels and Beyes, this volume).

Parallel to this, I teamed up with Antonio Strati (Strati 1999; Strati and Guillet de Monthoux 2002) to launch a series of academic summer schools exploring aesthetics as the missing link between art and management, and soon we had a network of management teachers, many of whom were also part of Daved Barry's Aacorn list, who were interested in experimenting with art in management teaching.

In classrooms, I noted that my students often felt imprisoned in narrow management science paradigms of decision making supported by algorithmic tools and quantitative modeling. When I told them Marcel Duchamp, Pablo Picasso, and Salvador Dali could be seen as super successful entrepreneurs, they liked the idea. And when I added that Freddy Nietzsche, Immo Kant, Gilles Deleuze, and Hans Georg Gadamer might help us understand why Andy Warhol, Ai Wei Wei, or Jeff Koons became such big business artists, my students began tackling real philosophical issues, perhaps without knowing it.

I was surprised at how easy the new artful management medicine went down as soon as my students saw old aesthetic philosophy as a cool way to inject energy into action and to grasp the role of passion and drive and get going on real "Schwung" – my term for the dynamic playful pendulum movement of aesthetics advocated by old German poet Friedrich Schiller (Guillet de Monthoux 2004). I felt particularly that avant-garde art transfigured the classroom discussions about enterprise from dry models to lived intensive experience. Art added flesh and blood to the skeleton of managerial reasoning (Statler and Guillet de Monthoux 2015) – the classroom became a stage for "aesthetic transubstantiation" when I opened the undergrad course by having each student recite excerpts from Friedrich Schiller's summary of Immanuel Kant's "Critique of Judgment" in a solemn voice. That kind of liturgy set a radically different tone in the classroom to that of the banal business PowerPoint presentations. Usually I received spontaneous support from students with artistic inclinations and experiences in conjuring the solemn atmosphere to maintain the delicate classroom-limbo between light playfulness and ridiculous pretentiousness. I particularly recall the impact on some top students who had left the world of classical dance and had turned to management education because of professional injuries. They had first-hand experience of that highly disciplined serious playfulness that I wanted to convey. To run a classroom discussion of enterprise and management using cases and inspiration from art became a way for me to challenge what I feared – the feeling that art would just offer an escape from hard work and that it was just a holiday trip using some new-age fuzzy touchy-feely toys.

My contempt for art instrumentalized as therapeutic consumption could stem from the fact that both my parents had been in business, but both had also been artists and gone through long schooling in music and theater. Yes, art is fun, but it is also hard work and should be respected as such. By trying to catch a glimpse of backstage art work, I used to attempt to convey the seriousness of play. I began collecting a small case archive with artist–managers–leaders to inspire students. One of my favorites is to open a course by showing what I regard as an art-management masterpiece: Wim Wenders' documentary of fashion maker Yoshi Yamamoto, *Notebook on Cities and Clothes*. This movie is an aesthetic documentary on an aesthetic trade starting/starring an entrepreneur–artist–designer. When we watch it, we do it with respect – and I use it, even though I have watched it over and over again, to focus my attention, to try to sink into the screen and rest in it. It has to do with experiencing the beauty of social organization (Ramirez 1991); it has to do with direct connection to the objects – the success of which we want to manage (Devin and Austin 2012); and it is a matter of teaching according to philosopher Susan Langer's (1967) motto: be presentational before you get discursive. It's a kind of "show, shut up and sink in" pedagogy where you present the case and then, quite contrary to case method debates, let it sink in. I usually do this using a kind of "sandwich" method, where I show the case – be it documentary, a visit to an art gallery, a talk with artists – and then, preferably not before the next day, reflect on what we have witnessed from an entrepreneurial or managerial point of view.

Then, and not before, we might turn to Andy Warhol as a consumer researcher (Schroeder 1997), Joseph Beuys for human resource management and strategy (Scharmer 2009), Michelangelo Pistoletto for corporate social responsibility (Guillet de Monthoux 2004), Christo and Jeanne Claude for entrepreneurship (Guillet de Monthoux 2008), Marina Abramovic for leadership (Guillet de Monthoux 2000), and even old Marcel Duchamp for design and marketing (Björkman 1998). For such an aesthetic reflection, there are many models and an increasing number of management studies using art. But beware, do not start with that and keep up the tension between the presentations and the discourse. If it works, the aesthetic discussions will run parallel to watching, listening, and touching art – the sensuous experiences. If it works, there will be tension in between – and then you get classroom Schwung! Good luck!

## Stefan Meisiek: place

It happened one day that I sat in Daved Barry's kitchen in Portugal – a bottle of inky red wine on the table and Daved cooking his emblematic coq-au-vin. We talked, as we often did those days, about what would be needed to make art and management really meet at a business school. The business school that we were working for at that time, Nova School of Business and Economics (Nova SBE), was proud of its finance and economics heritage, and our courses complemented its overall profile in terms of creativity, innovation, and general "otherness." At times we felt like the resident weirdoes, and we thought that the finance and economics core could do well with an infusion of creative spirit. Little by little we discovered that our colleagues had interests that corresponded with this. A Harvard-trained economist wrote novels, the strategy professor played in a jazz band, the finance professor recited poetry, and the dean collected art. But how could the appreciated and tangentially invited become relevant?

Daved asked me that day, "If you could have anything you wanted, what would you have and do with it?" After some hesitation, I said: "A business studio." I wanted a place that would naturally afford the way we wanted to work with students: egalitarian, developmental, visual–haptic, and driven also by curiosity, not only curriculum; a place and process that would complement lectures or case discussions; where teacher and students could meet face-to-face for co-inquiry, conversation, artful approaches, and develop intellectually rich solutions to pernicious business problems.

We were looking for a bridge between academic knowledge and practice. The inspiration came from the art, architecture, design, and craft schools that we had visited, and where studio education was so natural that hardly anybody thought about it. To make it fit to a business school with a science-driven, rather than a vocation-driven curriculum, we had to figure out how academic knowledge and practice could mutually benefit each other whilst students worked on their projects. Up until then, we had created a number of pop-up studios by converting ordinary classrooms into temporary studio spaces; however, janitors, cleaning staff, colleagues, and the study administration eyed our activities skeptically, suspecting us of rendering the classrooms useless for their habitual uses. Architectural limitations such as tables bolted to the ground, terraced rooms, bad lighting, or unusable wall space added to our woes. If we were to foster a different kind of management education, it would have to happen in a dedicated space – a space inviting inquiry, workflow, conversations, and reflection (Barry and Meisiek 2015).

Over the previous decade, design-thinking courses were sprouting up in numerous business schools across the world. In some schools, like Stanford, Rotman, or Sauder, there are even dedicated spaces for it. These spaces were really nice, and the courses that took place there were engaging and energizing, but the associated rhetoric was often dismissive of scientific endeavor, work, and theory. Most business schools, however, are located inside universities, and their promotion system is based on academic titles, output, and research funding. Rather than taking an antagonistic position, studio education – when migrating from art, design, and crafts schools to business schools – should be using and enhancing what is already there.

We secured 70,000 Euros in funding for a studio at Nova SBE, but space was scarce and the concept untested. A year later, Daved and I joined CBS, and through a number of fortuitous accidents I found myself in charge of a 300-square-meter villa in Frederiksberg where we began developing a physical studio environment and suitable educational processes. In spite of its lovely stucco ceilings, wooden floor, fireplace, kitchen, and balconies, it was a failed office space with terrible acoustics. But it was a great start nevertheless. I could experiment with my courses, and invite everyone from across the school to come and experiment with theirs. Further, administrative staff would use the studio for workshops on developing solutions for student needs. Soon, I thought, we would discover the foundations of studio pedagogy for business education.

Some years have passed since the studio at CBS opened its doors to students, faculty, staff, and managers, and it has grown from a small experiment into an educational concept accompanied by faculty development, a dedicated Master's programme, several studio-based minors and electives, a student organization, and student-led events. An imminent move to larger, custom-built premises is set to establish the studio at CBS as a continuous element of education at CBS. The studio is an ideal place for student-led inquiry. It invites students to explore, revise, and enrich their personal assumptions in view of pernicious problems and academic knowledge. The students develop a sense of their personal style of problem solving and decision making.

But what exactly is a business studio? At a basic level, "studio" is a deliberately underspecified method. It gives the learners space for curiosity, imagination, and discovery, and it decenters the teacher. Common elements of the studio method are a place, practice, process, and community. To many of my colleagues, a studio is a space with interesting furniture that they could book for their classes, but probably won't because they would find it cumbersome to lecture or facilitate discussions in it. And they are right. Merely changing the scene from a lecture hall to a studio space won't help if the learning process stays the same.

The longer we worked in the studio, and the more we observed colleagues work there, the more we realized that the physical studio is primarily a symbol, although a powerful one. It creates expectations in students and faculty that things are different there. This makes a search for a "correct" studio setup futile. For example, Doorley and Whithoft (2012) provide useful ideas on what a basic studio setup might look like. High tables and couches on wheels, lots of whiteboards, flip charts, Post-its, markers, throwaway prototyping material, and similar items come to mind. It is the setup for the tried-and-tested design thinking classes at the Stanford d-school (Institute of Design) and elsewhere. But many other setups are equally conductive to studio methods and afford associated behaviors and processes. Every studio teacher that we spoke to has his or her preferences regarding the physical environment. Some draw inspiration from visual art studios, some from black box theaters, and some have the craftsmen workshops in mind. We might say that a good studio signifies difference and possibility, and enables as many interpretations as possible of what a physical setup could be.

From this, it follows that a studio space doesn't work by itself: it has to be made to work. And the degree to which it works depends on the ability of the teacher just as much as on the experience of the students. An able studio teacher and studio-proficient students can make do with next to nothing to turn a studio class into an exceptional learning experience. Less experienced teachers and students might – in contrast – benefit from funky furniture and flexible setups to get started, develop habits of mind, test their ideas, and get used to how studio works for them. In the process, the studio space becomes a place to be and to work in. "Going to the studio" suggests working in a different way than "going to the group workroom, the library, or to the Bloomberg terminal."

The "habits of mind" of the studio are the link to practice. Learning these habits of mind whilst working on a project in a studio is sometimes referred to as the hidden curriculum. Based on a study of New England art colleges, Hetland *et al.* (2013) name eight specific habits of mind that students develop whilst working in a studio setting. They develop craft, learn to commit, think in images, find meaning, observe, reflect, stretch, and explore. When business students work on their first studio project, we often observe a lack of these studio habits of mind and a struggle to move ahead. In the Master's programme with consecutive studio projects, these habits develop more and more from one studio class to the other over the year.

Studios are process based. Instead of thinking how one piece of information and theory might enable students to understand the next piece in the buildup to a good lecture course, the studio process runs from the introduction of the issue and forming teams to the reporting of a possible solution at the end. In between these two points are iterative activities where the issue at hand is revisited time and again under introduction of further information, new techniques, acquired knowledge, and new ways of looking at it. The standard design thinking process is a good example of an explicit studio process with its iterative moves, but many other forms are possible as well.

Coming together around place, practice, and process, teachers, students, and issue stakeholders form a community of inquiry for the duration of the project. In this community, students help each other and learn from each other as they are trying to solve the problem at hand, and they learn in a self-guided way. Often, students in studio classes tell us that they have never discussed so much and so intensively with their fellow students about something they worked on. The community has to organize itself. It decides on decision rules, collaborative elements, and cooperative work. The teacher becomes one learner amongst others, facilitating the process, without exactly knowing how far the students will get and what else, other than the ascribed theories, they will learn in their projects.

With place, practice, process, and community, we have scratched the surface of what business studio can be, and how it draws inspiration from art, architecture, design, and craft education. The explorative, co-creative studio processes are a vehicle for acquiring techniques, developing skills, and learning, reflecting, and applying theory. In Jack Mezirow's terms of adult education (Mezirow 1991), the studio is a space for transformative, emancipatory learning, and it complements the learning in lectures and case discussions.

## Conclusion

Where does all of this take us? We don't know, because none of the stories are finished yet. Much is still to be done for altering the management classroom by inviting in the arts and humanities. That said – it is clear to us that simply making the invitation can be a fine and fruitful way to begin transforming management education.

## References

Austin R.D. and Devin, L. (2003) *Artful Making: What Managers Need to Know About How Artists Work*. Upper Saddle River, NJ: Financial Times Prentice Hall.

Austin, R.D. and Short, J.C. (2009) *iPremier (A): Denial of Service Attack (Graphic Novel Version)*. Boston, MA: Harvard Business School Publishing, Harvard Case #609-092, 2009.

Austin, R.D., Nolan, R.L. and O'Donnell, S. (2009a) *Adventures of an IT Leader*. Boston, MA: Harvard Business Press.

Austin, R.D., Nolan, R.L. and O'Donnell, S. (2009b) 'The technology manager's journey: an extended narrative approach to educating technical leaders', *Academy of Management Learning and Education*, 8, 337–55.

Austin, R.D., Nolan, R.L. and O'Donnell, S. (2012) *Harder Than I Thought: Adventures of a 21st Century Leader*. Boston, MA: Harvard Business Review Press.

Barry, D. and Meisiek, S. (2015) 'Discovering the business studio', *Journal of Management Education*, 39(1), 153–75.

Becker, H.S. (1982) *Art Worlds*. Berkeley, CA: University of California Press.

Björkman, I. (1998) *Sven Duchamp expert på auraproduktion*. Dissertation. Stockholm University.

Campbell, J. (1949) *The Hero with a Thousand Faces*. New York, NY: Pantheon.

Carroll, S. and Flood, P. (2010) *The Persuasive Leader: Lessons from the Arts*. Chichester, UK: Wiley and Sons.

Davies, S. (2007) *Philosophical Perspectives on Art*. Oxford: Oxford University Press.

Devin, L. and Austin, R. (2012) *The Soul of Design*. Palo Alto, CA: Stanford Business Books.

Doorley, S. and Whithoft, S. (2012) *Making Space*. Hoboken, NJ: Wiley and Sons.

Ericsson, K.A. and Simon, H.A. (1980) 'Verbal reports as data', *Psychological Review*, 87, 215–51.

Goldratt, E.M. and Cox, J. (1984) *The Goal: A Process of Ongoing Improvement*. Croton-on-Hudson, NY: North River Press.

Guillet de Monthoux, P. (2000) 'Performing the absolute; Marina Abramovic organizing the unfinished business of Arthur Schopenhauer', *Organization Studies*, 21, 29–52.

Guillet de Monthoux, P. (2004) *The Art Firm*. Palo Alto, CA: Stanford University Press.
Guillet de Monthoux, P. (2008) 'Opening the gates to the art firm'. *In:* D. Hjorth and C. Steyaert (eds.) *The Politics and Aesthetics of Entrepreneurship*. Cheltenham, UK: Edward Elgar, pp. 146–61.
Guillet de Monthoux, P., Gustafsson, C. and Sjöstrand, S.-E. (2007) *Aesthetic Leadership*. Houndmills, UK: Palgrave Macmillan.
Hetland, L., Winner, E., Veenema, S. and Sheridan, K. (2013) *Studio Thinking 2*. 2nd edn. New York, NY: Teachers College Press.
Kirkeby, O.F. (2000) *Management Philosophy. A Radical–Normative Perspective*. Heidelberg, Germany: Springer Verlag.
Langer, S. (1967) *Philosophy in a New Key*. Cambridge, MA: Harvard University Press.
Mezirow, J. (1991) *Transformative Dimensions of Adult Learning*. San Francisco, CA: Jossey-Bass.
Ramirez, R. (1991) *The Beauty of Social Organization*. Munich, Germany: Accedo.
Scharmer, O. (2009) *Theory U. Leading the Future as it Emerges*. San Francisco, CA: Berett Koehler Publishers.
Schroeder, J.E. (1997) 'Andy Warhol: consumer researcher', *NA – Advances in Consumer Research*, 24, 476–82.
Statler, M. and Guillet de Monthoux, P. (2015) 'Humanities and arts in management education: the emerging Carnegie paradigm', *Journal of Management Education*, 39(1), 3–15.
Strati, A. (1999) *Aesthetics and Organization*. London: Sage Publications.
Strati, A. and Guilllet de Monthoux, P. (2002) 'Organizing aesthetics', *Human Relations*, 7, 55.
Taylor, S.S. and Statler, M. (2013) 'Material matters: increasing emotional engagement in learning', *Journal of Management Education*, 38(4), 586–607.

# 25

# Playing and the performing arts

## Six memos for the future classroom

*Chris Steyaert, Patrizia Hoyer and Bernhard Resch*

Italo Calvino, invited as the first Italian to hold the Charles Eliot Norton Poetry Lectures at Harvard University in 1985–86, was meticulously preparing them when destiny hit hard. Ready to follow in the footsteps of famous artists such as Thomas Stearns Eliot, Igor Stravinsky, Jorge Luis Borges, Northrop Frye and Octavio Paz, Calvino, in a dramatic turn of events, died just before he was about to leave for the US. His wife – Esther Calvino – discovered the preparations on his desk, a series of folders, each one of them containing one of the planned lectures. These *Lezione Americane* were posthumously edited as 'six memos for the next millennium' (Calvino 2002), which are actually only five lectures because the sixth one on *consistency* was never finished. There is something very appealing (see also Steyaert, Hjorth and Gartner 2011) regarding Calvino's idea of speaking about the future of literature in the form of short memos and the inspiring titles he gave them: lightness, quickness, exactitude, visibility and multiplicity. We will undertake a similar endeavour and try to imagine memos for how the future classroom of management education might look like – even if we are not aiming for the next millennium. But one memo will also remain unfinished.

Therefore, we will pretend, somehow naïvely, that we can imagine current educational practices differently and feel inspired to imagine such features – inventiveness, thirdness, playfulness, experimentalism, nimbleness and asceticism/athleticism – by turning to the performing arts (dance, theatre, opera). We will remember some performative events as well as referring to one or two discussions on (the future of) education in the (performing) arts. The upcoming memos are thus as much about witnessing other practices as they are a form of wishful thinking. Even if we give some examples from our own classroom practices – from three different master courses (with alternative angles) on the theme of entrepreneurship – in order to reflect on these ideas, this chapter is mostly oriented at the (im)possible. To situate the three courses held at the University of St Gallen in Switzerland briefly: the course Creativity and Entrepreneurship is part of the masters programme Management, Organization Studies and Cultural Theory, but it is also open for students of other masters programmes (if places are available); the two other courses scheduled within contextual studies (see Eberle and Metelmann, this volume) are Interfaces: Entrepreneurship and Aesthetics and also Organizing New Museums in the Entrepreneurial City. What these courses have in common is that they introduce a simple rule: students cannot use PowerPoint presentations in their group work (Gabriel 2008). They are asked instead to present (new) learning and knowledge in a performative, or as we would call it a 'post-dramatic' way (Beyes and Steyaert 2006).

## Inventiveness

A future pedagogy is probably not mono-dimensional but might interweave many strings of pedagogical thinking that come together – some complementary, some compromised, some contradictory. Maybe one way to indicate a minimal feature or condition is to point to its inventiveness. Such pedagogy of invention has been stated most provocatively by Michel Serres:

> The goal of instruction is the end of instruction, that is to say invention. Invention is the only true intellectual act, the only act of intelligence. The rest? Copying, cheating, reproduction, laziness, convention, battle, sleep. Only discovery awakens. Only invention proves that one truly thinks what one thinks, whatever that may be. I think therefore I invent, I invent therefore I think.
>
> *Serres 1997 [1991]: 92–3*

If you ask us, this is a wonderful, witty paraphrase of the more famous Cartesian proposition. It is also outspoken, drawing a circle around 90 per cent of our teaching practices and calling them laziness or even sleepiness. However, Michel Serres is also affirmative and out to invent alternatives – as he documents in *Le Tiers-Instruit* (meaning the 'third-instructed' but translated as *The Troubadour of Knowledge*, 1997 [1991]) in which he explores the consequences an ontology of the multiple has for the inventive force of education (see Brown, this volume). The book forms 'an educational manual' for learning how the third-instructed – or the figure that learns in the third space (Steyaert 2006) – can become inventive by promoting 'Harlequin' as the conceptual persona of this pedagogy. This figure emphasizes that knowledge is interdisciplinary – even specialists have understood that 'each portion of their knowledge looks like Harlequin's coat, because each works at the intersection or the interference of many other disciplines and, sometimes, of almost all of them. In this way, their academy or the encyclopedia formally joined commedia dell'arte' (Serres 1997 [1991]: xvii).

Furthermore, learning equals invention as the body mediates the possibility of new practices and movements. Learning is a process that Serres compares with swimming, where learners have to risk leaving the shore, encounter strange currents in the ocean, and abandon all reference points. 'Depart, take the plunge,' Serres (1997 [1991]: 5) urges us, because learning requires a body that leaves the security of the shore and moves towards the middle where the real passage can occur. After this initiation into a third space, the body will never be home again; instead, it will live in the intermediary, in the middle, forming a hyphen that connects different sides. Make no mistake, he says, learning is a process that evokes and enacts the multiple (Steyaert 2014).

Serres has recently rephrased this 'emerging inventive pedagogy' (Dey and Steyaert 2007: 452) in a booklet entitled *Petite Poucette* (translated as *Thumbelina: The Culture and Technology of Millennials*, 2012) where he 'updates' his mantra on invention by connecting it to the upcoming new technologies and social media (see Bachmann and Shah, this volume). We do not have to fill the heads of students, Serres (2012) remarks, because students – like the decapitated St Denis of Paris who holds his head in his hands – carry their heads in front of them, albeit in the form of a computer or other communication devices. Students can swiftly access data and social networks. They do not need teachers-in-front who transfer their expertise and unload their knowledge upon students. Instead, the voice of teachers becomes increasingly drowned out by the noise that comes from the uproar of students who desire something different. It is not only a desire for new ways of relating through technology and social media, but a matter of transforming conventional practices. Thus, as Serres claims, we have to change the institution of the university and with it, we would add, its classrooms. This will require experiments. And swimming.

## Thirdness

We need to explore the conditions that assist experimentation and make us eager to swim because we can easily be caught up at the protected shores of disciplines. In order to prevent this, Serres proposes 'thirdness' as the primary generative condition, with swimming and other activities of passage as its main practices. Thirdness is the water (see Parker, this volume) or the boat that crosses it, named by Foucault (1986) a heterotopia par excellence (Beyes and Michels 2011; Steyaert 2006). The third space has been well enacted by the British theatre maker Peter Brook in his concept of the empty space (Brook 1990 [1968]) – his way to overrule conventions, traditions and rules of the institution of theatre, increasingly called a 'creative industry' (Henry 2007). 'Anyone interested in processes in the natural world would be greatly rewarded by a study of theatre *conditions*' (Brook 1990 [1968]: 111, emphasis added). We are therefore encouraged by Brook who, for a long time, has been a master in experimenting and resisting the ways in which theatre is produced and commercialized. In a similar way to Calvino, he gave lectures (at universities) and wrote about it (Brook 1990 [1968]: 157) – calling writing 'an exercise'. *The Empty Space* (Brook 1990 [1968]) features theatre spelt out in a Calvino-esque way as Brook distinguishes between four kinds of theatre he calls 'deadly', 'holy', 'rough' and 'immediate'. He fulminates against the so-called deadly theatre, a condemnation we could also apply to most classrooms:

> In a living theatre, we would each day approach the rehearsal putting yesterday's discoveries to the test, ready to believe that the true play has once again escaped us. But the Deadly Theatre approaches the classics from the viewpoint that somewhere, someone has found out and defined how the play should be done.
>
> *Brook 1990 [1968]: 17*

Classrooms in management education can be as 'deadly' – repeating existing truths kept up through a theatre of prescribed methods, fixed routines and tacit norms. What, therefore, is Brook's remedy? Sweeping, emptying, cleaning out, dusting, questioning the theatre. Testing its assumptions and its habitus. Or simply leave it and explore other spaces because any space can become an empty space for playing: 'I CAN take any empty space and call it a bare stage. A [wo]man walks across this empty space whilst someone else is watching him [her], and this is all that is needed for an act of theatre to be engaged' (Brook 1990 [1968]: 11, emphasis in original). However, emptying a space, in our view, does not have to imply the abandoning of all experience for the sake of the 'new'; instead, there may be many ways of altering the atmospheres of a classroom (Michels and Beyes, this volume) and allowing it to resonate with the possibilities of thirdness.

Such a third activity of 'emptying' we do in a masters course entitled Entrepreneurship and Creativity, where we try to immediately influence the conditions for experimenting. Picture it like this: students entering the classroom in a laid-back passive mode, searching for a comfortable place in the U-formation of tables and chairs where they can hide behind their screens. They are perfectly ready to allow yet another lecturer wash the contents of yet another course over them. What they are encountering instead, however, is an empty room with chairs next to each other against the walls, almost forming a circle. Not to mention the effort it takes to empty the classroom (for every session) and the negotiations with the technical staff to implement this set-up.

This mundane rearrangement seems to be deeply unsettling to the administration as well as to most students (see Vince, this volume). Their irritated facial expressions are revealing: where is the lecturer? Where can I sit down? Where should I put my belongings, especially the electronic gadgets? As the lecturer (who has been sitting amidst them 'incognito') is starting to speak, the trouble continues: 'Welcome to the second session of our class and thanks again for your active engagement in last week's introductory session. Let us move directly on to this week's agenda.' Although some students keep a poker face, others start gazing anxiously at each other, silently asking, 'Were you at that one?' As soon as this opening is unmasked as a somehow silly teaser alluding to the idea of 'starting in the middle', some students exhale in relief, whilst others become suspicious.

The effects are varied, and for some it was too much: 'When I walked out of the room after the first session, I was ready to quit. Not knowing what to expect, I had been taken aback by the unusual format of the course. It certainly was a jump in the pool ...' (from student learning paper 2012). For others, it gave a kick:

> The first class was amazing, since the moment I crossed the door everything was different, no tables, everyone with his or her name stapled, no barriers between professor–student. [...] No matter how shy, how uncomfortable and insecure I was finding myself to be, I really wanted to take the risk. I really wanted to experience something different and that's why I decided to continue with the course after the first class.
>
> *From student learning paper 2014*

And some connected comfort with uneasiness:

> The entire afternoon I felt an unusual combination of uneasiness and comfort. The uneasiness is self-explanatory; I had never before taken a course that was anything like this, and naturally felt a bit out of place. The comfort, however, is much more interesting. I cannot say that I understood it on the day, but looking back now I believe I can explain it. Subconsciously, I told myself that there were two possibilities. Either my classmates were just as uncomfortable as I was, or they felt that there was no reason to be.
>
> *From student learning paper 2015*

As the course moves on, we try to hold on to the atmosphere of the course as an intermezzo. When students decide to bear this tension between uneasiness and comfort, and thus to continue the journey, we take them to different playgrounds including a city walk through an artistic/entrepreneurial neighbourhood of Zurich, to the university sports hall for an improvisational dance workshop, and sometimes also to the local theatres to see an evening show. When we prepare the various 'parts' of a session, we try to consider how we can change the rhythms and intensities, possibly leave a thread and pick up an interrupted line instead, and so we cut through the 'lecturing' and make abrupt changes to an improvisation, an exercise, a video fragment or a case example.

As an inspiration (and maybe confidence boost) for their own group projects and group work dynamics we provide an unusual case example of an entrepreneurial team illustrated in the movie *The Full Monty* (Steyaert 2014). In this movie a group of former steelworkers in Sheffield, UK, reinvent themselves as strippers based on a collective learning process of collaboration turning creativity into an exercise of going 'all the way'. In order to prepare students for their final projects, which is a creative group performance around a chosen eminent creator, team, organization or urban setting, we allow them to live through a range of exercises that remain 'strange' within the business school: drawing, diary writing, role playing and acting out genres of drama (like thriller or comedy). Once they have developed a solid storyline for their group performance, we interrupt them again and ask for the integration of random objects or unusual perspectives, such as that of a clown, angel or a blind man. As students leave the classroom on the last day, we have to resist the other challenge of not getting trapped by the (upcoming) 'ending' of the course. We try to emphasize once more that this is not really the end, just like we did not stage a proper beginning in the first place. Therefore, we speak of the final group performances in terms of 'dress-rehearsals' or 'avant-première' to underline that there could be yet another session after our last session.

Following Deleuze (1988), our attempt is to depart and remain in the 'middle', emphasizing that creativity, just as the act of playing, has no real beginning and ending. Even if there are conventional markers of a beginning, such as the first session of a course, '[i]t is never the beginning or the end which are interesting; the beginning and end are points. What is interesting is the middle' (Deleuze and Parnet 1987: 39). Going even a step further, Deleuze (1988: 123) argues: 'One never commences, one never has a tabula rasa; one slips in, enters in the middle; one takes up or lays down rhythms.' This is how we imagine the students to 'perform': they sneak in, lay off their (usual) tools and pick up at a different speed to the one they have been working at so far – usually a break with the very sedentary mode of being a student.

This idea of entering (and leaving) in the middle is not only a 'guiding principle' (Marks 1998: 32) and practical tool to reframe the timing and spacing of classroom practice, but it also gives away our idea of creativity as consisting of practices of the middle. Thus, we immediately challenge the mainstream understanding of being creative as coming up with something 'new', 'original' and 'out of the box', which then results in something 'useful' that meets the promise for economic success (see De Cock, this volume). In this regard, we also refer in the opening session to a text by Rehn and De Cock (2009) who speak of a binary construction along the lines of 'old' as a signifier for 'bad' versus 'new' as the acme of 'good'. And yet, whenever we start something new, we are already in the midst of a complex and messy situation charged with individual experiences, institutional constraints and societal patterns of interpretation. For Deleuze, the middle is also a way to overcome such abundant use of binary or either/or thinking (Marks 1998) and to replace it with thinking that keeps increasing the connections: an 'and, and, and . . .'.

## Playfulness

And . . . we connect to the opera stage, in particular the Brussels opera house De Munt/La Monnaie where the 2015–16 season, referring to Huizinga's *Homo Ludens* (1955), is concentrated around play. The Brussels opera has earned a reputation for innovative and creative approaches to opera since the early 1980s. At this time Gerard Mortier initiated a renewal of the genre of opera between Brussels and Antwerp, between Salzburg and the Ruhr region, and between Paris and Madrid. This innovative force has been maintained in Brussels over the past decennia, illustrated, for example, by *La Monnaie* becoming 'European Opera House of the Year' in 2011.

Play is undoubtedly the word that best summarizes the new season, taking on at least three different connotations:

> [P]laying with locations and matching them with the appropriate projects and also playing with budgets and balancing them against the resources available in terms of time, staff, and money. And especially playing in the creative sense: because the building works have been

> repeatedly postponed over the last few years and we face, moreover, a serious and unexpected reduction in our subsidy, we have continued 'playing' with our programme right up to the deadline for this presentation of the season. In the circumstances under which this season has taken shape, it is already a minor miracle that we can 'keep on playing'.
>
> *de Caluwe 2015: 19*

An institution that is known for its creativity needs to maintain a mode of 'playing', especially when the setbacks are at their greatest. The budget cuts referred to relate to the austerity measures (Eeckhout 2014) of a conservative, federal coalition government (with a nationalist, Flemish party as its most powerful coalition partner) that is not very eager to support a federal institution like the Brussels opera house.

To choose play as its seasonal theme is thus a form of resistance, in a similar way as Johan Huizinga (1955) understood the force of play when he wrote his treatise on play sensing his worries and frustrations with upcoming national socialism and what he called 'this world-wide bastardization of culture' (1995: 205). *Homo Ludens* began as the theme of Huizinga's annual address as Rector of Leyden University in 1933. And as he publicly spoke against Nazism repeatedly in his function of Rector, the situation became increasingly precarious – the university was closed and Huizinga was deported to a hostage camp where he stayed in internal exile until his death in 1945. Playing is not (just) something leisurely; it can become a matter of life and death. In Brussels, playing is also an element of institutional survival.

The opera building has not been restored in thirty years and is in danger of collapse, and hence the whole season is to be played at outside locations – 'extra muros' as it is called so nicely. The choice of play not only seems vital, but also becomes positioned as participatory: citizens as much as cultural colleagues are encouraged to take part in the action to 'keep the lights on', to stop what is called 'the cultural blackout' and to counter this form of politics and policy. Indeed, Rancière's ignorant schoolmaster (see Huault and Perret, this volume) and his ideas on emancipation are drawn upon in the seasonal programme book for a chapter called 'Empowerment', where people are invited to 'the art of giving' and 'to help us avoid a cultural blackout' (de Caluwe 2015: 191) because 'any individual can always, at any moment, be emancipated and emancipate someone else, announce to others the *practice* and add to the number of people who know themselves as such and who no longer play the comedy of the inferior superiors' (Rancière 1991: 98).

Even if three productions have to be cancelled and personnel have to be laid off, the opera house will not withdraw, but rather invade the city and join its rhythms because 'the city never stops playing' (Lada 2015: 42). The programme is enacted in eight or so locations in Brussels, complemented with several urban activities, such as sonic bikes to tour the city, and a range of social programmes that target different communities and give them a chance to join opera or other events. The different locations become connected in a series of multi-layered photo collages and slogans by the Dutch-Croatian photographer Sanja Marusic that express the ongoing coming and going of a city in flux (Lada 2015) and encourage the audience to 'stop arriving', 'get lost', 'wander around', 'go nowhere' and 'find nothing'. In short, to suspend any interest in results and answers and give in to the city's invisibilities and questions as it befits the mode of play.

And playing happens. Take, for instance, Donizetti's opera buffa *L'elisir d'amore*, which opens the 2015–16 season in the Royal Circus in Brussels, a nineteenth-century building that was initially a permanent space for circus and horse riding shows and that now houses all kinds of cultural and entertainment activities. The opera is therefore played in a circular arena, a big circle that forms centre stage around which the audience is seated. The opera is restaged as a day on the beach and so the arena is filled with (fake) sand, and everything is redecorated likewise: there is an Adina beach bar with its cocktail drinks, summer deckchairs, beach towels and plastic sunbeds, a shower to cool down or tease some sun worshippers and occasionally people turn up on a Vespa or in a Jeep, the latter transporting oversized cans with new energy drinks as the 'love elixir'. Even the chairs of the audience are redesigned with blue and white striped covers. The singers – and the numerous choir members – run around in their swimming trunks or bathing suits, and the orchestra has 'dressed down' in beach shorts, colourful shirts and flip-flops. In the second act, the arena is filled with a big, plastic bath in the form of a wedding cake that, when fully blown up, becomes the location for a foam party, turning the event into a 'soap opera'.

Even if we have all the accessories that are associated with how beach life has become tamed and commercialized in recent decennia, the scene also refers to everything that makes a day at the beach a 'holiday' far away from work, duties and daily routines. 'The only order the beach knows is one of playing,' says the sociologist Weyns (2015) in the programme book of *L'elisir d'amore*. The beach is a playground, an in-between sandscape between low and high tide. Nothing, no form, no rule, no position will be fixed for very long. Against the four elements – sea (water), sun (fire), wind (air) and sand (earth) – assembled together at the beach, the atmosphere is one of freedom, possibility and lightness (Weyns 2015). As Huizinga (1955) remarks – and as quoted in the programme book – '[f]or seriousness seeks to exclude play, whereas play can very well include seriousness' (de Caluwe 2015). Play has a force as it can balance seriousness with lightness, and search for something utopian with frivolity.

Play is a core force in the management and organization of this opera house as well as a red thread through the staging of its season's opera. But how is it connected to our interest in education and learning? The link might be found in another quote from the extensive programme book that accompanies *L'elisir d'amore*: 'you can discover more about a person in an hour of play than in a year of conversation' (de Caluwe 2015: 43). This is paraphrased from a seventeenth-century courtesy manual by Richard Lingard (1907 [1670]) who wrote a letter of advice to young men leaving the university. Although this type of advice concerning manners and etiquette has been abandoned in academic education (see O'Doherty, this volume), it might be a good idea to take up this tradition again and write such letters to our students when they are about to leave our universities. Surprise them with a memo on playfulness.

Such a memo is needed because playing becomes banned in school when children reach the age of six or seven, and is something that becomes increasingly jeopardized even before that age, making place instead for a focus on skills such as reading and writing (Overbeek 2013). Afterwards, play is increasingly practised outside school or university. In *Playing and Reality*, Donald Winnicott also refers to the relationship between the beach and play as he introduces his ideas on potential space. For this he quotes the profoundly sensitive and beautiful verse by the Indian poet Rabindranath Tagore: 'On the seashore of endless worlds, children play' (Winnicott 1971: 95). Winnicott observes that somehow we all stop playing whilst growing up and thus he notices that the question is not whether but when children have stopped playing in the process of becoming an adult. However, when children or adults were soliciting therapy, for Winnicott, who was as much a therapist as a theorist (Tuber 2008), play became a remedy, a core activity to reopen processes of psychological closure or blockage. The question, therefore, is 'when we have unlearned to play, can we relearn to play, and can we also adopt and reintroduce practices of playing in the classroom'?

Anne Harris (2014), playwright and pedagogic scholar in the arts, interestingly notes a 'creative turn' where ideas from arts and arts education are entering management and business and are constantly connecting to innovation and profit. She also observes a trend towards commodification when she states that 'creativity is parting ways with arts practice in education, signaling a "creative turn" in understanding the commodity value of education' (Harris 2014: 5). The notion of play has also become commodified in the popular management literature, which we do not consider a suitable basis for educational philosophies and practices. A commodity focus brings with it, above all, an increasing attention to efficiency and measurement (Dey and Steyaert 2007; Parker and Jary 1995). Gielen (2015) argues that the only way play can be maintained as part of arts education is when it forms a 'dismeasure', a creative disruption that brings confusion to current standards and that even bends the rules that an educational regime imposes. If playful (arts) education is to teach its students anything, it is how to stretch the rules or measure of play: 'this is precisely how arts education may use (or, in the spirit of the avant-garde should use) play: play as disrupter of play' (Gielen 2015: 149). Even if disruptions often come with a sense of frustration, affecting smooth processes, agreed upon timeframes and linear storylines – things that are usually valued in management education – we still try to cultivate a 'routine' of disruption in our courses in how we push ourselves to alter some course elements each year and also in how we give disruptive input and feedback to student projects, which usually results in more varied and previously unimagined outcomes.

## Experimentalism

We said that inventiveness depends on 'experimenting'. If we want to reinvent educational institutions, experimenting cannot be ignored. At this point, enter some of the experiments in contemporary dance theatre. On this Sunday morning with a weak but upbeat autumn sun, there was a steady stream of people arriving at Wiels, a cultural art centre located in a former beer production factory in Brussels. Most people headed for the three-day Art Book Fair or queued for a ticket to the dance performance entitled 'Work/Travail/Arbeid' by the dance company Rosas, which was taking place on the last day of its reprise. In a back room on the first floor, there was also a book launch where a four-part catalogue of this production was presented to a small audience in a conversation between four participants from this performance: the choreographer Anne Teresa De Keersmaeker, who had started the dance company Rosas; Jean Luc Plouvier, pianist of the ensemble Ictus, which plays avant-garde music during the performance; Michaël Pomero, one of the Rosas dancers; and Dirk Snauwaert, the director of Wiels who also acts as host and moderator.

Each represented the various disciplines that are 'remixed' in this production: choreography, music, (dance) performance and exhibition (space). De Keersmaeker said she was happy that this catalogue was published and could be finally presented to the audience because it marked the outcome of a long 'work' process, and would form probably one of its main (but rare) traces – even if a movie of this production process (by Babette Mangolte) was still on its way as well. Although announced in English, the conversation alternated between French, Flemish and English and gave a glimpse of how significant this experiment had been for all parties involved, and probably would be in the years to come, for example the production will travel to the Centre Pompidou in Paris and Tate Modern in London.

The term 'Work' refers first of all to the work – dance oeuvre – by De Keersmaeker that stretches over more than thirty years ever since her first dance production entitled 'Fase: four movements on the minimal music of Steve Reich' – a production that one of the authors saw when he was an undergraduate student, and the performance's maxim, 'Dance is like life itself. It goes on and on, and suddenly it stops', printed on a postcard hung for years above his desk. It referred to the (post-)minimalist dance genre De Keersmaeker co-initiated and pioneered, characterized by a 'sustained combination [...] of iteration and variation, sameness and difference' (Laermans 2015: 84), which made her 'a revolutionary innovator in the aesthetic language of dance' (Snauwaert 2015: 7). Now this oeuvre is 'interrupted' by engaging with yet another new experiment.

The dance performance – or maybe rather dance diffusion – entitled 'Work/Travail/Arbeid' is based on an experiment about interdisciplinarity, organizing a meeting between dance, music and (exhibition) space. This experiment is focused on an analysis of work as performance and of the performance of work and its conditions, done in such an extensive and intensive way that would make most scholars interested in the study of work and organization envious, and 'bringing together parameters, questions, and possible answers to thirty years of taking dance and choreography seriously as ways of organizing movement in time and space' (De Keersmaeker 2015: 38). The book launch ran over the allocated time, and the dancer Michaël sneaked out of the press conference because he had to 'work' and dance his part(s) on the third floor.

The experiment was going on two floors up, in the post-industrial open space of the Wiels building, with white-painted walls and large windows through which the light entered differently depending on the hour of the day. The space was empty, except for a few chairs loosely spread along the walls; there was no stage, no light effects, only a range of circles and pentads drawn in chalk on the floor, regularly renewed by the dancers. This was what a museum space without any sculptures, paintings or installations looked like – the only objects to watch were moving dancers and musicians. When Rosas was invited to develop a dance performance to take place in this art centre – 'to make an exhibition as a performance, and a performance as an exhibition' (De Keersmaeker 2015: 36) – the idea was not just to change locations from the usual black box of the theatre to the white cube of the museum, as had often been done before, but to translate a dance performance 'tailored to the exigencies of an exhibition' (Crimp 2015: 103) and to explore how an exhibition can itself become a performance. As a consequence, the dance performance was 'reorganized' in a way that any other exhibition would be programmed: for nine weeks, ongoing everyday between 11.00 and 18.00 – the opening hours of Wiels. The structure of such continuing performance is closely connected to the way the music – a composition entitled *Vortex Temporum* by Gérard Grisey – had become de-composed in the single parts of each instrument to which a dancer was connected:

> Vortex is built with seven voices. When I took them apart, I realized that the voices were just as beautiful apart, and this allowed for combinations of sound and movement. As it happens, this is precisely what Grisey's piece does. Starting with a very basic motif, Grisey goes on to expand and condense time, and this idea of expanding and condensing time or harmonic space is what I wanted to work with.
>
> *De Keersmaeker 2015: 37*

When one of the authors entered the space on a late afternoon, there was one wind instrument being played and one dancer. This was a new experience for a spectator: usually a dance performance is intense and compact – because it does not take longer than an hour, everything is compressed in a density that cannot be taken in at one glance. Here, there was a kind of slowness, which gave everyone the time to observe at his or her own pace, similar to walking through a gallery or museum room and enjoying a particular sequence whilst looking for small differentiations. A spectator could follow the dancer or the music player as they moved through the various parts of the vast space, or just lean against the wall or sit on the floor. The audience could 'see this piece, not as it would be performed onstage, but as [they] worked (or are working) on it: the different perspectives and layering of the work process, etcetera' (De Keersmaeker 2015: 38).

And so it went on and on, hour by hour. 'Each hour [. . .], *Vortex Temporum* is played and danced anew, now with a duet of winds, now with a trio of strings, now with the piano and winds, now with the clarinet or the cello or the viola alone – and every so often the *tutti*' (Crimp 2015: 101–2). Later that day, there was a 'tutti' section where all dancers and music players were performing. Viewers were suddenly part of the movements, spirals and twirls, because several times a dancer passed skin-close or stopped, and there was a moment of eye-to-eye exchange before she or he moved on, undisturbed. But it worked also the other way around. As Michaël put it, he and his colleagues had become used to dancing amongst the audience and to adapting their 'routines' depending on how the audience was moving around in space. He remarked that they already 'missed' the audience when they were doing the 'usual' performance on stage, separated from spectators by a black curtain. That also explains why it was so hard to leave the space – it felt liberating to not have to wait for some ending, or to wait to applaud.

A viewer entered another time and found a new intensity of attention: taking part in (observing) the process of (everyday) work, with its repetition and variation, with its seriousness and dedication. The role of the audience had dissipated: we were no longer the divided mass each with one seat allocated, but performing our own collective movement, a kind of loose, clumsy shadow dance, mirroring Rosas's trust in dance and their 'sincere and intense conviction that dance matters, that it is worthy of exhibiting its own effort, excellence, and speechless ritual', reflecting 'a choice to believe that the broken link between the body, movement, music, time, and attention can be constructed again, with joy and insight' (Cvejic 2015: 21).

This process of making the work process visible is something we attempt in the Organizing New Museums in the Entrepreneurial City course, where we try to understand the contemporary work of the museum and its practices of exhibiting. It is a course with a triple, performative logic. First, based on a list of critical literature, we study the new performativity of museums because they have become the flagship cultural institutions of the entrepreneurial city (Michels *et al.* 2014). Second, we engage in onsite visits and interviews to understand how museums organize their daily work and activities. Third, the course participants prepare and execute an exhibition of the specific theme they have prepared – if museums have exhibited everything thinkable (even dance), they never exhibit themselves; there is no museum of museums.

The course is run as a five-day workshop, between an introductory meeting to frame the course and its literature and a post-workshop reflection session, where we discuss the various individual learning papers. The scenario of this workshop is roughly as follows: on day one, we discuss the problematics of the relationship between museums and urban entrepreneurialism, invite a museum director to talk about the daily 'running' of a museum and finish by exploring the campus as an exhibition space that is crowded with artwork – from Giacometti to Richter. On the second day, we walk through the city and, helped by an empirical doctoral study (Michels *et al.* 2014), we look at the range of different museums the city has from a classical museum to a post-industrial multi-art centre. We also visit artists who refuse to exhibit in a museum location and who organize their own space. On the third day, we split up the group and travel to museums in nearby cities, for example Zurich, Basel or even Bregenz in Austria, and we undertake a series of guided museum visits (not guiding us so much into their collections as into their behind-the-screen activities of organizing). The fourth day is project work where each group develops their upcoming exhibition.

After a morning (and usually some late evening if not night work) of attending to the pragmatics and aesthetics of exhibition making and its detailed finishing touches, on day five we invite a (small) audience to attend the preview. Each group has a guiding concept for the audience and a programme booklet with thematic and conceptual background to their exhibition. When we give students a suggestion for where to locate their exhibition, it is fascinating, but yet not surprising to see how students prefer to find their own space (usually a complete classroom), which they eagerly dismantle and redesign as an exhibition space (with us mediating with the technical staff). What students can learn here when trying to understand the organizing of museums is the embodied differences and relationships between reading/discussing texts on organizing museums, empirically studying the work of organizing museums and practising the everyday complexities of enacting a style of exhibiting.

As teachers of the course, we also send each project group a short reflection, almost a small notice that one could find in the next day's paper or indeed a letter of courtesy that would remind students of their own inventive potential. This is a shortened version of what we sent back (in 2014) to one of the projects entitled 'Glass and stones: are museums foundations or projections?':

> This exhibition is about moments of aesthetic reflection which you can encounter in a museum. It is sober and precise, yet also with rapid changes as you walk through it. The space is reshaped like a long, turning corridor where you have no choice as an audience but to 'follow'. The main vehicle is projection: projections of a classical fresco, a gallery of video screens, and even a small room where reflection becomes the 'real' object(ive). The exhibition gives the visitor several experiences of how you can walk through a museum and 'feel' time differently: first, you feel you can do the usual museum-thing by looking at 'things on walls' but soon one becomes confused as projections compete for your attention and for multiple versions of (in)attention. Questions on time and experience elicit further questions on the spaces which museums need: are they better served when their buildings resemble solid temples or are they better off now with their shiny glass-reflectors where the audience is more than ever narcissistically looking at itself? Or are museal experiences possible everywhere, as long as we are open for moments of surprise and meditation? In the end, you as a visitor are wondering: 'Am I back in the classical museum? Or will I forever look for another time in other spaces?'

## Nimbleness

Whatever masters programme one is studying nowadays, as a student (and teacher) one has to be a master of time, schedule and programme management. Simons and Masschelein (2013) therefore suggest returning to the 'original', etymological meaning of school, namely the Greek word 'scholè' which means 'free time' – not so much leisure time but rather the time to study and exercise. School – as it comes with the practices of suspension, profanation and attention – forms another time and space, which reminds us of the heterotopic quality of thirdness. Indeed, Simons and Masschelein refer to Serres's swimmer to underline that *scholè* is

> the time and space of attention, which is the time of regard for the world, of being present to it (or being in its presence), attending to it, a time of surrendering to the experience of the world, of exposure and effacing social subjectivities and orientations, a time filled with encounters and opportunities to study and exercise.
>
> *Simons and Masschelein 2013: 74*

With 'nimbleness', or nimble thinking that matches the lightness of playing, a different time of learning is entered, one where not-knowing as a legitimate position of the reflection process brings one to a border zone from where new thinking or doing may emerge, but also where it may not. This respect for impossibility is in strong contrast to the usual tempo at which teachers and students need to be so productive that they never seem to have time to explore, to think differently or to play abundantly without expectation of any return. Here again, one can draw inspiration from De Keersmaeker for how to reinvent the business school and its classrooms. In 1995, De Keersmaeker started her own dance school called PARTS, the acronym for Performing Arts Research and Training Studios. During the past twenty years, PARTS has not only developed a pool of well-trained and talented dancers from which Rosas can recruit, but it has also attracted a critical community of people interested in dance – a 'dance scene' comprising not only dancers but also critics, teachers, other (experimental) dance groups and choreographers (often students staying on after their study) and an audience increasingly familiar with new dance forms. This dance scene is making Brussels a capital for interdisciplinary artistic experimentation (Laermans 2015; Snauwaert 2015). Whether we need studios everywhere in management education (see Meisiek, Guillet de Monthoux, Barry and Austin, this volume) is not our argument, but what this Brussels-based international dance school seems to accomplish is a kind of minoritization of education itself.

First, it has circumvented (so far) the principles of the Bologna reform (Laermans 2013), and thus not given in to the fragmentation of education and its 'supermarket' model, where the collection of credits often becomes a goal in itself rather than the construction of an individual and yet integrated learning trajectory. The main educational purpose is 'to train "thinking dancers", as the school's founding documents state' (Laermans 2015: 286), aiming for a self-reflexive stance towards dance and choreography. The study is structured along two cycles of two years and is research-driven around the question 'what can dance be today?' This leads to a constant rearticulation of the curriculum (Laermans 2015) and, therefore, the ideal graduate 'combines artistic versatility – a feature befitting the conceptual de-definition of dance – with an inquisitive attitude that takes nothing for granted about the activity one actually engages in or prepares for' (Laermans 2015: 287).

Second, the programme is interdisciplinary and is also concerned with theory. The study, therefore, is more than training in movement and dance – it also requires that students study music analysis because, in De Keersmaeker's view, dancers should be able to read a music score and also engage with theatre training and understand its different forms of theatricality. Future dancers must be able 'to firmly articulate choreographic choices and frame their practice by means of general ideas or theoretical insights as well as informed references to dance history or the principal stakes of contemporary art' (Laermans 2013: 155).

This brings us back to the notion of nimbleness. When Rudi Laermans, a sociology professor at a Belgian university, teaches theory to students of PARTS, he reflects on the differences between both teaching situations, and he contrasts them as 'disciplinary instruction' versus 'nimble thinking', respectively. 'Nimbleness' – with its connotation of liveliness, agility and alertness – appears inspirational when thinking of the future (management education) classroom because it also underlines the importance of questioning and reflecting up to the point of not-knowing, which is called 'the heartbeat of PARTS' pedagogical project' (Laermans 2015: 157). 'Doing theory' has its own performativity because it is often a 'playful "doing with" (critically scrutinizing the consecrated insights of others, discussing actual facts, etc.), but when the teaching really goes well it is dominated by nimble action with/by words and concepts – something like linguistic choreography, minus any poetic slant' (Laermans 2015: 158).

Third, PARTS combines a transnational community, virtually networked and volatile in its composition, with an almost dated form of 'presence'. The dance school is almost 'schoolish' because students (accepted after an intensive audition week following pre-auditions in several locations across the globe) are 'subjected to a demanding educational regime. Except on Wednesdays, weekdays last from 9.15 to 17.15 or even 18.00; moreover, students are confronted with the implicit expectation that they explore personal ideas or projects further after school hours and over the weekend' (Laermans 2013: 155). Learning is also living together, as uninterrupted as possible, even sharing meals and lunches together. This reminds us of the kind of practice of living that comes with invention and creation according to Serres (1997 [1991]: 92), 'thus there exists a hygienics, yes, a diet of the work. High-level sportsmen live like monks, and creators live like athletes'. To anyone who seeks to invent, Serres therefore has these suggestions:

> Begin with exercise, seven regular hours of sleep, and a strict diet. The hardest life and the most demanding discipline: asceticism and austerity. Resist fiercely the talk around you that claims the opposite . . . Do not resist only narcotics, but especially social chemistry, by far the strongest and thus the worst: the media, conventional fashions. Everyone always says the same thing and, like the flow of influence, descends the steepest slope together.
>
> *Serres 1997 [1991]: 92*

## Asceticism/athleticism

In the course Interfaces: Entrepreneurship and Aesthetics, we try out aesthetic practices of theatre, movement and dance in relation to exploring the movements that constitute entrepreneurship. Framed between introductory sessions to focus attention and a reflection session to look back on the 'middle part', the bulk of this masters course forms a week of intensive bodily training, exercises and also developing in small groups a work-in-progress performance in front of an invited audience. The classroom is not the campus but the performance space of the city's dance theatre or (on one occasion) the rehearsal space of the masters in theatre at the Zurich University of the Arts (Steyaert and Grand 2009). With its very regulated and strict time schedule of working between 9.00 and 17.30, and also with its physical and embodied series of activities and a rising tension before the public performance, this is a time where nobody can 'hide' or remain on the surface – these are times of trial (and error), of confrontation (with one's limits, anxieties), of feelings of breakthrough or blockage.

The dance choreographer (who acts as co-teacher of this course), with his own practice of (work out) exercises and playful experiments, quick feedback circles that lead to even more attempts and improvisations without (verbal) preparations, confronts management students with a new form of attention, concentration and intensity that makes them often question the years of passive studying they have been doing or, in some cases, regain confidence through learning what their bodies can do in the connection between body, thinking and presence. Most of all, they enjoy the adrenaline of performing in front of an audience, moving between the loading up before and unloading during and after the performance and its applause. In the Entrepreneurship and Creativity course, we also invite the dance choreographer for a full afternoon session, which prompted one of its participants during a debriefing to feel rather disconcerted because she said: 'I have been four years at this university, and this is the first time my body also gets something to do. I ask myself why this university gives so little attention to embodied learning.' In one of the learning papers (from 2015), a student described his experience as he went through some of the exercises:

> A very intense experience was the improvisation workshop, which truly changed how I look at things. The space – the Lokremise, the old locomotive depot in St Gallen, offered a really inspiring and engaging space. By acting out the exercises, I truly enjoyed being in this space and feeling this. In a first exercise we went through the space blindfolded. By doing so I intensely began to realize my body, my surrounding area and the aura of the other people. In the next exercise, we needed to entrust our fate to an unknown person in

> the room. With him guiding me through the room – an unconscious connection of trust and empathy emerged, even though we did not talk. In the next exercise we stopped in front of the most proximate person, whom I did not know, and needed to stare into his eyes. This was a truly weird experience. It was like exchanging information on a meta-level – without talking. Here again, I first felt awkward and kind of naked, but after some minutes of assimilation, I did find this connection. Scary.

If there is one practice that is therefore core to the future classroom and the institution of the business school more broadly, it would have to be the practice of practising (see Gherardi, this volume), of doing exercises, of rehearsing. This is the sense of learning that respects, particularly through performing, that learning is embodied and not solely a cognitive activity. Practice, trying out and rehearsal are the core practice of the performing arts and their use of improvisation: 'the aim of improvisation in training actors in rehearsal, and the aim of exercises, is always the same: it is to get away from Deadly Theatre' (Brook 1990 [1968]: 126). If we want to get out of the 'deadly classroom', we therefore need to turn to a pedagogy of exercises and turn classroom spaces into zones of exercise based on a kind of 'anthropotechnics'.

For this – besides the writings of Serres – we can take inspiration from Sloterdijk's adage 'du musst dein Leben ändern' (you must change your life), which Sloterdijk (2009) borrowed from a poem by Rainer Maria Rilke, which has been translated into 'a philosophy of the acrobat' (Ansell-Pearson 2013) that mixes asceticism with athleticism. Seeing human beings as creatures of habits, Sloterdijk's summarized position suggests that if the nineteenth century can be viewed as standing under the sign of production and the twentieth century under the sign of reflexivity, then we need to grasp the future under the sign of the exercise (Ansell-Pearson 2013). Taking the anthropological character of human beings as practising, Sloterdijk's book is devoted to an analysis of anthropotechnical acrobatics (Schinkel and Noordegraaf-Eelens 2011) that is based on those mental and physical forms of exercise that can optimize people's cosmic and social immunity in the face of vague risks of life and acute certainties of death (Sloterdijk 2009).

If we start to think about the consequences of Sloterdijk's ideas, then turning the classroom into a zone of exercises would imply that the whole world is to become a 'school' brought closer by an education of practising. If so, the question therefore becomes, as Beyes (2014: 576) points out, 'How do we relate to the fundamental problematic of life-formation today and enact our own training regimes as scholars and educators?' In this regard, Serres (1997 [1991]: 80) asks: 'Have you noticed, in classrooms, in schools and lecture halls, the absence of true exercise?' And, with Serres, we could reply: don't copy, but live, taste, leave, do, practise, play . . .

## References

Ansell-Pearson, K. (2013) 'Philosophy of the acrobat: on Peter Sloterdijk', *Los Angeles Review of Books*, 8 July.

Beyes, T. (2014) 'Peter Sloterdijk'. *In:* J. Helin, T. Hernes, D. Hjorth and R. Holt (eds.) *Handbook of Process Philosophy and Organization Studies*. Oxford: Oxford University Press, pp. 567–84.

Beyes, T. and Michels, C. (2011) 'The production of educational space: heterotopia and the business university', *Management Learning*, 42(5), 521–36.

Beyes, T. and Steyaert, C. (2006) 'Justifying theatre in organizational analysis: a carnivalesque alternative?', *Consumption, Markets and Culture*, 9(2), 101–9.

Brook, P. (1990 [1968]) *The Empty Space*. London: Penguin Books.

Calvino, I. (2002) *Six Memos for the Next Millennium*. London: Penguin Books.

Crimp, D. (2015) 'Relocating Rosas'. *In:* E. Filipovic (ed.) *Anne Teresa De Keersmaeker. Work/Travail/Arbeid*. Vol. 3. Brussels: Mercatorfonds, Wiels, Rosas, pp. 81–103.

Cvejic, B. (2015) 'Dance in earnest: on time and attention in Work/Travail/Arbeid'. *In:* E. Filipovic (ed.) *Anne Teresa De Keersmaeker. Work/Travail/Arbeid*. Vol. 3. Brussels: Mercatorfonds, Wiels, Rosas, pp. 9–27.
de Caluwe, P. (2015) *Extra Muros: 2015–2016. Programme Brochure*. Brussels: De Munt.
De Keersmaeker, A.T. (2015) 'Taking the time for time'. *In:* E. Filipovic (ed.) *Anne Teresa De Keersmaeker. Work/Travail/Arbeid*.Vol. 1. Brussels: Mercatorfonds, Wiels, Rosas, pp. 35–40.
Deleuze, G. (1988) *Spinoza: Practical Philosophy*. San Francisco, CA: City Lights Books.
Deleuze, G. and Parnet C. (1987) *Dialogues II*. New York, NY: Columbia University Press.
Dey, P. and Steyaert, C. (2007) 'The troubadours of knowledge. Passion and invention in management education', *Organization*, 14(3), 437–61.
Eeckhout, B. (2014) 'There will be blood: Kunstensector staat voor zwaarste besparing ooit', *De Morgen*, 25 September.
Foucault, M. (1986) 'Of other spaces', *Diacritics*, 16(1), 22–7.
Gabriel, Y. (2008) 'Against the tyranny of PowerPoint: technology-in-use and technology abuse', *Organization Studies*, 29(2), 255–76.
Gielen, P. (2015) 'Lessons in disproportion: the role of play in arts education and the role of art in education'. *In:* B. van Heusen and P. Gielen (eds.) *Arts Education beyond Art: Teaching Art in Times of Change*. Amsterdam: Valiz, pp. 133–50.
Harris, A. (2014) *The Creative Turn: Toward a New Aesthetic Imaginary*. Rotterdam, Sense Publishers.
Henry, C. (2007) *Entrepreneurship in the Creative Industries*. Cheltenham, UK: Edward Elgar.
Huizinga, J. (1955 [1950]) *Homo Ludens. A Study of the Play Element in Culture*. Boston, MA: The Beacon Press.
Lada, K. (2015) 'A portrait of the city as a desert it opposes'. *In:* P. de Caluwe (ed.) *Extra Muros: 2015–2016. Programme Brochure*. Brussels: De Munt.
Laermans, R. (2013) 'Disciplining thought vs. nimble thinking'. *In:* P. Gielen and P. De Bruyne (eds.) *Teaching Art in the Neoliberal Realm: Realism versus Cynicism*. Amsterdam: Valiz, pp. 145–62.
Laermans, R. (2015) *Moving Together: Theorizing and Making Contemporary Dance*. Amsterdam: Valiz.
Lingard, R. (1907 [1670]) *A Letter of Advice to a Young Gentleman Leaving the University Concerning his Behaviour and Conversation in the World*. New York, NY: McAuliffe & Booth.
Marks, J. (1998) *Gilles Deleuze: Vitalism and Multiplicity*. London: Pluto Press.
Michels, C., Beyes, T. and Steyaert, C. (2014) 'Another new museum? Imagining the space of art in the creative city', *Scandinavian Journal of Public Administration*, 3, 9–28.
Overbeek, T. (2013) 'Extremes embodied: contemporary circus and education in Sweden'. *In:* P. Gielen and P. De Bruyne (eds.) *Teaching Art in the Neoliberal Realm: Realism versus Cynicism*. Amsterdam: Valiz, pp. 201–26.
Parker, M. and Jary, D. (1995) 'The McUniversity: organization, management and academic subjectivity', *Organization*, 2(2), 319–38.
Rancière, J. (1991) *The Ignorant Schoolmaster. Five Lessons in Intellectual Emancipation*. Stanford, CA: Stanford University Press.
Rehn, A. and De Cock, C. (2009) 'Deconstructing creativity'. *In:* T. Rickards, M.A. Runco and S. Moger (eds.) *The Routledge Companion to Creativity*. Abingdon, UK: Routledge, pp. 222–31.
Schinkel, W. and Noordegraaf-Eelens, L. (eds.) (2011) *In Medias Res: Peter Sloterdijk's Spherological Poetics of Being*. Amsterdam: Amsterdam University Press.
Serres, M. (1997 [1991]) *The Troubadour of Knowledge*. Ann Arbor, MI: University of Michigan Press.
Serres, M. (2012) *Petite Poucette*. Paris: Edition Le Pommier, Manifestes.
Simons, M. and Masschelein, J. (2013) 'School – a matter of form'. *In:* P. Gielen and P. De Bruyne (eds.) *Teaching Art in the Neoliberal Realm: Realism versus Cynicism*. Amsterdam: Valiz, pp. 69–83.
Sloterdijk, P. (2009) *Du musst dein Leben ändern: Über Anthropotechnik*. Berlin: Suhrkamp.
Snauwaert, D. (2015) 'Foreword'. *In:* E. Filipovic (ed.) *Anne Teresa De Keersmaeker. Work/Travail/Arbeid*. Vol. 1. Brussels: Mercatorfonds, Wiels, Rosas, pp. 7–9.
Steyaert, C. (2006) 'Cities as heterotopias and thirdspaces: the example of ImagiNation, the Swiss Expo02'. *In:* S.R. Clegg and M. Kornberger (eds.) *Space, Organization and Management Theory*. Copenhagen: Liber and CBS Press, pp. 248–65.
Steyaert, C. (2014) 'Michel Serres', *In:* J. Helin, T. Hernes, D. Hjorth and R. Holt (eds.) *Handbook of Process Philosphy and Organization Studies*. Oxford: Oxford University Press, pp. 549–66.
Steyaert, C. and Grand, S. (2009) 'Inventive pedagogy and aesthetic practices: embodying learning', *MPP LEADS*, 12, 20–1.

Steyaert, C., Hjorth, D. and Gartner, W.B. (2011) 'Six memos for a curious and imaginative future scholarship in entrepreneurship studies', *Entrepreneurship and Regional Development*, 23(1/2), 1–7.
Tuber, S.B. (2008) *Attachment, Play and Authenticity*. Lanham, MD: Jason Aronson.
Weyns, W. (2015) 'Strand, spel en het wonder van de liefde [Beach, play and the wonder of love]', *Programme book L'elisir d'amore*. Brussels: De Munt, pp. 109–18.
Winnicott, D. (1971) *Playing and Reality*. London: Routledge.

# Part V
# Programmes

# 26

# 'Permission taking'

## The humanities and critical pedagogy in the MBA

*Carl Rhodes*

## Introduction

The MBA has been under significant critique in recent years, most saliently in relation to its narrow functional focus, instrumental orientation and lack of attention to the ethical dimensions of business (Mintzberg 2004; Navarro 2008; Muff *et al.* 2013). Although it is common for responses to these issues to focus on broad-based programmes and curricular change (for example, Moldoveanu and Martin 2008; Datar *et al.* 2010), with this chapter I want to explore ways in which individual educators can respond and have responded to these issues in the classroom. In so doing I am not dismissing the importance of changes to the structure of education at the level of either policy or practice; clearly what happens at such lofty levels has a significant impact on teachers and students. Commentary on, for example, changes to government funding arrangements, the widespread vocationalization of management education, or universities focusing on using management programmes in a way that puts revenue generation above education is critical to maintaining democratic debate over the future of education. However, for most of us who toil away in the classroom our influence on such matters is for the most part limited, rendering us almost passive in our receipt of changes that eventually trickle down to us. We might engage with them in a similar manner to how we care about national politics, but our position is as citizens (in this case of the university) rather than as politicians. Moreover, if as individual educators we become enthralled solely with general debates at the expense of considering the possibilities of our own professional practice, then we risk avoiding taking action in the very location where we can make a difference. Although it may be the case that changes to the structure and governance regimes of universities have augmented managerial power at the expense of that of individual academics (Parker and Jary 1995), the classroom is a prime site where such encroachments can be resisted.

Focusing specifically on the classroom, I want to use this chapter to consider what modes of MBA pedagogy can emerge from the longstanding relationship between management research and the humanities. Moreover, I do so from an affirmative position that considers the possibilities of what one can do, rather than (just) bemoaning the forces that constrain those possibilities. As part of this, I hope to dismantle the very idea that pedagogy in the MBA classroom can and should be disciplined by functionalist and managerialist forces, a dismantling that creates a space for the enactment of critical pedagogy in the MBA (see Grey and Mitev 1995). In approaching this, I retain the idea that the vocational character of the MBA demands that this form of education be 'relevant' to managers; however, it is what is understood to be 'relevance' that needs to be questioned in order not to fall into the trap of uncritically accepting that only technocratic and instrumental skills and knowledge are what matter (see Bridgman 2007). The particular possibility I will discuss involves reformulating the meaning of 'relevance' in a liberal–critical tradition – one where what is relevant is that which enables students to reflect on, question and reformulate their own professional practice in the context of their own position as people, managers and citizens. Perhaps most importantly I will argue that pursuing this type of relevance, as an educator, does not require managerial decree within universities; it is at the disposal of educators without recourse to bureaucratic approval. In many senses, what is marked out here is a pedagogy that resists such authority and attests to the agency of the educator. It is suggested that critical pedagogy (Currie and Knights 2003) is a vehicle for this if the goals are less about handing over an approved bag of tools to students and more about providing opportunities for developing an enhanced understanding of managerial practice through an engagement with the dilemmas, ideas and contradictions that are inherent to management.

The chapter begins by exploring the central idea of 'permission taking' and what it means in relation to the practical limitations imposed by the disciplining of the academic subjectivity of the teacher. This is explored in the specific context of MBA education as it has been brought into question on account of its narrow and functionalist approach to teaching management. It is argued that responses to this critique have been dominated by proposals for structural and curricular changes and in so doing have largely ignored the role of syllabus and pedagogy. The result of this is that in all the talk of a 'crisis' of the MBA, the role and value of the educator has been sidelined. Resisting this tendency, the chapter notes that management itself can be understood as a 'field without discipline' in that throughout its history it has been characterized by an inter-disciplinary borrowing from more established fields of study, including the humanities (see Parker, this volume). Having concluded that as a body of knowledge management does not have to constitute an established, home-grown discipline, possible other forces of discipline are considered: the management textbook, the governing institutions of MBA programmes and the students themselves. Reviewing these reveals that their power and influence is overstated and the subjective limitations they impose do not have to be great, at least not in the actual classroom. This is illustrated by a personal example of teaching parts of the philosophical work of Jacques Derrida to MBA students and how this reflects a more general idea that the enactment of pedagogy exceeds the limits imposed on it by design and structure (Danby and Lee 2012). This opens up a broader set of subject positions for the educator to operate from. Moreover, it is through this pedagogy that these positions can be adopted and that permission can be taken. Such a pedagogy, the chapter goes on to argue, can enrol the humanities into 'critical management education' as a means to critique managerial dogma both theoretically and through a reconsidered relationship between student, teacher and subject matter.

## Permission taking

As a point of beginning, I would like to acknowledge how my ideas in this chapter are indebted to the late Professor Alison Lee who sadly passed away in 2012. Alison was my doctoral supervisor. A gifted scholar and educator, she influenced my own life and career in more ways than she knew. I will tell a small anecdote about one of these things she didn't know, and sadly I never took the time to tell her when I could. Several years after completing my doctoral studies I received a phone call from Alison. We were both working at the University of Technology Sydney but in different faculties, she in Education and me in Business. Alison asked me if I would come over to talk to a group of her then-doctoral students about the research I was doing and the approach I was taking. I felt that this was an odd request. These students where all studying education, and my own work, as it still is, concerned the goings-on in business and work organizations.

I asked Alison why she wanted me, rather than anyone else, to talk to these students. In response she explained how she felt that the students' work was too conservative and that she hoped that they might consider a broader set of theoretical and methodological possibilities in their studies. She wanted me to talk about my own doctoral research and some of the work that followed it. She suggested that the experimental writing and methodological work I was doing at the time would serve, to use Alison's words, as an act of 'permission giving'. Or more precisely that it might lead her students to a position of 'permission taking'. The issue she was raising was that these students had become restricted in the options and opportunities that they were considering for their own research because they had somehow the impression that they had to do things within the bounds of a limited and archaic set of scientifically and academically prescribed bounds. Alison's issue was that the seemingly overpowering authority that they felt they had to submit to was at best illusory, if not more likely to be nebulous. She suggested that the limitations that they believed were being imposed on them from an unidentified structure of authority within the university were actually self-imposed, at least in the sense that the projection of an external authority had been interiorized.

The power relations that were going on, Alison was suggesting, were therefore self-disciplining. Her comments were about the very nature and formation of academic subjectivity. She was keenly attuned to the manner in which university education served to shape and reshape people's sense of who they are in alignment with various narrow subject positions. In contrast, Alison's own work, as well as her pedagogical practice, had explicitly sought to 'allow for a more democratic and inclusive definition of the [academic] Subject' (Johnson *et al.* 2000: 146; see also Green and Lee 1995) that extended beyond the powerful image of the emotionally closed, masculine, autonomous and rational academic (Lee and Williams 1999). Such are the dominant and collusive modes of subjectivity that academics must contend with if they seek more than to just do as they are told by a spectre of authority; that is if they seek to 'negotiate a positionality "inside" those collusive spaces' of academic literacy (Fuller and Lee 1997: 411). In this particular case, Alison was concerned that the students would make particular choices because they felt that they had to in order to attain academic legitimacy. Moreover, alternative and less traditional choices were being dismissed because the students did not feel that they had permission to do otherwise. Despite this, as Alison explained to me, in the context of the degree they were doing and the location in which they were doing it, there was no real potential exercise of power or authority to prevent them from engaging in non-conventional or experimental work, either theoretically or methodologically. What Alison was encouraging them to do was to overcome and resist those disciplinary mechanisms that had embedded themselves. In other words, they were emboldened to take permission in place of self-imposed limitations projected on to a figment of authority.

Ever since that conversation with Alison, this issue of permission is something that has stayed with me and guided much of my own approach to academic work. The lesson that she wanted me to help pass on to the students ended up, in part, being the lesson that I myself learned from this experience. It is on that basis, and with respect for Alison's comments all of those years ago, that with this chapter I want to consider the question of management education (especially the MBA) and the humanities in relation to the (self)disciplining of teaching practice. It is an implication of this whole volume that bringing management education, humanities and social sciences together is fraught with problems and complexities – problems heightened in the MBA where the focus on instrumental, discipline-based knowledge is primary (Bridgman 2007). In pointing to such difficulties, the more specific questions I am interested in are: what are the disciplinary limitations around what and how we teach management in the MBA? More importantly, what might be the opportunities to resist this discipline; to resist ourselves, so to speak, through acts of 'permission taking'?

## The MBA in crisis

What does this talk of permission taking have to do with practising humanities and social sciences in management education? 'Business and liberal learning must be woven together to prepare students for their professional roles and work and also prepare them for lives of social contribution and personal fulfilment,' so says the Carnegie Report *Rethinking Undergraduate Business Education* (Colby *et al.* 2011: 2; Sullivan, Ehrlich and Colby, this volume). In the increasingly vocationalized university, the report distinguishes undergraduate from MBA education, suggesting that a first degree should be a preparation for life that does not mirror the more functionally focused MBA curriculum. For the undergraduates, they evince, what must be cultivated is 'a sense of professionalism grounded in loyalty to the mission of business to enhance public prosperity and well being' (Colby *et al.* 2011: 3). This statement of value directly opposes the idea that education should train students to be managerial technocrats mining the seam between corporate and self-interest. The American notion of liberal education that they refer to would expand students' perspective beyond the 'logic of the marketplace' (Colby *et al.* 2011: 5) through non-vocationally oriented training. In a seemingly anti-neoliberal stance the problem with undergraduate business education, the authors aver, is that it is too much like the MBA.

But the MBA is not without its detractors either – it faces criticism that in many cases echo the issues that the Carnegie Report surfaces about undergraduate education. The MBA has been said to be a vanilla course that reinforces 'functional silos' of business knowledge (Navarro 2008). It is managers that we need, not MBAs, heralds Henry Mintzberg (2004) such that the 'craft and art of managing' is built into management education, as opposed to the currently dominant practice of 'specialist training in the functions of business' (Mintzberg 2004: 4; see Srinivas, this volume). Even worse, this functionalism has been held to account for 'propagating ideologically inspired amoral theories' that serve as a 'pretence for knowledge' (Ghoshal 2005: 75). Such matters are not internal debates within universities where deals over curriculum change are hammered out; instead, they have become a matter of public concern. The dominant view is that 'management education has contributed to the systemic failure of leadership that led to the [global] financial crisis' not the least because it has privileged function over values (Podolny 2009: 63).

Beyond the details of the critique of business education there are two interesting features of these dialogues. The first is that they are couched in the language of crisis and the need for fundamental change, just as it has been in both the recent (for example, Beck 1994; Thomas 1997) and the more distant past (Gordon and Howell 1959; Pierson 1959). At present, this crisis is constructed as one where 'both academics and management practitioners criticize MBA programmes for their lack of relevance to practitioners, the values they impart to students, and their teaching methods' (Dunne and Martin 2006: 512). The MBA has faced 'intense criticism for failing to impart useful skills, failing to prepare leaders, failing to instil norms of ethical behaviour and even failing to lead graduates to good corporate jobs' (Bennis and O'Toole 2005: 96). MBA programmes, it is asserted, are at the crossroads; they need to leave the solitary path of developing analytical business functionaries and embark on the enlightened road of managerial 'values, attitudes and beliefs' (Datar *et al.* 2010: 7). The epochal vision is for fundamental change such that at this very moment fate demands that it is uniquely us, here and now, who stand at the crossroads that will determine the future direction of the world as enabled by management education (Muff *et al.* 2013).

The second feature is that the solution – the road out of the crisis – is most commonly found through structural and curricula changes to business education programmes, with scant attention to syllabus and pedagogy. We are told of the need to revisit the whole organization of the programmes, refocusing the entire ethos of our endeavours to this or that (Mintzberg 2004; Navarro 2008). It's all very macho. Big changes implemented by big men ... the others will follow.

I am reminded of Michel Foucault's statement that,

> one of the most harmful habits in contemporary thought [. . .is. . .] the analysis of the present as being precisely, in history, a present or rupture [. . .] we should have the modesty to say, on the other hand that [. . .] the time we live in is not *the* unique or fundamental or irruptive point in history where everything is completed and begun again.
>
> *Foucault 1988: 36*

Indeed crisis-mongering in business education seems to have fallen victim to such a self-centred narrative time and time again. But with stinging irony, the chief protagonist of this narrative, the one who can navigate the crisis, is still that character who is the hero of the MBA narrative – the manager – and in this case the educational manager. Answers lie, we are advised, in the management and organization of business education such that the required changes can be boldly implemented and the problems of the past be cast asunder in the awe of the new.

## Teaching in a field without discipline

Other than its convenient simplicity and managerial hubris, one thing especially notable about this narrative of crisis is the relative absence of the educator as anything but a receiver of managerial imperatives. If there is a role for that lonely person who inhabits the classroom, it is just to be beholden to the whims and fancies of those epochally minded managers who thrive on the crisis as the *raison d'etre* of their own leadership prowess. For each and every putative response it would seem as if there is no alternative but for the educator to be a support actor in a story starring the manager in the lead role. Management education might get questioned, but managerial self-importance and the grand pretensions of its own agency escape unscathed. The educator who teaches in a classroom is cast as a minor character in a managerial narrative. Is the figure of the educator to be accepted as an epiphenomenon swept away by the all-encompassing narrative of crisis and progress? Is the educator to be considered only in terms of how he or she can implement the curriculum that is handed down from a masterful authority? Are the limits of the educators' prerogative set at being only to do what they have authoritative permission to do?

Clearly my answer to such questions is an emphatic NO! Moreover, as I will turn to now, it is through teaching management with the humanities that this emphasis can be made practical. It is worth noting that the humanities, understood as those subjects concerned with non-vocational matters, such as literature, philosophy, art and culture, have never been far from the study and teaching in management education. In the MBA they are present, not so much at the level of curriculum, but within the specifics of syllabus and pedagogy – these latter areas being within the purview of the teacher. On the one hand, this is an educational matter. Back in 1959, Gordon and Howell's *Higher Education for Business* was recommending 'a more effective liberal arts component in the programme of degree candidates in business administration' (1959: 115). Little seems to have changed as far as the response is concerned. On the other hand, we can see that scholarship in management and organizations has always been infused with the humanities. Who is it that has inspired the development of management and organizational studies? Early examples include classical sociologists such as the holy triumvirate of Marx, Durkheim and (especially) Weber. This is a formidable counterpoint to the more managerially oriented Barnard, Taylor and Fayol (see O'Connor, this volume). Would we understand management the same way if it had not been for Schütz, Goffman and Geertz? Or more recently, Foucault and Derrida? Sociologists, philosophers, anthropologists, literary theorists, political scientists, as well as thinkers from other disciplines, have all been central in the development of the seeming cacophony that constitutes contemporary management knowledge. Doesn't this suggest that what can be referred to as the humanities already infuses the field of knowledge within which management teaching is located? This infusion is also about how scholarship and teaching is approached, with the humanities bequeathing a tradition characterized by 'searching critical thought, daring imagination, empathetic understanding of human experiences of many different kinds, and understanding of the complexity of the world we live in' (Nussbaum 2010: 7).

We can go further and suggest that management and organization studies (MOS) is actually a field without any discipline. With its youth there is no established way of doing things, or paradigmatically fixed approach (Westwood and Clegg 2003; Pullen and Rhodes 2009). Although it may be the case that scientific approaches have historically dominated business school education, especially in the US (Mulligan 1987), this is not a feature of research knowledge about management and organizations more generally. MOS is, theoretically, a borrower who travels afield to established disciplines bringing home ideas to inform its own loosely coupled body of knowledge. Less a well-organized system, MOS is a mixing pot of disciplinary knowledge on loan from elsewhere and brought to bear on how we might understand the phenomena of organization and the practice of management. It is indeed the case that 'what is called organization studies defies formal definition because of the breadth and incommensurability of what goes on under its name' (Pullen and Rhodes 2009: 11). Failure to recognize this is borne less out of an awareness of theoretical developments in this field, and more out of a narrow-mindedness that exacts the 'repeated exclusion of difference and sanctioned ignorance' (Jones and Munro 2005: 3). Indeed, a review of what has been going on in contemporary management and organization studies reveals that its main characteristic is diversity and lack of cohesion or agreement, married to a certain one-sided 'politic of prescribing what is "proper" to organization theory' (Jones and Munro 2005: 7).

Those who once wished to be denizens of an organization studies that could be identified by its pursuit of science without recourse to the variety of inspirations that can arise from the arts and humanities (see Pfeffer 1993; Donaldson 1996) might recoil at the fact that Burrell and Morgan's (1994 [1979]) *Sociological Paradigms and Organizational Analysis*, and its encouragement of paradigm diversity in organization studies, is 'one of the most referenced works in organization theory (OT) of the last half-century' (Hassard and Cox 2013: 1701). Empirically it has been noted that despite recent tendencies for powerful specialisms within MOS to be developing, it still remains the case that overall the field is characterized by 'theoretical and methodological diversity' (Vogel 2012: 1036) and the 'proliferation of diffuse and diverse goals and standards with little common background in terms of theories and methods' (Vogel 2012: 1020). The point taken from this is that MOS has no singular set of rules, procedures or theoretical orientations to which those operating under its name feel compelled to adhere. MOS is taught in a field with no discipline. Moreover, it is this lack of discipline that is an enabler of permission taking in the classroom, as well as a means through which the dominance of the educational manager can be resisted.

## Disciplining the educator

Given this undisciplined heterodoxy, how then might management knowledge be accused of blinkered functionalism when it comes to its teaching? As was just discussed, we can discount scholarly knowledge about management as being a singular force of discipline. Brocklehurst *et al.* (2007: 380) confirm that 'it is very difficult to point to an agreed body of knowledge upon which the MBA should be based'. So where, therefore, does the presumed dominance of functional knowledge in teaching arise? Where is this discipline coming from? As we saw earlier, the heterodoxy of management research itself is not a source of such discipline. As another contender we can consider the management textbook. Although the variety of topics and approaches to studying management might be a shifting sea of vaguely interrelated bits and pieces (Pullen and Rhodes 2009), the textbook seems to virtually canonize what counts as management knowledge.

Let's take for example the topic of 'organizational behaviour'. In terms of textbook knowledge, this topic coalesces around understanding organizations at the level of the individual (personality, perception, motivation and so forth), the group (teamwork, group dynamics, leadership, communication and so forth) and the organization (structure, culture, etc.). On top of this there may also be something about management practice. Whether you use the fifteenth edition of Robbins and Judge's *Organizational Behaviour* (2012), the eighth edition of Buchanan and Huczynski's *Organizational Behaviour* (2013), the third edition of Mullins's *Essentials of Organizational Behaviour* (2011), or even a critically oriented book like Fiona Wilson's *Organizational Behaviour at Work* (2014), the basic topics and research themes that are said to constitute how we might understand organizations are remarkably consistent.

Such textbook approaches serve to bolster the fantasy that we work in a field that has achieved consensus. Concurrently, it acts to limit management knowledge, most often in a functional manner, in order to squeeze out the beauty and variety of what constitutes the actual stock of knowledge. This knowledge is violently reduced into the virtually indistinguishable tables of contents of textbooks, or even more authoritatively through the provision of 'standardized OHPs and lecture scripts' by the textbook publisher (Lilley 1999: 33). To use these books, to feel compelled to use these books, releases a powerful normalizing and disciplining force on what goes on in the classroom. The study of management and organizations might have no discipline, but the teaching of it certainly does. Just like with Foucault's (2002 [1966]) infamous Chinese dictionary, the ordering seems largely arbitrary. Even worse, this ordering is isomorphic across the different books to the point of virtual hegemony. Perhaps, but only if one feels compelled to teach with and from these books. But that is not necessary. Why not just teach from research rather than textbooks in order to easily sidestep the disciplinary apparatus they erect? This is a well-established practice amongst educators who are in a position to not prescribe a textbook or to teach alongside it rather than remaining true to it.

Other candidates for the locus of discipline are, of course, the management of the departments that run the MBA programmes and the various accreditation bodies that anoint them. But discipline here, often imposed with seemingly sovereign authority, is largely at a high-level curricular level. The accrediting body Association of Masters in Business Administration (AMBA) provides a good exemplar of this. Their formally published *Criteria for Education* (2010) stipulates the curriculum through thirteen very briefly articulated topics. For each, however, there is no mention of what these mean or how they should be elaborated. There is also no real detail on syllabus or pedagogy. This might create the appearance that many different universities' MBA programmes look remarkably similar when reviewed from the website or prospectus, but beneath that, detailed prescriptions are hard to find. If one takes for example item three from the AMBA list: 'organisation theory, behaviour, HRM issues and interpersonal communications'

(AMBA 2010: 7) the breadth of possibilities, most especially as it concerns the humanities, is enormous. Foucault or Fayol, deconstruction or decision making, Marx or motivation, organizational dynamics or organizational rhizomatics: all can be incorporated (as long as you don't rely on a textbook).

There is another possible source of discipline and that is the students themselves and their expectations. But again this seems overstated. Of course students enrol in an MBA with at least some sense that it should be relevant to the practice of management, and that seems quite reasonable a request to be made of those who teach such a degree. But the nature of this relevance is not fixed such that it need not mean teaching some falsely assumed techniques for successful managerial control. A reason for avoiding this is its very impossibility, given that 'the fact that after a century or more of effort we have little in the way of generally applicable formulae' for how management should be practised (Grey 2004: 181). Or more positively, 'MBA students are likely to perceive as relevant those pedagogic practices that encourage them to critically reflect on the often unexamined mental models that inform managerial action' (Currie and Knights 2003: 44) rather than those that provide 'reliable techniques' (Grey 2004: 181).

## Teaching Derrida in the MBA

I can reflect here on a personal anecdote. For years I have drawn directly on the philosophy of Jacques Derrida in teaching MBA students on organizational theory and business ethics courses (see also Learmonth, Humphreys and Griffin, this volume). In particular, I have used some of Derrida's ideas to inform centrally how we might understand and practise management. I have never encountered any resistance either from students or from university managers; quite the contrary – this teaching has been quite successful with the students and they report that they find it both interesting and useful. I recall specifically a course I taught in Sydney a few years ago as part of a part-time MBA where I invoked Derrida's (1992, 1995, 1996) notion of undecidability in relation to how we might understand responsible decision making. The key point was that in the end – and after however much thinking, planning and research – decisions always advance into an unknowable future such that decision making is inherently non-rational, and that it is this non-rationality that renders us responsible for our decisions. About six months later I ran into one of the students. During the time the class was running this person had recently taken up a managerial position in a bank. He hated the job, largely on account of the processes of corporate management limiting individual initiative. He just didn't fit the corporate mould and what he saw as its expectation of conformism and devotion. This clearly troubled him, something he spoke about regularly in class. He felt, however, that he needed to stay in the job because it was secure and provided a predictable income for him and his family. He had previously been self-employed. He was suffering from what Derrida calls the ordeal of undecidability: a not-knowing what to do when all choices of action balance out in terms of what is appealing and not appealing about them. What he explained to me those six months later was that the class had successfully helped him understand his personal career predicament and had led him in the end to take the leap of faith and leave his bank job in order to pursue a different career in small business, outside of the corporate world. It had worked for him. He was visibly happier and no longer had an anxious and pained expression. He told me that after six months he now knew that he had made the right decision. He also said that had it not been for the class he would not have had the courage to make this decision. This seems to me to pass the test of relevance.

This example reflects on my own MBA teaching. I do teach management in a way that I position as relevant. But I also recognize that the possibilities for how relevance might be rendered are broad. If one teaches from research rather than textbooks, the opportunities are seemingly endless. This is the case as long as one takes the permission to do so. As I said before, despite the confines of the business school, what we teach is without discipline. Management is a phenomenon and a practice, not a scholarly discipline. Thus although people may be disciplined by various forces and perceptions, these can (quite easily) be resisted. A key mode of this resistance is taking permission to let the humanities in, as was the case in the example just recalled. For MBAs, if one is teaching management, then one must teach it (rather than teaching philosophy, literary criticism, etc.). There is considerable freedom in how one does so, however, as long as one assumes one's own permission and takes responsibility for it. Even more generally, we can assert that although there are clearly forces that seek a certain model of business school education based on an assumed canon of knowledge, people do not have to wait until these are changed from on high in order to 'practise the humanities' in management education. It is from the locus of the classroom that we can actually influence the direction of management education. It is through syllabus and pedagogy and with individual students that things can be done differently.

These issues more generally relate to the enactment of pedagogy in university settings. As Danby and Lee (2012) explain, we can consider pedagogy as the space between a designed plan and a practice. When we think of pedagogy we often think exclusively of design understood in terms of the selection, arrangement and scheduling of different teaching and learning activities; the people and relationships that are involved in the teaching and learning; and the way that the subject matter is translated and enacted through institutionalized norms and subject positions. All of these things are planned ahead of time with lecture schedules, class activities, allocation of teachers and tutors and so forth. The operationalization of such design denotes what Danby and Lee call 'pedagogy in action': the cultural reproduction of pedagogy through its practice. If pedagogical design is conducted by planning activities through which the textbooks' discipline of management is reproduced, understood and even indoctrinated, the practice here is therefore one of working to recreate particular forms of managerial subjectivity as dictated by dominant knowledge structures.

What the engagement with the humanities offers is the possibility of what we might call a pedagogy of critique where the design of activities serves to question the dogma of that managerialism as well as to provide less institutionalized alternatives. For example, this was what I was doing by bringing Derrida into my MBA classroom. With this practice, different modes of subjectivity can be opened up to students; modes that need not sacrifice managerial relevance, but instead reformulate relevance in a critical tradition – in this case, the critique of managerial prerogative, privilege and dogma. Moreover, all of this is within the purview and power of the educator who chooses to use it, as indeed many do. There is no need to wait for permission from accreditation bodies, curriculum committees or textbook authors. When pedagogy is seen as localized social action, it is always particular to the context in which it is performed. Moreover, this is not just pedagogy in terms of the design of different forms of learning activities, but rather a pedagogy that is practised through relationship between the shifting subject positions of teacher and student. I did not, and would not, ask my student to quit his job – doing so was entirely his initiative and responsibility. However, insofar as I can impute meaning to his actions, he was moved by a critique that brought corporate and managerial dogma into question such that he could reformulate it on his own terms.

## Attesting to critical pedagogy

The type of teaching I have been referring to aligns with what some call critical pedagogy (see Perriton and Singh, this volume; Vince, this volume). This is an approach to teaching and teacher–student relations where the university is regarded as a space for 'counter-hegemonic practice' (Boyce 1996: 1). In this case, it is the hegemony of the dogmatic managerial knowledge epitomized in the genre of the textbook that is being countered. In the example discussed earlier, this is manifested in how using Derrida to teach decision making enabled a particular student to re-evaluate his position as a corporate employee and in so doing to pursue different options in his own life in relation to himself and his family. This was quite different both in intent and in effect to standard approaches to the topic, which focus on normative or descriptive theories whereby 'organizational decision making is the process to make decisions following the protocols, rules and conventions defined by an organization' (Adam and Humphreys 2008: 71). Key to this difference is an approach that uses theory to promote freedom, choice, responsibility and opportunity rather than using it to train people in the technical skills required to do a job. This speaks to two very different conceptions of 'relevance'. On the one hand, management education has been thought to be relevant when it is pertinent to achieving business goals and solving business problems. On the other hand, and in the way it has been formulated here, relevance is about locating management education in a tradition that values and promotes freedom and responsibility (rather than skills and effectiveness) as the most important outcome of the educational process.

Critical pedagogy applied to the specificities of management education is, however, different from how it has been applied elsewhere. What is different is that although critical pedagogy has been traditionally aimed at the emancipation of dominated and subordinated groups, critical management pedagogy is directed at those who seek or have careers in management. To these aspirants to the managerial class, it is their potential for superordination rather than subordination that can inform teaching. As Grey and French (1996: 2) explain: 'the fact that management is socially important means that it is vital that it be exposed to critical interrogation. And since management education is such a significant arena for the reproduction of management, it follows that it is a primary site of such interrogation.' Applying critical pedagogy to management education, whilst exemplified in the story of my MBA student, is in fact much broader in its possibilities. The general ethos is to enact a pedagogy that suggests that existing ways of doing things are always open to question and reformulation, and that habituated or institutionalized management practice and knowledge is invariably subject to contestation. This is pedagogy not of providing different answers, but of formulating different questions, of 'generating openness to alternative ways of thinking' (Currie and Knights 2003: 33). The purpose of this, as Currie and Knights make clear, is to 'help arrest the drift, on the part of both teachers and students, towards an instrumentalism that easily collapses into indifference' (2003: 28) and to 'problematize rather than validate management theories and assumptions' (2003: 31). Such education is not so much about gaining relevant skills as about shifting identities and subjectivities through pedagogic interaction (Chappell *et al.* 2003). Turning again to the example of my student, this meant him coming to acknowledge the confines that the corporate world inflicts on identity, to realize that working and being within those confines was causing personal unhappiness, and being prepared to take the chance to do something different and to be someone different.

The pedagogy-in-action that led the student to this was not one that was designed for this specific result as a predetermined goal or intention. The pedagogy-in-action that was at play involves relinquishing the assumed canon of textbook management knowledge and rendering it open to critique, with the humanities serving as an ideal way to guide that opening. It was this, at least in part, that provided an opportunity for the student to rethink his own life and, as a result, make different decisions. What came with this pedagogy too was my relinquishing the expert position of the lecturer in that I had no specific expectation of what students might take or learn from the teaching. With critical pedagogy, the subjectivity of the lecturer must also be open to question such that a 'changed relationship between the management teacher and student' (Currie and Knights 2003: 31) is also required. But opportunities to do this are rife in that 'there is room for us as educators to reform the MBA and to start a debate with managers and many others about the nature of management and how it needs to be rethought' (Brocklehurst *et al.* 2007: 368) and re-lived.

The possibilities for MBA education offered by an engagement with the humanities are ones that afford a reformulated and extended notion of relevance for management education. We take heed here that conventional approaches have been questioned on these very grounds with 'management education generally and MBA programmes in particular, [having] been persistently criticized for failing to speak adequately to management practice' (Hay and Hodgkinson 2008: 21; see Landfester, Tofte Brenneche and Prat-i-Pubill, this volume). One response might be to try harder in pursuing this kind of relevance. Another one, as argued here, is to reconsider what we mean by relevance and to take the permission to do so. MBA education has a vocational and professional nature and is aimed specifically at those who do or want to manage. This is not a liberal education in any traditional sense, but that does not mean that the humanities cannot have a place. Critical pedagogy is a vehicle for this, given 'its call to broaden management education into the domains of philosophy, ethics, politics and social sciences' (Grey 2004: 185). This does not simply mean just switching allegiance away from management and organizational theory to a more ancient and supposedly more credible set of academic disciplines; instead, it means engaging with a form of education intended to open up opportunities for people to reflect on their own professional practice, in the context of its relationship to their own lives and the lives of others, and in so doing enable them to make different, better and more responsible decisions about how to live as people, managers and citizens.

## Conclusion

When managers are asked about the importance of their MBA education, they do not respond saying that they have gained a new bag of tools; instead, we hear that they have engaged with new perspectives, gained an enhanced sense of credibility and self-esteem, and acquired a different appreciation of managerial practice through an engagement with academic ideas. For them, education is relevant in that it contributes 'to their on-going learning to manage through a broadening and challenging of their understanding of practice' (Hay and Hodgkinson 2008: 32). Accepting this, the humanities – whether it is, amongst others, literary studies, philosophy or social theory – are prime candidates to contribute to such a model of relevance. Moreover, if it is management research and its connection with the humanities rather than management textbooks that provide the basis of knowledge from which to teach, all of these subjects are well-documented in the management and organization studies literature. The possibilities of connecting with the humanities and engaging in a critical pedagogy that is personally and practically relevant are already well accounted for – there is nothing new to this. All that has to be done – and as many already do – is to take the permission to enact it in the classroom.

By way of conclusion, what I have been working towards in this chapter is the elucidation of an approach to using the humanities in management education that is primarily driven by the individual educator in the spirit of critical pedagogy. This is informed by a focus on student relevance without recourse to the structures of institutional approval, strategy or imprimatur. Education is far too important for all of the decisions to be handed over to an increasingly bloated managerial class within universities, especially when it concerns decisions regarding what is taught and how it is taught. As individual academics, we can retain hope that we are employed to teach based on our experience and expertise in our fields and also as educators.

To not take charge of or take responsibility for the classroom is a retreat from professionalism that shifts accountability for education and learning from the academic specialist to the managerial generalist. This is nothing less than an affront to that profession. The argument I have made in this chapter is that involving the humanities in management education is a practice that is immediately possible, as well as one that supports a thinking, questioning and debating (rather than functional and instrumental) approach. But that does not mean that I am suggesting with false hubris and imagined power that everyone who teaches management *should* do this. More democratically, what I am suggesting is that people who teach management *can* do this if they choose to and, moreover, that there are some good reasons for making that choice. Permission is there for the taking.

## References


Adam, F. and Humphreys, P. (2008) *Encyclopaedia of Decision Making and Decision Support Technologies*. New York, NY: Information Science Reference.

Association of Masters in Business Administration (AMBA) (2010) *Criteria for the Accreditation of MBA Programs*. London: Association of Masters in Business Administration.

Beck, J.E. (1994) 'The new paradigm of management education revolution and counter-revolution', *Management Learning*, 25(2): 231–47.

Bennis, W.G. and O'Toole, J. (2005) 'How business schools lost their way', *Harvard Business Review*, 83(5): 96–104.

Boyce, M.E. (1996) 'Teaching critically as an act of praxis and resistance', *Electronic Journal of Radical Organization Theory*, 2(2): 1–14.

Bridgman, T. (2007) 'Reconstituting relevance exploring possibilities for management educators' critical engagement with the public', *Management Learning*, 38(4): 425–39.

Brocklehurst, M., Sturdy, A., Winstanley, D. and Driver, M. (2007) 'Introduction: whither the MBA? Factions, fault lines and the future', *Management Learning*, 38(4): 379–88.

Buchanan, D.A. and Huczynski, A. (2013) *Organizational Behaviour*. 8th edn. Harlow, UK: Pearson.

Burrell, G. and Morgan, G. (1994) [1979]) *Sociological Paradigms and Organisational Analysis*. London: Heinemann.

Chappell, C., Rhodes, C., Solomon, N., Tennant, M. and Yates, L. (2003) *Reconstructing the Lifelong Learner: Pedagogy and Identity in Individual, Organisational and Social Change*. London: Routledge.

Colby, A., Ehrlich, T., Sullivan, B. and Dolle, J. (2011) *Rethinking Undergraduate Business Education: Liberal Learning for the Profession*. San Francisco, CA: Jossey-Bass.

Currie, G. and Knights, D. (2003) 'Reflecting on a critical pedagogy in MBA education', *Management Learning*, 34(1): 27–49.

Danby, S. and Lee, A. (2012) 'Researching doctoral pedagogy close up: design and action in two doctoral programmes', *Australian Universities' Review*, 54(1): 19–28.

Datar, S.M., Garvin, D.A. and Cullen, P.G. (2010) *Rethinking the MBA: Business Education at a Crossroads*. Boston, MA: Harvard University Press.

Derrida, J. (1992) 'Force of law: the mystical foundation of authority'. *In:* D. Cornell, M. Rosenfeld and D.G. Carlson (eds.) *Deconstruction and the Possibility of Justice*. London: Routledge, pp. 3–67.

Derrida, J. (1995) *The Gift of Death*. Chicago, IL: Chicago University Press.

Derrida, J. (1996) 'Remarks on deconstruction and pragmatism'. *In:* C. Mouffe (ed.) *Deconstruction and Pragmatism*. London: Routledge, pp. 77–88.

Donaldson, L. (1996) *For Positivist Organization Theory*. London: Sage Publications.

Dunne, D. and Martin, R. (2006) 'Design thinking and how it will change management education: an interview and discussion', *Academy of Management Learning and Education*, 5(4): 512–23.

Foucault, M. (1988) *Politics, Philosophy, Culture: Interviews and Other Writing 1977/1984*. London: Routledge.

Foucault, M. (2002) [1966]) *The Order of Things: Archaeology of the Human Sciences*. London: Routledge.

Fuller, G. and Lee, A. (1997) 'Textual collusions', *Discourse: Studies in the Cultural Politics of Education*, 18(3): 409–23.

Ghoshal, S. (2005) 'Bad management theories are destroying good management practices', *Academy of Management Learning and Education*, 4(1): 75–91.

Gordon, R.A. and Howell, J.E. (1959) *Higher Education for Business*. New York, NY: Columbia University Press.
Green, B. and Lee, A. (1995) 'Theorising postgraduate pedagogy', *Australian Universities' Review*, 38(2): 40–5.
Grey, C. (2004) 'Reinventing business schools: the contribution of critical management education', *Academy of Management Learning and Education*, 3(2): 178–86.
Grey, C. and French, R. (1996) 'Rethinking management education: an introduction'. *In:* R. French and C. Grey (eds.) *Rethinking Management Education*. London: Sage Publications, pp. 1–16.
Grey, C. and Mitev, N. (1995) 'Management education: a polemic', *Management Learning*, 26(1): 73–90.
Hassard, J. and Cox, J.W. (2013) 'Can sociological paradigms still inform organizational analysis? A paradigm model for post-paradigm times', *Organization Studies*, 34(11): 1701–28.
Hay, A.J. and Hodgkinson, M. (2008) 'More success than meets the eye: a challenge to critiques of the MBA. Possibilities for critical management education?', *Management Learning*, 39(1): 21–40.
Johnson, L., Lee, A. and Green, B. (2000) 'The PhD and the autonomous self: gender, rationality and postgraduate pedagogy', *Studies in Higher Education*, 25(2): 135–47.
Jones, C. and Munro. R. (2005) 'Organization theory, 1985–2005'. *In:* C. Jones and R. Munro (eds.) *Contemporary Organization Theory*. Oxford: Blackwell, pp. 1–15.
Lee, A. and Williams, C. (1999) 'Forged in fire: narratives of trauma in PhD supervision pedagogy', *Southern Review*, 32(1), 6.
Lilley, S. (1999) 'Dr Deadpan's box of tricks', *Times Higher Education Supplement*, 26 February, 33.
Mintzberg, H. (2004) *Managers, Not MBAs: A Hard Look at the Soft Practice of Managing and Management Development*. San Francisco, CA: Berrett-Koehler Publishers.
Moldoveanu, M. and Martin, R. (2008) *The Future of the MBA: Designing the Thinker of the Future*. Oxford: Oxford University Press.
Muff, K., Dyllick, T., Drewell, M., North, J., Shrivastave, P. and Haertle, J. (2013) *Management Education for the World*. Cheltenham, UK: Edward Elgar.
Mulligan, T.M. (1987) 'Two cultures in business education', *The Academy of Management Review*, 12(4): 593–99.
Mullins, L. (2011) *Essentials of Organizational Behaviour.* 3rd edn. Harlow, UK: Pearson.
Navarro, P. (2008) 'The MBA core curricula of top-ranked US business schools: a study in failure?', *Academy of Management Learning and Education*, 7(1): 108–23.
Nussbaum, M.C. (2010) *Not for Profit: Why Democracy Needs the Humanities*. Princeton, NJ: Princeton University Press.
Parker, M. and Jary, D. (1995) 'The McUniversity: organization, management and academic subjectivity', *Organization*, 2(2): 319–38.
Pfeffer, J. (1993) 'Barriers to the advance of organizational science: paradigm development as a dependent variable', *Academy of Management Review*, 18(4): 599–620.
Pierson, F.C. (1959) *The Education of American Businessmen: A Study of University-College Programs in Business Administration*. New York, NY: McGraw Hill.
Podolny, J.M. (2009) 'The buck stops (and starts) at business school', *Harvard Business Review*, 87(6): 62–7.
Pullen, A. and Rhodes, C. (eds.) (2009) *Bits of Organization*. Copenhagen: Liber.
Robbins, S.P. and Judge, T.A. (2012) *Organizational Behaviour*, 15th edn. New York, NY: Prentice-Hall.
Thomas, A.B. (1997) 'The coming crisis of western management education', *Systemic Practice and Action Research*, 10(6): 681–701.
Vogel, R. (2012) 'The visible colleges of management and organization studies: a bibliometric analysis of academic journals', *Organization Studies*, 33(8): 1015–43.
Westwood, R. and Clegg, S. (eds.) (2003) *Debating Organization: Point-counterpoint in Organization Studies*. Oxford: Blackwell.
Wilson, F.M. (2014). *Organizational Behaviour and Work: A Critical Introduction*. 4th edn. Oxford: Oxford University Press.

# 27

# Knowledge you can't google

## Teaching philosophy at the business school

*Rasmus Johnsen, Morten Sørensen Thaning and Michael Pedersen*

### Introduction

The critique of higher education for its increasingly shortsighted focus on profitable skills rather than on the education of competent democratic citizens (for example, Nussbaum 2010) is prominently directed at business schools. Did they not create the kind of graduates whose focus on being ever more economically productive led to the most recent financial crisis? In turn, it has been suggested that if there is any positive aspect to this crisis, it is perhaps the opportunity it offers to bring business studies and the humanities into a fruitful dialogue. Integrating liberal learning with business education can 'enable students to make sense of the world and their place in it, preparing them to use knowledge and skills as means toward responsible engagement with the world' (Colby *et al.* 2011: 4; Sullivan, Ehrlich and Colby, this volume). If such a promise is to be realized, however, it demands a break with the way in which the humanities and business education are typecast.

The critique of business education often comes with the implicit assumption that the humanities have the moral high ground. From such a position they can come to act as the shepherds of the business world, ensuring that the economic logic does not lead to actions of moral, social and economic irresponsibility. In such a light, the humanities are reduced to a kind of moral super-ego working to promote a fairly predetermined set of ethics codes and social responsibility charters (Hoffmann 2009; Jones *et al.* 2005; Spoelstra 2007). As such, the promise of integration between the humanities and business studies ends up in an age-old dualism, which places critical explorative thought on one side and calculative instrumental economic rationality on the other.

Accepting the tempting offer of moral superiority not only leaves the image of business studies as morally doubtful untouched, it also misses the opportunity to realize the potential of the humanities as a practical form of knowledge, the purpose of which is to facilitate real change in its students (Gadamer 2004). Taking such an ambition seriously requires a proper dialogue between the different stakeholders in the field, that is an open debate about what business and management studies is or may become, which articulates the problems and dilemmas of this field from within the field itself. Engaging in such a process, business must not only learn from the humanities; the humanities must also learn from the logic of business studies. This means engaging with the emphatic focus on action and utility, which is a traditional hallmark of this sphere. It also requires acknowledging the immense practical importance of the forms of knowledge produced to the contemporary world. Developing education around the question of how to assume responsibility in a non-moralizing way may work to free the humanities from a two-fold trap: first, the illusion that what humanities represent is the ideal description of the world; second, the unfortunate tendency to wallow in critical or deconstructive debunking that comes with this illusion, which often fails to take responsibility for how we should act and decide.

In this chapter we will present the study programme in Philosophy and Business Administration (FLØK) at Copenhagen Business School (CBS). This programme, which in many ways can be seen as an academic and pedagogical response to the challenges described earlier, is one of only a few examples in higher education worldwide of academic programmes that not only integrate elements of philosophy in teaching traditional business disciplines, but also teach philosophy as an academic discipline in a business school setting. In this manner the programme represents a higher education experiment that continuously – now in its twentieth year – tackles the challenge of creating reciprocal integration between the central dimensions of the humanities and business education. We will share some of the experiences that we have had in this process and ponder their implications for teaching philosophy at the business school.

The chapter begins with a short introduction to the context of the study programme, explaining in a little more detail the vision of CBS as a 'business university' and providing some insights into the history of the programme at the institution. Following this, the chapter will give a more general reflection on the method of teaching philosophy at CBS. After this, we will move into a more practical exploration of three of the compulsory undergraduate courses that are taught in the programme. To us, they present examples of firmly establishing the humanities in management education that we would like to see multiplied and translated into new attempts to integrate philosophy and business studies. The chapter will end with a brief summary of our findings.

## FLØK: philosophy at the 'business university'

CBS is the largest business school in Northern Europe, but despite its name and the fact that it provides education in the traditional management and business disciplines it is not a conventional business school. If most business schools are faculties, colleges or departments, CBS has the distinct profile of a 'business university', hosting around 20,000 students and 690 full-time academic researchers with backgrounds not only in business and economics, but also in the social sciences and the humanities. The aim is to provide research and teaching in traditional business disciplines and in disciplines that place business in a wider social, political and cultural context. This sets CBS apart from more tightly focused business schools as well as from the 'full universities' (CBS 2011). When the programme in philosophy and business studies was first launched in 1995, it was one of the first examples of what has now developed into an array of programmes at CBS designed to fulfil such an interdisciplinary purpose. Today, the so-called 'combination-programmes' work to combine business studies with philosophy and also, for example, with psychology, sociology, communication, languages or IT.

FLØK is offered as a three-year undergraduate programme (BSc) that can be combined with a two-year master's programme (MSc). Since 2014, the MSc in Philosophy and Business Administration has been taught in English. Roughly 25 per cent of the students who complete the undergraduate programme also enrol on the master's programme. The main part of the remaining students go on to complete their master's in other academic programmes, mostly at CBS itself, and only a small number take jobs outside the university after their bachelor degree. In this chapter we will focus on the undergraduate programme (see Table 27.1 for an overview).

Divided into six semesters, the three-year undergraduate programme consists of seventeen courses, all of which integrate, in some way, philosophical themes like ethics, epistemology, politics or aesthetics, and business-related themes like management, finance, economics, marketing and organization. Students prepare two large integrative projects: a first-year project that focuses on philosophy of science and method, and a third-year bachelor's project, which completes the programme. The projects are mostly prepared in groups of two to four students.

It is the intention of the programme that the whole curriculum reflects the integration of philosophy and business studies, even if some courses are more oriented towards such integration than others. In general, this means that every course, no matter how it has been taught traditionally, should seek to maintain a pedagogical balance between familiarizing the student with the philosophical tradition and the interpretive endeavour of exploring how problems and dilemmas that surface in its texts play out in managerial or organizational practices. In practice, this means taking seriously the economic realm as a sphere of life and understanding its models and theories as cultural practices that can be the subject of philosophical reflection. Rather than being restricted to 'applying' philosophy to 'relevant' areas, which are more or less predetermined, such as ethics in corporate responsibility – a method that has been criticized for its tendency to foreclose reflection and philosophical thinking (Jones *et al.* 2005) – this means methodically broadening the area of interest to also include practical and theoretical spheres such as the aesthetics of marketing, the epistemology of finance and economics and the politics of organization. Ultimately, the pedagogical goal of the curriculum is to invite students to perceive *philosophical* subjects and dilemmas in management practices, rather than just obstacles that must be overcome or done away with. It is the aim of the programme to maintain that such reciprocal integration must be constantly provided through an interpretative effort.

*Table 27.1* An overview of FLØK (HA(fil))

| | | | | |
|---|---|---|---|---|
| 1st Semester | Economic philosophy (7.5 ECTS) | The Business in Society (7.5 ECTS) | Microeconomics (7.5 ECTS) | Cultural Analysis & Concept Development (7.5 ECTS) |
| 2nd Semester | Ethics & Responsibility (7.5 ECTS) | Marketing & Aesthetics (7.5 ECTS) | Accounting & Financial Management (7.5 ECTS) | 1st Year Project (with Scientific Method) (7.5 ECTS) |
| 3rd Semester | Epistemology and metaphysics in business studies (7.5 ECTS) | Philosophy of Management (7.5 ECTS) | Finance (7.5 ECTS) | Organization Theory (7.5 ECTS) |
| 4th Semester | Organizational Philosophy (15 ECTS) | Method (7.5 ECTS) | Macroeconomics & Social Responsibility (7.5 ECTS) | |
| 5th Semester | Elective (7.5 ECTS) | Elective (7.5 ECTS) | Strategy (7.5 ECTS) | Elective (7.5 ECTS) |
| 6th Semester | Philosophy of the Present: Human Capital (15 ECTS) | | | Bachelor Project (15 ECTS) |

Note: ECTS, European Credit Transfer and Accumulation System credits.

## A short history of FLØK

When the plans for a programme in philosophy and business studies at CBS emerged in the early 1990s, the ambition was to create an education combining the rigorous methodological aspects of conceptual thinking with general training in the more traditional business school disciplines (Siggaard 2014). Hans Siggaard, who was one of the people behind the programme's first curriculum, said in an interview that the idea to launch the programme came in response to a more general diversification at that time of what kinds of discourses could and should qualify for the business school curriculum. The educational 'momentum' that this diversification resulted in was perhaps not unlike the contemporary call to business schools and universities in the wake of the most recent financial crisis to diversify the content and the methods of their education in business skills and economics (for example, Colby *et al.* 2011; International Student Initiative for Pluralism in Economics (ISIPE) 2014). In an international perspective, the institutional trends that led people at CBS to launch a philosophy programme were the same type that led to the gradual emergence of business ethics, which became established as an academic field in its own right in the 1980s and 1990s. To begin with, business ethics was clearly interdisciplinary, with the lines between philosophy and business research often blurred (de George 2011). Likewise, the architects behind the programme in philosophy and business studies envisaged an interdisciplinary field that was to be pedagogically equipped to meet the need, as they put it, of 'rendering visible and useful the philosophical – including the moral philosophical – postmodernism also for business administration' and of 'creating a vocabulary with which we are equipped to conceptualize practical experiences, instead of leaving them tacit' (Siggaard and Pruzan 1995). To Siggaard, who names the controversy around the dismantling of Brent Spar – the North Sea oil storage and tanker loading buoy in the Brent oilfield operated by Shell UK – as a source of inspiration, the challenge was of a very practical nature. It emerged from the concern that the accepted body of knowledge, theories and methods represented in the business school curriculum did not contain the diversity of discourses necessary to engage with society's problems and to understand, account for and provide real solutions to them (Siggaard 2014).

In contrast to business ethics, which as a discipline has had an important impact on the body of knowledge that can be taught and reflected upon in a business school context, the ambition of the programme in philosophy and business studies at CBS was never limited to an ethical concern. Rather, in addition to the ethical interest, the programme from the beginning had a broader focus, drawing also on epistemology and inquiring into the production of knowledge that dominates the economic sphere in general and its microeconomic subfields (finance, accounting, marketing) in particular. The first curriculum contained integrative courses in aesthetics and in the philosophy of language designed to inquire into rhetoric and communication strategies. Rather than seeking a narrow definition of what counts as 'the ethical' and designating certain things as 'ethical' issues, students at FLØK were challenged to render core themes in business studies 'philosophically resilient' (Siggaard 2014) and to think and reflect on such notions as creativity, innovation, entrepreneurship, sustainability or responsibility in order to elucidate them as philosophical concepts. Another way to put this is to say that since the establishment of business ethics as a field, it has gradually come to rely less and less on its interdisciplinary relationship with philosophy – the fundamental ambition of the programme in Copenhagen was always to strengthen this bond.

Seen from an education perspective, the programme extended the relatively newfound interest within business schools in an ethical understanding of business behaviour into other themes that may just as easily qualify as philosophically interesting. During the first years of the programme, three themes were especially pertinent in this respect. First, there was the epistemological enquiry into the production of knowledge in economics, business and management that challenged the reliance in business studies on mostly mainstream pedagogical material, such as the textbooks and academic courses in business administration, which tend to have a largely reductionist, objectivist and positivist conceptualization of knowledge (Siggaard 2014). The epistemological inquiry reflected on the kinds of knowledge that the field produces and on the consequences for the decision maker and for their understanding of the world in which they live. Second, by turning to the field of organization, it was the ambition of the programme to challenge the traditional understanding in business studies of the organization as a discrete entity. Instead, taking a philosophical perspective meant conceiving of organization as an embedded social and cultural practice and to begin asking questions about what defines *organizing* in terms of, for example, physical limitations, ownership or the market. Finally, the question of management and leadership (and the differences between the two) was then – and still is – seen to lend itself strongly to philosophical analyses, not only because there is a strong tradition in Western philosophy concerned with the governing of oneself and the governing of others, but also because both the concept of management and that of leadership are imbued with characteristics that call for investigating their normative foundations.

## Philosophical 'method': teaching in the FLØK programme

A story goes that the early Greek philosopher Thales (*c.* 585 BCE) was so lost in thought that he fell down a well, before deciding eventually to go into business and use his philosophical observations to make a fortune. This anecdote is often used as an example of how philosophy can be integrated with the business world. It is thought to be a positive reminder that philosophical abstraction *can* have its use and even cash-value if it is only *applied* in the right manner. Philosophy, in such a popular perspective, must be put to work as theory and be applied to practice in order to achieve real use value.

The problem with such an idea of 'applied' philosophy is that it tends to reproduce a distinction between thought and life, between the existence of concepts and the lives we live with them, which ends up foreclosing reflection rather than furthering it and which distorts the pedagogical and educational responsibility of the teacher in the classroom (see Rhodes, this volume). In such a view, philosophy is essentially foreign to practice and, in turn, not only forfeits its own practice of thinking, but also 'forgets' to ask any real questions about the field that it is applied to. The result is most often a pragmatic division of labour that is played out in the classroom as a *fait accompli*: the philosophy teacher takes on the role of providing 'theories' to practise, while the so-called field of practice – in this respect the sphere of business studies – is represented by other teachers who are not meant to engage with philosophy. Philosophy and business studies therefore come to be taught in parallel worlds. Consequently, the important pedagogical and educational task of reciprocal integration is left wholly to the students themselves.

The pivotal point of the reciprocal integration of philosophy with business studies, in our view, lies in taking ownership of this task, both academically and pedagogically, and in meeting it head on in the classroom as a challenge. In our view, the first, serious step towards doing this lies in the acceptance, by philosophers and business academics, that philosophy lacks a predefined domain of application and general methodological presuppositions. This means that philosophy can make all aspects of reality subject to investigation. When philosophy takes up a problem, or a phenomenon that is a paradigmatic object for a specific science, and subjects it to philosophical inquiry, it is not committed to the methodological framework of the respective science. This is the reason why the general scope of philosophical practice is intrinsically open to interdisciplinary research and teaching (perhaps all the more so in the case of the undisciplined field of management research).

A look at the latest Gottlieb Duttweiler Institute ranking of so-called globally leading thinkers reveals that philosophy still plays an important role in shaping today's discourse on the future of society and the economy (Frick *et al.* 2014). Notably, the philosophers who have made the list are thinkers whose ideas are used and discussed across a plethora of different fields.[1] This reflects philosophy's resistance towards an exclusive focus on specialized knowledge production. The vocabulary of business and management today plays an important constitutive part in the overarching discourse of contemporary society and subjectivity in Western societies, linking the norms and techniques of the economic sphere to larger societal developments. As an 'open-minded' discipline, philosophy is well equipped – especially in a business school setting – to take this situation as a teaching opportunity and to meet the need to reflect critically upon its epistemic, ontological and anthropological implications, both for business and for society in general.

## *Problematization and responsibility*

To think of philosophy as an intrinsically 'open-minded' discipline should not be taken to mean that it is bound by nothing. On the contrary, the programme in philosophy and business studies is characterized by combining the general scope and relevance of a philosophical analysis of business practices with an emphasis on the fundamental practical origin of philosophy. Philosophy can be seen to originate in two questions of acute and practical nature: what should we think and how should we act? Questions like these are neither academic nor theoretical – they arise more or less emphatically in everyday life. As such, they are also implicitly and explicitly raised and replied to in all kinds of business practices. The conception of philosophy with which we work at FLØK is rooted in the idea that business, like all other forms of cultural and social practice, is inherently susceptible to the question of responsibility and is in this quite fundamental sense a normative practice. The problem of responsibility in relation to thought and action was already philosophically articulated forcefully in classical Antiquity by Socrates in the Platonic dialogues and by Aristotle in his practical philosophy (Plato 1995; Aristotle 1962). But this problem of responsibility also shapes contemporary philosophical thinking within a number of different traditions across the so-called analytic and continental divide (McDowell 1996; see Thaning 2015; ten Bos, this volume). FLØK draws on this tradition in its broadest sense, insisting that the problem of responsibility is not only relevant to ethical and political issues, where it is immediately apparent, but is actually pervasive in all practices in which standards of judgement and norms of action are at stake.

We insist that using philosophical reflection can excavate the assumptions at work within business practices and fields of knowledge. The philosophical hypothesis is that the fundamental assumptions underlying business and management practice have the irreducible character of questions or problems rather than answers or solutions and, therefore, bringing them to light is potentially a critical and creative enterprise that is valuable for philosophy and also for the practice of business itself. Rather than a philosophy that responds on the level of (an ideal) theory, this type of problem demands a philosophical practice that confronts us with what is fundamentally at stake in the practices of business in order to facilitate our capacity to creatively develop different modes of responding to the problem examined. With such a method of *problematization* (Raffnsøe *et al.* 2016), we insist, on the one hand, that a traditional virtue of philosophical reflection is to ascribe a certain 'logical' or theoretical primacy to questioning rather than to working out solutions. On the other hand, the aim of the programme is to confront students with the demands for taking action. We have developed exercises and assignments that also commit philosophical reflection to the practical demand to pass judgements and make decisions. Students of business – like all other students – must learn that they must steer and that despite the open-mindedness of philosophical reflection, the first-personal (plural) perspective from which we make decisions is ultimately unavoidable.

From a theoretical perspective, these two aspects – the virtue of questioning and the virtue of taking action – may appear incompatible. From a more practical standpoint, the attempt to intensify the dialectic between two such irreducible aspects constitutes an important pedagogical aim of the programme. It is precisely by insisting that the problem or question remains a fundamental reflective category – even as decisions have to be made – that a pedagogical space is opened in which students can perceive and produce new possibilities for thinking and acting within the concrete business practices. Such an approach does not exclude critique, but it challenges the critic to 'translate' their criticism into the horizon of practice.

### *The use of 'eminent texts'*

An important pedagogical instrument, which further anchors such a philosophical 'method' within the philosophical tradition and also complements the interplay between philosophical questioning and engagement with contemporary problems described earlier, is the programme's strong insistence on the use of classic or eminent texts from philosophy and also from business studies. A focused reading of classics relevant to the interdisciplinary field opened between philosophy and business studies is an effective way to critically access the fundamental assumptions of both fields. Such texts can come from political philosophy (such as Hobbes, Locke, Rousseau and Hegel) and from political economy (such as Smith and Marx), where they work to support the exploration of the contours of 'economic man' (*Homo oeconomicus*) within contemporary economic theory and practice. They can also constitute parts of a philosophy of management, which is based on readings of classical and contemporary philosophical texts on leadership, management and power, for example in the works of Plato, Aquinas, Machiavelli, Bodin, Hobbes or Foucault. The aim with such reading is not only to rethink the contemporary debates within management practice but also to place more recent works on management theory in a philosophical perspective. Most importantly, such a pedagogy based on a curriculum that mixes problem-based teaching with the reading of eminent texts from both fields works to gain the advantage of both approaches: the engagement of the students in debate about urgent challenges and dilemmas, and the distinct philosophical idea of *Bildung*, which contributes to the understanding of such challenges by analysing them from the perspectives of the classical and contemporary great works of the philosophical tradition.

## Reciprocal integration in practice: three examples

In this section, we will briefly present three compulsory courses from the BSc in philosophy and business studies at CBS. These courses represent examples of how we engage with reciprocal integration.

### *First semester: Economic Philosophy*

The course Economic Philosophy is the first of three courses that introduce students to the history of philosophy and, in the process, allow them to practise some of the various ways in which knowledge about this tradition can be integrated with business studies. Based on twelve lectures, combined with seminars offering text studies in smaller groups of about twenty students, the course revolves around a pedagogical model designed to meet the challenge of reciprocal integration. This model introduces students to the great texts of the philosophical tradition by engaging with the problems that emerge in a practical business study context. It also introduces the students to ways of 'making the link', which makes this tradition relevant to the dilemmas of contemporary business practices. The course works historically with the emergence of the logic of 'economic man' (*Homo economicus*) in the writings of Hobbes, Locke, Rousseau and in the political philosophies of Smith, Hegel and Marx. Using such classic texts, it explores themes such as the concept of the market, with its distinctive logic, the emergence of the 'human resource' and the meaning of the ideas of work and labour. To this end, it also draws on the works of more contemporary economic philosophers, like Albert Hirschman and Amartya Sen.

The philosophy of economics is traditionally concerned with the conceptual and methodological issues that arise in the discipline of economics and in economic practices, for example by dealing with the ethical dilemmas of economic reasoning or with the epistemological assumptions that economists make. Although such concerns are also central to Economic Philosophy, the aim of the course is to explore the logic of the economic sphere in a broader sense and to understand how this logic is created and applied to contemporary business practices and theories, rather than to focus narrowly on economics as a discipline.

Pedagogically, the central challenge of Economic Philosophy remains the integration of primary readings in the history of philosophy with contemporary issues in business studies. Such a task is made particularly difficult because of the large historical gap between the texts and today's problems. Another way to phrase such a challenge is to say that, even if the study of the history of philosophy often entails some exploration of how philosophical texts from prior historical eras can be understood today, such a perspective (in our experience) frequently fails to address and pedagogically develop the *contemporaneity* of the dilemmas and the philosophical responses that emerge.

In response to this, a central aspect of Economic Philosophy (and indeed of the two following courses in the history of philosophy, which follow a similar model) is a pedagogical model that takes on such a challenge by insisting hermeneutically that what characterizes eminent texts of the philosophical tradition is the manner in which they engage with problems and concepts on a level that is universal enough to be 'translated' into a contemporary context – and thus also into the theories and assumptions made in business studies. This means that although Hegel's idea of 'the market' as 'a remnant of the state of nature' in his political writings (Hegel 1999; see also Herzog 2013) can be read in historical context as a fairly peripheral part of his statement of legal, moral, social and political philosophy, it can also be given a more central meaning when it is reflected in Amartya Sen's understanding of market mechanisms as a part of how human beings in society live and interact with each other (Sen 1999). This may open up a philosophical discussion of the role and possibility of the market beyond the narrow understanding of it as a fundamentally *capitalist* construction, which sheds light on the works of Hegel and Sen. The pedagogical value of this lies in reading, understanding and discussing classical, philosophical texts alongside the ideas that shape and make out business studies as an emerging field. Elton Mayo, to give another example, is viewed by many as the father of modern human resource management (HRM). He was also a prolific writer and (in his own eyes) a philosopher who was profoundly inspired by Hobbes and Freud in his view of business administration and management (O'Connor 1999). Exploring Mayo's ideas of the manager's role in relation to the human being at work and of industrial unrest (for example, Mayo 1923) offers a pedagogical opportunity to teach Hobbes and also the notion of the fundamentally irrational nature of the human being in a practical context. Similarly, Douglas McGregor's management classic *The Human Side of Enterprise* (2006) offers invaluable insight into what it means to think of the human being in terms of the potential for development. Such a practical context may shed light on Rousseau's view of the human being in his *Discourse on the Origin and Basis of Inequality Among Men* (2010 [1754]). It also opens the question about the value of the capital H in HRM in philosophical reflection. By way of such hermeneutical 'encounters', the course trains students in the capacity to analyse and evaluate the assumptions that shape business, management and organization as cultural practices. In the process, the importance of the ability to articulate the fundamental values and problems that are at stake within these fields of practice and knowledge are brought to light.

## *Third semester: Management Philosophy*

Like Economic Philosophy, the third semester Management Philosophy course draws on the philosophical tradition in order to put the sphere of business administration into context. But if the first course uses problems and dilemmas in contemporary business practices to introduce students to the history of philosophy, then this course focuses on how the philosophical tradition can deepen insight into and understanding of management practices and the role of the manager today. The history of philosophy is full of thinking about leadership, from Plato through St Augustine and Machiavelli to Hegel, and in this way it can be said to constitute a history of 'management' thinking. Management Philosophy draws on this philosophical tradition by focusing on the identification of the various 'typologies' of management in philosophical discussions on ideal political governance, and on the dimensions of leadership that emerge with them.

To do so, the course draws on the works of Plato, Aquinas, Machiavelli and Foucault, for example, and combines these readings with central texts in the history of management theory, such as texts by Taylor, Follett and Drucker. The syllabus consists of three parts that represent different historical periods and works to excavate typologies of leadership in each of them: management before the twentieth century, management in the twentieth century and contemporary management.

Rather than exclusively taking a history of ideas perspective, as this approach might suggest, the course engages with the tradition in order to work out and analyse within a practical horizon the challenges of management and the role of the manager in contemporary organization. If there is one aspect that challenges management today, especially in a Northern European context, it is the invitation to the individual employee to contribute to the realization and improvement of her own needs, whilst at the same time anticipating how such needs and desires contribute productively to the various needs of the organization. Management Philosophy works with this paradigmatic dilemma by placing management theory and philosophy within the same horizon. In doing this, it challenges students to see the call for management and leadership – also historically – as a *response* to a specific social and cultural dilemma. Whether this applies to the Platonic polis, to the Machiavellian princedom, to Hegelian institutions or to Taylor's factory floors, the learning opportunity lies in the excavation of the specific form of practice that such responses produce and the image or 'figure' of leadership that they concurrently come to represent. In this way, the course addresses three aspects of contemporary management as a practice: first, it challenges students to identify the paradigmatic ways in which management becomes important as a response to the problem of the intertwinement of subjectivity and productivity. Second, it asks how historical images of leadership (that is, the leader figure as 'the shepherd', 'the role-model' or 'the engineer', etc.) can assist in understanding this type of dilemma. Third, it works with students to identify modes in which such knowledge can be put to use and improve our understanding of the expectations of managers in contemporary organizations.

A central aspect of the course is the explorative interviews with contemporary business leaders that students conduct to gain an understanding of how such leaders perceive their roles as managers. The students are asked to integrate their findings with the readings in the syllabus as they work with these interviews in groups to conceptualize the challenges and conflicts that emerge when leading others in organizational settings. In this way, an integrative learning space is opened that is historically informed by the ethical, aesthetical, political and epistemological ideas of management that emerge in the philosophical tradition. This learning space trains the ability to perceive more clearly the different courses of practical action in light of philosophical analyses and arguments.

### *Sixth semester: Philosophy of the Present: Human Capital*

Philosophy of the Present: Human Capital is the capstone course of the BSc programme in Philosophy and Business Studies and brings together themes and aspects from the whole curriculum. The idea behind the course is an investigation of the phenomenon of 'human capital' in theory and as a social practice. To this end, the course engages with Foucault's investigation of twentieth-century neoliberalism and its historical roots, and with the work of the Chicago School of Economics on human capital theory, especially by economist Gary Becker. Led by instructors recruited from the master's programme, students read Foucault's *Birth of Biopolitics* (2010 [1979]) in smaller reading groups as part of the course. The pedagogical aim with this endeavour is to engage intensely with Foucault's text and to develop its concepts and methods philosophically in relation to (neo)liberalism, as a governmental and managerial practice, and also as an economic–theoretical discourse. Similarly, Becker's extensive responses to Foucault's interpretation of his theories provide a learning opportunity to critically discuss the foundations of human capital theory (Becker *et al.* 2012, 2013; see Nussbaum 1997).

The course not only revolves around the epistemological authority of human capital theory in contemporary social life, but also highlights its implicit anthropology. To this end, it focuses especially on the concepts of work and labour presupposed by Becker's theory, comparing them with alternative conceptions that are formulated within the Western philosophical tradition. The pedagogical aim of this is to train students in the critical use of philosophy in relation to fundamental assumptions within the dominant theoretical paradigm of economy, and to give them a better grasp of the particularity of this paradigm in relation to a wider historical and philosophical horizon.

One of Foucault's key assumptions is the existence of an intrinsic interplay between 'procedures of veridiction' in economic analyses and corresponding modes of government or management rationality. To both liberalism and neoliberalism, this means that in order to express their predictive power, they are dependent on the kind of practices of government, leadership and management that conditions its subjects to optimize investments in their human capital. This is the reason for Becker's understanding of his own theory as a 'useful fiction' (Becker *et al.* 2012). We capture this phenomenon of 'conditioning' in an empirical context by emphasizing its influence on contemporary Danish educational institutions. The purpose of the educational efforts at all levels of the Danish educational system is shifting towards facilitating and promoting individual investments in human capital (see Pedersen 2011). The field provides an exemplary context for studying empirically how the anthropology of human capital theory is becoming more pervasive as an assumption about human nature and also as the goal of governmental rationality. The questions that we pursue in this connection are: how do paradigmatic juridical discourses and managerial practices within the education system employ and presuppose central elements of the conceptual framework of human capital theory and its anthropological assumptions?

How does the increased emphasis on optimizing investments in human capital affect the traditional purposes of education, notably the furthering of democratic citizenship as well as the autonomous and critical pursuit of insight? What expectations concerning the ability to measure and predict the effect of investments in human capital can be found and how do these align with the scientific authority of the theory? What types of theoretical and practical problems are encountered within the contemporary education system in the attempts to measure what counts as proper investments in human capital?

In answering such complex questions, the case-based exam format of the course plays an important methodological and pedagogical role. Turning the traditional idea of case-based teaching around, Philosophy of the Present: Human Capital works with students to write cases (including teaching notes) that relate to the subject matter they have engaged with. The task for them is to develop a convincing scenario within an organizational or institutional framework that illustrates how decisions or judgements related to human capital take place (compare with Barinaga, this volume). This format helps students to choose between and translate (some of) the philosophical and economic concepts and methods they have come across during the course in a concrete scenario of their own choosing. In the accompanying 'teaching note', students are challenged to describe the core philosophical and economical problem at stake in the case, using relevant literature from the course. At the oral exam, they 'defend' their case and discuss the underlying philosophical problem, reflecting upon their choices of economic and philosophical concepts and methods in light of the case scenario.

The purpose of case writing as an exam format in this respect is to train students in their ability to articulate and communicate complex problems. The format works to support their awareness of questioning as a fundamental philosophical skill and facilitates an understanding of problems and dilemmas as categories to which practical solutions may be found, even if the dilemmas themselves remain irreducibly problematic. In this way, the format works as a practical way of training the philosophical capacity for pursuing and articulating questions in relation to economy, business and management, which is a general aim of the FLØK programme.

## Furthering integration: some concluding remarks

In higher education today, the desire for widely applicable and agreed upon methods is evident, and the race is on to develop new ways of measuring learning and determining specifically what students should learn. There is no doubt that the abilities and skills that a student learns in an educational programme should also be helpful in the workplace, but measuring such competences in terms of applicability and evidence of effectiveness remains a challenge because it is difficult to decide beforehand how a student should be different after the completion of a course or a programme.

In this chapter, we have provided an example of how reciprocal integration between philosophy and business education can address this challenge of utility in a way that remains true to a fundamental insight of the humanities: the kind of change that learning brings is open-ended and for life. Throughout the six semesters of the programme described, we aim to teach our students four core competences that we believe could not be accomplished in a corresponding period of actual business experience. First, the capacity to analyse and evaluate the assumptions that construct management and organization as cultural practices enables our students to see business as embedded in society. Second, the ability to articulate the fundamental values and problems that are at stake within business practice and knowledge allows them to work with such values within a wider historical and cultural horizon. Third, the competence to communicate knowledge of such values and problems in a vocabulary that focuses on questioning and diagnosis, rather than directly on solutions, encourages the students to take the freedom to step back from their professional practice and reflect on it in cooperation with others. Finally, these competences all comprise part of the ability to contribute to a discussion about different courses of practical action in light of philosophical analyses and arguments.

In sum, as the examples of courses illustrate, the programme in philosophy and business studies aims at developing philosophy as a practice of analytical questioning. As such, its specificities might be contingent upon the social and institutional contexts of Northern Europe, Denmark and CBS. We hope it has become apparent that the programme's aims, implications and structures are not tied to these contexts. We believe that they can be translated easily into further attempts to integrate philosophy and business studies – after all, studying the assumptions of the world of business practices and considering them in context is also a way of learning to assume responsibility and to make decisions.

## Acknowledgements

The authors would like to thank Hans Siggaard, Bill Sullivan and the faculty of the program for philosophy and business studies at Copenhagen Business School for valuable comments, suggestions and critique in the process of writing this chapter.

## Note

1 Although a list like the Gottlieb Duttweiler Institute 'Global Thought Leaders' index may arguably constitute little more than an advanced joke, the high concentration of philosophical thinkers on it does show that philosophy is not only viewed as an academic discipline taking place behind the closed walls of the university, but also fosters public intellectuals, who play an important part in shaping public opinion across a plethora of fields.

## References

Aristotle (1962) *Ethica Nicomachea*. Oxford: Oxford University Press.

Becker, G., Ewald, F. and Harcourt, B. (2012) *Becker on Ewald on Foucault on Becker: American Neoliberalism and Michel Foucault's 1979 'Birth of Biopolitics' Lectures* (5 September 2012). University of Chicago Institute for Law & Economics Olin Research Paper No. 614; University of Chicago, Public Law Working Paper No. 401, 1–20.

Becker, G., Ewald, F. and Harcourt, B. (2013) *Becker and Foucault on Crime and Punishment* (6 September 2013). University of Chicago Coase-Sandor Institute for Law & Economics Research Paper No. 654; University of Chicago, Public Law Working Paper No. 440; Columbia Law and Economics Working Paper No. 456 (2013), 1–25.

Colby, A., Ehrlich, T., Sullivan, W. and Dolle, J.R. (2011) *Rethinking Undergraduate Business Education: Liberal Learning for the Profession*. San Francisco, CA: Jossey-Bass.

Copenhagen Business School (CBS) (2011) *CBS Strategy: Business in Society*. Available from: http://www.cbs.dk/files/cbs.dk/call_to_action/strategy_0.pdf (accessed 28 January 2016).

de George, R. (2011) 'A history of business ethics'. *In:* OpenMind (ed.) *Values and Ethics for the 21st Century*. OpenMind, BBVA, pp. 337–62.

Foucault, Michel (2010 [1979]) *The Birth of Biopolitics: Lectures at the Collège de France, 1978–1979*. London: Picador.

Frick, K., Gloor, P. and Gürtler, D. (2014) 'Thought leaders 2014: the most influential thinkers', *GDI Impuls*, 2014(4), 10–21.

Gadamer, H.-G. (2004) *Truth and Method*. London and New York, NY: Continuum.

Hegel, G.W.F. (1999) *Hegel: Political Writings*. Cambridge: Cambridge University Press.

Herzog, L. (2013) *Inventing the Market – Smith, Hegel, and Political Theory*. Oxford: Oxford University Press.

Hoffmann, T.S. (2009) *Wirtschaftsphilosophie: Ansätze und Perspektiven von der Antike bis heute*. Wiesbaden, Germany: Marix Verlag.

International Student Initiative for Pluralism in Economics (ISIPE) (2014) *International Student Initiative for Pluralism in Economics*. Available from: http://www.isipe.net/ (accessed 28 January 2016).
Jones, C., Parker, M. and ten Bos, R. (2005) *For Business Ethics*. London: Routledge.
McDowell, J. (1996) *Mind and World*. Cambridge, MA: Harvard University Press.
McGregor, D. (2006) *The Human Side of Enterprise* [ebook]. McGraw-Hill Education.
Mayo, E. (1923) 'The irrational factor in human behavior. The "night-mind" in industry', *Annals of the American Academy of Political and Social Science*, 110, 117–30.
Nussbaum, M. (1997) 'Flawed foundations: the philosophical critique of (a particular type of) economics', *University of Chicago Law Review*, 64(4), 1197–214.
Nussbaum, M. (2010) *Not for Profit – Why Democracy Needs the Humanities*. Princeton, NJ: Princeton University Press.
O'Connor, E. (1999) 'Minding the workers: the meaning of "human" and "human relations" in Elton Mayo', *Organization*, 6(2), 223–46.
Pedersen, O.K. (2011) *Konkurrencestaten*. Copenhagen: Hans Reitzel.
Plato (1995) '*Phaedo*'. *In: Platonis Opera I*. Oxford: Oxford University Press.
Raffnsøe, S., Gudmand-Høyer, M.T. and Thaning, M.S. (2016) *Foucault – A Research Companion*. London: Palgrave Macmillan.
Rousseau, Jean-Jacques (2010 [1754]) *Discourse on the Origin and Foundations of Inequality among Men*. Boston, MA: Bedford/St Martin's.
Sen, Amartya (1999) *Development as Freedom*. New York, NY: Alfred A. Knopf.
Siggaard, H. (2014) 'Interview with Hans Siggaard', conducted by Rasmus Johnsen, Copenhagen Business School.
Siggaard, H. and Pruzan, P. (1995) *Erhvervsøkonomi og filosofi: overvejelser over et grænseland i relation til oprettelse af en uddannelse i filosofi og økonomi ved Handelshøjskolen i København*. I Filosofi. Copenhagen: MN Monograph.
Spoelstra, S. (2007) 'What is philosophy of organization?'. *In:* C. Jones and R. ten Bos (eds.) *Philosophy and Organization*. London: Routledge.
Thaning, M.S. (2015) *The Problem of Objectivity in Gadamer's Hermeneutics in Light of McDowell's Empiricism*. Contributions to Hermeneutics 1. Berlin: Springer Verlag.

# 28

# Liberal arts in business and business in liberal arts

## The view from Bocconi

*Paola Dubini and Elena Raviola*

## Introduction

This chapter describes and explores the history, pedagogy, positioning and outcomes of Bocconi University's degree in Management for the Arts, Culture and Communication (CLEACC). The programme, based in Milan, started in 1999 as a four-year degree and was in Italian. In 2004, following the Bologna Reform, it was transformed into an undergraduate three-year programme of the same name (CLEACC) and a graduate course (CLEACC LS), both in Italian. In 2006, CLEACC LS became a Master of Science in Management and Economics of Arts, Culture, Media and Entertainment (ACME) and has since then been taught in English. Starting from the academic year 2016–17 one of the two classes of CLEACC will be held in English.

Since the establishment of a 3 + 2 CLEACC + ACME programme, each year approximately 240 students are admitted to the undergraduate programme (CLEACC) and 90 to ACME, nearly half of whom come from CLEACC. In connection to these study programmes, in 2004 Bocconi established a research centre for Art Science Knowledge, known as ASK Bocconi. It carries out both theoretical and empirical research and promotes cultural planning and management activities in cultural institutions. Research at ASK is therefore focused on contexts characterized by the meeting of the arts and the economy, and it covers a wide range of topics, such as cultural policies, the transformation of cultural industries and the often uneasy relationships between socio-technological (market) pressures and cultural production, as well as the interplay between emerging business models and intellectual property regimes.

The authors of this chapter have experienced teaching in CLEACC and ACME, as well as research at ASK in different roles. Paola, a Bocconi graduate and faculty member for almost 30 years, has been part of the core group that started CLEACC in 1999 and is the current Director of the programme. Between 2009 and 2013, she was also Director of ASK and is currently leading a number of its research projects. Elena is a CLEACC graduate from the class of 2000 and taught in several courses at CLEACC after that. She is affiliated with ASK and has collaborated with Paola on different publications and research projects.

This chapter synthesizes a series of reflections on the specificity of the degree and its validity, both as a management degree with a particular sensitivity to the humanities and as a degree preparing for a career in arts management. In doing so, we tentatively derive some 'lessons' from our experience for the establishment and development of study programmes that integrate the humanities and social sciences into management education.

The first section in this chapter focuses on the history and founding principles of CLEACC in order to highlight its specificity and its perceived difference from other undergraduate programmes as an educational project within management studies. The second section discusses the implications of these principles and choices in terms of curriculum design. The third section focuses on the outcomes and examines the characteristics of graduates and their careers.

## History and founding principles

Bocconi University is a leading university for the study of management and economics in Italy. The university was founded in 1902 as a school of commerce and for many years it offered a degree in management, a degree in economics and a degree in economics and social sciences. A degree in languages was also offered between 1946 and 1972, and in 1999 Bocconi opened a School of Law. Currently, the school offers six three-year bachelor programmes (of which two are in English), ten two-year master of science degrees (of which eight are in English), eight one-year master programmes (mostly for students who did not take an undergraduate degree in management), a law degree and two graduate programmes in law, and five PhD programmes. A four-year triple bachelor degree (the so-called World Bachelor in Business) in partnership with the Marshall School of Business, University of Southern California, and the Hong Kong University of Science and Technology complements the study architecture.

Within the Italian education landscape, Bocconi University is characterized by an international vocation and a strong link with practitioners. The school started offering career and placement services to its students and developed a series of programmes with companies well before the other universities in Italy, and many students choose to attend Bocconi for its placement prospects. According to university statistics, around 95 per cent of graduates are employed six months after graduation. Internally, programme directors are measured on the performances of their students, on their evaluation of teaching quality and on students' employability. This milieu has shaped CLEACC from its inception – the programme has struggled with being evaluated on the same measures as other programmes at Bocconi and also with representing a unique and different offering at this university.

The initial idea behind the establishment of CLEACC emerged in the beginning of the 1990s, when a group of faculty members started discussing the idea to create a programme addressing the management needs in cultural sectors and the 'cultural' needs in other industrial and service sectors. In the current official presentation of the programme to the students, it is emphasized that Italy has a unique, diverse and distinctive cultural heritage, which also has significant economic potential. 'Its experimental and creative nature makes this programme a peculiar educational experience, a bridge between the world of numbers, finance, organization and marketing and the world of art, performing arts, tourism and communication' (Bocconi corsi, 2015). The programme was therefore designed by focusing equally on management and economics courses (of which Bocconi has wide expertise) and liberal arts courses, which are taught by experts and teachers from other universities and institutions.

The term 'liberal arts' is difficult to place in the Italian context because in the Italian educational system there is no parallel to what this term actually includes in English-speaking countries. Management and economics curricula favour courses that provide tools and technical know-how and stimulate students to choose a specialism early on. In the design of CLEACC, the idea of bringing liberal arts into the curriculum was that management and economics should be accompanied not only by human sciences (*scienze umanistiche* – humanities), as is the case for the courses on philosophy of art or music, but also by other social sciences, like cultural anthropology, visual culture or design. The conception and design of these 'other' courses, which are not management and economics, in the CLEACC curriculum has gradually moved from humanities, which has a strong tradition in Italy, towards liberal arts. As an example, when the programme first began, there were courses on literature and poetry. These courses have disappeared over the years and other courses, such as cultural anthropology, have been added to the curriculum. The question of what to call these 'other' courses that are not appearing in the other Bocconi programmes is still unresolved. Some faculty talk about 'arts and culture' – as some of the courses are called in the official programme's study plan; some use the term 'human sciences'; whilst others prefer to speak of 'cultural consciousness'.

The discussions around what to include in the CLEACC curriculum as far as liberal arts are concerned and how to conceive, design and successively reform the study programme have revolved around two principles: to educate managers for the arts and to offer a liberal arts education to future managers. First, students interested in artistic and cultural organizations, in terms of potential career opportunities as managers or entrepreneurs, should be aware of the specificities of these domains in order to develop the necessary and complementary skills. As Guido Guerzoni, teacher of economic history and core CLEACC faculty, put it at the tenth anniversary celebrations, 'we believed and still believe that for a good manager it is important to get a sense of the content or object of management in the specific domains'. It seems fair to say that management and economics are not subjects typically chosen by students and their families for a specific intellectual curiosity or passion. Cultural institutions, not-for-profit organizations and the so-called 'creative industries' seem to be an exception, perhaps because they exude a more glamorous aura and because the arts often become prominent interests, hobbies or passions at a young age. This seems particularly true in countries like Italy, where arts and heritage are often mentioned as a distinctive feature of the economy and where the corresponding institutions are surrounded by a Bourdieu-like aura of cultural capital and elitism (Bourdieu 1984). Unlike other Bocconi students, CLEACC students would not choose typically to go to Bocconi if they could not attend this particular study programme. Since its inception, CLEACC has strongly benefited from this level of motivation and interest from the students, and has, for example, involved students in activities and provided contacts in companies and institutions.

Moreover, with regard to the first principle – to educate managers for the arts – the idea of specific management skills for cultural organizations was in line with the rising attention in public and academic debates on the creative industries. In fact, the managerial and economic specificities of these organizations had caught the attention of scholars since the 1960s and increasingly during the 1990s. From Baumol and Bowen's (1966) cost disease in the performing arts, to Caves's (2000) creative industries and Hesmondhalgh's (2012) cultural industries, these kinds of organizations have been portrayed as complex organizations whose sustainability requires solid, and yet specific management skills (see Baecker, this volume). Cultural organizations are challenging workplaces for managers because of the lack of slack resources, the difficulty of balancing costs and revenues, the prominence of fixed costs on total costs and the fundamental difficulty of assessing the quality of an artistic or cultural project in terms of common categories in managerial professions. Managers therefore need to develop an understanding and a curiosity concerning cultural phenomena and artistic processes, cost-control practices, good fundraising skills and a skill for team building and consensus management. CLEACC was designed with the awareness that the interplay between artistic and managerial positions may be conflictual and problematic, and was hence aimed at educating managers who are able to engage in meaningful interactions with the 'creative crowd' (Florida 2002; O'Doherty, this volume).

In order to do so, it is important for the students to invest time and energy in some form of artistic education. Given the increasing importance of visual culture in shaping public opinion and everyday life, specific attention was given to courses training students in these domains. Thus, cinema, TV, contemporary art and architecture are among the themes and fields on offer. As an undergraduate degree in management, CLEACC should give its students a proper basis for graduate studies in arts management and encourage those interested in investing in the field to complement and enrich their university education.

This brings us to the second principle, namely the liberal arts for future managers. CLEACC was designed with the idea that any manager should have the liberal arts as part of her curriculum, no matter which professional path she will pursue in the future. Notwithstanding the generic assumption that a varied background is important in any profession (which is the equivalent of the rather commonsensical expression that spinach is good in your diet or that an apple a day keeps the doctor away), and besides the elitist and traditional view of the importance of liberal learning for a gentleman's education (see Parker, this volume), the liberal arts become a fundamental component of a managerial education, as are accounting, statistics, marketing or law. Managers are no longer trained to become technocrats – and even the capability to play the multiple tasks theorized by Mintzberg (1973) seems inadequate to face the increased diversity and instability of the environment in which they operate. In their edited volume on *Management Education and Humanities*, Gagliardi and Czarniawska (2006) argued that humanism and the humanities might play an important role in the formation of new managerial elites in three different ways: in the conception of management as a profession; in offering a humanistic worldview; and in inspiring management curricula in new ways. According to this line of argument, the humanities can both enrich the ways in which managers educate themselves (Gagliardi and Czarniawska 2006) and offer new ways to read economic and management theories (Czarniawska and Guillet de Monthoux 1994). The exposure to a variety of disciplines, theories, models and languages is a way in which CLEACC students are taught to assume different perspectives, to critically reconcile often conflicting points of view, to develop the capacity to listen and to master different scientific languages and methods. Liberal arts complement a traditional curriculum in management and economics that prepares managers who are able to accept the ambiguities and complexities intrinsic to the current social cultural and economic world, and who are also exposed to economic theories and models aimed at maximizing effectiveness and efficiency of decision making under rationality constraints, and to the business schools' 'typical toolbox'.

As Gino Zaccaria, teacher of philosophy of art and part of the core CLEACC faculty, put it at the celebration of the tenth anniversary: 'CLEACC is a degree in management that acknowledges the possibility that arts can make explicit the limits of the economic thought. To see to it that the arts could modify the very economic thought was one of the main hypotheses for CLEACC.' This hypothesis presented by Zaccaria, remains to be evaluated and specified, but seems to point in the direction of putting management/economics and liberal arts at the same level, and therefore to be able to influence each other. This intuition of CLEACC's faculty became increasingly pertinent over the years and anticipated what the authors of the Carnegie Report wrote in 2011: 'the current troubles of the world economy . . . may stem in no small part from blind trust in an exclusively economic view of business and the world' (Colby *et al.* 2011: 29; Sullivan, Ehrlich and Colby, this volume). The publication of the Carnegie Report, and the subsequent discussion on the integration of liberal arts and humanities in management curricula, has therefore made the second principle of CLEACC's design ever more timely. In addition, the parallel and sometimes related debate on the creative economy and the need for Western countries to educate for innovation has also supported the increasing weight of this second principle (see, for example, the discussion on educating for creativity in Araya and Peters 2010; De Cock, this volume).

The two principles of 'liberal arts for managers' and 'managers for the arts' on which the programme is based give a certain ambiguity to CLEACC. The question whether it is a programme specifically directed solely at students who are interested in working in the cultural sector, or whether it is a broad education for all kinds of future managers, remains open and has never been answered clearly. In the shift to the 3 + 2 design, the curricula have been reformatted. The bachelor programme has become a generalist programme for future managers, whereas ACME is targeted more specifically at students interested in developing a managerial or entrepreneurial career in cultural industries and organizations.

## Pedagogy

Teaching at CLEACC has been inspired by the same two principles that guide the design of the programme – liberal arts for managers and managers for the arts – and it has evolved over the years according to the balance between the two principles. As a forum for discussing the programme's pedagogy, the debate around the name of the programme was important. Should it be 'management *of*' or 'management *for*' the arts, culture and communication? And should students of CLEACC learn to manage arts, culture and communication as cultural products and services or should they learn management as a support for arts, thus acknowledging a different 'status' for the arts, calling for specific norms, governance structures and practices?

Part of the faculty felt that Bocconi, as a leading university specializing in economics and management, should contribute to the managerialization of cultural institutions in Italy. Museum or theatre directors in Italy did not have an economic background and often people in administrative positions did not even hold an economics or business degree. The overall perception amongst practitioners in cultural organizations was that art is a sort of '*zona franca*', a special site in which a market logic does not apply. The argument, therefore, was that Bocconi should 'bring management to the arts' and adapt tools and theories developed for manufacturing and service firms to cultural institutions, much in the same way as new public management. The curriculum should focus on management and economics and courses should involve guests from the field and discuss cases from the cultural industries. In a university traditionally concerned with the placement of its students, the scope of the programme (that is, which industries should be included and what would be the professional destiny of CLEACC graduates compared with the other Bocconi graduates) was of paramount importance. The job market in cultural institutions is very peculiar, particularly in Italy: entry is limited, stability of employment is hard to reach, a graduate in business administration is typically not a choice in job postings for theatres or museums. On the supply side, the arts and the cultural fields are characterized by very limited opportunities and are not a good job market, in principle, for a graduate in business. Why, after all, would a smart graduate whose job market is open for six-digit salaries in finance apply for a job in the arts? To compensate for the limited amount of placement opportunities for management graduates, the programme should embrace a wide spectrum of industries, from the arts to media, tourism and communication.

Another part of the faculty considered art as a form of knowledge in itself and looked for a programme addressing contemporary economic and cultural challenges to 'restore the cultural dimension of societies that are too often represented simply as economies and to restore the calculative dimension to societies that are too often simply portrayed as solidarities' (Appadurai 1986: 12). A programme in management and economics for the arts should therefore help to build an economy supportive of the arts instead of transforming them into products or services and artists into brands. By including the liberal arts in the curriculum, the programme should explicitly address the often problematic relationship between markets, the cultural sphere and society. Although the curriculum would be particularly suitable for managers willing to work in specific industries and business contexts, the programme should not be designed as a vocational course. The experience of art should provide a possibility of modifying our view on the economy and opening up opportunities for research, innovation and experimentation.

Although eventually the name of the programme came to express the decision of a more challenging positioning for Bocconi, the tension between these two views has never been fully resolved; it is a constant element of discussion – and sometimes a bone of contention – within the faculty, between faculty and students, and amongst the students themselves. However, we contend that it is precisely this tension that makes the programme more innovative and unique. The transition to a 3 + 2 programme has somewhat smoothed the intrinsic contradiction of being a management programme targeting specific industries and also a mind-opening programme that is broad in its scope. In its current configuration, the graduate programme is specialized in specific industries and is closer to an arts management programme, whilst at the bachelor level CLEACC opens up a broad spectrum of choices because of its liberal arts elements.

A number of implications followed from this decision. First of all, CLEACC is in its structure an undergraduate programme in management, compliant with the Italian state legislation for a curriculum in management studies at undergraduate level, with limited differences in the traditional curriculum. But there are differences. Specifically, our management courses address the difference between market and non-market logic, between consumers, audiences and citizens. Unlike the other undergraduate courses offered by Bocconi, economic history classes include the history of economic thought. Immaterial assets are looked upon in accounting. In terms of pedagogy, students are encouraged to write essays (as opposed to multiple choice texts) and to carry out project and field works. Most importantly, the liberal arts are given equal weight to economics, management, law and quantitative methods in characterizing the programme.

Today, the specificity of CLEACC curriculum, as opposed to general management programmes, consists of five courses, three of which are compulsory: philosophy of art; theories and methods in artistic research; and cultural anthropology. Students choose the two remaining courses from a choice of ten options ranging from Italian renaissance art, theatre, design, and information and power. The three compulsory courses set the conceptual and methodological bases for the students to appreciate the specificity of the programme. The other ten courses privilege visual arts and contemporary visual forms over other forms of arts or historic periods. The options result partly from the availability of excellent faculty, partly from interest from students, and partly from the weakness of Italian high schools as far as education in the visual arts is concerned.

## Outcomes: professional and institutional results

In terms of student interest and numbers, the launch of CLEACC was far more successful than had been imagined by its founders. Students and their families appreciated the innovative approach of the programme, and applications outnumbered the rosiest expectations. Even today, after the programme doubled its initial size of 120 students and there is now a variety of other universities starting to offer degrees in arts management at national and international level, the interest in the programme is very high and, it seems to us, the presence of liberal arts in a management degree is far more appreciated than the insertion of management courses in liberal arts degrees.

CLEACC brought to Bocconi a new kind of student. Compared with other Bocconi teaching programmes, students who chose humanities as a major in high school are overrepresented, as are those playing an instrument or dancing at professional level and those who are regular consumers of cultural goods (exhibitions, literature, performances, films, and so on). Typically, students attending CLEACC would not have chosen Management and Economics as a degree (or Bocconi) if it were not for CLEACC. Moreover, their participation in campus and community life is very strong, as the setup of the university radio and the students' web TV testifies. In 2015, the Bocconi Arts Campus was launched in order to offer students even more opportunities to practise the arts and to be exposed to the challenges of cultural management and entrepreneurship.

CLEACC graduates have a broad set of educational and professional alternatives after completing the programme. The broad scope of CLEACC is mirrored in the choices after graduation. Twenty-five per cent of graduates choose arts management for their graduate studies, 18 per cent management, 18 per cent marketing and 14 per cent international management. Five per cent of graduates stop studying and get a job and 15 per cent split their time between master's courses in content production, tourism, service or fashion management and communication studies. Interestingly, 5 per cent choose to work as artists. Among CLEACC graduates there are professional music and jazz players, a composer and several art scholars at PhD level. Twenty-five per cent of graduates work abroad. Analysis of career patterns of CLEACC graduates after graduate studies reveals – not surprisingly – that graduate studies influence job choices much more than undergraduate studies. Given the broad spectrum of alternatives open to CLEACC students at the end of the degree, it is not a coincidence that they work in all kinds of organizations, industries and functions in managerial positions and that some of them do work in cultural organizations or firms straight out of university or after a few years of managerial experience in various sectors. Although a CLEACC graduate is considered a Bocconi graduate by any employer in the business community, it is difficult to be hired in a cultural institution with a degree in management and economics other than ACME (and CLEACC).

An important aspect of the students' education, often underestimated by the students before they come to Bocconi, is the building of a strong peer community. CLEACC students have common interests in the relation of art and the economy, and throughout their education they initiate a number of activities outside their regular university curriculum. The arts, for many of the students, are a passion and not just a school duty, and CLEACC students develop many art-based initiatives that bond them together during the university years and afterwards in what could be called an art-and-economy community. The lively cultural life of Milan offers several opportunities for students and alumni to meet and share common interests and professional opportunities.

More than sixteen years have passed since the first group of students started CLEACC. Since then, we have experienced a number of changes in the institutional context, and, consequently, CLEACC has adapted to and transformed within this framework. First, we would like to reflect on the outcomes of CLEACC amongst practitioners in the arts and cultural sectors and also in the business community at large. The programme has gradually established its reputation in the artistic and cultural community. In spite of – or perhaps because of – the many changes in the past sixteen years, the world of scholars and practitioners in the arts and within cultural organizations is culturally and ideologically far removed from the neoliberal approach of Bocconi. The acceptance of the school and of CLEACC amongst the professional communities in the arts has therefore been a long process. In the business and academic communities in Europe, and increasingly worldwide, Bocconi has a solid reputation as a research university characterized by a quantitative approach. On the contrary, artistic and cultural organizations were unaware of Bocconi. Generally speaking, these organizations constitute fairly closed communities that are quite suspicious about the supposed role of managers. Moreover, the world of cultural and artistic institutions is very heterogeneous: museums and opera houses are worlds apart from each other, and contemporary art museums face different challenges from the big institutions hosting collections from the past. As far as cultural industries are concerned, the faculty has developed a specific know-how and close relations along with the development of the programme. This is because, in all of these cases, the managerialization of cultural practices and organizations is a shared and recent phenomenon.

The other significant result of the programme has been the development of a strong sense of CLEACC community during university years and after. CLEACC is perceived as unique within Bocconi, and CLEACC students (and faculty) do feel a strong sense of belonging to the programme, more than to the school. Graduates – particularly those working in cultural institutions and creative industries – share this unity even after college years and make up a vibrant alumni community, with strong links to their Alma Mater and its students. A number of firms and cultural institutions have thus become enclaves of former CLEACC students, and CLEACC has had a significant impact on shaping the new generation of hires in those industries, at least in the Milan area where Bocconi is based. As a result, the feeling of belonging to a special and successful community spreads from the school to the profession and back to the school through the engagement of alumni in university courses in different forms, from single lectures to entire courses.

The second field of outcomes on which we would like to reflect concerns the institutional sphere at Bocconi University. The most visible result is that an applied research programme was put in place in parallel with the development of CLEACC in order to develop teaching materials and also to get faculty acquainted with different cultural industries. Over the years, the initial investment led to the creation of the multidisciplinary ASK Research Centre in 2004, which hosts research in the areas of cultural policy, intellectual property management and policies, sustainability and transformation of cultural firms and institutions. The centre is small and the nature of the issues addressed, as well as the methodologies used, makes it difficult to comply with Bocconi academic rules in terms of publications. It is therefore difficult for the centre to attract as many researchers as the breadth of the industries/topics covered would suggest. A lot of work still needs to be done for the humanities and management to understand each other as academic fields. From a research viewpoint, arts and cultural industries were not a typical field of research for management scholars at Bocconi until very recently. The high specialization and competence required to address each professional field, the limited average size of companies and their fragility from an institutional and economic sustainability point of view made these industries not particularly appealing for research or consulting purposes. At the same time, a lack of systematic data and the extreme specificity of each business model made it very challenging to set up research projects building on heavy and powerful generalizations. Moreover, the interdisciplinarity of research in these fields, praised in theory in the university discourse, is challenged in practice by the disciplinary logic of research journals, grant applications and departmental recruitment and promotion policies.

Another visible result of the institutional changes brought by CLEACC is the increasing engagement of CLEACC students in campus life, thus spreading and practising CLEACC life through the university. In Spring 2015, an open space entirely managed by CLEACC students and supported by the faculty was opened on campus, focusing on the arts and education. This project is called 'openside' and is part of the activities of Bocconi Arts Campus. Its programme, curated by the ASK Research Centre, will concentrate on the moulding of artistic practices and the education of artists.

## Concluding remarks

The culture–commerce debate so extensively addressed in cultural economic literature (Appadurai 1986; Caves 2000) has been internalized by CLEACC. Since the study programme's inception, management practices and jargon have gradually entered cultural institutions, blurred the boundaries between cultural and creative industries, and, for better or worse, brought market logic into fields that used to be dominated by a very different sense of urgency. However, the programme, although a management degree, has not completely embraced market logic applied to art; instead, it has sought to educate future managers to be aware of the risks and limits of market logic applied to the arts. At the same time, in spite of legitimate concerns over the possibility of a programme like this to adequately prepare good and competent managers, the track record of CLEACC graduates proves the validity of the programme in preparing open-minded responsible managers, academics, professionals and cultural entrepreneurs.

We would argue that the experience of the programme over the past sixteen years has been characterized by what could be framed as a productive ambiguity. In fact, the debate on whether this is a programme for cultural managers or a programme for managers that need to increasingly understand the world through the liberal arts and humanities (Araya and Peters, 2010) is not resolved. The balance between the two principles has changed through the years, partly following the climate in the public debate (see the Carnegie Report, for example) and partly adjusting to the experience of teachers and graduates.

I, Elena, have experienced a shift from being interested in cultural management as the management of cultural institutions to being interested in a liberal arts-inspired management of all kinds of organizations. I entered CLEACC because I wanted to marry my interest in ballet with some kind of useful management skills. I graduated from CLEACC, entered a PhD in Business Administration and pursued my research work, willing to draw on liberal arts to enrich management and organization studies and yet remaining deeply interested in the peculiarity of the cultural sectors. The ambiguity between the two principles setting up CLEACC has been frustrating at times during my education studies, not least in relation to the unpleasant rumours of other graduates accusing CLEACC of being an easy programme for dancers. At the same time, it is precisely this ambiguity that has produced a very interesting base for learning to approach current societal challenges with transdisciplinary and uncomfortable methods.

We, Paola and Elena, as teachers and researchers of CLEACC and ASK, are convinced of the educational quality of the programme, although it is evident that it needs to be continuously updated and supported. It is somewhat surprising to us that when confronted on the programme by families of prospective students or by the business community, CLEACC is still perceived as very innovative because of the presence of liberal arts in a management and economics curriculum – only CLEACC and a handful of other programmes worldwide have them. As markets and private logic are gaining ground over communities and public spaces, managers and entrepreneurs need to be more attentive to diversity, more responsible and more concerned about long-term sustainability. Liberal arts and humanities are the disciplines that teach us to search for the woman (and the man), to develop critical thinking and to be able to learn from others.

We would like to summarize three lessons from our experience in Bocconi. First, the context of the programme is very important in its design and realization. In a globalized education landscape with increasingly homogeneous generalized programmes, we want to stress the importance of rooting education in the local context. The fact that CLEACC is in Bocconi and not at another university or school has shaped the possibilities and the constraints of CLEACC's development. One of the greatest challenges in this matter is the choice of liberal arts courses to offer in the programme. This offer is constantly under revision and has undergone significant changes since the launch of the programme. The realization that it is not possible to cover all liberal arts, but it is necessary to choose, has meant that the direction of this choice has been influenced by a number of contextual elements. One element is the location of Bocconi in Milan and the relationship with the local cultural and artistic community. This has meant that a number of courses have been prioritized based on the available faculty from the local community and their appreciation by CLEACC students. A second element is the Italian high school curriculum, which values literary studies over visual arts. This has led to priority being given to the visual arts in order to improve students' knowledge and familiarity with this field. The third element is the Bocconi culture, which has deeply influenced how the programme looks and what type of students it attracts. Just to mention one illustration of this influence: CLEACC, like all the other programmes, is subject to a strong pressure on the employability of all graduates and is measured on this. This has shaped the character of CLEACC and its struggles for legitimacy.

A second lesson from our experience is the importance of keeping the programme alive and being ready to make changes, small and big, in a continuous dialogue between faculty, students and the surrounding community. Throughout its reforms, CLEACC has been able to increase its relevance and build its reputation internally in Bocconi and externally in the cultural and business communities. The challenge is to balance between changing the programme and keeping its core.

The third lesson is that the multiplicity and ambiguity of goals and perspectives enrich the programme – if embraced and organized around the common effort of an educational programme. The struggles amongst different perspectives and goals of CLEACC faculty, for example educating cultural managers as well as managers with a liberal arts sensitivity, might produce anxiety at times, but they contribute to keeping the programme alive by continuously questioning its shape and its relevance. The close collaboration between university faculty and practitioners teaching on several courses gives the opportunity to always challenge the relevance of the whole programme in the changing 'real' world.

In conclusion, we believe that CLEACC is such a wonderful, strong and innovative programme because it is in a business school with the prestige and solidity of Bocconi and is in a lively culturally and economically diverse city like Milan. We hope that in the coming twenty years, the whole of Bocconi University will become more like CLEACC.

## Acknowledgements

The authors acknowledge the support of ASK research centre in Università Bocconi.

## References

Appadurai, A. (1986) 'Introduction: commodities and the politics of value'. *In:* A. Appadurai (ed.) *The Social Life of Things: Commodities in Cultural Perspective*. Cambridge: Cambridge University Press, pp. 3–63.

Araya, D. and Peters, M.A. (2010) *Education in the Creative Economy: Knowledge and Learning in the Age of Innovation*. New York, NY: Peter Lang.

Baumol, W. and Bowen, W. (1966) *Performing Arts, the Economic Dilemma: A Study of Problems Common to Theater, Opera, Music, and Dance*. New York, NY: Twentieth Century Fund.

Bocconi corsi, Servizio Orientamento Universitario (2015) *CLEACC, Economia per le Arti, la Cultura e la Comunicazione*. Available from: www.unibocconi.com (accessed 5 August 2015).

Bourdieu, P. (1984) *Distinction*. London: Routledge.

Caves, R. (2000) *Creative Industries. Contracts between Art and Commerce*. Cambridge, MA: Harvard University Press.

Colby, A., Ehrlich, T., Sullivan, B. and Dolle, J. (2011) *Rethinking Undergraduate Business Education: Liberal Learning for the Profession*. San Francisco, CA: Jossey-Bass.

Czarniawska-Joerges, B. and Guillet de Monthoux, P. (1994) *Good Novels, Better Management: Reading Organizational Realities*. Chur, Switzerland: Harwood Academic.

Florida, R. (2002) *The Rise of the Creative Class: and How it's Transforming Work, Leisure and Everyday Life*. New York, NY: Basic Books.
Gagliardi, P. and Czarniawska, B. (2006) *Management Education and Humanities*. Cheltenham, UK: Edward Elgar.
Hesmondhalgh, D. (2012) *Cultural Industries*. 3rd edn. London: Sage Publications.
Mintzberg, H. (1973) *The Nature of Managerial Work*. New York, NY: Harper and Row.

# 29

# Integrating humanities and social sciences

## Institutionalizing a contextual studies programme

*Thomas S. Eberle and Jörg Metelmann*

At the University of St Gallen in Switzerland, rethinking business education and integrating the humanities, social sciences and liberal learning was being implemented and practised long before the Carnegie Report was published (Colby *et al.* 2011; and Sullivan, Ehrlich and Colby, this volume). When the so-called Bologna standardization reform was agreed upon by the European nations, the University of St Gallen moved fast and initiated a fundamental reform of the whole architecture of its study programmes. It aimed at a strategic repositioning in the international field and at being a forerunner amongst European universities. One of the key innovations was the so-called 'contextual studies' programme, which makes up 25 per cent of the study time and is mandatory for every student at our university, at first year and Bachelor level as well as at the Master level. The basic idea is that students of business administration and economics must be aware of the complex sociological, cultural and historical contexts in which economic and managerial processes take place. Therefore, the study of humanities and social sciences now constitutes an integral part of their study programme.

This contextual studies programme was established in its present structure in 2001. Such an all-encompassing institutionalization of humanities and social sciences into business education is, to our knowledge, still unique, not only in Europe and the US but also on a global scale. Now, our university and particularly the executive board of this programme have more than fourteen years of experience with it. Both authors have been members of this board, Thomas since its inception in 2001 to his retirement in 2015 and Jörg since 2009. The goals of our chapter are, therefore, first to describe the ideas and aims of our reform and the institutional framework in which it was implemented; second, to depict the major challenges we had to deal with and how we attempted to come to terms with them; and third, to discuss some crucial and fundamental issues that may be inherent to any cooperation between management and economics on the one hand and humanities and social sciences on the other. They refer in particular to the educational model, the question of integration and the university culture on which a shared perspective should be developed.

## Business in context: an integrative perspective

### *History*

The University of St Gallen was founded as a commercial academy ('Handelsakademie') in 1898, in the same year as similar institutions in Leipzig, Aachen and Vienna and a few years before those in Frankfurt am Main (1901), Cologne (1901), Berlin (1906), Mannheim (1907), Munich (1910), Königsberg (1915) and Nuremberg (1919), and it opened its doors in 1899 (see Thürer 1974; Burmeister 1998). All over Europe as well as in the US, a growing consensus had been formed in the second half of the nineteenth century that institutions of higher education were also needed in the area of commerce and business administration. The Wharton school of finance and commerce was founded as a branch of the University of Pennsylvania in Philadelphia in 1881 (see O'Connor, this volume), in the same year as the École des Hautes Études Commerciales (HEC) in Paris. To mark its academic aspirations, the teachers at St Gallen were called 'professors' and the academy was soon renamed the 'Handels-Hochschule (HH)' ('graduate school of commerce'). However, commercial academies were different from universities: their aim was not scientific specialization but rather to convey well-founded practical knowledge and skills to their students. Mathematical calculation and accounting skills, legal norms and knowledge about cost effectiveness and commerce were considered crucial, but equally important were foreign language skills and knowledge about culture, history and literature as well as chemical, physical and technological insights into industrial products and commercial goods.

Business administration has retained this split identity up to the present day. *Is it an art form,* as Eugen Schmalenbach (1911/12) – one of the founders of German business administration as an academic discipline – had contended early on, *or is it a scientific discipline?* Although many universities often reserved newly founded chairs for business administration with acknowledged scientists, like micro-economists, commercial academies such as St Gallen preferred a practice approach and also maintained close relations with business corporations, public and non-profit institutions. But at the same time the HH also strived for academic recognition, which was finally granted in the 1930s. At the beginning, the majority of professors did not have a doctorate, and hardly anyone had a habilitation, a higher doctorate. In 1936 the first habilitation took place, which endows a lecturer ('Privatdozent') with a 'venia legendi' for a particular discipline or area of expertise. This paved the way for making academic careers. A crucial milestone happened in 1939 when the HH, after long deliberations, was accepted as equivalent to the seven other universities and the two Federal Institutes of Technology in Switzerland. In the same year it was granted the right to award doctoral degrees (which occurred in 1942 for the first time). In 1962, it changed the name into 'Hochschule St Gallen', and thereby created the brand 'HSG' that still prevails today. The full name in English was 'St Gallen graduate school of business administration, economics and social sciences'; later on, 'law' was added (after 'economics') when a law degree was created in 1988. When eventually other, less academic graduate schools of business administration ('Fachhochschulen') emerged, the official name was changed in 1995 into 'University of St Gallen' (whilst the brand name 'HSG' was kept).

The institutional development of the HSG reflects the *processes of scientification and professionalization* that are characteristic of the twentieth century. After the first three decades, business administration strived – in spite of its persisting goal to be applicable in business practice – for acceptance as an academic discipline, which its big brother economics had already reached. Taylor's (1947 [1911]) 'scientific management' helped establish this idea, which sparked the *rationalization movement* in the 1920s and acquired wide recognition. Although at first this was primarily conceived as a business engineering project, the social sciences soon gained significant relevance. In his illuminating research on the evolution of management knowledge, exemplified by the case of the St Gallen graduate school, Walter-Busch (1998) shows that the process of scientification can be best illustrated by the *rise of the behavioural sciences at business schools.* In the pioneer phase (1899–*c.* 1920), human behaviour was considered a moral topic that was treated by invoking practical virtues, like merchant's honour, acquaintance with human nature, life experience and wisdom, self-control and self-discipline (Jahresbericht 1911/12: 64 et seq.). In phase 2 (1920–*c.* 1950), research results from the behavioural sciences were increasingly adopted and propagated as superior to common sense knowledge – in particular, concepts from the human-relations-movement were incorporated. In phase 3 (since 1950), research on organizational behaviour was produced and published, carried out by the chairs of business administration and management, but also by newly founded professorships of psychology, sociology and human resources in the 1950s and 1960s, political sciences in the 1970s and business ethics in the 1980s. By 1962, when the name of the graduate school was changed from HH to HSG, the social sciences were considered so important that they were explicitly mentioned in the new name.

A milestone in the development of business administration at our graduate school was the *St Gallen Management Model* that was conceived by Hans Ulrich (1968) and his collaborators. Ulrich decoupled business administration from its restrictive focus on economic aspects; its object of discovery is rather the corporation in all its aspects, the corporation as 'a productive social system'. He drew on social sciences and especially the systems theory and cybernetics of Stafford Beer (1959) in order to systematically organize business and management knowledge and to promote systems thinking. The St Gallen Management Model (Ulrich and Krieg 1972) distinguished economic, technological and social dimensions of management intervention and identified nature, society, technology and economy as relevant environments of organizations. It proclaimed therefore an *integrative perspective* and a *transdisciplinary approach*. For the past four decades, concepts like 'holistic thinking', 'holistic problem solving', 'network thinking', 'holistic management' and 'integrated management' were predominant and are still considered crucial nowadays, as exemplified by 'the new St Gallen management model' (Rüegg-Stürm 2005) and its current, updated revision (Rüegg-Stürm and Grand 2014). Although this management model increased the *degree of scientification* in our business education, the HSG maintained close relations with business corporations as well as public institutions and non-profit organizations. The institutional infrastructure was laid by the foundation of *institutes* (of business administration, marketing and sales, banking, insurance, etc.) that offered workshops and seminars as well as consulting, thereby also funding themselves. This way, the St Gallen Management Model became a success story and for some time it was a *unité de doctrine* internally but it also gained wide recognition in the business world. In Switzerland, management became seen as a profession that can be learned. The more this view disseminated in society, the more students came to study in St Gallen (400 in 1950, 2,000 in 1980, 4,000 in 1990, 8,000 in 2014) and the more practitioners applied for advanced vocational training and professional development. Despite an increasing scientification and academic credibility, the University of St Gallen has kept a good reputation in business practice.

Although the *social sciences* have increasingly gained importance and even figure in the name of the HSG, the *humanities* remained somewhat in the shadow of the other disciplines; however, they were included as a relevant part of the St Gallen graduate school's programme from the outset. The First Annual Report (Jahresbericht 1900) declares the goal of a comprehensive formation that encompasses, besides business administration, lectures in humanities and natural sciences. Mastery of foreign languages was considered important for merchants. In the first year, there were courses in eight foreign languages offered (Arabic, English, French, Dutch, Italian,

Portuguese, Spanish and Russian). In addition, there were lectures held about cultural history, the history of the nineteenth century, as well as about German, English, French and Italian literature. In other words, the *humanistic ideal of the nineteenth century that higher education should not only procure technical expertise but foster general knowledge* was adhered to from the very beginning. When the graduate school was organized into departments in 1919, there was a department of business administration, of economics and law, of languages and history, of technology and natural sciences, and of pedagogics and philosophy. The departments were reorganized in 1937, and the humanities were regrouped into the Department of Languages, History and Philosophy. In 1975 this was renamed the Department of Cultural Sciences. It remained, compared with the other departments, rather small. The even smaller Department of Technology and Natural Sciences was dissolved in 1989.

In the course of the increasing scientification, specialization and professionalization and the rise of the social sciences, the *relative importance of the humanities has considerably declined.* If we compare the numbers of professors *(ordinarii et extraordinarii)* over the past hundred years, the total has significantly soared whilst the number of professors in the humanities has remained remarkably stable: at the end of the twentieth century, the same chairs of 'German and German literature' still existed, and likewise of English, French, Italian, Spanish (and Portuguese) and Russian language and literature, as well as a chair of philosophy and one of history. Table 29.1 illustrates the development. Although 36 per cent of all the professors represented humanities in 1920, nowadays their share has declined to 8 per cent – although the longstanding policy that our students have to achieve degrees in two foreign languages remained unchanged.[1] This development reflects in a nutshell what happened to the humanities in general in the twentieth century – and also at other Swiss, and presumably other European and US, universities. Public policies favoured the funding of natural sciences, technology and medical science – and later economics and political science – because of their evident utility, whilst the share and the acknowledged importance of the humanities shrunk (see Honegger *et al.* 2007).

To summarize, at the dawn of the Bologna Reform, we had a longstanding tradition that the humanities constituted an important part of business education, particularly because foreign language skills were considered important but also because the humanities represented 'general education'. The humanities survived; technology and natural sciences did not. The social

*Table 29.1* Number of professors per department

| | *WS* | | *WS* | | *WS* | | *WS* | | *WS* | | *WS* | |
|---|---|---|---|---|---|---|---|---|---|---|---|---|
| | *1920–1*[1] | | *1938–9*[1] | | *1954–5*[1] | | *1978–9*[1] | | *1999–2000*[2] | | *2014–15* | |
| | *%* | *No.* | *%* | *No.* | *%* | *No.* | *%* | *No.* | *%* | *No.* | *%* | *No.* |
| Business Administration | 25 | 4.5 | 25 | 4 | 21 | 4 | 27 | 12 | 38 | 29 | 42 | 39 |
| Economics | 6 | 1 | 13 | 2 | 21 | 4 | 20 | 9 | 17 | 13 | 12 | 11 |
| Law | 11 | 2 | 13 | 2 | 16 | 3 | 20 | 9 | 19 | 15 | 14 | 13 |
| Humanities | 36 | 6.5 | 31 | 5 | 32 | 6 | 13 | 6 | 9 | 7 | 8 | 7[3] |
| Nat. & Techn. | 17 | 3 | 13 | 2 | 11 | 2 | 2 | 1 | 0 | 0 | 0 | 0 |
| Finance[4] | | | | | | | | | | | 9 | 8 |
| Others[5] | 6 | 1 | 6 | 1 | 0 | 0 | 18 | 8 | 17 | 13 | 15 | 14 |
| Students | 217 | | 211 | | 542 | | 1,833 | | 4,553 | | 8,020 | |

*Notes:* [1] years of major reforms implemented; [2] at the dawn of reform 2000; [3] without the social sciences that became part of the same department in 2001; [4] founded in 2011; [5] including social sciences, business ethics, computer science, mathematics. WS: Winter Semester.

sciences became ever more important in business administration since the human-relations movement – and particularly since the St Gallen Management Model.

## *The Bologna Reform – the 'reform 2000'*

At the University of Bologna in 1999, 29 European Ministers of Education signed the so-called Bologna Declaration. Its main goal was to create a European Higher Education Area until 2010, in which students and graduates could move around freely. This required a harmonization of formal teaching structures and mutual acknowledgement of degrees between universities. It was agreed to introduce the Anglo-Saxon model of two consecutive study cycles, an undergraduate programme of three years with a Bachelor degree (BA) and a graduate programme with a Master degree (MA) and/or Doctoral degree. The European Credit Transfer System (ECTS) should help to make achievements and qualifications of students comparable. In addition, a European collaboration in quality development was decided, and employability and international competitiveness became declared goals. Finally, a European Research Area should be established.

The Bologna Declaration prompted the rectorate of the University of St Gallen to initiate the most fundamental reform in its history. The rectorate attempted to find a balance between corporate management techniques and the traditionally democratic constitution of a university. It imposed basic formal structures, like the BA–MA cycles, and invited every member to collaborate and define the contents. In two-day workshops, all the professors were invited to collaboratively reinvent their university, and many project teams were formed that subsequently further discussed and gave substance to the new ideas. By a rather unconventional change-management technique that used new forms of collaboration, much creative energy was released.

Any institutional change requires a change of its legitimating discourse. To let go of the old and focus attention on the new, the same management tools that have been already propagated for corporations for several decades were applied to our own university: analysing the changing environment, recognizing future trends, identifying strategic success potentials and formulating a vision, a mission statement and guiding principles (Gomez and Spoun 2009). In 2000, the Vision 2005 was agreed upon:

> We are acknowledged as one of the leading business universities in Europe, in science as well as in practice. We are united by an integrative perspective of economic science, law, and social sciences.

This vision was substantiated by a mission statement and guiding principles and each department was required to define which strategic aims they wanted to have achieved by 2005. There followed a Vision 2010, and current goals and activities orient towards the Vision 2020:

> As one of Europe's leading business universities, we are recognised globally as a place for thought leadership on current economic, business, and societal matters and for the development of talent able to integrate perspectives and act both entrepreneurially and responsibly.
>
> *http://www.unisg.ch/en/universitaet/vision (retrieved on 1 January 2004)*

The Reform 2000, which started in 1999 and was implemented in 2001 and following years, resulted in a fundamentally *new study architecture with three levels and three pillars* (see Figure 29.1). The three levels consist of the assessment level (first year), the Bachelor level (second and third year, which together make a three-year Bachelor programme), and the Master level (three or four semesters). The three pillars consist of classroom activities (lectures and seminars; 50 per cent),

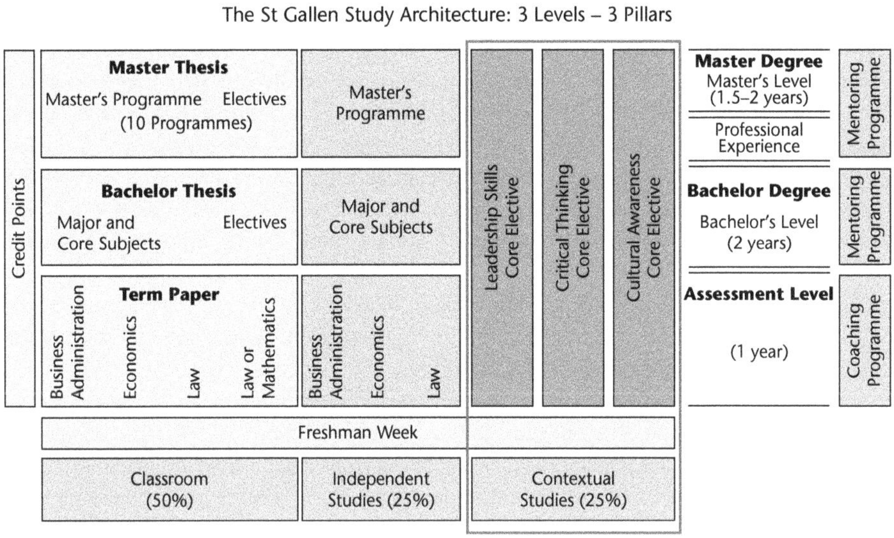


*Figure 29.1* Study architecture

(http://www.unisg.ch/en/studium/darumhsg/einzigartigestudienarchitektur)

self-study (reading; 25 per cent) and contextual studies (25 per cent of study time). The calculated average study time is forty hours per week.

Let us first consider the three levels. The goals of the assessment level are to introduce new students intensely and effectively into scientific study, but also to shorten the selection process that previously lasted two or even three years. Students should realize quickly if they have chosen the appropriate subject and if they are capable of meeting the requirements. After passing the exams of the assessment level, students enter the Bachelor level where they have to choose one of the four majors (business administration, economics, law or international affairs, each with a programme committee), with the possibility of choosing a double degree. They have to achieve the required ECTS credits in their major and core subjects as well as in some electives, plus in the contextual studies. The Bachelor thesis may be written on any topic, including one of the contextual studies. The Master level consists of three semesters, but many students use a fourth semester to write their Master's thesis. The former study programme had allowed for specializing in one of more than twenty areas. Now this scope was greatly reduced to a few programmes (each with a programme committee of its own). The reform aimed at a reduction to eight core areas and finally ended with ten. At the time of writing (in 2015) there are thirteen.

The new study architecture has three pillars. The reduction of lectures and seminars and the increase of time for self-study had already been aims of previous reforms, but it was time to carefully sort out once more for which kind of competences classroom activities are needed and what students can learn on their own. In view of the rapid development of new technologies and web-based learning, this will remain a challenge for the future. The most innovative pillar was, however, the contextual studies programme.

## *Contextual studies*

The most visible institutional innovation of the Reform 2000 was undoubtedly the creation of contextual studies, where 25 per cent of the study time, from the assessment level up to the

Master level, is dedicated to perspectives of other disciplines and topics that concern the context of business, economy, law and international affairs. At a time when most business schools had restricted their programmes predominantly or even exclusively to their core subjects, the University of St Gallen decided to devote 25 per cent to general formation. This is a really substantial share of the overall study time, and it indicates that the contextual studies programme was designed to become a competitive advantage on an international scale. A crucial guideline of the reform was 'to demand and foster personalities' and it was carefully discussed how the university could effectively contribute to 'develop students' personalities' (Spoun and Wunderlich 2005).

Contextual studies also consists of three pillars, which were defined in line with modern pedagogics as different competences: cultural competence, reflection competence and action competence. They were defined in the following way:

- Cultural competence is 'the capacity to understand other cultures, their standards and values, lifestyles and concepts of order, institutions and history, language and art. For respectful contact with other cultures and for successful intercultural communication, foreign language skills are a necessity. Our courses include instruction in various foreign languages as well as cultural seminars, opening up access to the culture of the respective language'.
- Reflection competence is 'the capacity to develop sound systematic analyses of intellectual problems and cultural issues. The lectures and seminars of the elective courses of history, philosophy, business ethics, psychology and sociology in the critical thinking pillar provide an introduction to the conceptual models and instruments of these disciplines'.
- Action competence is 'composed of knowledge and application of interdisciplinary methods of scientific and practically oriented work and learning. We teach you problem-solving skills and practically oriented requirements for social competence, strategic and well-conceived action for your education and your career'.

*Contextual Studies at Bachelor's Level (n.d.)*

We face an interesting problem of translation here, which reflects the pervasive reference of conceptual definitions to a specific cultural and linguistic context: everybody who masters more than one language knows that many notions of one language cannot be translated exactly, and often not even adequately, into terms of another language. The three competences were originally formulated in German; however, because some Master programmes were designed in English from the outset, we also used English terminology from the outset. The English terms may be well chosen for an English-speaking community, but they do not exactly convey what the German definitions mean. The German term 'Kulturelle Kompetenz' literally means 'cultural competence' in English, but it was translated as 'cultural awareness'; the German term 'Reflexionskompetenz' means 'competence to pursue elaborate reflections', but was translated as 'critical thinking'; the German term 'Handlungskompetenz' means the 'competence to act (in any respect)', but was translated as 'leadership skills'. We chose to use a literal translation because the concrete measures of implementation and substantiation, which we are going to discuss later, are difficult to understand using the official English terminology.

The Reform 2000 brought a massive challenge for the institution as almost overnight 25 per cent of the curriculum of every major on Bachelor and Master level for about 6,000 students had to be provided for with interesting and relevant courses in the newly established contextual studies. The pillar *cultural competence* could draw upon what the humanities had offered already in the past. The pillar *reflection competence* could integrate diverse social sciences, history and philosophy, but was too vast to be filled by the sparse local faculty only, which opened the opportunity to employ external lecturers and guest professors from other universities in order to introduce additional disciplines and themes. The pillar *action competence*, however, had to be built up largely from scratch. This pillar formed the bridge between business administration or management and the humanities and social sciences and was aimed at helping students to develop practical action skills. These courses should train people in specific activities and therefore should be smaller in size (thirty-five participants maximum) and scale (two ECTS credits in contrast to four ECTS credits of the other courses). It meant that there was a greater variety of offers for the students as well as an increased need to hire external lecturers and trainers to meet the demand.

To translate these competences into concrete courses was, and is, the task of the programme committee for contextual studies (which will be discussed later). Its members were proposed by the rectorate and approved by the senate. This committee was composed of members of different departments and was organizationally subordinated to the rectorate. When the University of St Gallen reorganized its departments into schools in 2011, the programme committee for contextual studies became a committee of the school of humanities and social sciences. The task of this committee was, and is, to create a programme of contextual studies every year to concretely define which kind of courses make up the programme. Let us recall that this programme takes up 25 per cent of the overall curriculum, which leaves 75 per cent for the respective study programmes of the other schools (primarily the school of management and the school of finance, and also the school of economics and political sciences and the school of law). Each of these schools has an elected representative in the programme committee. There is also, as in all our committees, a student representative. Because this committee is much larger than other programme committees, we call it an 'executive board'.

There were some institutional innovations beyond the reach of this executive board. A crucial idea was to test not only intellectual capabilities but also personal behaviours at the assessment level, such as communication skills, collaborating in a team, conflict resolution, self-presentation, and so on because this is crucial in the business world. When the idea was rejected saying that these criteria would be too soft for student selection, it was decided to create other vessels. One is the *coaching programme* that still is unique amongst universities and business schools, which offers the opportunity to a limited number of students to develop competences like self-reflection, self-responsibility and social and leadership skills with a personal coach (Eberle 2012; Eberle and Spoun 2012). Another one is the *mentoring programme* that offers students a personal mentor from the corporate world for further study and career planning (Spoun and Müller 2012). Both programmes persist and have their own programme director. Another innovation took the form of a cooperation with the Haniel Foundation in Germany, which supports and co-develops educational initiatives and was involved soon after the reform. The Haniel Seminars (now the European Haniel Programme on Entrepreneurship and the Humanities) enabled experiments with theme-based learning opportunities and new pedagogics that were specifically situated in contextual studies.

## Experiences and major challenges

After covering this delineation of the new study architecture created by the Reform 2000, we will now discuss *our experiences with implementing contextual studies*. Concrete problems pop up whilst you attempt to implement ambitious ideas. In this section we focus on some major challenges that we have been facing that may be symptomatic of any attempt to integrate humanities and social sciences with business education, and which therefore may be of interest to the readership of this book.

On the *assessment level*, contextual studies have a special shape and there is less choice for the students. Cultural competence consists exclusively in languages because every student has to learn at least two foreign languages. Reflection competence is represented by four basic disciplines: the students choose between sociology and psychology in one semester, and between philosophy and history in the other. Action competence consisted of an introduction to academic work. In the autumn semester, the students study academic writing, and in the spring semester they attend a course in Integrative Problem Solving, a complex business case that has to be analysed from different perspectives and solved by a holistic approach. Although there is not much choice, all these competences are mainly taught in comparatively small groups of thirty to fifty students.

The contextual studies at the Bachelor and Master level are much more multifaceted and there are now 350 courses to choose from. In order to structure our experiences and the implied challenges, we discuss them from *three perspectives*: first, the view of the executive board, then the position of the faculty and finally the students' perspective.

## *Perspective of the executive board of contextual studies*

The executive board of contextual studies has the task of implementing the basic ideas of the reform into a concrete course programme. This implied multiple subtasks, such as the selection of suitable course topics; ensuring diverse teaching methods; negotiations with in-house faculty and appointment of lecturers and guest professors from other universities; managing offer and demand as well as growing student numbers; and much more. The board had a *considerable influence on defining which course topics and designs would fit the three competences.* Cultural competence would encompass foreign language classes, but above all, it would increase the cultural awareness and the cultural conditions of economic practice. Course examples include 'Public sphere, economy and power in Putin's Russia', 'May 68 in France in its political and cultural contexts' and 'Political Islam'. Although our professors in the humanities were appointed as professors of (French, English, etc.) language and literature, they widened their scope to a broader concept of culture. Reflection competence should enable students to reflect the philosophical, ethical, sociological, psychological or religious context of economic activity but also incorporate courses on arts and media. Some examples of courses include 'Escape, mission, tourism: on the cultural poetics of travelling', 'Philosophy of money' and 'Innovation and tradition: radical change and its historical foundations'. Action competence should empower people in regard to concrete activities, such as presentation techniques, team development, conflict resolution, but also programming or empirical research methods. A different approach to learning where students are actually involved was crucial. Our course examples in this situation include 'Asperitas – organizational development in a simulated business company' (Eberle and Steyaert 2013), 'Cities and creativity' (see Michels and Beyes, this volume) and 'Visual storytelling: from first idea to final film'.

To realize such an ambitious programme the collaboration of (nearly) everybody was needed. The board invited the faculty of the humanities and social sciences to submit concrete course proposals with aims, structure, literature and exam requirements, and explain how the proposed course would contribute to the goals of contextual studies. This initiated a wide and prolific reflection process among the faculty, but the board also negotiated face-to-face with many colleagues and insisted on adjustments to the new profile; on course topics that were either too narrow or too broad; and course requirements that were comparable to those of other courses. Regarding course contents, the board decided to favour disciplinary approaches at the Bachelor level and multi- or interdisciplinary courses at the Master level, and it kept a kind of 'firewall' from the core disciplines in order to ensure that the contextual studies would address the context of business administration, economics and law and not consist of 'ordinary' courses of these disciplines. The board also introduced a new tool to manage numbers: in order to restrict the maximum number of students per course, a bidding system was developed. Each student received 500 points and could bid for the courses he or she would like to attend. The students who set most points for a specific course would be admitted (sixty students for a Bachelor course, forty-five for a Master course). Besides scrutinizing the course proposals, the board also observed how many students bid for a certain course and how many dropped out during the semester. These numbers were interpreted as indicators for the attractiveness of a course to the students. In addition, regular evaluations in the form of student feedback were collected by the university's quality development services. All these results were taken into account in the board's future decision making.

Twenty-five per cent is a considerable share of the teaching load, and the amount of courses outnumbered the in-house faculty by far. This gave the board the option to think about additional topics and specialities that were not represented and offered in-house, and invite lecturers and guest professors from other universities. We also attempted to regularly invite some 'big shots' who would endow the contextual studies with significant public recognition and appreciation. Every year, we had a contextual studies programme that offered a wide array of interesting courses; however, the board was very small during the first decade (one person in charge of each competence, one representative of another department, a student representative and an administrative officer) and was extremely busy in face of the rapidly increasing course numbers – from about 80 in 2001 to 350 in 2014. The programme became ever more complex and opaque, with no clear profile, and for an outside observer it could give the impression of a 'hodge podge', an unsystematic conglomeration of too many topics. The board attempted to deal with this problem and did more proactive agenda setting by introducing a 'topic of the year'. The faculty were invited to design new courses that covered the topic of the year, for example 'Old worlds, new worlds' in 2011 and 'Responsibility' in 2012. Although announced fifteen months in advance, and although lower participant numbers were offered as incentives, this initiative proved unsuccessful – it often led to a cosmetic rewording of already existing formats. The 'topic of the year' tool was given up in 2013 and gave way to an ongoing reform process that sought to achieve a more transparent and plausible structure by clustering contents and developing clearer profiles.

## *Perspective of the faculty*

All the chairs in the school of humanities and social sciences have been professors of disciplinary origin, for example philosophy with a trained philosopher (and not a person from business administration with some expertise or a second book in philosophy). This assures a high competence with regards to the debates in the proper discipline, but poses questions for the dialogue with the core studies. Almost all the colleagues report a longer phase of adjustment to the students' background knowledge and expectations. This *train-the-trainer problem* is partially dealt with in further education offers, such as the supplementary university teaching certificate organized by the institute of business pedagogics at the university. The exercises in this training help the teacher to understand the huge potential of teaching tools, but do not cover explicitly the broader range of questions of interdisciplinary *content* exchange. Here further research, such as the presidential project 'humanities' business' (that tries to map the Europe-wide programmes, initiatives and courses regarding integrative business education), as well the dialogue between faculties can increase collaboration between the disciplines (Landfester, Tofte Brenneche and Prat-i-Pubill, this volume).

Another way of bridging different disciplinary approaches is *co-teaching of faculty from different disciplines*, like sociology and business administration; philosophy and economics; or a Latin America specialist and a professor of international management. The University of St Gallen rewards co-teaching by granting double the amount of hours of the teaching load for the first performance, but less if a course is repeated. Although we had a number of innovative and rewarding interdisciplinary courses, co-teaching did not become common practice in contextual studies. The reason for this may be found, more and more, in the primacy of research and publishing over teaching. Although there is distinct appreciation for good teaching, such as awards by the student union, the institutional incentives are not as rewarding as a good publication list. This primacy of research is particularly relevant for younger faculty with international career plans, something that the Bologna process encourages. Increasingly, and clearly intensified by ranking measures, journal publications and third-party-funded research have become primary criteria for academic careers and personal as well as institutional reputation. This means that teaching engagement and commitments to community-building activities are considered as 'nice-to-have' but not as really relevant. In career terms, interdisciplinarity and a broad knowledge in various fields – a precondition for efficient and plausible integrative courses – become an obstacle instead of an incentive. To counter this development, new institutional incentives like extra allowances of teaching hours for co-teaching or special career tracks based on teaching quality could encourage new ways of cooperation and shift the balance (back) towards teaching; otherwise, teaching will continue to be considered an 'add-on', which counteracts any initiative to introduce and foster the humanities and social sciences in management education.

There is also still some latent *internal resistance* to the idea that 25 per cent of the students' time and engagement should be dedicated to non-core studies, especially at the Master level. Although there might be good arguments, the institution's commitment to integrative education demands compromises and reasonable cooperation, for example, as in the shape of courses in contextual studies that show close ties to the core studies. Here again, a particular difficulty often gets in the way. The contextual studies, although formally under the responsibility of the school of humanities and social sciences, are not 'owned' by anyone. They can be positioned as a 'third space' open to all the schools and their faculties to offer courses with an inter- or even transdisciplinary ambition and learning objective – a 'third space' indicating that it's neither the core nor the context disciplines that rule this kind of vessel for integrative thinking (Beyes and Michels 2011: 524 *passim*; and Steyaert, Hoyer and Resch, this volume).

As for the students, meeting in the classroom is the elementary way of experiencing the contextual studies. Due to the constraints mentioned earlier, there's relatively *little investment* in *innovative teaching formats*, although the willingness might be high. Nonetheless, there are formats for more experimental teaching that enable changes in the setting. For example, the Haniel Seminars and the European Haniel Programme, mentioned earlier, can rely on special funds, for example for using alternative spaces (such as ateliers, see Johnsen, Sørensen Thaning and Pedersen, this volume) and/or the invitation of multiple guests. These relatively small changes – space, more guests, different didactics – can have a significant effect, as the evaluations show. Students like different settings that point to another kind of learning experience – in contrast to the PowerPoint presentation 'industry' that rules the classroom and is often also in contextual studies.

## *Perspective of the students*

The most important outcome after almost fifteen years of contextual studies at the University of St Gallen is the *support for this type of structure by the students*. The recent survey *HSG Student Monitoring* of the Research Institute of Sociology in July 2014 (Egger 2014) showed that over

50 per cent of all Bachelor students ($n$ = 233) consider the contextual studies 'very important' or 'important'; the action competence was the most appreciated pillar (62 per cent), followed by reflection competence (51 per cent) and cultural competence (48 per cent). The results at Master level are a bit weaker (51 per cent action competency; 45 per cent reflection competence; 43 per cent cultural competence) but still add up to 46 per cent of the students with a high esteem of contextual studies. Along with this positive notion is the fact that about 50 per cent of the Bachelor students think that 25 per cent of the whole curriculum is an adequate size, with another 35 per cent of the student corpus answering that it should even be expanded. This appreciation goes along with the fact that their courses in the contextual studies receive, on average, better evaluations than classes or electives in the core disciplines, as the regular standardized evaluations by the Department of Quality Management show.

The *HSG Student Monitoring* survey also offers insight into the *sociocultural factors* that enhance appreciation for this kind of integrative education. A *privileged family background/social status and a privileged study situation* are the most significant factors here. Students who are most in favour of contextual studies are from families familiar with education who live close to campus, don't have to work much in side-jobs to earn their living (see Śliwa and Sørensen, this volume), study longer, go abroad more often and engage more intensely in the student associations and initiatives. On the other hand, *social deficits* (as the survey calls them), such as poorer family background, purely job-focused education as well as strong regional anchoring, seem to contribute to an attitude that considers the contextual studies as an indifferent, partially negligible or even disturbing feature of the university. The survey concludes that these two positions – the first being close to the ideal imaginary of the institution, the second closer to a business *school* rather than a business university – are 'relatively clear, almost antithetical' and so deeply grounded in the social background that a change in motivation will hardly be achieved during the study time. This distinction goes along with another, not asked for in the report but recurring in student feedback, that positions the wish for *alternative* courses in the sense of a 'humanist supplement' more at the Bachelor level, whereas the demand for core study focus is more often found at the Master level.

Apart from these deep-rooted attitudes, the habit is partially also homemade. The challenging requirements of the first year force students into surface instead of deep learning and therefore into economizing on their efforts in order to obtain the best degrees in the shortest amount of invested time. This spirit of optimization is fostered by the fact that about 40 per cent of the students won't make it to the second year. Phenomena such as 'bulimia learning' – a term used by our colleagues in the Institute of Business Education to describe short-term learning results (learn–reproduce–forget) – or 'memory clear parties' (student slang) after the central block of exams indicate a learning culture that is based on strict avoidance of interesting, but (potentially) time-consuming courses and a clear-cut culture of delivery. However, as experienced by the authors numerous times, it is not impossible to reopen the students' attention to a broader perspective, and yet this entails didactic changes from ex-cathedra teaching and PowerPoint presentations to more dialogical formats and variations of exam formats.

## What can contextual studies teach us about integrative education?

What can we learn from our institutional experiences in regard to the larger debates on integrative management education within the context provided by the second Carnegie Report on undergraduate management education (Colby *et al.* 2011)? We focus on three challenges that we believe every business university will have to deal with when starting or fostering an integrative education approach. Our guiding question is therefore 'what are the crucial issues that may be inherent to any cooperation between management and economics, on the one hand, and humanities and social sciences on the other?' One challenge is located on a meta-level framework; the second concerns faculty and disciplinary-related problems; and the third the concrete ground of learning culture and student learning behaviour.

## *The Humboldt paradigm versus the alignment model*

The aim of an integrative business education, as stated in the mission of the University of St Gallen, is an *open-minded, socially responsible and entrepreneurial personality*. Referring not only to the instrumental transfer of knowledge, but also to the transformative character of higher education inevitably leads back to Wilhelm von Humboldt who called for the unity of research and teaching (Thomä 2005) and for whom education (*Bildung*) was an act of free self-formation (*freie Selbstbildung*) in the spirit of autonomy and maturity. In his report to the King of Prussia in 1809, Humboldt defined education accordingly as the 'inspiration of all potencies of man' through the 'appropriation of the world' in order to develop a self-determining individuality and personality (quoted in Ellwein 1985: 116; translated by authors; see also Hofmann 2010). For the University of St Gallen, this ideal was revitalized by the reform in 2000. Although the renaming from graduate school (*Hochschule*) to university in 1995 suggested a turn towards a broader notion of education, the core of the institution's self-image as well as public reputation remained strictly business oriented. With the explicit reinvention of the university in light of an institutionalized strand of contextual studies, an interesting constellation came into place. Humboldt's ideal was present now, but the institution slowly had to learn how to 'live it' – on both the side of the faculty and the side of the students.

This challenge became even bigger due to the *institutional need for accreditation*. The contextual studies were implemented as a competitive advantage of the university, but paradoxically weren't considered an essential part of the university when it came to external audits. In recent years the presidency, also under the pressure of the accreditation agencies, has therefore requested the reform of contextual studies through clearly defined learning objectives and reports documenting at which level they have been achieved. The underlying assumption of this logic is the accessibility of every outcome in education, based on a more instrumental approach to learning and teaching. This model could be called the *alignment model* and its implementation, on the one hand, might be necessary to conform to the rest of the European university system. On the other hand, it opens the more general question of *how to assess reflection competencies, creativity and personal development*. Humboldt's ideal leaves much room for the unexpected, the potential. If the contextual studies are considered to be working in this spirit, but should also be fully accredited and normalized according to fixed rules – as the internationalization strategy and the global competitiveness might urge us to – there might be a danger of increasing standardization that is rather antithetical to the humanities and the social sciences.

The challenge exists not only for the ongoing reform process in contextual studies, but also for all related initiatives on improving integrative management thinking. How is it possible to find equilibrium between required homogeneity and necessary deviance – in topics, approaches, methods and teaching styles – in order to open a space of possibilities for students willing to develop themselves? This is a need that has strong support in the findings of the Carnegie Report and its results could provide a strong value basis for a Humboldtian engagement because only a campus university with teaching in face-to-face interaction seems to be able to activate the individuals' potential for sustainable change in their personalities (*Economist* 2015: 4, 8; see also Panda 2004: 79 *passim*). This argument, however, often remains distant from the new and persistent habits of our students, such as multitasking and a focus on grades and certificates, if it is only used as a claim for a humanistic refinement in morals as the Carnegie Report often does (see Parker, this volume; O'Doherty, this volume). The real impetus of our experience is to open the discussion about the valid contributions of the humanities and social sciences into business education, and morals are only one aspect here. Although business ethics and cultural refinement are important, it would be too narrow a perspective if the impact of integration was not more core-relevant and *essential for the business of tomorrow* (Chia and Nayak, this volume), that is beyond the classical division of labour in the education of the next generation.

## The 'integrative management education' topic

It is this persistence of *silo thinking* – a kind of essentialism that claims to define stable boundaries between different disciplines with the strong emphasis on privileging one over the other – that could be considered the most prominent feature of ongoing debates not only in theory, but also at our institution. In the wording of the HSG study architecture, this is articulated in phrases like 'context is not necessary, we only need the text, i.e. core business', a statement that is rarely heard in public any more but is still prevalent amongst some of our colleagues. It reflects a completely different take on the expected relevance of certain fields of knowledge. The average humanities' and social sciences' scholar might claim to clarify the cultural framework and societal embeddedness of any market and business academy, but some representatives of economics, finance and accounting might state that these reflections only waste time that is otherwise needed urgently for an increasingly complex curriculum in the 'core studies'. These different perspectives surely stem from a long tradition of disciplinary self-description and status, but they are also partially produced by the 'integration' topic itself because the term suggests a clear direction 'from–to' instead of pointing to the interrelatedness of many questions and problems especially in management education with the humanities and social sciences.

One way to reframe this could be the improvement of *relational thinking* that overcomes 'silo mentality' and, relying on problem-based teaching methods, explores new perspectives on crucial topics of today's (business) world. The central twist would be to avoid the disciplinary problem definition with subsequent interdisciplinary exchange about these definitions. Instead of thus potentially reducing the phenomena, the challenge would consist in a reflexive transdisciplinary process of staying with the problem of constructing a problem (see Johnsen, Sørensen Thaning and Pedersen, this volume). The focus shifts from the application of solution tools to multiple reframings of the many facets of the phenomena in question that could be a problem. It is necessary to add that this shift in perspectives requires openness and willingness in institutional terms. Are there incentives in both research and teaching to engage in relational thinking? Or do the paradigms of publication rankings and instrumental alignment models favour mainstreaming and still hinder such initiatives? The HSG experience shows the resistance of the established faculty structure as well as the possibilities of contextual studies as a 'third space', for example in the more experimental course design – which leads to our final consideration.

## Teaching culture and student learning behaviour

If the question related to Humboldt's ideal is how to reinvent it in the twenty-first century facing digitalization and accreditation, the related question regarding the concrete situations of teaching and learning could be 'how can we encourage the faculty to do really new things in the classroom?' In the contextual studies the pillar of action competence was the only place to systematically invite internal and external lecturers to *experiment with innovative teaching formats*, often with the help of the Haniel Foundation. There was and is too little discussion about the radical nature of claims towards integrative education with the related demand to train the trainer and to get into *real contact with the students*. This should become an objective in itself and not just part of the workload or even a potential obstacle in an increasingly publication-driven career system. Within the given institutional framework, this remains a persistent problem even for faculty at the HSG who are truly committed to innovative teaching methods and fostering students' personalities.

There is, of course, a widespread change in the expectations and the behaviour of students at universities, and also in higher education in general. Semi-frustrated teacher statements like 'I'm not in the education business, I'm in the diploma business' point to a development amongst younger people to focus on the institutional imprint on a certain period of their lives that is understood not in terms of personal growth but in terms of survival and final victory, fun and a lot of networking. This could also be seen against the background of the megatrend of the new millennium because *digitalization* has generally changed the status of content and learning (see Bachmann and Shah, this volume). We all know that our students are online during our lessons and regard the courses as a multitasking challenge, and that this might reduce their curricular engagement and attention. Besides, if any of the taught material is available for free online, why should students meet on campus? One position strengthens the need for dialogue and face-to-face contact for real learning and personal growth, another one puts networking and certification in the foreground. Of course, a degree from a prestigious institution has always been attractive, but this is not the point (although it is still valid). One central challenge of an integrative management education with regards to MOOCs (Massive Open Online Courses) and the like will therefore be *to make the class an experience*, a space of transformation and not the physical form of knowledge otherwise available.

This might also make a difference when it comes to the selection of courses by the students. We do have feedback from student representatives that their fellow students do not bid on courses with, for example, three exam formats or long reading lists. To put it bluntly (and almost a bit like a caricature): the executive board of the contextual studies might be interested in content and relevant topics, the students are not – they want to get their credit points as easily as possible and nothing more. Without exaggerating the impact of the university in general, to start over in the spirit of Humboldt could therefore mean to pick up the students where they are – a cultural era in the transformation away from the 'Gutenberg galaxy' and canon knowledge, but with an emphasis on experience and usability. We have to revitalize the core idea. We should do and teach what is relevant for the students, not for the teachers (particularly, it seems, for those academics in the old 'Ordinarii university' (chair) tradition, as well as the scholars in the humanities). The *business university of the future* will therefore have to reinvent the institution as *a laboratory that fosters change, creativity and personal transformation*. This might not be necessary in all fields, but definitely in the way students are encouraged to think of themselves as potentially different from what they had expected to become. This encouragement to constantly change holds true for the teachers as well because they should be enabled not only to accompany students but also to help themselves in ensuring that the university stays as one of the most important institutions in society.

## Conclusion

To briefly sum up, in this chapter we have looked back upon and made sense of our experiences of many years in conceptualizing and realizing what – as far as we can see – is a unique endeavour: an institutionally integrated programme of the humanities and social sciences at a business university and 'for' management education. We believe that this programme can or should inspire institutional 'followers'. The analysis of our experiences gained with and through the contextual studies offers pitfalls (for example, behaviours, practices, expectations in conflict with visions and incentives) and advantages (for example, the huge innovation potential in contextual studies at the interface of different disciplines, enabling critical and relational thinking). From what we have learned, having a clear understanding of and a shared perspective on the three issues – educational model, integration paradigm and university culture – is an indispensable prerequisite for any attempt to reinvent business education in the name of the humanities and social sciences.

## Note

1 The number of professors is only a crude indicator: first, the early lists of employed professors also contain persons who were additionally employed at other institutions; second, it does not mirror the number of lectures that are actually taught in each field – in 2014 there were 92 professorships but a total of 600 persons who teach. Nevertheless, professorships are a good indicator of a university's institutionalization policies.

## References

Beer, S. (1959) *Cybernetics and Management*. London: English Universities Press.
Beyes, T. and Michels, C. (2011) 'The production of educational space: heterotopia and the business university', *Management Learning*, 42(5), 521–46.
Burmeister, K.H. (1998) *Geschichte der Universität St Gallen*. Bern: Stämpfli.
Colby, A., Ehrlich, T., Sullivan, W.M. and Dolle, J.R. (2011) *Rethinking Undergraduate Business Education: Liberal Learning for the Profession*. San Francisco, CA: Jossey-Bass.
Contextual Studies at Bachelor's Level (n.d.) University of St Gallen, Switzerland. Available from: www.unisg.ch/en/studium/bachelor/allgemeineinformationen/kontextstudium (accessed 1 January 2015).
Eberle, T.S. (2012) 'Das Coaching-Programm der Universität St Gallen'. *In*: T.S. Eberle and S. Spoun (eds.) *Durch Coaching Führungsqualitäten entwickeln. Kernkompetenzen erkennen und fördern*. Zurich: Versus Verlag, pp. 115–36.
Eberle, T.S. and Spoun, S. (2012) *Durch Coaching Führungsqualitäten entwickeln. Kernkompetenzen erkennen und fördern*. Zurich: Versus Verlag
Eberle, T.S. and Steyaert, C. (2013) 'OE lehren an der Universität: Ein erfahrungszentrierter Ansatz mit Organisationssimulation', *Organisations Entwicklung. Zeitschrift für Unternehmensentwicklung und Change Management*, no. 2, 54–63.
Economist, The (2015) 'The future of universities: the digital degree', *The Economist*, 28 June 2014. Available from: www.economist.com/node/21605899/print (accessed 17 August 2015).
Egger, S. (2014) 'HSG Student Monitoring: Kontextstudium an der HSG – Merkmale der Akzeptanz', Research Institute of Sociology (internal report), July 2014.
Ellwein, T. (1985) *Die deutsche Universität vom Mittelalter bis zur Gegenwart*. Königstein, Germany: Athenäum.
Gomez, P. and Spoun, S. (2009) 'Vision and strategy: instruments for building individual university profiles'. *In*: E. Frament, J. Kohler, L. Purser and L. Wilson (eds.) *EUA Bologna Handbook: Making Bologna Work*. Stuttgart, Germany: Raabe, pp. 1–22.
Hofmann, J. (2010) 'Welche Bedeutung hat das Humboldt'sche Erbe für unsere Zeit?', Presentation at the 225th Conference of the Humboldt-Gesellschaft, 8 January 2010. Available from: www.humboldtgesellschaft.de/inhalt.php?name=humboldt (accessed 17 August 2015).
Honegger, C., Jost, H.-U., Burren, S. and Jurt, P. (2007) *Konkurrierende Deutungen des Sozialen. Geschichts-, Sozial- und Wirtschaftswissenschaften im Spannungsfeld von Politik und Wissenschaft*. Zurich: Chronos.
Jahresberichte (Annual Report) (1900) *Erster Jahresbericht über die Handels-Akademie St Gallen (1900)*. St Gallen, Switzerland: Zollikofer'sche Buchdruckerei.
Jahresberichte (Annual Report) (1911/12) *13th Jahresbericht der Handels-Hochschule St Gallen*. St Gallen, Switzerland: Zollikofer'sche Buchdruckerei.
Panda, S. (2004) 'People: staffing, development and management'. *In*: H. Perraton and H. Lentell (eds.) *Policy for Open and Distance Learning: World Review of Distance Education and Open Learning*. Vol. 4. London/New York: Routledge Falmer, pp. 115–36.

Rüegg-Stürm, J. (2005) *The New St Gallen Management Model: Basic Categories of an Approach to Integrated Management*. Basingstoke, UK: Palgrave Macmillan.

Rüegg-Stürm, J. and Grand, S. (2014) *Das St Galler Management-Modell: 4. Generation – Einführung*. Bern: Haupt Verlag.

Schmalenbach, E. (1911/12) 'Die Privatwirtschaftslehre als Kunstlehre', *Zeitschrift für handelswissenschaftliche Forschung*, 6, 304–16.

Spoun, S. and Müller, J. (2012) 'Mentoring an der Universität: Legitimation – Ziele – Gestaltung'. *In*: T.S. Eberle and S. Spoun (eds.) *Durch Coaching Führungsqualitäten entwickeln. Kernkompetenzen erkennen und fördern*. Zurich: Versus Verlag, pp. 213–26.

Spoun, S. and Wunderlich, W. (eds.) (2005) *Studienziel Persönlichkeit. Beiträge zum Bildungsauftrag der Universität heute*. Frankfurt am Main, Germany: Campus.

Taylor, F. (1947 [1911]) *Scientific Management*. New York, NY: Harper.

Thomä, D. (2005) 'Drei Prinzipien und drei Phasen der "Humboldt-Kultur". Erfindung, Krise und ein Leben nach dem Tod'. *In*: S. Spoun and W. Wunderlich (eds.) *Studienziel Persönlichkeit. Beiträge zum Bildungsauftrag der Universität heute*. Frankfurt am Main, Germany: Campus, pp. 49–70.

Thürer, G. (1974) *Hochschule St Gallen für Wirtschafts und Sozialwissenschaften 1899–1974*. St Gallen, Switzerland: Verlag Zollikofer & Co.

Ulrich, H. (1968) *Die Unternehmung als produktives soziales System: Grundlagen der allgemeinen Unternehmungslehre*. Bern: Haupt.

Ulrich, H. and Krieg, W. (1972) *Das St. Galler Management-Modell*. Bern: Haupt.

*Vision and General Principles* (n.d.) University of St Gallen, Switzerland. Available from www.unisg.ch/en/universitaet/vision (accessed 1 January 2015).

Walter-Busch, E. (1998) 'Wandel oder Fortschritt der Erkenntnis? Beiträge der Hochschule St Gallen zur Verwissenschaftlichung sozialer Betriebsführungskonzepte, 1898–1998'. *In*: T. Geiser, H. Schmid and E. Walter-Busch (eds.) *Arbeit in der Schweiz des 20. Jahrhunderts. Wirtschaftliche, rechtliche und soziale Perspektiven*. Bern: Paul Haupt, pp. 535–605.

# 30

# Survivors of an endangered species

## Doctoral programmes of the future

*Barbara Czarniawska*

### The way we live now

Depending on one's ideological stance, the present developments of the institution of university can be deplored or hailed. There is no doubt, however, that mass universities turn into professional schools – partly because mass higher education does not have the resources to keep it at the level envisioned by Humboldt, and partly because new digital technologies allow it to be turned into mass higher education. Doctoral and postdoctoral studies will likely become the equivalent of the university of the old vision – an elitist development for some, an obvious result of democratization for others. In what follows, I abstain from such judgments, focusing on possible desirable directions such a development may take. Accordingly, my first assumption is that candidates to our doctoral courses will not have a university education in the sense of *Bildung* as Humboldt understood it – a first step in the lifelong development, rather than acquisition of specialized knowledge and skills – and that the courses will have to complete their education in that way.

My second assumption is also related to the present developments concerning university education. The current reforming of universities (see, for example, Tuchman 2009; Grafton 2010; Collini 2012) is generally seen as an attack on the humanities, which are the victims of cutbacks, savings and other attacks. Consequently, there is a choir of voices defending the humanities (four languages have just been defended at my university), and yet as I see it, the humanities are not in real danger. They are, as Italian sociologist Marco Marzano put it (personal communication, 26 August 2013), like pandas: perhaps not directly useful, but rare and cute and to be protected. As to their utility, who knows? Some authors are suggesting that it is only the humanists who can interpret big data (Aiden and Michel 2013). Being neither fish nor fowl (not to mention the cuddly bears), it could be the social sciences that are in real danger.

Having separated from the humanities in the twentieth century (Lepenies 1988), the social sciences run after the natural sciences. Whereas some of them simply joined natural sciences, creating disciplines like neuropsychology, others created a convincing simulacrum, like in the science fiction of economics (in the sense of analyzing events into a modeled world). As Khurana put it,

> The turn toward neoclassical economics, with its combination of parsimonious theory, elegant models, and reliance on mathematics, enabled the discipline to begin cultivating an image in the academy as the most complete of the social sciences and the one closest to high-status scientific disciplines such as physics and chemistry.
>
> *Khurana 2007: 162*

Another social science presenting itself as a natural science is the mainstream of political science. Both economics and political science refuse to admit their own performativity, achieved by economists through their modeling and by political scientists through their opinion polls. Interestingly enough, their imitation of natural sciences takes two forms. Economics is obsessed with ever more sophisticated measurement methods, which results in advanced econometrics applied to such metaphors as "intrinsic motivation" (Bénabou and Tirole 2003); whereas most political scientists have no deep interest in method, and assume that answers to a survey hold a perfect mirror to reality. What joins the two areas of study is a definite rejection of disciplinary reflection.

It could be claimed that the tendency to reflect over the objects of our research and the methods used to study them was the undoing of management and organization studies, in the sense that it weakened their political position compared with economists and political scientists. Although physicists are allowed to express doubt in their own research methods and results, social scientists are apparently not allowed such luxuries. Thus, together with other social scientists prone to reflection, management and organization scholars have been skating on thin ice since politicians and the managers discovered that we are no longer willing to produce simple prescriptions or legitimize their plans. Indeed, to paraphrase a quote in Khurana's book, management and organization studies is branded – together with the classics, Egyptology, and other branches of the humanities – as interesting to many able people, but not bases for public policy making (Khurana 2007: 221). Well, if we are branded together, why not join forces?

My conclusion, therefore, is that if we do not want to abdicate our reflective stance, and if we want to give our doctoral students a proper education, the road to take would be a reconnection to the humanities (for the reasons and history of separation, see Lepenies 1988; Latour 1993; but see also Latour 2010, on reconnection).

## Becoming friends with pandas (again)

As the situation is now, it will not be easy to renew our friendship with pandas. The humanities are not eager to join forces with the social sciences again, especially not with management studies, suspected of enormous resources and general administrative support at the expense of the humanities. Luckily for us, some anthropologists and ethnologists did discover that we are not dangerous and are quite prepared to share the money that we still have. This also goes for some philosophers, as the departments of philosophy are becoming fewer and smaller. Thus future doctoral education could be based on a close cooperation between management scholars and those representatives of the humanities who consider the world of management and organization central to contemporary cultures and therefore worthy of study.

Let me then make a tentative list of courses that should be included in the curriculum of future doctoral studies in management and organization:

1 A propaedeutic of philosophy. At present, many doctoral students and young researchers show great interest in philosophy, but this interest is focused primarily on some fashionable philosophers. No problem there, but a general philosophy course would give them a frame into which they could situate those philosophers who are currently in fashion, and would

even help them to choose their own favorites (see Johnsen, Sørensen Thaning, and Pedersen, this volume). Well-chosen philosophers, such as Martha Nussbaum (1997), will help students to live – and to think.

2 A course in formal logic. It does not always need to be followed (the world is not arranged logically, but an argument should be), but it is certainly helpful to know at least the basic logical fallacies – if only to avoid them. As Nussbaum (2010) has demonstrated,[1] even children and young adults can learn the rules of formal logic (see, for example, *An Illustrated Book of Bad Arguments* by Ali Almossawi (2013)).
3 A course in rhetoric and a course in photo and video elaboration – to choose from or to take both. Doctoral students need to learn how to paint with words, but also how to use pictures because contemporary culture (including management) relies more and more on visual persuasion.
4 A course (or several) in cultural studies. The contents can vary, depending on local resources, but it should include gender studies, diversity and integration studies, and studies of popular culture.
5 A course in the historio*graphy* of business and administration, in the spirit of Hayden White (1973), to learn how business and administration history was written in various epochs.
6 A course in the latest advances in science. This course could actually follow the suggestion given by Michel Serres (2006; also see Brown, this volume) at our conference on Management Education and Humanities at Fundazione Cini in 2003:

> As the *hard sciences* have already achieved universality, we will take them on board as a whole and according to the general evolution of the world which the contemporary encyclopedia describes:
>
> - Elements of physics and astrophysics: the formation of the universe, from Big Bang to the cooling of the planets.
> - Elements of geophysics, chemistry and biology: from the creation of the earth to the appearance of life and the evolution of the species.
> - Elements of general anthropology: the emergence, spreading and prehistory of humankind.
> - Elements of agronomy, medicine and the transition to culture: the relations between Human Beings, the Earth, Life and Humanity itself.
>
> *Serres 2006: 231–32*

This science course cannot be taught at a very high level, of course. Bill Bryson's *A Short History of Nearly Everything* (2004) will do, but a general orientation in those matters is necessary for a person doing postgraduate studies, no matter what the discipline – a strategy opposite to that followed by economists and political scientists: we are not to imitate natural sciences, but learn *about* them.

7 Finally, a course that Serres (strangely) did not mention: a course in the latest advances in technology. Aspiring scholars in organization and management must know what use is being made of big data, whether robots will bring welfare or a divided society, and the relationship between the newest means of transportation and ecology, to mention the most obvious topics relevant to organizations and management.

Observe that I do not suggest a course in business ethics. It may be the remnant of my own life experience: I could have joined a doctoral programme in ethics, but I did not believe what my professor did. He was truly convinced that formulating a codex of socialist ethos and teaching it would construct a socialist morality. At any rate, I share the opinion of Harlow Person, Dean of Tuck School of Business (1906–19), who said:

> We do not attempt any formal instruction in business ethics. We believe that the formality and artificiality of a formal course in business ethics would defeat its very purpose. But in every course it is the aim of every instructor, I know, to inspire in his students a conception of the nobility of the profession of the business man and of his responsibility to his fellow-men and to society.
>
> *Quoted in Khurana 2007: 153; see also O'Connor, this volume*

Neither do I mention courses in specific topics within the discipline because I assume that the advances in appropriate research topics are dealt with, as before, in doctoral seminar series. Then there are workshops training practical skills, which will be discussed later.

Apart from specific courses in the humanities, natural sciences, technology, and social sciences close to the humanities, certain more general attitudes need to be shaped as well – many of them in opposition to the trends prevailing at the moment.

## The method mania and how to curb it

> Some speak greedily and urgently about method. It never seems rigorous or formal enough to them. Method becomes Law, but as this Law is deprived of any effect that would be outside of itself (no one can say, in the "human sciences," what a "result" is) it always falls short [. . .] As a result, a work that unceasingly declares its will-to-methodology always becomes sterile in the end. Everything takes place inside the method, nothing is left to the "writing," [. . .] the searcher repeats that his text will be methodological, but this text never arrives. There is nothing more sure to kill research and sweep it off into the leftover of abandoned works, nothing more sure, than method. At some point one has to turn against method, or at least to treat it without any founding privilege.
>
> *Barthes 1971: 9*

There are quite a few things to be noticed about this quote from an interview with Barthes. To begin with: the date. Is what he is saying of any relevance for the second decade of the twenty-first century? Strangely enough, during the almost half century that has passed, the wheel of fashion made a complete turn. After a movement "against method" (Feyerabend 1975 – four editions between 1975 and 2010) wiped out this "method fetishism" in the 1980s and the 1990s (forever, it seemed), it quietly returned in the new century. As it happens, Barthes's quote is relevant again, not least in relation to the "human sciences," which also decided that they needed a method and possibly a "scientific" one. The results of counting literary works are sometimes intriguing (for example, Moretti 2013) and sometimes absurd. Why this re-turn? Apart from the general tendency of fashions to go around in circles, or rather in spirals because the next turn is never identical, I believe that method texts play the critical role of a tranquilizer for anguished young researchers. As with tranquilizers, though, there is always a danger of addiction. Indeed, at present, when publishers compete with one another in the number of method manuals and handbooks of method, the danger is stronger than ever.

These statements may sound hypocritical because I contributed to the method frenzy myself. In defense, I can say that I see method texts not as providing a key contribution to "real science" (indeed, because "rigor" means "stiffness," it is no wonder that, as Barthes pointed out, the works on method have to become sterile in the end), but as an equivalent of cookbooks (also recently popular[2]). A good cookbook will start with general dietary information and then present a variety of recipes. A beginner will follow them slavishly; an experienced cook will make variations, combine, and make changes to suit the situation. But the main analogy lies in this: the proof of the pudding is in the eating. Good cooks don't defend their products by waving the pages of their cookbooks – either their dishes taste good or they don't (and tastes differ, as do cookbooks). A rigorous method may lead to trite results; it deserves no founding privilege indeed.

One question is still open: can the social sciences – management and organization included – claim to have any *method* or methods in the literal sense of the word? There can be no doubt, however, that there is a need for a better understanding of *methodology* to be completed by a familiarity with a great many techniques and technologies: in the form of both hardware and software.

The point of stressing methodology[3] rather than method is an emphasis on the well-considered study design and choice of techniques to be used, depending on the character of the research question and the character of the researcher. At present, the reason for choosing a given approach is only too often that "everybody uses it" or that "in marketing/accounting/leadership [take your pick] this is what we usually do." Whatever can be said of positivists, and however wrong we may judge them to be, they at least knew what they were doing and why. Especially visible in recent times is a "positivism lite," whereby researchers count and correlate (commonly mistaking correlations for causality) their own metaphors or the uses of certain words.

In brief, I see a great need of workshops or, as the French call it "laboratories" (same word, after all), in which the doctoral students will be trying out different field study techniques and various analytical approaches. This is in contrast to the present emphasis on training in the capacity for long discourses on ontology and epistemology, developing impressively long list of references to method books, accompanied by the lack of argumentation for the choices made and an incomprehensible description of the actual actions taken. Such workshops on field study techniques should be complemented by writing workshops. Here, yet another quote from the 1970s seems appropriate:

> No doubt owing to the desire to cash in on the prestige of the natural sciences, the concern with methodology has become unduly slanted towards quantification at the cost of such essential skills as textual criticism, literary flair and semantic sensitivity, which every social scientist, not excluding the economists, ought to possess.
>
> *Andreski 1972: 123*

## Writing workshops

Flexibility in choosing and perfecting writing forms could be greatly facilitated by rekindling contacts with the humanities and learning from them how to read and how to write. A closer familiarity with the literary workshop will help to reveal to our students that fiction writers do research too (sometimes much more systematic and ambitious research than scholars), but that they attend more to the ways they write, differentiating among genres and audiences. Please observe that I am not speaking of courses in "academic writing." In order to know how academic writing differs from other types of writing, students must first know something about writing in general. Thus, something like "creative writing courses" (if the pretentious name can be forgotten), which would combine some general orientation in genres and styles with actual "textwork," as John Van Maanen (2006) called it. Nothing will better teach young people academic writing than attempts to write non-academically – and such courses would, of course, be given by our friends from the humanities. Our friends from education departments are now doing quite well giving obligatory courses in higher education pedagogy[4] – could language and literature people join them in an effort to improve the writing skills of management scholars?

As I have said many times, this does not mean that management scholars should turn themselves into fiction writers. There are some social scientists who are *also* fiction writers – John K. Galbraith, Richard Sennett, Umberto Eco; and in our circles Fabrizio Battistelli and Mariusz Czubaj who both write detective stories, to name a few[5]; however, none of them present their fiction work as scientific. Whereas experiments in social science writings should continue, the purpose should be to develop and embellish the genre, rather than move to competitors. Few of us will ever become philosophers or *literati*, which does not mean that we cannot learn from them.

I should add that, in my opinion, there should be two such workshops in non-English-speaking countries: one in the native language, the other in English. There is never too much textwork.

## Resisting the publishing frenzy

> A basic challenge is that PhD programmes have fostered a culture that glorifies arcane unintelligibility while disdaining impact and audience. This culture of exclusivity is then transmitted to the next generation through the publish-or-perish tenure process. Rebels are too often crushed or driven away.
>
> *Kristof 2014: 11*

The present frenzy of publishing articles has several reasons: the ranking of universities, whereby publications are one of the easiest ways to evaluate research; the modeling role of the UK Research Excellence Framework; and the publishers' financial gain from starting new journals (Monbiot 2011).

As to ranking based on citations, the somewhat irritated mathematicians and statisticians, whose opinions on the matter had never been asked, produced a report from the International Mathematical Union in cooperation with the International Council of Industrial and Applied Mathematics and the Institute of Mathematical Statistics, in which they say, amongst other things, that "*Numbers are not inherently superior to sound judgments*" (Adler *et al.* 2008: 166, italics in original). And they continue:

> We do not dismiss citation statistics as a tool for assessing the quality of research – citation data and statistics can provide some valuable information. We recognize that assessment must be practical, and for this reason easily-derived citation statistics almost surely will be part of the process. But citation data provide only a limited and incomplete view of research quality, and the statistics derived from citation data are sometimes poorly understood and misused. Research is too important to measure its value with only a single coarse tool.
>
> *Adler et al. 2008: 167*

In case of rankings and the Research Excellence Framework, it is easy to see that these are fashionable trends and, therefore, like all fashionable trends, will vanish or be transformed in time. Judging from the usual duration of fashion trends, which may be shortened nowadays due to general acceleration, it is likely that they will change during the course of the career of today's doctoral students. Those trained only in article writing will be as helpless as those who were trained only in the writing of monographs. It is commonsense that young researchers should acquire familiarity with various forms of writing because the fashion may change or even a period of a tolerance for diversified forms of writing may ensue. Such a general preparation would also permit them to discover where their own talents lie or do not lie. It is also possible that it will again be acknowledged that good teachers are not necessarily good researchers or writers. Good teachers *read* a lot.

Is it possible, however, to resist the publishing pressure? As Michael Billig formulated it, bitterly but truthfully, at present ". . . the rewards do not go to those who only write when they have something to say and who then take trouble to write as clearly as possible. This is an age of academic mass publication, and certainly not a time for academic idealists" (2013: 13). Perhaps the times are never good for academic idealists; academic realists, however, would do well to try to understand the role of fashions, in research as well as in university management. As to the ways of relating oneself to research fashion, I would recommend two: to become either a fashion leader or a moderate follower. Choosing the former inevitably involves great risk – of many who try, only few will be chosen. This unpleasant lesson must be taught because young scholars are presently shocked by the fact that their originality is not always rewarded and that their experiments may fail. In relation to the latter – moderate followership – the way to do it is like with any fashion: try whether it fits, if you can afford it, and if the result is aesthetically pleasing.

I am fully aware, however, that it is not the task of doctoral students to combat the publishing mania because it is not their task to start opposing the growing demands of publishers who shove more and more work (and therefore costs) on to the authors. This, I think, is a task for tenured academics, a task that we should consider in all seriousness. It may take some time, but if successful, it would permit young researchers to follow their interests widely and freely. After all, the texts of the most revered social scientists would most likely never be accepted for publication in top journals of our times. It could be claimed, however, that one thing was common to most of them – they were keen on cultivating humanity.

## Cultivating humanity

> The study of history allows us to come to terms with the achievements as well as the depredations of our collective past so that we might experience a future that is free from injustice. The study of rhetoric furnishes us with the capacities of self-expression in order that we might persuade our fellow citizens about the worth of our most cherished beliefs and convictions. The study of literature introduces us to imaginary worlds and new experiences, so that our conceptions of human possibility transcend the boundaries and limitations of what was heretofore conceivable. The study of philosophy instructs us in the virtues of reasoning and moral judgment [. . .].
>
> *Wolin 2011: 15*

A skeptical reader may ask, where in this litany is a place for natural sciences and technology, praised by me on the equal level with history, rhetoric, literature, and philosophy? As Todorov (2002) reminded his readers, the point is that the term "humanist" was coined to denote the specificity of human affairs, in contrast to those of God – not in contrast to those of animals and things. Although Wolin is hostile toward "technologically administered somnambulance" (2011: 20), the way out is not to revert to Luddism, but to harmonize technology and the humanities – indeed, to cultivate "humanism amidst our machines," as the editorial to the same issue of *The Hedgehog Review* would have it. *Techne* in Greek means both technique and art – and for good reason. As Richard Sennett pointed out, the modern laboratory has its origins in the medieval guild workshop, which developed in the Renaissance as the result of belief in "the human being as a work in progress" (Sennett 2011: 25). The problem is – and was – that "technical innovations run ahead of people's ability to use the innovations well" (Sennett 2011: 28). This applies to both material technologies and quasi-material technologies, such as management; and this is why humanist education is so important – to managers and engineers.

I borrowed the title of this final section from Martha Nussbaum's book (1997). At that time, she was extremely optimistic about what she called "the new liberal education," and quoted several experimental programs, all aimed at turning higher education into preparation for citizenship and not merely preparation for a career. By 2010, she was speaking of the "silent crisis," by which she meant the US cuts in humanities and arts education. Her reasoning confirms my initial observation: she mentions the social sciences once (with addition "particularly economics"; Nussbaum, 1997: 177) and political science five times through the whole book.[6] But it is in her 2010 book, *Not for Profit: Why Democracy Needs Humanities*, that she made a powerful connection between education in the humanities and business. This is how she summarized it in an interview:

> . . . for commerce and technology to succeed, they need the humanistic imagination and the ability to think critically and rigorously.
>
> Science at its best is closely allied to the humanities because it is creative, highly rigorous and critical. So what the world needs is an alliance between the humanities and creative basic science to foster the skills that produce good citizenship and healthy business cultures.
>
> *Nussbaum 2011*

Nussbaum's plea (like that of many of the chapters in this book) is to reintroduce the humanities and arts into all undergraduate education but, if my second assumption as mentioned in my introduction is correct, this is unlikely to happen, at least in Europe. It is doubly important, therefore, that future university teachers – our doctoral students – receive such an education.

Her plea is supported independently by Umberto Eco (2013), who claims that education in the humanities helps people in all professions (his examples are engineers). An education in the humanities helps to develop, again in Nussbaum's (1997) words, a "narrative imagination," and this, says Eco, permits a foreseeing of the future. A well-educated electrical engineer should be able to imagine what would happen if the illumination and heating of tomorrow did not depend on electricity. Philology, philosophy, and "a bit of logic" will prepare computer specialists for the tasks of tomorrow.

His text, like mine, is likely yet another item on a list of wishful thoughts to be realized in a Utopia – but as long as Utopia is not treated as a blueprint to be followed religiously, it may at least be a starting point for a conversation.

## Notes

1 Her example is the program "Philosophy for Children," initiated by the late Mathew Lipman and his book *Harry Stottlemeier's Discovery* (1974).
2 My friend and language editor, Nina Lee Colwill, was several times invited to Cranfield School of Management to teach a course in Cookbook Statistics, which confirms the correctness of my analogy.
3 Michael Billig (2013) ridicules the latest fashion of extending the word "method" to a longer and more impressive "methodology." I completely agree: calling the description of a field technique a methodology is ridiculous, but arguing for one's choice of methodology is not.
4 I am speaking of Sweden and contradicting Nussbaum's (2010) statement that there are no such courses here – they have been obligatory for university lecturers since 2003.

5 At present, only Czubaj has been translated into English (*21.37*, 2013). Czubaj is an anthropologist and his novels depict the present Poland in an incomparable way. Battistelli's detective novels are historical.

6 She does quote experimental psychology, even though she calls Auguste Comte a "cosmopolitan French thinker" (Nussbaum, 1997: 964), as if to avoid calling him a sociologist.

## References


Adler, R., Ewing, J. and Taylor, P. (2008) 'Joint committee on quantitative evaluation of research: citation statistics', *The Australian Mathematical Society Gazette*, 35(3), 166–88.

Aiden, E. and Michel, J.-B. (2013) *Uncharted. Big Data as Lens on Human Culture*. New York, NY: Riverhead Books.

Almossawi, A. (2013) *An Illustrated Book of Bad Arguments*. New York, NY: Jasper Collins.

Andreski, S. (1972) *Social Science as Sorcery*. London: Penguin.

Barthes, R. (1971) An interview for *Tel Quel*, 47, 9–10.

Bénabou, R. and Tirole, J. (2003) 'Intrinsic and extrinsic motivation', *Review of Economic Studies*, 70, 489–520.

Billig, M. (2013) *Learn to Write Badly: How to Succeed in the Social Sciences*. Cambridge: Cambridge University Press.

Bryson, B. (2004) *A Short History of Nearly Everything*. London: Black Swan.

Collini, S. (2012) *What Are Universities For?* London: Penguin Books.

Czubaj, M. (2013) *21.37*. London: Stork Press.

Eco, U. (2013) Elogio del classico. *L'Espresso*, 10 October, 162.

Feyerabend, P. (1975) *Against Method. Outline of an Anarchist Theory of Knowledge*. New York, NY: New Left Books.

Grafton, A. (2010) 'Britain: the disgrace of the universities', *New York Review of Books*, 8 April, 57(6).

Khurana, R. (2007) *From Higher Aims to Hired Hands: The Social Transformation of American Business Schools and the Unfulfilled Promise of Management as a Profession*. Princeton, NJ: Princeton University Press.

Kristof, N. (2014) 'Smart minds, slim impact', *New York Times*, 16 February, 11.

Latour, B. (1993) *We Have Never Been Modern*. Cambridge: Cambridge University Press.

Latour, B. (2010) 'Coming out as a philosopher', *Social Studies of Science*, 40(4), 599–608.

Lepenies, W. (1988) *Between Literature and Science: The Rise of Sociology*. Cambridge: Cambridge University Press.

Monbiot, G. (2011) 'Academic publishers make Murdoch look like a socialist', *The Guardian*, 29 August.

Moretti, F. (2013) *Distant Reading*. London: Verso.

Nussbaum, M. (1997) *Cultivating Humanity. A Classical Defense of Reform in Liberal Education*. Cambridge, MA: Harvard University Press.

Nussbaum, M. (2010) *Not for Profit: Why Democracy needs Humanities*. Princeton, NJ: Princeton University Press.

Nussbaum, M. (2011) 'Our world needs humanities', *The Australian* (an interview by Jennifer Oriel), 13 July.

Sennett, R. (2011) 'Humanism', *The Hedgehog Review*, 13(2), 21–30.

Serres, M. (2006) 'The great narrative of the sciences and the history of humanities'. *In*: P. Gagliardi and B. Czarniawska (eds.) *Management Education and Humanities*. Cheltenham, UK: Edward Elgar, pp. 227–32.

Todorov, T. (2002) *The Imperfect Garden: The Legacy of Humanism*. Princeton, NJ: Princeton University Press.

Tuchman, G. (2009) *Wannabe U. Inside the Corporate University*. Chicago, IL: University of Chicago Press.

Van Maanen, J. (2006) 'Ethnography then and now', *Qualitative Research in Organizations and Management: An International Journal*, 1(1), 13–21.

White, H. (1973) *Metahistory. The Historical Imagination in 19th Century Europe*. Baltimore, MD: Johns Hopkins University Press.

Wolin, R. (2011) 'Reflections on the crisis in the humanities', *The Hedgehog Review*, 13(2), 8–20.

# 31

# The researcher's duties

## Continuing the conversation

*Marton Racz*

### We, reflexive, academic, intellectuals

The dystopia we live in now makes Czarniawska's 'starting point for a conversation' about the future of doctoral programmes in the previous chapter very timely.[1] Naturally, the present always seems dystopian compared with any utopian future, but the way we live now is different. Our institutional position in academia limits what we, as intellectuals, can say under the current neoliberal regime of excellence. Reimagining doctoral education, Czarniawska urges us not to stop reflecting on this situation. Sharing in this quest, I propose to mess with it. In this chapter, after reviewing the current academic context of and students' experiences in doctoral programmes in management, I present my utopian vision underpinned by the idea of reading and practising scholarship politically.

Let me briefly summarize Czarniawska's argument. She claims that mass education drives the professionalization and degradation of universities, especially regarding management education. Hence, only doctoral programmes can provide the *Bildung* necessary for forming, what I would call, 'public intellectuals'. If undergraduate education is inevitably lost, we should save the higher levels. The problem is that the social sciences cannot reflect on their objects and methods of study because they are 'suspended [...] between the detailed unintelligibility of science and technology, and the cultural legitimacy of the arts and humanities' (Parker 2014: 266). Unlike the sciences, they can't confidently afford a reflective stance undermining their hard-earned legitimacy, and unlike the humanities, they haven't pleaded guilty to being insignificant enough to be defended for their cuteness. As social scientists of management, today we are largely unimportant because we are not equipped to inform policy making, and also businesses do not care much about what we say. To retain our reflexive capability and refusal to make conclusive claims, we should join forces with the humanities. Ultimately, this may prove difficult because they despise us for the money and power we currently possess.

I agree with Czarniawska that education has professionalized, necessitating a rethink of doctoral programmes. To this end, in the next section I outline how Western academia has changed recently. My assumption is that we are trying hard to (re)connect to worlds outside and are encouraged by calls for demonstrating impact, but it's proving hard because hardly anyone listens. Had we studied medicine or science, were designers or comedians, we could speak more widely. It is therefore important to rekindle a relationship with the humanities and gain similar social status and learn to tell better stories. In the second part of this chapter, I reflect on postgraduate management researchers' published accounts to highlight how changes in academia affect them.[2] I argue that we need to push our thinking beyond reflection. The political context shapes our experiences and, consequently, PhD researchers must actively engage with the politics of their own practices too.

I conclude by arguing that management doctoral students should take both the humanities and social sciences more seriously. Research insights in these fields can be inconvenient and challenging, hence politically difficult to act on. I propose that as intellectuals in academia, it is the arena of doctoral education that we should imagine acting on first and develop a critical consciousness of its fertile grounds. We should embody change here and now instead of waiting for it to happen in an imagined outside world. This is certainly not a new idea, but we should entertain it more.

## We must never be complacent

> [O]lyan nem jók a kilátások, / nem nagyon van hova menni, / nem nagyon van tovább, ennyi.
>
> *Kafkaz: Panda (Kardos-Horváth n.d.)*[3]

The expression 'neoliberal university' is often used as a general derogatory term for the evils currently befalling academia. For instance, Flew (2014: 52) condemns critics of neoliberalism for using the term 'as a rhetorical trope' to invite already interested readers, which makes the expression empty. Consequently, it becomes impossible to engage with the concept, especially for those whose thinking we'd like to see changed. To make such discussions possible, let me outline some crucial neoliberal processes in higher education. As a caveat, keep in mind that there are historically specific variants of neoliberalism, in order to warrant caution with treating it 'simply as an expression of the *zeitgeist* of global capitalism or as a conspiracy of ruling elites' (Flew 2014: 67). It doesn't start as an ideological project of Thatcher and Reagan (Connell and Dados 2014) and it isn't necessarily an enforced rightist political project, like in the case of Australia (Cahill 2013) or the Central Eastern European post-socialist countries after 1989 (Bohle and Greskovits 2007).

Particular manifestations of neoliberalism have been challenged over the years, and this chapter intends to suggest further ways that this can be done. However, there also is a certain tendency across the globe for a combination of the processes described in this section to materialize in academic life – with variations I can't fully account for in detail here. Even Flew (2014: 64) concludes on some generalizable characteristics and claims that '[a]s a political philosophy, neoliberalism has been sufficiently practical in its recommendations to constitute what Michel Foucault terms an "art of government" that serves to shape institutions'. Amongst those institutions is the university. As Connell and Dados (2014: 132) argue, 'the worldwide extension of market logic continues, with education currently at the cutting edge – through international league tables for schools, corporatization of universities, restructuring of teaching workforces, and the redefinition of education systems as export industries pursuing comparative advantage'. This pursuit drives university visions, at least in the UK.

At the global scale, local universities have to outperform foreign ones. '[A]s (then British Prime Minister) Tony Blair warns us, "we can't be complacent ... [w]e are determined to stay ahead of our competitors"' (cited alongside other government officials in De Angelis and Harvie 2009: 8–9). Nationally, '[a]cross the sector, the allocation of resources is driven by the consideration of where particular universities can best compete: high-flying research-institutions get more research-money, whilst "lowly" institutions get funding tied to "widening access"' (De Angelis and Harvie 2009: 9). Exacerbating this internal differentiation, universities increasingly rely on research grants as the state shifts its financial support from the institution to the individual student. Companies and powerful charities, which adhere to carefully selected criteria and attach strings, award such grants (Newell *et al.* 2001; Newfield 2004). In the spirit of entrepreneurship, scholars are transformed from public intellectuals into professional academic service providers (Giroux 2013) whose research outputs are often made inaccessible to the public by patents and pay walls. Public goals are fulfilled supposedly through private corporations, and higher education therefore becomes a means to further these private interests. Marketing events and job fairs are commonplace on our campuses.

For faculty, the general movement has been from academic freedom, 'the intra- and inter-psychic freedom to exercise defiant imagination' for a restricted group of people (mostly white and male), towards wider access 'into highly managed and controlled spaces that produce docile bodies with compliant imaginations' (Boden and Epstein 2011: 478). Performance measurement using quantifiable indicators has been an important element in this process. Such audit exercises dismantle academic collegiality by introducing individualized performance review and they also lead to a loss of academic freedom by defining valuable knowledge externally (Craig *et al.* 2014). Contrary to its espoused values, 'extreme regulation' (Harney and Dunne 2013) is an important feature of neoliberalism. Measurement produces 'individual outcomes, differentiation, and hierarchy', which by introducing 'competition, individualism, and most importantly precariousness and uncertainty' impedes attempts at solidarity (Harney and Dunne 2013: 339). It's easier to keep individuals in fear of losing their jobs should they underperform (Jump 2013). Even more so for the multitude of teaching-only adjuncts in the US, zero-hour faculty in the UK and forced-entrepreneur tutors in Hungary, who are only paid for the classes they teach on fixed contracts as second-rate academic citizens.

For instance, in the UK, a select panel of experts provides accountability by evaluating academics' outputs through the Research Excellence Framework. The common objective of four at least 'internationally excellent' (Research Excellence Framework 2014) articles published in each five-year chunk of knowledge-production cycle facilitates an often mindless churning out of repetitive, unoriginal or artificially bloated publications. Growing importance is also placed on demonstrating the impact of research beyond academia. Impact, however, mostly translates into meeting the needs of business by increasing students' employability, giving a bigger role to vocational practice and nurturing relationships with companies – masking the corporate truths of unaccountability and masculine domination (Edmonds 2013). Impact only counts when recognized as such, and researchers must therefore submit to the discipline of those who can grant recognition. As a result, defiant imagination is undermined again.

The outcome of the UK research evaluation determines the small amount of state funding each department receives, but even more importantly it provides the basis for calculating league table rankings. This is (financially) important because it serves as students' first and often only point of reference in deciding which institution to favour. Students are implicated in the discourse of choice as consumers who don't actively engage with their education. The main goal becomes to train a good workforce for participation in the market economy (Giroux 2013) after being temporarily 'warehoused' in the university (Harney cited in Dunne *et al.* 2008a) and having amassed a debt that makes them financially dependent on finding any (precarious) job whatsoever.[4]

All this raises the question as to whether a management PhD programme is possible, using the resources we currently enjoy, which nurtures future public intellectuals and develops the common social good. Taking forward the Humboldtian sense of *Bildung*, as many chapters in this volume do, proper education should open up trajectories of learning about organization from multiple perspectives rather than focusing on the acquisition of a skill-set or toolbox of solutions to managerial challenges, problematize its social embeddedness and, importantly, be open-ended rather than orientated towards perfecting one's self. And if we're hopeful enough to answer the question positively, then we might ponder what we need to do to achieve this goal. I want to suggest an ambitious path. But before that, I turn to what we already know about existing doctoral programmes in management.

## The future arrived a while ago

> Como dijo mi amigo el gato, el futuro llegó hace rato.[5]
>
> *Manu Chao: Merry Blues (2001)*

Czarniawska describes the humanities as pandas who are few but protected. I think management studies are like cats on the Internet. It could be cute, but right now it's an annoying colonizer of social life. Management is impossible to ignore, just like web-cats. Cats can explain anything from 'social meowdia' (Avalaunch Media 2013) to gender performativity (Binarythis 2013), just as how (more) management has become the one-stop solution to *any* personal, institutional or global problem (Hancock and Tyler 2008). Management encloses, patents and brands anything it finds, even Grumpy Cat®. I don't have a problem with cats (or management) as such, rather with how pervasive they have become. Critical management studies (or hard to resist, *catical* management studies) has been good at explaining this phenomenon – critiquing cat owners and managers, and paying attention to dogs and other commoning species.

The doctoral programmes I base my discussion on exhibit an intention to realize our chance to be cute again – by joining forces with the panda-humanities and social sciences (at least in the form of a supervisor). Through these accounts I explore connections between neoliberal academia, as discussed previously, and management PhD students' experiences. These examples represent more general problems with doctoral programmes and highlight that a critical orientation doesn't in itself resolve these wider challenges – it may even exacerbate doctoral students' cognitive dissonance. In short, if such problems exist even in these supposedly better programmes, then that is rather worrisome. Relying on published accounts and personal experience is obviously partial. These disillusioned accounts represent situated knowledges about particular programmes, which may not be generalizable. Experiences of happiness and ease of navigating a PhD programme receive much less publicity. Nevertheless, some overarching dispositifs turn these existing accounts into something more-than-itself.

Doctoral programmes have characteristics potentially hard to cope with. Gardner (2008) and Lovitts (2008) highlight the frustration involved in moving from the taught element to the more unstructured years of independent study. Being left 'alone' may be exponentially challenging if the programme is critically oriented and full of obscure concepts for the uninitiated (Batchelor and Fulop 2003). Students often struggle to map the field until their internal defence or comprehensive exams (McLaren *et al.* 2014). Academics' and senior peers' knowledge can look overwhelming, triggering the anxious question of 'do they think I'm good enough?' (McLaren *et al.* 2014: 18). I've heard of supervisors advising their students, to calm them down, to take other examiners' comments on their progress with a pinch of salt – pressurizing them is just the kind of thing anyone in that position has to do.

Coming to terms with social theory may produce anxiety, and seeking to build on these theories can have a similar effect. Doctoral students in management often have a background in social sciences or humanities. Particularly in the US and Canadian context, this entails a more critically oriented approach than one is faced with in most business schools, and hence Prasad (2013) talks about the PhD programme as a panoptic institution where (internalized) disciplinary mechanisms ascertain either conformation to the accepted managerialist ideology or being marked out. Beyond Foucauldian disciplinary techniques, Deleuze's (1992) 'society of control' is also reflected in academia in the forms of 'standardisation, quantification and surveillance' (De Angelis and Harvie 2009: 7). Some universities now have 'tone of voice' guides (see Newey 2015) that by defining *how* things can be said take an aim at *what* can be said by any 'citizen' of the university on or off-campus at any time. One is never off work because the constitutive fabric of academia is sewn beyond the regular working hours. 'Peer reviews?', I was recently told, 'I usually do those on Sundays'. PhD students, the main providers of small group teaching in numerous countries, also participate indirectly in validation exercises, whereby international bodies benchmark and certify schools and programmes using semi-standardized forms.

The neoliberal principle of 'trickle down' makes itself felt when it comes to publications. Compared with even ten years ago when PhD students were told not to worry about publishing during their doctoral studies, now it is commonplace to discuss how journal articles can be chiselled off the draft thesis, and whether a 'revise and resubmit' in one journal is more valuable than a published article in another. In the US, this often means being 'surrounded by driven academics including a few dominant (male) voices who have a Tayloristic approach to publishing' (Kweder 2014; see also Prasad 2013). In Hungary, a meticulous publication point system is in place with a minimum score set as an award criterion. In the UK, publishing is an informal but essential requirement for a chance at an academic job. Increasingly, doctoral 'publication hatcheries' render 'intellectual pregnancy', the invisible labour involved in the barely controllable birthing of an idea, unacceptable (Bristow 2012).

After all, academia is a performative masculine playground. Professor Tim Hunt, Nobel laureate in medicine, recently brought this to public attention, claiming there is a 'trouble with girls. [. . .] three things happen when they are in the lab [. . .] You fall in love with them, they fall in love with you, and when you criticise them, they cry' (Ratcliffe 2015). Not surprisingly, female PhD students may find little support and an unwelcoming future in academia (Lober Newsome 2008). There are fewer women the higher one looks in the hierarchy (Equality Challenge Unit 2014) – an organizational aspect that in itself exhibits a masculine political choice (see Acker 1990). Parenting responsibilities, still mostly done by women, are hard to harmonize with job requirements (Murray 2014). Academic competition may result in postponing having children or losing out because of maternity leave, whereas children may induce guilty consciences due to the lack of separation between work and leisure time. Even the authoritative *Oxford Handbook of Critical Management Studies* (Alvesson *et al.* 2009) has only seven female contributors out of forty-five altogether, which at 15.5 per cent is worse than the share of women at professorial grade in the UK.

At a more symbolic level, academia is aimed at perfect mastery of knowledge, which can be scary for doctoral students, as we saw earlier. Similar to how organizations eschew emotionality (Burrell 1997), academia prohibits appearing vulnerable, ignorant or hesitant, even when one doesn't have in-depth knowledge. This happens as much in the classroom as at conferences, where one is often judged by how convincingly they can flaunt their being-in-the-know. Voice training, the academic equivalent of assertiveness training in corporate practice, can help with conforming to this world. It also helps if one is able to fulfil traditional gender requirements reproduced inside the university. For instance, Westerlund (2014), in a relentless stream of consciousness, complains about having to perform a range of tasks beyond her legally contracted hours during her doctoral studies. She reports being exhausted because of teaching duties, largely undercompensated, whilst also 'naturally' being tasked with performing care by organizing a social event for the doctoral community.[6]

The presence of a few isolated critical scholars cannot really change the overall situation if, in certain circumstances, '"[c]ritical" just adds another identity which potentially makes you vulnerable in a long, unnecessary "hazing process" which we rebrand as "doctoral education"' (Kweder 2014: 10). Award of the PhD degree is just an artificial milestone, and it's not surprising that early-career academics in critical management studies often grapple with very similar conditions (Bristow *et al.* 2014). As Foucault (2008) reminds us, such an initiation process is more than a repressive mechanism imposed by the state or the market. The government of individuals requires that they accept and internalize the need for being governed. Even seasoned academics rationalize the contradictions of playing the publication game, thus inadvertently tricking themselves into acting in line with neoliberal requirements (Butler and Spoelstra 2012, 2014; Clarke, Knights and Jarvis 2012). Doctoral students (as this very chapter attests) are not outside this playing field.[7]

Reflection on these experiences might make us feel hopeless – which brings me to the researcher's duties. In another piece, Czarniawska declares that she doesn't believe that 'attempting to overthrow the dominant institutional order [which is to say] starting a revolution is included among a researcher's duties' (2014: 5). Here we disagree. I don't think serious change can occur otherwise in a university that is neither innocuous nor amicable towards its citizens at the present. To continue the conversation about the 'list of wishful thoughts, to be realized in a Utopia' (Czarniawska, this volume), let me turn towards the revolutionary duties to which doctoral researchers in management should attend.

## The real world is not out there

FATHER: One day, lad, all this will be yours!
HERBERT: What, the curtains?
FATHER: No, not the curtains, lad. All that you can see! Stretched out over the hills and valleys of this land! This'll be your kingdom, lad!
HERBERT: But, Mother –
FATHER: Father, I'm Father.
HERBERT: But Father, I don't want any of that.

*Monty Python and the Holy Grail, 1975*

Let's stop bringing the 'real world' into classrooms – alleged places of the less-than-real, the imitated. It's precisely the other way around. The world is the surreal place where the Law of the Father dictates social order, where the immediately visible is curtained in favour of something farther away, where the promise of 'one day' makes sense. If we want to live up to the Humboldtian ideal, we could start by reasserting the role of the university and doctoral studies in critiquing society as it currently exists. Although this may prove difficult in undergraduate mass education, reflection is still possible at PhD level. Doctoral education should emphasize that it isn't about preparing student-researchers for something *else*, for example to be proper scholars one bright day or to be successful managers. Nor is it about preparing for something *later* – when as well-established academics we dare speak truth in the face of power – because if those times are not here now, they'll likely never be.

Recall Czarniawska's thesis that we, (critical) management researchers, have a reflexive intent that differentiates us from some other strands of social research. If we don't want to lose this intent, it's high time we got serious about reflection. For a start, we could look at problems that research in management, organization or business studies, or even in finance, logistics or strategy, could address but doesn't quite do (Dunne *et al.* 2008b). But instead of stopping there or waiting for the right moment to change the world, we (including both 'staff' and 'students') could redress that which is closest to home – the PhD programme.

Czarniawska invokes the idea of the laboratory to resolve the apparent antagonism of humanist education and technology. I find her Renaissance laboratory too closely related to the idea of the self-made man and his reflections in contemporary management literature. His posture, of not being motivated by God, was radical in its own social context but has since been co-opted in the process that rendered superficial difference as the only unique selling proposition in town. Nostalgia for 'Man as his own Maker' in a medieval guild workshop (Sennett 2011) invokes the masculine desire for perfect creation, as if in order not to be unmade and lose out (Kimmel 1996). But man is hardly his own maker, let alone woman hers. Only in a liberal world does it sound plausible that through cooperation 'different parties all gain by exchanging, rather than one part gaining at the expense of others' (Sennett 2011: 26). Social reproduction does not level the playing field for all to gain – some will have 'to give up individual and family privilege for the collective good, and [...] recognize that inaction is action and that there may be no better place to address the overlapping and persistent problems of poverty, inequality, and injustice than in business schools' (Kweder 2014: 10).

The guild workshop, in a process with a predetermined end-state in mind, aims at perfecting the individual who then exercises impact. I imagine a PhD laboratory that articulates its own proposition of the world (Latour 2010). The real world is not brought into the laboratory to be subsequently analysed; rather, scientists interacting in the laboratory create a politically interested reality through various steps of translation (Latour 1999; see also Johnsen, Sørensen Thaning and Pedersen, this volume). What deters us therefore from using this process in the laboratory that is a doctoral programme? Do we not do the same with samples from the jungle we call society? Business schools are often assumed to affect business life (Ghoshal 2005; James 2009) similarly to how Pasteur's method of controlled experimentation influenced social engineers in nineteenth-century Paris (Burrell 1997). This happens less through scholarship and more through the production of a particular mentality spread by experts (who have a vested interest in maintaining the status quo) and students (who stand a better chance to be hired if they readily accept contemporary management theories). But if there really are affective similes between the business school as lab and society at large, then we could do something else, something good. In a dirty lab where the real world is made, where 'proletarian insurrection [is not] Pasteurized out of sight and out of existence' (Burrell 1997: 209), where contamination is the norm, I'd be happy to be one of the 'lab Racz'.

A laboratory could also provide a means to sneak labour back into the business school. Labour in academia – academic labour – means 'study' (Harney and Moten 2009). Under the conditions of neoliberal capitalism, study should mean precisely the study of labour. Change of perspective for the worker, rarely discussed as underprivileged in management studies, could start at the PhD level. This may offer the prospect of doctoral students grasping the de-skilling consequences of extreme regulation/extreme externalization (Harney and Dunne 2013). We could then hope that, as future educators, current doctoral students would also embed this perspective into their teaching. If we're concerned with teaching future generations, even in a vocational university, then we should appreciate the conditions students have to face in the global organizations that so many of them aspire to work for.

A PhD programme that successfully draws in applicants from other disciplines should not normalize their differences, but encourage research into diverse forms of organizing, management, business, capitalism and so on. I fully agree with Czarniawska that to this end, we have to dampen the publishing frenzy and stop insisting on acceptable methods. But more than that, we have to advocate for:

> organizations that are at the same time laboratories for the collective elaboration of new projects and new mass forms of critical political intellectuality, and experimental sites for new social and political relations. In this sense, they have to be more democratic, more egalitarian, more open, less hierarchical and less sexist than the society around them.
>
> *Sotiris 2014*

Addressing these concerns could start in the PhD programme by taking seriously social science and humanities research, our own projects and also those of other scholars. Serious scholarship starts with reflection on the political nature of knowledge, but it cannot stop there. We must practise being academics politically. By doing so we would deconstruct the immobilizing spatio-temporal separation between the presence of academia and the externalized future (see Barinaga, this volume). Questions about what *else* it is that we do as critical scholars and how we impact the world would not make sense any more. We impact it by being critical scholars.

Quoting Harlow Person, erstwhile Dean of Tuck Business School, Czarniawska argues for management scholars who personify their ethics. I couldn't agree more. However, I think the kind of ethics that one practises is of utmost importance. Person was 'a protégé of Fredrick Taylor' and believed that the biggest public service Tuck Business School provided was achieved through individual students' 'career preparation and status', as well as networking with (lecturing) business*men* (Khurana 2007: 153–4). Embodying their ethics, these businessmen seem to have fostered the kind of 'illiberal and unprogressive' professionalism (Tinker 2004: 74) that draws upon theoretical principles looking for practical solutions to managerial problems leaving aside the consideration of the wider context, the foundations of those principles or ethical issues. What embodying *our* ethics means in terms of selecting which insights of the humanities and social sciences to incorporate into our practices is inherently a political decision. It is the researcher's duty to reflect on their politics and, I believe, also to imagine and enact radical alternatives to the present. As PhD students we have a vested interest in not abandoning the university in neoliberal times, but if we're stuck with (and in) it for years, why shouldn't we collectively exercise our hope that it can be transformed?

Let me then offer some ideas for initiating the change we want to see. To begin, we should practise a sense of collegiality to resist control mechanisms. Some form of 'ontological empathy' (Prasad 2013) could replace judging each other simply by research outputs. It could also mean resisting bureaucratic regulations of the university by running cooperative projects with the aim of maximum participation for the benefit of sharing ideas. This would require discussions about the value of knowledge and how this relates to an openly accessible reservoir of half-formed or abandoned projects (Marquez-Gallardo and Checchi 2014).

We should continuously remind ourselves of the racist and classist origins of our discipline (Cooke 2003; Prasad, this volume) – not as an expiating exercise in Western academic masochism (Cheresheva and Racz 2013) but to be aware of the dangers of imposing universal (read 'white male') standards. Recordkeeping – of progress meetings, completion rates, publications and conference spending – is a way to organize knowledge, which 'requires the death or at least the mutilation of that which is analysed' (including ourselves) (Burrell 1997: 19). We might ally ourselves with museum studies, given its interest in organizing historical records for various audiences, to re-enliven displays and challenge representations. Organizational microhistories can help reformulate local politics by (re)discovering the conflict-ridden past of our workplace in contrast to the sanitized corporate histories of royal visits, Nobel prize winners, national Cycle Parking Awards and symbolically erected statues. Working with historians, we have a chance to excavate struggle and petrify vice-chancellors in a different way. On the other hand, longer-term histories, which Guldi and Armitage (2014) call for, might help shed new light on the dark side of management's relationship with workers (Hanlon 2015).

We can also discuss current research on the culture of drug use, including alcohol and tobacco, in doctoral studies. Literary fiction abounds with stories about and by users. This can lead us to social research on the use of drugs to enhance imagination. Correspondingly, insights from psychology can highlight drug abuse and mental illness in neoliberal academia (Shaw and Ward 2014). Criminology may help us understand the relevant context and offer some solutions. Its feminist strands have reflected on the constellation of academic power, political economy of the job market, and cases of rape and harassment in PhD supervision (Lee 1998), fieldwork (Clancy *et al.* 2014) and elsewhere (see Pullen, this volume). Further, we should insist on practising childcare as a community and use this as a route into studying how capitalism proliferates a gendered and sexed social order. Cultural studies of fictional representations of culture at work (for example, Tyler and Cohen 2008; Bell and Sinclair, this volume) illustrate that gender performances are not immutable. Cultural studies could also dissect the relationship between the culture of producing output and the production of impact culture in academia. Once we uncover this relationship, we could rearticulate the current frenzy.

Geography and politics, combined with the study of transnational corporations, has produced scathing accounts of the world's food system (Patel 2007). To battle the grip and greed of profit-hungry food giants on a local scale, we could create allotments on our campuses and use their seasonal produce for non-profit university catering. Public accounting coupled with educational policy could see whole universities transformed into cooperative trusts (Boden *et al.* 2012). Education, critical pedagogy in particular, should help reform our teaching methods (Perriton and Singh, this volume; Vince, this volume).

We could experiment with writing creatively, as Czarniawska suggests, in different tones and languages. Become better writers by producing dirty accounts (Pullen and Rhodes 2008) that express a different libidinal economy. Use theatre studies to bring speech and voice back into academic scholarship – not as the spoken writing of conferences or speech as pure presence-to-self (Derrida 1997; Learmonth, Humphreys and Griffin, this volume) but as an embodied way of doing scholarship. Explain cultural and conceptual differences through languages. Dance. Listen – to an 'unknown' language for its expressiveness, beyond the confines of any one system of language games (Anzaldúa 1991).

If you are still interpellated by the 'we' running through this chapter, then you might want to treat the entanglements between management, social science and the humanities I've listed here as a springboard of ideas for future doctoral programmes in management to be reworked and expanded at will. Some of the interactions mentioned in this chapter point beyond the PhD and can be reimagined easily in other fields. Such is the nature of entanglements between arbitrarily separated disciplines.

## On aftershocks and afterlife

As a teenager in my native Hungary, we used to joke that *utópia*, translated literally, would mean *afterbooze* – in the same notional category with afterword, aftershocks, afterlife. Undoubtedly, some ideas developed in conversation with others, possibly over half-empty glasses. This text is what remains – part of it is hazy; another gives me a headache; whilst the rest may be overly ludicrous. But we could play, because this volume will likely make libraries bigger, and make some money for the publisher, rather than generating waves of aftershocks. My argument has precisely been that this is what happens to most writing in the humanities and social sciences. If we can hope for an afterlife, that should be about living our utopias in the now, not postponing them to some mythical future, not de-positing them on a hidden shelf of an unknown library.

The possibility of an afterlife in the present primarily depends on what we think the humanities and social sciences can do in management education or otherwise. I'm hopeful, although I don't see how there could be space and time for my suggestions in the academic environment of the near future. As academic intellectuals, we should be equipped to change what lies before us using the political explanations of the world we normally produce. Much like pandas. Because they spend most of their time chewing bamboo shoots, it's even scarier when they suddenly embrace the human(ist) form they've been given and speak up about being in a cage (Matthews 2014). Students from Amsterdam to Montreal, from Bulgaria to Chile, have recently demonstrated their belief in changing the world by changing our own institutions and work collectives (Baker 2015; Bor *et al.* 2015; Debnath 2014; Junes 2013; Vrousalis *et al.* 2015). Politics should be reclaimed. And there's no better place to start a revolution than amidst the relative freedom of our own doctoral programmes.

## Notes

1 I thank Irina Cheresheva and all PhD students who have been kind enough to discuss my ideas, and the editors for their valuable comments on the manuscript.

2 My own experience comes out of researching business and management schools that bring management, social sciences and humanities together. What I say here should be understood against this background and my more detailed knowledge of the UK, US and Hungarian situation. It is admittedly partial but hopefully applicable to other contexts.

3 'the outlook isn't quite good, / there isn't really anywhere to go, / there isn't really a way forward, this is it'.

4 Students buy educational services on loan and (in theory) repay the costs from their future salaries – only this will not actually happen in the UK, thus making the rhetoric of austerity empty but its grip more pervasive (see McGettigan 2013; Śliwa and Sørensen, this volume).

5 'Like my friend, the cat, has once remarked, the future arrived a while ago.'

6 I have to add that not all is absolutely grim when it comes to gender issues in academia, only that positive examples are more isolated. Moreover, they clearly don't support my argument here. I'll get back to potential solutions to the problems listed here in the next section.

7 It is beyond mere coincidence that one of the editors of this book happens to be my PhD supervisor. This is bothering because what if this fact – and not my nascent scholarly virtues – has led to my becoming a published author? A group of PhD students at the last CMS conference reassured me that such opportunities don't come easy and I wouldn't have been chosen without having 'objective' qualities in support. However, the passive voice conceals that my supervisor actively chose to ask me and that I accepted his invitation. At present my discomfort alerts me to how exclusive this offer was, but I can also see how one can easily slip into the comfortable explanation of being a worthwhile scholar whilst forgetting the role that personal–professional networks play in academic knowledge production and the nodes of power (of exclusiveness) they create.

## References

Acker, J. (1990) 'Hierarchies, jobs, bodies: a theory of gendered organizations', *Gender and Society*, 4(2), 139–58.

Alvesson, M., Bridgman, T. and Willmott, H. (eds.) (2009) *The Oxford Handbook of Critical Management Studies*. Oxford: Oxford University Press.

Anzaldúa, G. (1991) *Borderlands: The New Mestiza = La Frontera*. San Francisco, CA: Aunt Lute Books.

Avalaunch Media (2013) Social meowdia explained. *Avalaunch Media*. Available from: http://avalaunchmedia.com/infographics/social-meowdia-explained (accessed 23 April 2015).

Baker, J. (2015) 'Montreal students occupy CEGEP with call to occupy everything', *Revolution News*, 21 April. Available from: http://revolution-news.com/montreal-students-occupy-cegep-with-a-call-to-occupy-everything/ (accessed 27 January 2016).

Batchelor, L. and Fulop, L. (2003) 'You can do it! Critical management research'. Paper presented at the 3rd International Critical Management Studies Conference, 7–9 July, Lancaster University, UK. Unpublished. Available from: www.mngt.waikato.ac.nz/ejrot/cmsconference/2003/proceedings/activism/Batchelor.pdf (accessed 27 January 2016).

Binarythis (2013) 'Judith Butler explained with cats', *Binarythis*. Available from: http://binarythis.com/2013/05/23/judith-butler-explained-with-cats/ (accessed 11 April 2015).

Boden, R. and Epstein, D. (2011) 'A flat earth society? Imagining academic freedom', *The Sociological Review*, 59(3), 476–95.

Boden, R., Ciancanelli, P. and Wright, S. (2012) 'Trust universities? Governing post-capitalist futures', *Journal of Co-operative Studies*, 45(2), 16–24.

Bohle, D. and Greskovits, B. (2007) 'Neoliberalism, embedded neoliberalism and neocorporatism: towards transnational capitalism in Central-Eastern Europe', *West European Politics*, 30(3), 443–66.

Bor, E.-G., Wilson, B. and Harper, A. (2015) 'Free university: the new wave of student occupations', *Transformation*, 10 April. Available from: https://www.opendemocracy.net/transformation/evagrace-bor-ben-wilson-aidan-harper/free-university-new-wave-of-student-occupations (accessed 27 January 2016).

Bristow, A. (2012) 'On life, death and radical critique: a non-survival guide to the brave new higher education for the intellectually pregnant', *Scandinavian Journal of Management*, 28(3), 234–41.

Bristow, A., Ratle, O. and Robinson, S. (2014) 'Resistance as institutional entrepreneurship in unsettled times: the case of early-career academics in critical management studies'. Paper presented at the 30th EGOS Colloquium, 3–5 July, Rotterdam, The Netherlands.

Burrell, G. (1997) *Pandemonium: Towards a Retro-Organization Theory*. London: Sage Publications.

Butler, N. and Spoelstra, S. (2012) 'Your excellency', *Organization*, 19(6), 891–903.

Butler, N. and Spoelstra, S. (2014) 'The regime of excellence and the erosion of ethos in critical management studies', *British Journal of Management*, 25(3), 538–50.

Cahill, D. (2013) 'Ideas-centred explanations of the rise of neoliberalism: a critique', *Australian Journal of Political Science*, 48(1), 71–84.

Chao, Manu (2001) 'Merry Blues'. *On Próxima Estación: Esperanza (CD)*. Virgin Records.

Cheresheva, I. and Racz, M. (2013) 'What's in your head, zombie, zombie, zombie . . .'. Paper presented at the CPPE@10 Conference, 16–18 December, Leicester, UK.

Clancy, K.B.H., Nelson, R.G., Rutherford, J.N. and Hinde, K. (2014) 'Survey of academic field experiences (SAFE): trainees report harassment and assault', *PloS one*, 9(7), 1–9.

Clarke, C., Knights, D. and Jarvis, C. (2012) 'A labour of love? Academics in business schools', *Scandinavian Journal of Management*, 28(1), 5–15.

Connell, R. and Dados, N. (2014) 'Where in the world does neoliberalism come from? The market agenda in southern perspective', *Theory and Society*, 43(2), 117–38.

Cooke, B. (2003) 'The denial of slavery in management studies', *Journal of Management Studies*, 40(8), 1895–918.

Craig, R., Amernic, J. and Tourish, D. (2014) 'Perverse audit culture and accountability of the modern public university', *Financial Accountability and Management*, 30(1), 1–24.

Czarniawska, B. (2014) *A Theory of Organizing*. 2nd edn. Cheltenham, UK: Edward Elgar.

De Angelis, M. and Harvie, D. (2009) '"Cognitive capitalism" and the rat-race: how capital measures immaterial labour in British universities', *Historical Materialism*, 17(3), 3–30.

Debnath, N. (2014) 'Chilean activist destroys student debt papers worth $500m', *The Independent*, 18 May. Available from: www.independent.co.uk/news/world/americas/chilean-activist-destroys-student-debt-papers-worth-500m-9391907.html (accessed 27 January 2016).

Deleuze, G. (1992) 'Postscript on the societies of control', *October*, 59(1), 3–7.

Derrida, J. (1997) *Of Grammatology*. Baltimore, MD: Johns Hopkins University Press.

Dunne, S., Harney, S., Parker, M. and Tinker, T. (2008a) 'Discussing the role of the business school', *ephemera*, 8(3), 271–93.

Dunne, S., Harney, S. and Parker, M. (2008b) 'Speaking out: the responsibilities of management intellectuals: a survey', *Organization*, 15(2), 271–82.

Edmonds, J. (2013) 'Should we envision the future or help to create it?' Paper presented at the Reclaiming Impact Conference, 18 September, Durham Business School, UK.

Equality Challenge Unit (2014) *Equality in Higher Education: Statistical Report 2014*. Equality Challenge Unit: London. Available from: www.ecu.ac.uk/wp-content/uploads/2014/11/2014-08-ECU_HE-stats-report_staff_v19.pdf (accessed 11 June 2015).

Flew, T. (2014) 'Six theories of neoliberalism', *Thesis Eleven*, 122(1), 49–71.
Foucault, M. (2008) *The Birth of Biopolitics*. Basingstoke, UK: Palgrave Macmillan.
Gardner, S.K. (2008) '"What's too much and what's too little?" The process of becoming an independent researcher in doctoral education', *The Journal of Higher Education*, 79(3), 326–50.
Ghoshal, S. (2005) 'Bad management theories are destroying good management practices', *Academy of Management Learning and Education*, 4(1), 75–91.
Giroux, H.A. (2013) 'Public intellectuals against the neoliberal university', *Truthout*, 29 October. Available from: www.truth-out.org/opinion/item/19654-public-intellectuals-against-the-neoliberal-university (accessed 12 March 2015).
Guldi, J. and Armitage, D. (2014) *The History Manifesto*. Cambridge: Cambridge University Press.
Hancock, P. and Tyler, M. (2008) 'Beyond the confines: managerial colonization and the everyday', *Critical Sociology*, 34(1), 29–49.
Hanlon, G. (2015) *The Dark Side of Management*. London: Routledge.
Harney, S. and Dunne, S. (2013) 'More than nothing? Accounting, business, and management studies, and the research audit', *Critical Perspectives on Accounting*, 24(4–5), 338–49.
Harney, S. and Moten, F. (2009) 'The university and the undercommons'. *In:* The Edu-Factory Collective (ed.) *Toward a Global Autonomous University*. New York, NY: Autonomedia, pp. 145–50.
James, A. (2009) 'Academies of the apocalypse?' *The Guardian*, 7 April.
Jump, P. (2013) 'UCU uncovers high price of failure to hit REF targets', *Times Higher Education*, 3 October.
Junes, T. (2013) 'Students take Bulgaria's protests to the next level. Can they break the political stalemate?', *Tr@nsit online*. Available from: www.iwm.at/read-listen-watch/transit-online/students-take-bulgarias-protests-to-the-next-level-why-the-student-protests-could-break-the-political-stalemate/ (accessed 15 July 2014).
Kardos-Horváth, János (n.d.) 'Panda'. Performed by Kafkaz. Self-released.
Khurana, R. (2007) *From Higher Aims to Hired Hands*. Princeton, NJ: Princeton University Press.
Kimmel, M. (1996) *Manhood in America: A Cultural History*. New York, NY: The Free Press.
Kweder, M. (2014) 'Can I have some social change? Using autoethnography to explore a CMS-ish doctoral program in the US'. Paper presented at the What's So Critical About Your Critical Management Studies PhD? Conference, 16–17 September, University of Leicester, UK.
Latour, B. (1999) *Pandora's Hope*. London: Harvard University Press.
Latour, B. (2010) 'Coming out as a philosopher', *Social Studies of Science*, 40(4), 599–608.
Lee, D. (1998) 'Sexual harassment in PhD supervision', *Gender and Education*, 10(3), 299–312.
Lober Newsome, J. (2008) *The Chemistry PhD: The Impact on Women's Retention*. The Royal Society of Chemistry and UK Resource Centre, London. Available from: www.rsc.org/images/womensretention_tcm18-139215.pdf (accessed 11 June 2015).
Lovitts, B.E. (2008) 'The transition to independent research: who makes it, who doesn't, and why', *The Journal of Higher Education*, 79(3), 296–325.
McGettigan, A. (2013) *The Great University Gamble: Money, Markets and the Future of Higher Education*. London: Pluto Press.
McLaren, P.G., Campbell, S., Rostis, A. and Murray, W.C. (2014) 'Analyzing terse stories: socialization into the academy', *Global Review*, 1(2), 1–32.
Marquez-Gallardo, S.L. and Checchi, M. (2014) '"Resistance my ass!". Reflections on the strange encounter of "resistant" academics and dinner at the yacht club'. Paper presented at the What's So Critical About Your Critical Management Studies PhD? Conference, 16–17 September, University of Leicester, UK.
Matthews, D. (2014) 'Thomas Docherty to face insubordination charge in tribunal', *Times Higher Education*, 24 July.
Murray, D.E. (2014) Parenthood and academia: an impossible balance? *Times Higher Education*, 4 September.
Newell, S., Swan, J. and Kautz, K. (2001) 'The role of funding bodies in the creation and diffusion of management fads and fashions', *Organization*, 8(1), 97–120.
Newey, G. (2015) 'Mind your tone', *London Review of Books blog*, 10 April. Available from: www.lrb.co.uk/blog/2015/04/10/glen-newey/mind-your-tone/ (accessed 11 April 2015).
Newfield, C. (2004) 'Jurassic U: the state of university–industry relations', *Social Text*, 22(2), 37–66.
Parker, M. (2014) 'Writing: what can be said, by who, and where?' *In:* E. Jeanes and T. Huzzard (eds.) *Critical Management Research: Reflections from the Field*. London: Sage Publications, pp. 257–76.
Patel, R. (2007) *Stuffed and Starved: Markets, Power and the Hidden Battle for the World's Food System*. London: Portobello.

Prasad, A. (2013) 'Playing the game and trying not to lose myself: a doctoral student's perspective on the institutional pressures for research output', *Organization*, 20(6), 936–48.

Pullen, A. and Rhodes, C. (2008) 'Dirty writing', *Culture and Organization*, 14(3), 241–59.

Ratcliffe, R. (2015) 'Nobel scientist Tim Hunt: female scientists cause trouble for men in labs', *The Guardian*, 10 June.

Research Excellence Framework (2014) Assessment criteria and level definitions. Available from: www.ref.ac.uk/panels/assessmentcriteriaandleveldefinitions/ (accessed 27 January 2016).

Sennett, R. (2011) 'Humanism', *The Hedgehog Review*, 13(2), 21–30.

Shaw, C. and Ward, L. (2014) 'Dark thoughts: why mental illness is on the rise in academia', *The Guardian*, 6 March.

Sotiris, P. (2014) 'How can we change the world if we can't change ourselves?' Paper presented at the 11th Annual Historical Materialism Conference, 6–9 November, SOAS, London. Transcription available from: http://rs21.org.uk/2014/11/ 13/how-can-we-change-the-world-if-we-cant-change-ourselves/ (accessed 27 January 2016).

Tinker, T. (2004) '"The end of business schools?" More than meets the eye', *Social Text*, 22(2), 67–80.

Tyler, M. and Cohen, L. (2008) 'Management in/as comic relief: queer theory and gender performativity in *The Office*', *Gender, Work and Organization*, 15(2), 113–32.

Vrousalis, N., Celikates, R., Hartle, J. and Rossi, E. (2015) 'Why we occupy: Dutch universities at the cross-roads', *OpenDemocracy*, 2 March. Available from: https://www.opendemocracy.net/can-europe-make-it/nicholas-vrousalis-robin-celikates-johan-hartle-enzo-rossi/why-we-occupy-dutch-un (accessed 8 March 2015).

Westerlund, D. (2014) 'Critical university studies: being a PhD student and still staying in academia?' Paper presented at the What's So Critical About Your Critical Management Studies PhD? Conference, 16–17 September, University of Leicester, UK.

# Part VI
# Futures

# 32

# Notes on feminist management education

*Alison Pullen*

> If we are to achieve a richer culture, rich in contrasting values, we must recognize the whole gamut of human potentialities, and so weave a less arbitrary social fabric, one in which each diverse gift will find a fitting place.
>
> *Margaret Mead 1963: 147*

## Situating

When I became a university teacher I felt out of place. I remember my first lecture teaching on a research methods course to MBA students in the UK. Despite being prepared and dressed in the most professional way I could muster, I felt exposed. At every lecture at the beginning of every semester since then, across two continents and across many different courses, I experience the same exposure. But this is not negative, and in this chapter I want to start by considering the value of this exposure.

When I was a management student I always valued the lectures that I could identify with. This identification was with the research that informed the teaching and with the organizational and management practice that I understood. From these early days, I became fascinated by the ways in which the relationships that developed between lecturers and students could become the platform for bringing about personal change. Despite this occasional fascination, I spent most of my own education bored by the content, uninspired by the people pushing information on me, and yet too obedient to quit. When I did voice interest (usually through disagreement), I was too often labelled obstructive and overly questioning. As I reflect back on these times now, it seems that traditional and well-established power relations that create distance and detachment between teachers and students promote too much emphasis on information transfer, following rules and regulations, and on polite gesturing between autonomous people. It was a long time before I came to the realization that the reason I wanted to teach was to teach differently to how I was, by and large, taught. I think my students would agree that when the relationship between pedagog and student is open and vibrant, then critical learning can take place as collaboration. However, to achieve this participative space, the 'I' has to be exposed. Moreover, this process is not without problems because of the anxiety that the exposure entails. Furthermore, these open learning spaces can invoke resistance, especially when they depart from students' expectations and prior experiences of teaching and learning. I often think it would be much easier to pick up a repeat lecture every session and address the class without any real sense of engagement. But I never do! Instead, I find myself doing every session anew with an inbuilt commitment to encourage thought and critical reflexivity. This is another factor that exposes me.

As a woman, I have been held *to account* for my ideas, critiques and concerns in different ways to my male colleagues. Naming myself as a feminist management educator has exacerbated this imposed accountability. Although feminism offers a critical platform from which to speak, and enables me to speak from a particular sense of self, it also enhances my visibility. Despite this, and more practically, feminism enables a theoretical and political foundation that carries an inbuilt potential for change. This is the case regardless of whether it is challenging dominant frameworks of management and organization studies, or of academe more generally. Yet, as time passes, I am becoming more open and further committed to the radical possibilities that feminism offers. The possibilities range from emphasizing change in micro-interactions between individuals to challenging oppressive societal structures that create and sustain inequality.

Despite a growing literature on feminism and management and organization studies (Calás and Smircich 2006; Vachhani 2012; Harding *et al.* 2013) with which to work, management students still think of feminism in its radical sense. Most students find it confronting rather than liberating. I struggle with this. In organizations, sexism is deeply entrenched in the structural and cultural fabric. Whilst feminist writers have long challenged gendered cultures that sustain gendered discrimination and organizations have introduced proactive measures to redress this discrimination, as Gill (2014) testifies sexism has become more mobile, subtle and revitalized. Feminism enables this sexism to be spoken, challenged and resisted through a critical vocabulary and political movement, as well as an interdisciplinary spirit. But despite this value, feminism also exposes its proponents.

Teaching puts me at the centre of this exposure. In the classroom I become political – my body and words convey an identity politics. It carries the politics of feminism.

## Introducing management education and neoliberalism

The institutional context in which we practise management education is important in shaping the ways in which we think, teach, work and live. Neoliberal modes of governance, which aim to secure profits and emphasize market competition, affect universities and academic work in radical ways (Leonard 1998). Even though there is much rhetoric around greater entrepreneurialism and autonomy for academics, the reality is that academics have become increasingly constrained. McNay (2009) reminds us that neoliberalism involves permanent vigilance, activity and intervention. Neoliberal managerialism has informed conventional business school teaching where (in the UK in particular) the proletarianization of labour and the diminishing of trade union power has created a fervour for market managerialism (Parker 2014). On a social level, this threatens democracy and citizenship, especially in contexts where surveillance and control are heightened. For business school academics it threatens to limit academic freedom by demanding knowledge and teaching that is managerially relevant. 'New managerialism' has produced new audit cultures through the Research Assessment Exercise (RAE) and then the Research Excellence Framework (REF) in the UK and the Excellence in Research Assessment (ERA) in Australia. This managerialization (and resulting corporatization) of universities is an achievement that is measured by league table positions. All of this greatly influences academic performance management in increasingly stratified universities (McRobbie 2015a). Referring to UK universities, McRobbie writes:

> The RAE/REF introduced a rankings system whereby departments are measured and funds distributed according to the quality of the publications produced over a period of time by faculty. Alongside this there are other criteria that have to be met, including getting the research into the public realm and creating a rich research 'environment'.
>
> *McRobbie 2015a*

McRobbie raises the problem for what counts as a 'normal' academic career and the implications this has for women, especially those who want a family. She suggests that there is an idealized academic career replete with the winning of awards and prizes, the appointment to fellowships and the capture of prestigious grants. Moreover, this career is 'tailored around the image of the brilliant young man untrammelled by any of the fine details of domestic life' (McRobbie 2015a). This idealized career is by now part of the everyday sense of what it means to be successful as an academic.

For the academic in the neoliberal university, McRobbie convincingly argues that the masculine model of success that impinges on us all

> means not just fulfilling endless benchmarks against a grid of criteria which include leadership and achievement in teaching, administration and management (i.e. setting up new degrees) and in research, scholarship and publication, but also keeping a strict diary of everything that happens, all events attended, all papers given, all targets met with students, all the citations, radio slots etc., these too should be noted to be duly referred to in all annual performance reviews which in turn are connected to promotions and pay increments.
>
> *McRobbie 2015a*

From my own experience working in business schools, the individualistic demands of neoliberal subjectivity and auditing cultures threaten research culture, collegiality and cooperation. The obsession with university rankings and the measurement of academic labour and performance has implications for the nature of academic work and scholarship. Competition is a key feature of contemporary neoliberalism and, following McRobbie (2015b: 3), this 'construes the violent underpinnings of the perfect' which emerges as 'a horizon of expectation'. Even more damningly, this striving for perfection and self-definition for young women stifles 'the possibility of an expansive feminist movement' (2015b: 3). The success of the market-driven model of the business school has been eagerly promoted by universities as a means of cross-subsidizing other disciplines that have not benefited from burgeoning international and domestic markets. The pressure on this cash generation weighs heavily on both education and scholarship. Student recruitment is central to success. Class sizes are becoming larger and there is an intensification of the work of academics. In such contexts we witness greater reliance on adjunct and contract staff, budget cuts for permanent academics and administrators, the devolvement of administrative duties to academics, and a cut in research budgets.

It is not surprising that as academics we are surrounded with uncertainty, anxiety and overwork. Greater controls and surveillance through performance monitoring results in further exposure. These changes to the higher education sector in Australia and the UK (the two countries where I have worked) are intrinsically connected to gendered subjectivities at work (Leonard 1998; Clarke and Knights 2015). Some academics have spoken out against these work regimes, but there are punitive measures for those who fail to follow the doctrine and there is an aggressive policing of dissent (Parker 2014). Moreover, in this highly stratified university, women (especially those in the early stages of their careers and those with children) are too often marginalized and discriminated against.

In effect, these changes widen inequalities and corrode democratic and collegial academic work, as well as enacting symbolic and material violence to academic values and scholarship. In some cases academics become disposable objects or wasted humans (Bauman 2004). With this background, the lack of recognition of the multidisciplinary nature of business and management scholarship in universities, and the increased competition between academics, women become visible and vulnerable. As one blog captures it:

> This has been exactly the situation in my department. For years, women have been silenced by the institutional structures that have supported and enabled harassment and bullying to continue. When women have sought advice or spoken to other members of staff about the situation, there has been overwhelming complacency and, in many cases, a will to protect the institution by making the problem go away. Until very recently, there has been very little – or no – will to actually address the issue or intervene in the ongoing abuses of power.
>
> *A neoliberal university blog 'Strategic Misogyny', 31 May 2014*

The institutional structures and cultures and ongoing abuses of power that many of us face influence the ways in which any form of management education is done, especially if that education takes as its goal the questioning of power structures and ideology. Inherent bullying is fast becoming an epidemic in management contexts and as Ford *et al.* (2010) ask: what are we as critical scholars doing about it? The widening inequalities – especially between male and female careers, pay awards and career recognition – require much more scrutiny and action.

In addition to the silencing and marginalization of women, feminist research and pedagogy is not acknowledged in the mainstream managerialist agenda of most business schools. Feminists and those who employ feminism and feminist management education face particular pressures within the dominant, normative and mainstream environment in which we are located. On the one hand, given that feminism has long held the conviction that 'the personal is political' we should find comfort in feminism as a means to bring about changes in the schools we work in, challenge the fields that oppress critical thinking in management and combat the inequalities and abuses of power that we endure. On the other hand, there is a backlash against taking feminism into the classroom (hooks 2014). Being a feminist educator means taking a stand and the ensuing exposure and vulnerability risks becoming too dangerous in the current climate.

Will we see business school feminists go underground? Will we see the neutralization of feminism in an increasingly post-feminist classroom where students are unaware of gender pay gaps, discrimination and harassment at work and sex role bias? Post-feminist culture (McRobbie 2009), where perceptions of equality between men and women are assumed, presents its own dangers to feminist management educators, especially when other women don't see feminism as a necessary practice and theory in the business school classroom. The ways in which feminist management educators work requires thought especially in terms of either the direct and overt acknowledgement of feminist pedagogy, or a subtler integration of feminism.

There are continued stereotypes that women and feminist management educators face. Students' expectations of women as being kinder, more approachable, caring and empathic than their male counterparts often result in increased workloads. Working as a feminist also involves participation and collaboration, and student expectations run high in classes that engender an emotional connection and response. Many women experience sexism, fatigue, burnout, embarrassment and discrimination working as feminists. In my own case, my motivation for educating management students is to incorporate critical, multi-disciplinary thinking into dominant mainstream, managerialist, uncritical and unreflexive management education. Associated with this, there is personal satisfaction in getting people to see phenomena differently and to experience the classroom as a collaborative, safe space where learning can take place. Using feminist values challenges the oppression and marginalization that many women experience in university and in their working lives. Embodying feminist values in the classroom and providing a critique of gender-neutral management and organization theory enables educators to advocate and represent those who are silent in the class. Consequently, feminist management educators have greater responsibility to work against the grain in order to teach management knowledge, skills and practices that equip managers and organizational members with ways of thinking that don't repeat the failure of management and leadership that we are seeing on a global scale.

To expose gender-based power imbalances, developing principles of social justice and addressing inequalities, feminism has a long history of promoting the broadening of people's consciousness of the oppression they are embroiled in and also (often inadvertently) contribute to. In neoliberal contexts, which corrode freedom and equality, feminism is more important than ever in raising marginal voices and surfacing unnamed forms of discrimination. Feminism gives licence to take the private into the public by ensuring that the personal is political, especially in the classroom.

The points that I have been making so far start with the conviction that management education in current neoliberal contexts and the constituent audit culture creates an individualized academic subjectivity based on the ideal of the independent man. The resultant pressures that women face within the highly stratified, gender-neutral academy makes working with feminism in the business school particularly challenging and potentially oppositional. This challenge is, however, one worth accepting. This chapter will now continue to outline the key tenets of feminism and feminist pedagogy and its potential for management education.

## Feminism in the classroom: values and pedagogy

> Feminist education – the feminist classroom – is and should be a place where there is a sense of struggle, where there is visible acknowledgement of the union of theory and practice, where we work together as teachers and students to overcome the estrangement and alienation that have become so much the norm in the contemporary university.
>
> *bell hooks 1989: 51*

All teaching is political, whether it is acknowledged as such or not. Feminist classrooms explicitly acknowledge that doing management education involves doing gender (West and Zimmerman 1987), as well as questioning the assumed gender-neutrality of organizations (Acker 1990). Feminism makes a difference in the way that classrooms are formed, the way that we work in them, as well as the content of the syllabus. Despite such generalizations, feminist education, values and pedagogy start with 'us'. Women academics have choices whether to neuter ourselves in university and business school life by striving for masculinist images of perfection and excellence. There is indeed a temptation for women to adopt strategies to become competitive in the manly academic market through the mimesis of masculine or androgynous ways of working.

For feminism to thrive and strive as an 'expansive feminist movement' (McRobbie 2015b), we need to take up our gender positioning in university life. In doing this we claim our space in a politics of knowledge and work with an identity politics that is essential for progressing women's equality in organizations and redressing their continued bias and discrimination at work, home and in organizations. To consider this in terms of a personal example, in my post-graduate class on leadership, we consider examples of elite women who have achieved exceptional levels of corporate success (such as Sheryl Sandberg of Facebook and Marissa Mayer of Yahoo!). The demands of corporate culture and the striving for excellence as women leaders required for such success, however, can seem impossible for working women to even aspire to, especially if they are, or want to be, mothers.

Recognizing that power, knowledge and gender are intimately intertwined (see Gherardi 2011 for a review) enables critique of high-profile examples that reinforce women's continued striving for masculine models of perfection in corporate life (McRobbie 2015b). Moreover, this allows for the emergence and consideration of alternative gendered possibilities in organizations. It also promotes the need to work for better working conditions for women. Without creating feminist spaces in classrooms, students are not likely to become familiar with the ways that organizations are gendered, and how men and women in organizations experience gender with all the multiplicity, fragmentation and contestation that this involves. Feminist education is essential to enable women to make choices in organizations, with all the resistance that this involves.

Through direct and indirect engagement with feminism, classrooms can become re-politicized to enable greater participation, build communal values, work with local knowledge, provide spaces for grounding the authority of corporeal and affectual experience, and encourage critique of dominant power relations and associated forms of control in management and organization studies. Students have the opportunity to acquire politico–intellectual tools that can supplant hand-me-down political doctrines. They can also enhance their skills and become aware of the greater social and political responsibilities that might inform their working lives.

Different feminisms emphasize different identity politics because they relate, for example, to issues of intersectionality, queering and associated claims of inclusion and exclusion. Recognizing that there are philosophical and political variations within feminism, feminist scholarship can still be collectivized as a project of political advocacy that enables 'an activist agenda of social justice' (Dill *et al.* 2007: 636 cited in Patai 2012: 676). Decades of feminist theory, praxis and activism have left a rich legacy in terms of social justice and of challenging dominant knowledge structures, working with local knowledge and recognizing the authority of experience. In a general sense, feminism has given voice to the estranged, alienated and marginalized experiences of women. It has empowered women and has campaigned against capitalism and for social change in the status of women in society. From groundbreaking and agenda-setting work of de Beauvoir (1972 [1949]), Woolf (1956 [1928]) and Friedan (1963), the focus has been on investigating women's social, cultural, economic and political exclusion and exploring avenues of knowledge building. For management students, what can be highlighted is how the political, social and cultural context in which we understand organizations, management and leadership is gendered. Moreover, an awareness of this relation between gender and work is vital to convey the differences between how people experience their working lives, especially the lives of those subordinated.

As educators we can ask directly: who is feminism working for and who is it not working for? Given the 'links between feminism, activism, and the academy and women's every day lives' (Hesse-Biber 2012: 3), with feminist education women students are given space to surface their own politics and take charge of their futures, and given licence to think and work differently. Women students, whether they are from the Middle East or Scandinavia, can speak out, giving voice to their experiences of being a woman, whether it is surrounded by democracy and equality or by alienation and oppression. Given that women are largely excluded from management thought, writing and practice, feminist perspectives carry 'messages of empowerment that challenge the encircling of knowledge claims by those who occupy privileged positions' (Hesse-Biber 2012: 3). To engage in feminist education, theory and praxis means challenging knowledge that excludes whilst seeming to include. Feminists ask 'new' questions that 'place women's lives and those of "other" marginalized groups at the centre of social inquiry' (Hesse-Biber 2012: 3). Feminism enables women to speak from their own social, cultural, political and economic location, erasing the universality of women's experiences in favour of acknowledging and attending to difference, and it challenges the academic authority that some women find oppressive and obstructive to their learning.

Feminism encourages less-advantaged members of the classroom to speak, especially when the access to power of privileged subject positions becomes explicit. It is within the classroom that we as educators have the responsibility for what becomes visible and not. Harding (1991) contends that the emancipatory goal of feminist teaching needs to result in democratic ends. I have often observed, even in large management classes, women working together to experience collective and participative collaborations. Through an engagement with feminism in the classroom, the boundaries that mark who can be the knower and known become visible and broken down. Naturally, feminism 'strives to speak to women' (hooks 1994: 70) but because it recognizes 'being other' it has the potential to challenge those taken-for-granted assumptions for men and raise the marginalization of sexuality in workplaces. In so doing, feminism challenges knowledge that excludes and questions what counts as legitimate. In questioning the authority structures inherent in management knowledge and practice, feminism creates a space for doing and redoing management education differently, and by pushing to create change. Feminism carries 'inclusive, anti-oppressive, and transformative' values (Patai 2012: 677). Patai (2012: 677) stresses that to enact feminist education and

> To justify and defend the introduction of feminist as a legitimate modifier of their teaching and research, feminists have had to emphasise and greatly exaggerate the flaws of the pre- or non-feminist models they are contesting.

Feminist teaching fosters change through advocacy and provides a context for understanding situations (Lather 1991), and yet given that it involves considerable critique of the mainstream and the non-feminist there can be a backlash in the classroom as students resist politically charged critique that can threaten their prior knowledge or assumptions. To effect or mobilize classroom participation relies in part on the ability of the educator to convey the personal.

Reinharz (1992: 243) usefully states that 'feminism supplies the perspective and the disciplines supply the method'. Feminist teaching is therefore driven by feminist values. In relation to management, it works across disciplines to bring cases and theory that challenge dominant knowledge. Processually this involves being active, showing and telling your own experiences, and engaging with social change and women-centred activism. Class members are encouraged to be open to the co-construction of knowledge. In management education non-corporate case studies in a variety of media expose students to alternatives to the corporate mainstream accounts. The power gained from following feminist research and writing provides the space to speak and write for yourself in the hope that others will follow.

There are as many variations within feminist pedagogy as there are within feminism. A key element of this variation revolves around the extent to which feminist educators envisage their commitments to pedagogy as being informed by academic and/or political motives. In the context of management education, where neoliberalism and managerialism prevail, the extent of political intervention requires special consideration. For example, Kaufman and Lewis (2012) ask students to reflect on the degree to which they are political subjects. Although management students do not often disclose their politics explicitly, in my classes what has been important is the delivery of critical and political thinking as a way to challenge the gender neutrality of the mainstream. To illustrate, I often use films of political and leadership speeches so that students can critically assess the ways in which language articulates power, control and knowledge. In this way, students can conduct a gendered critique of, for example, feminine leadership or masculine workplace cultures through accessible material.

This process asks students (with their peers) to acknowledge their values and to question how they think differently to others, whether those others are the exploited, the unemployed, the poor or the elite. Subsequently the relationship between corporate success and historical and political inequalities in organizations is interrogated. The combination of personal reflection and multidisciplinary research is used as the foundation of student learning and becomes the means to develop critical thinking. Adopting feminist research and feminist management studies that reveal the existence of power relationships in society and organizations and associated marginalization and oppression is key (see, for example, Fletcher 2001). An awareness of structural inequalities enables students to question whether we take women's working lives for granted and whether we falsely assume aspects of progress towards equality. Incorporating reflexive learning and knowledge building is key for students to recognize their place in established power relations.

## Feminism in (critical) management education

> . . . as the margin or 'outside' enters an institution or teaching machine, what kind of teaching machine it enters will determine its contours. Therefore the struggle continues in different ways, after the infiltration.
>
> *Spivak 2012: ix*

The focus on power relations, political advocacy and social justice in feminist pedagogy has led some management and organization studies feminist academics to consider critical management studies (CMS) as a position to work from. CMS has interrogated the political and philosophical basis of management. Grey (2002: 496), for example, questioned the 'socialisation of managers and their ideological functions' in order to raise issues of power and voice in what has been called the 'messiness and suffering that characterizes management practice' (2002: 509). Grey also recognizes 'other problematic features of management' (2002: 509) such as gender, ethnicity, power and the environment. The political basis for this critique of management is assisted by feminism because it provides one avenue for what Grey (2002: 509) calls the 'freedom that presents critically orientated academics with both the possibility, and perhaps duty to articulate dissent'. CMS provides a shared location to work with feminist theory and practice in the classroom, where teaching and research, and education and politics come together. The pedagogical goals of feminism within critical management are united in standing 'against hegemonic educational practices that tacitly accept or more, forcefully reproduce an oppressively gendered, classed, racialized, and androcentric social order' (Crabtree *et al.* 2009: 1 cited in Patai 2012: 677).

Sinclair (1997, 2000) and Simpson (2006) illustrated the masculine nature of management programmes and syllabi, and show how this presents particular challenges for female students and teachers alike. Given that feminist education has as its goal women's emancipation and advocacy, it has the potential to rewrite management education and theory anew. Teaching is political and the female body carries an identity politics. To further understand how teaching is embodied and political, Sinclair (2005) demonstrated how bodies shape teachers and students, particularly in how they act, think and what is taken away. Bodies shape relationships and offer the means whereby solidarity between women can develop against hegemony. Sinclair explores how different repertories of disembodied and embodied pedagogical styles unfold in classrooms, and how management pedagogy celebrates particular bodily performances through which specific bodies become visible. Awareness of this in/visibility can be a source of oppression/liberation for students and teachers alike (see Bell and Sinclair, this volume).

Feminism enables the body to be present and provides a place from which to speak and act. It also allows the disembodiment of management theory and practice to be challenged. Further, observers of classroom dynamics see the ways in which women's bodies are sexualized and materialized as they are fashioned through the feminine, and feminism also shows how the masculine body is read and taken up differently with regard to power to effect relationships and learning. The feminine body is stereotypically recognized as caring and subordinate compared with the masculine body. Swan (2005: 317) reminds us that there is more to women's bodies in the management classroom than 'nurturance, learner-centredness or disembodied rationality'. Given that management has long been associated with masculinity (Knights 1992), the management classroom similarly creates a space where those lacking masculinity lack embodied authority. Akin to Swan, I suggest that women's bodies in management classrooms are a source of political resistance.

Feminism enables a critical appraisal of taken-for-granted management concepts and principles, and assists with the critical project within management studies and education. Given the importance of social justice and activism against women's marginalization in management practice and academia, feminism is once again gaining traction, not only as a social movement and identity politics but also as a critical pedagogy. In relation to management, this may involve getting participants to engage in critical, anti-managerialist syllabi and creating alternative spaces in which to speak out against oppressive workplace practices. For feminist pedagogy, this encompasses intersectionality and it becomes 'inclusive, anti-oppressive, and transformative' (Crabtree *et al.* 2009: 17). Feminism is a political imperative to address the question of marginalization in the context of management. In this sense, feminist scholarship re-politicizes every classroom participant's role. This engenders corporeal relationships that enable the political transformation of how management is perceived.

The use of feminism in management classrooms is starkly different to working with feminist pedagogy in other disciplines such as sociology, women's studies and politics. The assumed motivation of many business and management students is employability and career progression in the business world, and many of the ambitions and desires underlying this stand in contrast to feminist ways of working. In practice, however, students are not limited to such one-dimensional assumptions. In my mixed-sex multicultural classes, my drive is to make some difference. In some classes, this means encouraging women's participation and relying on a politics of empowerment (Collins 2002). To achieve these basic aims, I use alternative readings and case studies that do not fall into the confines of mainstream management. Incorporating women and gender studies into management education provides rich sociological, cultural and philosophical insights that challenge mainstream management. Judith Butler's (2002) ideas on gender performativity are useful, for example, to show how gender gets done and undone in organizations and thus challenges normative accounts of leadership, management and work. In considering this, students are able to challenge stereotypes and assumptions surrounding working identities in organizations. Hélène Cixous' (see Sellers 1996) radical questioning of patriarchy, hegemony and masculine ideologies can be brought to bear to rethink the ways in which we reinforce problematic dualities in organization theorizing. Cultural theorist Judith Halberstam (1998), whose queer performativity challenges dominant masculinity, offers a way to reconsider organizational models of leadership, success and effectiveness. Using such ideas, alternative realities can be engaged with that defy the corporate focus of much management education. Through multidisciplinary thought, such as that explored in this volume, new possibilities open up for the teaching of alternative forms of organizing and of understanding organizations. In the process, avenues for social justice and advocacy become visible.

In my own teaching practice, I encourage students to take concepts such as leadership and unpack them in relation to what they assume and know by raising the historical development of taken-for-granted ideas, particularly women's presence or lack thereof in history. Here it becomes important to surface the tensions between global and local knowledge and students' participation in questioning the homogeneity of management knowledge. Realizing students' own cultural experiences is central. Additionally, encouraging storytelling is a non-confrontational way to enable students to engage. The classroom becomes a space where hierarchy is challenged through collaborative and transparent thinking, experiencing and reflecting. It starts by asking 'what do you think?', and careful attention to individual experience and individuality of students is valued.

As an illustration, I recall a recent class where a white male Australian student asked if he could start my leadership class with a story about speaking to a senior female manager from the professional service firm PricewaterhouseCoopers at a university engagement event. He recalled how women were reluctant to name inequality and didn't want to be associated with feminism. We discussed the multiple ways that women's experiences could be interpreted. At the end of the session, a female accountant from China working in Australia stood up and argued for equality being the responsibility of us all. This openness and debate was only enabled by six weeks of building trust and dialogue.

My own classroom experiences in business schools can be thought of in terms of the feminist practice of 'consciousness-raising'. Consciousness-raising is a term rooted in feminist history and writing. Collins (2002) notes that consciousness-raising starts by acknowledging the double burden experienced by black women and identifying avenues for their empowerment. Collins is important in reminding us that women's role and status within the economy are not equal. A large amount of women in management literature focused on the barriers to progression and the image and dress of women managers, but I am mindful that these bourgeois debates do not carry the same political incentive as a black woman's experience of being arrested on her way to work in the US or a Kuwaiti woman driving a car and breaching social and cultural norms (see Prasad, this volume). I also note that although CMS has located feminism at the heart of its project, feminist consciousness has not been present or debated recently. This is remiss given that critical reflection and 'self-knowledge is an important dimension of our understanding of management as a practice' (Townley 1995: 271). More radically, Martin's (1990) research on feminist organizations illustrates feminist alternatives to bureaucratic organizations, concluding that women need to take responsibility for the women's movement and the creation of feminist organizations. Reflecting on my classroom interactions, I have been reminded of Trethewey's (1999) idea that irony can be used to understand how ambiguities and paradoxes structure organizational reality. Exposing the ironies and contradictions can be achieved by introducing cases from popular culture into the classroom. Comedy is particularly useful, and there are research papers that can be drawn on for inspiration. The animated television programme *Futurama* (Pullen and Rhodes 2013) and the comedy serial *The Office* (Tyler and Cohen 2008), for example, can be used to question and undermine the patriarchal heterosexism of organizational life.

Although acknowledging that consciousness-raising may have gone out of fashion in culture at large, its role in the classroom is still important. This is particularly so given these post-feminist times where young women too often find feminism a movement of the past and not relevant to their lives. Thinking of Stanley and Wise's (1983) classic book *Breaking Out: Feminist Consciousness and Feminist Research*, we can ask: what work are we doing and in the name of what? Perhaps, following Reger (2004: 205), we can still acknowledge that 'consciousness-raising serves as the organizational process that helps transform personal emotions into a collectively defined sense of injustice'.

## Feminist possibilities in critical management education

> I thought how unpleasant it is to be locked out; and I thought how it is worse, perhaps, to be locked in.
>
> *Virginia Woolf 1945 [1928]*

In feminist management research, attention to power, authority, reflexivity, ethics and difference have been given significant attention (see Calás and Smircich (1989 for an early review). Feminism enables alternative readings to those that result from the dominance of male authors in the key texts recommended to students. In turn this challenges the gender-neutrality of management and management education. It also creates opportunities to question the work we engage with and what becomes subjugated knowledge. In part, CMS has assisted with this development, and yet CMS has *incorporated* feminism into its own project and, with this, feminism's radical aims have been dissipated. The question I am left with is what influence can feminist scholarship and activism have on social and educational transformation? This journey starts with the continuing need to politicize education, and for women, the need to engage with feminist politics in order to stand against misogyny and to work for women's rights.

Feminism recognizes the multiple voices and fractured identities that surface exclusion and discrimination. It also provides a platform for resistance to the ensuing injustice. In the context of management, feminism provides a critique of organizational rationality, phallocentrism and the violent relations inherent in organizational gender inequality (Acker 1990; Pullen and Rhodes 2015). When working well, classrooms from large lecture halls to small seminar groups cultivate *social sensitivity* that requires a commitment to politics that emerges through intercorporeality (Medina 2012). Medina writes: 'insensitivity involves being cognitively and affectively numbed to the lives of others; being inattentive to and unconcerned by their experiences, problems, and aspirations; and being unable to connect with them and to understand their speech and action' (Medina 2012: xi). Conversely, feminism creates intellectual, physical and pedagogical spaces for engagement and sensitivity and reminds us that insensitivity prevents us from resisting oppression, inequality and injustice. It forces us to look at the contexts of organizations and recognize the ways in which contemporary management and organizations affect women and how women in particular must take ownership of these escalating inequalities as they graduate from university and move into professional and management roles.

In this chapter, I have attempted to show how feminism, despite its divided history, can be brought to bear on how we can understand, resist and even change organizational life and management practice, and what this means for management education. Using insights from across the humanities and social sciences, feminist management education can be transformative. In some cases, this might be about disturbing the taken-for-granted canon that re-inscribes a gendered neutrality and particular notions of reason and rationality in philosophical thinking and writing (Phillips *et al.* 2014). In other cases, it might involve examining the possibilities and practices of a gendered philosophy of organization and its effects on gendered subjectivities and knowledge. Feminist epistemologies explore different ways of knowing (Lennon and Whitford 1994) such that working with feminism means being 'committed to opening the space for new symbolic representations of women' (Deutscher 1997: 59). Questioning issues of exclusion, power, equality, difference and voice, Gatens (1991) contests the status quo found in most management courses and texts. We can ask: how can feminism advance management education? Does feminism pose a threat to educators in neoliberal times? How does feminism organize/disorganize differently? What are the possibilities for new workplace relations if feminist principles are taken on board? What are the effects of the male dominance of management education? What are the potential traps for feminists? What are our ethical responsibilities to challenge the taken-for-granted norms of the field of work and organization?

Feminism urges me to think that one's life, work and politics cannot be divorced from each other. On many occasions within the male-dominated realm of management, the academy and society, I neuter and silence my work and self because the *F-word* is still dirty! In neoliberal, post-feminist times many women have discounted feminism, and it seems that the attendant failure to name feminism shapes the ways in which women engage (or don't engage) in everyday politics. This exacerbates women's social, economic and political subordination; however, although feminism is dismissed by some women, it still retains the ability to instigate response and stimulate debate; to develop relationships between class members; and expose the abhorrent global inequalities for women. Despite progress, feminism is still on the margins of management and organization studies and even critical management studies. Perhaps this margin is the place for transformative change beyond preoccupations concerning which feminist camp, with their clashes and contradictions, one should assign oneself to?

Change can start in the classroom and with us as management educators. The experiences shared in these potentially safe spaces enable people to shape their working lives and to be reflexive about those work practices and cultures that breach equality and freedom. This very question harbours within it a desire for change and for a politics of becoming and potential. I am personally implicated in this as well, of course. In one sense, I am grateful that my work on gender is acknowledged in the field of critical management studies, but perhaps this acknowledgement aids complacency in that such work, and the life and politics it reflects, becomes assigned to a respectable place? This tendency is also evidenced in the multiple handbooks of CMS and organization studies, where there is a devoted space for the female writer, the feminist contribution, the gender chapter. How can we change this? Has feminism become a ghetto in the mainstream? Has it been depoliticized?

I, like others, have employed feminist theory as activism, but this is not enough without an everyday politics that is informed by feminist ethics and practice marked by defiance to counteract a notable complacency with women's progress, women's representation, women's discrimination. I am angry and frustrated. But feminist politics is a politics that aims to bring about change; it does not shirk at making trouble both inside and outside the academy. Care needs to be taken that feminism is not cleansed and incorporated, not just theoretically but also as each and every one of us that needs to manage the political contexts in which we work. Could it not be the case that in the neoliberal business school, on a day-to-day basis, feminism is allowed in only to immunize against its more radical potential? But we must not forget that feminism provides a platform for exploring the ways in which education is an ethically motivated act of resistance. In the classroom, feminist politics and resistance may emerge through relationships between each other, as an intercorporeal affect between bodies (Pullen and Rhodes 2015). Feminist management education, which recognizes the sociality between individual bodies, can create spaces where generous acts surface. This is management education as an embodied and reflexive practice. Solidarity represents a radical openness to the other and forms generous relationships through collaboration and participation. It is in these encounters that imaginations are seized and the potential for change becomes present. Thinking this way asks us all to question our privilege and how it shapes how we see and behave in the world. It is the opportunity for self and other knowledge. The very basis of education.

For those who aspire towards revolutionary changes through feminist movements, we must consider the questions: what 'openly femocratic transformations inspired by feminist principles' (Deem and Ozga 2000: 163) are possible given neoliberal pressures? How can a radical politics of life (Butler 2005) and an affirmative politics that places transformation at the centre (Braidotti 2010), which challenges male dominance, work to benefit women's lives within the academy? A radical politics of life means working outside of the systems of oppression that govern/oppress. Resisting the neoliberalized institutionalization that organizes us is important. This means defying pressures to pursue a career measured against male ideas. As McRobbie (2015a) states: 'only a truly exceptional young woman, one who was also lucky in her life-planning with a partner could have children and could survive this new style of university governmentality without falling apart'. The same holds for so many other occupations and professions. Feminist education needs to raise both ours and others' consciousness and work against regimes that hold us back from living a liveable life.

## References


Acker, J. (1990) 'Hierarchies, jobs, bodies: a theory of gendered organizations', *Gender and Society*, 4(2), 139–58.

Bauman, Z. (2004) *Work, Consumerism and the New Poor*. London: McGraw-Hill.

Braidotti, R. (2010) 'On putting the active back into activism', *New Formations*, 68(1), 42–57.

Butler, J. (2002) *Gender Trouble*. London: Routledge.

Butler, J. (2005) *Giving an Account of Oneself*. New York, NY: Fordham University Press.

Calás, M.B. and Smircich, L. (1989) 'Using the f word: feminist theories and the social consequences of organizational research', *Academy of Management Proceedings*, 1, 355–9.

Calás, M.B. and Smircich, L. (2006) 'From the "woman's point of view" ten years later: towards a feminist organization studies'. *In:* S.R. Clegg, C. Hardy, T.B. Lawrence and W.R. Nord (eds.) *The Sage Handbook of Organization Studies*. London: Sage Publications, pp. 284–346.

Clarke, C.A. and Knights, D. (2015) 'Careering through academia: securing identities or engaging ethical subjectivities?', *Human Relations* 68(12), 1865–88.

Collins, P.H. (2002) *Black Feminist Thought: Knowledge, Consciousness, and the Politics of Empowerment*. London: Routledge.

Crabtree, R.D., Sapp, D.A. and Licona, A.C. (2009) *Feminist Pedagogy: Looking Back to Move Forward*. Baltimore, MD: Johns Hopkins University Press.

de Beauvoir, S. (1972 [1949]) *The Second Sex*. Harmondsworth, UK: Penguin.

Deem, R. and Ozga, J.T. (2000) 'Transforming post-compulsory education? Femocrats at work in the academy', *Women's Studies International Forum*, 23(2), 153–66.

Deutscher, P. (1997) *Yielding Gender: Feminism, Deconstruction and the History of Philosophy*. London: Routledge.

Fletcher, J.K. (2001) *Disappearing Acts: Gender, Power, and Relational Practice at Work*. Boston, MA: MIT Press.

Ford, J., Harding, N. and Learmonth, M. (2010) 'Who is it that would make business schools more critical? Critical reflections on critical management studies', *British Journal of Management*, 21(1), 71–81.

Friedan, B. (1963) *The Feminist Mystique*. London: Penguin.

Gatens, M. (1991) *Feminism and Philosophy: Perspectives on Difference and Equality*. Cambridge: Polity Press.

Gherardi, S. (2011) 'Ways of knowing: gender as a politics of knowledge?' *In:* E.L. Jeanes, D. Knights and P.Y. Martin(eds.) *Handbook of Gender, Work and Organization*. Chichester, UK: Wiley, pp. 37–49.

Gill, R. (2014) 'Unspeakable inequalities: post feminism, entrepreneurial subjectivity, and the repudiation of sexism among cultural workers', *Social Politics*, Winter, 509–28.

Grey, C. (2002) 'What are business schools for? On silence and voice in management education', *Journal of Management Education*, 26(5), 496–511.

Halberstam, J. (1998) *Female Masculinity*. Durham, NC: Duke University Press.

Harding, N., Ford, J. and Fotaki, M. (2013) 'Is the "f"-word still dirty? A past, present and future of/for feminist and gender studies in organization', *Organization*, 20(1), 51–65.

Harding, S G. (1991) *Whose Science? Whose Knowledge?: Thinking from Women's Lives.* New York, NY: Cornell University Press.
Hesse-Biber, S.N. (ed.) (2012) *The Handbook of Feminist Research: Theory and Praxis.* 2nd edn. London: Sage Publications.
hooks, b. (1989) *Talking Back: Thinking Feminist, Thinking Black.* London: Sheba.
hooks, b. (1994) *Outlaw Culture: Resisting Representations.* London: Routledge.
hooks, b. (2014) *Teaching to Transgress.* London: Routledge.
Kaufman, D.R. and Lewis, R. (2012) 'From course to dis-course: mainstreaming feminist pedagogical, methodological and theoretical perspectives'. *In:* S.N. Hesse-Biber (ed.) *The Handbook of Feminist Research: Theory and Praxis.* 2nd edn. London: Sage Publications, pp. 659–74.
Knights, D. (1992) 'Changing spaces: the disruptive impact of a new epistemological location for the study of management', *Academy of Management Review*, 17(3), 514–36.
Lather, P.A. (1991) *Getting Smart: Feminist Research and Pedagogy with/in the Postmodern.* London: Routledge.
Lennon, K. and Whitford, M. (eds.) (1994) *Knowing the Difference: Feminist Perspectives in Epistemology.* London: Routledge.
Leonard, P. (1998) 'Gendering change? Management, masculinity and the dynamics of incorporation', *Gender and Education*, 10(1), 70–83.
McNay, L. (2009) 'Self as enterprise dilemmas of control and resistance in Foucault's "The Birth of Biopolitics"', *Theory, Culture and Society*, 26(6), 55–77.
McRobbie, A. (2009) *The Aftermath of Feminism: Gender, Culture and Social Change.* London: Sage Publications.
McRobbie, A. (2015a) 'Women's working lives in the "new" university', *The Guardian*, 19 August.
McRobbie, A. (2015b) 'Notes on the perfect: competitive femininity in neoliberal times', *Australian Feminist Studies*, 30(83), 3–20.
Martin, P.Y. (1990) 'Rethinking feminist organizations', *Gender & Society*, 4(2), 182–206.
Mead, M. (1963) *Sex and Temperament in Three Primitive Societies.* New York, NY: Morrow.
Medina, J. (2012) *The Epistemology of Resistance: Gender and Racial Oppression, Epistemic Injustice, and the Social Imagination.* Oxford: Oxford University Press.
Parker, M. (2014) 'University, Ltd: changing a business school', *Organization*, 21(2), 281–92.
Patai, D. (2012) 'Feminist pedagogy reconsidered'. *In:* S.N. Hesse-Biber (ed.) *The Handbook of Feminist Research: Theory and Praxis.* 2nd edn. London: Sage Publications, pp. 675–92.
Phillips, M., Pullen, A. and Rhodes, C. (2014) 'Writing organization as gendered practice: interrupting the libidinal economy', *Organization Studies*, 35(3), 313–33.
Pullen, A. and Rhodes, C. (2013) 'Parody, subversion and the politics of gender at work: the case of Futurama's "Raging Bender"', *Organization*, 20(4), 512–33.
Pullen, A. and Rhodes, C. (2015) 'Is becoming-woman possible in organizations?'. *In:* A. Pullen and C. Rhodes (eds.) *The Routledge Companion to Ethics, Politics and Organizations.* London: Routledge, pp. 355–67.
Reger, J. (2004) 'Organizational "emotion work" through consciousness-raising: an analysis of a feminist organization', *Qualitative Sociology*, 27(2), 205–22.
Reinharz, S. (1992) 'Feminist interview research'. *In:* S. Reinharz and L. Davidman (eds.) *Feminist Methods in Social Research.* Oxford: Oxford University Press, pp. 18–45.
Sellers, S. (1996) *Helene Cixous: Authorship, Autobiography and Love.* Cambridge: Polity Press.
Simpson, R. (2006) 'Masculinity and management education: feminizing the MBA', *Academy of Management Learning and Education*, 5(2), 182–93.
Sinclair, A. (1997) 'The MBA through women's eyes: learning and pedagogy in management education', *Management Learning*, 28(3), 313–30.
Sinclair, A. (2000) 'Teaching managers about masculinities: are you kidding?', *Management Learning*, 31(1), 83–101.
Sinclair, A. (2005) 'Body and management pedagogy', *Gender, Work and Organization*, 12(1), 89–104.
Spivak, G.C. (2012) *Outside in the Teaching Machine.* London: Routledge.
Stanley, L. and Wise, S. (1983) *Breaking Out: Feminist Consciousness and Feminist Research.* London: Routledge.
Swan, E. (2005) 'On bodies, rhinestones, and pleasures: women teaching managers', *Management Learning*, 36(3), 317–33.
Townley, B. (1995) '"Know thyself": self-awareness, self-formation and managing', *Organization*, 2(2), 271–89.
Trethewey, A. (1999) 'Isn't it ironic: using irony to explore the contradictions of organizational life', *Western Journal of Communication*, 63(2), 140–67.

Tyler, M. and Cohen, L. (2008) 'Management in/as comic relief: queer theory and gender performativity in *The Office*', *Gender, Work and Organization*, 15(2), 113–32.
Vachhani, S.J. (2012) 'The subordination of the feminine? Developing a critical feminist approach to the psychoanalysis of organizations', *Organization Studies*, 33(9), 1237–55.
West, C. and Zimmerman, D.H. (1987) 'Doing gender', *Gender and Society*, 1(2), 125–51.
Woolf, V. (1945 [1928]) *A Room of One's Own*. London: Harmonds.
Woolf, V. (1956 [1928]) *Orlando: A Biography*. London: The Hogarth Press.

# 33

# The fact of otherness

## Towards liberating the subaltern consciousness in contemporary management education

*Ajnesh Prasad*

> [P]ostcolonial intellectuals from and in formerly colonized countries [must] critically analyze and dissemble imperialist forms of knowledge that insidiously occupy a space both in their political and cultural unconscious as well as in representations of the non-Western produced through Eurocentricism.
>
> *Persram 2007: xxiii–xxiv*

> When our lived experience of theorizing is fundamentally linked to the processes of self-recovery, of collective liberation, no gap exists between theory and practice.
>
> *hooks 1994: 61*

### Prologue

Almost a century ago, Saratcandra Chattopadhyay published his powerful novel, *Devdas* (2002 [1917]). *Devdas* narrates the tragic story of its title character, a young Bengali man whose socio-cultural position requires him to negotiate his gendered identity at the liminal juncture that is constitutive of colonial India. Devdas has a longing affection for his childhood playmate Parvati, and yet is ultimately unable to pursue a relationship with her because of a set of complex psycho-sexual dynamics engendered by British imperialism; namely, in attempting to discursively subvert the essentialized depictions of the identity of the colonized Bengali man as being 'effete, promiscuous, and degenerate', Devdas must negate his libidinal desires to contravene the stereotypes cast upon him by his colonial masters (Arora 1995: 269). In doing so, his love goes forever unconsummated.

### Introduction

Recognizing the Westocentric disposition in mainstream organizational theories (Frenkel and Shenhav 2006), the aim of this chapter is to adopt a postcolonial theoretical perspective to illustrate how contemporary management education can move towards a future that recognizes the voice-consciousness of members of non-Western subaltern classes who have been systematically rendered invisible in scholarship and teaching in the field of management and organization studies. Moving towards achieving this objective will better serve those individuals who consider themselves as being colonial subjects or who otherwise possess some lingering remnants of the colonial legacy. To animate the abstract claims found in this chapter, I revisit Abraham Maslow's hierarchy of needs – as an indicative example of ethnocentricism in the extant literature in the field – in an effort to illuminate the necessity for more cultural situatedness in management and organization studies. In doing so, I hope to contribute to the debunking of the tacit assumption of universality that is the hallmark of mainstream research in the discipline. It is only in repudiating the universality in management and organization studies research that management education, informed by the humanities, can be transformed into a site that holds the potential to liberate the subaltern consciousness of colonized subjects.

Before proceeding, a proviso is warranted. Although the ideas in the chapter have broad implications for the field of management and organization studies, I seek particularly to contribute to some of the ongoing discourses occurring in the critical management studies (CMS) community. CMS scholars have long problematized the ethnocentric prejudices embedded in management scholarship. They observe that although these theories have their contextual – and, certainly, their empirical – roots in the West, many management researchers have tacitly, though rather erroneously, afforded such theories a level of universal applicability. It is precisely this assumption of universality that has largely provided epistemological hegemony to the Western academy. A CMS perspective is particularly well versed for a postcolonial interrogation of ethnocentric organizational theories insofar as it represents 'a branch of management theory that critiques our intellectual and social practices, questions the "natural order" of institutional arrangements, and engages in actions that support challenges to prevailing systems of domination' (Cunliffe *et al.* 2002: 489; see also Perriton and Singh, this volume). More precisely, the ideological commitment of CMS is to present, specifically from the discipline of management and organization studies (which draws necessarily and extensively on works from the humanities and the social sciences), a 'radical critique' against social patterns of oppression, particularly those stemming from capitalism, patriarchy and imperialism (Adler *et al.* 2007: 120; also see Fournier and Grey 2000; Prasad and Mills 2010).

One important site where Western epistemological hegemony, sponsored by specious claims to universality, has profound repercussions is contemporary management education; namely, the ethnocentric biases that are found in mainstream scholarship serve to discursively construct and reify a system of marginalization against those subjects with colonial legacies who are engaged with or are in management education. In rendering a postcolonial critique against the Westocentric biases that pervades much of management education (Joy and Poonamallee 2013), the phenomenological experiences and the situated knowledge(s) of the systematically disenfranchised are therefore prompted to emerge and to be duly recognized by those responsible for delivering management education (see Durepos *et al.* forthcoming; Haraway 1988).

The remainder of this chapter is organized into four sections. First, I provide a brief sketch of postcolonial theory, inspired originally by thinkers from the humanities, with a particular emphasis on the concept that is the focus of this chapter, the subaltern (Spivak 1988). This section also includes some consideration of how postcolonial theory has been applied in management and organization studies – and specifically CMS – research thus far. Second, I describe Abraham Maslow's (1943, 1970) hierarchy of needs, a mainstream organizational behaviour theory of motivation and, thereafter, critique it in an effort to elucidate how Western theorizing in the field of management and organization studies is often inadequate to address the idiosyncrasies in the forms of organizing and the organizational practices that prevail across different parts of the non-Western world. Indeed, in building on the critiques on the hierarchy of needs already posited by several CMS scholars, I highlight the Westocentric and ideological currents that undergird this theory. Third, drawing on different postcolonial concepts, I discuss the possibilities for future management education to serve as a site of liberation for colonized subjects/ students. Finally, I conclude the chapter with some postcolonial caveats – that is, thoughts on what conscientious management educators ought to avoid when attempting to transform scholarship and the classroom into an emancipatory arena.

## Postcolonial theory

Moving beyond overly simplistic analyses of geopolitical expansion by Europe into Africa, Asia, Latin America and, what are today known as, *white-settler* countries – Canada, Australia and New Zealand – postcolonial thought turns its analytical gaze most prominently to the cultural, the political and the economic imperialism that occurred during the colonial phenomenon (Childs and Williams 1997). As such, this line of critique has provided scholars with an important lens from which to critically appraise the cultural production of such ideas as race, nation, empire, migration and ethnicity (Cooppan 2000; Moore-Gilbert 1997). Its relevance and applicability for understanding these concepts has made postcolonial theory a mainstay in research in the social sciences and the humanities (for an excellent overview, see Childs and Williams 1997).[1]

In its broadest conceptual scope, postcolonial theory seeks to identify, problematize, and ultimately deconstruct Western epistemological and capitalist hegemony that emerged and became codified through the myriad repertoires of the colonial experience (for classic works, see Bhabha 1994; Fanon 1967; Nandy 1983; Said 1978; Spivak 1988). It endeavours to elucidate the processes of Western knowledge construction, which pivots on the stereotyping and the subordination of the 'Other' (Lorbiecki and Jack 1999: S25). Most fundamentally, therefore, postcolonial theorists repudiate the assumed universality in Western language, knowledge claims and value systems that functioned – and continue to function in various manifestations – to stringently demarcate the identities of the colonizer and the colonized (Frenkel 2008) and, thereby, to establish the ideological justification that would permit the former to govern the peoples and the territories of the latter (Ashcroft *et al.* 1989). Said (1978) contends that it was, in part, the hegemonic authority encapsulated by Western epistemology – and the complementary negation of other ways of knowing – during the colonial period that engendered the ideological construction and the deployment of 'Orientalism' (for excellent discussions of the psychological elements of colonialism, see Fanon 1967; Nandy 1983). For Said, a hierarchical mode of thinking was enacted, informed by a system of ethnocentric myths, racist beliefs and the Western post-Enlightenment canon, in which the Orient was juxtaposed as the cultural opposite of the ideologies represented by the colonizers. The colonial powers ultimately created and reified the perverse discourse that rendered the Orient as the mirror opposite of the Occident, although still an 'inferior, exotic, and degenerative culture that requires acculturation and modernization' (Frenkel and Shenhav 2006: 857). In this way, the ontological othering of the colonized by the colonizers not only denigrated the former but also provided the very rationale upon which the colonial project was founded and maintained (Said 1978).

Amongst the most dispiriting outcomes of colonialism were the cultural and the economic construction of the subaltern class. The origins of the concept of the subaltern rests in the works of Antonio Gramsci (1971). Adopting Marxist vernacular, Gramsci explained that the subaltern could be considered as the working-class constituents who lacked class consciousness and whose narratives were systematically written out of the bourgeois' writing of history (Ashcroft *et al.* 2000).

Postcolonial studies adopted the concept to 'challenge elitist historiography and to illuminate aspects of subaltern history as they relate to class, caste, age, gender, and so forth' (Green 2002: 16). Working from this framework, Gayatri Spivak (1988) appropriates Gramsci's notion of the subaltern to offer a feminist reading of the Indian practice of sati during British imperialism. This cultural practice involves a widow self-immolating by ascending her deceased husband's pyre. During colonialism, the British banned the practice, which launched a highly polemical debate. In rationalizing their decision, imperial elites made recourse to perennial themes of colonialism and accused the practice of being uncivilized and barbaric; in contrast, Indian bourgeois-nationalist elites valorized the practice by claiming that it was a religious mandate that served the spiritual interests of Hindu women and of Hindu society more broadly (Spivak 1988). Spivak (1988: 297) explains that the corollary of the debate was the production of the colonialist discourse: 'White men saving brown women from brown men'. She further articulates that although this discourse was performed on the body of the sati, her body merely functions as the site upon which acrimonious and paternalistic ideologies of competing masculinities were contended. Indeed, her voice becomes silenced because the debate occurs between two sets of masculine elites – between the British imperialists on the one hand and the Indian bourgeois-nationalists on the other. This leads Spivak to conclude that the subaltern is the subject who has had her voice-consciousness silenced in prevailing socio-cultural discourses and, by extension, lacks access to exercise institutional hegemony (also see Ashcroft *et al.* 2000). Interestingly, the discourse posited on the body of the sati is analogous to the bifurcated discourse of the Indian *babu*, labelled by British imperialists as 'effeminate and degenerate' whilst seen by Indian bourgeois-nationalists as 'straying from the social and religious values of Hindu orthodoxy' (Arora 1995: 259).[2]

Akin to Spivak's analysis of the subaltern, CMS scholars have long noted how organizational theories have written out or have otherwise hidden certain marginalized members of society (Calás and Smircich 1991; Cooke 1999; Dye *et al.* 2005; Ibarra-Colado 2006; Prasad 2009). For example, in their excellent critique of the leadership literature, Calás and Smircich (1991) demonstrate how researchers have ostensibly negated the 'problem' of seduction, which had led to leadership acquiring a gendered meaning. The negation of seduction within the context of leadership is, for them, tantamount to the negation of femininity. For its focus on the written out, the hidden and the negated, postcolonial theory shares many ontological and epistemological affinities with members of the CMS community and is, as a result, gaining purchase within the field of management and organization studies (for example, Banerjee and Prasad 2008; Prasad 2014; Ulus 2015; Westwood and Jack 2007).

## *Postcolonial theory in management and organization studies*

Management studies scholars, particularly those working within the CMS tradition, have made significant strides in incorporating postcolonial theory into organizational analyses (for example, Banerjee 2003; Frenkel 2008; Jack *et al.* 2011; Prasad 1997; Westwood and Jack 2007).[3] The seminal figure for the introduction of postcolonial thought into management and organization studies research is Anshuman Prasad (1997, 2003, 2006, 2012). Nearly two decades ago, Prasad (1997: 286) insightfully remarked that postcolonial theory could potentially serve as a useful conceptual framework from which to critically '[analyse] the cultural dynamics of control and resistance in the period of colonialism and its aftermath'. In suggesting the link between the colonial and the postcolonial, Prasad emphasizes how the colonial subject's experience in contemporary organizations is informed by her history. In making this observation, he illuminates the need for future management and organization studies scholarship to diligently adopt postcolonial perspectives.

Extending Prasad's line of critique, several insightful organizational analyses have since emerged from CMS scholars that invoke a postcolonial theoretical lens. One noteworthy example is a study by Bobby Banerjee (2003) in which he illustrates how the meanings, the practices and the policies of sustainable development have problematic consequences for Third World states. Drawing explicitly on postcolonial theory, he elucidates how the discourse of sustainable development is informed by a colonial ethos, which ultimately perpetuates the imperialistic process by which Third World citizens are subjugated. Elsewhere Banerjee and Linstead (2004) further develop this theme by highlighting how management research that studies members of indigenous communities is endemically fraught with/in the (neo-)colonial mentality. They conclude that this stream of literature 'ignores histories of colonialism with which indigenous peoples have had to contend' (Banerjee and Linstead 2004: 225). Banerjee and Linstead's claim has resonance with the broader postcolonial discourse, which asserts that indigenous communities have had their culture grossly misrepresented or entirely ignored in historical narratives.

The purposeful erasure of certain histories is a prevalent concern for postcolonial theorists because they recognize that it is the erasure of history that marks the ontology of the subaltern (Ashcroft *et al.* 2000). Its attention to history is precisely what marks the utility of postcolonial theory for advancing theory and practice. Because it is foregrounded in the study of the colonial, this strand of theory is necessarily historical and, thus, is able to substantively engage with historical processes that engender contemporary social inequalities. Indeed, as Childs and Williams (1997: 8) argue:

> Since the West has a deplorable record of simultaneously denying the existence of any worthwhile history in areas it colonized and destroying the cultures which embodied that history, an important dimension of postcolonial work has been the recovery or revaluing of indigenous histories.

Threading along this current, Frenkel and Shenhav (2006: 859) show how certain theories and practices that materialized during the colonial encounter were systematically and purposefully 'edited out of MOS [management and organization studies] canon and its historiography'. They further observe that when management texts did consider colonial and postcolonial knowledge they were marked by certain Orientalist predilections, which effectively called into question the trustworthiness of that knowledge.

With this in mind, CMS scholars have a timely opportunity. They can conscientiously engage with historiography in order to render visible the cultural idiosyncrasies that are embedded in different modes of organizing and in different manifestations of organizational behaviour (Rowlinson and Proctor 1999). A project of this scope moves beyond simply demonstrating the cultural variance in organizational phenomena; it also begins to duly recognize the consciousness of those subjects previously rendered subaltern. The following section invokes a particular organizational behaviour theory in order to illuminate the potential utility for repudiating the universality that apportions unwarranted privilege to Western epistemology.

## Challenging universality in management research

Thus far, this chapter has drawn upon postcolonial theory to elucidate how the Orientalist mentality concurrently undermined colonized voices and afforded epistemological supremacy to the Western canon. It comes as no surprise, therefore, that the field of management and organization studies is entrenched in a set of institutionalized ethnocentric biases, which sustains intellectual hegemony through a self-fulfilling prophecy wherein knowledge created in a particular time and space discursively proclaims its own universal applicability. Indeed, much of the theory development in management and organization studies encapsulates a set of Westocentric biases (Frenkel and Shenhav 2006; Prasad 2009). Owing to the voluminous literature available for critique, this chapter cannot exhaustively chronicle all the areas of management and organization studies that are undergirded by problematic colonial assumptions (for a more comprehensive overview, see Prasad 2003). Rather I use an illustrative example – motivation theory – to explain that although management theories habitually assert universality, either explicitly or implicitly, they usually emanate from, and have their contextual roots, in the West.

Although other theories are available for critique within the extant management literature, motivation theory offers an exceptionally well-known example with which to illuminate the Westocentric biases endemic in the field. Moreover, for the purposes of the present chapter, motivation theory is invoked for two particular reasons. First, motivation theory has been posited largely as a dispositional trait that is indifferent to the effects of time and space. Consequently, it provides a glimpse into the problematic ways that the corpus of mainstream management and organization studies scholarship tacitly and discursively normalizes Western experiences and Western bodies. Second, critical examination of motivation theory serves as a useful conceptual site from which to understand the manifestations and the dynamics that underlie other management ideas. As Cooke *et al.* (2005) conclude, motivation theory – and particularly the branch of the theory that will be under scrutiny here – offers an informative canvas from which to study the analogous development of other management and organizational theories.

Motivation theory was one of the earliest theories to develop within what was, during the time of its conception, the embryonic field of management studies. Several mainstream theories for conceptualizing motivation have since developed, including equity theory (Adams 1965), expectancy theory (Vroom 1964) and goal-setting theory (Locke and Latham 1990). Although a postcolonial, deconstructionist analysis can be applied to show the Westocentric biases undergirding each of the theories, for brevity, the focus here will be on Abraham Maslow's (1943, 1970) hierarchy of needs. The hierarchy of needs is employed for the present analysis because (1) it has had, arguably, the most enduring influence in accounting for (workplace) motivation (Cullen and Gotell 2002) and (2) it is a theory that is inherently codified in exploitive workplace relations (Knights and Willmott 1974), a phenomenon which scholars invoking postcolonial thought would be necessarily interested in redressing.

Maslow's hierarchy of needs suggests that human behaviour is motivated by needs and desires. Maslow delineates these needs into five categories ranging from low-level to high-level needs: the physiological needs, the safety needs, the love needs, the esteem needs and the need for self-actualization. According to Maslow (1943: 370), '[h]uman needs arrange themselves in hierarchies of pre-potency. That is to say, the appearance of one need usually rests on the prior satisfaction of another, more pre-potent need'. Working from this claim, for individuals to achieve esteem needs they must have first satisfied their physiological, safety and love needs.

Since the publication of Maslow's hierarchy of needs, it has come to be adopted in virtually all introductory level management texts (Dye *et al.* 2005) – the hierarchy has become institutionalized as a dominant explanation for human motivation.[4] One scholar notes that 'Maslow's hierarchy is so pervasive that it has almost become invisible, in that its basic framework and concepts are accepted without question' (Cullen 1997: 355–6). Notwithstanding its influence, it is a theory that has been critiqued by CMS scholars for the empirical research upon which it is based and also for the conceptual claims that it advances.

Two lines of criticism should be emphasized for the present discussion. First, Albert Mills and colleagues have gone to great lengths to situate Maslow and his hierarchy of needs within the broader discourses of the day (Cooke *et al.* 2005; Dye *et al.* 2005). In so doing, they describe the social and the political conditions that profoundly informed the scope and the content of Maslow's theory. In juxtaposing Maslow's theory with the Cold War context, they insightfully underscore the socially constructed origins of the hierarchy of needs. Indeed, Cooke *et al.* (2005) suggest that the institutional pressures and the cultural dynamics that manifested as a result of the Cold War served, with varying degrees of effectiveness, the ideological determinants for the management ideas presented by Maslow and his contemporaries. Through a careful deconstructionist analysis, they find that the hierarchy of needs became reflective of the underlying assumptions about modernity in which realization of motivational needs was conflated with corresponding levels of political progress; that is, Maslow's theory came to serve as an ideological means by which to order nation-states from ideal to deviant – the US, as the archetypical Western state, was of course asserted to be the 'ideal social state' (Cooke *et al.* 2005: 148).

Second, Dallas Cullen (1994, 1997; Cullen and Gotell 2002) describes the androcentric basis for Maslow's theory of motivation. Cullen and Gotell (2002) revisit and carefully deconstruct the empirical evidence upon which Maslow developed the hierarchy of needs. They find that the hierarchy of needs was predicated on Maslow's study of women's sexuality, which was fraught with methodological and ideological concerns. This study, although providing the empirical foundation for Maslow's conceptualization of motivation, naturalized men's dominance and women's submission in 'healthy' socio-sexual relations – women who did not adopt submissive tendencies qualified, for Maslow, as aberrations (Cullen and Gotell 2002). Given the attributes associated with masculinity and femininity, Cullen (1994) observes that the hierarchy of needs is ontologically gendered insofar as it privileges masculinity and relegates femininity to peripheral spaces. Indeed, there is a ubiquitous 'conflation of self-actualization with masculinity' (Cullen and Gotell 2002: 553). Cullen further applies a liberal feminist reading of gender emancipation to the position of women in the hierarchy of needs:

> [The] argument that women should take their place in the male world in order to achieve their full human potential [is] an argument that women should become like men, accepting male values and behaviors and rejecting female values and behaviors.
>
> *Cullen 1994: 135*

Hence, for Cullen, although Maslow's theory is portrayed as being humanistic, it harbours a series of gendered prejudices (see also Pullen, this volume). As such, the hierarchy of needs works for women only under those circumstances in which they are willing to relinquish feminine characteristics and embrace masculine behavioural attributes and value systems.[5]

These dual streams of critique 'demonstrate the usefulness of contextualizing theory development in the field of management and understanding the types of theoretical explanations that come to dominate the field' (Konrad 2005: 127). Indeed, by contextualizing theory as done by Mills and colleagues and also by Cullen, some of the pivotal concerns with Maslow's hierarchy of needs are foregrounded. Taken collectively, these critiques illuminate the fact not only that Maslow's theory of motivation is problematic, but also that it has been interpreted in problematic ways by management researchers. Much akin to myriad other management theories, the hierarchy of needs is erroneously viewed as being 'ahistorical, universal and unchanging' (Cullen 1994: 128).

Similar to how postcolonial theorists have described how the hegemonic assumption of universality in Western epistemology consigns Others' knowledge claims to the margins, so too Maslow's hierarchy of needs declares universality in one breath, but it overtly excludes certain constituents in another. For instance, within this theory, 'the voices of gay men and blacks are visibly suppressed' (Dye *et al.* 2005: 1389). Other silenced groups within Maslow's conceptual purview include colonized subjects of subaltern classes; indeed, nowhere does Maslow discuss the idiosyncrasies in motivation and how it discursively manifests in non-Western societies, much less the determinants of motivation amongst those who have been systematically oppressed.[6]

Through the diligent work of CMS scholars, it is apparent that Maslow's theory of motivation was predicated on a set of Westocentric and ideological values. However, this phenomenon was not limited to Maslow alone – other scholars who contributed to the development of, what are today, foundational management ideas also exhibited similar predilections (Cooke *et al.* 2005). As such, there continues to be a need for studying the forms of organizing and expressions of organizational behaviour that occurred during different periods and in different societies.

## Postcolonial contributions to management research and education

This chapter has sought to illuminate the potential for management and organization scholars – the same individuals who are also responsible for delivering management education – to engage with the study of the voice-consciousness of members of non-Western subaltern classes. Indeed, much of the management research produced thus far has been ethnocentric in that it has been predicated on Western assumptions, values and ideals (Prasad 2003). As such, due to the largely monolithic grounding of management scholarship – in that it is based on and reflective of Western knowledge systems – current understanding of human behaviour in organizations and the possibilities in modes of organizing are insufficient for capturing the complexities and the nuances of different groups and cultures around the world. Critical approaches to management studies – especially those perspectives foregrounded in postcolonial thought – permit scholars to account for the idiosyncrasies that are found in different cultures and contexts, and to explain how these idiosyncrasies manifest in particular organizational settings. This therefore allows management educators to teach increasingly diverse cohorts of students using more holistic and less ethnocentric curricular and pedagogical approaches (see Joy and Poonamallee 2013; see also Perriton and Singh, this volume).

This chapter contributes to three interrelated areas of scholarship. Each contribution poses implications for management education. I will consider these implications in relation to subjects of colonized regions.

First, this chapter identifies a path by which to emancipate the subaltern consciousness. To reiterate, the ontological markings of the subaltern refer to that subject who has had her voice-consciousness erased in the prevailing discourses of the day (Spivak 1988). It represents those subjects who have not been represented – or who have been silenced – in the construction of history by various elite classes (Ashcroft *et al.* 2000; Gramsci 1971). As discussed earlier, the silencing of the sati is the corollary of the process in which the imperialist and the bourgeois-nationalist elites engaged in the masculinist project of debating the rights/rites of her body (Spivak 1988). Extending this idea, by critically examining the subjectivity of the colonized subaltern with regards to her participation in organizing and within organizations, new insights will develop that will be germane for creating alternative organizational theories. At a minimum, such a project can reveal how subaltern epistemologies contest, confirm or edit traditional theories in the field.

Spivak's (1988) important contributions to critical historiography create spaces for opportunity – allowing consideration of how individuals who have not been represented in management and organization studies thus far can be heard (Durepos *et al.* forthcoming ). Namely, by conceptualizing how the different expressions of organizational behaviour and the diversity in forms of organizing, the cultural vicissitudes of difference, particularly between Western societies and non-Western societies, and within each, are elucidated. Moreover, as the late Eduardo Ibarra-Colado observed, by further focusing scholarly analysis on the subaltern, there is a move to '*reclaim the reality of organizational knowledge from* [the perspective of the historically subjugated], which has been hidden for too long' (2006: 465, emphasis in original). This process of reclaiming provides new meaning and dignity for identities of colonized subjects that were ideologically rendered – as part of the justification for imperialist conquest – as being subversive, uncivilized and morally bankrupt. In this way, management educators who are invested in hearing the voices of the subaltern will afford students with colonial legacies spaces to articulate their own voice-consciousness. Indeed, it will bring into awareness how colonized subjects approached myriad organizational phenomena.

Second, this chapter engages with debates in the field of management and organization studies on culture and politics. Postcolonial theorist Homi Bhabha (1994) has described the constitution of culture. Bhabha believes that culture is necessarily a hybrid construct emanating from the politics of liminality, the discursive engagements that manifest between and amongst different social systems (also see Childs and Williams 1997; Frenkel, 2008). He clarifies this claim by explaining that culture is an 'ongoing process of interpretation and reinterpretation, rather than a fixed feature of a given society' (Frenkel 2008: 927). For Bhabha, there is no possibility of *authentic* culture, which can be retrieved through a diligently executed ethnohistorical study (Yuval-Davis 1997). Through liminal and intersubjective processes, cultural hybrids have formed that are incessantly involved in discursive redefinitions of meaning and power. Bhabha's postulation of culture requires management scholars to abandon the idea of universality because culture is situated in the liminal forums of time and space. Returning to the field of management studies, because culture is not constant, theories professing universality are not attuned to analysing the dynamics of organizations and systems of organizing across different spaces.

These insights compel management and organization studies scholars to consider the question of power within liminal contexts. By critically studying imperialism, insights might emerge regarding how social and governance systems in South America, Africa, Asia and elsewhere were transformed or mediated as a consequence of the colonial experience. It has the potential to show how new institutional arrangements resulted in the emergence of new forms of colonized agency. It might explain, for instance, how colonized subjects responded differently to the British colonial policy of indirect rule versus the French colonial policy of associationalism. Beyond the question of resistance, such studies can serve as an important source for conceptualizing early forms of cross-cultural knowledge transfer (Frenkel 2008; Mir *et al.* 2008), that is it can show how the colonial encounter was the site at which the epistemological structures of Western and non-Western cultures were substantively (re)negotiated. This can serve an important purpose for colonized subjects engaging with contemporary management education because it illustrates the fallacy of the idea that organization and management knowledge is predicated purely on knowledge ascertained from a monolithic cultural source. It shows how the colonial experience had some sort of (tacit) impact on the development of even mainstream management and organization studies research.

Third, and in a related vein, these arguments extend the recent discourse regarding mimicry and epistemic coloniality. There is an imminent need to address the postcolonial subject's mimicry complex. Returning again to Bhabha's work (1994: 86, emphasis in original), he writes: '[c]olonial mimicry is the desire for a reformed, recognizable Other, *as a subject of a difference that is almost the same, but not quite*'. For Bhabha, mimicry is 'the sign of double articulation', that is to say, it is wedded in ambivalence between reform and recalcitrance (Frenkel 2008). Eduardo Ibarra-Colado (2006) has explored the mimicry complex as it materializes within the neo-colonial organizational setting. Applying his analysis to Latin America, Ibarra-Colado asserts that nations situated at the global periphery have a tendency to imitate the knowledge that has been constructed and institutionalized at the hegemonic centre. Through this phenomenon, which he labels epistemic coloniality, indigenous and parochial knowledges become appropriated in such perverse ways that they become a reflection of the centre, with all the ethnocentric biases that the centre embodies.

Tracing subaltern or precolonial knowledges of different societies allows the subjects of the postcolonial developing world to move away from, or wholly reject, the mimicry complex. Scholarship of this scope is not interested in developing knowledge that ideologically caters to the centre, but rather in identifying epistemological structures that were suppressed during colonization. Understanding the past can identify new directions for the field of management and organization studies (Westwood and Jack 2007). Likewise, it can also provide some insight into organizational differences amongst colonized societies – it can demonstrate, for example, how organizational structures differed between a particular community in Africa and a community in Oceania. Management education that establishes pedagogical space in order for these differences to be considered offers colonized subjects/students an understanding of how organizations and organizing were assembled in various parts of the non-West. Indeed, this form of management education may become a source for self-realization for these students, highlighting how things were done in different indigenous lands, including perhaps their own.

## Conclusion

To conclude, it is perhaps useful to offer three 'postcolonial' caveats or words of caution to researchers genuinely interested in transforming management education informed by the humanities into a site of liberation for colonized subjects.

First, management researchers ought to heed the advice of scholars in the field influenced by postcolonial theory, which asserts that organizational practices – and organizational realities more broadly – should be studied and taught without ethnocentric predilections that concurrently normalize Western experiences and render as deviant the experiences of Others (Prasad 2003; Westwood and Jack 2007). That is, management researchers should redirect attention from invoking Western knowledge bases to make appeals to universality and instead devote greater energies to conceptualizing how organizational practices manifest in idiosyncratic ways and are context specific. On this point, rather than using Westocentric measures by which to render axiological or moral judgements on organizational practices in non-Western contexts, scholars should more substantively endeavour to understand – empirically, conceptually and pedagogically – the specificities of localized organizational experiences (Boyacigiller and Adler 1991). With the political, the economic and the social transformations engendered by globalization, this postcolonial ethos will become of increasing significance for understanding the value of, and diversity within, organizational practices across different cultures. Undertaking such consideration will illuminate how organizational realities in non-Western contexts diverge from, or correspond with, extant theories in the field that have been predominantly developed in the West.

Second, management educators must be conscientious not to exploit their privileged status as members of the 'intellectual elite'; namely, scholars in the field who are studying or teaching different forms of organizing and organizational practices who perpetually risk committing cultural misappropriation and misrepresentation (Ball and Janyst 2008; Kim 2008; Patai 1987). It is therefore crucial to honour Spivak's (1988) provocative assertion that scholars do not *speak for*, but rather, *speak with* constituents of the subaltern class. This means affording subaltern informants the space and the agency to be the authors of their own narratives.

Third, although related to the previous point, even conscientious management educators who account for the colonization phenomenon in their teaching may risk essentializing subaltern identities and experiences. That is, in keeping with Said's (1978) and Nandy's (1983) instrumental ideas, scholars should not construct subaltern identity on the deterministic logic of it being a binary or relational opposite to Western identity. Indeed, this is precisely the rationale upon which postcolonial culture has been constructed and monolithically defined by Third World elites (Norton 2002). As Frenkel and Shenhav (2006: 872) suggest, '[r]aising the subaltern voice does not imply that it represents an alternative truth to that represented by hegemonic culture'; instead, management educators should ensure that when conducting research or teaching about colonial phenomena they are diligently open to recognizing the cultural and the individual nuances that existed across the colonial experience. This will judiciously 'encourage a multiplicity of voices and possibilities, which might challenge the assumptions upon which our perspective of the world is built' (Frenkel and Shenhav 2006: 872).

In short, the future of management education can function as a pivotal site in moving towards emancipating the subaltern consciousness. It can begin to repudiate the assumptions of universality that presently govern knowledge construction in the field and it can better recognize the voices silenced through the colonial legacy. As scholars in the field begin to think of management education in this spirit, inspired by thinkers from the humanities, there will be – to borrow the words of bell hooks (1994: 61) – a substantive intellectual and pedagogical engagement with 'the processes of self-recovery' and with 'collective liberation'.

## Epilogue

The story of Devdas introduced at the onset of this chapter alludes to the intricacies marking the ontology of a colonized subject. Although he is a literary character, Devdas is illustrative of how the colonial experience implicated the situated identities of those individuals under imperialist governance. Indeed, Devdas's tragic demise – and specifically his unconsummated love – is the corollary of the 'colonized subject [being] compelled to choose between the social ideal of manly self-control and his desire for Parvati' (Arora 1995: 260). It poignantly illuminates the idea that colonized subjectivities reside within the spatial complexities of liminality, which continues to be owed deconstruction and understanding.

## Notes

1 The corpus of postcolonial theory is constituted by rich and diverse traditions, which have engendered a wide gamut of claims (Lewis and Mills 2003). Although it is certainly not feasible to exhaustively chronicle the many nuanced arguments that have come from scholars who adopt this theoretical position, it is important to briefly identify how postcolonial thought is deployed here. Stated briefly, for the present chapter, postcolonial theory is used to conceptualize and critique the social hierarchies that were constructed and reified during and through cultural imperialism (Prasad 2003).

2 As Arora (1995: 274) notes, '[t]he *babu* was a term the British used to refer to the educated Bengali male, who often functioned as the intermediary between the colonial administration and the Indian populace' (emphasis in original).

3 The use of postcolonial theory in business schools has not been limited to the field of management and organization studies. In accounting, for example, Dean Neu (2001; also see Gallhofer and Chew 2000; Neu amd Heincke 2004) uses the concept of the subaltern to explain how large tranches of accounting scholarship lack relevance and applicability for the majority of the global population, particularly for significant parts of the developing world. Equally, in marketing, postcolonial theory has been referenced to conceptualize the complexities of expatriate professionals to construct cosmopolitan identities (Thompson and Tambyah 1999).

4 Interestingly, although management texts have habitually presented the idea that Maslow was clear in his suggestion that humans have five categories of needs that can be hierarchically arranged from basic to complex needs (Dye *et al.* 2005), Maslow was never this simple. Indeed, in his groundbreaking article,

'A theory of human motivation', Maslow stated that although it might appear that 'this hierarchy were a fixed order . . . actually it is not nearly as rigid as . . . implied' (1943: 386). Maslow then goes further to describe a series of hypothetical circumstances under which the hierarchy of needs might be problematized. For instance, he says of 'innately creative people in whom the drive to creativeness seems to be more important than any other counter-determinant [that] their creativeness might appear not as self-actualization released by basic satisfaction, but in spite of basic satisfaction' (1943: 386). Maslow's slightly nuanced reading of motivation has been almost wholly ignored in management texts.

5 The requirement for women to become like men to 'achieve their full human potential' engenders the classic double bind. Indeed, the moment a woman adopts masculine characteristics – for Maslow, the most important masculine characteristic would be dominance – she would be transgressing from her natural mandate, which is 'the desire to be an ideal mother' (Maslow cited in Cullen and Gotell 2002: 553). As Maslow's logic goes, women's biology ensures that they cannot achieve their full human potential (in the sense that men can), and if they do elect to exhibit the behavioural characteristics of men, they are abandoning their feminine destiny and should be considered aberrations.

6 There has been an abundance of cross-cultural research on the determinants of motivation. For instance, it has been shown that in Japan employees were motivated by their work tasks, opportunities for self-improvement and financial reward, whereas American employees placed much more emphasis on affiliation, social concern and recognition. Similarly, it has been reported that achievement motivation is more socially orientated in East Asian collectivist culture than in Western culture. What is apparent is that determinants of motivation are directly contingent upon the values of a culture (see Bond and Smith 1996).

## References


Adams, J.S. (1965) 'Inequity in social exchange'. *In:* L. Berkowitz (ed.) *Advances in Experimental Social Psychology*. Vol. 2. New York, NY: Academic Press, pp. 267–99.

Adler, P.S., Forbes, L.C. and Willmott, H. (2007) 'Critical management studies'. *In:* J.P. Walsh and A.P. Brief (eds.) *Academy of Management Annals*. Vol. 1. Mahwah, NJ: Lawrence Erlbaum, pp. 119–79.

Arora, P. (1995) 'Devdas: Indian cinema's emasculated hero, sado-masochism, and colonialism', *Journal of South Asian Literature*, 30(1/2), 253–76.

Ashcroft, B., Griffiths, G. and Tiffins, H. (1989) *The Empire Writes Back: Theory and Practice in Post-colonial Literatures*. London: Routledge.

Ashcroft, B., Griffiths, G. and Tiffins, H. (2000) *Key Concepts in Postcolonial Studies*. New York, NY: Routledge.

Ball, J. and Janyst, P. (2008) 'Enacting research ethics in partnerships with indigenous communities in Canada: "doing it in a good way"', *Journal of Empirical Research on Human Research Ethics*, 3(2), 33–51.

Banerjee, S.B. (2003) 'Who sustains whose development: sustainable development and the reinvention of nature', *Organization Studies*, 24(1), 143–80.

Banerjee, S.B. and Linstead, S. (2004) 'Masking subversion: neocolonial embeddedness in anthropological accounts of indigenous management', *Human Relations*, 57(2), 221–47.

Banerjee, S.B. and Prasad, A. (2008) 'Introduction to the special issue on "Critical reflections on management and organizations: a postcolonial perspective"', *Critical Perspectives on International Business*, 4(2/3), 90–8.

Bhabha, H. (1994) *The Location of Culture*. New York, NY: Routledge.

Bond, M.H. and Smith, P.B. (1996) 'Cross-cultural social and organizational psychology', *Annual Review of Psychology*, 47(1), 205–35.

Boyacigiller, N.A. and Adler, N.J. (1991) 'The parochial dinosaur: organizational context in a global context', *Academy of Management Review*, 16(2), 262–90.

Calás, M. and Smircich, L. (1991) 'Voicing seduction to silence leadership', *Organization Studies*, 12(4), 567–601.

Chattopadhyay, S. (2002 [1917]). *Devdas*. New Delhi: Penguin.

Childs, P. and Williams, P. (1997) *An Introduction to Post-Colonial Theory*. London: Prentice Hall.

Cooke, B. (1999) 'Writing the left out of management theory: the historiography of the management of change', *Organization*, 6(1), 81–105.

Cooke, B., Mills, A.J. and Kelley, E.S. (2005) 'Situating Maslow in Cold War America: a recontextualization of management theory', *Group and Organization Management*, 30(2), 129–52.

Cooppan, V. (2000) 'W(h)ither post-colonial studies? Towards the transnational study of race and nation'. *In:* L. Chrisman and B. Parry (eds.) *Postcolonial Theory and Criticism*. Cambridge: D.S. Brewer, pp. 1–36.

Cullen, D. (1994) 'Feminism, management and self-actualization', *Gender, Work and Organization*, 1(3), 127–37.
Cullen, D. (1997) 'Maslow, monkeys and motivation theory', *Organization*, 4(3), 355–73.
Cullen, D. and Gotell, L. (2002) 'From orgasms to organizations: Maslow, women's sexuality and the gendered foundations of the needs hierarchy', *Gender, Work and Organization*, 9(5), 537–55.
Cunliffe, A., Forray, J.M. and Knights, D. (2002) 'Considering management education: insights from critical management studies', *Journal of Management Education*, 26(5), 489–95.
Durepos, G., Prasad, A. and Villanueva, C.E. (forthcoming) 'How might we study international business to account for marginalized subjects: turning to practice and situating knowledges', *Critical Perspectives on International Business*.
Dye, K., Mills, A.J. and Weatherbee, T. (2005) 'Maslow: man interrupted: reading management theory in context', *Management Decision*, 43(10), 1375–95.
Fanon, F. (1967) *Black Skin, White Masks*. New York, NY: Grove Press.
Fournier, V. and Grey, C. (2000) 'At the critical moment: conditions and prospects for critical management studies', *Human Relations*, 53(1), 7–32.
Frenkel, M. (2008) 'The MNC as a third space: rethinking international management discourse on knowledge transfer through Homi Bhabha', *Academy of Management Review*, 33(4), 924–42.
Frenkel, M. and Shenhav, Y. (2006) 'From binarism back to hybridity: a postcolonial reading of management and organization studies', *Organization Studies*, 27(6), 855–76.
Gallhofer, S. and Chew, A. (2000) 'Introduction: accounting and indigenous peoples', *Accounting, Auditing and Accountability Journal*, 13(3), 256–67.
Gramsci, A. (1971) *Selections from the Prison Notebooks*. New York, NY: International Publishers.
Green, M. (2002) 'Gramsci cannot speak: presentations and interpretations of Gramsci's concept of the subaltern', *Rethinking Marxism*, 14(3), 1–24.
Haraway, D. (1988) 'Situated knowledges: the science question in feminism and the privilege of partial knowledge', *Feminist Studies*, 14(3), 575–99.
hooks, b. (1994) *Teaching to Transgress: Education and the Practice for Freedom*. New York, NY: Routledge.
Ibarra-Colado, E. (2006) 'Organization studies and epistemic coloniality in Latin America: thinking otherness from the margins', *Organization*, 13(4), 463–88.
Jack, G., Westwood, R., Srinivas, N. and Sardar, Z. (2011) 'Deepening, broadening and re-asserting a postcolonial interrogative space in organization studies', *Organization*, 18(3), 275–302.
Joy, S. and Poonamallee, L. (2013) 'Cross-cultural teaching in globalized management classrooms: time to move from functionalist to post-colonial approaches?', *Academy of Management Learning and Education*, 12(3), 396–413.
Kim, S.N. (2008) 'Whose voice is it anyway? Rethinking the oral history method in accounting research on race, ethnicity and gender', *Critical Perspectives on Accounting*, 19(8), 1346–69.
Knights, D. and Willmott, H. (1974) 'Humanistic social science and the theory of needs', *Interpersonal Development*, 5(4), 213–22.
Konrad, A.M. (2005) 'Editorial comment', *Group and Organization Management*, 30(2), 127–8.
Lewis, R. and Mills, S. (2003) 'Introduction'. *In:* R. Lewis and S. Mills (eds.) *Feminist Postcolonial Theory: A Reader*. New York, NY: Routledge, pp. 1–22.
Locke, E.A. and Latham, G.P. (1990) *A Theory of Goal Setting and Task Performance*. Englewood Cliffs, NJ: Prentice Hall.
Lorbiecki, A. and Jack, G. (1999) 'Critical turns in the evolution of diversity management', *British Journal of Management*, 11(S), S17–31.
Maslow, A.H. (1943) 'A theory of human motivation', *Psychological Review*, 50(4), 370–96.
Maslow, A.H. (1970) *Motivation and Personality*. New York, NY: Harper and Row.
Mir, R., Banerjee, S.B. and Mir, A. (2008) 'Hegemony and its discontents: a critical analysis of organizational knowledge transfer', *Critical Perspectives on International Business*, 4(2/3), 203–27.
Moore-Gilbert, B. (1997) *Postcolonial Theory: Contexts, Practices, Politics*. New York, NY: Verso.
Nandy, A. (1983) *The Intimate Enemy: Loss and Recovery of Self under Colonialism*. New Delhi: Oxford University Press.
Neu, D. (2001) 'Banal accounts: subaltern voices', *Accounting Forum*, 25(4), 319–33.
Neu, D. and Heincke, M. (2004) 'The subaltern speaks: financial relations and the limits of governmentality', *Critical Perspectives on Accounting*, 15(1), 179–206.
Norton, A. (2002) *Bloodrites of the Poststructuralists: Word, Flesh and Revolution*. New York, NY: Routledge.
Patai, D. (1987) 'Ethical problems of personal narratives, or, who should eat the last piece of cake?', *International Journal of Oral History*, 8(1), 5–27.

Persram, N. (2007) 'Introduction: pushing politics'. *In:* N. Persram (ed.) *Postcolonialism and Political Theory*. Lanham, MD: Rowman & Littlefield, pp. xi–xlii.

Prasad, A. (1997) 'The colonizing consciousness and representations of the other: a postcolonial critique of the discourse of oil'. *In:* P. Prasad, A.J. Mills, M. Elmes and A. Prasad (eds.) *Managing the Organizational Melting Pot: Dilemmas of Workplace Diversity*. Thousand Oaks, CA: Sage Publications, pp. 285–311.

Prasad, A. (2003) 'The gaze of the other: postcolonial theory and organizational analysis'. *In:* A. Prasad (ed.) *Postcolonial Theory and Organizational Analysis: A Critical Engagement*. New York, NY: Palgrave, pp. 3–43.

Prasad, A. (2006) 'The jewel in the crown: postcolonial theory and workplace diversity'. *In:* A.M. Konrad, P. Prasad and J.K. Pringle (eds.) *Handbook of Workplace Diversity*. Thousand Oaks, CA: Sage Publications, pp. 121–44.

Prasad, A. (2009) 'Contesting hegemony through genealogy: Foucault and cross-cultural management research', *International Journal of Cross Cultural Management*, 9(3), 359–69.

Prasad, A. (2012) 'Working against the grain: beyond Eurocentricism in organization studies'. *In:* A. Prasad (ed.) *Against the Grain: Advances in Postcolonial Organization Studies*. Frederiksberg, Denmark: Copenhagen Business School Press, pp. 13–31.

Prasad, A. (2014) 'You can't go home again: and other psychoanalytic lessons from crossing a neo-colonial border', *Human Relations*, 67(2), 233–57.

Prasad, A. and Mills, A.J. (2010) 'Critical management studies and business ethics: a synthesis and three research trajectories for the coming decade', *Journal of Business Ethics*, 94(S2), 227–37.

Rowlinson, M. and Proctor, S. (1999) 'Organizational culture and business history', *Organization Studies*, 20(3), 369–96.

Said, E.W. (1978) *Orientalism*. New York, NY: Pantheon.

Spivak, G.C. (1988) 'Can the subaltern speak?'. *In:* C. Nelson and L. Grossberg (eds.) *Marxism and the Interpretation of Culture*. Urbana, IL: University of Illinois Press, pp. 271–313.

Thompson, C.J. and Tambyah, S.K. (1999) 'Trying to be cosmopolitan', *Journal of Consumer Research*, 26(3), 214–41.

Ulus, E. (2015) 'Workplace emotions in postcolonial spaces: enduring legacies, ambivalence, and subversion', *Organization*, 22(6), 890–908.

Vroom, V.H. (1964) *Work and Motivation*. New York, NY: Wiley.

Westwood, R.I. and Jack, G. (2007) 'Manifesto for a post-colonial international business and management studies: a provocation', *Critical Perspectives on International Business*, 3(3), 246–65.

Yuval-Davis, N. (1997) *Gender and Nation*. New York, NY: Routledge.

# 34

# Engaging with the contradictions of capitalism

## Teaching 'sustainability' in the business school

*Christopher Wright and Daniel Nyberg*

### Introduction

We live in an era of environmental and social crisis. Humanity's inventiveness has over the past two centuries created unimaginable wealth for a small part of the world's population; however, this has come at a huge environmental cost in terms of biodiversity loss, ocean acidification and climate change – degrading the very ecosystems upon which we depend as a species. In order to be relevant in the future, business schools need to play a central role in confronting this most critical of issues; however, much of what passes for 'sustainability' education remains wedded to a defence of the system that has generated this crisis – free-market capitalism. Naïve best-case scenarios are promoted to justify continuous economic growth and consumption, albeit in a marginally less unsustainable fashion. In this chapter we argue that we are facing a far more profound sustainability challenge.

The chapter explores how sustainability education might contribute to a reimagining of our economic system and the role of business. Based on our experience in developing and teaching sustainability curricula in business schools, we highlight some of the challenges such a concept highlights. For instance, sustainability defies the hierarchy of our thinking in business schools by placing the environment, not the economy or even society, at the centre of our understanding. How might we then reimagine a new hierarchy in which nature sets the boundaries for what is doable and desirable? Genuine sustainability also confronts the idea of a simple market justification for human action. How can we imagine other values and justifications where relations between individuals, society and nature are based on more than market fetishism? Tomorrow's citizens will also need to understand how to manage organizational and social change in an era of unprecedented environmental and social crisis. How can we teach the concept of managing the unmanageable? Although these ideas are heretical to the established order of business education, and hence require that we use materials from the broader arts and social sciences, we argue that they are central to the future relevance of the business school in our changing world.

## Sustainability: the problems we confront and how we got here

Humanity's impact upon nature and the environment has become increasingly evident as a product of our technological innovation, the expansion of consumption and our growing population. Dubbed the 'Great Acceleration' (Steffen *et al.* 2007), human activities since 1950 have not only brought improved health and living standards to many millions around the world, but also irrevocably changed our planet, resulting in an unprecedented degradation of natural resources (McKibben, 2010). In the words of the United Nations Millennium Ecosystem Assessment:

> Over the past 50 years, humans have changed ecosystems more rapidly and extensively than in any comparable period of time in human history, largely to meet rapidly growing demands for food, fresh water, timber, fiber, and fuel. This has resulted in a substantial and largely irreversible loss in the diversity of life on Earth.
>
> *Millennium Ecosystem Assessment 2005: 2*

The dominant factor underlying such environmental degradation has been our species' economic and technological inventiveness, such that we now have the power to fundamentally change the very nature of our atmosphere and ecosystem, with likely catastrophic effects (Anderson and Bows 2008). Indeed, we are currently poised to cross a number of interdependent 'planetary boundaries', including climate change, biodiversity loss, changes to the nitrogen cycle, ozone depletion and ocean acidification (Rockström *et al.* 2009; Whiteman *et al.* 2013). Crossing these boundaries is likely to result in irreversible environmental changes limiting human development. Despite increasing discussion of climate change 'adaptation' and even 'geo-engineering' as a solution to some of these problems (Hamilton 2013), scientific projections emphasize likely catastrophic outcomes from a continuation of 'business as usual'. We are on the track for 3–6 degrees Celsius average global warming by 2100, resulting in a significant rise in sea-levels and likely societal breakdown, with much of this locked in within the next decade or so (Intergovernmental Panel on Climate Change (IPCC) 2013; Stafford Smith *et al.* 2011).

Clearly there is little that is 'sustainable' in our current economic and environmental trajectory. Graphs of greenhouse gas emissions, aggregate consumption patterns and population growth all demonstrate an almost exponential increase over the past four to five decades. The disconnect between our economic imaginary of endless economic growth and the natural limits of our ecosystem is at the heart of the debate about sustainability. Indeed, harking back to Karl Marx's original observations about capitalism's reliance on the unending exploitation of nature (Foster 2000), the current destruction of the environment is not so much an unfortunate by-product of industrialization, but rather an essential feature of our dependence upon continued economic growth and the expansion of consumption (Schnaiberg and Gould 1994). This process of environmental destruction aligns with the depiction of capitalism as based upon crises and the 'enforced destruction of a mass of productive forces' (Marx and Engels 1998 [1848]: 42). Later conceived by Schumpeter (2003 [1943]) as a process of 'creative destruction', the technological innovation and entrepreneurship that characterize capitalist dynamism also involve the destruction of previous forms of capital accumulation and natural resources.

Given what is at stake (the future of our society and indeed the existence of our species), you would think this would be an issue of major concern for governments and forward-thinking companies. However, you would be wrong. What has perhaps been even more shocking than the procession of increasingly dire scientific projections of our future has been the collective denial exhibited by governments and industry over the crisis that we now face. Climate change and the broader environmental catastrophe that awaits us is the biggest issue of our time and yet the response from government and business has been to largely ignore the threat. This has partly been the product of the orchestrated misinformation that vested interests (such as the fossil fuel industries) have promoted (Dunlap and McCright 2011); however, it is also the result of the nature of the problem – the hegemonic belief that we are dependent on the global economic system for our quality of life. Perhaps not surprisingly, therefore, the debate over climate change (the most prominent manifestation of our unsustainability) has very quickly become a political lightning rod in a broader culture war (Hoffman 2012).

It is this broader context that informs many of the challenges of teaching sustainability in a university business school. This is the most critical issue we will face in our life-times – and yet it is also hugely controversial, political and ultimately threatening to our conventional view of business, economics and our self-identity as consumers, employees and citizens. So how have business schools responded to the challenge of sustainability we now face?

## What role for the business school in sustainability research and teaching?

Businesses have of course played a key role in the creation of many of the environmental problems we now face. For instance, one recent study has found that nearly two-thirds of the greenhouse gas emissions generated since the dawn of the Industrial Age were caused through the activities of just 90 large companies, including such well-known brands as Chevron, ExxonMobil, Shell, BP and ConocoPhillips. Half of these emissions were produced in the past 25 years, a period in which governments and companies have been well aware of the dangers of anthropogenic climate change (Heede 2014). However, just as businesses have been the major (and knowing) contributors to our current environmental crisis, so many observers look to business as the actor best placed to respond to these threats through technological innovation and economic reinvention. Indeed, concepts of 'ecological modernism' and 'corporate environmentalism' in which businesses are seen as contributors to environmental well-being have become increasingly evident, not only in academic circles (Mol and Sonnenfeld 2000; Mol and Spaargaren 2000), but also amongst consultants and businesses themselves (Esty and Winston 2006; Orsato 2009).

For business schools, consideration of social and environmental issues has traditionally been given short shrift. In reviewing the history of the business school as an institution, its purpose was seen in largely instrumental terms: to educate future managers in the technical and functional skills central to their future role as custodians of shareholder capital. Invariably this led to a focus on the teaching of finance, accounting, operational efficiency, strategy and organizational behaviour. Echoing the concerns of neoclassical economist Milton Friedman (1970: 33), business schools concurred that 'the social responsibility of business is to increase its profits' (see also Siegel 2009). Where controversy did exist, this focused less on the business school's social impact and more on the relative weighting of applied skills as opposed to management theory (Khurana 2007). For example, recent critics of the burgeoning Masters of Business Administration (MBA) programmes argued that US business schools focused too much on the teaching of the 'science' of management to inexperienced young graduates, ignoring the need for organizational experience and reflection (Mintzberg 2004; see Srinivas, this volume). Although these are important insights, simply getting managers to reflect on their experience says little about the substance of such reflection beyond better ways to maximize profits and shareholder value.

Rather than change coming from within business education, in the past decade or so a range of external factors have driven a reconsideration of the need to better consider social and environmental concerns in business school curricula. For instance, a procession of corporate corruption scandals (for example, Enron, WorldCom, Northern Rock, Lehman Brothers), human rights abuses (for example, Nike and Apple supply chains, Raza Plaza) and the ongoing global economic crisis, have led many to point the finger of blame at deficiencies in the way business leaders are themselves educated (Podolny 2009). In addition to a recognition of the need to better address issues of business ethics, business educators have also focused increasing attention on corporate social responsibility (CSR) and sustainability (Christensen *et al.* 2007). Evidence for such change can be seen in the growing number of business schools that now promote CSR and sustainability courses in their MBA programmes. Initiatives include the development of new courses on sustainability and social entrepreneurship (some programmes even seek to embed a minimum percentage of sustainability issues in all core programmes), as well as specialist degree programmes, such as so-called 'Green MBAs' (Runnalls 2013; see Barinaga, this volume).

Sustainability issues therefore appear to have become fashionable in many US and European business schools, and some have sought to make business ethics and sustainability a point of differentiation in their marketing to potential students and corporate sponsors. Indeed, there are influential backers for such a trend. In responding to the growing social criticism of global capitalism, leading management authorities such as Professor Michael Porter from Harvard and Dominic Barton, Managing Partner of leading management consultancy McKinsey & Co., have argued for a new approach to corporate–social relations. In Porter's case, this has involved a focus on corporate environmental concerns (Porter and van der Linde 1995), as well as his more recent promotion of the concept of 'creating shared value' (CSV), billed in *Harvard Business Review* as the answer to 'how to fix capitalism – and unleash a new wave of growth' (Porter and Kramer 2011). For management consultancy, the need for a new approach is driven by the fear that 'Business leaders today face a choice: We can reform capitalism, or we can let capitalism be reformed for us, through political measures and the pressures of an angry public' (Barton 2011). These calls have been matched by activity within corporations worldwide, evident in the growth of new sustainability functions and practices within corporations (Hoffman 2007; Wright *et al.* 2012). This is not simply 'greenwashing' and 'spin' but often strategic and operational programmes aimed at improving efficiencies and supply chain synergies, reducing costs and carbon footprints, attracting and retaining staff, and developing new products and markets (Dauvergne and Lister 2013; Lash and Wellington 2007). This has extended to increasing political activity as 'corporate citizens' seeking to shape legislative outcome, and the promotion of business as a 'leader' in social and environmental action (Barley 2007; Nyberg, Spicer, and Wright 2013).

However, there is also much about the 'mainstreaming' of sustainability in business schools that is problematic for critical scholars. In particular, in embracing sustainability, business gurus and educators are often explicit about the limits of such engagement. Businesses need to do this, we are told, in order to respond to the critique of their activities, to restore their 'social licence to operate' and, most importantly, as a source of future value creation (Porter and Kramer 2011). Business engagement with sustainability, therefore, is essentially a form of risk management. Much as corporations sought to incorporate earlier forms of social criticism by accepting and then adapting critique for their own purposes (Boltanski and Chiapello 2005), so we can see the incorporation of sustainability in a similar manner. Capturing the terminology of sustainability allows for some level of definitional closure and a limiting of the true potential of a sustainability critique (a theme we return to in the next section of this chapter).

Second, in promoting 'sustainability', businesses and business schools explicitly frame this as a source of value creation. This caveat is evident in the dominant discourse of the 'business case'. Although promoters stress the many 'win–win' outcomes that are being achieved by major companies through their sustainability initiatives (Esty and Winston 2006; Orsato 2009), this raises the question of what happens when there is no 'business case' for action (Banerjee 2008).

Although sustainability texts make much of the 'three pillars' of sustainability (economic, social and environmental), in practice these are rarely accorded parity and the economic is implicitly defined as the dominant concern. Indeed, in our own research we have found that where the interests of the market conflict with the environment (or society), the former invariably wins out (Nyberg and Wright 2013). As a result, the enactment of corporate sustainability involves a steady 'corruption' of the good of the environment in favour of the market. This is despite the obvious fact that as environmental economist Herman Daly (1992: 25) noted many years ago, 'what use is a sawmill without a forest?' (see also Brown, this volume). Indeed, as John Ehrenfeld argues, what we are often really talking about in the corporate re-conceptualization of sustainability is being just a little less 'unsustainable':

> It is encouraging to see firms show that they are thinking about sustainability, but they have got it mostly or completely wrong. My concern is not that this new awareness is the wrong thing to do, but it can, at best, produce only incremental Band-Aids ... At worst, they are creating harm by fooling us into thinking we are solving the problem.
>
> *Ehrenfeld and Hoffman 2013: 50–1*

In this sense Milton Friedman, if he were alive today, would probably be fairly happy with the direction of corporate actions regarding social and environmental 'responsibilities' and even perhaps business schools' embrace of sustainability as a subject of study. Sustainability as conceived of within corporate environmentalism aims at improving business profitability whilst potentially being a 'little less unsustainable'. There is no danger that these corporate initiatives will harm shareholder value, but their positive social and environmental impacts remain at best a useful coincidence. Change from such initiatives remains incremental and based on existing understandings of 'business as usual'; however, in claiming some greater impact, this vision of sustainability is also potentially harmful in convincing civil society that it is sufficient to deal with the critical social and environmental problems we now face (Wright and Nyberg 2014).

## Towards a critical teaching of sustainability in business schools

So what might alternative possibilities in teaching sustainability in the business school look like and how might we move forward in building a genuine critical approach to this issue? We don't pretend to have the answers here; however, we can reflect on our own experience in developing specialist masters courses on organizational sustainability in business schools at the University of Sydney and the University of Nottingham. In developing these programmes we have used a number of methods to both frame our focus on sustainability in ways that placate faculty gatekeepers, and yet also build student enthusiasm for the empirical specifics of social and environmental challenges, as well as deeper conceptual complexities.

Our first point is that sustainability, if taken seriously, is potentially a heretical and even possibly a revolutionary concept. Clearly this comes back to how 'sustainability' is defined and how the implications of this definition are drawn out. Indeed, this is often where we have started our sustainability teaching: going back to a very basic understanding of the concept of sustainability and then unpacking what this might mean for our understanding of business and capitalism more broadly. For instance, in contrast to the mainstream interpretation of 'sustainability' in which social and environmental values are compromised in favour of the market, we suggest sustainability is better understood as the ability of humanity and its economic activities to live within the carrying capacity of the planet. This framing draws on the classic definition of sustainable development proposed by the Brundtland Commission in 1987, '... development that meets the needs of the present without compromising the ability of future generations to meet their own needs' (World Commision on Environment and Development 1987: 44). However, we also stress the growing scientific evidence that we are now exceeding planetary boundaries (Whiteman *et al.* 2013). For instance, humanity globally is consuming the equivalent of one and a half planets' worth of resources every year (and for those in the developed economies like the US, the equivalent of four planet Earths!) (Global Footprint Network 2011). This ecological overshoot continues to grow as our population and consumption expand. Moreover, our current economic thinking is reliant on ever-continuing growth; hence, the concept of living within the carrying capacity of the plant is, despite its physical necessity, revolutionary. It challenges the very basis of our economic system (Jackson 2009).

Given this, a common opening discussion in our sustainability teaching is whether 'sustainability', as we are defining it, is in fact possible in an economic system reliant upon 'unending' material economic growth. Core concepts we include here are Kenneth Boulding's metaphor of 'spaceship Earth' (Boulding 1966), the 'tragedy of the commons' (Hardin 1968), the limits to growth (Meadows *et al.* 1972) and a more realistic depiction of the 'triple bottom-line' conception of sustainability in which environmental well-being underpins the existence of society and within that, an economy (Elkington 1997). Beginning the teaching of sustainability from these basic, and interdisciplinary, concepts is essential in breaking the established paradigms of 'business as usual' and also questioning the assumptions that we uncritically accept in business education. This therefore opens up space to query other features of global consumer capitalism, in particular the normalization of hyper-consumption and how this blinds us to the broader connectivity of our actions (Hamilton and Denniss 2005; Wood 2012). Going to the heart of what 'sustainability' means forces students to reconsider the nature of our economic system and the inherent unsustainability of our way of life. If anything, this is perhaps the long-term objective of our teaching in these types of courses: allowing students to go to a more fundamental questioning of business and capitalism and relate this back to their own personal values and goals.

Pointing out the limits to finite resources limits the possibility to promote sustainability within the conventional 'win–win' optimism of corporate environmentalism. Framing the social and economic within environmental boundaries also enables us to delve deeper in exploring the contradictions of sustainability as popularly understood. For example, one exercise we often use to demonstrate the problem of a neoclassical economic understanding of the 'tragedy of the commons' is the 'fishing game' (Hardin 1968; Prothero 2011). Here students in groups act out the role of atomistic businesses competing with their colleagues for a finite fish stock under time pressure (they are racing to collect paper clips on a table that represent fish in the ocean). In the context of a game in which they first believe the winner takes all, they quickly deplete the 'fish' on the table and then realize there is little left to enable regrowth for the next 'season' (round two of the game). By allowing students to then talk to one another and collaborate, students realize some of the advantages of collaboration and the need to manage scarce resources. We supplement this activity with videos, readings and social media on fisheries management, the debate over 'sustainable fisheries' and other relevant examples. Considering planetary boundaries, this particular example can then be used to discuss a range of sustainability issues, such as climate change, ocean acidification, fresh water and land use. Following Hardin (1968), the key lesson is that there are no easy technical solutions *deus ex machina*. Moral and social developments are required to live sustainably in a resource-constrained world.

Considering that there are no technical solutions, how can we think differently about the dire state we are in? This arguably requires shifting our understanding away from the impersonal, apolitical and technical thinking underpinning business schools towards the 'subjective, situated and normative imaginations of human actors' (Jasanoff 2010: 235). Considering the grip of free-market capitalism, it is as Jameson (2003: 73) noted 'easier to imagine the end of the world than to imagine the end of capitalism'. Taking our cue from Jameson, is it possible to engage in alternative imaginings of the present, both from the future and the past? In challenging students to imagine an alternative present, the history of science and fiction provide useful resources (see De Cock, this volume). For instance, Oreskes and Conway (2014) blend science fiction with history to imagine a future historian looking back on a climate-changed past that is our present. The future historian concludes that the ideological fixation on free-market capitalism disabled any action on climate change with disastrous results. The view from the future is a powerful heuristic device to imagine alternative presents. Another alternative is to use fiction to imagine a future. For instance, Margaret Atwood's *MaddAddam* (2003, 2009, 2013) trilogy is speculative fiction about environmental destruction that allows students to imagine the future of the present trajectory. Atwood is adamant that she is not writing science fiction because everything that happens in the trilogy is possible and parts of the events she depicts may already have happened (Atwood 2011). This is how creative arts can help a student to extrapolate imaginatively from current trends and stretch these to a near future. Other novels that fulfil a similar purpose for students are Cormac McCarthy's *The Road* (2006) and Kim Stanley Robinson's trilogy (*Forty Signs of Rain* (2004); *Fifty Degrees Below* (2005); *Sixty Days and Counting* (2007) on a climate-changed future.

The alternative to imagining a different present is to use the past. In doing this, we have found Jared Diamond's (2005) *Collapse: How Societies Choose to Fail or Succeed* helpful. Diamond (2005) uses the history of previous civilizations (from the Polynesian cultures on Easter Island to the flourishing American civilizations of the Anasazi and the Maya, to the doomed Viking colony on Greenland) to forecast our current suicidal tendencies on a societal scale. The parallels between previous collapses and our present situation can help students to think and talk about, current issues such as climate change. The past can be used as a resource to imagine the devastating consequences of current environmental destruction, but also to challenge that which blinds us from seeing the obvious parallels. What are the functions of present stories and narratives in 'hiding' what is in plain view – that we are heading towards environmental and social crisis?

Using these alternatives to imagine the present, students are equipped to challenge our narrow thinking in business schools in regards to the workings of capitalism and corporate strategies. With an emphasis on the role of business, the programmes and courses can then set out to answer the question: why, despite evidence of emerging sustainability crises, has humanity been so reticent to respond in some meaningful way to avert disasters? Following this, sustainability requires us to rethink or reimagine how we conceptualize business at different levels of student experiences: societal, organizational and individual. The topicality of sustainability, with examples emerging daily from media, ensures that students recognize the challenges and complexities these issues bring to each of these levels of reflections. Using creative arts and other disciplines allows a broader horizon in understanding these complexities. Since space does not allow us to discuss curricula in detail, the following paragraphs are indications of issues raised in teaching sustainability courses.

On a societal, or even global level, sustainability challenges, such as climate change, ocean acidification and freshwater usage, represent truly complex problems. Sorting out the distribution of responsibility and consequences on a global scale in terms of present and future generations, developed and less developed nations, and biodiversity loss without a global jurisdiction or consensus, requires compromises with disastrous effects. For business students it is essential that they understand corporate roles in adapting to and influencing societal and global constraints in dealing with sustainability. For example, corporations are increasingly facing carbon emission targets and trading schemes (Newell and Paterson 2010). These are frameworks affecting business decisions, both in terms of adapting to the external environment and influencing it through political activities, such as lobbying, funding think-tanks, astroturfing and media campaigns (Dunlap and McCright 2011; Nyberg *et al.* 2013). The evaluations of these types of activities are well suited for class debates and group discussions. We have also engaged students in acting out multi-stakeholder meetings and deliberations over proposed legislation, developments (for example, fracking, tar sands) and distributions (for example, quotas, tax, market mechanisms), with students playing corporate, government, regulatory and community roles.

On an organizational or industry level, it is possible to frame the course from the perspective of mainstream business strategy: what are the key business risks and opportunities that businesses face in the next 10 to 20 years? As we pointed out earlier, it is not hard to make the case that issues such as climate change, planetary boundaries and population growth pose profound risks for businesses. Sustainability shapes the resource-constrained world that businesses operate in, and here we engage students in classifying different risks that corporations and industries are facing. For example, using the case of anthropogenic climate change, how might some of the second- and third-order impacts of different 'climate change' scenarios impact on different industries and businesses? Here we have used brainstorming and scenario planning exercises around examples such as:

- risk management for resource, manufacturing and insurance companies for projected increases in extreme weather events such as hurricanes, typhoons and superstorms (for example, Superstorm Sandy, the 2012 Bangkok floods and Typhoon Haiyan) (C2ES 2013; Linnenluecke *et al.* 2013);
- strategic planning for defence and national security contractors of climate change as a 'threat multiplier' regarding increasing geopolitical conflict over scarce resources such as water, climate refugees or access to newly available fossil fuels (Dyer 2010);
- implications for the health industry from changed disease vectors and potential pandemics via a warming climate (Martens 2013);
- scenario planning for major financial institutions of 'stranded assets' and risks to investments in fossil fuel extraction and use (Carbon Tracker Initiative 2012).

The conclusion of this type of exercise is that all corporations and industries are facing major strategic challenges in regards to their own and others' sustainability.

On an individual or community level, we are reluctant to promote 'green consumerist' discourses because this reinforces a simple green capitalism message (Hamilton 2010). Rather, we engage students in identifying dissonance between individual practices and beliefs and the identity crises that occur in seeking to narrate a coherent self in a period of ecological crisis (Festinger 1962; Ricœur 1991). Considering the possible fragmentation of our beliefs, identities and interests within consumer society, class discussion often surfaces a variety of sustainability issues around consumption, transportation and energy and water usage. Here we also allow for self-reflection in terms of how students themselves justify their consumption patterns despite understanding the importance of sustainability. Students are also given 'tools' to analyse how they reconcile cognitive dissonance and identity fractions. Examples of frameworks for reflection include Hirschman's (1970) model of 'exit, voice and loyalty'; how we tamper with or disregard information (Hamilton 2010); the development of narrative genres or plots (Wright *et al.* 2012); and the use of metaphors and metonyms in bridging identity fragmentation (Nyberg and Sveningsson, 2014).

The discussion of identity work allows students to explore how they can act as change agents within corporations and through social movements, link their personal values with their professional lives and decode some of the ethical dilemmas we face in an age of resource scarcity. Indeed, the emergence of sustainability discourses has also led to the formation of new roles and departments within organizations dealing explicitly with sustainability issues. Although positions such as environmental managers and sustainability consultants are now legitimate within business settings, engaging with sustainability challenges the dominant and privileged discourses of shareholder value and economic growth (Wright and Nyberg, 2012; Wright *et al.* 2012). These positions, similar to engaging with social movements, are therefore political positions in personifying change and influencing others. The aim of these discussions is to prepare students for challenging mainstream business 'thinking', meeting criticism and dealing with doubts and uncertainty in an emotional and volatile organizational and political context.

Finally, developing this more critical understanding of sustainability requires an inherently eclectic academic orientation that goes well beyond the usual business framings. Although we have developed a critical political–economy perspective on business sustainability linked to critiques of capitalism and neoliberalism (Wright and Nyberg 2015), in our teaching we also emphasize insights from the fields of environmental politics, geography, sociology, history and critical social theory. Engaging with the broader social sciences and humanities is essential in challenging business students' often limited understandings of the world and exposing them to a very different form of writing and sense making. In contrast to the beloved Harvard case method with its formulaic approach, we believe far greater value lies in exposing students to works such as Rachel Carson's *Silent Spring* (1962) or Aldo Leopold's *A Sand County Almanac* (1966). These works not only address sustainability, but they do so through a personal style that blends literature and political advocacy. Getting students to read these founding classics in parallel with contemporary activists such as Bill McKibben (1989, 2010) and Naomi Klein (2014), or viewing films such as *Gasland* (Fox 2010) or *Bidder 70* (Gage 2012) offers insights into a world that business studies rarely comprehends – the world of wonder, beauty, compassion, loss, fear and anger as our environment is exploited and degraded. These works offer the opportunity to promote a very different subjectivity to that encouraged in traditional business studies: less a concern with the self and provoking a greater awareness of community.

## Future challenges in teaching sustainability in the business school

There continue to be significant constraints and challenges to the teaching of a more critical conception of sustainability within the business school. Unlike an arts or social science faculty, the business school purpose is often defined in narrower terms: educating managers, or those who aspire to be managers, and undertaking research that benefits the business community. Sometimes it can be even more instrumental: as a former Dean stated to one of the authors, 'it's all about how we make businesses more efficient and effective'. Often there will be some acknowledgement that this also includes other social actors such as government, not-for-profit organizations and non-government organizations; however, in practice most business schools seem to focus their attention on the big graduate employers – financial and professional service firms, manufacturing, resource and fast-moving consumer goods companies – the 'big end of town' (see Parker, this volume). A first constraint to consider is therefore the extent to which the purpose of the business school allows space for (or tolerates) challenging and critical perspectives of sustainability?.

In practice, the degree to which such heretical thinking is allowed in the curriculum varies from institution to institution. As we have seen, there are many business schools worldwide that are now focusing on sustainability as a central feature of their teaching and research and use this as a point of differentiation in their marketing and promotion. Moreover, individual academics may be able to develop a consideration of sustainability in their teaching of individual courses. Against this, however, is the increasing tendency towards centralized control over curriculum design, evident in the process of business school accreditation, and the potential for direct intervention by more senior colleagues regarding what should be taught. This can become particularly vexed in the 'turf wars' that often accompany curriculum discussions over 'core' courses (see Eberle and Metelmann, this volume). Here discussion will often come back to debates over 'what is nice to know and what students need to know'. A topic such as 'sustainability', which lacks a defined disciplinary home, is often at a marked disadvantage in the competitive battle for 'core' programme space. This is even more likely when it proposes a fundamental critique of the institutions and economic system that the business school is charged with upholding!

Beyond the potential marginalization of sustainability in business school curricula, it is likely that when sustainability is taught, Deans and senior administrators will prefer a soothing message and ideally one that emphasizes the 'win–win' outcomes that dominate 'green business' and corporate environmental messaging (Wright and Nyberg 2014). Here, the business school fulfils the ideological purpose of political myth narration – that we can have economic growth and hyper-consumption and that technological innovation and market mechanisms will solve any resulting environmental and social problems. This is of course an appealing message but, as we suggested earlier, ultimately counter-productive in dealing with the urgent environmental crisis we are now facing. One strategy to counter this slippage is perhaps to broaden our imaginations in confronting where this view leads us. It is important to situate the current narrow thinking in an expanded temporality. It is only then that students can confront the implications of current trajectories. For specific industries and businesses, using the language of business 'risk' and 'opportunity', although potentially problematic, does provide a framing that can potentially engage business people and students of business. The 'burning platform', so beloved of organizational change theorists (Kotter 1995), becomes a very apt metaphor for broader social and political change.

Finally, there are individual constraints upon business school academics embracing a more critical view of sustainability. In particular, as the academic labour market has become increasingly competitive (and determined largely on individuals' abilities to publish in so-called 'top tier' journals), so the risks for younger academics of researching and teaching outside the mainstream increase. Within the 'top-tier' (largely US) business and management journals, sustainability issues remain fringe areas of interest. For instance, business academic discussion of critical environmental issues such as climate change is rare and, despite the significant business implications, often limited to journal special issues (Okereke *et al.* 2012; Wittneben *et al.* 2012; Wright *et al.* 2013). Where sustainability issues are addressed, these invariably take the form of buying into the 'mainstreaming' of sustainability as a contributor to business success (that is, improved profitability and shareholder value). Indeed, the growing adoption of journal rankings and academic assessment exercises, such as the UK Research Excellence Framework (REF) or the Excellence in Research for Australia (ERA) are having a profound impact on even critical management scholars, who in the chase for a 'top-tier' publication often tone down the critical intent of their work (Butler and Spoelstra 2014).

Moreover, the few journals that do publish critical research on sustainability appear endangered under the commercial imperative of publishers seeking to maximize their 'impact factors'. A good example of this process occurred recently at the journal *Organization and Environment*. Founded in 1987, *Organization and Environment* was one of the leading journals bridging the fields of environmental sociology, critical social theory and organization studies. In 2012, the journal's publisher, SAGE, announced a revamp of the journal and the replacement of its editors with the aim of increasing submissions and the journal's impact. For the previous editors, these changes came as a surprise and led to accusations that the publisher had undertaken 'an editorial coup designed to displace environmental sociology and a leftist critique of environmental issues with an emphasis on the more business-friendly concept of sustainability'. Indeed, the publisher's actions led to the wholesale resignation of the journal's broader editorial board (Angus 2012). As one-time co-editor and contributor to the journal John Bellamy Foster lamented:

> *O&E* is being transformed from a self-designated 'eco-social' journal with strong links both to critical organizations theory and environmental sociology to one in which environmental sociology will be excluded, in favor of a sustainability-management (or green-capitalist) policy orientation . . . This represents a major setback for environmental sociology, if not environmental social science as a whole.
>
> *Jaschik 2012*

This example highlights how mainstream 'business-friendly' depictions of sustainability can in fact result in a further narrowing of critical thinking and the potential of sustainability teaching to challenge business as usual. One response to this narrowing of publication outlets for a critical understanding of sustainability in business and management is to look to other disciplines such as critical social theory, sociology, politics and geography, although the career implications of such choices are unclear.

## Conclusion

Our experiences in teaching sustainability in a business school have evolved from our research interests in areas such as climate change and business ethics and, as a result, are somewhat idiosyncratic. Nevertheless, they are driven by a strong belief that sustainability is a critical issue for students to be aware of, think about and hopefully act upon in their roles as managers and citizens. Moreover, we think sustainability is an ideal space to expand critical management studies in the business school because the concept lends itself to deeper questioning of the nature of our economic system and its relationship to society and the natural environment. Sustainability challenges the hierarchy of our thinking in the business school. Sustainability places the environment in the centre of analysis, rather than the economy, or even society. Although the market has a role to play and human ingenuity can help, the best responses to the numerous environmental crises we face, such as biodiversity loss, ocean acidification and climate change, would be to reduce our consumption of the environment; however, with an increasing world population and affluence, this solution is not imaginable. How can we reimagine a business school where economics, or even human beings, are not in the centre of decision making?

This type of question provokes numerous challenges in understanding the role of societies, business schools and ourselves as employees, consumers and citizens. We need to reimagine the hierarchies where nature, rather than the economy or society, sets the boundaries for what is doable and desirable. We need to reimagine production and consumption where relations between individuals and society, as well as people and nature, are not based on the ever-increasing consumption of natural resources. And we need to reimagine the role of the business school, and the knowledges produced by the wider university, in managing the unmanageable. Environmental crisis has illustrated clearly that we cannot 'manage' the environment – we need to build new relations based on new verbs where human mastery of nature is not taken for granted. The role of business schools, therefore, would be to understand the limits to growth, how to let the environment 'manage' the market, provide meaning to identity projects and relations that are not based on material consumption and develop truly sustainable businesses. Less unsustainable is not sustainable. Are we up for the challenge?

## References


Anderson, K. and Bows, A. (2008) 'Reframing the climate change challenge in light of post-2000 emission trends', *Philosophical Transactions A*, 366(1882), 3863–82.

Angus, I. (2012) 'Environmental journal editors reply to publisher', *Climate and Capitalism*, 1 November. Available from: http://climateandcapitalism.com/2012/11/01/environmental-journal-editors-reply-to-publisher/ (accessed 21 March 2014).

Atwood, M. (2003) *Oryx and Crake*. London: Bloomsbury.

Atwood, M. (2009) *The Year of the Flood*. London: Bloomsbury.

Atwood, M. (2011) 'The road to ustopia', *The Guardian*, 15 October. Available from: www.theguardian.com/books/2011/oct/14/margaret-atwood-road-to-ustopia (accessed 30 October 2014).

Atwood, M. (2013) *Madd Addam*. London: Bloomsbury.

Banerjee, S.B. (2008) 'Corporate social responsibility: the good, the bad and the ugly', *Critical Sociology*, 34(1), 51–79.

Barley, S.R. (2007) 'Corporations, democracy, and the public good', *Journal of Management Inquiry*, 16(3), 201–15.

Barton, D. (2011) 'Capitalism for the long term', *Harvard Business Review*, 89(3), 84–91.

Boltanski, L. and Chiapello, E. (2005) *The New Spirit of Capitalism*. London: Verso.

Boulding, K.E. (1966) 'The economics of the coming spaceship earth'. *In:* H. Jarrett (ed.) *Environmental Quality in a Growing Economy*. Baltimore, MD: Johns Hopkins University Press, pp. 3–14.

Butler, N. and Spoelstra, S. (2014) 'The regime of excellence and the erosion of ethos in critical management studies', *British Journal of Management*, 25(3), 538–50.

C2ES (2013) *Weathering the Storm: Building Business Resilience to Climate Change*. Arlington, VA: Center for Climate and Energy Solutions.

Carbon Tracker Initiative (CTI) (2012) *Unburnable Carbon: Are the World's Financial Markets Carrying a Carbon Bubble?*. London: Carbon Tracker Initiative.

Carson, R. (1962) *Silent Spring*. Boston, MA: Houghton Mifflin.

Christensen, L., Peirce, E., Hartman, L., Hoffman, W.M. and Carrier, J. (2007) 'Ethics, CSR, and sustainability education in the Financial Times Top 50 Global Business Schools: baseline data and future research directions', *Journal of Business Ethics*, 73(4), 347–68.

Daly, H.E. (1992) 'From empty-world economics to full-world economics: recognizing an historical turning point in economic development'. *In:* R. Goodland, H.E. Daly and S. El Serafy (eds.) *Population, Technology, and Lifestyle: The Transition to Sustainability*. Washington, DC: Island Press, pp. 23–37.

Dauvergne, P. and Lister, J. (2013) *Eco-Business: A Big-Brand Takeover of Sustainability*. Cambridge, MA: MIT Press.

Diamond, J.M. (2005) *Collapse: How Societies Choose to Fail or Succeed*. New York, NY: Viking.

Dunlap, R.E. and McCright, A.M. (2011) 'Organized climate change denial'. *In:* J.S. Dryzek, R.B. Norgaard and Schlosberg, D. (eds.) *The Oxford Handbook of Climate Change and Society*. Oxford: Oxford University Press, pp. 144–60.

Dyer, G. (2010) *Climate Wars: The Fight for Survival as the World Overheats*. Oxford: Oneworld.

Ehrenfeld, J.R. and Hoffman, A.J. (2013) *Flourishing: A Frank Conversation about Sustainability*. Stanford, CA: Greenleaf Publishing.

Elkington, J. (1997) *Cannibals with Forks: The Triple Bottom Line of 21st Century Business*. Oxford: Capstone.

Esty, D.C. and Winston, A.S. (2006) *Green to Gold: How Smart Companies Use Environmental Strategy to Innovate, Create Value, and Build Competitive Advantage*. Hoboken, NJ: John Wiley & Sons.

Festinger, L. (1962) *A Theory of Cognitive Dissonance*. Stanford, CA: Stanford University Press.

Foster, J.B. (2000) *Marx's Ecology: Materialism and Nature*. New York, NY: Monthly Review Press.

Fox, J. (2010) *Gasland*. New York, NY: International WOW Company.

Friedman, M. (1970) 'The social responsibility of business is to increase its profits', *New York Times Magazine*, 33.

Gage, B. (2012) *Bidder 70*. New York, NY: First Run Features.

Global Footprint Network (GFN) (2011) *What Happens When an Infinite-Growth Economy Runs into a Finite Planet? Global Footprint Network 2011 Annual Report*. Oakland, CA: Global Footprint Network.

Hamilton, C. (2010) *Requiem for a Species: Why We Resist the Truth about Climate Change*. London: Earthscan.

Hamilton, C. (2013) *Earthmasters: Playing God with the Climate*. Sydney: Allen & Unwin.

Hamilton, C. and Denniss, R. (2005) *Affluenza: When Too Much Is Never Enough*. Sydney: Allen & Unwin.

Hardin, G. (1968) 'The tragedy of the commons', *Science*, 162(3859), 1243–48.

Heede, R. (2014) 'Tracing anthropogenic carbon dioxide and methane emissions to fossil fuel and cement producers, 1854–2010', *Climatic Change*, 122(1–2), 229–41.

Hirschman, A.O. (1970) *Exit, Voice and Loyalty: Responses to Decline in Firms, Organizations and States*. Cambridge, MA: Harvard University Press.

Hoffman, A.J. (2007) *Carbon Strategies: How Leading Companies are Reducing their Climate Change Footprint*. Ann Arbor, MI: University of Michigan Press.

Hoffman, A.J. (2012) 'Climate science as culture war', *Stanford Social Innovation Review*, 10(4), 30–7.

Intergovernmental Panel on Climate Change (IPCC) (2013) *Climate Change 2013: The Physical Science Basis*. Geneva: Intergovernmental Panel on Climate Change.

Jackson, T. (2009) *Prosperity without Growth: Economics for a Finite Planet*. London: Earthscan.

Jameson, F. (2003) 'Future city', *New Left Review*, 21(May–June), 65–80.

Jasanoff, S. (2010) 'A new climate for society', *Theory, Culture and Society*, 27(2–3), 233–53.

Jaschik, S. (2012) 'Coup at environmental journal?' *Inside Higher Ed*, 29 October. Available from: www.insidehighered.com/news/2012/10/29/editorial-board-quits-protest-changes-environmental-journal (accessed 21 March 2014).

Khurana, R. (2007) *From Higher Aims to Hired Hands: The Social Transformation of American Business Schools and the Unfulfilled Promise of Management as a Profession*. Princeton, NJ: Princeton University Press.

Klein, N. (2014) *This Changes Everything: Capitalism vs the Climate*. New York, NY: Simon & Schuster.

Kotter, J. (1995) 'Leading change: why transformation efforts fail', *Harvard Business Review*, 73(2), 59–67.

Lash, J. and Wellington, F. (2007) 'Competitive advantage on a warming planet', *Harvard Business Review*, 85(3), 94–102.

Leopold, A. (1966) *A Sand County Almanac: With Other Essays on Conservation from Round River*. New York, NY: Oxford University Press.

Linnenluecke, M.K., Griffiths, A. and Winn, M.I. (2013) 'Firm and industry adaptation to climate change: a review of climate adaptation studies in the business and management field', *Wiley Interdisciplinary Reviews: Climate Change*, 4(5), 397–416.

McCarthy, C. (2006) *The Road*. London: Picador.

McKibben, B. (1989) *The End of Nature*. New York, NY: Random House.

McKibben, B. (2010) *Eaarth: Making a Life on a Tough New Planet*. New York, NY: Times Books.

Martens, P. (2013) *Health and Climate Change: Modelling the Impacts of Global Warming and Ozone Depletion*. London: Routledge.

Marx, K. and Engels, F. (1998 [1848]) *The Communist Manifesto: A Modern Edition*. New York, NY: Verso.

Meadows, D.H., Meadows, D.L., Randers, J. and Behrens, W.W. (1972) *The Limits to Growth*. New York, NY: Potomac Associates.

Millennium Ecosystem Assessment (2005) *Ecosystems and Human Well-Being: Synthesis*. Washington, DC: Island Press.

Mintzberg, H. (2004) *Managers not MBAs: A Hard Look at the Soft Practice of Managing and Management Development*. San Francisco, CA: Berrett-Koehler.

Mol, A.P. and Sonnenfeld, D.A. (2000) 'Ecological modernisation around the world: an introduction'. *In:* A.P. Mol and D.A. Sonnenfeld (eds.) *Ecological Modernisation around the World: Perspectives and Critical Debates*. London: Frank Cass, pp. 3–14.

Mol, A.P.J. and Spaargaren, G. (2000) 'Ecological modernisation theory in debate: a review', *Environmental Politics*, 9(1), 17–49.

Newell, P. and Paterson, M. (2010) *Climate Capitalism: Global Warming and the Transformation of the Global Economy*. Cambridge: Cambridge University Press.

Nyberg, D. and Sveningsson, S. (2014) 'Paradoxes of authentic leadership: leader identity struggles', *Leadership*, 10(4), 437–55.

Nyberg, D. and Wright, C. (2013) 'Corporate corruption of the environment: sustainability as a process of compromise', *British Journal of Sociology*, 64(3), 405–24.

Nyberg, D., Spicer, A. and Wright, C. (2013) 'Incorporating citizens: corporate political engagement with climate change in Australia', *Organization*, 20(3), 433–53.

Okereke, C., Wittneben, B. and Bowen, F. (2012) 'Climate change: challenging business, transforming politics', *Business and Society*, 51(1), 7–30.

Oreskes, N. and Conway, E.M. (2014) *The Collapse of Western Civilization: A View from the Future*. New York, NY: Columbia University Press.

Orsato, R.J. (2009) *Sustainability Strategies: When Does It Pay to Be Green?* London: Palgrave Macmillan.

Podolny, J.M. (2009) 'The buck stops (and starts) at business school', *Harvard Business Review*, 87(6), 62–7.

Porter, M.E. and Kramer, M.R. (2011) 'Creating shared value', *Harvard Business Review*, 89(1/2), 62–77.
Porter, M.E. and van der Linde, C. (1995) 'Green and competitive: ending the stalemate', *Harvard Business Review*, 73(5), 120–34.
Prothero, W.A. (2011) 'Tragedy of the commons fisheries management simulation game', American Geophysical Union, Fall Meeting 2011, abstract #ED21D-0602,
Ricœur, P. (1991) 'Narrative identity', *Philosophy Today*, 35(1), 73–81.
Robinson, K.S. (2004) *Forty Signs of Rain*. London: HarperCollins.
Robinson, K.S. (2005) *Fifty Degrees Below*. London: HarperCollins.
Robinson, K.S. (2007) *Sixty Days and Counting*. London: HarperCollins.
Rockström, J., Steffen, W., Noone, K., Persson, Å., Chapin III, F.S., Lambin, E.F., Lenton, T.M., Scheffer, M., Folke, C., Schellnhuber, H.J., Nykvist, B., de Wit, C.A., Hughes, T., van der Leeuw, S., Rodhe, H., Sörlin, S., Snyder, P.K., Costanza, R., Svedin, U., Falkenmark, M., Karlberg, L., Corell, R.W., Fabry, V.J., Hansen, J., Walker, B., Liverman, D., Richardson, K., Crutzen, P. and Foley, J.A. (2009) 'A safe operating space for humanity', *Nature*, 461, 472–5.
Runnalls, J. (2013) 'Charting a new course', *Corporate Knights*. Available from: www.corporateknights.com/report/2013-global-green-mba-survey/charting-new-course (accessed 21 March 2014).
Schnaiberg, A. and Gould, K. (1994) *Environment and Society: The Enduring Conflict*. New York, NY: St Martin's Press
Schumpeter, J. (2003 [1943]) *Capitalism, Socialism and Democracy*. Taylor & Francis e-Library.
Siegel, D.S. (2009) 'Green management matters only if it yields more green: an economic/strategic perspective', *Academy of Management Perspectives*, 23(3), 5–16.
Stafford Smith, M., Horrocks, L., Harvey, A. and Hamilton, C. (2011) 'Rethinking adaptation for a 4°C world', *Philosophical Transactions of the Royal Society A*, 369(1934), 196–216.
Steffen, W., Crutzen, P.J. and McNeill, J.R. (2007) 'The anthropocene: are humans now overwhelming the great forces of nature?', *AMBIO: A Journal of the Human Environment*, 36(8), 614–21.
Whiteman, G., Walker, B. and Perego, P. (2013) 'Planetary boundaries: ecological foundations for corporate sustainability', *Journal of Management Studies*, 50(2), 307–36.
Wittneben, B.B.F., Okereke, C., Banerjee, S.B. and Levy, D.L. (2012) 'Climate change and the emergence of new organizational landscapes', *Organization Studies*, 33(11), 1431–50.
Wood, G. (2012) 'It's not easy being green: anti-environmental discourse, behavior, and ideology'. *In:* T. Theis and J. Tomkin (eds.) *Sustainability: A Comprehensive Foundation*. Houston, TX: Connexions, pp. 478–83.
World Commision on Environment and Development (1987) *Our Common Future*. Oxford: Oxford University Press.
Wright, C. and Nyberg, D. (2012) 'Working with passion: emotionology, corporate environmentalism and climate change', *Human Relations*, 65(12), 1561–87.
Wright, C. and Nyberg, D. (2014) 'Creative self-destruction: corporate responses to climate change as political myths', *Environmental Politics*, 23(2), 205–23.
Wright, C. and Nyberg, D. (2015) *Climate Change, Capitalism and Corporations: Processes of Creative Self-Destruction*. Cambridge: Cambridge University Press.
Wright, C., Nyberg, D. and Grant, D. (2012) '"Hippies on the third floor": climate change, narrative identity and the micro-politics of corporate environmentalism', *Organization Studies*, 33(11), 1451–75.
Wright, C., Nyberg, D., De Cock, C. and Whiteman, G. (2013) 'Future imaginings: organizing in response to climate change', *Organization*, 20(5), 647–58.

# 35

# Classroom diversity, infinite potential and the *Bildung* of debt

*Bent Meier Sørensen and Martyna Śliwa*

## Introduction

The deployment of the humanities and social sciences in management education has by now become, if not common, then at least sufficiently frequent for it to constitute a 'body of pedagogic interventions' that takes place across business schools in different countries (see Sullivan, Ehrlich and Colby, this volume). The purpose of our chapter is to problematise the use of humanities in management education in the context of a number of phenomena underlying education within the contemporary business school, and in particular against the increasingly prevalent phenomenon of student debt. Debt already 'weighs' upon students as they enter the world of work, itself infused and changed by 'the new spirit of capitalism', which has brought with it, for example, the passionate body and the assertive bodily comportments as central to labour on account of this passion's connection to creativity and excess; the eschewing of routines and the production of scenic emergence and unique character; and the shift from discipline to control, that is from the confined body to excessive and continuous modulation. These changes in the world of work, combined with the ubiquity of debt amongst individuals who hope to successfully function and build livelihoods within this world, have raised questions about which kind of subjectivity is deemed appropriate for such new labour market premises, and what role the business school can play in the formation of this subjectivity of an indebted, passionate, flexible worker.

In addition to the expectations that the 'brave new world of work' imposes on the 'working body', and the possible implications this has for the form and content of management education, the composition of the 'student body' has also changed. Globalisation, economic growth and commodification of education have resulted in previously unprecedented flows of rather diversely educated students in need of what they believe to be a CV strengthening master's degree from Western management schools. The past four decades of various economic crises have only accelerated this tendency. Many business school courses nowadays are therefore culturally diverse and, in some cases, filled with students coming from a social and educational background very distant from the one in which they have come to study for their management-related degree. This presents those management educators who nurture the ambition to draw on the humanities and social sciences in their educational practice with an additional dilemma.

They need to ponder the relevance of their pedagogy not only in the context of the contemporary labour market, but also in relation to a population of students, who have not previously been exposed to education in the spirit of *Bildung* (or 'self-cultivation') or to universities of the Humboldtian tradition, that is institutions which claim to integrate the arts and sciences with research to achieve general learning.

In our chapter, we take as the point of departure a management course given at a UK university, in which we deployed novels as vehicles of insights into the world of organisation. During the course and the assessment of students' work, it became obvious that the inherently biopolitical frame of this endeavour was by no means clear to the educators. The 'values' of the European humanistic tradition are not part and parcel of everybody's tradition, and the immanent attempt to enforce these values upon the students did to a certain extent happen without either the students or the educators being aware of this process. The chapter will reflect on these insights in the context of the Western tradition of *Bildung* and a Rancièrian 'pedagogy of dissensus' built on 'radical equality'. We argue that Jacques Rancière's ideas about radical equality (see Huault and Perret, this volume) and his emphasis on the need for dis-identification offer the possibilities for problematising and potentially escaping the expectations imposed upon subjectivities by the current structures within the broader society and economy and also work organisations.

## The pedagogic intervention

The idea of drawing on humanities and social sciences in management education is by no means new. In fact, it is not unusual for educators to encourage students to develop their understanding of management and organisation with reference to philosophical texts or popular culture, for example. Our own pedagogic intervention consisted in using literary fiction on an introductory management and organisation course taught to a group of management master's students, the majority of whom did not have a first degree in a management-related discipline and had never worked in an organisation (for a full analysis, see Śliwa *et al.* 2015). Although the content of the weekly lectures drew on chapters from a critical management textbook – specifically Linstead *et al.* (2006) – to familiarise the students with key concepts and theories surrounding organisational culture, structure, power and change, the seminar discussions revolved around material taken from literary novels. We had designed the course based on the assumption that engagement with literary texts would lead to the creation of a learning environment in which management theories and concepts would become better understood and more meaningful to the students compared with a course where assigned readings are a compilation of academic journal articles and purpose-written case studies.

The particular novels from which we had selected extracts as the basis of seminar discussions included Huxley's *Brave New World*, Lodge's *Nice Work* and Orwell's *Animal Farm*. To pass the course, the students were asked to choose a novel, possibly one they knew very well and found suitable for discussing one of the core management concepts explored during the teaching sessions. In addition to analysing their chosen novel through the lens of management and organisation theory, the students were asked to submit, as part of their coursework, a short essay containing their reflections on the course we taught, specifically on the use of literary fiction as a vehicle for learning about management and organisation.

Students' responses varied in relation to the weekly sessions and to the assignment task. For the majority of students, discussing novels in a management course turned into an intellectual and perhaps even transformational adventure. In their reflective essays, they emphasised the advantages of this approach to learning, as illustrated in the excerpts below:

> Using a novel to relate theory to the real world and human nature introduces an element of reality into the context in which the learning is taking place which I feel helps aid a deeper understanding of what it is to manage and to organise.
>
> The most important learning outcome for me is the ability to 'read between the lines'... My views about what it means to manage and organize have changed since there is no 'right' answer, by which all others are 'wrong'. In addition, my attitude to other cultures, professions and individuals has also changed ... I discovered the existence of interaction between management, sociology and psychology.

In the classroom, however, there were also individuals for whom learning about management through literary fiction was not at all an obvious way of knowledge building and sense making. For example, one student stated from the very beginning that he had 'never read a book in (his) life' and that he'd rather choose a film as the basis of his final assignment. We refused to fulfil his request, and not until much later did we reflect on our implicit assumption that there is supposedly something superior about books, as opposed to films, as a vehicle for learning about organisations, and that students enrolled on postgraduate taught programmes should be well accustomed to reading novels. Another student, in her reflective essay, described the problems she faced, as a result of her prior educational experience, with the pedagogic approach adopted in the classroom:

> In fact, as a Chinese student, it is difficult for me to put these theories into practice because of the spoon-feeding education. It is a common phenomenon that we just memorise the theories in the book without any thinking.

This variety of students' responses, including expressions of reluctance or perhaps inability to engage with literary fiction for the purposes of the course, created for us the opportunity to problematise our image of ourselves as progressive educators and to reflect on what ends our pedagogic approach actually served. We realised that from the beginning of the course there was a danger, even if unintended, of an attempt to colonise the students' thinking through a set of presumptions we held as educators (see Perriton and Singh, this volume). These presumptions stemmed from a combination of our belief in the relevance of novels as a medium of learning for present-day management students and our lack of knowledge about the students we taught: their backgrounds, motivations, needs and expectations. Reflecting on our own presumptions posited for us broader dilemmas regarding how to employ humanities in the management classroom. The pedagogic process demonstrated to us that, despite us being critical management educators, our intervention was part of what Foucault (2008) refers to as a biopolitical regime of power. This is understood as a way of governing the desires and interests of the population and exercising 'governmentality' whereby subjects are 'steered' towards self-development as resources through being urged to manage their lives and learning capabilities to their fullest (Simons and Masschelein 2008).

In the end, the biopolitical problem that we encountered was that today's university lecturers might have little knowledge about the labour market conditions that their students will have to confront and navigate. Driven by the wish to better understand our students and in this context to assess the suitability of pedagogic interventions drawing on the humanities and social sciences in management education, we decided to first explore who it is that our pedagogic practice is addressed to.

## The students

An important – and striking – characteristic of the contemporary management education classroom, particularly in Anglophone educational contexts, is its diversity. The student population in the UK is highly internationalised because universities direct a lot of their recruitment efforts at attracting overseas students. This is because with the gradual withdrawal of government funding for higher education, British universities have been charged with the task of securing their own economic survival, primarily through generating income from tuition fees, especially those paid by the premium fee-paying overseas students (Brown 2013). This, unsurprisingly, has led to redefining the relationship between higher education institutions and those they teach: students have become paying customers and universities 'mega-businesses' (Coman 2014). Concomitantly, university recruitment activities have turned into the art of implementing marketing strategies to compete within the global market for educational services. Indeed, higher education is currently UK's seventh largest export industry, with one in six of the students enrolled at British universities coming from outside the EU (Collini 2013).

On postgraduate taught programmes offered by business schools, the proportion of non-British students tends to be much higher, and the majority of the master's students are likely to come from China. This was also the case with the course we taught. Prior to our pedagogic intervention, however, we had only acknowledged it to a limited extent. We had recognised that the students had come from diverse cultural backgrounds, and therefore might have had different experiences of education, and especially of exposure to literary fiction, before enrolling on the course; however, we had not actually reflected on the various dimensions of this diversity and its implications for the students' motivations, needs, hopes and plans for the future. In other words, we had not considered carefully who it was that we, as educators, were engaging with and aspiring to 'transform' through our pedagogic approach, drawing on novels to discuss concepts and issues pertaining to management and organisation. Moreover, we had not thought about whether and in what way our use of literary fiction as a vehicle for learning about management and organisation might be relevant to our students in light of their hoped-for and probable future trajectories. Neither had we considered in advance whether our students had to face any difficulties or make sacrifices in order to be able to study, or what labour market conditions they would be confronted with upon the completion of their degree.

Our realisation of the implications of classroom diversity along with the contemporary economic conditions under which the students gain education and apply for jobs only developed throughout the course as we gradually got to know our students and, in particular, as we read their final assignments. This gave rise to broader reflections about the composition of the student 'body' that is nowadays subject to the biopolitical project of higher education, particularly its management education-related variety, and also about the students' present and potential future place within the constellation of global economic and labour market relations.

For example, one thing we had not considered in advance was that in the case of some of the students, their main interest, as far as the content of the curriculum was concerned, was primarily oriented towards management practice rather than familiarisation with management theories and concepts. They wanted to learn from us about how to manage in order to be able to help out with running family businesses or applying for jobs in multinational companies upon return to their home countries. Moreover, many overseas students came to study management in the UK with the assumption that their future employment was likely to involve collaboration with Anglophone business partners and clients; therefore, to them, at least as important as the applicability of the subject content of the degree was the fact that participating in it would allow them to improve their English language skills.

In advance of teaching on the course, we also had not realised that regardless of their level of proficiency in English, some students had little pre-university experience of reading and writing and found the requirement to write an assignment based on a combination of their reading of a novel, their analysis of management-related theories and concepts, and their own reflections on using literary fiction as a way to facilitate learning taxing. Altogether, the experience of studying on our module was certainly challenging to a number of our students and did not, in a direct way, correspond to the expectations they had had of the master's degree.

The fact that we had not reflected on the relevance of our course to those who studied on it resulted in difficulties experienced by those who struggled not only with the mode of learning we presented them with, but also with covering the expenses associated with the degree programme fees and the costs of living. In fact, a closer look at the students taking our course points to an important 'feature' that the majority of them shared, despite the cultural diversity among them and despite the differences between their pre-master's levels of knowledge and skills: to most of the learners, studying also meant having to borrow money.

Aside from very few who came from wealthy backgrounds and had both their tuition fees and living expenses covered by their families, the rest of the students financed their education through a combination of loans, part-time work and savings. Their specific circumstances differed, but they all viewed education as an investment in the future and a route into employment rather than as an intellectual journey, at least primarily. On listening to the stories students told us about how they covered the costs associated with their master's programme, the realisation dawned upon us that the common denominator within these stories was debt, and that the complex link between education, debt and employment was a source of stress and anxiety for many of the learners. We now present a few examples of students from our course to illustrate this point.

One student was Yan whose parents belonged to the aspiring new middle class of Chinese citizens. In order to enable their daughter to study in the UK, they had taken out a bank loan in China to pay for the tuition fees of Yan's master's programme and for her living expenses in the UK. Paying back the loan constituted a burden for the family, and in order to contribute to the repayments, throughout the degree Yan was working three times a week in a Chinese restaurant. Although helpful in financial terms, Yan's part-time work took up a lot of her study time and exacerbated the difficulties she was experiencing with reading and writing in English. At the same time, Yan felt under a strong pressure to successfully complete the programme because her family had sacrificed a lot to create for her the opportunity to study in the UK. She also saw the master's degree as a condition of securing a junior management position in a multinational company back in China and of subsequently climbing up the company ladder; a career she was intending to embark on upon graduation.

Another participant in our course was Harriett, a mature British student with more than 20 years' experience in the corporate sector. In her early 50s, Harriett's decision to enrol on the master's programme was triggered by having been made redundant from work. She saw the degree as a route towards a career change and was hoping that upon its completion, she'd be able to secure employment. As far as the programme was concerned, she enjoyed it and when participating in the module we taught, had no difficulty engaging with literary fiction and drawing on novels to discuss matters related to management and organisation. Indeed, in her reflective essay she expressed appreciation of this mode of learning:

> I have found reasons and explanations which have greatly helped me to re-evaluate and justify matters which before were often, by necessity governed by the immediate demands of the job in hand and guided by instinct as well as reflection.
>
> *Harriett, UK*

Harriett was complimentary about and interested in the content of her master's programme curriculum, and considered the cost of her new qualification as an investment that one day will see a return. Studying towards a postgraduate qualification also put her into a relationship of debt – in her case with herself – because she used her own pension savings to pay for the degree. Harriett was therefore finding it stressful to be taking the risk of borrowing money from what she had previously saved for her long-term future in order to secure her livelihood in the years between her graduation and retirement.

Slightly different to Yan's and Harriett's was the situation of another participant in the course we taught, Troels, a student from Scandinavia who came from an affluent middle-class background. He graduated with a first degree from a university in his home country and travelled to the UK to study for his master's degree. Up until the end of his bachelor's degree, the costs of Troels's education had been partially covered by the welfare state, which provided free university tuition to its citizens, and partially by his parents who had paid for Troels's accommodation and subsistence. His parents also covered the costs of his tuition fees and living in the UK. In addition, throughout his bachelor's and master's degree, Troels had been working part-time in a coffee shop. This work did not constitute an obstacle to Troels's academic performance: his proficiency in English was high, he was a keen reader of literary fiction and was familiar with engagement with novels as a mode of sensemaking. As the following excerpt from his assignment illustrates, he found it easy to make connections between his favourite novel and the theories and concepts from management and organisation that were discussed throughout the course:

> In my book, *Blindness*, I was fortunate to witness all of the above [leaders and followers, strategy, power and politics] and the material was endless.
>
> *Troels, Scandinavia*

In our conversation with Troels, we found out that despite his relatively privileged financial position, this student was also going to graduate with a debt that he would need to pay back as an employee because, in addition to the money received from the state and his parents, throughout his university education Troels had taken out bank loans in order to cover the expenses associated with his desired – and expected – level of lifestyle. His hope following the master's programme was to apply for a job in a big multinational organisation and, in the future, become a successful management practitioner.

Although getting to know our students' backgrounds and plans, as educators we were also confronted by the question of whether the fulfilment of their aspirations regarding future employment would be facilitated by the programme they studied on, and by drawing on the humanities, in particular through the application of literary fiction, in studying management and organisation. How many of them will manage to secure a full-time job upon graduation? Will they be in the position to pay back the money they had borrowed throughout their degree? Will they be able to build careers that will translate into sustainable livelihoods for them and potentially for their families?

## Debt as *Bildung*

As we have seen, our students had very different backgrounds and circumstances, and yet they also shared a certain economic horizon. In their 'professional' future, they will have to negotiate a particular relationship, regardless of whether they indeed become attached to something we may meaningfully term a 'professional' context or not – they will have to manage a long-term debt relation. This is a premise that along with its related condition – short- and long-term graduate unemployment (Śliwa and Sørensen in Falkenberg 2013; Williams 2006) – has been left rather unaddressed with few exceptions in the 'humanities in business' discourse. The fact that we are currently experiencing what Agresto (2011) refers to as an 'education bubble', where private, commercially based suppliers of education aggressively market their 'products' and enrol ever increasing numbers on their programmes, only exacerbates the relation between debt and unemployment. This relation is of course intimate and critical. On the back of the higher education boom, debt is becoming not only a pedagogy (as Williams (2006) argues in his important essay 'The pedagogy of debt') but also a *Bildung* of debt, that is a total cosmology and ideology forming the entire subjectivity of the students and graduates. A young Italian law school graduate expresses this *Bildung* forcefully:

> I don't think I will be able to pay back the debts I owe for my education. Sometimes I think that when I die I will still have monthly payments to make for university. I currently have a repayment plan spread over 27 and a half years, but that is too ambitious since the interest is variable and I am only able to pay it back at a certain rate. I am very careful with my spending; I note any expense, from coffee to a bus ticket . . . Everything has to be planned . . . The thing that worries me the most is that I am incapable of saving, and my debt is always there looming over me.
>
> *Repubblica, 4 August 2008, cited in Lazzarato 2011: 187, no. 17*

This Italian graduate does not appear overwhelmingly gloomy, but rather sober and realistic. Recent data show invariably that the various job markets for graduates globally are characterised by growing unemployment, rapidly growing debt and an ever increasing inequality (Dorling 2014). In Italy, 40 per cent of young people are currently unemployed, whereas in the UK, according to one survey, 47 per cent of recent graduates were working in jobs classified as 'non-graduate' (Coman 2014). Rather than a linear career development, throughout their (non-)working lives, graduates are likely to face a mixture of employment, unemployment, part-time employment, project employment and so on. This is the 'brave new world of post-employment' described by Boltanski and Chiapello (2005). Although more and more students enter universities, they will leave them – either as drop-outs or graduates – heavily in debt because of the amounts of money they borrow to cover the costs of tuition fees and also due to widespread practices of credit card use and what seems to be excessive spending amongst students. As a result, in the US alone, student loans have also grown exponentially because tuition fees have skyrocketed, for example in 2011 the total outstanding student loan debt passed 1 trillion USD (Touryalai 2013). In the UK, it is estimated that the average amount that a student graduating in 2015 is going to owe is £44,000 (Coman 2014).

Altogether, this confirms the growing precariousness of the subjectivity of graduates, and we as university educators will have to ask ourselves – because our university's career centre is unlikely to ask such questions – what is the role of the educator and the curriculum in a situation where perhaps more than half of the graduates will not get a permanent job, and the job they might get will most probably not be in line with their education and qualifications? We actively refrain from saying 'our' students because once they have produced their last value for the university through paying the final instalment of their tuition fees and collecting their graduation certificate, they are no longer in any sensible way 'our' students – if they ever were beyond the financial and status relation. However, their post-graduation trajectories are closely connected to what they experience in the business school or other higher educational settings.

Higher education institutions are by now inadvertently practising a pedagogy of debt – what we term a *Bildung* of debt. To formulate it in a Nietzschean style: *debt is a teacher*. Debt will – as we are following Williams's (2006: 162; emphasis in original) argument in this section – teach the student population that '*higher education is a consumer service*'. This is important for any attempt to revitalise humanities in business. A realisation of the existence of pedagogy of debt may point out to us that the notion of humanities in business encompasses an understanding of humanities *as* business. *Bildung* is not, in this perspective, a room for spiritual growth sheltered from the listlessness of business. On the contrary, *Bildung*, through the debt it generates, teaches students '*career choices*' – and this perhaps explains why in the US the liberal arts have faded and business has tripled its part of the student population since the mid-1990s. Debt even teaches a '*worldview*' and '*civic lessons*' that include the dogma of the market as a fair dealer of options and rewards, and the individuality of the graduate's economic fate. In fact, debt teaches the very '*worth of a person*': 'You are how much you can make, minus how much you owe' (Williams 2006: 165). Such precariousness induces a permanent 'fear of falling' (Ehrenreich 1989) or even of being haunted by Sennett's (2006) 'specter of uselessness'.

There is a whole new anthropology here, which is why we term this a *Bildung* of debt, and it is more profound than the dogma of *Homo economicus*: the modern human is no longer 'man enclosed, but man in debt' (Deleuze 1992: 6). This is the insight that is further developed in Lazzarato's 2011 book, *The Making of the Indebted Man*. What the past three decades of university politics have taught us is that the basic social relation is neither 'the gift' nor 'exchange' but, as Nietzsche has argued, debt. When meeting 'the other', the measure is really one of credibility: can this individual pay back what I now may invest in him or her?[1] Etymologically, credit is concerned with trust, whilst the debtor is concerned with what they 'must do' as debtor. 'Man in debt' is referring to not only a situation of day-to-day debt, but a debt that today must be understood as infinite. Debt defines men and women in terms of their personal debts like student loans, house mortgages, but also collectively through, for instance, national debt.

Debt therefore makes the future of humans, the future that is the horizon of expectation for action – to actually belong to the creditor instead of, theologically, God. And here we have the reason for scholastic Christian theology to reject the creation of debt and the taking of interest because this way human appropriated what ontologically belonged to God, namely time. Although usually downplaying the risk of unemployment, we (that is, the university and its career consultants) promise infinite possibilities that a degree will give. We promise to the students that the degree will supposedly give them infinite productivity and the ability to modulate its working force to all situations – unemployment, again, not being part of this scheme of modulation. In the employability discourse deployed by universities in the so-called knowledge societies, work becomes the site where the graduate is to fulfil her very humanity. A university degree, as the first step towards future employment, gains the status of a qualification pursued out of necessity rather than choice. Coman (2014) quotes a 'warning' issued by a graduating student to an imaginary 18-year-old considering whether, in light of the compulsory tuition fees within the UK system, to enrol on a university degree scheme or not:

> Just imagine if you chose not to go to university. Then what would you do? Work full time or even two part-time jobs, both for the minimum wage, where you will just scrape by and become trapped in a dead-end, demeaning job? Even then, there's no guarantee to get work

> so you might have to sign on, getting a measly £56.80-a-week, forced to work any job, no matter how dirty, embarrassing or dangerous, in fear of losing benefits.

Through promising to protect students from such a grim prospect, the university constructs the students' view of themselves as one of infinite potential in a direct exchange for the mortgage. This ties in closely with the infinity of the debt; infinity in the sense that it cannot be paid back in one's own life time. In other words, at the university the question of money 'is replaced by the ethical machine of potentiality' (Costea *et al.* 2012: 34), and yet on the other side of the relation – the debt side after graduation (that is, after payment) – *money prevails as measure.* In other words, 'student debt' and 'potentiality' are mediated by money: the infinity of the debt is what motivates the students' desire for infinite potentiality and agility on behalf of the worker-*to-be*.

The result is not a *Homo economicus* taking rational decisions; rather the result of the '*Bildung* of debt' is a new social character we may term the 'manic depressive debtor'. This is a character who suffers a nervous oscillation between absolute serfdom (owing to the infinity of the debt) and absolute freedom (owing to the infinity of the potentiality fantasy) sustained by internal rivalry in the labour market or workplace. Of course, this nervous oscillation is not what you take with you to your bank. You do not even take your creativity with you to the bank. Actually, to be a credible paying-back bank customer you must construct a future in which you do not come up with any ideas other than to go to the same work every day and do the same as you did yesterday. Debt, in other words, is a vaccine against creativity and change, and a lesson in acting in certain ways (Lazzarato 2011). Although the business school now appears fully integrated with this type of *Bildung* by debt, one crucially needs to consider ways to negotiate this and how the humanities could play a role. We turn to these issues in the remainder of this chapter.

## The challenge for humanities and social sciences

How should the humanities and social sciences deal with this predicament – that is, the scenario of indebting the majority of the student population even beyond the scope of their ability to pay back in exchange for high pitched expectations of future rewards? Bearing in mind our pedagogical intervention in the course on organisation and management, one could ask which kind of interventions would be adequate in those students' case? Although we obviously do not possess the definitive answer to these questions, we insist on the necessity of posing them, not least in a book inspired by questions about what humanities may do for (the) business (of) education. Our hypothesis is that the heart of the problem persists in the neoliberal ideology's gospel: nothing is impossible as long as you 'will' it – and just a little more than the will of your peer (that is, your competitor). Installing a hitherto unseen 'sound rivalry' (Deleuze 1992), the university uses *envy*, as argued by Bloom and Cederström (2009: 173), to 'affectively "seize" employees [students] with promises of future individual freedom and respect [i.e., income] as it extols the virtue of the person who envies today through hard work will be the person envied tomorrow'. The winning discourse is one of potentiality and infinity – but this utopia collapses not only because of decreasing job opportunities, but also because the debt of the graduates is overwhelming and it impedes their incentives to *actually* experiment with their future and their future productivity. The race forecloses other options, for example in Denmark each year around 30 per cent of the population are accepted into a university programme. As Dorling (2014) argues:

> One reason that more young people apply is that other options are becoming more limited and less desirable. As income inequalities escalate, the cost of failing to secure a place in the top half of society rises, and so the perceived benefits of a university education rise in turn.

Here Dorling clearly points out that university applicants are attracted by the *perceived* benefits of higher education, and these tend to rise *even though* the job market for graduates is deteriorating at a high and accelerating pace.

However, we are not willing to give in to defeatist thinking, which would suggest that there is nothing we can do. On the contrary, we believe that the university has an important mission to fulfil and we subscribe to the ideal of *Bildung* as the overall formation of the individual, rather than education understood as training in skills and equipping students with 'tools' for becoming better managers. *Bildung* should have a transformative capacity and the question is what kind of *Bildung* can we offer in order that it is relevant to culturally diverse groups of students, as well as to the current socioeconomic environment in which those entering the labour market will experience both employment and unemployment? We ponder this important question, drawing on ideas from the original German *Bildung* tradition and from Jacques Rancière and the French pedagogy of dissensus, where the premise is that every individual has the capacity to 'transform' and 'liberate' themselves within a horizon of 'radical equality'.

## The possibilities of *Bildung*: building radical equality

As discussed at the beginning of our chapter, there existed throughout our pedagogic intervention a misalignment between our understanding of the purpose of higher education, of prior socialisation of the learners and of what might be considered a valuable approach to developing knowledge about management and organisation, and the actual circumstances, needs and aspirations of the students. We wanted to find out why our presumptions had turned out to be inadequate and what alternatives exist for applying humanities and social sciences in management education.

An important aspect of the inadequacy of our presumptions and understandings in the context of present-day management education was associated with our belief in a model of higher education stemming from the *Bildung* tradition and a commitment to the ideal of the university conceived in Humboldtian terms. A brief overview of the concept of *Bildung* and its historical roots will help bring out the idealistic and normative, as well as specific political connotations of *Bildung*.

Although the very concept of *Bildung* (understood as self-cultivation) can be traced as far back as sixteenth-century theology and the idea of 'forming' oneself in the image of God, the roots of Humboldt's theory of *Bildung* can be found in Hegel's (1977) *Phenomenology of Spirit* – through a constant process of disintegration and coming to itself, the Spirit achieves a higher state. The notion of *Bildung* therefore has a strong normative flavour. It denotes a process in which the creative and intellectual capacities of an individual unfold, leading to a virtuous life and to the 'enrichment' of the individual. This enrichment, as explained in von Humboldt's (1980: 235–6) definition of *Bildung*, takes place through the 'most general, most intensive and most free' interaction between the individual and the world. The individual develops through experiencing the world and through relations with others.

Arguably, Humboldt uses the concept of the 'world' in universalist terms, as an 'indefinable centre', a core unifying all languages and cultures. Although no particular language or culture is capable of grasping the 'world', the bringing together of alternative cultures and perspectives on reality serves the objective of approaching the world, of grasping 'universal meanings by transcending any particular and contextual horizons of reality perception and interpretation' (Stojanov 2012: 3).

Centred on the development of the creative and intellectual capacities of individuals, the general objective of *Bildung* is close to our hearts as educators, and it was indirectly the reason why we decided to draw on the humanities in teaching about management and organisation. *Bildung*'s universalist undertones, however, are more problematic when the diversity – and its implications – of the group of students we taught is seriously reflected upon. Aiming to transcend the contextual horizons that underpin each of the student's *Weltanschauung* or world-view is not helpful to the present-day educator or to the learner. It is precisely the specific background – the cultural, economic, ethnic and class context of the student's origin, as well as her or his future aspirations, plans, opportunities and constraints – that provides the lens through which knowledge is constructed and interpreted, and thanks to this it becomes meaningful to the individual.

Another problematic dimension of a conception of higher education in the spirit of *Bildung* relates to the presumptions of *Bildung* regarding the formation of citizens. As an educational paradigm, *Bildung* implies directing efforts at the maturation of the learner in a personal and cultural sense. The aim of *Bildung* is the lifelong growth of the human who, through achieving a higher level of self-reflection, becomes more free. A more self-reflective individual, in turn, has the capacity to engage in the critique of her or his society, to reject the status quo and to mobilise her or his abilities to contribute to the society's fulfilment of its ideals. In the case of our pedagogic intervention, asking the students as part of their assignments to submit reflections on participating in our course (which used novels as a vehicle for learning about management) constituted an attempt at facilitating the formation of such self-reflective and thus freer citizens. The ideal of citizen formation underlying the concept of *Bildung*, however, was not based on an abstract notion of society; in fact, as Massumi (1992) points out, it was tied to a historical process of state formation, with a particular reference to the Prussian state. As such, Humboldt's ideas about the contribution of citizens to society were closely connected to specific historico-political conditions of nineteenth-century Prussia: the increase in significance of the nation state; the understanding of society confined within state borders; and an industrialising, strongly growing economy. Unsurprisingly, concomitant with this conception of society was a universalist notion of education as a social good, necessary in order to facilitate the formation of the politically strong and economically expanding state's citizens and represented by the ideals of *Bildung*.

Although we agree with *Bildung*'s conception of education as a social good, it is necessary to reflect upon it in the context of contemporary political economy of education: the economic conditions the students face on graduation will not be framed in terms of growth and expansion, but rather, graduates will need to find ways of building their livelihoods under the conditions of post-growth and recurring economic and environmental crises. It is therefore imperative for us as educators to realise the pressures and challenges that the students face. As illustrated earlier, using examples of the students on the course we taught, these challenges often mean that the students' conception of education has less to do with the objective of self-searching and more with the desire to achieve a return on the very tangible and often burdensome investment that education is to them, and to cover the debt incurred through being a student.

However, according to Rancière, transformation should not aim at fulfilment of society's ideals but at transforming it according to a different set of ideals. The discourse of Critical Management Education seems at this point somewhat bogged down between two positions (Huault and Perret 2011). The first is more 'critical' in the Frankfurt School tradition, in which the teacher as expert is supposed to reveal to the students their alienation and subjugated positions by pointing to dominant power structures and hegemonic discourses. The danger of this position is that one (market) discourse is just substituted with another, namely the critical one (Grey *et al.* 1996). The other position tries to abolish the distance between the 'expert' and the 'novices', in order to further deeper collaboration between teacher and the audience in order to reach a consensus.

We want to take issue with this impasse by introducing the pedagogical – or perhaps anti-pedagogical – concepts from Rancière's philosophy (see also Huault and Perret, this volume). In his magnificent *The Ignorant Schoolmaster: Five Lessons in Intellectual Emancipation* (1991) Rancière argues that the founding 'myth of pedagogy' is 'explication':

> Before being the act of the pedagogue, explication is the myth of pedagogy, the parable of a world divided into knowing minds and ignorant ones, ripe minds and immature ones, the capable and the incapable, the intelligent and the stupid.
>
> *Rancière 1991: 6*

Such instruction creates a distinction between the 'groping animal' and the 'learned little man', continues Rancière (1991: 8). This creates, in turn, a hierarchy of intelligence through which the fate of the 'learner' is destined – in time and with labour – to potentially become equal to the 'teacher' by subjugating to this superior intelligence. But Rancière shows through analysing the story of the early French pedagogue Joseph Jacotot (who taught French to Flemish students without being able to speak Flemish himself) that this does not have to be the point of departure. Jacotot's emancipatory pedagogy was based on the principle that all humans are endowed with the same intelligence and with an ability to instruct themselves; one can even 'teach what one doesn't know if the student is emancipated, that is to say, if he is obliged to use his own intelligence' (Rancière 1991: 15). This pedagogy focuses on the learner's concrete and historical situation and takes, to frame it in Deleuze's words (1988: 119 cited in Dey and Steyaert 2007: 444), the following question as its starting point: 'what can I see [tomorrow], and what can I say today?' This question is clearly taking issue with the ongoing futurisation of life that happens through indebtedness – but one is not in need of anything to become emancipated. In our context, the student does not need the professor as the ignorant would need the learned, but the student would need to reveal her or his intelligence to herself or himself. In Rancière's (1991: 28) view, the problem is fundamentally

> to reveal an intelligence to itself. *Anything* can be used . . . a prayer or a song that the child or the ignorant one knows by heart. There is always something the ignorant one knows that can be used as a point of comparison, something to which a new thing to be learned can be related.

In essence, this was the idea that we sought to deploy in our course, in which we had the students select books from their own history or material archive. Following from our experience and the discussion presented in this chapter, we encourage management educators to use novels in their pedagogic practice, as well as other popular culture genres that are part of the students' socialisation and are chosen by them as easy to relate to (see Bell and Sinclair, this volume). Drawing on literary fiction or films rather than exclusively on academic texts creates a context in which teaching becomes less of an 'expert explanation' that inevitably establishes 'an order of inequality' (Dillon 2005: 444) and more of a process whereby the students may be 'emancipated' through the obligation to use their 'own intelligence' (Rancière 1991: 15). A pedagogic encounter of this kind ideally allows for the emergence of 'a society of equals' (Rancière 1991). Instead of erecting what Rancière considers a fraudulent 'hierarchy of intelligence', in which evaluators enforce examinations in order to judge 'go' or 'no go' (Deleuze and Guattari 1988: 177), the 'ignorant schoolmaster' (Rancière 1991) departs from a premise of an already given equality: the teacher says 'go with us' (Deleuze and Guattari 1988: 177). This, of course, clashes with today's university system that is increasingly focused on assessments, evaluations and tests. It also clashes with the infinite potential of the employability discourse, in which the student, prior to receiving their degree, stands in need of the teacher's expert knowledge in order to realise their potential. Finally, it clashes with a whole *Homo economicus* discourse, in which human ability is basically measurable and quantifiable. Indeed, the very notion of intelligence as a measure is highly problematic through its association with phrenology and the way in which, until today, the use of intelligence tests is understood by some as a tool to legitimise the spread of an inherently racist ideology.

However, instead of establishing a pedagogical consensus around such a hierarchy of intelligence, Rancière argues for a radical equality, although not as 'a goal to strive for, but a hypothesis to actualize' through a search for 'polyphony and polemic spaces' (Huault and Perret 2011: 292, 300; this volume). It is the same strategic cynicism that allows for measuring humans in terms of intelligence that allows for measuring them in terms of debt. There is a fundamental cruelty in such an operation. To Nietzsche, the labour of man on himself that produces the subject answerable and indebted to the creditor is a 'self-torture' (Nietzsche cited in Lazzarato 2011: 42). Moreover, it is inscribed on to the body to such an extent that, as Shakespeare's Jewish Shylock (the moneylender in the *Merchant of Venice*) insists, one may take an amount of flesh from the guilty party if they cannot pay. Entire accounting systems developed that specified legally what each limb and body part was worth, based on a logic that has its extreme manifestation in the human body parts industry in which you *sell* a body part to regain your credit worth. The debt-identity is, in other words, as ingrained in the human as the intelligence-identity, and they often work in tandem: one is poor *because* one is stupid and, in the schoolyard, one is simply *guilty* of being stupid. Insult is here not *added* to injury: it is the insult itself that creates the injury.

Pedagogy now becomes a matter of disconnecting the installation of intelligence-identity and debt-identity from the practice of *Bildung*, a practice in which they have resided with pride and effective domination. In Rancière's words:

> What counts is to dis-adapt, to dis-identify with regard to a form of identity, with regard to a form of being, feeling, perceiving and speaking, which effectively corresponds to ordinary sensible experience as it is organised by domination.
>
> *Rancière 1991: 491, cited in Huault and Perret 2011: 300*

This way, one may dismantle *Bildung* from the hierarchy with which it is imbued and which is inherent in state thinking: intelligent–stupid, creditor–debtor, centre–periphery, citizen–foreigner, etc. Davis (2010: 184), reading Rancière, explicates the teacher's role as one of placing

> the student in a situation from which they can only escape by using their own intellect. Teaching in such a way as to promote intellectual emancipation thus involves a paradox: if emancipation is something which can never be given but only taken, to teach is to construct a series of puzzles from which the student can only escape by seizing knowledge.

Moreover, having done away with the transcendent position of the university teacher, a new *Bildung* should incorporate a critical stance towards the assumed anthropology forged on the debt relation both financially, as a relation of money (German *Geld*), but also as a relation of guilt (stemming from *Geld*). The specific 'human' in this, argues Graeber (2011: 79), lies in altogether 'refusing to make such calculations ... [since we by] doing so would [reduce] each other to slaves or dogs through debt'. Such a *Bildung* should also encompass preparing students for unemployment/part-time employment by facilitating the articulation of the following message: waged work will not bring you out of your stupidity nor out of your debt somewhere in a fantastic future. You will be better off rejecting such anthropology altogether and focusing on the present.

Intelligence and debt are all about the development of rivalry, competition and the fear of not making it. The course we developed and taught features novels in teaching – this will not, in and of itself, provide an alternative anthropology devoid of hierarchies of intelligence and debt. However, because it would have the ability to integrate various life areas into its curriculum, it may create a *Bildung* that is not so much directed towards future fantasies as directed towards the present – that is, what you (as Deleuze mentioned earlier) can see tomorrow and what you can say today. *Bildung* may therefore slow down the ecstatic movement towards a potential future where you are not stupid anymore and (hence) are going to repay your debt.

Of course, in our multicultural classroom, each student experiences very different problems and has very different needs. What we in particular learned through our pedagogic intervention is that the students' need and our need did not match. Our assumptions are changing about what the university or the business school is and also what the role of higher education is, and as a result the acuteness of the students' new predicaments and problems and the fact that these will be very different from ours is beginning to become clear. The students' debt situations certainly differ, and yet they will all tend to align in time with the experience of the Italian graduate quoted earlier: a life of debt and, hence, in the system of higher education, a *Bildung* of debt. It is this dominant *Bildung* that students and teachers must 'dis-adapt' from or 'dis-identify' with as Rancière (1991: 491) advises. This implies, following Huault and Perret's (2011: 301) reading of Rancière, that a new paradigm of *Bildung* must refuse 'to align education about management and its institutions simply with the interests of private enterprise and the values associated with the market economy' – that is, refuse to align education with the value of debt and the ensuing debt habitus.

Although this would involve restructuring university pedagogy around more classical ideals of *Bildung* and incorporating Rancière's ideas of equality of intelligence and the need for dis-adaption, our pedagogic intervention may also point in this direction. One way to address the challenges of the contemporary diverse classroom and of the debt–labour market relationship that the graduates face, is through literary fiction that draws attention to the finite, perhaps even tragic, bounded nature of life's choices. And this is how we see the role of the humanities and the social sciences in the 'new spirit' of management education: to bring into the curriculum the 'narrative of finitude' (see also Brown, this volume; Wright and Nyberg, this volume), and point to the already given aspects of our (working) lives. This would form a necessary counter-narrative to the ideology of 'modulation', 'infinity' and 'potentiality' in which you are 'never finished with anything', as is the case in Deleuze's (1992) societies of control. A new (ancient) ideal concomitant with such a 'narrative of finitude' could be one of a certain asceticism in which the universities play the role of separating educational practice from the rivalry of the market and, through practising a radical equality, position themselves firmly in the business of slowing down the ecstatic movement towards the future.

## Note

1 Although Graeber (2011: 76–80) rejects this as a traditional *anthropological* fact, he praises it for being a necessary, imaginative exercise, which elaborates what bourgeois capitalism would need as an anthropology to make sense of its own political economy of debt.

## References

Agresto, J. (2011) 'The liberal arts bubble', *Academic Questions*, 24(4), 392–402.
Bloom, P. and Cederström, C. (2009) 'The sky's the limit: fantasy in the age of market rationality', *Journal of Organizational Change Management*, 22(2), 159–90.
Boltanski, L. and Chiapello, E. (2005) *The New Spirit of Capitalism*. London: Verso.
Brown, R. (2013) *Everything for Sale? The Marketisation of UK Higher Education*. London: Routledge.
Collini, S. (2013) 'Sold out', *London Review of Books*, 35(20), 3–12.
Coman, J. (2014) 'Have England's universities been privatised by stealth?' *The Observer*, 12 October. Available from: www.theguardian.com/education/2014/oct/12/have-universities-been-privatised-by-stealth (accessed 12 October 2014).
Costea, B., Amiridis, K. and Crump, N. (2012) 'Graduate employability and the principle of potentiality: an aspect of the ethics of HRM', *Journal of Business Ethics*, 111(1), 25–36.
Davis, O. (2010) 'The radical pedagogies of François Bon and Jacques Rancière', *French Studies*, 64(2), 178–91.
Deleuze, G. (1988) *Spinoza: Practical Philosophy*. San Francisco, CA: City Lights Books.
Deleuze, G. (1992) 'Postscript on the societies of control', *October*, 59, 3–7.
Deleuze, G. and Guattari, F. (1988) *A Thousand Plateaus: Capitalism and Schizophrenia*. London: Bloomsbury Publishing.
Dey, P. and Steyaert, C. (2007) 'The troubadours of knowledge: passion and invention in management education', *Organization*, 14(3), 437–61.
Dillon, M. (2005) 'A passion for the (im)possible: Jacques Rancière, equality, pedagogy and the messianic', *European Journal of Political Theory*, 4(4), 429–52.
Dorling, D. (2014) 'Tuition fees: a bonanza for the 1%', *The Guardian*, 30 September. Available from: http://theguardian.com/education/2014/sep/30/tuition-fees-bonanza-for-one-per-cent-danny-dorling/print (accessed 1 October 2014).
Ehrenreich, B. (1989) *Fear of Falling: The Inner Life of the Middle Class*. New York, NY: Knopf Doubleday Publishing Group.
Falkenberg, C. (2013) 'Fairy tales of the future – educated for unemployment', *GRASP*, 7 July 2013. Available from: http://graspmag.org/education/rethink-mgmt-edu/fairy-tales-of-the-future-educated-for-unemployment/ (accessed 10 November 2015).
Foucault, M. (2008) *The Birth of Biopolitics: Lectures at the Collège de France, 1978–79*. Basingstoke, UK: Palgrave Macmillan.
Graeber, D. (2011) *Debt: The First 5000 Years*. New York, NY: Melville House.
Grey, C., Knights, D. and Willmott, H. (1996) 'Is a critical pedagogy of management possible?' *In:* R. French and C. Grey (eds.) *Rethinking Management Education*. London: Sage Publications, pp. 94–110.
Hegel, G.W.F. (1977) *Phenomenology of Spirit*. Oxford: Clarendon Press.
Huault, I. and Perret, V. (2011) 'Critical management education as a vehicle for emancipation. Exploring the philosophy of Jacques Rancière', *M@n@gement*, 14(5), 281–309.
Lazzarato, M. (2011) *The Making of the Indebted Man*. Los Angeles, CA: Semiotext(e).
Linstead, S., Fullop, L. and Lilley, S. (2006) *Management and Organization. A Critical Text*. Basingstoke, UK: Palgrave Macmillan.
Massumi, B. (1992) *A User's Guide to Capitalism and Schizophrenia: Deviations from Deleuze and Guattari*. Boston, MA: MIT Press.
Rancière, J. (1991) *The Ignorant Schoolmaster: Five Lessons in Intellectual Emancipation*. Stanford, CA: Stanford University Press.
Sennett, R. (2006) *The Culture of the New Capitalism*. London: Yale University Press.
Simons, M. and Masschelein, J. (2008) 'The governmentalization of learning and the assemblage of a learning apparatus', *Educational Theory*, 58(4), 391–415.
Śliwa, M., Sørensen, B.M. and Cairns, G. (2015) '"You have to choose a novel": the biopolitics of critical management education', *Management Learning*, 46(3), 243–59.
Stojanov, K. (2012) 'The concept of *Bildung* and its moral implications'. Paper presented at the Annual Conference of the Philosophy of Education Society of Great Britain, 30 March–1 April, Oxford, UK.
Touryalai, H. (2013) 'More evidence on the student debt crisis: average grad's loan jumps to $27,000', *Forbes.Com*, 31.
von Humboldt, W. (1980) 'Theorie der *Bildung* des Menschen'. *In:* A. Flitner and K. Giel (eds.) *Wilhelm von Humboldt. Werke in fünf Bänden. Bd. 1*. Darmstadt, Germany: Wissenschaftliche Buchgesellschaft, pp. 234–40.
Williams, J. (2006) 'The pedagogy of debt', *College Literature*, 33(4), 155–69.

# 36

# 'This is water'

## Labours of division, institutions and history

*Martin Parker*

*Nottingham's New University*
In Nottingham, that dismal town
where I went to school and college,
they've built a new university,
for a new dispensation of knowledge.
Built it most grand and cakeily
out of the noble loot
derived from shrewd cash chemistry
by good Sir Jesse Boot . . .

*Lawrence 2002 [1929]*

The complaints voiced within the Carnegie Report (Colby *et al.* 2011) and related discussions, and extensively echoed in this book, do concern the specifics of the business school but can just as easily be more widely framed in terms of the ideas and politics that govern the modern university.[1] It makes sense to do this because the standoff between liberal humanism and utilitarianism, one with a long history in some countries (Newman 1907 [1852]; Lawson 1998; Collini 2012), has shaped academics, disciplines and institutions. Lawrence's catty complaints about 'a university where smart men would dispense doses of smart cash-chemistry in language of common-sense' don't sound as if they are a century old, but could be echoed by anyone who nowadays bemoans the massification and marketization of higher education. Universities, it seems, have been accused of 'dumbing down' for quite a long time.

Lawrence's allusions refer to 'Boots the Chemist', a national chain of shops in the UK and previously a big employer in Nottingham. Jesse Boot's piles of money helped the university establish a new campus, one that, for Lawrence, was then already contaminated by the busyness of industry. The perception of a gap between business and culture is therefore not a new one. Demands for cultural literacy and high-minded waffle about citizenship, civilization and democracy have long been counter-posed to compelling arguments about efficiency, usefulness and markets. 'Why should universities be subject to the dull disciplines of the market?' roar the brave defenders of the best that has been thought and said. 'What is the point of spending public money teaching people poetry?' reply the fish-eyed modernizers before turning back to their spreadsheets.

The growth of the business school has made what Andrew Lawson called 'the agon of culture and utility' (1998: 273) even more dramatic because this fat cuckoo in the nest is predicated on selling knowledge about how to make money for large amounts of money. There is normally very little breast-beating within the business school, beyond the whining émigrés of critical management studies, because the ducks are so nicely aligned in terms of institutional and professional desires. The quality of any given business school is reflected in the price that students pay – so get the brand offer right and the money will keep sloshing in. Within the carpeted halls and the atria hung with inoffensive art, utility is defined as what the punters want, so give it to them. But this is not primarily a chapter about the intellectual contents of the business school, nor an attempt to encourage people to use films in the classroom or philosophy in the boardroom, interesting and worthy though such practices are. Rather, I want to think about the relationship between the business school and the humanities as a historical and organizational matter because I think that classification is at the heart of the problem here. It seems to me that universities are classification machines, institutions designed to keep things separated, and it seems entirely predictable that the arts and the business school won't be encouraged to mix. Labours of division have placed subjects in boxes, preventing contamination and ensuring purity, for example the *Methodenstreit*, which is the long standoff between *Naturwissenschaft* and *Geisteswissenschaft* that shaped German university education, or in the UK, Snow's (2001 [1959]) much discussed 'two cultures' of science and art. Wherever we look, we can find the interminable distinctions between quantitative and qualitative, positivism and interpretivism, modern and post, social sciences and humanities, this and that. It's almost enough to make us believe that these dotted lines are to be found in the world, rather than in our institutions.

The US writer David Foster Wallace, in his celebrated talk 'This is Water', encourages us to be aware of things that we don't normally see very clearly. He begins the commencement address to the 2005 graduates of Keynon College, a liberal arts college in Ohio, with this 'didactic little parable-ish' story.

> There are these two young fish swimming along and they happen to meet an older fish swimming the other way, who nods at them and says 'Morning, boys. How's the water?' And the two young fish swim on for a bit and then eventually one of them looks over at the other and goes 'What the hell is water?'
>
> *Foster Wallace 2008*

Of course, Foster Wallace says, this is a story about the value of a liberal arts education and that it teaches you how to see, how to think, how to understand other people's points of view, 'to be just a little bit less arrogant' and so on. Foster Wallace claims that these clichés contain some real truths because the 2005 class of Keynon will hopefully have learnt how to be 'conscious and aware enough to choose what you pay attention to and to choose how you construct meaning from experience'. He committed suicide before the Carnegie Report was published, but it seems at first glance that he might have agreed with much of its implicit promise of the arts as being good for helping to make good people.

But he might not have agreed with it all, because there is something oddly convenient about the way that Colby, Ehrlich, Sullivan and Dolle line up their ducks. Throughout their book, they suggest that the liberal arts teaches exploratory and integrative thought – and, luckily enough, this is also what twenty-first-century knowledge businesses need (Colby *et al.* 2011; see also Sullivan, Ehrlich and Colby, this volume). The 'multiple framing', which they find to be characteristic of the liberal arts, maps nicely on to the achievement motivation of entrepreneurs, the concern for social responsibility and the team-oriented stakeholder value approach that contemporary 'leaders' are said to require. And so on. The idea that the liberal arts might criticize business itself, or even that there might be a fundamental problem with the way that business operates, is flattened to a convenient agreement that the point of the liberal arts is to be a resource for the cultivated business person. I don't think Foster Wallace would like that because his scenes from working life in novels like *Infinite Jest* (1996) and *The Pale King* (2011) present organizations as labyrinths of confusion and misunderstanding, places of boredom and fear. Dignity and bravery also, but not the sort of tidy story about enterprise and character that we find in Carnegie. Foster Wallace seemed to dislike neat explanations and, just like his sentences, footnotes and endnotes, preferred baroque involution.

In this chapter, I will try to understand the ways in which the differences between the business school and the arts and humanities can be understood historically and institutionally. It seems to me that it is inadequate to assume that we can think about such matters without seeing them as organizational questions, as forms of classification practice which have become concrete in the buildings of the university. I think the problem is in the university itself, and is not something that is unique to the business school – although it is in the business school that this problem finds a rather intense expression. I will begin with some brief remarks on the history of the university, before moving on to consider the university as a machine for classifying, separating and distributing knowledge. Spatially and epistemologically, the university produces disciplines. I then move on to consider the ways that the business school has grown and produced its own divisions which themselves discipline thought. After a consideration of the relationship between the practical and the liberal justifications for education, I conclude by rejecting (with a certain sadness) the idea that the humanities can either civilize or radicalize the business school. I think the problem is the classification that produces the business school, and it is that which needs to be dissolved in order that any interdisciplinary project can flourish.

A note before I start. This is an essay written from the perspective of the UK and many of its assumptions might seem rather alien to readers based in other university systems. I currently work somewhere where state support is disappearing, and the business school is both the engine and symptom of the dominance of utility over culture. I offer no apologies for writing from where I am because what else can I do, but I wanted to remind you that I am aware of this. That is the point – for a goldfish who is trying hard to see the water.

## The idea of a university

The most impressive part of the Bodleian library in Oxford, UK, is the Old Schools Quadrangle, which dates from 1613. It's a gorgeous golden stone structure and looks like it has always been there, emplaced solidly in the cobbles and harbouring generations of scholars. For the clicking tourists and the self-consciously busy students who rush impatiently across the square, there is no question that it belongs, that it deserves to always be here. Setting aside its unshakable confidence as a building, there is something else that catches the eye as you stand in the courtyard, a series of beautiful doors with a golden serif lettered sign above them in Latin. *Schola Moralis Philosophiae, Schola Logicae, Schola Naturalis Philosophiae* and so on. They look like props from the Harry Potter films, so much mystery do they promise. Their reason for being there was that each discipline once had a single room and the doors are still marked with the subject. On the ground floor: Moral Philosophy, Grammar and History, Metaphysics, Logic, Music, Natural Philosophy. On the first floor: Law, Greek, Arithmetic and Geometry, Astronomy, Rhetoric, and Anatomy and Medicine. Doorways to knowledge, set in institutional stone.

How could it be otherwise? We need to know what we are going to get in the lecture theatre so that we know which lecture theatre to go to. Universities, like libraries, must advertise their classifications. How could we have a library in which all the books were jumbled up in piles, like a crazy second-hand book shop with no logic, no filing system, no way of finding what you want to read? Knowledge could be lost in such places, put aside one day and not found for decades. Classification matters to the university. You can't just go to one and study, because you have to study something that has already been identified as a field of study. That is to say that the structure of the institution prefigures what is knowable, and allocates space and resources accordingly. Not that these categories are timeless. Those that made sense four hundred years ago are different to those we recognize now. So some subjects have grown and divided, such as Natural Philosophy and Astronomy, whilst others have shrunk and congealed, like Moral Philosophy, Metaphysics and Logic. Still other areas are entirely new – Anthropology, Geography, Psychology, Sociology and so on.

Other things haven't changed. In order to collect the books and build the library, Sir Thomas Bodley – son of a merchant, career diplomat and husband to a wealthy wife – had to collect a lot of money. Like most of the ancient universities of Western Europe, the generosity of kings, bishops and merchants was required in order that stone and wood could be carved and pheasants cooked for table. And, just like nowadays, generosity often likes to be noticed – and so Bodley ensured that it would be.

> He had prepared a handsome Register of Donations, in vellum, in which the name of every benefactor should be written down in a large and fair hand so all might read. And he kept the Register prominently displayed so that no visitor to the library could escape seeing the generosity of Bodley's friends. The plan, as it deserved, was a success, for its originator found that, 'every man bethinks himself how by some good book or other he may be written in the scroll of the benefactors'.
>
> *Wright 1939: 357–8*

The money and books poured in, from the Earl of Essex, Lord Buckhurst, Lord Hunsdon, Lord Lumley and many others. Universities have always been dependent on benefactors, on flattering the powerful of any given age. Although they have occasionally been places where dissent has been sheltered, or even revolution fomented, for most of their history they have been places that responded enthusiastically to those with money and power, naming buildings, lecture theatres and chairs after those who open their purses.

## The door to knowledge

The point is that the door to knowledge is a particular door, not a general one, and it requires money and power to build it. Furthermore, the university isn't a door in itself, but it contains many different doors. They don't go to anywhere and everywhere, but to particular places. Indeed, the spatial map of any university is a guide to its classification systems, to what it collects together and what it keeps apart, with science areas and arts areas, social science towers, and floors or corridors for other specialisms. The spatial and temporal distribution of knowledge is written across the campus, with ivy-clad stone for the old and glass-clad concrete for the new. Probably the most significant addition to most universities in the global north in the past fifty years has been the *Schola Commercia*, the business school. Often lodged in one of the newer buildings of the campus, it might have its own coffee bar for students who pay a lot of money, well-paid academics and lecture theatres with ample carpeting. It might also be named after someone who gave rather a lot of money and wants to be known as a benefactor.

So what do we find on the other side of the business school door? One example will suffice – that of Warwick Business School in England, a place that appears to have embraced the idea that theirs is a form of knowledge that changes the world and that should therefore be sold for premium prices. In a text with echoes of medieval theology in its 'visions' and 'missions', we find a description of what we can find if we open this door.

> ***Our Vision and Mission***
>
> Our vision is straightforward. What underlies everything is academic excellence, and the impact it has on society.
>
> Our vision.
>
> - To be the leading university-based business school in Europe.
>
> Our mission.
>
> - To produce and disseminate world-class, cutting edge research that is capable of shaping the way organisations operate and businesses are led and managed.
> - To produce world-class, socially responsible, creative leaders and managers who think on a global scale, regardless of the size of their organisation.
> - To provide a lifelong return on investment for our students and alumni.
>
> *www.wbs.ac.uk/about/difference/mission/ (accessed 15 September 2014)*

Some features of this knowledge are worth drawing attention to. First, we might observe that 'academic excellence' is asserted to be the practice that underpins everything that takes place within this business school, although this has been qualified (with an insertion that was edited several years after the original 2010 version of this statement) with the idea of 'impact on society'. Quite apart from the political good sense of nodding to the UK Government's introduction of 'impact' as a measure of excellence in the current state audit of research, this insertion might also be taken to qualify the previous clause, and also to suggest that the academic excellence which matters is that which has impact, and not that which is speculative or ivory tower. Further qualification is provided by the 'vision', which suggests that the institution is in competition with other 'university-based business schools' in Europe, and specifies that it is going to be the best one in the region. On what criteria is unclear, but we can probably assume that this will be measured by league tables and the like because some sort of metric must be used if the term 'leading' is to have anything other than rhetorical force. The 'mission' section further qualifies the claim about competitive and impactful research because it tells us who the customers are – 'leaders' and 'managers'. These are people who think on a global scale and who consequently require research that is up-to-date and amongst the best in the world in order to support their leadership and managing of organizations. The final sentence suggests a particular orientation to this knowledge because it is articulated as an investment that will provide a return. That is to say, the customer will purchase the knowledge with their money and time, and it will repay them. It seems safe to assume that this return will be economic, given the tone of the rest of the text.

In a text like this, we find a particular understanding of the relationship between knowledge and students, an assumption about who those students are, an implication about the market that business schools trade in, and a series of qualifications which allow us to understand that research is excellent when it helps leaders and managers (and the order is significant) have an impact on the world. Reading this statement as a series of claims about what the school *does not do* (which might be the only way to give it some distinctive meaning), it is clear that business schools do not teach knowledges or practices as an intrinsic good; do not teach workers, citizens or activists;

do not collaborate with other schools; and do not pursue research that helps workers, citizens and activists to have an impact on the world. If you want those other forms of knowledge, go elsewhere.

The point of this rather extended textual torture is to underline the idea that there is a relationship between forms of knowing and the structure of institutions. That is to say that the idea of the university as a timeless institution where certain liberal values *should* be taught is evidently misleading because the university does not have one orientation to knowledge, but many. Probably the only generalization we can make is to say that it is a machine for generating divisions and distinctions, made concrete in the long walk from the physics department to the philosophy department or the ramifications of the committee structure. As Mary Douglas (1987) has suggested, institutions can be treated like brains, structures that encourage certain forms of thinking whilst quietly making other connections difficult, even heretical. The mere fact that the Warwick Business School is on the edge of campus and has its own café is itself a way for an institution to think. So is the fact that the last time I was there, on the ground floor of one of its clinically white atria there was a large etched plastic plaque on the wall that lists its corporate benefactors. It also has links with the Royal Shakespeare Company in Stratford-upon-Avon. In 2012, Professor Mark Taylor, the then Dean of Warwick Business School, commented:

> This collaboration brings together two world-class organisations located in Shakespeare's Warwickshire in a unique creative partnership between a leading business school and a leading artistic company. WBS [Warwick Business School] brings the business acumen and academic experience of a top business school to the partnership, while the RSC [Royal Shakespeare Company] brings the creativity and performing experience of the world's greatest theatre company. This is in line with the WBS policy of looking at things differently. At WBS, creativity is our business.
>
> *Warwick University n.d.; see Taylor and O'Hanlon 2013*

Shakespeare, it seems, is going to be good for business, and D.H. Lawrence is turning in his grave.

## The labour of division

Daniel Defoe's posthumously published *The Compleat English Gentleman*, probably written in 1728–9, is in part an attack on the entrenched privileges of the day, and makes the seditious suggestion that anyone, regardless of parentage, can become a gentleman. One of his targets throughout the text is the 'meer scholar', someone he contrasts with 'the man of polite learning'.

> I think our meer scholars are a kind of mechanicks in the schools, for they deal in words and syllables as haberdashers deal in small ware. They trade in measure, quantityes, dactyls, and spondaes, as instrument-makers do in quadrants, rules, squares, and compasses; etymologyes, and derivations, prepositions and terminations, points, commas, colons and semicolons, etc. are the product of their brain, just as gods and devils are made in Italy by every carver and painter; and they fix them in their proper stations in perspective, just as they do in nitches and glass windows.
>
> *Defoe 1890: 201*

The scholar, for Defoe, was someone who administered narrow forms of knowledge, who didn't know how to do things themselves, but could scorn people who didn't understand Latin grammar. Defoe was on the side of utility, a dissenter who had run businesses and earned a living with his pen (Hamilton and Parker 2016). He saw no particular merit in learning for the sake of learning, but – perhaps like Mark Taylor – wanted people to be taught useful things.

Whatever we make of Defoe's impatience with conservative institutions that he felt were irrelevant to real lives, educated as he was within a dissenting academy, he does point to a crucial issue for my argument here. Organizations classify and place things in boxes. Nonetheless, there is often enough disagreement concerning what should go in which box, or what counts as learning within a particular discipline. Knowing is shaped by where we know from, by our location within the structures that make matters knowable. Our thought is situated, located, shaped by the questions that we are encouraged to ask, and the questions we are discouraged from asking. Foucault shows us that, particularly in *The Order of Things* (1989) but also in other works, to ask questions of classification is also to ask about epistemology because the connections and separations made are constitutive of the things themselves. As Foucault puts it, disciplines allow 'thought to operate on the entities of our world, to put them in order, to divide them into classes, to group them according to names that designate their similarities and differences' (1989: xix; see also Hjorth and Holt, this volume). I think this means that we can't understand the distinction between 'the humanities' and 'the social sciences' in terms of the *contents* of the domains because their separation is an *effect* of the way that classification systems operate. That is to say, it is the question of organization (in both its entity and process senses) that is so often missing from this account of two cultures, and that Foucault – institutional structuralist that he so often is – puts back in. This means that business school knowing is a particular form of knowledge – one that trades in words like 'leaders', 'management' and 'relevance'. As Douglas puts it in *How Institutions Think* (1987), the structures and processes of an organization tell us how people classify knowledge. They produce what is thinkable. We have a whole series of categories of people and things that are literally unimaginable without an institution to make them – professionals, alumni, car parking permits, managers, executives, students, hierarchies, departments, pay scales, professors, examinations, pigeonholes, administrators, deans, employees, reports, disciplines, degrees, programmes, committees, agendas, reports, targets, vice chancellors and so on. If we look at the organization charts of the university, we can see in boxes and lines how it chops up the world. Indeed, the words used are telling, speaking as they do of the separations that bring things together – faculties, colleges, schools, departments, divisions, units, groups, centres, institutes, hubs, areas, fields and classes. As Cooper (1993, 1989) observed, the boundary between this and that is what makes the system because there is no vision without division. So difference is manufactured, a dotted line is emplaced and it brings new knowing into the world.

## Seeing the B School

So the business school was made by acts of organizational classification. We could tell a story about student demand for the knowledges that might be used to run capitalism and a technocratic state, or (in some states such as the UK) the need for income for universities facing gradual withdrawal of state support and strong encouragement to find income streams from elsewhere. There are some excellent accounts of the growth and development of the business school, particularly in the US (Khurana 2007; O'Connor 2012; O'Connor, this volume), but any intellectual history must also tell a story about how a particular field of *knowledge* was demarcated through deploying new divisions of the old and unities of the new. From the late nineteenth century onwards, we therefore have the beginnings of a productive differentiation in much of the global north, which produces 'management' (and related terms) as a topic, although this assemblage is made with different components in different places at different times. In the

UK, the whole thing happens quite late, with a curriculum produced with bits and pieces from pre-existing fields – including 'the humanities' such as sociology, psychology and economics (all of which are categories of knowing that we don't find in the Old Schools Quadrangle).

The establishment of a new disciplinary area – Management, Commerce and Business – could never be something that happens rapidly because it involves many elements becoming aligned. Teaching and research staff must first come from elsewhere and then establish the infrastructure that supports a discipline. This includes workshops, conferences, journals, textbooks, websites, a professional association, prizes, publishing lists, endowed chairs, buildings, degrees, PhD students and so on. After a while, the infrastructure is experienced as timeless, as being a necessary part of the way in which the practice of the discipline is conducted. When the PhD students graduate to teaching and research positions, the business school is staffed by people who have not come from elsewhere and who do not have personal experiences of a different configuration of knowledge (Parker 2015). Students are in turn taught by people who have done business school PhDs, and people inside and outside the institution begin to recognize the B School as a particular sort of place that deals in particular kinds of knowledge.

But the labour of division doesn't end here, because the knowledge in the B School is further divided into departments – strategy, marketing, finance, accounting, operations, information systems – each of which become recognizable as a distinct concern, often with its own conferences, journals, textbooks and so on. Within the new building, each domain has its own corridor and perhaps a group, division or department. The granularity of knowing doesn't end there either because fine internal distinctions become deployed to understand the particular orientation that individuals or groups might have towards their subject matter, such as those who operate to distinguish organizational behaviour, organizational theory, organization studies, human resource management, organizational psychology, industrial relations, employee relations and so on. As Defoe suggested, 'meer scholars' will often find it hard to explain to outsiders just what these distinctions mean and why they matter at all.

There is a further context here as well because the business school, as it solidifies and becomes a distinctive place concerned with its own continuation, tends to become somewhere that produces knowledge *for* management rather than knowledge *about* management. As the professional assemblage hardens, it tends to exclude ideas and practices that do not fit easily into the classification systems that have been established. If a form of knowledge cannot be emplaced, like a misplaced book in a library, it ceases to become useful knowledge and instead falls between the cracks. The knowledge that is hegemonic in the business school is that which assumes hierarchical organization, market-based forms of exchange (including a marketizing state) and the need for 'management' as occupational group, academic discipline and practical skill. It is knowledge about how to make capitalism and markets work – and that relies on flattering those in power, just as Thomas Bodley did, four centuries earlier. The inhabitants of the business school therefore teach about 'leadership' as if it were a form of grace and host lectures from the rich and powerful, perhaps in the hope that some of their gold might pay for the chicken dinner.

Academic knowledge is made by institutions and the story I have suggested here is one that could be echoed in the rise of any discipline during the past four hundred years. Such assemblages allow us to do all sorts of interesting things, things that would be much more difficult without the supports and scaffolds of the discipline, but we also need to be aware of the constraints that this produces. The B School makes things possible, but quietly makes others things difficult too. Discipline can be defined in at least three ways: as a form of training that involves following rules; as an activity that improves a skill; and also as a form of punishment that corrects inappropriate behaviour. These are not contradictory because if you want to learn something, you must also learn what *not* to do and what practices or habits to avoid. This means that certain methods, authorities and evidence become constitutive of what it means to practise a certain discipline. In terms of the concerns of this book, it suggests that the sort of things that go on in the arts and humanities have to be shaped to fit the assumptions of the business school if they are to be recognizable, that the materials and practices that are admitted tend to be used for their utility, and the materials and practices that can't be co-opted easily tend to be pushed away. Shakespeare is being used to sell Warwick Business School when, ironically, Thomas Bodley was assiduous in keeping 'riff-raff' books and plays – including Shakespeare – from getting into his library at all (Wright 1939: 360). That is what all the divisions within the university do – not just the business school. Doors are there to keep people out too.

## Practical education

In 1827, Thomas Carlyle remarked of one of his contemporaries, Dugald Stewart, that he

> does not enter on the field to till it: He only encompasses it with fences, invites cultivators, and drives away intruders; often . . . he is reduced to long arguments with the passers-by, to prove that it is a field, that this so highly prized domain of his is, in truth, soil and substance, not clouds and shadow.
>
> *Carlyle cited in Beer 1989: 78*

There is something rather timeless about the idea of scholars fighting over trivia, over the ownership of fields, and this whole book could easily be seen as another example of it. But whatever side we take in Lawson's wrestling match between culture and utility (1998: 273) we must never forget that these are very often institutional matters. The practice of dividing this from that must eventually come down to deciding what is in and what is out through the machineries of promotions, exam boards, course reviews, set texts and so on. Making grand pronouncements about the importance of the arts and humanities for management education is a bit pointless if it doesn't connect squarely to the ways that institutions think. But it also helps if we understand something about history, and know that we are not the first people to have these worries.

Defoe's utilitarian complaints about the pointlessness of the 'meer scholars' were echoed by Adam Smith (now the *eminence grise* of the neoliberals) fifty years later. In Smith's 1776 *The Wealth of Nations*, he complains about the lack of teaching, the Latin and Greek, the refusal to change and the poor preparation for life that the universities of the time provided. He famously complained that they were a 'sanctuary in which exploded systems and obsolete prejudices find shelter and protection after they have been hunted out of every corner of the world' (1990: 360). Given such hostility, no wonder that a version of Jonathan Swift's celebration of 'sweetness and light' was put forward loudly as a defence of liberal education by various cultured commentators during the nineteenth century because the utilitarians (the progenitors of the business school, remember) were noisily on the march.

To use a British example, *Practical Education* was a treatise published in 1798 by Maria Edgeworth and her father, Richard Lovell Edgeworth. Influenced by Locke and Rousseau, they encourage hands-on learning, experimentation and precision in words. The idea was to ensure that education 'endeavoured to suggest the easiest means of inducing useful and agreeable habits, well-regulated sympathy and benevolent affections' (1815: iv). That meant no fairy tales or discussions of religion, but a clear, practical and useful set of well-defined tasks that would lead to the development of skill. Edward Copleston, Provost of Oriel College, Oxford from 1814 to 1828 and later Bishop of Llandaff in Wales, took exception to such educational instrumentalism.

> In his [Mr Edgeworth's] system, the value of every attainment is to be measured by its subserviency to a calling. The specific duties of that calling are exalted at the cost of those free and independent tastes and virtues which come in to sustain the common relations of society, and raise the individual in them. In short, a man is to be usurped by his profession. He is to be clothed in its garb from head to foot. His virtues, his science, and his ideas are all to be put into a gown or uniform, and the whole man to be shaped, pressed, and stiffened, in the exact mould of his technical character. Any interloping accomplishments, or a faculty which cannot be taken into public pay, if they are to be indulged in him at all, must creep along under the cloak of his more serviceable privileged merits. Such is the state of perfection to which the spirit and general tendency of this system would lead us.
>
> *Copleston 1811: 174*

Copleston was quoted approvingly by one of the famous English defenders of the university, John Henry Newman, in his 1852 lectures *The Idea of an University* (1907 [1852]: 170). Newman is defending a free but Catholic university in Ireland, and appears to quite like Copleston's idea that a good education

> without directly qualifying a man for any of the employments of life, it enriches and ennobles all. Without teaching him the particular business of any one office or calling, it enables him to act his part in each of them with better grace and more elevated carriage.
>
> *Newman 1907 [1852]: 169*

With a few amendments, it seems to me that this is an assertion that could also have come from the Carnegie Report, if we add some echoes of the British class system and the sort of cultural capital that allowed one to believe that the Empire was won on the playing fields of Eton. But there is a darker side to Copleston and Newman's understanding of the university, a romantic critique of industrialism, and a clear reference to Smith's complicity with the dark satanic mills.

> 'It is an undisputed maxim in Political Economy', says Dr Copleston, 'that the separation of professions and the division of labour tend to the perfection of every art, to the wealth of nations, to the general comfort and well-being of the community. This principle of division is in some instances pursued so far as to excite the wonder of people to whose notice it is for the first time pointed out. [. . .] But, while [the worker] thus contributes more effectually to the accumulation of national wealth, he becomes himself more and more degraded as a rational being. In proportion as his sphere of action is narrowed his mental powers and habits become contracted; and he resembles a subordinate part of some powerful machinery, useful in its place, but insignificant and worthless out of it'.
>
> *Newman 1907 [1852]: 168*

Lawson (1998) describes this long standoff between classifications, between the humanities and the utilitarians, as a *differend* in Lyotard's phrasing (1988). This is a dispute that can never be solved because the parties don't agree on the terms, to which Lawson adds the suggestion that the distinction is productive on both sides. As Cooper (1993, 1989; see also Brown, this volume) suggests, the work of making a boundary is the important issue here. The distinction between the two sides is an effect of classification, something made by the organization, and hence by the organization of knowledge. The business school, it seems to me, is predicated on assumptions that make it very difficult indeed to do anything other than *use* the humanities. The questions must always be, what is this for, what does it do, what does it add? How can Shakespeare help me get things done by Monday morning?

## Conclusion

The argument I have been leading to here is one that might be described as institutionally structuralist or historically determinist, with systems of classification determining the genesis and reception of ideas. It does seem to me that it is necessary to make this argument in order to push back against two tendencies: the first that assumes the utility of culture and the second that assumes that culture can put utility in its place. The first is the convenient magical resolution that we find in Colby *et al.* (2011), in which the contradiction between culture and utility is dissolved by insisting that the cultivated intellect is exactly what twenty-first-century business needs (see also Chia and Nayak, this volume). The guest workers, shipping container parks and the financialization of everything disappear behind a beguiling account of the synergies between knowledge capitalism and human capital. Ironically, we can find pretty much the same disregard of structures from the opposite side of the argument, from those who wish to use the humanities to civilize managers, or even as a battering ram to smash down the gates of the neoliberal dream factory. Of course, this is not a new argument and the echo of Newman is there still.

> The Philosopher, indeed, and the man of the world differ in their very notion, but the methods, by which they are respectively formed, are pretty much the same. The Philosopher has the same command of matters of thought, which the true citizen and gentleman has of matters of business and conduct. If then a practical end must be assigned to a University course, I say it is that of training good members of society. Its art is the art of social life, and its end is fitness for the world. It neither confines its views to particular professions on the one hand, nor creates heroes or inspires genius on the other.
>
> *Newman 1907 [1852]: 177*

Many of the chapters in this book end with this sort of wilful optimism, more radical than Newman's but still shaped by the idea that studying the humanities is good in itself, that it helps form character and sympathy, produce critical citizens and questioning subjects.

To my mind, both of these positions fail to engage with the university as an institution, and with the ways in which the very construction of the B School is an act of classification that asserts utility against culture. There will always be leaks and gaps, of course, but the *Schola Commercia* cannot be wished away as if a hopeful insistence could dissolve the epistemological and financial imperatives which built the thing in the first place. To put it simply, the business school teaches capitalism, and although this way of shaping the human and its potentialities is dominant, the business school will continue to exist. The management of an Amazon warehouse will not change because the manager has learned multiple framing and integrative thought from reading Shakespeare on their MBA. Neither will capitalism be undone by using films in the classroom, or writing about radical art practice or selected philosophers in books like these.

This is a conclusion I don't like very much, and I would very much like to pull a rabbit out of the hat at this point and show how agency trumps structure, how the humanities will vanquish the utilitarians and the B School produce revolutionaries inspired by art. As one of my co-editors reminded me, I haven't thought much here about the 'social sciences' as a category, which confuses my too tidy binary between art and business. Neither have I written anything about the ways that the actual practice of teaching with a humanities sensibility – documented in many of the chapters in this volume – allows boundaries to be blurred and new spaces to emerge (see, for example, Michels and Beyes, this volume). It would be comforting for someone like me to be able to say these sort of things, a lullaby that soothes the conscience and allows me to feel righteous when I confront the hopeful masses in Management 101, or my employer's demands for more financial 'contribution' that prevents the closure of departments of philosophy, sociology, history and so on. But let's be clear what I am concluding here. It's simply that the business school cannot be civilized or radicalized by the arts and humanities, not that the arts and humanities can't in themselves civilize or radicalize. I think that the problem is the business school, and it will continue to be the business school, whether it has art on the walls or plays in the atrium.

David Foster Wallace expresses the value of a liberal education in much more personal ways. In encouraging us to see the water, he is encouraging us to see, to notice what happens around us and prevent ourselves falling into easy habits and patterns of thought. For the purposes of my argument here, this means seeing the historical structuring of the *differend* between culture and utility, and seeing the ways in which institutions do thinking for us. It means noticing that universities are machines for dividing up knowledge, and that they have long been in the business of dispensing qualifications for money. But knowing this doesn't make the arts and humanities any the less important. It's just that I think their importance can only be understood in rather personal terms, unless we really think hard about restructuring the university itself, and that probably means getting rid of the business school.

There is a paradox here in that I have told a gloomy story about the monolithic business school from inside it – indeed from inside the UK version of it, which is perhaps more neoliberal than many other European examples (Parker 2014). Perhaps this is a performative contradiction, in terms of my institutionally structuralist argument, and I am in fact demonstrating (with my smattering of history, literature and social theory) that which I claim to be disallowed by the ways that institutions think. This 'humanities sensibility' informs all of the chapters in this volume, after all. I think David Foster Wallace would like this sort of paradox and the way it demonstrates that thought often exceeds the buildings we place it in. As he concluded, to the liberal arts graduates of Keynon,

> It is about the real value of a real education, which has almost nothing to do with knowledge, and everything to do with simple awareness; awareness of what is so real and essential, so hidden in plain sight all around us, all the time, that we have to keep reminding ourselves over and over: 'this is water'.
>
> *Foster Wallace 2008*

## Note

1 Thanks to my co-editors for comments on an even gloomier version of this chapter.

## References


Beer, G. (1989) *Arguing with the Past*. London: Routledge.

Cooper, R. (1989) 'The visibility of social systems'. *In:* M.C. Jackson, P. Keys and S. Cropper (eds.) *Operational Research and the Social Sciences*. New York, NY: Plenum Press, pp. 51–9.

Cooper, R. (1993) 'Technologies of representation'. *In:* P. Ahonen (ed.) *Tracing the Semiotic Boundaries of Politics*. Berlin: Mouton de Gruyter, pp. 279–312.

Copleston, E. (1811) 'Art.X. Essays on professional education,' *The Quarterly Review*, VI. London: John Murray, pp. 166–91.

Colby, A., Ehrlich, T., Sullivan, W. and Dolle, J. (2011) *Rethinking Undergraduate Business Education*. San Francisco, CA: Jossey-Bass.

Collini, S. (2012) *What are Universities For?* London: Penguin.

Defoe, D. (1890) *The Compleat English Gentleman*. London: David Nutt.

Douglas, M. (1987) *How Institutions Think*. London: Routledge and Kegan Paul.

Edgeworth, M. and Edgeworth, R. (1815) *Practical Education*. Providence, RI: J. Francis Lippitt.

Foster Wallace, D. (1996) *Infinite Jest*. New York, NY: Little, Brown.

Foster Wallace, D. (2011) *The Pale King*. New York, NY: Little, Brown.

Foster Wallace, D. (2008) 'This is water'. Available from: http://bulletin.kenyon.edu/x4280.html (accessed 29 January 2016).

Foucault, M. (1989) *The Order of Things*. Abingdon, UK: Routledge.

Hamilton, V. and Parker, M. (2016) *Daniel Defoe and the Bank of England: The Dark Arts of Projectors*. Winchester, UK: Zero Books.

Khurana, R. (2007) *From Higher Aims to Hired Hands*. Princeton, NJ: Princeton University Press.

Lawrence, D.H. (2002 [1929]) *Pansies*. Amsterdam: Fredonia Books.

Lawson, A. (1998) 'Culture and utility: phrases in dispute'. *In:* D. Jary and M. Parker (eds.) *The New Higher Education*. Stoke-on-Trent, UK: Staffordshire University Press, pp. 273–87.

Lyotard, J.-F. (1988) *The Differend*. Minneapolis, MN: University of Minnesota Press.

Newman, J.H. (1907 [1852]) *The Idea of an University. Defined and Illustrated*. London: Longmans Green and Co.

O'Connor, E. (2012) *Creating New Knowledge in Management*. Stanford, CA: Stanford University Press.

Parker, M. (2014) 'University, Ltd: changing a business school', *Organization*, 21(2), 281–92.

Parker, M. (2015) 'Between sociology and the B School: critical studies of organization, work and employment in the UK', *Sociological Review*, 63(1), 162–80.

Smith, A. (1776 [1990]) *The Wealth of Nations*. London: Penguin.

Snow, C.P. (2001 [1959]) *The Two Cultures*. London: Cambridge University Press.

Taylor, M. and O'Hanlon, J. (2013) 'WBS and the RSC – teaching Shakespeare'. YouTube, 19 April. Available from: https://www.youtube.com/watch?v=7aA9TpJquRA (accessed 29 January 2016).

Warwick University (n.d.) 'Warwick Business School and Royal Shakespeare Company announce joint venture for the teaching of Shakespeare'. Available from: http://www2.warwick.ac.uk/newsandevents/pressreleases/teaching-shakespeare/ (accessed 29 January 2016).

Wright, L. (1939) 'Some early "friends" of libraries', *Huntingdon Library Quarterly*, 2/3, 355–69.

# 37

# Management education and the humanities

## A future together?

*Bogdan Costea and Kostas Amiridis*

The Carnegie Report of 2011 marked a very public reopening of the debate about the nature of business education (see Sullivan, Ehrlich and Colby, this volume). Targeted at the more or less typical structure of undergraduate programmes in US schools, the report discloses certain fundamental limitations of the current dominant curriculum and its general intellectual constitution. The focus on the undergraduate level is quite apposite: not only are they not inferior to postgraduate programmes, but their formative influence is also perhaps even more noteworthy because their much longer duration inevitably gives them a more intimate and nuanced place in the general personal and professional evolution of the participants. The report develops a picture that captures, far beyond the sample of institutions surveyed in the text itself, a series of difficult areas of inquiry that show how business and management programmes have become less able to engage with complex problems derived from the increasingly central place of business and management in the cultural, social, economic and political processes of our age. There are not many empirical findings presented in the report that do not characterise, to a greater or lesser extent, any undergraduate programme in any business school.

One apparently coincidental aspect, however, brings into sharp focus what is really taking place – in intellectual terms – in undergraduate business education. Although the research and publication of the text would have taken place anyway, it is highly illustrative that its unfolding around the onset of the global financial and economic crisis in 2008 allowed the team, led by Anne Colby, to focus amongst other things on how business schools came to treat, understand and represent the nature, origins and sense of the powerful process that has been taking place ever since all over the world and in every sphere of global business and economy, as well as affecting global society as a whole. It is perhaps the most troubling and revealing finding that mobilised the team: the most important event and process that ought to concern academics in business and management schools turned out to be the least explicit topic of debate in lecture halls and seminar rooms. What Colby and her colleagues realised, with legitimate surprise and indignation, was the paradox that the very core event of the business world – the 'signal event of the time' (Colby *et al.* 2011: 11) as they rightly call it – had somehow become unteachable and almost unthinkable in business schools themselves. They note their reaction with explicit intensity:

> Many [students and faculty] we spoke with seemed to hope that it would all somehow be corrected so they could resume business as usual. Their previous understandings of the workings of the business world were so strong that, even in the face of massive problems, neither business faculty nor students cracked open those understandings to reveal the need for alternative points of view and new approaches.
>
> *Colby et al. 2011: 11*

As they encountered it repeatedly throughout the empirical phase of the research, this troubling silence seems to have had significant importance for the report, explicitly and implicitly – and it is indeed a remarkable and undeniable occurrence: what ought to have been a most eminently 'teachable moment' (Colby *et al.* 2011: 10–12) is met with an almost inexplicable intellectual silence, with a suspect conceptual resistance precisely in those disciplines that should be most interested in it. Even after 2011, this silence has remained a feature of the pedagogy of business education: it is almost as if the now multiple and deep crises of business, economy and finance have the power to embarrass rather than interest those respective disciplines. Altogether, the general diagnostic of the report is at once straightforward and compelling: business schools have become increasingly isolated from the other domains of inquiry into the social, cultural, economic and political processes of our time. This isolation has left business schools in a position of conceptual and intellectual vulnerability and impoverishment to such an extent that even the most important historical events in which business plays a central role are hard to analyse and understand in the very places where business is studied.

What the Carnegie Report suggests is that the solution is to open up business education to the resources of what is carefully termed 'liberal learning' – a notion that comes to stand as a general reference to the broad domains of the social sciences and humanities. This rapprochement would add the necessary ingredients for a pedagogical synthesis leading to the formation of an 'integrative consciousness' (Colby *et al.* 2011: 6), a completed manner of 'being' a business person or manager: endowed with mastery over calculative rationality, with the ability to synthesise self-reflective control over personal will and drive with the sensibility for multiple possible contexts of meaning outside oneself, as well as with the capacity for more responsible ethical and social deliberation in, and for, the world (Colby *et al.* 2011: 60). This is indeed a noble quest for a kind of business education whose aim is the perfection of the character of the professional who embodies the agency of business and management as the axes of the process of value creation in the contemporary world. Perhaps not another coincidence, the emergence in 2009 of the 'MBA Oath' outlined a similar set of aspirations and also carried the perceptive and suggestive subtitle of 'Responsible Value Creation' (Anderson 2009). This is an equally, if not even more, ambitious statement of the desire that business education would lead to the formation of the manager as a professional character able to secure in 'business' that place of value creation, distribution and exchange where the contradictions between prosperity, profitability and growth would finally come to be reconciled with the imperatives of balance, justice, the well-being of all, as well as the sustainability of humanity's existence within the limits of nature.

Notwithstanding the legitimacy of all these desiderata and of the imperative that these contradictions ought to be recognised and resolved, the question remains: is it really possible to believe that such a Promethean character can exist and, moreover, be brought about through a system of education? Is this incontestably positive agenda not a utopian statement that begins to obscure rather than disclose what might actually be at stake in business education? And, on the other hand, would the humanities and social sciences, as they are struggling with their own intellectual identities, be able to deliver the enlightenment necessary for the emergence of this new 'integrative consciousness' – in other words, would the humanities have the power to humanise to such an extent? And is that even their task?

Whilst appearing entirely reasonable and opportune, we argue that the programme outlined in the Carnegie Report might not be as intellectually productive as it seems. As an expression of what might be termed an ethical 'neo-Enlightenment' (the synthesis of its programme bearing an unmistakable resemblance to Kant's philosophical system), it is an attempt to seek the resolution of a series of contradictions whose formulations require a more detailed reading. This chapter will highlight several aspects that are problematic in the Carnegie diagnosis of business education, and – more importantly perhaps – of 'business' as a general historical phenomenon. Our argument is contrapuntal: we do not contest at all the conclusion that highlights the intellectual isolation of business schools within universities and their apparent impoverishment, but we do contest the manner in which this conclusion is derived. Perhaps a better understanding of the power and cultural force of business schools would shed light on why they can carry on despite their intellectual avoidance of the complex contradictions of the epoch. The question of a possible contribution from the humanities might then appear in a different light. To anticipate, our suggestion is that the humanities might not be the miraculous, humanising cure for the actual and purported limitations of business education. Rather, the humanities may still have access to major sources of thinking that could bring students of business into a closer connection with the complexity of the contemporary world as a whole and also to a better understanding of the central, determining place that business, as a historical process, occupies within it. In other words, instead of the formation of a perfect character, business education might benefit from a deeper investigation of business itself, provided it can subject itself to an analysis that might reveal an uncomfortable image. Despite its historical centrality, business and management are places of irreducible contradiction, of unanswered and unanswerable questions that now form the very ground of business conduct.

It is important to note that these questions are publicly explicit in the concerns of the business domain itself. From a recent and extensive survey (CarringtonCrisp 2014) emerges a synthesis that grasps the essence of the dilemmas generated by the essential place of business in the world today. The survey reveals four major dimensions marking the expectations of the kind of understanding and ability to think that business schools ought to provide. Graduates of business schools should be able to understand that:

1 Business models need to change to better engage with society.
2 Business needs to be about more than just maximising shareholder value.
3 Business needs to take a stronger lead on sustainability.
4 Business leaders should behave ethically at all times.

In these apparently simple statements, something very important is said about the intellectual demands facing business education. First, new forms of engagement with society indicate the capacity to understand the permanent question and struggle concerning the place of 'business' in contemporary society and politics. To conduct business is not merely a matter of 'new products and services' or of 'creativity and innovation'. It is a matter of understanding what kind of forces management and business are. Second, the ability to think about new forms of value entails another struggle: the struggle to claim power over the creation of value in new ways, to find new forms of social, cultural, political and economic legitimation of what counts as value. It is not simply a question of 'rethinking money' or 'products' or 'economics'. It means the capacity to understand that business has become a place where value is continuously displaced and destroyed in order for anything that might be called 'new' to emerge at all. In other words, it is a matter of understanding how business becomes increasingly unsettled by the demands for the production of the 'new' and how it becomes preoccupied with the permanent destruction and destabilisation of all values. Third, the call to think about 'sustainability' means the ability to understand that the power of nature has become the embodiment of a permanent danger to the current mode of life and that it shows the incapacity of contemporary societies and cultures to think about limits (Brown, this volume; Wright and Nyberg, this volume). Finally, the permanent call to 'be ethical' shows the equal difficulty faced in understanding what is binding in contemporary social and political relationships: what does it mean to 'be good'? When does the pursuit of legitimate business – that is, the pursuit of the production of 'value' – become a danger? And what is to be done when the genuine ethical conflict arises: when the collision of 'good' with 'good' is irresolvable and entails radical sacrifice?

We have reformulated these four areas as examples of the depth and ambiguity of the questions that face business – questions that ought to find their expression in business education itself, but also questions that explain why it is worth setting out the task we formulate in the title: could business education and the humanities have a future together in any substantive sense at all? Our argument is that the heritage of the humanities and social sciences, especially the rereading of major classical sources in a historical key, could be potentially mobilised if 'business' and 'management' are opened up for investigation in the most profound sense. It is not impossible to envisage interdisciplinary programmes that would attempt to explore the complexity of the contemporary historical condition in which business and management are so central; it is, however, in our opinion less viable to think of the humanities and social sciences as devices for the production of a perfected human character, of a figure that would tower above the dilemmas of its own condition.

## What the Carnegie Report does not see: an alternative reading

The Carnegie Report is a rich and multifaceted text. Whilst it is not a normal academic monograph, it is an articulate volume that operates as a diagnostic of the present situation of undergraduate business education, as a revisiting of elements of its history, as an empirical investigation and also, perhaps most importantly, as a programmatic document (see Landfester, Tofte Brenneche and Prat-i-Pubill, this volume). Nonetheless, its mission is clear throughout: it aims to elaborate a normative programme, a vision of how business education *ought* to be oriented, an 'ought' defined in critical contradistinction with a current state of imperfection and educational deficit.

For us, of central interest is how the report constructs this deficit, this lack of liberal learning in business education and what are its most basic assumptions for this diagnostic. This means trying to understand and decipher the text itself, but also some of the elements behind or between its lines. Some of its major conceptual aspects (indeed the very categories of 'business' and 'liberal learning'), certain fundamental definitions and deep assumptions, as well as the ground of core contrasts set up to sustain the argument, are not analysed explicitly. Rather they are simply sustained by powerful general statements that appeal with ease to a sense of indignation with the 'business way of thinking' as a force that subverts a more genuine, 'liberal' humanity. Thus, the analytic and conceptual material, the empirical data and the historical sources, as well as the programmatic, normative ideas, are all interwoven in a dense texture that is not easy to penetrate.

To understand the deeper currents flowing through the report, the reader must pause and actively force apart some of its assumptions, as well as having to separate the content from the various tonalities in which the text is written. The main reason lies in the difficult manner in which programmatic (or 'curative') strategies, however well intended, intersect and overlap with analysis and diagnosis. As is often the case with complex programmatic documents, the silent premises and conceptual sources for the diagnosis provide just as much insight into the subtle but essential architecture of the argument as the text itself. We will consider several of these aspects here, recognising that we run the risk of brevity and could have devoted a full chapter to each.

### *Business*

The report opens with a strong statement: 'Business has never mattered more' (Colby *et al.* 2011: 1). It seems to express *ab initio* the recognition that the place of 'business' in the world today is to have become that kind of historical force that connects and determines destinies and directions at planetary level; however, throughout the text, one of the truly decisive premises is the manner in which 'business' (as a general domain of human existence) is then set up in a radical antinomy to the rest of the social world. Perhaps the most emphatic iteration of this position states that:

> it is especially important that business students learn to recognize and distinguish between the dominant logic of business and the marketplace, on the one hand, and, on the other, the very different values and ways of acting that hold sway in the family and the domestic sphere, the worlds of science and education, the arts, and within a democratic government. Business graduates will need facility in moving among these different spheres of value and logics of action. They will benefit from learning to see business and its logic from the outside as well as from within.
>
> *Colby et al. 2011: 5*

This passage marks the essential gesture through which 'business' is configured as a separate sphere of social life but, more importantly, as a sphere in which values are produced that stand over and against the private lives of individuals and families, the public life of the polis and government itself in its democratic constitution, as well as against different modes of thinking, valuation and expression in science, arts and education. Business thinking is moreover the marker of a specific mentality that '... overlook[s] the different values represented by families, religious congregations, and communities' (Colby *et al.* 2011: 5).

So what is 'business' then? What exactly is its place in the current historical process? And why does it stand in such a stark antagonism in terms of foundational values from all the other spheres in which values are decided, individually or collectively? The category of 'business' and the domain subsumed under this label are never actually defined. Throughout the text they remain in an open-ended, undecided and permanently ambiguous condition. In spite of its stated importance, the sphere of this core category is not substantiated through a systematic exposition, neither at the outset, nor elsewhere in the text. Without precise conceptual contour, the word 'business' appears as a kind of general historical force that may, and indeed does, take on any sense required in the formation of the argument: at times business means 'corporations' or sectors of activity, at other times it refers to an economic process taking the general form of the 'market'. Sometimes it comes to mean a way of thinking contaminating other sectors of activity, as well as being used to refer to a 'utilitarian', self-absorbed mindset characteristic of students or academics in business education. The key element we seek to highlight here is that because the concept of business does not settle in the text, the directions and consequences deriving from its varied incarnations begin to merge in a rather amorphous and fluid aggregate whose role is to carry and represent one constant feature: that business is accompanied always by a shadow of danger, by a kind of darkness and guilt that have the power to subvert humanity in its more genuine and innocent manifestations.

'Business' – and by extension business education – appears to hide a form of anti-humanism, in other words a thinking that disrupts the humanity of the human and destabilises processes of value creation in their authentic human character. The tendency to place business in the role of a bad, subversive, treacherous, greedy, destructive character of history becomes an underlying feature of the text – and this simplification becomes a fundamental question about the validity of the historical interpretation that underlies the report. The concern that arises immediately is if business carries inextricably in itself the seeds of evil, why would it make sense to rescue its educational system at all? How could it still be part of a perfected future if its real power is to arouse the worst forms of valuation and become destructive of the true values of the family, community and the democratic state? Interpreting the report's underlying direction in these precise terms is important because it is this tendency that becomes decisive if we are to understand the viability and substance of its programme. Is it productive to simplify the historical meaning of 'business' to this extent? Does this position really capture what 'business' represents in this epoch: the source of humanity's general malaise, a place for the predication of a kind of inhumanity? Our argument is that this premise, even if it were a mere intellectual exercise, delivers a conceptual reduction that cannot but haunt the overall argument itself. It seems to us that this simplification leaves out the real problem with 'business' as a mode of human existence that claims power over the dynamic of contemporary history (for better or worse), namely the problem that the business enterprise is not only a source of human malevolence, of a will structured by dark values.

The problem for thinking about 'business' is that since the dawn of modernity it has also been the domain claimed by the modern subject for the expression of its freedom. The sense of the word 'freedom' and the way in which it comes to be linked to business is quite essential: modern freedom is grounded in the claim to self-determination and this means that it is understood as a struggle to secure a position from which the self comes to determine the way in which everything is, and in which everything is taken to be, with respect to his or her life. In other words, freedom itself becomes an act of production and self-production: setting up everything that is, making and remaking everything into objects as well as subjective states. Acting, deciding for oneself and ultimately risking oneself is the dynamic of contemporary society – it pertains to all spheres of life: individual, family, civil society, state and world as a whole. What is obscured in a purely negative moral interpretation of 'business' is perhaps its most important character. It seems to us a crucial starting point to recognise that the historical condition of a business is as the machinery of human production, as a claim to human self-expression. In other words, business has to be understood in more essential terms, namely representing the historical process of modernity as an expression of the place of value production for the modern subject as fabricator, but above all as valuator.

This is what makes 'business' such an important part of contemporary society and why commerce becomes the central stage where the characters of our epoch try to work out the sense of existence: because 'business' and 'commerce' come to occupy the place where values are determined and thus where the essential confrontations and contestations take place. Both 'good' and 'bad' will are expressed on this stage, for better or for worse. Perhaps this makes it easier to understand why the language of 'finance' and 'economics' started to attract enormous interest for prospective students precisely when the crises of finance and economy erupted on the public scene. It became clear that current generations are instinctively attracted to the place of value production – going to business school and studying 'finance' is not merely a circumstantial gesture, but a process that has to be understood in its true depth if the educational process is to begin to consider ways of expanding its intellectual reach. The appeal of business education to students cannot be taken as superficial. Indeed, the report's own findings emphasise this: '. . . we found it distressingly common, even in high-quality programs, to hear students say that their business courses had taught them that "everything is business"' (Colby *et al.* 2011: 5). In fact, this formulation perhaps hides the fact that choosing to go to business school in the first place has been increasingly bound up with this mentality: business courses cement it, for sure, but they add to an existing mindset. If business is a dangerous mode of thinking about the world, this is actually because it has come to permeate all spheres of value judgement – and in the way in which it does indeed hold sway over contemporary orders of life, it is just as dangerous to deny its fundamental historical effectiveness.

## *Liberal learning*

Let us now turn to another antinomy set up in the report, one that arises as an extension of the separation of business from other spheres of human self-expression that comes to be mirrored in the contrast set up between business education and 'liberal learning'. Several elements establish this contrast. Two are important to explain here. On the one hand, business education is profiled as a kind of 'disintegrating', fragmentary type of education based exclusively upon a 'highly technical model' (Colby *et al.* 2011: 12), in contrast to the possibility of 'an integrative vision' (Colby *et al.* 2011: 6) with its roots in the powers of liberal learning. This is the vision of the completed and perfected minds of

> integrative thinkers [who] have developed the ability to hold conflicting strategies and imperatives together at the same time. This capacity to find integrative solutions to problems created by the messy conjunction of conflicting opposites is a cardinal feature of a high-quality liberal education.
>
> *Colby* et al. *2011: 31*

To posit this high ideal for the kind of education business and management ought to become, it is necessary to elaborate an image of the current state as distant from and opposed to this ideal. It is through the way in which this sub-ideal state is constructed that the report creates a rather distorted image of the thematic and ethos of business education in its current form. The choice is to focus upon certain elements of the business curriculum that allow the argument to characterise business education as 'highly technical'. The focus falls, unsurprisingly, upon the disciplines that always appear to be devoid of 'human content', preoccupied exclusively with the construction of calculative regularities and 'one-way causation', in other words with 'linear thinking' (Colby *et al.* 2011: 30–1). The domains in question are accounting, financial modelling and economics. They are and have been, of course, much maligned in multiple critical assessments of the limits of business thinking.

But is it really sufficient to assume that the content and disciplinary dynamic of these domains is disconnected from a general conception of humanity? Moreover, is it possible to consider such disciplines as subverting human purposes and ideals characteristic of this – our – historical period? The danger here lies in the following assumption: that characterising business education as 'technical' and 'calculative' is a sufficient critique demonstrating its deficit of human concern. The reason why this assumption is dangerous is because it obscures the very centrality of technical thinking, of technology as a mode of human engagement with the world. The implication that technical thinking leads to a dissolution of an ideal unity of human existence poses a significant risk, a risk that is taken in the report but not resolved. This risk is that an interpretation of the relationship between technology and modern humans as an opposition misses entirely the fact that technology and calculative thought are the core manifestation of modernity as the era of human self-assertion. Technology itself has come to be precisely the core mechanism through which modernity seeks to pursue its core human value: freedom, understood as liberation from constraints, dangers, unpredictability and as security against the possibility of violence (Jaspers 1951; Jünger 1993; Heidegger 2010). The assumption that technical thinking is soulless is not hard to make – it is in fact an easy position to adopt for a contemporary audience. However, it is also a weak approach to technology and its direct and unambiguous relation with the soul of the modern epoch.

## *The market and the person*

The report introduces two additional reductions in its general tendency to portray business education as incomplete. First, the argument pursues the trope of a 'market mindset' (Colby *et al.* 2011: 26) as the exclusive cultural frame of reference for the business classroom. The question is not whether this portrayal is wrong, but whether it is sufficient to invoke 'the market' in order to have secured an unequivocal image of an inhuman or dehumanising order of values. The positing of the market as a place that releases the worst in human attitudes is, similar to criticisms of technology, an effective rhetorical device that relies on justified moral objections. Just as in the case of technology, moral objections or a position of moral reservation cannot eliminate the historical reality of the market as an institution of human exchange, which in itself expresses a particular humanity, however problematic it may appear from certain angles. The 'market mindset' functions in the report in a particular manner: its exposition builds up to a general picture in which human interactions are fraught with cruelty, selfishness, exploitative instincts, distrust and fraudulence (Colby *et al.* 2011: 26–9). Indeed, this portrayal may be legitimate, but the 'market' form of human exchange is but an outcome of certain historical processes whose condition of possibility lies in the cultural character of the epoch. If the market mindset were to disappear or be reduced, would selfishness, possessiveness, desire, the sense of entitlement, also disappear?

Finally, there is one more element in the structure of business education presented in the Carnegie Report that is worth noting. The authors do not analyse the other half, as it were, of management education: the body of disciplines, motifs and ideas that engage with the affirmation and cultivation of a particular image of human subjectivity not as an additional, but as a central dimension of business writ large. Organisational behaviour is mentioned once (Colby *et al.* 2011: 64); human resources twice (Colby *et al.* 2011: 17, 83) – both in passing. As we will show in the next section, this is not a simple oversight. This is, in our estimation, a major omission of an entire family of disciplines, subdisciplines and themes that have become firmly established in the business curriculum and whose constitution actually reproduces and repeats many of the pedagogical tactics and devices of 'liberal learning'. It is hard to explain how these elements have been elided in the analysis, but it is not hard to imagine that the inclusion and analysis of essential and radical transformations of the business vocabulary of subjectivity in the past three decades would have posed decisive problems for the dynamic of the argument. The logic of 'liberal learning', as a contrasting framework to that of business education, would not have been so easy to establish.

The essence of the report, its proposed programme of liberal learning for the reform of business education, offers an image that is initially unsurprising (the entire text prepared the reader for it), and yet on closer reading the internal dynamic of the argument is remarkable. The figure supposed to emerge from the integration of business education with 'liberal learning' takes on startling Promethean proportions. The graduate of such a programme would be the locus, in one person, where all the imperatives of our age would find their reconciliation and resolution, and their contradictions would be fully overcome. This figure would gather in its mental and intellectual constitution, as well as in its ethos, the possibility of reconciling almost impossible conflicting demands, the embodiment of an ultimate humanism that would deliver both a complete human and better 'business'. The strength of this model of reform takes on proportions that are not dissimilar in their systematic ambition from the Kantian programme of system of philosophy. The image of the Kantian system is strikingly clear in its mirrored form for the programme proposed and synthesised in Chapter 4 of the report (Colby *et al.* 2011: 60). This model, which cannot be analysed in detail here, presents an image of a full affirmation and resolution of the power of reason and the overcoming of all its possible limits. The principle of 'integrative thinking' – from which the programme derives – takes on an impossible expression in the report's proposals. Taken in turns, all these suggestions are of course legitimate, and certainly legitimate with respect to core anxieties of our age (such as pluralism, diversity and permanent invocations of the dangers of their neglect). However, when presented in this systematic and total connection, the principles and imperatives of the model appear questionable with regard to the remotest possibility of their delivery.

An irony here is that this model of person (anticipated at the beginning of the text) originates not in sources of liberal learning, but from popular business literature itself (Martin 2007, 2009). There is something of a lesson emerging in this interesting detail: that the field of business, with its ways of thinking, is the source that provides the paradoxical path to a salvation of business education towards the affirmation of the power of humanity to take control over its destiny. 'Liberal learning' moves sideways and away from its traditional sources in the liberal arts, humanities or social sciences, and returns to business's continuous preoccupation with its own perfectibility and reaffirmation.

The recourse to business literature itself as a source for the report's own programme of reform is not merely a circumstantial occurrence: business circles themselves provided a particular 'enlightened' vision of a manager with qualities emerging from a broadened conception of the nature of the human subject at the core of business processes. It is symptomatic of the cultural power acquired almost explosively by business and management in the past three decades or so (especially since 1989) not just as modes of thinking about 'firms' or 'structures of trade', but also as modes of conceiving of how value is produced in the modern world. As we will discuss later, this is perhaps the most surprising aspect of the report to emerge: it does not seem to investigate in any depth how business and management ideas have expanded the range of motifs, tropes, references and sources that sustain and legitimise historically the principle of business as the core 'engine' of the current order. Far from remaining distant, business and management thinking and education currently construct a set of ideals capable of mirroring and reproducing the core sensibilities and values that sustain modern subjectivity. This occurs in the so-called technical–calculative domains and even more emphatically in the new domains in which the power of the human subject is projected as the ultimate strategic platform. However problematic we may want to consider business imperatives to be, it is a high risk to overlook their connection with the ground of the modern age as the self-assertion of the human subject through the promises of *human production*. And this is perhaps where the most dangerous misinterpretations in the Carnegie Report occur.

## *Technical calculation*

One of its key oversights is that technical–calculative business disciplines are not neutral mechanisms but contain a very strong and powerful interpretation of both the past and the future world that is grounded in a powerful idea of human control. In other words, the technical–instrumental mentality of the calculative and administrative disciplines always presupposes the mobilisation of the human power to understand and control its own engagement towards a perfected future. The calculative disciplines rely on an idea of human capability to disclose a future that is always amenable to technical manipulation in the attempt to shed the burdens of crises, interruptions and limits.

Technical modelling of management and organisational functions, and its pedagogical approach, are centred upon calculative models of optimisation. Their purpose is *optimal* resource allocation with the 'firm' as a unit of concern. Associated with this framework is a specific logic of study – accounting, finance, economics, operations management and marketing – that advances the ability to project and sustain, through calculative models, a fantasy of unlimited value production in an imaginary future horizon. Although it requires a complex analysis, the dominance of this technical mindset can be briefly synthesised as an attempt to set the future on a path of unlimited perfectibility. Technical thought contains a promise that through the continuous improvement, optimisation and refinement of calculative models, the future appears as a horizon of endless production. It appears as a thought that can actively produce 'results' that can permanently enhance 'value' in the economic process by linking 'means' to 'ends' in an instrumental rationality (Roberts 1996: 55). Thinking technically carries with it an ethics of optimism in which lie the premises of continuous progress: the affirmation of possibilities of always breaking boundaries in a quest for a more perfected, more efficient, more productive technique. In this respect, technical thought is the thought of hope, one that students become intensely attached to, finding it very hard to see its limits, as Colby and the team recognise themselves (Colby *et al.* 2011: 62).

Moreover, technical management thought is articulated through mathematical constructions that seek to contain complex processes. Multiple factors are reduced to equations that provide univocal relationships that exclude and close down ambiguity. They objectify the future into a set of knowable alternatives, and thus the future itself comes to be disclosed exclusively as 'this' finite set of 'options' for human decision that appears to 'tame' unpredictability, ambiguity and risk. The purpose of mathematical thinking is to discover the steady state of the operational optimum and bring it under human control. The mathematical can then act as a code that can be perpetually performed by individuals and organisations. Optimisation is the core intellectual outcome of technical thought – models that promise the possibility of always finding sources to increase value in whatever form it is conceived. Calculative and mathematical modelling of management processes points to a horizon in which limits can always be surpassed. Management conceived and taught in technical terms carries a pedagogical promise that any process of production can be appropriated and manipulated in the name of perpetual optimisation and perfectibility.

This explains perhaps why the typical response to crises in such systems is to consider them as 'accidents' requiring only the further refinement of those management techniques that had caused them in the first place. The basis of mainstream business responses to its crises lies in the assumption that the self, institutions and society, nature and the economy are resources that can sustain business and production towards growth, manipulation and progress. Management techniques need only refine further their frameworks in order to sustain the promise of delivering unlimited production and exchange of 'goods' and value. The technical disciplinary core of management and business education (for example, accounting, finance, economics or operations management) is in itself a world-historical narrative that lays claim to the power to explain and absorb apparent 'anomalies' in the flow of historical events because they can be controlled by human agency. This is perhaps the reason why the current global economic and financial crisis is not seen as a radical threat in business schools. Rather, its 'resolution' already lies within the logic of the system of 'business' itself and in its power to overcome any internal crisis simply through its self-perpetuation.

## *Subjectivity*

But the power of the technical–calculative optimism in the core structure of business education is only half of the story. As we noted earlier, there are themes in management education, and more broadly management discourses, which have been almost completely overlooked in the Carnegie Report. These themes relate to conceptual elements that have become established and entrenched as core currency of the management imaginary in the past two or three decades. They form an overarching umbrella that encompasses the most effective promissory engine of managerialism in relation to the human subject: the explosive growth of a new culture of self-expression and self-realisation in business and management since the 1980s.

Interestingly, this turn in management towards the expression of subjectivity in the domain of production was also the outcome of a deep economic crisis that spanned the 1970s and 1980s. During those decades, both US and UK economies found themselves in genuine decline and their managerial frameworks stuttered and faltered faced with the advance of both Germany and Japan, quickly followed by other Asian economies and culminating in the 'Chinese Miracle'. Scrambling for an answer, top academic management circles felt the pressure to explain and respond to this process of decline. More or less grudgingly, academics from top business schools began to produce a new kind of programme for the re-articulation of America's ability to manage productively, to regain some sense of direction towards survival and, possibly, growth. The outcome was that management thinkers (Harvard was the first place to go public) felt that they had to teach new things in new ways, to invent new managerial objects and new modes of intervention. They began to accept that the rationalist paradigm of the 1950s and 1960s had to be complemented by new motifs that quickly became central and visible. Western interpretations of the 'Japanese Miracle' saw the core success factor in a specific *culture* of Japanese organisations. Japanese work cultures seemed to place the human subject, the 'self', at the centre of all systems of production, from the micro-controls of details of work to the general macro-institutional framework. And not just any sense of 'self', but an empowered, participative, committed, expressive self. In Total Quality Management (TQM), in Kaizen or Quality Circles, the participative-committed subject seemed to be the key ingredient. This appeared as a radically new kind of relationship in the workplace that had to be captured in new core elements of the educational curriculum.

New cultural resources therefore began to enter the business educational framework: organisational cultures, participation, TQM, empowerment, commitment, teamwork, organisational learning and self-development, excellence, performativity, human resource management, entrepreneurship, enlightened leadership, creativity, knowledge, innovation, talent, self-actualisation or wellness to mention but a few. They became central to a new management idea, namely that there is a deep correspondence between performance and personal affirmation through work. When organisations began to affirm that 'People are our most important asset' this was not an empty slogan; rather it led to the emergence and development of a sophisticated new system of ideas whose centre of gravity was (and is) the increasing importance given to attributes of subjectivity. The human subject and its attributes became a core structural element of managerial vocabularies and practices. In response, business education itself began to foreground and cultivate precisely these human attributes in order to prepare students to understand a new principle of production systems: that productivity, profitability, efficiency, effectiveness have become dependent upon a new economy of subjectivity.

The classroom itself has now become a complex stage for the exploration and expression of this new direction: only if human subjects intensify their contribution as selves can they enhance the production process and lead an organisation to success. This set of ideas is not a marginal element of the curriculum but is now actively integrated and connected with strategic thinking about management and business as a whole. The integration of subjectivity entails the development of new structures of involvement, participation, evaluation, development and care. If maximising productivity is a function of intensifying the contribution of people's committed efforts then new ways of organisation-wide human integration are required in order to mobilise the resourcefulness of the 'self'.

The projection of the human subject as one of the central dimensions of organisational performance has led to the formation of a new synthesis of indispensable themes: organisations as communities of culture and commitment to common values; individual participation and work as platforms of self-expression; the duty of organisational 'care' and therapeutic concern for the wellness, health and 'happiness' of employees; and performativity as an essential expression not just of 'production' but also of personal worth. So how does this relate to the Carnegie Report and why is it absent?

## Conclusion: does business education need the humanities?

Our purpose in rereading Colby *et al.* (2011) is not to resolve or close the question we pose in this heading. Neither are we seeking to provide an alternative programme. Rather the aim is to show that business education has become a truly complex cultural ensemble whose articulation needs to be understood in the most profound sense before we can diagnose its limits, deficiencies and possible future needs. We do certainly concur with the Carnegie Report in more than one way: undergraduate programmes in business schools have indeed become almost entirely detached from the humanities and social sciences in dangerous ways. It is equally clear that a certain kind of dogmatism of 'positivity' traverses the various disciplines now taught in these faculties and that their self-confidence is not intellectually or pedagogically productive. On the contrary, it seems that we are witnessing an increasing intellectual withdrawal from the most complex problems of the current period, problems from which business itself is utterly inseparable. Despite the prominence of critical economic, ecological and ethical questions facing business, there is indeed a troubling systematic silence in the kind of thinking that underpins business education.

The more uncomfortable truth, however, seems to be that business education is not perceiving itself as endangered in any way – perhaps quite the opposite – and we have tried to show that it is dangerous to overlook the reasons why business education feels culturally secure. Its isolation from other disciplines might be not a sign of a deficiency but rather the outcome of a highly powerful and complex cultural apparatus that believes in its own self-reliance and believes it needs no further input when it is able to participate directly in the production, exchange and dissemination of ideas, mentalities and promises that are nowadays the most desirable. Why would business education turn to the humanities and social sciences? Is there anything to be found in this kind of interdisciplinarity?

The answer might be no if all there is to be found in the humanities and social sciences is a kind of moral condemnation of 'business' based on judgements that end up in isolating business as the sphere where various forms of malevolence hold sway. Indeed, moral programmes are in themselves dangerous, which is why the Carnegie Report can be read both as a very productive chance to open up debate about the limits of business education and also as a possible instrument of blunt and unproductive criticism.

On the other hand, there may be another avenue for thinking about bridges between business education and the humanities. Our suggestion is that these connections can come from another way of asking the central question: don't the humanities and social sciences need to understand business more? Perhaps the two domains should not encounter each other in a relationship of correction in which the humanities are called in to repair the ethical deficiencies of business schools, but rather should be brought together by a renewed intellectual curiosity about the place of business in the contemporary world. The fact that business is so integral to the core questions that face humanity today is a fundamental reason why it should be one of the most researched themes in the social sciences and humanities. In fact until the middle of the twentieth century, it was one of the most researched themes – understanding business, work, production and the economy were core themes for understanding how humanity expresses its relationship to the world, to itself and to nature since the dawn of modernity with Machiavelli and Hobbes. The conduct of business was a common central concern in philosophy, theology, history, social theory and the study of politics, and this was not only true of Euro-Atlantic cultures.

The emergence of business schools has indeed changed this relationship – a deep intellectual rift has emerged with other faculties. However, nothing has changed. On the contrary, the need to understand business as a core historical process is even more emphatic. The call for this kind of understanding is perhaps the basis for thinking about a possible future re-engagement between the immense heritage of the humanities and social sciences and the study of business and management. It is – even though not explicitly stated – the essence of the outcome of the 2014 survey mentioned earlier: an understanding of the place of business in society, in the general order of values, in the troubled relationship between humanity and nature, and in the order of the relationships of human beings to themselves.

## References


Anderson, M. (2009) 'Why we created the MBA oath', *Harvard Business Review*, [online]. Available from: https://hbr.org/2009/06/why-we-created-the-mba-oath (accessed 26 April 2015).

CarringtonCrisp (2014) *See the Future 2014*. CarringtonCrisp Ltd. [online]. Available from: www.carringtoncrisp.com/images/PDFs/See_The_Future_2014.pdf (accessed 25 January 2016).

Colby, A., Ehrlich, T., Sullivan, W. and Dolle, J. (2011) *Rethinking Undergraduate Business Education*. San Francisco, CA: Jossey-Bass.

Heidegger, M. (2010) *Basic Writings* (edited by D.F. Krell). London: Routledge.

Jaspers, K. (1951) *Man in the Modern Age*. London: Routledge & Kegan Paul.

Jünger, E. (1993) 'On danger', *New German Critique*, 59, 27–32.

Martin, R.L. (2007). *The Opposable Mind: How Successful Leaders Win Through Integrative Thinking*. Boston, MA: Harvard Business School Press.

Martin, R.L. (2009) *The Design of Business: Why Design Thinking is the Next Competitive Advantage*. Boston, MA: Harvard Business Press.

Roberts, J. (1996) 'Management education and the limits of technical rationality: the conditions and consequences of management practice'. *In:* R. French and C. Grey (eds.) *Rethinking Management Education*. London: Sage Publications, pp. 54–75.

# 38

# Manners, taste and etiquette

## New practices of 'politesse' in business and management

*Damian O'Doherty*

### Introduction

Imagine an MBA lecture theatre. You're a little hungover after the excesses of last night's revelries but you are managing to sit dutifully in the back row of the theatre, performing the role of 'heard it all before' disinterest in an effort to ingratiate yourself with fellow students.

Ping! Your iPad. An invitation to attend a graduation ball. A banner advert pops up at the same time. It is from the farfetch.com website with the banner headline 'Tom Rhys Harries: The Welsh actor rocks an evening look as dark as his new television show'. You think about whether you need a new outfit to attend the graduation ball but the words of the lecture catch your ear . . . 'So let me begin by saying that students do not know how to dress correctly . . .'. You might be wondering, 'Have I stepped into the wrong class? I'm supposed to be studying an MBA, not fashion and textiles'. The lecturer continues '. . . and ultimately they will fail in business . . .'. Maybe he now has your attention.

It might be considered rude and bad manners to begin with such a bald claim but we are going to mobilise all the resources of the self-righteous and inveterate snob and take this a little further. *Your table manners are atrocious.* While we are at it, let us note the offence caused by the fact that you do not know whether the chief executive of BP would prefer red or white wine with his Hereford Rib-Eye, or whether the Burgundy taken by the chief operating officer of the Lloyds Banking Group has been well served in a Bordeaux glass. One can easily imagine how a situation such as this might develop for the average graduate of an MBA programme:[1] as the conversation turns to, let's say, the recent exhibition at the Institute of Contemporary Arts, our student will be unable to tell the difference between Goya and the Chapman brothers. Beethoven might as well be a German car-advertisement, and 'musique concrete'? Well, that sounds like dental surgery. When asked what they are reading, we would not be surprised if they were to respond with Dan Brown's *Inferno* 'on Kindle', perhaps even declaring it to be the greatest piece of writing (ever). *Seriously.* At which point we might begin to wince in embarrassment as we realise they don't even know how to talk effectively. No doubt silence will descend upon the table as our recent graduate of your typical 'European Business School' (see Parker 2014) is invited to comment on the announced merger of the UK Investment Management Association with the investment arm of the Association of British Insurers. Summoning up all he can recall about 'The Strategic Focus Wheel' (Roberts and MacLennan 2003), he barely notices the embarrassment on the faces of his fellow dinner guests. Glasses clink, a few people cough discretely into their hands, while someone suggests they ask for the dessert menu …

We systematically fail our students at the business school as we cast them into situations such as this one described – ill-equipped and ill-resourced to cope with the demands of polite dinner table conversation. In order to address some of these issues the burden of this chapter is devoted to finding the right tone that will encourage future teaching and research to seize the importance of managers as 'amateurs' of taste, etiquette and manners (Gherardi 2009). By amateurs we mean to draw on the newly emerging sociology of 'passionate attachments' (Gomart and Hennion 1999; Hennion 2001, 2004, 2007) and its analysis of the 'pragmatics' of taste. However, where these studies examine the practices of amateur music fans, wine tasting, flute-making (Cook and Yanow 1993), cooking, walking, or other domestic and predominantly bourgeois practices, we look at the (semi) public world of business and management, which we might characterise as made up of a more aspirational class of actors than the comfortable and established gentry. Moreover, Hennion's important and influential work tends to focus on interests and passions and the cultivation of taste that are formed *outside* of work: cooking, walking, music listening, etc. In this chapter we address manners, taste and etiquette as practised in the workplace by managers and business executives of corporate organisations.

Our concern is to begin to lay out a *political diagnostics* of the competitive and often violent realm of jousting that takes place in the name of taste and manners as it is played out in business. Business and management studies has neglected these features of business practice, and even where certain strands of organisation studies have shown a greater interest in that which is deemed to be the non-rational, the social, the symbolic and cultural, they have in the main preferred to *apply* the arts and humanities. Whether anthropology, literature, art, history or theology, scholars of organisation have mobilised, or we might say ransacked, the arts and humanities as intellectual resources for re-describing or theorising the world of business and management, often in ways deemed alternative and more imaginative than mainstream quasi-natural science. By contrast, our interest in manners, taste and etiquette forms part of a strategy that seeks to acknowledge that the arts and humanities form a reflexive and constitutive practice that is *inextricably a part of the way in which business and management gets done*. In other words, there is no separation between business and art, or business studies and the humanities.

The chapter also tries to do two things, simultaneously, which is important in terms of the pedagogic lessons of this text.[2] I want to try and *talk about* those spaces in the practice of business and management where a good grounding in the humanities is of vital importance for graduates of business school seeking to navigate the corridors of power and through which they might want to know how to succeed. This is important because it is absent from the current MBA curriculum and also neglected in some of the most rampant but also academically respectable texts offering prescriptive advice on how to succeed (for example, Pfeffer 2010). Even the homespun homilies of Dale Carnegie's (2010 [1936]) *How to Win Friends and Influence People* fail to adequately address the topic of manners and taste. But if the arts and humanities are already reflexively constitutive of the world of business, I also need to work out of a space that is *in neither the humanities nor the business school* – that is, I must seek to speak out of this space if I am not to fall into tautology – that is, use the same intellectual or linguistic resource as that for which I am trying to offer a diagnosis. In brief, a diagnostics cannot proceed in the same terms as that which the diagnosis is aimed towards. Moreover, the desire for a return to the humanities – to its presumed rigour, intellectual range or inspiration to the imagination – or an interdisciplinary alliance to revise the MBA curriculum – is possibly retrograde. My sense is that we need to cultivate and practise a form of thinking that is beyond and outside these categories. Only then can we understand how to deploy manners, taste and etiquette.

First, we need to know how the practitioners of business *do* manners, taste and etiquette. This is hard to do because it is a world that is so familiar that we have become immune to it. Hence, prior to this, the main body of the chapter turns to a close reading of certain sections of Jane Austen's *Pride and Prejudice* (2008 [1815]) to show that manners, taste and etiquette are simultaneously obscure to their contemporary practitioners and historically contingent. Moreover, tastes are subject to sudden eruptions of change that dislodge established expertise and purveyors of discrimination and judgement, and a reading of Austen should be sufficiently unfamiliar to remind us of this historical contingency. Austen is important because she shows the hidden 'violence' of everyday Georgian society, violence that is committed through the competitive and mutual trade of judgements and assessments that inhere in social intercourse. Such violence is easy to see in a society other than our own, but it is something that we are too quick to consign to history and/or others whilst celebrating that which we assume to be the more relaxed and liberal regimes in which we live. We feel ourselves to be the beneficiaries of a liberal-freedom in manners, taste and etiquette, but the otherness of Austen's late-eighteenth century should alert us to the possible otherness of our own world. It is possible that we are able to laugh at the customs and practices of the characters portrayed in Austen because we avoid the deeper lesson of her literature, namely that we all live subject and agent to a mundane violence that we perpetuate through the snares and circuitous strategies of denial and resistance. The chapter then introduces ethnographic material that is currently being worked up in an extended study of the Manchester Airport Group in the UK to show that the competent practitioner of manners and etiquette is not one who simply has the capacity to *exercise* correct 'aesthetic' discernment and application. A more consummate embrace of manners and taste is that of someone who can explore and then tolerate a more basic *aporia* in organisation. We identify this aporia as the demands placed on the member of management and work organisation to resolve the existence of both competition and cooperation in social relations at work. It deserves the concept aporetic because this is an impossible task, but also one in which it is impossible to finally sever the terms into a clearly demarcated opposition – that is, competition and cooperation are often difficult to distinguish. To explore this, the final part of the chapter focuses on the proceedings of an annual industry dinner that resonates with the ethnographic work of people like Rosen (1988).

## The business of taste

These days it is taken for granted that business executives know how to calculate net-present value, they know the difference between a joint venture and a merger and acquisition, and they are simply expected to be conversant about proposed changes to tax regulations or how different multipliers can skew comparative shareholder value. More precisely, an accounting graduate is presumed to know the various methods of calculating net present value, taxation and liabilities. A human resource graduate, on the other hand, will know how to set out a job description form and how to observe equal opportunities legislation. Often this knowledge is exercised with a certain degree of diffidence that borders on chagrin, of course, but most significant is the fact that this kind of knowledge has long been black-boxed into software programs, Apple apps and cloud technology business dashboard calculators. However, it is a simple but often neglected truth that business is conducted over dinner and deals are often struck in the private members' club. Here, the human has not been quite so displaced and marginalised. A round of golf is often the prelude for a contract exchange; new business is negotiated during an industry awards ceremony; and a three-day industry conference in Abu Dhabi provides opportunities for 'networking'; and 'entertainment' for a visiting delegation of Chinese businessmen becomes the most-pressing problem for colleagues in a UK financial services head office.

How are we to adequately prepare our students for the rigour of these spaces and the terrifying bouts of intellectual testing and cultural interrogation that take place in them? And made more terrifying by the fact that most of the time these events pass unnoticed, in what appears to be the benign and mundane everyday. What the chief executive officer (CEO) of a rival company will doubtless be more interested in hearing about as one shares his or her dinner table is your reaction to the recent 'Disasters of War' exhibition by the Chapman brothers. Does it represent inspired vandalism, he or she might ask, or maybe postmodern irony? *What do you think*? On the other hand, he or she may well ask if you have happened to see the new production of Wagner's *Parsifal* at the English National Opera. Questions may go along the following lines: did the new staging by Stephen Langridge really manage to convey the spiritual qualities of the Grail? Were the medical uniforms and the ubiquitous Francis Bacon cube a little too heavy-handed in their symbolism, over-played to the extent that it detracted from its Wagnerian roots in nineteenth-century Germany? Did Langridge successfully conjure aspects of compassion in the libretto, or does it remain a work of perfidy, of vindictiveness, of a secret attempt to poison the presuppositions of life?[3] Our chief executive will not want to hear his or her guest pontificate about recent adjustments to the way net present value is calculated – which to the ears of the CEO is likely to sound like a precocious 5-year-old counting the three-times table, or reciting the names of all the Scottish professional football teams in reverse alphabetical order.[4] And if all you have at your disposal is the platitudes of the daily tabloid newspapers in which to form your contribution to the conversation, you are likely to be cast as a klutz or an ignoramus. Of course *you will not be castigated overtly in this way*, or indeed in any way that might offend you, but subtly, and executed with such guile and precision, according to the principles of the '1 in 5 is an idiot rule', that you are unlikely to spot the fact that you have been the victim of a reprimand. However, one should rest assured that reciting clichés from tabloid newspapers about art is likely to identify that idiot amongst the five sitting down for dinner.

Consider a further 'test' that is likely to be posed to our graduate of management studies during dinner. At some point, the graduate is no doubt going to be asked to express a preference for wine. Perhaps our student notices the waiter has poured a glass of 1961 Mouton Rothschild into the client CEO's Bordeaux glass. Do they notice the offence? The issues at stake here are complex and shifting where in both the professional world of the sommelier and the worlds of the amateur lay-practitioner, the etiquette of glassware has become a subject of considerable controversy (Fischer 2005; Parr and Mackay 2010). Rebecca Thomas (2013) in her introduction for beginners is fairly generous in her latitude of acceptable taste, but offers little beyond very general specifications: 'The type of wine glass you use depends on the type of wine you intend to drink from it. For red wines, the best choice is a wide glass' and 'the common shape resembles a bowl' (Thomas 2013: 25). The recommended size, she goes on, is somewhere between 10 and 20 ounces which will ensure that the glass holder has 'adequate room to effectively swirl the wine' (Thomas 2013: 25). The International Standards Organisation (ISO) provides classification and standards for a range of sizes for those perplexed by these casual generalisations. Peynaud's (1987) classic instructional treatise, on the other hand, provides far greater detail, arguing the case that a wine of distinction needs 'a stemmed glass made of fine crystal; smooth, transparent, colourless and without ornament or engraving' (1987: 97–8). There is often a delicate choice between glasses designed to intensify the flavour of the wine and those of modest ornamentation that intensify other sensorial tastes. A careful St Louis-style etching or crystal overlay on the stem and bowl helps capture and reflect table candlelight, for example, but there may be some sacrifice in terms of oral taste. No such dilemmas, however, will be present in public dining although it might often require delicate negotiation between the host and the restaurant staff.

Particular attention, however, should be devoted to the qualities and properties of the stem, which needs to be slender and of sufficient height to allow room for the thumb and finger to manipulate the glass. Peynaud goes further in his detailing and suggests that we should also devote attention to the properties of the rim of the glass, which can only achieve the required thinness if made out of crystal. The shape of the glass is important because each wine benefits from different sizes and shapes, each of which is distinctive in terms of the interaction between evaporation, surface tension and capillarity. Robinson (2000: 74) explains that one important feature of choosing the correct shape of glass is the degree to which it allows the bouquet to be trapped within the glass and concludes that 'glasses whose shape encourages the volatiles to escape into the atmosphere' make the bouquet far more evasive and less distinctive. Hence, the importance of a tulip shaped, slightly domed and enclosed glass. In the second edition of Jackson and Jackson's (2009) professional handbook, it is the 'Libbey's Royal Leerdam #9309RL', the 'Durand Viticole Tasting glass' or the 'Libbey Citation #8470' that are recommended to bring out the best in red wines (2009: 309). The location and time of day can also be important factors when judging the correct glass, but essentially in terms of glass shape the larger bowl of the Burgundy helps aerate the subtle aromas of wines, such as the pinot noir, and importantly directs the wine to the tip of the tongue where, according to some understandings of physiology, sweetness is best appreciated. This is not so important with a Mouton Rothschild, which is a more full-bodied wine that responds better when directed more quickly to the back of the mouth, a task discharged more efficiently by a tall and broad glass. Experimental laboratory science conducted by Delwiche and Pelchat (2002) confirms that the physical properties of the Bordeaux glass are particularly effective in reducing the intensity of the wine because the 'glass is both much taller and of greater overall capacity compared to that of the other glasses', which means that 'when the wine was presented in the Bordeaux glass, it was the furthest from the subjects' noses and the volatiles were possibly the most dilute due to the large cuppa' (Delwiche and Pelchat 2002: 26; see Venturi *et al.* 2014), hence the near ruinous treatment of the CEO's Mouton Rothschild that had been served in a Bordeaux glass.

There is a lot for our student to observe in this apparently trivial ritual of ordering wine. If offered the wine to taste, for example, should one actually drink a small amount of the wine, to taste – as they say in French – 'le gout'? Or do they offer this ceremony to the CEO? Care must be taken. Elaborate swirling of the glass followed by demonstrative inhalation through the nose will likely be a further cause of embarrassment. One might be well advised, however, to offer a few words of approval or a polite question or two to the sommelier, for example how long has the restaurant stored the wine? From which estate was it bought? Modern table manners have changed considerably (Elias 1969) since it was de rigueur *not* to taste the wine (Visser 1992). It was a considerable *faux pas* to *taste* the wine in the days of private dining when the person ordering the wine was usually requesting a bottle procured for their own cellars. This might imply that the taste or its suitability for the food is unknown to you, which means that you have in effect requested a 'guinea pig' bottle of wine, or more strictly that *your guests are the guinea pigs*. Nothing could be more damaging to one's reputation, and most diners of good breeding and manners would take extreme unction at this offence, prompting in some circles a demand for 'satisfaction' that might eventually lead to the blood-letting of a duel (Banks 2012). To avoid all this unpleasantness, one simply needs to *smell the cork of the wine*. All that needs to be established is whether the wine has been 'corked' during its time in the cellar, the traits of which can be discerned easily by the modest gesture of a quick 'inspiration' of the cork. The practice of tasting the wine in a public restaurant has not been clearly sanctioned or proscribed by the connoisseurs, and significant differences prevail amongst the amateurs. This can leave the diner in a quandary. The only elegant solution must be calculated by the triangulation of a series of known and partly unknown and contingent variables. Are you regular co-diners? If so, you may have shared the wine before and so there is no need to taste the wine. If your guests were relatively unknown to you, on the other hand, and the range of wines rather limited, the best course of action would be to invite approval of the proposed order, and then following the arrival of the bottle ask whether your co-diner would object to your tasting the wine.

Clearly these rituals of taste and manners will not concern everyone; the finer details of wine etiquette and the staging of high opera might only appeal to the tastes of a minority elite, for example, and further research is needed in order to help guide the perplexed. One way forward might be to classify business and management into different 'style paradigms'. Older, more conservative and established businesses might tend towards the elite of wine and opera; a new start-up web design or IT business, on the other hand, might favour the rituals of football, beer and pizza. One might imagine an industrial classification system based loosely on the old categories of manufacturing, light engineering, services, etc. Another system might seek to distribute business into 'highbrow' and 'lowbrow', with each sub-dividing into further important niches – classic, modern and contemporary, for example, or further, in terms of international, domestic and regional. The regional modern lowbrow might be companies in which one might expect to find the equivalent of pigeon-fanciers, those companies classified as highbrow, modern and international would be composed of people who tend towards the appreciation of world literature. This is of course hugely restricted by a European sensibility and would need considerable revision and nuance by those schooled in African cultures, Latin America, the Middle East and China. Then there are the hybrid worlds of taste and fashion in which it is acceptable to invest as much 'highbrow' intellectual endeavour into the understanding of boxing or football, for example, where it would be bad manners to dismiss an opposing team as simply 'crap', or to invest 'highbrow' forms with popular content. For example, Jocelyn Pooks's 2010 'Ingerland' staged at the Royal Opera House in London, featuring WAGs (wives and girlfriends of famous footballers), pregnancy tests and cosmetic surgery and a chorus that includes famous football terrace songs such as 'Steve Gerrard, Gerrard/He'll pass the ball 40 yards/He's big and he's f★★★★★★ hard/Steve Gerrard, Gerrard', is perhaps evidence of this hybridisation and indicative of a new world of 'postmodern' manners and taste (Hebdige 1979, 1982; Bauman 1995; Featherstone 1995).

How to navigate across this highly dynamic and patchwork quilt of hybrid forms, subcultures, anti-cultures and 'post-cultures' poses considerable problems for the management of manners, taste and etiquette. At its simplest, there are likely to be significant differences between a CEO working in the oil industry and the CEO of the Arts and Humanities Research Council, and different tests of manners, taste and etiquette can be expected to prevail. Manners, taste and etiquette will be no less complex, whether we regard the content as highbrow or lowbrow. The skills required, for example, to follow the intricate plot line of a broadcast television soap opera, which are equally as tortuous and baroque as any opera by Mozart, demands an attention to detail that competes with that of the wine connoisseur. The rituals of sharing and conversation turn-taking, the delicate politics involved in judging the behaviour or decisions of characters, the investments and identifications amongst audience members with certain characters, the revealing of plot lines and denouements, etc. all bespeak a complicated theatre of manners, taste and etiquette. When one adds that these worlds of taste and manner are variously constructed, negotiated and navigated, ranging from a knowing disregard through to militant and passionate commitment, and all inflected with elements of reflexivity, irony and pastiche, then the pedagogic challenge is a formidable one.

## Pride and prejudice[5]

Having sought to establish an appreciation of the importance of manners, taste and etiquette in business, the next important lesson requires the student to appreciate the particular and peculiar historical circumstances within which the world of business and management operates today. To make that which is contemporary appear worthy of consideration is the cause of considerable methodological and epistemological difficulties. Typically, we are so caught up in the everyday that either everything appears remarkable or nothing stands out as significant. Only with a degree of cultural or historical relativism can that which is potentially significant about our own world be made to stand out. For our purposes here it is sufficient to note briefly that that which is most familiar to us – the everyday – is so commonplace as to be accepted without question, forming a background of taken-for-granted assumption (Berger and Luckmann 1967). In other words, it is so close that, as Heidegger (1962) reminds us, it remains something that is 'ontologically' the furthest away. 'Ontological' means to Heidegger that which is available for philosophical consideration, that is in order to acquire a pure understanding of that reality in which we are placed, we must somehow be *outside* of it to be able to get some measure of it objectively. And this is a very tricky position indeed. To know about it as a possibility, let alone to assume that one might have achieved it as a position of knowledge, poses a formidable conundrum to the philosophy of modern social science. Hence, to gain some purchase on how strange our current practices might be, it is useful, and arguably even a necessity, to turn to the details of everyday life as revealed in texts of greater age and even antiquity (Duby *et al.* 1987). We turn to Austen's (2008 [1815]) *Pride and Prejudice* in part because Austen is widely known for the attention she pays to the subtle discretions and manners of the early modern Georgian society of the English landed gentry, but also because this world will be *partly* familiar to us. At least for those of us in broadly Anglo-Saxon cultures, the ways and mores of Austen's characters are still somewhat recognisable, despite the passage of some two hundred years.

Towards the end of Book 11 of *Pride and Prejudice*, Austen narrates the departure of Elizabeth and Maria as they take their leave from the Collins's in Hunsford:

> After an affectionate parting between the friends, Elizabeth was attended to the carriage by Mr Collins, and as they walked down the garden, he was commissioning her with his best respects to all her family, not forgetting his thanks for the kindness he had received at Longbourn in the winter, and his compliments to Mr and Mrs Gardiner, though unknown. He then handed her in, Maria followed, and the door was on the point of being closed, when he suddenly reminded them, with some consternation, that they had hitherto forgotten to leave any message for the ladies of Rosings. 'But,' he added, 'you will of course wish to have your humble respects delivered to them, with your grateful thanks for their kindness to you while you have been there'.
>
> *Austen 2008 [1815]: 166*

Certain things immediately stand out as worthy of comment. Elizabeth was 'attended' to, after an 'affectionate parting between friends'. The contrast established between the first two clauses of the opening sentence is telling and typical of Austen, where the style mimics that of the subtlety and oblique quality with which the characters she portrays reference the obligations of custom and decorum – what is significant is 'told' in the silences and gaps of conversations. The comma almost hangs like a pendulum between the clauses, marking a swing from one tone to another, in which it is precisely this swing, or the differential movement it marks, that we find most clearly the elegant genius of the novelist. It should be known to the reader at this stage that the status of Elizabeth to that of Collins is not clear; indeed, the relationship is awkward and difficult given that Collins had previously proposed marriage to Lizzy. They are not married, nor are they courting, they are not (quite) family, they are not strangers, and they are not friends – albeit its possibility seems to offer one route forward providing a set of fledgling rules and customs within which to conduct the relationship. In this passage, the conversation is mannered and stilted in a way that suggests both parties are trepidatiously stepping over the memory and legacy of their previous parting. In fact the relationship marks something akin to that of an 'empty signifier' – as understood in certain strands of semiotics and literary theory – and marks a certain moment of 'crisis' in the social fabric. Hence, although a blowhard in many respects, Collins is made to appear here just ever so slightly more anxious in his deference to formality and custom as he 'attended' Elizabeth to the carriage and 'commissioned' her with respects.

We could have picked any passage from Austen, but we see from this example how the surface and ostensible topics of conversation are freighted with reference and negotiation to underlying codes of behaviour and conduct – in this case the correct social procedures to enact at the point at which guests leave their hosts. The rules of conduct for hosting and reciprocal rules of behaviour for guests exist in the world of business and management today, as they did in Austen's time, but it is perhaps a little easier to appreciate in Austen given the distance of time between authorship and reading.

It is the underlying sense of threat and violence however that is so startling in Austen. Most critics focus on the apparent gentility and the peculiar idiosyncrasies of the contemporary landed gentry (Handler and Segal 1999); however, there is barely a sentence in Austen in which some kind of judgement is not being passed or formed. Personal reputation, status, dignity and integrity are permanently in crisis and are constantly being sifted, evaluated, performed and judged – a silent but persistent underlying violence of discipline, and one in which everyone colludes. In Austen's passage earlier, there are things that the host is expected to say, and vice-versa, and gestures and condescension the guests should observe in return. So finely calibrated and complex is the mesh of mutual obligation that one false move, one miscalculated gamble on the parameters of manners and etiquette, could spell disaster, and with implications and consequences rippling out into wider society like a fall of dominoes to evoke further rounds of (oblique) commentary, reflection and judgement.

What is most noteworthy in this passage, however, is the subtlety with which discipline and reprimand is conducted. Indeed, so subtle, that this reprimand might hardly be noticed. And this of course is the point. Such was the skill with which Collins delivers his rebuke that it would hardly have registered as a reprimand, and given the manner in which the articulation was shaped and crafted, it cannot be the cause of offence. One has to reprimand carefully, otherwise one is likely to fall foul of immodesty, poor taste and bad manners. Of further significance is the fact that Collins leaves his comment until the door of the carriage is almost closed 'when he suddenly reminded them, with some consternation, that they had hitherto forgotten to leave any message for the ladies of Rosings. "But," he added, "*you will of course wish* to have your humble respects delivered to them, with your grateful thanks for their kindness to you while you have been there"'. Note the emphasis – 'you will of course': naturally he doesn't want to presume that his guests had forgotten to observe etiquette. Such would not be etiquette itself in this elaborate and convoluted politics of manners and taste. Clearly Collins also wishes to have an excuse to hold court back at the Rosings where he will have another stage upon which to enact a finely crafted series of compliments to Lady de Bourgh. Collins seems more calculating and skilful and so we suspect he does more than simply note the failure of Lizzy Bennet to offer her thanks to the ladies of Rosings. However, it is important to note that Austen writes that Collins 'suddenly reminded them' and 'with consternation'. Thus on further reflection we might consider Collins in a different light. In a cruel paradox this moment marks either his innocence or his culpability in the Georgian codes of violence and leaves the reader in a difficult position as to whether Collins is to be liked or disliked – which is the genius and tremendous humanity of Austen.

The response by Lizzy to Collins is also significant. '*Elizabeth made no objection*.' She seems in other words to gently yield to his advance, and does not seek to recover or excuse her apparent failure to take the initiative; however, she clearly does not feel humbled or chastised. She simply makes no objection to compliments being passed on to Lady de Bourgh. This might be seen as having slightly underplayed her obligation, and for some contemporary readers of Austen might border on disregard and rudeness. Is Lizzy rude and obnoxious? This is a classic high school question in English literature exams. The point is, of course, that there are subtle calculations by all parties, which is revealing of the virulence of the competition of honour pursued through manners, etiquette and taste. However, we need to try and explain a little further to achieve a greater sense of what is going on here. Given the letter she has just read from Darcy, Elizabeth *does not have quite the same pressure of obligation*. In fact Darcy has just made a proposal of marriage and hence she may not need to prostrate herself and curry favour or maintain cordial relations at the Rosings as much as we might presume one in her position was obliged, or that Collins, with his over-anxious deference to do the correct thing, might similarly incline.

The past is a foreign country and they clearly do things differently there, as has been long observed, but there are two things here that we need to take forward. One is that manners and taste is an ongoing negotiation between actors who seem always-already about to teeter into a burlesque comedy of competition in which parties successively raise the ante in round after round of trial and error. We have already seen that there are many different systems and subcultures of taste and etiquette, and that power relations can shift as new cultures emerge with novel methods of performing and evaluating manners. Second, it is important to emphasise that taste is as much a *resource* through which established power *could* be challenged because it is a fixed system of classification and judgement. One only acquires taste by exploring it, and by exploring it one participates in its production, and as in any form of participation this will involve *change*, however minor. In other words, we can assume that every way of knowing is a way of changing that which is to be known. In Austen, we see characters that evolve and develop, or sometimes regress, but they are never puppets in a system of fixed roles that come complete with scripts. Although Bourdieu (1984) reduces taste to a vehicle of social distinction worked by abstract social forces that subjugate and reproduce power and inequality, Becker (1953) has shown how tastes do not refer to an objective reality that is prior to its construction and socialisation. In his famous case of the etiquette of marijuana use, he shows how users have to 'learn' that imbibing a drug is a pleasurable experience. Similarly Becker's full-length treatment of *Art Worlds* (1982) shows how we can extend this analysis to say that subjects are not fixed, they do not exist 'prior' to the acquisition of taste, they acquire new capacities as they explore tastes. However, most troubling is the fact that tastes do not inhere *within* a stable social but help us to understand 'the social'. Tastes are therefore partly constitutive of the social in a highly dynamic relation. As Hennion (2004, 2007) shows, subjects are always becoming co-constitutively with the objects of their taste and the techniques and methods through which taste is developed. More challenging still is the possibility that the particular method or manner in which enquiry and research is practised is also in part performative or, following Mol (2002), participates in what might be called the 'enactment' of tastes and the social, which raises questions of value, politics and the intention of one's enquiry.

## Bawdy humour: the cultivation of sensibility

We can better explore this reflexive and performative feature of our pedagogy of taste by turning to an episode worked up during a recent ethnography of airports in the UK to show how humour is also a vehicle for the management of taste and etiquette. This particular tale involves Martin Garnish who is a young senior project manager and is employed by one of the UK's largest design, engineering and project management consultancies, but seconded to work at Manchester Airport (in the UK) on terminal and commercial projects. He shares a similar history and a similar sense of humour to the ethnographer, the shared understanding of which is itself the product of a careful negotiation of manners between ethnographer and informant. Martin holds a postgraduate MSc degree, which marks him out in an office populated by a cadre of older and more established project managers who have served the airport for a long period of time. He is also marked by the fact that he is not from the North of England, but from the South, and his accent to some appears 'posh' and 'southern'. Again, like the ethnographer, he is trying to 'make his way', which is perhaps also significant. Martin is articulate and urbane and without fail wears a smart two-piece suit, which is always worn tight, perhaps to emphasise the sharpness of its cut. These objects are significant because it is through them that Martin negotiates manners, taste and fashion in the airport, but also because they form part of his 'performance' and through which the world of etiquette is revealed to him (see Goffman 1959). On occasion he will deploy these objects, but often cloaked in irony and tempered to the particular habits and tastes of his interlocutor (as he understands them), whom he will also be simultaneously 'testing' and exploring through the interaction. One rarely enjoys the privilege of 'knowing' a colleague at work and vigilance is exercised at all times lest one over-extends a familiarity that might induce one to indulge certain informalities and thereby leave one vulnerable to embarrassments at a later stage.

Hence, Martin is a particularly good informant because he shares with the ethnographer the status of 'outsider' and he is particularly sensitive to the nuances of judgement and evaluation that are an omnipresent feature of working life amongst project managers. On this occasion he is telling me about the timetable of seasonal and annual Royal Institute of Chartered Surveyors (RICS) networking dinners, which he is obliged to attend. These obligations are never explicit of course, but colleagues and partners, he tells me, will note one's absence. The dinners are formal, black-tie events and, consistent with the industry in general, are very masculine affairs, which is also typical of the world of construction. It is how they 'do' masculinity as part of their management of manners, taste and etiquette, however, which is of interest here. The annual dinner in Manchester attracts over 850 people and the seating plan is not known in advance, or at least it is supposed not to be known in advance. It is widely understood that a series of negotiations precede the event, particularly where important clients are being wined and dined by senior partners of the various construction firms positioned on a table with a large group of people from all levels of seniority, some of whom you will know, while others are strangers. Some seats are block-booked and companies offer them as 'corporates, to clients', as Martin tells me, but exact seating plans are published as a table-plan that is erected outside the main dining hall.

People sit at tables of ten to fifteen people. As the evening progresses, the humour becomes increasingly risqué, but the tempo and rhythm of this regression is a complex matter and demands astute attention and self-awareness. As Martin tells me, 'you don't want to up the stakes too early . . . but then you don't want to fail to participate at all', so you want to make the most-timely intervention you can. Remember this is also mixed up with drinking rituals and the pace with which the drinking proceeds. Like the carnivalesque 'roasting' rituals of

Christmas parties, in which senior management are made the object of satire and ridicule (Rosen 1988), the precise boundaries and gradation between the acceptable and the offensive are never known, but always contingently produced out of the orchestration performed by members. As Foucault (1977) famously showed in his preface to Bataille, transgression is only known at the 'impossible' moment when one has crossed what subsequently appears as a boundary or line in the sand. In these situations, no one seems in control, indeed the subject is more often the outcome of transgression than it is an author or agent in any conventional sense of those terms. Moreover, you cannot assume to take charge, but at the same time it is not acceptable to completely cede authority to anyone in the group. The apparent lottery-like nature of the seating means you can never entirely know your fellow dinner guests. Introductions are often a fine art as well. How much you might reveal of your seniority, or how much you might presume is known of you, involves a complex evaluation of a series of variables, some visual, some known, others upon which one has to speculate. It is part gamble and part calculation.

A treacherous but ubiquitous event in corporate management, these dinners are made more complex by the fact that everyone is trying to work out the precise contours of propriety as they are simultaneously trying to observe them whilst also pushing against them to display their skill and/or creativity. The real skill is how to improvise and fashion a joke that is just that little bit more extreme than the last one. We are now fairly late into the evening, it is post-dessert and a joke is told about a senior executive of a well-known firm who 'lost it' during an international stag weekend (that is, he fell victim to inebriation), falling down the steps off the aircraft on arrival. It is a double punch line. One might be induced to laugh at the contrast this casts between the (supposed) formality of the dinner with each diner wearing pressed black-tie outfits, and the rather colourful nature of the tale told. In other words, it is a possible example of the upside-down Bacchanalian nature of many corporate social events (Rosen 1988). But this is rapidly followed up by a comment that the said senior partner was never the same again, and he soon left the company and was never seen again. Laughter again. But as Martin explains, you can't help thinking what is given with the one hand is taken away in the other. Is there, in other words, a 'meta' (moral) commentary going on here in this joke? Is this a moral warning about the possible dangers that might be in store for those sitting around the table drinking and telling risqué jokes? Moreover, the joke is also a challenge and invites a further elaboration to up the ante. Martin continues his tale and tells me that 'as the laughter subsides around the table' – and he emphasises this for dramatic effect by slowing down his delivery (note how the ethnographer becomes embroiled in a similar meta- or meta-meta(!) level game of joking) – you realise 'this is your chance'. So, you might decide to venture a joke to add to the one just told. One can surely imagine an intake of breath as you voice the words 'So, I heard about this guy from Gleads, you may know him, and they hired a midget to accompany him on his stag weekend. The midget was handcuffed to the stag the moment they arrived in Amsterdam . . .' People are now laughing, you take confidence, faces are staring at you, eyes wide with astonishment, should you push it to the next level? '. . . and then they paid this prostitute £50 to perform oral sex on the midget . . .' You look around the table again. People's expressions have changed. It is unclear if they are still enjoying the joke. Remember, employers, clients, colleagues surround you – and people you don't know, and all of whom might make capital from a faux pas. Or . . . No! Maybe one of the people sat around the table is a midget? Did you check before telling the tale? Have we pushed it too far? Readers who remain uncertain about their response to this question – and can dwell in this incertitude for more than a few moments, or even cultivate a certain undecidability – will have achieved the space of learning towards which this chapter has tried to move.

## Conclusions: eating, listening, talking

Ping! It's your iPad again, advertising a new App. It is called 'APS', auto text-generated pithy summaries of difficult academic texts. As if responding to the lecture you have just sat through, banner adverts stream from right to left entitled: 'Fine wine', 'opera', 'literature', and 'bawdy humour'. Each subject is a perilous terrain within which manners, taste and etiquette are played out and, through its medium, job applicants are assessed, promotion decisions made and business affairs conducted. In each case, taste is not a stable rulebook that can be acquired and digested and then tactically deployed as each situation demands. This would reflect the dominant learning paradigm in the business school, but it captures none of the contingent, constructed, reflexive, emergent and contested nature associated with the conduct of manners, taste and etiquette. What is funny? What is good taste? What is it to have 'good taste'? Who has good taste? What is to be valued? These are all questions that reflexively form part of the conduct of manners, taste and etiquette. But can we both ask these questions and participate in the world of business? We cannot rely on the opposition between context and content, or structure and agent. In order to study those practices we have to 'de-sociologise' both our own thinking and that of our interlocutors in order to trace those properties that need to be mastered by the student of taste, manners and etiquette. In this term 'de-sociologise' we mean to indicate a tactic by which one tries to think *as if* there was no such thing as society. We routinely defer to this reification 'society', but it soon disseminates into multiplicity and contradiction when we try to define it, and so to de-sociologise might help us become more sensitive to features of the world that do not appear to yet form a part of a social. New manners, tastes and etiquette might not register if we are too inured to the idea of a fully composed and coherent social context, but might simply appear as noise or deviance, or even as insignificant. Becoming sensitive to more inchoate experiments and trials in new manners and tastes might heighten our sense of the contingency of the social and thereby encourage us to more fully participate in *making* a society – and one that might just stand a chance of survival beyond the current ravages of climate change and geopolitical realignments of East–West and North–South relations.

The burden of this chapter has not been directed to argue for a pedagogy for the elite, or the aspiring elite; instead, we have tried to find a mode of construction and diagnostics that displaces the opposition of high and low. With this in mind a plurality of styles have been deployed and intentionally exaggerated, from the bawdy and vulgar to the rarefied and elitist. In part the intention is to performatively unsettle and disorientate so that the text might provoke its reader. If the reader is left wondering, 'well, what the hell is taste and how should we best teach students?', then the conceit might have had some success. Of course, I'm offering you reassurance here, which might undermine this intention. However, stated in its most blunt form, teaching students how to order French wine is not going to ensure success. If, on the other hand, the brief oenological display has stimulated the mind and the senses into new ways of thinking and being that inspire further elaborations and cultivation, then there may be some value to the oenological arts – if nothing else than to spit in the eye of some pretentious corporate executive trying to lord it over you with their superior knowledge of wine. Likewise, if one can see the refined art and elaboration involved in the participatory practices of vulgar badinage and storytelling, in which one has to navigate a tantalisingly elusive line between the acceptable and the unacceptable, then you are perhaps well on your way to engaging with the world of business.

At times, these practices reflect the elements of a stage-play and the masquerade-ball, where nothing is what it seems. In order to participate in such a complicated game the consummate practitioner of business requires learning, cultivation and study, but also self-effacement, modesty and irony. A good grounding in Shakespeare, Beethoven and Gombrich's (1966) *History of Art* would seem to be preliminary to a full course of study that would include focused scholarship on the texts of food and table manners and the uses of literacy, humour and popular culture. This would seem consistent with many of the tenets of the post-Renaissance humanities with some of its most recent advocates suggesting that democracy itself relies upon the liberal tolerance taught by a competent humanities curriculum (see Nussbaum 2012; Czarniawska, this volume). However, where this places a premium on the dignity of the *humanitas* as something worth cultivating, principally through private individual study and contemplation, to fully master the lessons of tastes, manners and etiquette requires something *post* or even *in*-human (see Wolfe 2010). This means we cannot rely on scholastic or textual endeavour; instead, as teachers, we may need to *invent* modules in taste, manners and etiquette that take us outside our all too-human preoccupations. To invent requires us to step outside or to seize that in us which is outside of the figure of man, or 'the human', as it has been elaborated in what Foucault (1973) calls the modern episteme, so that we might elaborate what is currently dismissed as abhorrent or impossible. When reaching such paroxysmal heights, we also face the terrifying question as to why bother participating at all, why bother reinventing the wheel, elaborating ever more manners, tastes and etiquettes. No one can answer this question for someone else.

As a prelude to this vertiginous existential horror, we could do well to invest time developing practical exercises that facilitate multiple re-embodiments through which we are able to counter the dominant forms of crass technical training that are so popular in the business school. Elsewhere I have lobbied for a post-human 'art of walking' (O'Doherty 2013), but what is perhaps needed is to expand these experiments into a more diverse syllabus that might include a new corporeal calisthenics of business and management. We have in mind 'ceremonies of pleasures' (Hennion 2001), but also classes in cookery, dress, drinking and elocution, and perhaps elective modules that might promote idiosyncrasies that will add 'colour' to one's CV whilst also enhancing 'character' and individuality. The possibilities are endless. Virtual swordsmanship, human–animal cross-species agility training (Haraway 2008), 'how to talk dirty and influence people' (Bruce 1965), the history of murder considered as a fine art (de Quincey 2013), the artisanal practice of pencil sharpening, treated as an extreme sport (Rees 2012)...

## Notes

1 It is important to recognise the differentiated market for the MBA ranging from what some consider to be elite (Harvard, INSEAD) to the other end of the scale: local colleges running part-time evening courses staffed with part-timers and out of work consultants. So, Harvard might be considered a 'finishing school' for the wealthy and therefore – even though doubtless still regarded as 'new money' – one might expect Harvard and their alumni to enjoy a grounding in the classics of European/North American 'culture'. They will certainly have some knowledge of fine wine and Jane Austen.

2 In making such an ill-mannered claim, the text thereby steps outside of its self-declared strategy and, presumably, must fail. Such is the sacrifice for clarity. Hopefully only a momentary aberration and we will trust that the manners of good reading will return to the academy (Ulin 2010; Calvino 2014).

3 Lest this portrait of a cultured CEO appear somewhat exaggerated, survey data of arts sponsorship, investment and endowments in culture and arts is revealing, and across Europe trends show a huge increase over the twentieth century. Data in this area is fraught with dangers of course, but the BCA report in 2012 shows that 41 per cent of all businesses are deemed to provide some support to the arts, with some companies providing over USD50 million a year – amounting to 18 per cent of those businesses contributing to the arts (BCA Report 2013). Spedding's data (2012) for the UK shows that business investment in the arts increased from £114.4 million in 2001 to £134.2 million in 2011.

4 With apologies to John Hassard (personal correspondence).

5 At the risk of committing colonialist assumptions, we assume a familiarity with the work of Austen (see Prasad, this volume). This could be considered bad taste.

## References

Austen, J. (2008 [1815]) *Pride and Prejudice*. Oxford: Oxford University Press.
Banks, S. (2012) *Duels and Duelling*. Oxford: Shire Books.
Bauman, Z. (1995) *Life in Fragments: Essays in Postmodern Morality*. Oxford: Blackwell.
Becker, H.S. (1953) 'Becoming a marihuana user', *American Journal of Sociology*, 59(3), 235–42.
Becker, H.S. (1982) *Art Worlds*. Berkeley, CA: University of California Press.
Berger, P. and Luckmann, T. (1967). *The Social Construction of Reality: A Treatise in the Sociology of Knowledge*. Garden City, NY: Doubleday.
Bourdieu, P. (1984) *Distinction*. Cambridge, MA: Harvard University Press.
Business Committee for the Arts (BCA) (2013) *The BCA National Survey of Business Support for the Arts*. Washington, DC: Americans for the Arts.
Calvino, I. (2014) *Why Read the Classics?* Boston, MA: Houghton Mifflin Harcourt.
Carnegie, D. (2010 [1936]) *How to Win Friends and Influence People*. London: Vermillon.
Cook, S.D. and Yanow, D. (1993) 'Culture and organizational learning', *Journal of Management Inquiry*, 2(4), 373–90.
Bruce, L. (1965) *How to Talk Dirty and Influence People*. Chicago, IL: Playboy Press.
Delwiche, J.F. and Pelchat, M.L. (2002) 'Influence of glass shape on wine aroma', *Journal of Sensory Studies*, 17(1), 19–28.
De Quincey, T. (2013) *Confessions of an English Opium-eater and Other Writings*. Oxford: Oxford University Press.
Duby, G., Veyne, P., and Ariès, P. (1987) *A History of Private Life*. Vol. 1. Cambridge, MA: Belknap Press of Harvard University Press.
Elias, N. (1969) *The Civilizing Process. Vol. I: The History of Manners*. Oxford: Blackwell.
Featherstone, M. (1995) *Undoing Culture: Globalization, Postmodernism and Identity*. London: Sage Publications.
Fischer, J.W. (2005) *At Your Service: A Hands-on Guide to the Professional Dining Room*. Hoboken, NJ: Wiley.
Foucault, M. (1973) *The Order of Things: An Archeology of the Human Sciences*. New York, NY: Vintage.
Foucault, M. (1977) 'A preface to transgression'. *In:* M. Foucault (ed.) *Language, Counter-Memory, Practice: Selected Essays and Interviews*. New York, NY: Cornell University Press, pp. 29–52.
Gherardi, S. (2009) 'Practice? It's a matter of taste!', *Management Learning*, 40(5), 535–50.
Goffman, E. (1959) *The Presentation of Self in Everyday Life*. Garden City, NY: Anchor.
Gomart, E. and Hennion, A. (1999) 'A sociology of attachment: music, amateurs, drug users'. *In:* J. Law and J. Hassard (eds.) *Actor Network and After*. Oxford: Blackwell, pp. 220–47.
Gombrich, E.H. (1966) *History of Art*. London: Phaidon.
Handler, R. and Segal, D.A. (1999) *Jane Austen and the Fiction of Culture: An Essay on the Narration of Social Realities*. Lanham, MD: Rowman & Littlefield.
Haraway, D.J. (2008) *When Species Meet*. Minneapolis, MN: University of Minnesota Press.
Hebdige, D. (1979) *Subcultures*. London: Methuen.
Hebdige, D. (1982) 'Towards a cartography of taste 1935–1962'. *In:* D. Hebdige (ed.) *Popular Culture: Past and Present*. London: Croom Helm, pp. 194–218.
Heidegger, M. (1962) *Being and Time*. Oxford: Blackwell.
Hennion, A. (2001) 'Music lovers: taste as performance', *Theory, Culture and Society*, 18(5), 1–22.
Hennion, A. (2004) 'Une sociologie des attachements. D'une sociologie de la culture à une pragmatique de l'amateur', *Sociétés*, 85(3), 9–24.
Hennion, A. (2007) 'Those things that hold us together: taste and sociology', *Cultural Sociology*, 1(1), 97–114.
Jackson, R. and Jackson, R.S. (2009) *Wine Tasting: A Professional Handbook*. Waltham, MA: Academic Press.
Mol, A. (2002) *The Body Multiple*. Durham, NC: Duke University Press.
Nussbaum, M.C. (2012) *Not for Profit: Why Democracy Needs the Humanities*. Princeton, NJ: Princeton University Press.
O'Doherty, D.P. (2013) 'Off-road and spaced-out in the city: organization and the interruption of topology', *Space and Culture*, 16(2), 211–28.
Parker, M. (2014) 'University, Ltd: changing a business school', *Organization*, 21(2), 281–92.
Parr, R. and Mackay, J. (2010) *Secrets of the Sommeliers: How to Think and Drink Like the World's Top Wine Professionals*. New York, NY: Random House.
Peynaud, E. (1987) *The Taste of Wine*. London: Macdonald Orbis.

Pfeffer, J. (2010) *Power: Why Some People Have It and Others Don't.* New York, NY: Harper Business.
Rees, D. (2012) *How to Sharpen Pencils: A Practical and Theoretical Treatise on the Artisanal Craft of Pencil Sharpening for Writers, Artists, Contractors, Flange Turners, Anglesmiths, and Civil Servants.* New York, NY: Melville House.
Roberts, A. and MacLennan, A.F. (2003) *Making Strategies Work.* Upper Saddle River, NJ: Pearson Education.
Robinson, J. (2000) *How to Taste: A Guide to Enjoying Wine.* New York, NY: Simon and Schuster.
Rosen, M. (1988) 'You asked for it: Christmas at the bosses' expense', *Journal of Management Studies*, 25(5), 463–80.
Spedding, P. (2012) *Private Investment in Culture 2010/11.* London: Arts and Business.
Thomas, R. (2013) *Wine Tasting for Beginners: Ultimate Wine Tasting Guide.* Raleigh, NC: Lulu.
Ulin, D.L. (2010) *The Lost Art of Reading.* Seattle, WA: Sasquatch Books.
Venturi, F., Andrich, G., Sanmartin, C., Scalabrelli, G., Ferroni, G. and Zinnai, A. (2014) 'The expression of a full-bodied red wine as a function of the characteristics of the glass utilized for the tasting', *CyTA-Journal of Food*, 12(3), 291–7.
Visser, M. (1992) *The Rituals of Dinner.* Harmondsworth: Penguin.
Wolfe, C. (2010) *What is Posthumanism?* Minneapolis, MN: University of Minnesota Press.

# Index

For Product Safety Concerns and Information please contact our EU
representative GPSR@taylorandfrancis.com
Taylor & Francis Verlag GmbH, Kaufingerstraße 24, 80331 München, Germany

www.ingramcontent.com/pod-product-compliance
Ingram Content Group UK Ltd.
Pitfield, Milton Keynes, MK11 3LW, UK
UKHW052054230926
475702UK00031B/2797

* 9 7 8 1 0 3 2 2 4 2 4 3 9 *